L.V. Pienaar

**MANAGEMENT
SCIENCE FOR
BUSINESS
DECISIONS**

MANAGEMENT SCIENCE FOR BUSINESS DECISIONS

LAWRENCE L. LAPIN
San José State University

HARCOURT BRACE JOVANOVICH, INC.
New York   San Diego   Chicago   San Francisco   Atlanta

Copyright © 1980, 1976, 1975 by Harcourt Brace Jovanovich, Inc.

All rights reserved. No part of this publication may be reproduced or transmitted in any form or by any means, electronic or mechanical, including photocopy, recording, or any information storage and retrieval system, without permission in writing from the publisher.

Requests for permission to make copies of any part of the work should be mailed to: Permissions, Harcourt Brace Jovanovich, Inc., 757 Third Avenue, New York, NY 10017.

Much of the material in this edition was previously published in QUANTITATIVE METHODS FOR BUSINESS DECISIONS by Lawrence Lapin.

Printed in the United States of America

Library of Congress Catalog Card Number: 79-89522

ISBN: 0-15-554690-2

Preface

Management Science for Business Decisions provides an introduction to basic management-science methodology. This book is directed to the average college student; algebra is the only prerequisite. The book emphasizes the variety and power of the available management-science tools so that the reader will not be apprehensive of them and will be able to recognize on-the-job situations in which they can be successfully employed.

Much of the material in this book originally appeared in my earlier book, *Quantitative Methods for Business Decisions.* The present text has been shortened, largely by deleting the more advanced topics. One added feature is a completely new chapter on forecasting (Chapter 4). Several chapters have been improved; for instance, instead of one long chapter, two short chapters (Chapters 13 and 14) now cover the simplex method. The new chapter order improves topical flow and facilitates transitions.

This book is more intuitive than most other books on the subject. Good explanations are richly illustrated with relevant and interesting examples to provide more meaningful and *easier* learning experiences. For example, Chapter 13 thoroughly describes the underlying rationale of the simplex method in nonmathematical terms so that the student can learn why, as well as how, it works. Chapter 16 discusses network planning (PERT or CPM) in a broad context, including its management

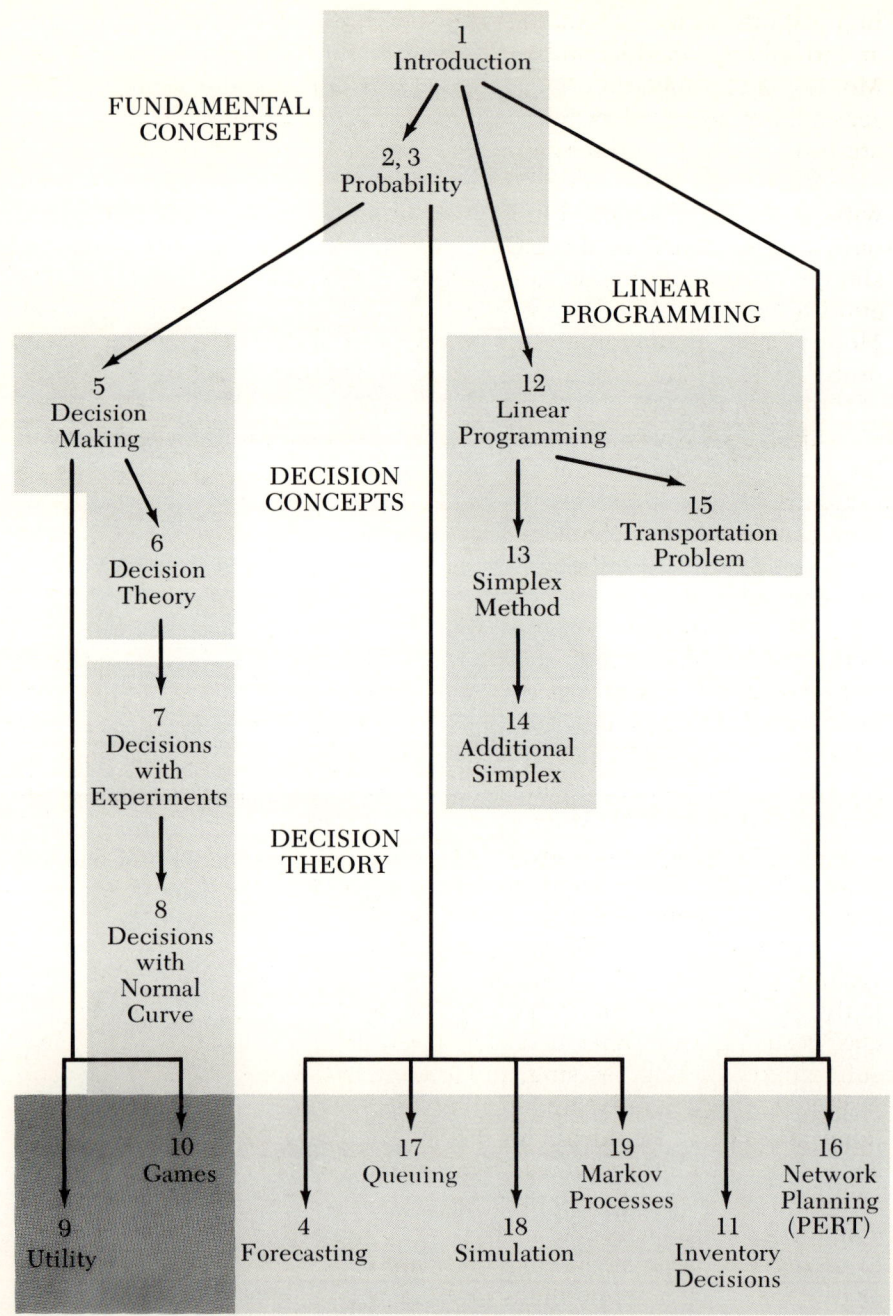

implications, milestone and activity scheduling, the time–cost tradeoff, and (in an appendix) its probabilistic aspects. Chapter 18 first introduces Monte Carlo simulation as a simple substitute for the stopwatch observation of an actual system operation. Highly intuitive decision trees are used extensively throughout to explain a variety of concepts.

This book also highlights the limitations and pitfalls associated with various mathematical models and algorithms. For example, some basic models, such as the EOQ used in inventory decisions and the simple queuing formulas, are based on assumptions that are rarely applicable to real life. Where practical, alternative approaches such as Monte Carlo simulation are indicated and fully described. Traditional probabilistic PERT assumptions are accompanied by a critical analysis of their applicability.

One difficulty in any quantitative methods course is the necessity for hand calculations. The problem material has been designed to minimize computational chores and to emphasize concepts and formulation. Sufficient coverage of the computer is provided, although specific programs are not described in detail. (This subject is properly relegated to a computer manual.)

The overall book design is modular, providing, as the tinted areas in the opposite figure indicate, maximum flexibility in adapting the book to the requirements of a particular course. All or portions of any part may be used. For example, Chapters 2 and 3 can be bypassed by students who have had a prior statistics course. The chapters on probability (or some prior knowledge of the subject) serve as the prerequisite to all the stochastic material. Much of the book follows directly from Chapter 5, which discusses the basic concepts of decision making and how to cope with uncertainty. There, expected-value and decision-tree analyses are applied to general problem solving.

The *Instructor's Manual* provides specific recommendations for various course designs, teaching suggestions, and detailed solutions to the over 200 problems in the text. The book itself has been thoroughly class tested several times in a variety of different courses, which has resulted in the culling, revising, and grading of the problem material. The problems are generally broken into distinct parts, both to benefit students and to give the instructor flexibility in making assignments. Brief answers to selected problems are also provided in the back of the book so that students can monitor their own progress. The *Instructor's Manual* contains an additional set of more than 120 solved problems, from slight to moderate difficulty, that may be used for supplementary homework or examinations. A comprehensive bibliography is included in the back of the book for students who wish to pursue a particular topic in greater detail.

I wish to thank my colleagues who were instrumental in helping me shape the manuscript: C. Randall Byers of the University of Idaho, Ke T. Hsia of California State University (Los Angeles), Ross Lanser of San José State University, William D. Whisler of the California State University at Hayward, and Zeb Vancura of the University of Santa Clara. I also wish to acknowledge the valuable assistance of my students.

LAWRENCE L. LAPIN

Contents

Preface   v

CHAPTER ONE   INTRODUCTION TO MANAGEMENT SCIENCE FOR DECISION MAKING   1

  1–1 MANAGEMENT SCIENCE—A CONTINUING STORY OF SUCCESS   2

      Managing Research and Development 2
      Determining the Number of Bank Tellers 2
      Locating Warehouses 3
      Choosing the Design for an Oil-Tanker Port Facility 3
      Deployment of Fire-Fighting Companies 5
      Advantages of Paper Recycling 5
      Satellite Communications Systems—An Investment Analysis 6
      Planning Political Campaign Strategies 7

1-2 MANAGEMENT SCIENCE AND OPERATIONS
     RESEARCH   8

1-3 HISTORY OF QUANTITATIVE METHODS   9

1-4 PROCEDURES AND APPLICATIONS   9

1-5 MODELS AND DECISION MAKING   11

1-6 IMPORTANCE OF STUDYING MANAGEMENT   13

CHAPTER TWO   PROBABILITY CONCEPTS   14

2-1 FUNDAMENTAL CONCEPTS   15

   The Event   15
   Basic Definition of Probability   18

2-2 EVENT RELATIONSHIPS   21

2-3 THE ADDITION LAW   24

   The Addition Law for Mutually Exclusive Events   25
   Events That Are Mutually Exclusive and Collectively
      Exhaustive   26
   Application to Complementary Events   27

2-4 CONDITIONAL PROBABILITY AND THE JOINT
     PROBABILITY TABLE   28

   Conditional Probability   28
   Joint Probability Table and Marginal Probabilities   29
   Computing Conditional Probability from Joint
      Probability   30

2-5 THE MULTIPLICATION LAW   33

   Joint Probabilities for More Than Two Events   35
   The Probability Tree Diagram   36
   Multiplication Law for Independent Events   38

2-6 COMMON ERRORS IN APPLYING THE CONCEPTS
     OF PROBABILITY   40

2-7 REVISING PROBABILITIES USING BAYES' THEOREM   42

    Bayes' Theorem 43
    Posterior Probability as a Conditional Probability 45

2-8 PROBABILITIES OBTAINED FROM HISTORY   48

2-9 SUBJECTIVE PROBABILITIES   49

    PROBLEMS   50

CHAPTER THREE   PROBABILITY DISTRIBUTIONS AND EXPECTED VALUE   58

3-1 THE RANDOM VARIABLE   59

    An Illustration from Roulette 59
    The Probability Distribution 61

3-2 EXPECTED VALUE   63

    The Meaning of Expected Value 63
    Variance of a Random Variable 65

3-3 THE BINOMIAL DISTRIBUTION   66

    The Bernoulli Process 69
    The Binomial Formula 70
    Cumulative Probabilities 72
    Using Binomial Probability Tables 73
    Mean and Variance of Binomial Distribution 77

3-4 THE NORMAL DISTRIBUTION   77

    Finding Areas Under the Normal Curve 79
    Standard Normal Random Variable 84
    The Normal Distribution and Sampling 86

3-5 POISSON AND EXPONENTIAL DISTRIBUTIONS   88

    PROBLEMS   89

CHAPTER FOUR — FORECASTING 84

4-1 FORECASTING USING PAST DATA: TIME-SERIES ANALYSIS 95

The Classical Time-Series Model 97

4-2 FORECASTING TREND USING REGRESSION 103

Determining Trend Using Least Squares 103
Forecasting Trend 105
The Trend Curve 105

4-3 FORECASTING USING SEASONAL INDEXES 107

Ratio-to-Moving-Average Method 108
Monthly Data 114
Deseasonalized Data 114
Making the Forecast 115

4-4 IDENTIFYING CYCLES 116

4-5 EXPONENTIAL SMOOTHING 116

Single-Parameter Exponential Smoothing 117
Two-Parameter Exponential Smoothing 118
Further Exponential Smoothing Procedures 120

4-6 FORECASTING USING CAUSAL MODELS: REGRESSION ANALYSIS 120

Simple Regression 121
Multiple Regression 122
Comparison of Simple and Multiple Regression 125
Further Considerations 126

4-7 FORECASTING USING JUDGMENT 126

Judgmental Probability Distribution: Interview Method 126
Finding a Probability Distribution from Actual/Forecast Ratios 130
Delphi Forecasting and Other Methods 132

PROBLEMS 133

CHAPTER FIVE   BASIC CONCEPTS OF DECISION MAKING   139

5-1 CERTAINTY AND UNCERTAINTY IN DECISION MAKING   139

5-2 ELEMENTS OF DECISIONS   140

Decision Table   141
Decision Tree Diagram   142

5-3 RANKING THE ALTERNATIVES AND THE PAYOFF TABLE   143

Objectives and Payoff Values   144
Reducing the Number of Alternatives: Inadmissible Acts   148

5-4 EXPECTED PAYOFF   149

Maximizing Expected Payoff: Bayes Decision Rule   149

5-5 DECISION TREE ANALYSIS   150

The Decision Tree Diagram   152
Determining the Payoffs   153
Assigning Event Probabilities   154
Backward Induction   156
Additional Remarks   159

PROBLEMS   160

CHAPTER SIX   ELEMENTS OF DECISION THEORY   166

6-1 DECISION CRITERIA   167

Maximin Payoff   167
Maximum Likelihood Criterion   170
Criterion of Insufficient Reason   172
Bayes Decision Rule Preferred   172

6-2 DECISION MAKING USING STRATEGIES   173

Extensive and Normal Form Analysis   176

6-3 BAYES DECISION RULE AND UTILITY 180

6-4 OPPORTUNITY LOSS AND EXPECTED VALUE OF
     PERFECT INFORMATION 181

   Opportunity Loss 181
   Bayes Decision Rule and Opportunity Loss 182
   Expected Value of Perfect Information 183

   PROBLEMS 187

CHAPTER SEVEN   DECISION MAKING WITH EXPERIMENTAL INFORMATION   191

7-1 REVISING PROBABILITIES 192

   Using Probability Trees 195

7-2 POSTERIOR ANALYSIS 198

   Obviously Non-Optimal Strategies 199

7-3 DECISION TO EXPERIMENT:
     PREPOSTERIOR ANALYSIS 200

   Role of EVPI 202

   PROBLEMS 203

CHAPTER EIGHT   DECISION MAKING WITH THE NORMAL DISTRIBUTION   209

8-1 A COMPUTER MEMORY DEVICE DECISION 209

8-2 DECISION STRUCTURE 210

8-3 DECISION MAKING USING OPPORTUNITY LOSSES 212

8-4 **PRIOR ANALYSIS WITHOUT SAMPLE INFORMATION** 215

    Minimum Expected Opportunity Loss Acts 216
    Determining the EVPI: The Normal Loss Function 218

8-5 **POSTERIOR ANALYSIS FOR A GIVEN SAMPLE SIZE** 219

    Posterior Probability Distribution for μ 219
    Finding the Critical Value 222

8-6 **DECISIONS REGARDING THE SAMPLE: PREPOSTERIOR ANALYSIS** 224

    Expected Value of Sample Information 225
    The Decision to Sample 226
    Determining the Optimal Sample Size 226
    The Optimal Decision Rule 227

8-7 **A SUMMARY OF THE PROCEDURES** 228

8-8 **CONCLUDING REMARKS** 230

    PROBLEMS 231

CHAPTER NINE   DECISION MAKING WITH UTILITY   235

9-1 **ATTITUDES, PREFERENCES, AND UTILITY** 236

    Decision to Buy Insurance 236

9-2 **NUMERICAL UTILITY VALUES** 238

    Saint Petersburg Paradox 239
    Validity of Logarithmic Values 240
    Outcomes Without a Natural Payoff Measure 240

9-3 **UTILITY THEORY** 241

    Assumptions of Utility Theory 241
    Gambles and Expected Utility 242
    Determining Expected Utilities 243
    Further Assumptions of Utility Theory 244

9-4 DETERMINING UTILITY VALUES 248

    Attitude Versus Judgment 251
    Utility and the Bayes Decision Rule 252

9-5 THE UTILITY FOR MONEY AND ATTITUDES TOWARD RISK 253

    Applying the Utility Function in Decision Analysis 253
    Attitudes Toward Risk and the Shape of the Utility Curve 256

PROBLEMS 259

CHAPTER TEN GAMES AND INTERACTIVE DECISIONS 266

10-1 INTERACTIVE DECISION MAKING AND GAME THEORY 266

    Example from the Battle of the Bismark Sea 268

10-2 TWO-PERSON ZERO-SUM GAMES 269

    Analyzing the Decision: Minimax Principle 270
    Saddle Points and Value of Game 271
    Other Features in Two-Person Zero-Sum Games 272

10-3 MIXED STRATEGIES IN GAMES WITHOUT A SADDLE POINT 273

    The Mixed Strategy 274
    Elimination of Inadmissible Acts 276

10-4 OPTIMAL MIXED STRATEGIES FOR ZERO-SUM GAMES 278

    Graphical Solution 279
    Algebraic Solution 282
    Solving 3×2 and Larger Games 282

10-5 NON-ZERO-SUM AND OTHER GAMES 286

Two-Person Non-Zero-Sum Games 286
The Prisoner's Dilemma 286
Games with Several Players 288

10–6 CONCLUDING REMARKS 289

PROBLEMS 289

CHAPTER ELEVEN   INVENTORY DECISIONS   295

11–1 FACTORS INFLUENCING INVENTORY POLICY 296

Inventory Cost Components 297
Structure of Inventory System 298
Types of Inventory Items 298
Nature of Demand and Supply 299

11–2 ECONOMIC ORDER QUANTITY MODEL 300

The Mathematical Model 300
Finding the Optimal Solution 303
An Illustration 306

11–3 OPTIMAL INVENTORY POLICY WITH BACKORDERING 308

11–4 INVENTORY POLICY FOR LOST SALES 312

11–5 FIXED PRODUCTION-RATE MODEL 312

11–6 INVENTORY DECISIONS WITH UNCERTAIN FACTORS 315

EOQ Model for Uncertain Demand 316
An Illustration 318
EOQ Model When Demand Is Normally Distributed 321
An Illustration 322

11–7 ANALYTIC AND NUMERICAL SOLUTION METHODS 324

PROBLEMS 325

CHAPTER TWELVE LINEAR PROGRAMMING: AN INTRODUCTION 330

12-1 A PROBLEM ILLUSTRATION 331

12-2 FORMULATING THE LINEAR PROGRAM 332

12-3 THE GRAPHICAL SOLUTION METHOD 334

> Plotting Constraint Lines 335
> Finding the Valid Side of the Constraint Line 337
> The Feasible Solution Region 338
> The Most Attractive Corner 339
> Finding the Optimal Solution 341

12-4 SUMMARY OF PROCEDURE 343

12-5 COST MINIMIZATION: A FEED-MIX PROBLEM 344

12-6 SPECIAL PROBLEMS IN CONSTRUCTING LINES 347

12-7 MIXTURE CONSTRAINTS 348

12-8 EQUALITY CONSTRAINTS 351

12-9 MULTIPLE OPTIMAL SOLUTIONS 353

12-10 CONCLUDING REMARKS 355

PROBLEMS 355

CHAPTER THIRTEEN THE SIMPLEX METHOD IN LINEAR PROGRAMMING 361

13-1 BASIC CONCEPTS 363

> Slack Variables 363
> Expressing the Linear Program in Terms of Slacks 364
> Algebraic Solution 364
> The Variable Mix 366

13-2 THE SIMPLEX METHOD 369

    The Simplex Tableau 370
    Summary of the Simplex Method 373
    Constructing the New Simplex Tableau 375
    Finding the Optimal Solution 378

13-3 COMPUTATIONAL ASPECTS OF SIMPLEX 381

13-4 SHORTCUTS IN CONSTRUCTING TABLEAUS 383

13-5 SPECIAL SIMPLEX CONSIDERATIONS 383

    PROBLEMS 384

CHAPTER FOURTEEN   ADDITIONAL SIMPLEX METHOD CONSIDERATIONS   387

14-1 SURPLUS AND ARTIFICIAL VARIABLES: THE BIG-M METHOD 387

14-2 COST MINIMIZATION PROBLEMS 391

14-3 SUMMARY OF SIMPLEX FORMULATION REQUIREMENTS 396

14-4 SPECIAL PROBLEMS IN LINEAR PROGRAMMING 397

    Infeasible Problems 397
    Unbounded Problems 399
    Ties for Optimal Solution 401
    Degeneracy and Redundant Constraints 403
    Variables Unrestricted As to Sign 404

    PROBLEMS 405

CHAPTER FIFTEEN   THE TRANSPORTATION PROBLEM   411

15-1 FORMULATING THE TRANSPORTATION PROBLEM 413

15-2 GETTING STARTED: NORTHWEST CORNER RULE   416

15-3 SOLVING THE PROBLEM:
      THE TRANSPORTATION METHOD   418

   The Simplex Analogy 418
   Finding the Entering Cell: Row and Column Numbers 419
   Finding the New Solution: The Closed-Loop Path 423
   Further Iterations to Find the Optimal Solution 425
   The Required Number of Non-Empty Cells 426
   Ties for Exiting Cell 427
   Determining the Optimal Solution 428

15-4 DUMMY PLANTS AND WAREHOUSES   429

15-5 SPECIAL PROBLEMS GETTING STARTED   431

15-6 OTHER APPLICATIONS
      OF THE TRANSPORTATION PROBLEM   433

15-7 ADVANTAGES OF THE TRANSPORTATION METHOD   435

15-8 CONCLUDING REMARKS   436

      PROBLEMS   437

CHAPTER SIXTEEN   NETWORK PLANNING
                           WITH PERT   442

16-1 THE IMPORTANCE OF TIME IN PLANNING   442

16-2 BASIC CONCEPTS OF PERT   443

   The PERT Network 444
   Dummy Activities 448
   Activity Completion Times 449

16-3 ANALYSIS OF THE PERT NETWORK   450

   Earliest Possible Event Times 450
   The Critical Path 453
   Latest Allowable Event Times 455
   Event Slack Times: Finding the Critical Path 457

16-4 PLANNING AND CONTROL USING THE PERT
      NETWORK   459

    Activity Scheduling 459
    Activity Slack Times 461
    Milestone Scheduling 461
    Managing with PERT 462

16-5 REPLANNING AND ADJUSTMENT WITH PERT   463

    The Time-Cost Tradeoff 463
    Regular and Crash Activity Plans 465
    Constructing the Time-Cost Tradeoff Curve 467
    Updating the PERT Network 470

16-6 CONCLUDING REMARKS   473

Appendix 16-1: Traditional PERT Analysis with
      Three Time Estimates   473

Appendix 16-2: The CPM Network   476

    PROBLEMS   478

CHAPTER SEVENTEEN   WAITING LINES (QUEUES)   484

17-1 BASIC QUEUING SITUATIONS   485

    Structures of Queuing Systems 486
    Queue Disciplines 488
    Arrival and Service Patterns 489

17-2 EXPONENTIAL AND POISSON DISTRIBUTIONS   490

    The Poisson Process 490
    The Exponential Distribution 491
    The Poisson Distribution 494
    Using Poisson Probability Tables 496
    Other Instances of Poisson Processes 497
    Practical Limitations of the Poisson Process 498

17-3 SINGLE-SERVER QUEUING MODEL WITH
EXPONENTIAL SERVICE TIMES   498

Some Important Queuing Results   499
Basic Queuing Formulas   500
An Illustration   502
Interpreting Queuing Formulas and Alternative
    Expressions   505

17-4 MULTIPLE-SERVER QUEUING MODEL   508

Queuing Formulas   508
An Illustration   510
Two Servers Compared to One Twice As Fast   512

17-5 CONCLUDING REMARKS   513

Appendix 17-1: Some Further Queuing Models   514

A Single-Server Model for a Finite Queue   514
A Single-Server Model for a Limited Population   515
A Single-Server Model with Poisson Arrivals and Any
    Service-Time Distribution   516
A Single-Server Model with Constant Service Times   516

PROBLEMS   517

CHAPTER EIGHTEEN   SIMULATION 522

18-1 THE NATURE OF SIMULATION   523

Other Kinds of Simulation   523
Features of Monte Carlo Simulation   524

18-2 CONCEPTS AND PROCEDURES:
A WAITING-LINE SIMULATION   525

A One-Man Barbershop Illustration   525
Duplicating Reality   526
Probability Distributions   527
Generating Events Using Random Numbers   528
Setting Up the Simulation   530
Conducting the Simulation   531
Transient Simulation States   536

Decision Making with Simulation 537

18-3 STATISTICAL ASPECTS OF SIMULATION 537

Required Number of Trials 538
The Confidence Interval Estimate 540
Further Statistical Considerations 541

18-4 SIMULATION AND PERT 542

Using Random Numbers with Continuous
 Distributions 543
The Simulation 545

18-5 SIMULATING INVENTORY POLICIES 547

18-6 SIMULATION VERSUS THE ANALYTIC SOLUTION 548

18-7 SIMULATION AND THE COMPUTER 550

Simulation Programs and Languages 550
Random-Number Generation 550
Disadvantages of Computer Simulation 551

PROBLEMS 551

CHAPTER NINETEEN DECISION MAKING WITH MARKOV PROCESSES 557

19-1 THE MARKOV PROCESS 557

Characteristics of Markov Processes 558
State and Transition Probabilities 559
How State Probabilities Change over Time 560

19-2 CALCULATION OF STEADY-STATE PROBABILITIES 562

19-3 DECISION MAKING WITH A MARKOV PROCESS 564

19-4 FINDING AN OPTIMAL MAINTENANCE POLICY 565

19-5 CONCLUDING REMARKS 570

PROBLEMS 573

BIBLIOGRAPHY 577

APPENDIX TABLES 583

- A CUMULATIVE VALUES FOR THE BINOMIAL PROBABILITY DISTRIBUTION — 584
- B AREAS UNDER THE STANDARD NORMAL CURVE — 589
- C LOSS FUNCTION FOR DECISION MAKING WITH THE NORMAL CURVE — 590
- D EXPONENTIAL FUNCTIONS — 592
- E CUMULATIVE PROBABILITY VALUES FOR THE POISSON DISTRIBUTION — 593
- F RANDOM NUMBERS — 595

ANSWERS TO SELECTED PROBLEMS 596

INDEX 605

**MANAGEMENT
SCIENCE FOR
BUSINESS
DECISIONS**

One

Introduction to Management Science for Decision Making

A quiet revolution has taken place in managerial decision making over the past several years. This has been largely due to successful implementation of *management science* and the widespread use of computers. The many techniques of management science are often called *quantitative methods*. The list of business problems solved by these procedures grows daily. Literally every functional area, from marketing to production, from finance to personnel, involves problems that have been successfully solved. All major industries provide examples of successful application. Indeed, quantitative methods may be applied to decision making in general and can be used by individuals or groups, in education, in the professions, and in every type of organization, including governments and nonprofit foundations.

1-1 MANAGEMENT SCIENCE —A CONTINUING STORY OF SUCCESS

A few short case histories demonstrate how management science has been useful in solving a variety of actual problems.

Managing Research and Development

In the late 1950s, the U.S. Navy was faced with the monumental task of equipping its nuclear submarine fleet with Polaris ballistic missiles. The ships and missiles were designed and built over a period of several years with the objective of reaching operational capability as soon as possible. In establishing schedules and coordinating and controlling the efforts of the hundreds of contractors involved, a new quantitative method called PERT (for Program Evaluation and Review Technique) was used. PERT has been credited with saving more than one year in getting the Polaris program implemented.

Determining the Number of Bank Tellers

All of us have spent a great deal of time waiting in line at banks. Quantitative methods have been applied to this and a variety of similar situations where the objective is finding the proper balance between customer annoyance and inconvenience resulting from waiting and the bank's operational efficiency. One result has been a major change in how customers are serviced. Today the little lines that used to form before each teller window are being replaced by a single line that feeds all the open windows; now customers need not feel guilty doing time-consuming chores, such as buying money orders, nor do they have to put up with nosey people eavesdropping on their transactions.

Many banks have used quantitative analysis to decide how many tellers are needed at various times during the week, so that these employees experience a smooth flow of work and the customers spend a tolerable amount of time waiting. One bank thus determined to open 10 windows on Friday afternoons, but only three during slow periods, such as Tuesday mornings. Previously, five tellers were used at all times. The new policy has further advantages because part-time employees can fill in during rush hours, and tellers are no longer bored standing at their windows with nothing to do for long stretches. The customers are happier too, and business has improved considerably, with far fewer defections to competing banks than before.

Locating Warehouses

A chemical company engaged in the fertilizer and pesticide business solved the problem of locating its warehouses. The resulting sites minimized the combined annual cost of transportation, storage, and handling. To achieve this, all the customers in each of several hundred sales territories were treated as a single demand center. Figure 1-1 shows a schematic representation of the distribution system to these centers, each of which could be supplied directly from a plant, from a regional warehouse, or from both.

Possible solutions ranged from having no warehouses (so that all customers received shipments directly from the plants) to having one warehouse in the largest town or city in each territory; both alternatives were prohibitively costly. Selection of those in-between warehouse combinations was a major task because of the astronomical number of possibilities. To begin with, a screening procedure eliminated all but the most attractive ones. Each of these alternative siting plans was evaluated thoroughly by a lengthy computer program that found the minimum-cost distribution pattern for the indicated warehouse locations. The final solution provided a plan capable of saving several million dollars annually over the former operation.

Choosing the Design
for an Oil-Tanker Port Facility

An international oil company committed several hundred million dollars to constructing a port facility in the Persian Gulf to service oil tankers. Various alternative configurations of loading and storage components were considered, and the potential capacities ranged from tiny to huge. A host of variables affected the design evaluation, many of them uncertain because of the long construction lead times. Such factors include future world demands for petroleum, level of reserves in those producing fields supplying the port, and size and characteristics of the oil tanker fleet. Other variables included prices for oil and operating costs of all kinds. Also, political ramifications had to be considered. (At that time, major oil-producing nations were neither nationalizing petroleum production, forming cartels, nor embargoing consumer countries—although such contingencies had been allowed for.)

Each alternative port facility was constructed and run "on paper"

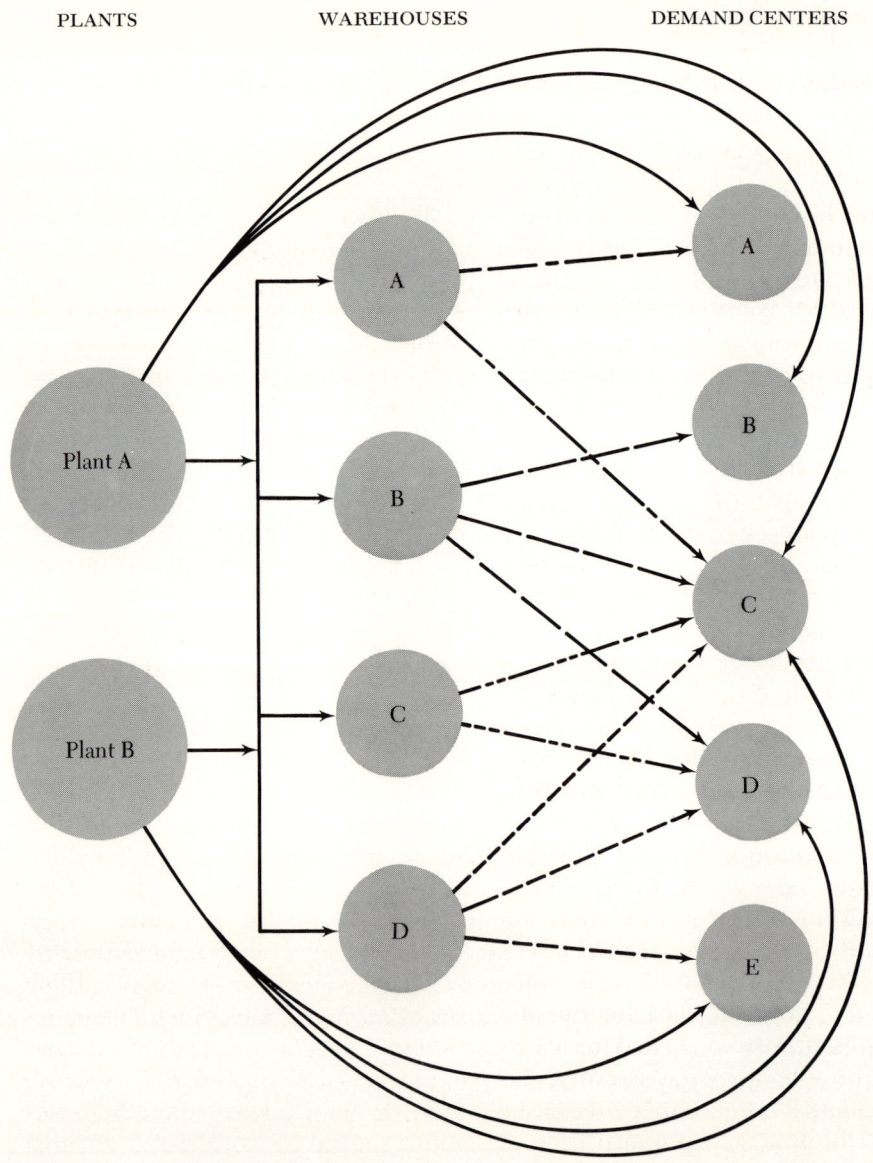

Figure 1-1
A schematic representation of a distribution system.

for a number of years to determine a statistical pattern for future profits. Through this computer simulation a design was selected which provided the greatest rate of return on invested capital at an acceptable level of risk.

Deployment of Fire-Fighting Companies

A recent study was conducted to determine how many fire companies were needed by New York City, where they should be located, and how they should be dispatched to alarms.* Traditional policy had been to dispatch the nearest available five companies (three engines and two ladders) for each alarm, with more units on call. Instead, a more flexible plan was evaluated that varied the number of companies sent for any given alarm, depending on the nature of the call. This would help prevent depletion of nearby units available for future calls.

A simulation of this adaptive procedure indicated that faster response times could be achieved while at the same time workloads could be substantially lowered. Further study identified imbalances in levels of service between various regions within the city which indicated how companies should be reallocated. When the results were implemented, six companies were eliminated, and total annual savings to the city exceeded $5 million per year.

Advantages of Paper Recycling

Paper production and consumption in modern societies have been increasingly criticized as excessive. The amount of virgin pulp used each year in the United States approaches 100 million tons, but much of our paper needs could be satisfied by using recycled paper. Figure 1-2 shows how waste recovery provides secondary pulp that can be used in making new paper. A study was made to determine how much paper could be recycled and what could be done to increase the amounts so treated.

The basic data for the study were developed from the chemical processes used in making various types of paper. Information relating to how, and in what quantity, each paper type is consumed was also used. A mathematical procedure based on one of the quantitative methods described in this book was then applied to the problem. The results indi-

---

* Ignall, E. J. et al., "Improving the Deployment of New York City Fire Companies," *Interfaces* (February 1975), pp. 48–61.

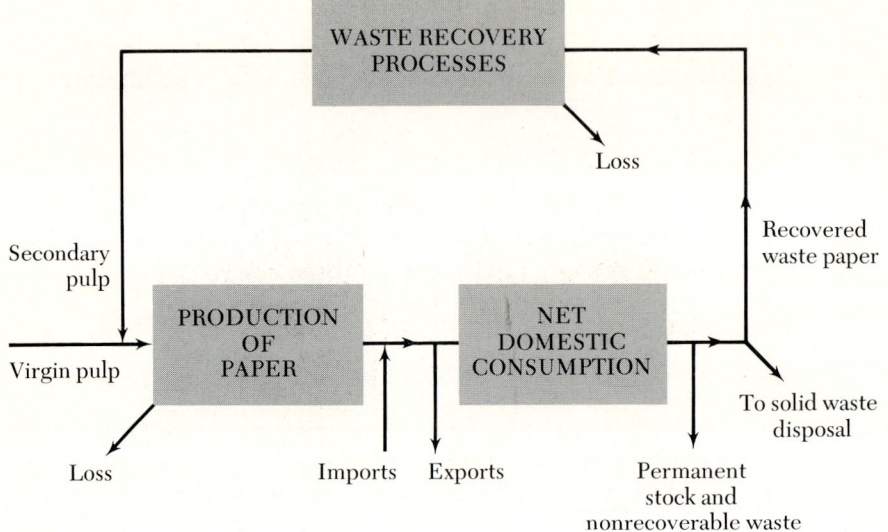

Figure 1-2
Paper production and consumption system.

SOURCE: Glassey, C. R., and V. K. Gupta, "A Linear Programming Analysis of Paper Recycling," *Management Science* (December 1974), p. 393.

cate that waste recovery methods can cut virgin pulp requirements almost in half. Even allowing for the cost of collecting and processing waste paper, the net savings throughout the economy would be substantial.

Satellite Communications Systems — An Investment Analysis

Satellites have become an increasingly important element in worldwide communications. In 1971, RCA Corporation decided to enter the satellite business for the private sector.* Because of new technology needs and the nature of the uncertainties involved, previous planning methods were found lacking in helping to establish an overall strategy for this new communications business. A variety of options were considered in three areas. The technical alternatives included type of satellite, kind of launch vehicle, and the equipment and location for

* Nigam, A. K., "Analysis for a Satellite Communications System," *Interfaces* (February 1975), pp. 37–47.

ground stations. Among the hardware choices were the following alternatives:

Satellite	Capacity	Weight
Spinner	12 transponders	1500 lb
Spinner	24 transponders	2800–3300 lb
Three-axis stabilized	12 transponders	1500 lb
Three-axis stabilized	24 transponders	2000 lb

Launch Vehicle	Synchronous Orbit Payload Capability
Thor Delta 2914	1550 lb
Thor Delta 3914	2000 lb
Atlas Centaur	4000 lb

Decisions also had to be made regarding the types of service provided (for example, television and several kinds of voice transmission). Finally, a number of financial alternatives were available.

A study team was formed to evaluate the various alternatives and to recommend the best strategy. Quantitative methods of various types from many different areas of application were brought into play. Alternatives were compared in terms of a variety of goals across operational and financial lines. A best strategy was found and eventually adopted by RCA management. One benefit of this effort was a greater level of cooperation between corporate staff analysts and line management.

Planning Political Campaign Strategies

A candidate running for high political office today must spend a great deal of money campaigning to win the election. One interesting application of quantitative methods was achieved during a U. S. Senatorial race. The problem was to select target precincts for various activities, such as registration drives, candidate appearances, mailings, and door-to-door canvassing. This was done by separating geographical segments of the electorate where a small gain could swing the district from those areas with such high loyalty that campaign efforts would be wasted. In doing this, voters were divided into more precise categories, as shown in Table 1-1, than were available on voter registration rolls. Applying

Table 1-1

PARTY IDENTIFICATION BY ELECTORAL LOYALTY OF PARTY REGISTRATION (SAMPLE RESULTS)

	ELECTORAL LOYALTY TO PARTY OF REGISTRATION		
Party Identification	Loyal Democrats	Defectors	Loyal Republicans
Strong Republicans	1%	5%	43%
Weak Republicans	1	8	36
Independents	25	51	21
Weak Democrats	33	33	—
Strong Democrats	40	6	—

SOURCE: Barkan, J. D. and J. E. Bruno, "Operations Research in Planning Political Campaign Strategies," *Operations Research* (September-October 1972), p. 928.

quantitative methods to identify the important characteristics of small geographical units throughout the state, the candidate was able to concentrate campaign expenditures on just a few of them.

1-2 MANAGEMENT SCIENCE AND OPERATIONS RESEARCH

This book is largely concerned with the specific techniques used in the above and similar situations. These quantitative methods fall into the broad category of *management science*, a field melding portions of business, economics, statistics, mathematics, and other disciplines into a pragmatic effort that focuses on helping managers make decisions. As an area of study, these quantitative methods are often identified as *operations research*. Regardless of the label used, the techniques of management science and operations research are concerned with selecting the best alternative for any decision where mathematics can be helpful. Many problem situations can be structured so that the possible choices can be ranked on a numerical scale. Common rankings are profit or cost. In such cases, an *optimal solution* is one that yields the maximum profit or minimum cost. Other yardsticks may apply in some applications, so that an optimal solution might be the most effective one in terms of time, reliability, or one of many kinds of measures. The particular quantitative method for finding the best answer is sometimes called a *mathematical optimization procedure*.

HISTORY OF QUANTITATIVE METHODS 1-3

We trace the beginnings of operations research to World War II. At that time the United States and Great Britain employed mathematicians and physicists to analyze military operations. The need for new thinking was created by the accelerating technological development of weapon systems and by the terrific pressures and strains of modern warfare. For example, radar and sonar were just coming into use, and long-range, high-altitude bombing required the efficient operation of sophisticated equipment. Operations-research groups were established to determine the most effective deployment and operation of these sophisticated systems. Notable success was achieved in a number of problems, especially in the vital area of antisubmarine warfare.

After the war, many of those same persons involved in military operations research retained their interest in analyzing decision making while in pursuit of peacetime endeavors. They developed new techniques directly applicable to business problems. Corporations formed operations-research groups, patterned after their military precursors. Schools of business and engineering began graduate programs in operations research, and the field evolved into a complete academic discipline, fostering further applications and theoretical developments. Concurrently, the wide-scale availability of digital computers, themselves being improved constantly, allowed the newly developed techniques to be applied quickly to large-scale optimization problems previously beyond human ability to solve.

PROCEDURES AND APPLICATIONS 1-4

As presently conceived, operations research is concerned with using available resources to find optimal courses of action. In its most general scope, the field is functional in nature, so that interdisciplinary teams (which sometimes include such disparate persons as historians, sociologists, and psychologists) are often used to attack decision problems. In this book we view operations research in terms of the tools historically associated with it, as they are applied to managerial decision making.

Operations-research methods have been cataloged by type of application and kind of procedure. One of the earliest applications, which predates modern operations research by several decades, is the analysis of *waiting lines* and gives rise to an area of mathematics referred to as *queuing theory.* It has been used in a variety of operational decisions and in helping to design facilities. Successful applications range from deciding the number of supermarket check stands to determining how large a parking lot should be. Quantitative methods have also been developed in *inventory control* and *equipment replacement.* Annual costs amounting to billions of dollars have been saved by businesses just by better management of inventories.

The most famous operations-research procedure is *linear programming,* a mathematical optimization tool that has been used in a tremendous variety of decision problems where scarce resources must be allocated. Linear programming is used today in oil refineries for determining how gasolines should be blended; similar applications apply throughout the chemical industry. It has been used also in determining how goods should be transported. Linear programming is even reputed to be largely responsible in establishing the successful tactics used by the Israeli Air Force during bombing missions in the 1967 Six-Day War. (Several times the usual number of sorties were flown by each aircraft, multiplying the effective number of available bombers.)

Related resource-allocation methods include the more general *mathematical programming,* which extends beyond linear programming to a much wider class of problem situations. For decisions that must be made at several successive points in time, such as budgetary investment decisions, *dynamic programming* is a procedure that might be used. Another important tool, mentioned earlier, is PERT; the Polaris program experience shows that it has proven useful for controlling large, long-run projects.

The list of operations-research procedures and applications is still growing.

Although the two fields are often confused and their borders are fuzzy, management science is somewhat broader in concept than operations research. Management science encompasses a variety of quantitative methods from older disciplines, especially economics, statistics, and industrial engineering, as well as from newer ones, such as cybernetics, systems analysis, organization theory, and computer and information sciences. It relies heavily on *statistical decision theory,* itself an amalgam of statistics, economics, and psychology. Also included in management science are the concepts of *game theory,* which is the province of mathematicians and economists. Both management science and operations research use elements of stochastic processes, areas of *probability theory;* important applications to business problems may be expressed as *Markov processes.* Another powerful tool is *Monte Carlo simulation,* used in the oil-tanker port facility study described earlier, which is essentially a form of statistical sampling usually carried out on a computer.

MODELS AND DECISION MAKING 1-5

Every decision situation involves *alternatives*. Quantitative methods are concerned with the selection of the alternative that best satisfies the decision-maker's goals. Identification of the possible alternatives and goals is an important task. Once the alternatives are identified, we begin quantitative analysis of a problem by comparing them in terms of how well they meet the objectives of the decision maker. Various yardsticks are used for comparison; the classical gauge in business is profit or cost, although we will encounter others as well.

This book is concerned with decision problems where quantitative methods apply. As a first step, we generally express the problem mathematically. Such a formulation is called a *mathematical model*. All such models consist of *variables* and constant terms sometimes referred to as *parameters*. The variables and parameters are usually tied together by algebraic expressions reflecting the decision-maker's goals and any special limitations on what kinds of alternatives might be considered.

As an example, consider a simple inventory problem where the goal is to determine the quantity of items to order periodically so that total operating cost is minimized. A simple mathematical model takes the form

Total annual cost = Ordering cost + Holding cost + Procurement cost

and the objective may be expressed as

$$\text{Minimize: Total annual cost} = \left(\frac{A}{Q}\right)k + hc\left(\frac{Q}{2}\right) + Ac$$

where Q is the order quantity and the single decision-variable for this particular problem. The variable Q can assume many different alternative values, such as 0, 1, 2, 3, . . ., 100, 101, ... The parameters are: A = annual number of items demanded; k = cost of placing an order; h = annual cost per dollar value for holding items in inventory; and c = unit cost of procuring an item. These parameters may be set at any levels that apply to a given situation, so that the same model applies regardless of the levels established for the parameters. This particular model is explained in further detail in Chapter 11.

Sometimes a mathematical model incorporates *constraints*, reflecting special limitations on the problem variables. Often these constraints may be expressed algebraically. For example, suppose that the storage facilities can accommodate only 300 units at a time. This constraint could be expressed as

$$Q \leq 300$$

which would then be an integral part of the model formulation. The above restriction disallows any order quantity such as $Q = 350$ units. In effect, this constraint separates the alternatives into two groups: *feasible solutions* (values for Q not exceeding 300 units) and *infeasible solutions* (values for Q greater than 300).

Quantitative methods are also concerned with solving the problem, that is, with finding the variable value meeting the requirements of the mathematical model. For the above inventory model, we must find the optimal value for the variable Q. In this illustration, the optimal solution may be found from

$$Q = \sqrt{\frac{2Ak}{hc}}$$

which was derived from a mathematical analysis. For example, suppose that each order costs $4 to place, that the annual demand is 1000 units, that it costs 20 cents per year for each dollar value of items held in inventory, and that they may be procured from the supplier for $1 each. Substituting the values $k = 4$, $A = 1000$, $h = .20$, and $c = 1$ into the above expression, we find the minimum-cost order quantity to be

$$Q = \sqrt{\frac{2(1000)4}{.20(1)}} = \sqrt{40{,}000} = 200 \text{ units}$$

The solution procedure used to solve the above problem is an example of an *algorithm*. Often algorithms are simple formulas, as above. But they may be very complex, requiring a series of involved steps. Sometimes a problem's mathematical model may exhibit certain undesirable features, or may be so complex or large that a solution arrived at by purely mathematical reasoning is impractical. It might be impossible in such cases to construct an algorithm that finds a truly optimal solution. In those cases it is still possible to apply quantitative methods to reach a reasonably good problem solution.

Throughout this book we consider two basic classes of models. The simplest, like the above inventory order-quantity model, involves no uncertainty. Such models have certain (known and fixed) constants thoughout their formulation and are referred to as *deterministic models*. More difficult to solve are problems with one or more uncertain quantities. In these cases, probability must be considered, and *stochastic models* may be used.

1-6 IMPORTANCE OF STUDYING MANAGEMENT SCIENCE

This book is not intended to create experts in quantitative methods. Rather, its goal is to familiarize readers with the more important quantitative method tools and to give them wide exposure to a variety of successful applications. No great skill in mathematics is demanded. Three main advantages accrue from exposure to quantitative methods. First, it should increase our confidence as decision makers, largely because we will see how vast and varied the problems are that have been solved through quantitative methods. Second, a study of quantitative methods creates problem-solving skills helpful when encountering an unsolved problem. These skills can be of tremendous help whether or not you are directly responsible for finding the answer. A final advantage pertains to our ability to cope with decisions, either as a manager or an employee, or in our personal lives.

Some knowledge of quantitative methods is especially crucial to the modern manager because of the nature of the decisions that must be made. Since an effective manager must make good choices, an exposure to quantitative methods devoted to making optimal decisions places the manager at a definite advantage. It will help him or her to know where, when, and how to use them. This doesn't mean that an effective manager must be mathematically skilled and has to personally develop models and solutions. Although a tremendous number of opportunities exist for the ordinary person to do exactly that, experts can be hired to take on the more demanding tasks. It is very important to know enough about this subject to guide those high-powered analysts (who too often stray into a mathematical "never-never land"). As a bare minimum, any exposure to quantitative methods will certainly help future managers to ask the right questions and to recognize when outside help might be useful.

Two

Probability Concepts

Probability plays a special role in all our lives, because we use it to measure uncertainty. We are continually faced with decisions leading to uncertain outcomes, and we rely on probability to help us make our choice. Think of the planned outdoor activities, such as picnics or boating, you cancelled because the chance of bad weather seemed too high. Remember those nights before examinations when you decided not to study some topics because they were not likely to be on the test. In business, probability is a pivotal factor in most significant decisions. A department store buyer will order heavily in a new style that is believed likely to sell well. A company will launch a new product when the chance of its success seems high enough to outweigh the possibility of losses due to failure. A new college graduate is hired when the probability of satisfactory performance is judged sufficiently high.

A probability is a numerical value that measures the uncertainty that a particular event will occur. The probability of an event ordinarily represents the *proportion of times under identical circumstances that the event can be expected to occur*. Such a long-run frequency of occurrence is referred to as *objective probability*. In tossing a fair coin, the probability is 1/2 for getting a head because this can be verified after tossing the coin many times and observing that heads appear about half the time. However, a probability value is often subjective, set solely on the basis of personal judgment. *Subjective probabilities* are used for events having no meaningful long-run frequency of occurrence. For example, an oil wildcatter may express his uncertainty about the presence of oil beneath a candidate drilling site in terms of a probability value such as 1/2. One attempt will be made at drilling on that site; since no two sites are identical, there are no other situations like the present one for which the frequency of oil strikes can be determined.

More than 300 years ago, several famous mathematicians initially studied probability scientifically in connection with gambling problems. The theory of probability has since evolved into one of the most elegant and useful branches of mathematics. Today devices ordinarily associated with gambling, such as dice and playing cards, are still useful in illustrating how to find probabilities.

FUNDAMENTAL CONCEPTS 2-1

The Event

Uncertain outcomes are called *events*. In the case of tomorrow's weather, the occurrence of precipitation would be one possible event. Even more specific events may be considered; for example, precipitation could be in the form of rain, hail, or snow. Or events may be quite detailed: 1.2 inches of rain may fall.

A preliminary step in finding an event's probability is to identify all possible outcomes of the uncertain situation. In cataloging possible outcomes or events, it is convenient to discuss them in groupings or *sets*. A complete listing of events is called the *sample space*. Exactly one and only one event on this master list will occur.

The sample space for tossing a coin contains just two events, head and tail, which may be conveniently expressed in set notation as

Sample space = {head, tail}

Head and tail are the *elements* of the sample space. Just one of these events must occur. We rule out such possibilities as the coin landing on its edge or perhaps being lost by specifying that these are not legitimate outcomes; that is, the toss is incomplete in such instances and must be repeated until either a head or a tail occurs.

As another illustration, consider the characteristics of a card drawn from a shuffled deck of 52 ordinary playing cards. Here we have

Sample space = {ace of spades, deuce of spades, . . ., king of diamonds}

It is convenient to represent the sample space pictorially as shown in Figure 2-1. Each point in the figure represents an element of the sample space, in this case the drawing of a particular card.

For many situations it is possible to construct more than one sample space. For instance, if we were interested only in the suit of the selected card, we might have used the set

{spade, heart, club, diamond}

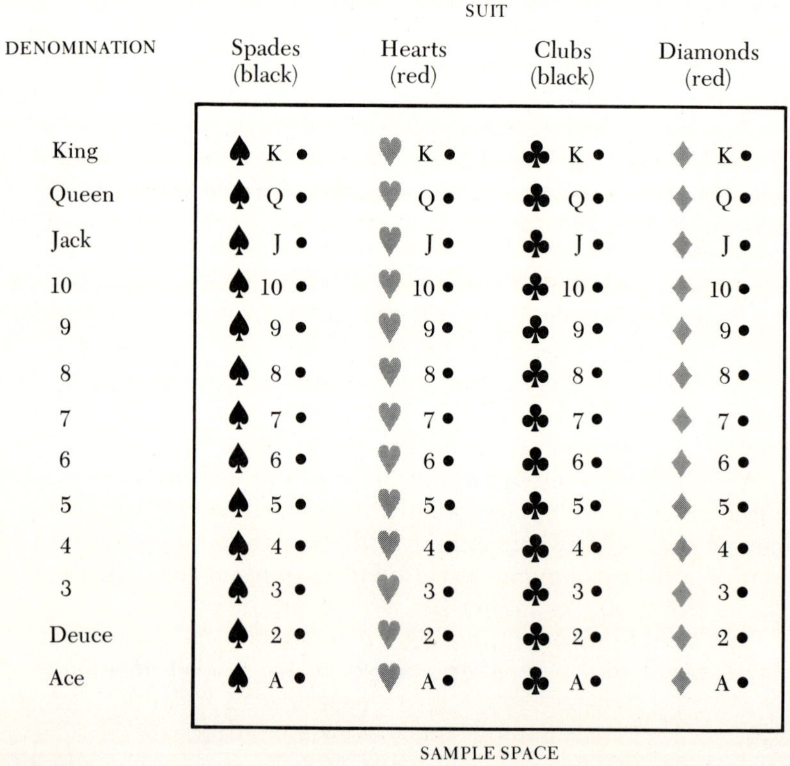

	SUIT			
DENOMINATION	Spades (black)	Hearts (red)	Clubs (black)	Diamonds (red)
King	♠ K •	♥ K •	♣ K •	♦ K •
Queen	♠ Q •	♥ Q •	♣ Q •	♦ Q •
Jack	♠ J •	♥ J •	♣ J •	♦ J •
10	♠ 10 •	♥ 10 •	♣ 10 •	♦ 10 •
9	♠ 9 •	♥ 9 •	♣ 9 •	♦ 9 •
8	♠ 8 •	♥ 8 •	♣ 8 •	♦ 8 •
7	♠ 7 •	♥ 7 •	♣ 7 •	♦ 7 •
6	♠ 6 •	♥ 6 •	♣ 6 •	♦ 6 •
5	♠ 5 •	♥ 5 •	♣ 5 •	♦ 5 •
4	♠ 4 •	♥ 4 •	♣ 4 •	♦ 4 •
3	♠ 3 •	♥ 3 •	♣ 3 •	♦ 3 •
Deuce	♠ 2 •	♥ 2 •	♣ 2 •	♦ 2 •
Ace	♠ A •	♥ A •	♣ A •	♦ A •

SAMPLE SPACE

Figure 2-1
Sample space describing the card selected randomly from a shuffled deck of 52 ordinary playing cards.

For our example, it is convenient to keep the sample space for drawing a card in the more detailed form, making it possible to describe any type of outcome in terms of the more detailed elements—the individual cards. For this reason, we refer to the elements of the sample space shown in Figure 2-1 as *elementary events*.

To extend these concepts, consider the outcomes when three different coins—a penny, a nickel, and a dime—are tossed so that each will show either a head or a tail. The sample space is shown in Figure 2-2. Notice that the events are ordered triples such as (H,T,H), which represents the outcome "head for the penny, tail for the nickel, head for the dime." Even though three coins are tossed, this may be viewed as a single random situation, and the outcome (H,T,H) is a single elementary event. The events (H,H,T) and (T,H,H) differ from (H,T,H), for in each case a different coin has the tail side showing. If we were describing the sample space for three tosses of the *same* coin, the elementary events would be represented in precisely the same manner—as eight ordered triples. In that case, the situation would have three *stages*, so that (H,T,H) would represent the event "head for the first toss, tail for the second toss, head for the third toss." (H,T,H) would be different from the event (T,H,H), because in each the tail appears on a different toss.

The elements in the sample space are the simplest outcomes or elementary events. We may, however, be interested in more complex outcomes. For example, consider the sample space for the outcome from tossing a six-sided die:

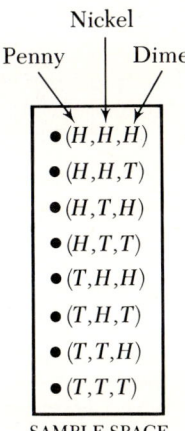

Figure 2-2
Sample space for the tossing of three coins.

$$\text{Sample space} = \{1, 2, 3, 4, 5, 6\}$$

where the elements represent the number of dots on the showing face. The outcome "an even-valued face" is a *composite event*, occurring whenever any one of the elementary events 2, 4, or 6 results. In keeping with our set representation, we denote the possible ways this event may occur by

$$\text{Even-valued face} = \{2, 4, 6\}$$

Such a partial listing is an *event set*. Notice that it is a *subset* of the sample space: all of its elements also belong to the sample space. An event set for an elementary event, such as the king of spades, will contain a single element:

$$\text{King of spades} = \{\text{king of spades}\}$$

For most uncertain situations many composite events are possible. Figure 2-3 shows a few that can be associated with drawing one card from a deck of 52 ordinary playing cards. Here, the respective event sets are pictured as groupings of those dots corresponding to the applicable elementary events.

Basic Definition of Probability

Classically, the probability of an event is the relative frequency that it occurs when the identical situation is repeated a large number of times. It is thus the ratio of the number of times the event occurs to the number of times the circumstances are faced. The notation used to express the probability of an event is the bracketed form shown below:

$$P[\text{event}] = \frac{\text{Number of times the event occurs}}{\text{Number of times the situation is repeated}}$$

The above expression indicates that a probability is an empirically derived value obtainable only after repeated experimentation. In practice, actual experimentation is unnecessary for a great many types of events. The probability of an event such as getting a head in a coin toss may be approximated by plausible reasoning with regard to the sort of outcomes that may be expected. Knowing that a coin has two sides, assuming that it is evenly balanced, and presuming that it is tossed

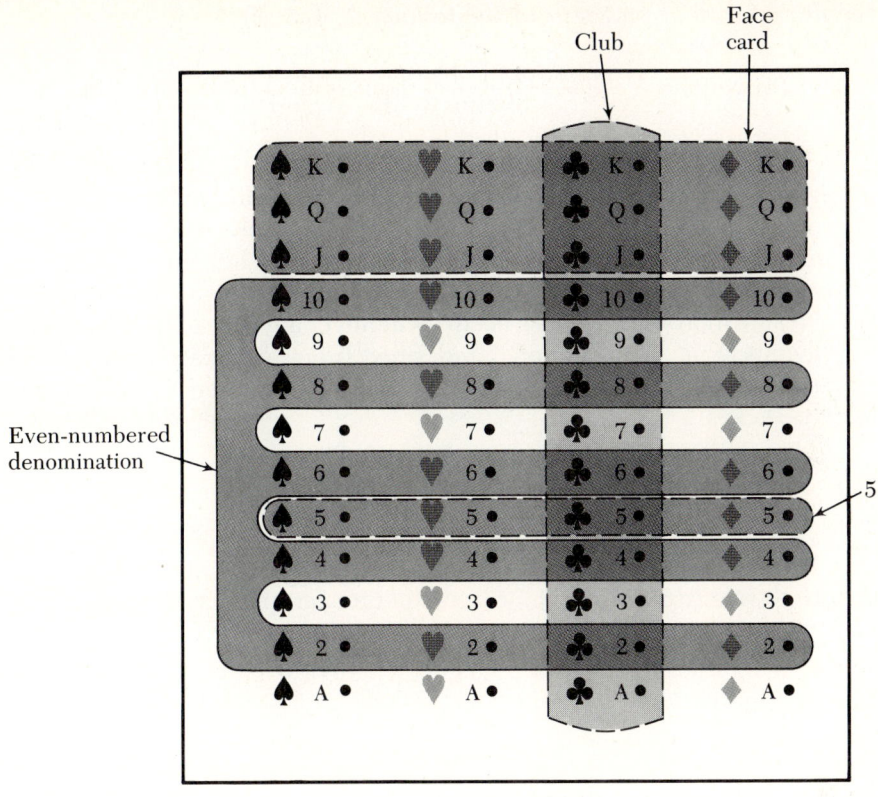

Figure 2-3
Composite events for drawing a card from a shuffled deck of 52 ordinary playing cards.

with no bias toward any particular face, we may reasonably expect a head to occur in about half of any number of tosses and, thus, that

$$P[\text{head}] = \frac{1}{2}$$

In a similar manner, we may reason that the probability of drawing the ace of spades from a shuffled deck of cards is 1/52, as there is no reason to suspect that certain of the 52 cards would be favored. Each card should appear with the same frequency in repeated shufflings. Each possible card is equally likely to turn up.

When all elementary events are equally likely, we may determine the probability of an event in the following manner:

$$P[\text{event}] = \frac{\text{Number of elementary events in its event set}}{\text{Number of equally likely elementary events}}$$

Thus, since there is a single way to achieve a head (that is, since its event set is of size 1, because head is an elementary event), the above expression tells us that $P[\text{head}] = 1/2$, where the 2 represents the size of the sample space for one coin toss. The same procedure applies for composite events. For example, since the event "even-valued face" resulting from a die toss occurs whenever any one of the 3 elementary events 2, 4, or 6 happens, and since there are exactly 6 possible elementary events, or showing faces, that are reasoned to be equally likely:

$$P[\text{even-valued face}] = \frac{3}{6} = \frac{1}{2}$$

We may use this definition to find the probabilities of the composite events shown in Figure 2-3 for drawing one card from a shuffled deck:

$$P[\text{club}] = \frac{13}{52} = \frac{1}{4}$$

$$P[\text{face card}] = \frac{12}{52} = \frac{3}{13}$$

$$P[5] = \frac{4}{52} = \frac{1}{13}$$

$$P[\text{even-numbered denomination}] = \frac{20}{52} = \frac{5}{13}$$

In each case, all cards (elementary events) are equally likely, and since there are 52 of them, the denominator in each case is 52 (the size of the sample space). The numerators are the sizes of the respective event sets (found by counting the number of elementary events—possible cards—in each set). The probabilities are therefore readily obtained by counting the number of elements in the respective sets and computing the ratios.

If the elementary events are not all equally likely, the basic definition of probability must be used: the probabilities here must be estimated by repeating the uncertain situation many times. For example, if a die is shaved until it is asymmetrical, it becomes more likely to roll some sides than others. Logical reasoning cannot tell us what the probabilities ought to be for the faces of a shaved die. Only after many tosses can they be estimated from the results actually obtained. Physicists could perhaps reason what the probabilities ought to be, but even they would be forced to rely on empirically derived constants, such as the force of gravity.

From our basic definition of probability, it may be noted that a probability will always be between 0 and 1, inclusively. This is because the numerator in the probability fraction can never be negative nor can it be larger than the denominator. Two important observations follow from the definition. First, an event that is certain to occur will have the same value in both the numerator and the denominator, for the same events will result from all experiments (that is, with frequency 1). Thus,

$$P[\text{certain event}] = 1$$

The event "the next President of the United States will be at least 35 years old" is a certain event and has a probability of 1, because the Constitution specifies a minimum age of 35. The event "food prices will rise, fall, or remain unchanged" likewise is certain and has a probability of 1.

At the other extreme, an impossible event's frequency ratio will always have a 0 in the numerator, for such an event will occur in none of the experiments. Thus,

$$P[\text{impossible event}] = 0$$

For example, the U.S. auto industry has limited capacity to produce cars and cannot make 50 million of them. This outcome for next year is impossible and we can state that

$$P[\text{50 million cars made}] = 0$$

EVENT RELATIONSHIPS 2-2

To ease our task in computing probabilities, it is often helpful to look at relationships between events. Several types of relationships are important. We first consider how events may be combined.

Some outcomes may be explained by the occurrence of more than one event. For example, getting at least two heads when tossing three coins is equivalent to obtaining exactly two heads or exactly three heads. Dealing yourself the ace of spades may be stated more precisely as getting a card that is both an ace and a spade. The basic event combinations important to probability are expressed in the logical connective sense of "or" and "and."

An outcome that occurs whenever any one of several more specific events happens is called the *union* of those events. This is expressed as

A or B

which represents the outcome when either event *A* occurs singly, event *B* occurs singly, or both *A* and *B* occur together. The importance of this relationship is that probability computations can often be simplified by first looking at *A* and *B* separately. Figure 2-4 illustrates how the union of the events "king," "queen," and "jack" provides the event "face card."

An outcome that arises only when both *A* and *B* occur is referred to as the *intersection* of events *A* and *B*. We express this as

A and B

We sometimes refer to *A and B* as a *joint event*. Figure 2-5 illustrates this concept for three coin tosses. There the event "all heads" is portrayed as the intersection of the events "dime is head" and "all coins show the same side."

Another type of event relationship involves properties exhibited by two or more events, whether or not they are combined. In developing laws of probability it is important to know if two events can occur jointly. We may also need to know if a collection of events is complete. Sometimes it is helpful to determine whether the occurrence of one event will make another more or less likely or if its effect is neutral.

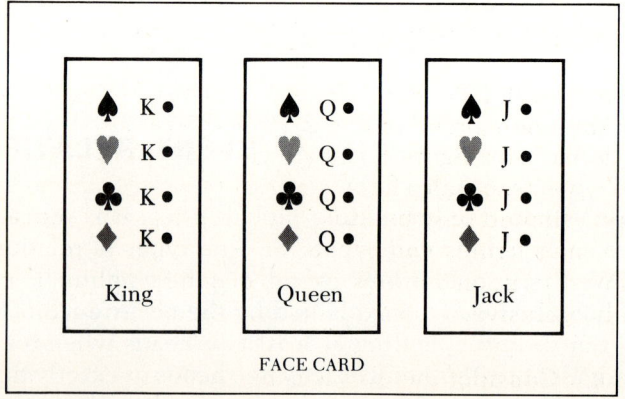

Face card = King *or* queen *or* jack

Figure 2-4
Portrayal of an event set comprising the union of three component events.

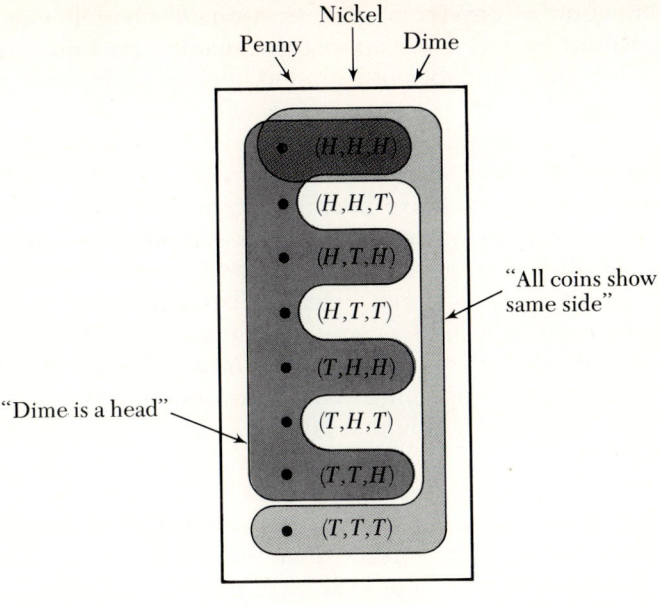

Figure 2-5
Portrayal of the intersection of two events.

Several events are *mutually exclusive* if the occurrence of any one event automatically precludes the occurrence of the others. Another way of saying this is that the joint occurrence of the events is itself an impossible event. The following examples illustrate this.

EXAMPLE Meat-T Pet Food Company is considering its advertising budget for a new brand of dog food. The event of primary interest is the dollar sales figure for next year's operation. The number of possible events, or sales figures, varies from a minimum of zero to a maximum limited only by Meat-T's plant capacity. Since only one of these sales figures will appear in the company's accounts at the end of next year, only one event can occur, and thus the events are mutually exclusive.

EXAMPLE Consider the events bankruptcy and profit that may result from the current year's operation of a firm. These events are *not* mutually exclusive, since it is possible for a business to make a profit and yet also be forced into bankruptcy by the claims of impatient creditors.

2-2 EVENT RELATIONSHIPS

A collection of events is *collectively exhaustive* if one of those events is bound to occur. For example, consider the following events describing the characteristics of a randomly chosen playing card:

red suit, black suit, spade

It is certain that one of these events will occur, since together they comprise all possibilities. Notice that the above events are not mutually exclusive, because the spades are also black cards. A collectively exhaustive grouping of events may be redundant.

Two events exhibit *independence* when the probability of one is unaffected by the occurrence of the other. As an example, consider two successive coin tosses. Assuming that one toss outcome has no influence on the other, we can conclude that getting a head on the second toss is independent of getting a head on the first, because the probability is 1/2 regardless of whether a head or tail is obtained first. But we cannot conclude that a randomly chosen person's education and income events are independent, since we know that education influences income levels; the probability of a high income is greater for a college graduate than for a high-school dropout.

2-3 THE ADDITION LAW

Several laws can ease our task of determining probabilities of complex events. They are used when it is convenient to find values for a complicated probability problem by breaking it into pieces that can be analyzed separately and then combined. The *addition law* serves this purpose for the combination form A or B. This law is predicated on the fact that, due to the logical nature of *or*, the number of ways in which the desired event may occur is the net sum of the ways in which the component events may occur. It states that

$$P[A \text{ or } B] = P[A] + P[B] - P[A \text{ and } B]$$

As an illustration, consider the event "ace *or* heart" describing the properties of a randomly chosen playing card. The addition law tells us that

$$P[\text{ace } or \text{ heart}] = P[\text{ace}] + P[\text{heart}] - P[\text{ace } and \text{ heart (ace of hearts)}]$$

$$= \frac{4}{52} + \frac{13}{52} - \frac{1}{52} = \frac{16}{52}$$

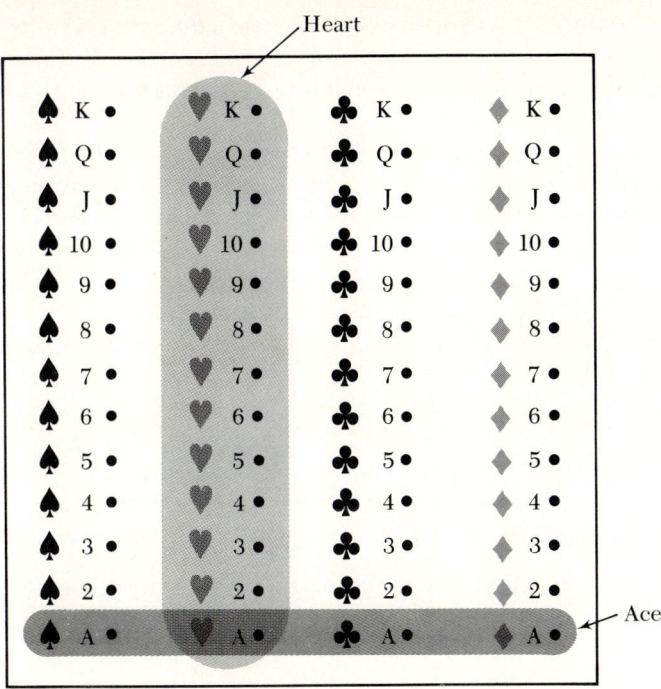

Figure 2-6
The union of events "heart" and "ace" is the entire shaded area.

Figure 2-6 shows that there are 16 elementary events in the sample space that are either ace or heart. Note that the event sets for ace and heart intersect at the ace of hearts. The sizes of the two sets are 4 and 13, respectively, and the ace of hearts is included in both. Therefore, the probability of ace of hearts must be subtracted from the sum of these probabilities in order to provide a result consistent with the basic probability definition. Since 16 cards in the deck are either ace or heart, the correct probability must be 16/52.

The Addition Law
for Mutually Exclusive Events

If A and B are mutually exclusive events, their joint occurrence is impossible and $P[A \text{ and } B] = 0$. This allows us to simplify the above law:

$$P[A \text{ or } B] = P[A] + P[B]$$

This simplified law applies only when the components are mutually exclusive events.

As an illustration, suppose that the number of customers arriving at a barbershop during the first 10 minutes it is open can be any value between zero and four, with the following probabilities:

Number of Persons	Probability
0	.1
1	.2
2	.3
3	.3
4	.1

The simplified addition law gives us the probability that two or three persons arrive

$$P[\text{two or three}] = P[\text{two}] + P[\text{three}]$$
$$= .3 + .3 = .6$$

since the two event components are mutually exclusive.

The addition law applies for any number of components. For example, the probability that at least one person arrives may be expressed as

$$P[\text{at least one}] = P[\text{one or two or three or four}]$$
$$= P[\text{one}] + P[\text{two}] + P[\text{three}] + P[\text{four}]$$
$$= .2 + .3 + .3 + .1 = .9$$

Events That Are Mutually Exclusive and Collectively Exhaustive

Many uncertain situations involve outcomes that are not only mutually exclusive, but also collectively exhaustive. We may use the following addition-law property *whenever the component events are both mutually exclusive and collectively exhaustive.*

$$P[A \text{ or } B \text{ or } C] = P[A] + P[B] + P[C] = 1$$

Although the above expression involves three events, in some situations more or fewer event components may be involved. These components sum to one because the two properties make the complex outcome *A or B or C* certain.

Returning to the barbershop example, we see that the five values representing the number of persons exhibit the properties of mutual exclusiveness and are also collectively exhaustive, since one of them is bound to occur (and five or more persons arriving is impossible for this particular barbershop). Thus,

$$P[\text{zero } or \text{ one } or \text{ two } or \text{ three } or \text{ four}]$$
$$= P[\text{zero}] + P[\text{one}] + P[\text{two}] + P[\text{three}] + P[\text{four}]$$
$$= .1 + .2 + .3 + .3 + .1 = 1$$

Viewed another way, we have

$$P[\text{zero } or \text{ at least one}] = P[\text{zero}] + P[\text{at least one}]$$
$$= .1 + .9 = 1$$

The outcomes "zero" and "at least one" have a very special relationship: they are complementary to each other. This feature can be very useful in finding probabilities.

Application to Complementary Events

The addition law can be very useful in dealing with *complementary events* (opposites). An event and its complement are collectively exhaustive, because either one or the other must occur. For example, a person chosen at random must be either male or female (which may be expressed as not male). Since these events are obviously mutually exclusive, for any event A with a complement that is not A, the addition law provides

$$P[A \text{ or not } A] = P[A] + P[\text{not } A] = 1$$

From this it follows that

$$P[A] = 1 - P[\text{not } A]$$

This principle can be useful when the event "not A" has a probability value that is easier to find than that of A itself.

Suppose that we wanted a faster way to compute the probability that at least one person would arrive at the barbershop. "At least one" means "some," and *the opposite of some is none*. The complementary event is therefore "zero" customers and, thus,

$$P[\text{at least one}] = 1 - P[\text{zero}]$$
$$= 1 - .1 = .9$$

2-4 CONDITIONAL PROBABILITY AND THE JOINT PROBABILITY TABLE

Conditional Probability

Some uncertain situations can result in the joint occurrence of two or more events. This may happen because several stages are involved, as in tossing a coin more than once, or it may be due to the simultaneous occurrence of several events, such as selecting a person at random who will be either male or female, married or single, and over or under 21 years old. In these cases, new questions arise about the relationship between separate events of a situation. In particular, do the conditions imposed by the occurrence of some events affect the probabilities of the other events? Thus, we may ask whether the probability of getting a head on the eleventh toss ought to be any different when the previous ten tosses had all been heads than if they had all been tails. Or we may question whether the probability that a female under 21 is married should be any different from the probability that an older woman is married. We refer to probability values obtained under the stipulation that some events have occurred or will occur as *conditional probabilities*.

Conditional probability may be illustrated for the outcome of drawing a card from a fully shuffled deck. Suppose another person draws the card without letting you see it, but in a brief glimpse you see that it must be a face card. The deck has only 12 face cards. What is the probability that the card is a king? Although the deck contains 4 kings, our answer is not 4/52, since our surreptitiously gained information indicates that some of the 52 cards are impossible. The sample space has been restricted to the 12 face cards, and the only remaining uncertainty is which of these 12 cards has been removed. In a sense, there is a new "sample space" having the 12 face cards as elementary events. Using basic concepts, we determine that the probability of a king is $4/12 = 1/3$. Thus, we may state that the conditional probability of a king *given* face card is

$$P[\text{king}|\text{face card}] = \frac{4}{12} = \frac{1}{3}$$

where the vertical bar stands for "given."

Joint Probability Table and Marginal Probabilities

To further illustrate how probabilities may be obtained when there are several simultaneous events, let us consider the following situation.

The credit applicants of a department store are classified in terms of home ownership and job tenure. Suppose that one application is chosen by lottery from 100, which are grouped into four categories in Table 2-1. The letters O, R, L, and M will be used to simplify the following discussion. Using the probability definition for equally likely events, we can determine the following probability values:

$$P[O \text{ and } L] = \frac{10}{100} = .10 \qquad P[R \text{ and } L] = \frac{40}{100} = .40$$

$$P[O \text{ and } M] = \frac{20}{100} = .20 \qquad P[R \text{ and } M] = \frac{30}{100} = .30$$

Table 2-1
NUMBER OF CREDIT APPLICANTS BY CATEGORY

	On Present Job 2 Years or Less (L)	On Present Job More than 2 Years (M)	Total
Owns Home (O)	10	20	30
Rents Home (R)	40	30	70
Total	50	50	100

The marginal totals may be used to determine the probabilities that the applicant has the respective attributes. For instance, the probability that the applicant owns a home is $P[O] = 30/100 = .30$. In a like manner, we can find $P[R]$, $P[L]$, and $P[M]$. Since only the numbers in the margins of Table 2-1 are needed to compute these probabilities, they are sometimes called *marginal probabilities*.

Construction of the *joint probability table* shown in Table 2-2 may be helpful. The joint events represented by each cell in a joint probability table are mutually exclusive. Thus, the marginal probabilities

Table 2-2

JOINT PROBABILITY TABLE FOR A RANDOMLY SELECTED APPLICATION

	On Present Job 2 Years or Less (L)	On Present Job More than 2 Years (M)	Marginal Probability
Owns Home (O)	.10	.20	.30
Rents Home (R)	.40	.30	.70
Marginal Probability	.50	.50	1.00

may also be found by applying the addition law for mutually exclusive events. For example, the event O has two mutually exclusive components: O and L, O and M. Hence, using the appropriate values from Table 2-2, we determine the probability that the applicant is a homeowner by

$$P[O] = P[(O \text{ and } L) \text{ or } (O \text{ and } M)]$$
$$= P[O \text{ and } L] + P[O \text{ and } M]$$
$$= .10 + .20 = .30$$

The probability values in the cells of the row (or column) corresponding to the event with the desired characteristic are added to obtain the other marginal probabilities using the addition law:

$$P[R] = P[R \text{ and } L] + P[R \text{ and } M] = .40 + .30 = .70$$
$$P[L] = P[O \text{ and } L] + P[R \text{ and } L] = .10 + .40 = .50$$
$$P[M] = P[O \text{ and } M] + P[R \text{ and } M] = .20 + .30 = .50$$

Computing Conditional Probability from Joint Probability

We are able to compute conditional probabilities by using the joint probability of two events, when it is known, and the probability for the given event. The following expression always applies for any two possible events:

$$P[A|B] = \frac{P[A \text{ and } B]}{P[B]}$$

Applying this property to the credit applicant illustration, we may compute the conditional probability that the applicant owns a home given job tenure of more than two years:

$$P[O|M] = \frac{P[O \text{ and } M]}{P[M]} = \frac{.20}{.50} = .40$$

Notice that the same result could have been obtained from the data in Table 2-1 by calculating the proportion of applicants on their present job more than 2 years who are also homeowners:

$$\frac{20}{20+30} = \frac{20}{50} = .40$$

Thus, we see *the conditional probability of A given B is the proportion of times that A occurs out of all the times B occurs.* This explains why we divide the joint probability by the probability of the given event to obtain $P[A|B]$.

Figure 2-7 shows how the same result could be obtained directly from a diagram of the sample space by noticing that the condition of being on the job more than 2 years limits the outcomes to a new, smaller sample space of size 50. The probability of obtaining a homeowner is now obtained by observing that 20 events out of 50 provide this outcome.

As further illustrations of conditional probability, we may use the preceding property to recompute the probability of getting a king given a face card:

$$P[\text{king}|\text{face}] = \frac{P[\text{king and face}]}{P[\text{face}]} = \frac{4/52}{12/52} = \frac{4}{12} = \frac{1}{3}$$

Notice that in both illustrations the conditional probabilities differ from the corresponding probabilities when there are no stipulations, which we call *unconditional probabilities*. We have

$$P[\text{king}|\text{face}] = \frac{1}{3} \neq \frac{1}{13} = P[\text{king}]$$

$$P[O|M] = .40 \neq .30 = P[O]$$

The unconditional and conditional probabilities do not always differ, but the comparative values may be used to establish independence, which exists when the probability of one event is unaffected by the occurrence of the other. In effect, *events are independent only when their conditional probabilities equal their respective unconditional probabilities.* Here we see that king and face are not independent; likewise O and M are dependent events.

2-4 CONDITIONAL PROBABILITY AND THE JOINT PROBABILITY TABLE

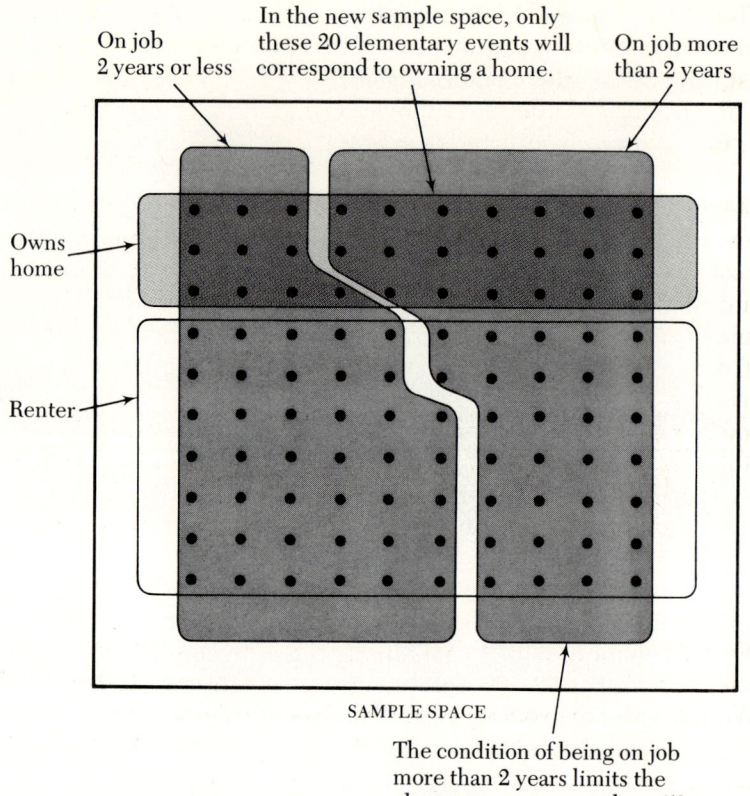

P [owns home | on present job more than 2 years] $= \frac{20}{50} = .40$

Figure 2-7
Portrayal of the concept of conditional probability.

Consider another example from playing cards. For a randomly selected card the events "ace" and "heart" are independent. To verify this, we compute

$$P[\text{ace}] = \frac{4}{52} = \frac{1}{13}$$

which is equal to

$$P[\text{ace}|\text{heart}] = \frac{1}{13}$$

The principles underlying conditional probability are extensively used in our daily decision making; for example, when the sky is heavily overcast, enhancing the chance of rain, you carry an umbrella. Conditional probability is often used in decision making. Insurance companies, for example, use it to determine their rates.

EXAMPLE Life insurance companies charge a sizable premium for covering the lives of steeplejacks, miners, divers, and others with hazardous occupations. The mortality tables on which insurance rates are based indicate that such persons have a shorter life expectancy than the population as a whole; in essence, their probability of dying in any year is higher. Additional information about an insurance applicant's occupation affects this probability; the likelihood of the event "untimely death" is affected by the occurrence of the event "applicant is a steeplejack."

THE MULTIPLICATION LAW 2-5

We have seen how the addition law may be used to find the probability for a complex event joining several component events with the "or." We now introduce the *multiplication law*, which is used to find the probability of the joint occurrence or intersection of two or more events. The multiplication law is especially necessary when the component events have probability values that can readily be found but the joint probability cannot be directly obtained through the basic probability definitions. For instance, the necessary information may not be summarized conveniently in a joint probability table, as it was in the credit applicant illustration presented earlier.

The multiplication law indicates that a joint probability may be obtained from the product of the individual probabilities

$$P[A \text{ and } B] = P[A] \times P[B|A]$$

This law is an immediate consequence of the property of conditional probability. (The above is obtained by multiplying both sides of the expression on page 30 by the given event probability, where the roles of A and B are interchanged.)

Continuing with the credit applicant illustration, we may apply the multiplication law. Recall that $P[O|M] = .40$ and also that $P[M] = .50$. Multiplying these values, we obtain

$$P[O \text{ and } M] = P[M] \times P[O|M] = .50(.40) = .20$$

This is the same joint probability value found earlier.

When the joint probabilities are already known, the multiplication law is not needed. But in some situations only conditional and marginal probabilities are available, and the joint probabilities may be obtained only by using the multiplication law.

EXAMPLE A highway commissioner has found that half of all fatal automobile accidents in the state may be blamed on drunken drivers. Only 4 in 1000 reported accidents have proved fatal, and 10 percent of all accidents in the state are attributable to drunken drivers. The commissioner wishes to summarize this information in a joint probability table relating to future accidents. Assuming that the present pattern prevails, we find that the joint probability that a reported accident happens to be fatal is

$$P[F] = 4/1000 = .004$$

whereas the probability that a drunken driver causes the accident (fatal or not) is

$$P[D] = .10$$

and the conditional probability that a drunken driver causes the accident given that it is fatal is

$$P[D|F] = .50$$

Table 2-3 is the joint probability table for cause and kind of accident events. Only the numbers shown in regular type are directly provided by the data given above. The boldface probability values were obtained in the following manner.

Table 2-3

JOINT PROBABILITY TABLE FOR CAUSE AND KIND OF AUTOMOBILE ACCIDENT

	Fatal (F)	*Nonfatal* (not F)	*Marginal Probability*
Drunken Driver (D)	.002	.098	.100
Other Cause (O)	.002	.898	.900
Marginal Probability	.004	.996	1.000

The multiplication law provides the joint probability that a fatal accident is caused by a drunken driver:

$$P[F \text{ and } D] = P[F] \times P[D|F]$$
$$= .004(.50) = .002$$

The marginal probabilities for the causes and the types of accidents must sum, respectively, to 1. It therefore follows that

$$P[O] = 1 - P[D] = 1 - .100 = .900$$
$$P[\text{not } F] = 1 - P[F] = 1 - .004 = .996$$

The remaining joint probabilities can be found by using the fact that the joint probabilities in each row and column must sum to the respective marginal probability values. Thus, subtracting the known joint probability value from the marginal probability, we find the unknown joint probability values:

$$P[\text{not } F \text{ and } D] = P[D] - P[F \text{ and } D] = .100 - .002 = .098$$
$$P[F \text{ and } O] = P[F] - P[F \text{ and } D] = .004 - .002 = .002$$
$$P[\text{not } F \text{ and } O] = P[O] - P[F \text{ and } O] = .900 - .002 = .898$$

Joint Probabilities for More Than Two Events

When we wish to find the joint probability of more than two events, the multiplication law may be extended.

Suppose that we have a box containing five marbles, each of a different color: yellow, red, green, orange, and purple. Three marbles are selected from the box at random, one at a time, so that all marbles remaining in the box have an equal chance of being selected at each drawing. Once drawn, a marble is not replaced. The following events are designated:

A = First marble is yellow
B = Second marble is green
C = Third marble is orange

It is easy to establish that $P[A] = 1/5$. If a yellow marble is selected, then only four remain, and one of these is green. Thus, the conditional probability that the second marble will be green given that the first is yellow is $P[B|A] = 1/4$. Likewise, should the yellow and green marbles be selected, then the third marble is equally likely to be one of the three colors red, orange, or purple, so that $P[C|A \text{ and } B] = 1/3$. The joint probability for A, B, and C may be determined by substituting these values into

$$P[A \text{ and } B \text{ and } C] = P[A] \times P[B|A] \times P[C|A \text{ and } B]$$

Thus,

$$P[A \text{ and } B \text{ and } C] = \frac{1}{5} \times \frac{1}{4} \times \frac{1}{3} = \frac{1}{60}$$

For a large number of component events, the same approach applies.

The Probability Tree Diagram

A very convenient arrangement for applying the multiplication law is provided by a *probability tree diagram*. To illustrate this concept, we consider a situation often encountered in quality control sampling. Suppose that a shipment of 100 parts received from a supplier contains exactly 5 defectives. Ordinarily, the inspector doesn't know this fact and, based on a sample of three items selected randomly, must decide whether to accept or to reject the entire shipment. We wish to consider various probabilities for the content of the sample.

Figure 2-8 shows the probability tree diagram for this situation. Here, each successive sample observation outcome is represented by a branch, and the probability of an outcome is indicated alongside its branch. Since there are two complementary events possible for each item observed, there are two branches for each item—one for defective and one for good. There is a different branching point or *fork* for each observation. Two forks are thus required for the second item—a different one for each possible attribute of the first observation. Because four distinct outcomes are possible for the quality of the earlier items, four forks are needed for the third observation. To distinguish the outcomes for each item, we use the subscripts 1, 2, and 3. For instance, D_1 means that the first item will be defective; G_2 means that the second will be good. Altogether there are eight paths through the tree, each representing different sample outcomes. Each path leads to a different elementary event for this random experiment, so that the eight end positions provide the sample space for the final sample results.

The results of each selection are *not independent,* because after one item is inspected it is not replaced back with the original ones, which makes the composition of the remainder of the shipment change each time. The proportion of defective items remaining increases or de-

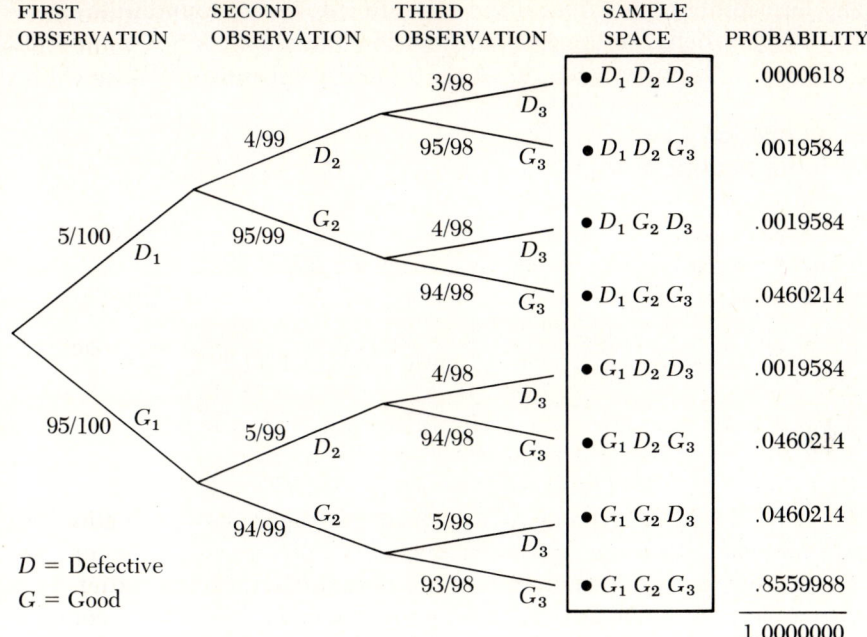

Figure 2-8
Probability tree diagram for selecting a quality control sample of three items without replacement from a population of size 100.

creases, depending on the quality of the prior selection. Thus, if the first item proves defective, so that D_1 occurs, there are only four defectives left out of 99 remaining items, and the probability that the second item is defective D_2 is 4/99. But if G_1 is the first event, then D_2 has a probability of 5/99, because any one of five remaining defective items could be chosen. These values are *conditional probabilities,* because D_2 has a different chance of occurring in each case.

The probabilities for each elementary event, each a *joint probability* for three successive events, may be found by multiplying the probability values for the branches on the path leading to that particular outcome. For instance, the multiplication law may be applied to find the probability that all three items are defective:

$$P[D_1 \text{ and } D_2 \text{ and } D_3] = P[D_1] \times P[D_2|D_1] \times P[D_3|D_1 \text{ and } D_2]$$

$$= \left(\frac{5}{100}\right)\left(\frac{4}{99}\right)\left(\frac{3}{98}\right)$$

$$= .0000618$$

2-5   THE MULTIPLICATION LAW

The joint probabilities for all the other outcomes are found in the same way and are listed in the final column in Figure 2-8.

Multiplication Law for Independent Events

Recall that two events are independent if the probability of one event is unaffected by the occurrence of the other. This means that the conditional and unconditional probabilities are identical. Thus,

$$P[A|B] = P[A] \quad \text{and} \quad P[B|A] = P[B]$$

The multiplication law is then simplified and takes the form

$$P[A \text{ and } B] = P[A] \times P[B]$$

only when A and B are independent events.

Earlier we established for a randomly selected playing card that the events "ace" and "heart" are independent events. Thus,

$$P[\text{ace and heart}] = P[\text{ace}] \times P[\text{heart}]$$
$$= \frac{1}{13} \times \frac{1}{4} = \frac{1}{52}$$

This concept extends to any number of independent events. For example, suppose that just as many men as women read a particular magazine, that married readers are just as predominant among males as females, and that proportionately there are just as many Democrats in each sex and marital status combination. For a randomly selected reader, his or her sex, marital status, and political affiliation characteristics yield combinations of three independent events. Thus, to compute the probability of selecting a married man who is a Democrat, we may use the multiplication law for independent events:

$$P[\text{man and married and Democrat}]$$
$$= P[\text{man}] \times P[\text{married}] \times P[\text{Democrat}]$$

To further illustrate this concept, let us return to the preceding quality control situation. Instead of the user, consider the analogous problem faced by the supplier of the parts, who produces them continuously. The production inspector wishes to use sample data to determine whether adjustments are required in plant machinery. Suppose that defectives actually occur 5 percent of the time (but the inspector does not know this). When three parts are randomly taken at separate times from the production line, the probability tree in Figure 2-9 applies. Here the successive events G_1 (first part is good), D_2 (second is defective), D_3, etc., for any tree path are independent because errors in such continuous processes are generally erratic. Therefore, the characteristics of an earlier item will not influence the incidence of defectives in future parts. The probability is thus .05 for a defective part, regardless of the sequence in which it is chosen, and it is .95 for a good one. The conditional probabilities equal the unconditional ones. The probability that all sample parts are defective is thus

$$P[D_1 \text{ and } D_2 \text{ and } D_3] = P[D_1] \times P[D_2] \times P[D_3]$$
$$= (.05)(.05)(.05)$$
$$= (.05)^3 = .000125$$

Compare the tree in Figure 2-9 with the one in Figure 2-8. These

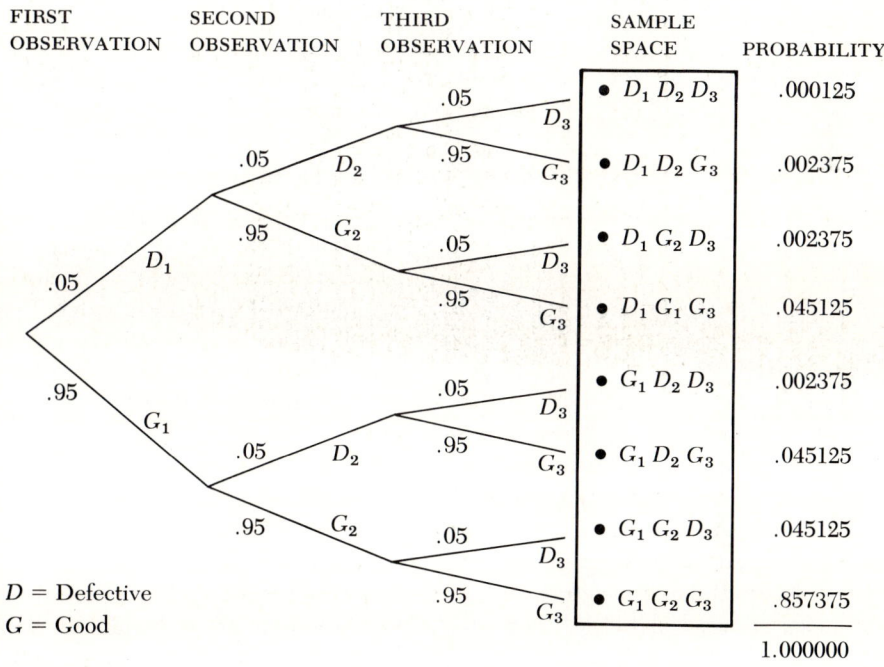

Figure 2-9
Probability tree diagram for selecting a quality control sample of three items from a production process.

2-5 THE MULTIPLICATION LAW

two situations illustrate some important probability concepts. The earlier tree pertains to sampling *without replacement* from a small population of parts; there successive events are dependent. The second tree applies to the same situation for a population of unlimited size; a probability tree identical to Figure 2-9 applies as well when sampling *with replacement* from a small population. Independence between successive events applies in either case. The latter two situations are analogous to a series of coin tosses, and they give rise to the very important binomial probability distribution discussed in Chapter 3.

2-6 COMMON ERRORS IN APPLYING THE CONCEPTS OF PROBABILITY

Some of the most prevalent errors made in finding probabilities are due to the improper use of the laws of probability. A few common mistakes are listed here:

(1) Using the addition law to find the probability of the union of several events when they are not mutually exclusive, without correcting for the double counting of possible occurrences.

For example, a casualty-insurance underwriter might establish that the probabilities of a city experiencing a natural disaster in the next decade are:

tornado	.5
flood	.3
earthquake	.4

We cannot say that the probability of suffering one of these acts is $.5 + .3 + .4 = 1.2$. Clearly, two or more of these disasters may occur over a ten-year period, and some may occur more than once.

(2) Using the addition law when the multiplication law should be used, and conversely. Remember that *or* signifies addition and that *and* signifies multiplication.

For example, the probability of drawing a red face card is the same as that for the event "red *and* face." Recall that $P[\text{red}] = 26/52$ and $P[\text{face}] = 12/52$. Adding these values we get 38/52, which is a meaningless result. Since red and face are independent events:

$$P[\text{red } and \text{ face}] = \frac{26}{52} \times \frac{12}{52} = \frac{6}{52}$$

(3) Using the multiplication law for independent component events when the events are dependent.

This error occurs, for example, when replacement is mistakenly assumed in calculating the probability of obtaining a particular sample result. As we have seen removal of an item from a group changes the group's composition and, hence, the probabilities that future selections will be of a certain type.

(4) Improperly identifying the complement of an event. For example, *the complement of none is some* (which may be expressed as "one or more" or as "at least one").

The following example, which actually happened, dramatically illustrates how ludicrous results may be obtained through the incorrect application of probability laws.*

EXAMPLE An elderly woman was mugged in the suburb of a large city. A couple was convicted of the crime; the evidence on which the prosecution rested its case was largely circumstantial. Probability was used to demonstrate that an extremely low probability of one twelve-millionth existed that any specific couple could have committed the crime. The probability value was determined by using the multiplication law for independent events. The events — the characteristics ascribed by witnesses to the couple who actually did the deed — are listed below, along with the assumed probabilities:

Characteristic Event	Assumed Probability
Drives yellow car	1/10
Interracial couple	1/1000
Blonde girl	1/4
Girl wears hair in ponytail	1/10
Man bearded	1/10
Man black	1/3

By multiplying the above values, the probability was obtained that any specific couple, chosen at random from the city's population, had all six characteristics:

$$\frac{1}{10} \times \frac{1}{1000} \times \frac{1}{4} \times \frac{1}{10} \times \frac{1}{10} \times \frac{1}{3} = \frac{1}{12,000,000}$$

* For a detailed discussion, see "Trial by Mathematics," *Time* (April 26, 1968), p. 41.

Since the defendants had all six characteristics and the jury was mystified by the overwhelming strength of the probability argument, they were convicted.

The Supreme Court of the state heard the appeal of one of the defendants. The defense attorneys, after obtaining some good advice on probability theory, attacked the prosecution's analysis on two points: (1) the rather dubiously assumed event probability values, and (2) the invalid assumption of independence implicit in using the multiplication law in the above manner (for example, the proportion of black men having beards may have been greater than the proportion of the population as a whole having beards; also, "interracial couple" and "black man" are definitely not independent events). The judge accepted the arguments of the defense and noted that the trial evidence, even allowing for its incorrect assumptions, was misleading on another score—namely, a high probability that the defendants were the only such couple should really have been determined to demonstrate a strong case. Using the prosecution's original figures and its assumptions of independence, one can demonstrate that the probability is large that at least one other couple in the area had the same characteristics.

2-7 REVISING PROBABILITIES USING BAYES' THEOREM

In this section, we will introduce a procedure whereby probabilities can be revised when new information pertaining to a random experiment is obtained. The notion of revising probabilities is a familiar one, for all of us—even those with no previous experience in calculating probabilities—have lived in an environment ruled by the whims of chance and have made informal probability judgments. We have also intuitively revised these probabilities on observing certain facts and have changed our actions accordingly. For example, think how many times you have left home in the morning with no raincoat, only to look up and notice a menacing cloud cover which sends you back for some protection in case it rains. On first charging outdoors, you behaved in a manner consistent with your judgment that the probability of rain was small. But the presence of clouds caused you to revise this probability significantly upward.

Our concern for revising probabilities arises from a need to make better use of experimental information. We begin here by establishing a fundamental principle that follows immediately from the laws of probability developed earlier in this chapter. This is referred to as *Bayes'*

Theorem, after the Reverend Thomas Bayes, who proposed in the eighteenth century that probabilities be revised in accordance with empirical findings.

Such empirical findings may result from very elaborate experiments; in science, for example, many man-years of effort and much expensive equipment are devoted to such activities as studying physical laws by observing solar eclipses. Empirical findings may also arise from a very minor effort, such as asking a person questions in order to become better acquainted. No matter what their scope, they have one feature in common: *experimental results provide information.* This information may serve to realign uncertainty. Data obtained by observing a solar eclipse can lend support to hypotheses regarding the effect of the sun's gravity on stellar light rays. A person's responses to your questions may help you decide whether or not it is worthwhile to become friends. Scientists can become more certain that the sun's gravity has an effect on light rays, and their observations can lead to finer choices for further experiments. The answers to your questions can tell you that an ugly person is really beautiful or that a physically attractive person is vain and selfish.

Most information is not conclusive. Any empirical test can camouflage the truth. For instance, some potentially good students will do badly on college entrance examinations and some poor students will score highly. A good example of how such information may be unreliable is illustrated by the oil wildcatter's seismic test. Not completely reliable, a seismic survey can deny the presence of oil in a field already producing it and can confirm the presence of oil under a site already proved dry. Still, such imperfect findings can be valuable. An unfavorable test result can increase the chance of rejecting a poor prospect—college applicant or drilling lease—or a favorable result can enhance the likelihood of selecting a good one.

The information obtained will affect the probabilities of those events that determine the consequences of each act. We can revise the probabilities of these events upward or downward, depending upon the evidence obtained. Thus, the geologist increases the probability that she will find oil if she obtains a favorable seismic survey analysis, and she decreases the probability if she obtains an unfavorable survey.

Bayes' Theorem

Consider a situation in which two uncertain events E and not E are possible. Suppose that $P[E]$ and $P[\text{not } E]$ have been obtained. These probabilities are referred to as *prior probabilities,* because they represent the chances of the events *before* the results from the empirical investigation are obtained. The investigation itself may have several possible outcomes, each statistically dependent on E. For any particular result, which we will denote by R, the conditional probabilities $P[R|E]$, $P[R|\text{not }E]$ are often available. The result itself serves to revise the probabilities for E and not E upward or downward. The resulting values are called *posterior probabilities*, because they apply *after* the factual result has been learned.

The posterior probability values are actually conditional probabilities of the form $P[E|R]$, $P[\text{not }E|R]$ that can be found according to *Bayes' Theorem*. This theorem states that the posterior probability of event E for a particular result R of an empirical investigation can be found from

$$P[E|R] = \frac{P[E]P[R|E]}{P[E]P[R|E] + P[\text{not }E]P[R|\text{not }E]}$$

The principle underlying Bayes' Theorem can best be explained in terms of the following example.

EXAMPLE A box contains four fair dice and one crooked die with a leaded weight that makes the six-face appear on two-thirds of all tosses. You are asked to select one die at random and toss it. If the crooked die is indistinguishable from the fair dice and the result of your toss is a six-face, what is the probability that you have tossed the crooked die?

The events in question are

$$C = \text{crooked die}$$
$$\text{not }C = \text{fair die}$$

The empirical investigation here is the toss itself, so

$$R = \text{six-face}$$

Since 1 out of 5 dice is crooked, the prior probabilities for the type of die tossed are

$$P[C] = 1/5$$
$$P[\text{not }C] = 4/5$$

Due to the weight inside, we are told that when the crooked die is tossed

$$P[R|C] = 2/3$$

If a fair die is tossed, we know that one of the equally likely sides is a six-face, so that

$$P[R|\text{not } C] = 1/6$$

The posterior probability that the die you tossed is crooked is therefore

$$P[C|R] = \frac{P[C]P[R|C]}{P[C]P[R|C] + P[\text{not } C]P[R|\text{not } C]}$$

$$= \frac{(1/5)(2/3)}{(1/5)(2/3) + (4/5)(1/6)}$$

$$= \frac{2/15}{4/15} = 1/2$$

Here, we see that the probability of tossing a crooked die must be revised upward from the prior value of 1/5, which applies when there is no information, to 1/2 after we know that the toss resulted in a six-face.

Posterior Probability as a Conditional Probability

Although it has a special interpretation, a posterior probability is merely a conditional probability when some relevant result is given, and it can be found in the same manner:

$$\begin{array}{c}\text{Posterior}\\\text{probability}\\\text{of event}\end{array} = P[\text{event}|\text{result}] = \frac{P[\text{event } and \text{ result}]}{P[\text{result}]}$$

A straightforward procedure for calculating an event's posterior probability is first to find the joint probability that the event will occur with the given result and then divide by the probability of that result. This is exactly what Bayes' Theorem accomplishes. The numerator is the joint probability found by using the multiplication law. The denominator is the probability of obtaining the particular empirical result and is basically the sum of all those joint probabilities for potential outcomes where that result might occur. In practice, Bayes' Theorem can be cumbersome to use when the data are given in such a way that the posterior probabilities may be found more directly.

For example, if a statistics class contains just as many men as women, then the prior probability that an examination paper chosen at random will belong to a man (*M*) would be 1/2. Now suppose that the exams have been graded and 20 percent of the papers received a mark of "C or better" (*C*) *and* were written by men; a total of 60 percent of the exams were scored "C or better." If a randomly selected test sheet was graded "C," we have sufficient information to calculate the posterior probability that it was written by a man:

$$P[M|C] = \frac{P[M \text{ and } C]}{P[C]} = \frac{.20}{.60} = \frac{1}{3}$$

Here, the information regarding the paper's grade causes us to revise downward the probability that it belongs to a man.

Typically, the probability values needed to make a simple calculation such as this are not immediately available. When we use evidence or empirical results to revise probabilities, our knowledge of the various events involved is usually structured so that some preliminary work is necessary to obtain the needed probability values. To accomplish this, it may help to construct a joint probability table first.

EXAMPLE A noted lawyer specializing in defending his corporate clients in personal-injury suits thinks that getting a sympathetic jury is half the battle. In large measure, he can winnow a jury panel down to a largely sympathetic group by preemptory challenges. Since a potential juror's leaning in a particular case remains largely concealed during the selection interview, superficial characteristics must be relied on in accepting or rejecting jury candidates. The lawyer has found that mature and stable persons, those who "made it on their own," are the most likely to be sympathetic to the defendant, while young people tend to have a "social worker attitude" which makes them likely to favor the plaintiff. From post-trial talks with jurors over the years, the lawyer has managed to identify their attitudes toward his clients. He has found that 65 percent of the sympathetic jurors have been older persons. A special bar study in his county has shown that only 30 percent of jury panel members are sympathetic to the defendant in a personal-injury suit.

In a negligence suit resulting from an elevator accident, all but one juror has been chosen, and both lawyers have no more challenges left. Of the available jurors, six are younger and four are older. Depending on alphabetical sequence, one of these ten will be the last juror.

Table 2-4 is a joint probability table constructed regarding this last juror. The probability values obtained directly from the data provided above are shown in lightface type. The boldface numbers were obtained from these data by first noting that

$$P[U] = 1 - P[S] = .70$$

The fact that we have been told the following conditional probability:

$$P[O|S] = .65$$

enables us to find the joint probability of obtaining an older, more sympathetic juror:

$$P[O \text{ and } S] = P[O|S]P[S] = .65(.30) = .195$$

The remaining values follow from this one and from the fact that the joint probabilities must sum to the respective marginal values.

Table 2-4
JOINT PROBABILITY TABLE USED TO ILLUSTRATE POSTERIOR PROBABILITY CALCULATION

	Older (O)	Younger (Y)	Marginal Probability
Sympathetic (S)	.195	.105	.300
Unsympathetic (U)	.205	.495	.700
Marginal Probability	.400	.600	1.000

The prior probability that a sympathetic juror will be obtained is only .30 (which is also the marginal probability for this event). Suppose that an older juror is chosen. The posterior probability that the juror will also be sympathetic is

$$P[S|O] = \frac{P[O \text{ and } S]}{P[O]} = \frac{.195}{.40} = .4875$$

The above example shows how we can calculate posterior probabilities by relying on basic concepts, instead of using the complicated expression of Bayes' Theorem. Nevertheless, as Table 2-4 shows, essentially the same steps are required in either case.

2-8 PROBABILITIES OBTAINED FROM HISTORY

Historical experience may be a convenient starting point for assigning probabilities. All that is necessary to calculate the historical frequency of an event is knowledge of how many times it has occurred in the past and the number of opportunities when it could have occurred. This is how fire insurance underwriters get their probabilities for determining expected claim sizes used to establish policy charges. With tens of thousands of buildings involved, *the event frequencies themselves define the probabilities,* because in the traditional sense probability fundamentally expresses long-run frequency of occurrence.

Difficulties do arise in using historical frequencies as probabilities. One is the limited extent of history—not enough data may be available for anything but a rather crude frequency estimate. Unless the number of similar past circumstances is large, statistical estimates of event frequencies may be unreliable. Past history may be suitable for setting fire insurance rates. But past frequency cannot be wholly adequate, indeed is unavailable, for finding probability distributions for a great many variables encountered in business, such as the demand for a new product.

Another serious difficulty arises as conditions change over time. The recent experience of automobile casualty insurance firms serves as an example of how changing conditions can make historical frequencies unsuitable for obtaining probabilities. Car insurers, who have consistently complained about losing money on collision and comprehensive coverage, have found that past experience has proven a poor predictor of the future levels of damage claims. The fault lies not with sampling error, virtually nonexistent because data obtained constitute a census, but rather in changing circumstances. Cars have been becoming steadily less sturdy, so that minor impacts that would hardly dent an older car can cause serious damage to a new one. The costs of repairs have also been rising in a pronounced inflationary spiral. More cars are sharing roads that are not increasing at the same rate, while driving habits are also changing; this affects the accident rate. Losses due to auto theft have been increasing as the result of new social pressures.

Using historical frequencies to estimate probabilities of future auto insurance claims may be compared to the random experiment of tossing a die, some side of which is shaved before each toss. We do not know which side is shaved nor by how much. Under these circumstances we can never obtain a reasonable probability distribution for the respective sides from historical frequencies alone.

SUBJECTIVE PROBABILITIES 2-9

In order to apply basic decision-making models based upon expected payoff or utility, probabilities must be employed. Past history can sometimes provide probability values that fit into the mold of long-run frequencies. But the applicability of such data is limited to events with a rich history, such as insurance claims. Even when they are available, these data can be misleading owing to the forces of change.

In many business decisions, there is ordinarily no recourse but to use subjective probabilities, which are not tied to a long-run frequency of occurrence, because so many decisions are "one shot" in nature and may be characterized by essentially nonrepeatable uncertainties. Good *judgment* may be the only recourse available for transforming such uncertainties into a set of probabilities for the various events involved.

We have seen that decision making under uncertainty is really analogous to gambling. Unlike card games, lotteries, dice, or roulette, most real-life gambles can be analyzed only with the help of subjective probabilities. As noted, these must reflect an amalgam of the decision-maker's judgment and experience.

How do we obtain a subjective probability?

We may consider subjective probabilities as "betting odds." That is, they can be treated just like the probabilities that the decision maker would desire in a lottery situation—of his or her own design—in which the payoffs are identical in every respect to those possible from the actual decision being evaluated. For example, suppose a contractor assigns a subjective probability of .5 to the event of winning a contract that will increase profits by $50,000, while losing will cause a $10,000 loss. The contractor then ought to be indifferent between preparing a bid for this contract and gambling on a coin toss where a head provides a $50,000 win and a tail results in a $10,000 loss. The subjective probability of winning the contract may be transformed directly into an "objective" .5 probability of getting a head from a coin toss. Assuming indifference between the real-life gamble and a hypothetical coin toss, we can substitute the latter into the decision analysis.

One practical benefit of such a hypothetical-for-real substitution is that subjective probabilities may be used in conjunction with the traditional long-run frequency type. In effect, apples and oranges may be mixed, thus providing for wider acceptance of the decision-theoretical analysis. More significantly, a hypothetical gamble or lottery can provide a convenient means of obtaining the subjective probability value itself.

PROBLEMS

2-1 A smoker has eight pipes, two of which are meerschaums. One of his meerschaums has a curved stem. He has a total of four curved-stem pipes. He asks his son to bring him the curved-stem meerschaum. The boy, not knowing rose briar from ivory nor calabash from hookah, selects a curved-stem pipe at random. What is the probability that the father will get the pipe he wants?

2-2 A coin is tossed exactly three times in succession. Here, the sample space has the same form as Figure 2-2. List the elements of the event set for each of the following events and then determine each event's probability:
(a) Exactly two heads appear in the three tosses.
(b) The same side does not appear twice in succession.
(c) The toss sequence ends with a head.
(d) An odd number of tails is obtained.

2-3 Determine the probabilities of the following events:
(a) A man chosen randomly from a group of ten men is a doctor, if the group contains two doctors.
(b) Winning a raffle with a single ticket out of 10,000.
(c) Getting both heads on one toss each of a dime and a penny. (First determine the sample space.)
(d) Getting a number greater than 2 for the value of the showing face from the toss of a six-sided die.

2-4 A consumer testing panel has 100 members, 40 women and 60 men. Of these, 15 of the women and 35 of the men are married. One panel member is chosen at random.
(a) Find the probabilities for each of the following outcomes:
    Man   Married man
    Woman   Married woman
    Married   Unmarried man
    Unmarried   Unmarried woman
(b) Using your answers to part (a), apply the addition law to find the probabilities for the following results:
    Woman *or* unmarried   Man *or* married
    Woman *or* married   Man *or* unmarried

2-5 The events listed below pertain to a card selected from a fully shuffled deck of 52 ordinary playing cards. Determine in each case the appropriate relationship (mutually exclusive, collectively exhaustive, both, neither).

(a) Heart, diamond, 10.
(b) 10, queen, ace.
(c) Face, nonface.
(d) Face, red, club, spade.

2-6 For each of the following situations, indicate whether the events are mutually exclusive, and if not, state why.
(a) Toss of a six-sided die: even-valued result, 1-face, 2-face, 5-face.
(b) Thermometers are inspected and rejected if any of the following is found: poor calibration, inability to withstand extreme temperatures without breaking, not within specified size tolerances.
(c) A manager will reject a job applicant for any of the following reasons: lack of relevant experience, slovenly appearance, too young, too old.

2-7 An antique car parts supplier has determined the following probabilities for the number of annual orders for Locomobile fuel pumps:

Number of Orders	Probability
0	.3
1	.2
2	.1
3	.1
4	.1
5	.1
6	.1
7 or more	0
Total	1.0

Find the probability that there will be:
(a) Less than 4 orders.
(b) Between 2 and 6 orders.
(c) At least 1 order.
(d) Between 2 and 4 orders.
(e) At the most 2 orders.

2-8 Events A, B, C are mutually exclusive and collectively exhaustive, each having a probability of 1/3. Find
(a) $P[A \text{ or } B]$
(b) $P[\text{not } C]$
(c) $P[\text{not } (A \text{ or } B)]$
(d) $P[A \text{ or } B \text{ or } C]$
(e) $P[\text{not } (A \text{ or } B \text{ or } C)]$

2-9 The antique car parts supplier in Exercise 2–7 has provided the probabilities on the next page for the annual number of orders for Pierce-Arrow, Duesenberg, and Silver Ghost carburetors:

Number of Orders	Probabilities for Pierce-Arrow	Duesenberg	Silver Ghost
0	.5	.4	.3
1	.3	.2	.2
2	.2	.1	.2
3	.1	.1	.1
4	.1	.1	.1
5	.1	0	.1
6 or more	0	0	0

For each type of car, determine whether the probability values have been assigned properly in accordance with the addition law for mutually exclusive and collectively exhaustive events. If not, state why (verbally).

2-10 An employment agency specializing in clerical and secretarial help classifies candidates in terms of primary skills and years of experience. The skills are bookkeeping, switchboard operation, and stenography (we will assume that no candidate is proficient in more than one of these). Experience categories are less than one year, between one and three years, and more than three years. There are 100 candidates currently on file, and their skills and experience are summarized in the following table.

| Experience | SKILL | | | Total |
	Book-keeping	Switch-board	Stenog-raphy	
Less than One Year	15		30	50
Between One and Three Years	5	10		20
More than Three Years			10	
Total		30		100

One candidate is chosen at random. Find the following:
(a) The missing numbers in the table.
(b) $P[$stenographer or bookkeeper$]$
(c) $P[$stenographer$|$more than three years experience$]$
(d) $P[$bookkeeper or less than one year experience$]$

2-11 A box contains 100 marbles, 60 red and 40 green. There are 30 striped; 70 are solid. There are 10 green-striped marbles. One marble is chosen at random from the box.

(a) Construct a joint probability table summarizing the events describing the properties (color, solid or striped) of the selected marble; include the marginal probabilities.
(b) Find P[marble is solid|marble is green].
(c) Is the event "marble is solid" independent of the event "marble is green"? Why?

2-12 You have drawn a card from a fully shuffled deck of 52 ordinary playing cards. Find:
(a) P[ace|red]
(b) P[ace of diamonds|red]
(c) P[diamond|red]
(d) P[face card|red]

2-13 A new family with two children of different ages has moved into the neighborhood. Suppose that it is equally likely that either child will be a boy or girl. Hence, the following situations are equally likely:

Youngest	Oldest	
boy	boy	(B, B)
boy	girl	(B, G)
girl	boy	(G, B)
girl	girl	(G, G)

(a) Find P[at least one girl].
(b) If you know there is at least one girl, what is the conditional probability that the family has exactly one boy?
(c) Given that at least one child is a girl, what is the conditional probability that the other child is a girl?

2-14 Two consumer testing panels of 100 persons each are used by a company in evaluating product design. One person is chosen at random from each panel.
(a) Panel A is half men and half women. Seventy percent of the panel are married, and just as many men as women are married. This makes any two sex and marital status events independent. Construct the joint probability table by first finding the marginal probabilities and then using the multiplication law to get the joint probabilities, which in this case may be expressed as the products of the two respective marginal probabilities.
(b) Panel B is also half men and half women, and 70 percent of the panel members are married. However, only 60 percent of the men are married, whereas 80 percent of the women are. Thus, any two sex and marital status events are dependent. This means that the product of the respective marginal probabilities does not equal the corresponding joint probability. Construct the joint probability table.

2-15 The following joint probability table represents the particular characteristics of a randomly selected retired military person.

Rank	COLLEGE EDUCATION Yes	No	Marginal Probability
Officer	.21	.13	____
Enlisted	.06	.60	____
Marginal Probability	____	____	1.00

(a) Find the missing marginal probability values.
(b) Find the joint probability that the selected retiree was both an officer and college educated.
(c) Find the conditional probability that the selected person was an officer, given that he graduated from college.
(d) Determine the percentage of college-educated persons who were officers.

2-16 A fruit inspector accepts or rejects shipments of bananas after performing tests on a few sample bunches. He rejects 15 percent of all shipments inspected. Thus far, he has rejected 95 percent of all bad shipments inspected, and 10 percent of all shipments have ultimately proved bad.
(a) Using the above experience as a basis, find the values for the probabilities regarding the outcome of any particular shipment handled by this particular inspector: $P[\text{reject}]$, $P[\text{bad}]$, $P[\text{reject}|\text{bad}]$.
(b) Find $P[\text{reject and bad}]$, using the multiplication law with the appropriate values found in part (a).
(c) Construct a joint probability table showing the joint probabilities and the marginal probabilities for the inspector's actions (accept or reject) and the quality (good or bad) of the banana shipment.

2-17 An experiment is conducted using three boxes, each containing a mixture of ten (R)ed and (W)hite marbles. The three boxes have the following compositions:

Box A
6 R
4 W

Box B
4 R
6 W

Box C
7 R
3 W

Two marbles are selected randomly. The first is selected from Box

54   PROBABILITY CONCEPTS

A. If it is red, the second marble is to be picked from Box B, but if the first marble is white, the second marble will be taken from Box C. Using R_1 and W_1 to represent the color of the first marble and R_2 and W_2 to represent the color of the second,
(a) Find the following probabilities:

$$P[R_1] \qquad P[W_1]$$
$$P[R_2|R_1] \qquad P[R_2|W_1]$$
$$P[W_2|R_1] \qquad P[W_2|W_1]$$

(b) From your answers to part (a), use the multiplication law to determine the following joint probabilities:

$$P[R_1 \text{ and } R_2]$$
$$P[R_1 \text{ and } W_2]$$
$$P[W_1 \text{ and } R_2]$$
$$P[W_1 \text{ and } W_2]$$

(c) Determine the probabilities that
(1) One red and one white marble will be chosen.
(2) Either two red or two white marbles will be chosen.

2-18 Of the ten employees in a particular branch office of XYZ Corporation, six are men. Suppose that two employees are successively selected at random without replacement. We are only concerned with the events: male, female.
(a) Construct a probability tree diagram for this situation, placing identifying labels and appropriate probability values on all branches. Indicate also the joint probability values for the end positions.
(b) Find the probability that the two employees are of the same sex.
(c) Are the events "first person is a man" and "second person is a man" independent? Explain.

2-19 Ten percent of the ball bearings in a lot of 50 are known to be overweight. Three bearings are randomly selected, one at a time, and weighed. Each in turn is returned to the lot and allowed the same chance of being selected as the unweighed items. Construct a probability tree diagram for this situation. Find the following probabilities describing the final results of the sampling procedure:
(a) No overweight items are selected; (b) All the items are found to be overweight; (c) Exactly one overweight ball bearing is found.

2-20 Repeat Exercise 2-19 if the successively weighed items are not replaced.

2-21 A local television weather reporter makes a daily forecast indicating the probability that it will rain tomorrow. On one particular evening, she announces an 80 percent chance of rain (E) the next day. The manager of the city golf courses has established a policy that he will only water the greens if the probability of rain is less than 90 percent. Using the local TV forecast as his prior probability, the manager also relies on his father-in-law's rheumatism: historically, he gets a "rain pain" (R) on 90 percent of all days followed by rain, but he also gets a pain on 20 percent of the days not followed by rain. The following probabilities therefore apply:

$$P[E] = .80 \quad P[R|E] = .90 \quad P[R|\text{not } E] = .20$$

(a) Assuming that the golf course manager's father-in-law is currently receiving pain signals, find the posterior probability that it will rain tomorrow. Should the manager water the greens?

(b) If the manager's father-in-law feels just fine, what is the posterior probability of rain tomorrow?

2-22 A marketing researcher wishes to determine from a given response to a question, whether a randomly chosen person will choose BriDent when next purchasing toothpaste. The question will reveal whether the selected person recalls the name BriDent, an event we will designate R. From previous testing, it has been established that 99 percent of those persons buying BriDent had previously recalled the name. It has also been found that only 10 percent of the nonbuyers of BriDent recalled this particular brand name. Since BriDent now has 30 percent of the toothpaste market, the researcher chooses .30 as the prior probability that the person will buy BriDent. Denoting this event by B, we have the following probabilities:

$$P[B] = .30 \quad P[R|B] = .99 \quad P[R|\text{not } B] = .10$$

(a) Suppose that the chosen person remembers BriDent. What is the posterior probability that BriDent will be purchased next?

(b) Suppose the person selected does not remember BriDent. Find the posterior probability BriDent will be picked when next buying toothpaste.

2-23 An oil wildcatter has assigned a .50 probability to striking oil on his property. He orders a seismic survey that has proved only 80 percent reliable in the past: given oil it predicts favorably 80 percent of the time; given no oil, it augurs unfavorably with a frequency of .8.

(a) Given a favorable seismic result, what is the probability of oil?

(b) Given an unfavorable seismic result, what is the probability of oil?

2-24 A life insurance company gives an aptitude test to new sales personnel in order to predict their success at selling. Like most aptitude tests, this one is imperfect. Some high scorers will be poor salespeople, lacking the necessary motivation. A few low scorers will turn out to be excellent sales representatives. Sacrificing justice for efficiency, the company has established a score of 80 as the minimum for hiring. This score was determined after a year of testing new hires, who were divided into two categories—satisfactory and unsatisfactory. The results of the tests are summarized below:

Performance	Proportion of People Who		Total
	Scored Below 80	Scored 80 or Above	
Satisfactory	.10	.40	.50
Unsatisfactory	.30	.20	.50
Total	.40	.60	1.00

Since the people tested represent a typical cross section of applicants, the above figures have been judged acceptable as probabilities for future candidates.

(a) What is the prior probability that a candidate will be satisfactory?

(b) What is the posterior probability that a candidate will perform unsatisfactorily if hired after scoring 80 or above?

(c) What is the posterior probability that a candidate *would have been* satisfactory (if hired) after scoring below 80?

2-25 For each of the following situations, discuss whether historical frequencies can be used meaningfully to estimate probabilities:
(a) For first-year salary levels of business-school graduates.
(b) For the faces obtained by tossing an asymmetrical die.
(c) Of dying during the next year, for persons in various age, health, sex, and occupational categories.

2-26 Using your judgment, assess the probability that you will receive an "A" on your next quantitative methods examination. To help you achieve this, imagine that your instructor will let you obtain your grade by lottery, so that 100 slips of paper — some saying A, the rest not A — will be put into a hat and mixed. You will then draw one of these slips at random. The letter obtained will be the grade you receive. How many A slips must there be to make you indifferent between letting your grade be determined by lottery and earning it?

Three

Probability Distributions and Expected Value

The preceding chapter provides the fundamental concepts of probability. We are now ready to study some of the tools used in analyzing business decisions when uncertainty is present. Often the outcomes of such decisions are numerical, and the particular result to be achieved may be expressed as a variable. Because the particular value is itself uncertain and determined by chance, we refer to it as a random variable. Probabilities assigned to each possible value for this variable constitute a probability distribution.

For instance, alternative locations for a new plant might be compared in terms of profitability, which also can be viewed as a random variable with a probability distribution. But how can the attractiveness of each candidate plant site be ranked? To do this we need a single profit figure for each. We will show how the expected level of profitability can be determined for the alternatives by using the respective probability distributions in arriving at an "average" figure.

This chapter first discusses random variables and probability distributions and then expected value. Finally, it presents two specific probability distributions: the binomial, which is one of the most common distributions encountered, and the normal, which is perhaps the most important distribution whenever sample information is used to help analyze decisions.

THE RANDOM VARIABLE 3-1

Consider the management decision of selecting among alternative projects for inclusion in the current budget. One such project may be to expand the plant capacity through purchase of new equipment. Various measures, such as cost or profit, may be used to compare the attractiveness of this purchase with competing projects. One common gauge is the investment's rate of return.

The actual rate of return will depend on the particular levels and timing of cash receipts and expenditures attributable to the new equipment. Except for the initial outlay, all these lie in the future and are therefore subject to uncertainties.

Many rate-of-return outcomes are possible from an equipment investment. Each outcome consists of groupings of potential cash flows, several of which may yield the same rate of return. A rate-of-return figure may be calculated for each, using the principles of compound interest. Since the rate of return may assume any one of a number of possible values, we may view it as a variable.

A variable whose level is determined by chance is known as a *random variable*. When a specific outcome is uncertain it is treated as a variable. The random variable assumes actual numerical value only *after* all relevant outcomes are known.

A single situation may give rise to many different kinds of random variables. In a budgeting decision, an alternative's net cost or net profit, instead of rate of return, could serve as the random variable. The values would be calculated in a different manner but from the same data. The elementary events in the sample space would be the same.

An Illustration from Roulette

Roulette, the internationally popular casino game, vividly illustrates the relationship between elementary events and random variables. The procedure is for the players to commit themselves to particular bets. A wheel with 38 slots is then spun, and a ball is set in motion. The outcome is determined by the slot the ball drops into. The sample space consists of the 38 slots, 36 of which are numbered from 1 to 36 (with half of these being red, the others black) plus two green slots numbered 0 and 00.

There are several ways of placing a roulette bet. For instance, a

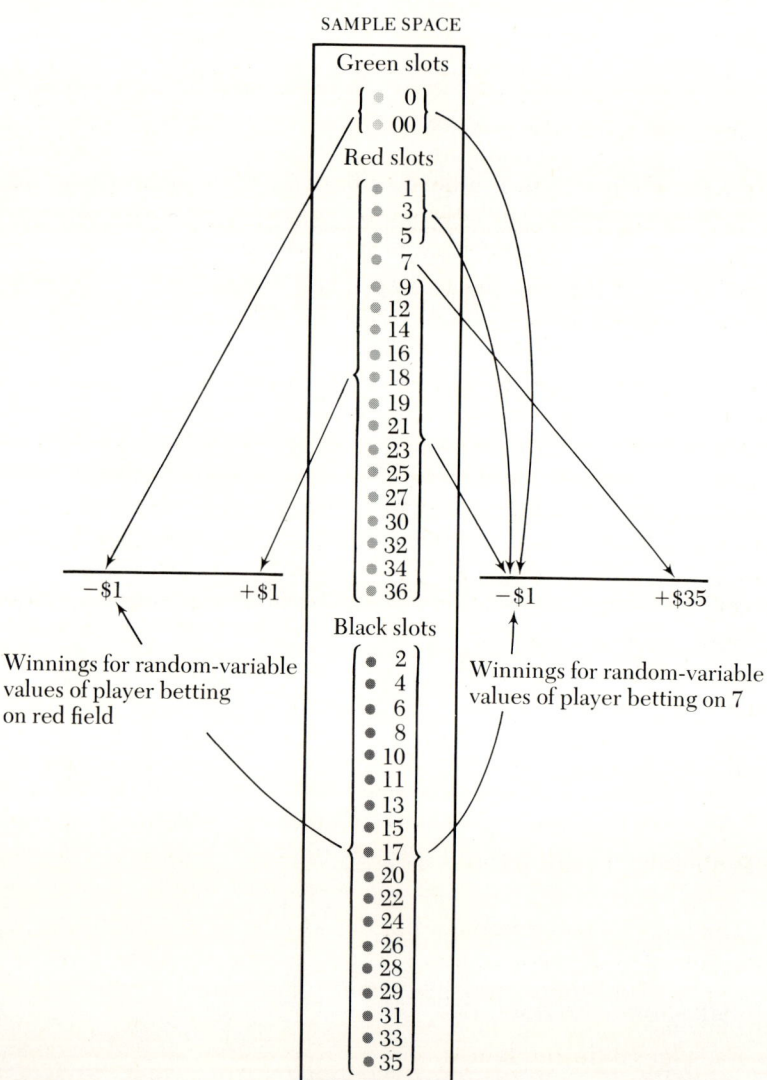

Figure 3-1
Portrayal of two different random variables for two types of roulette gambles.

60   PROBABILITY DISTRIBUTIONS AND EXPECTED VALUE

player may place a dollar on a particular number, say 7. If the ball drops into the 7 slot, the player receives a 35 dollar payoff;* otherwise the player forfeits the bet. Another way to play is to bet a dollar on the red field. If the ball drops into a red slot, the player receives a dollar; the bet is lost if a black or green number appears. In either case, the sample space for the outcome of the spin of a roulette wheel comprises 38 equally likely elementary events.

For each player, the random variable of prime interest is the winnings. The 7-player's random variable has two values: +35 (if 7 comes up) and −$1 (if the ball drops into any of the other slots). For the game there are two distinctly different random variables, *depending on the type of gamble made.*

Figure 3-1 shows how each of the roulette random variables is defined in terms of the same sample space. The values of the respective random variables are determined on each play by the elementary event that occurs. The arrows match each elementary event to a particular point on a numerical scale, depending on the gamble chosen. Mathematically, we interpret a random variable to be a function mapping the elementary events onto their corresponding points on the numerical scale.

A random variable must assure numerical values. For example, the outcomes of a coin toss, head and tail, are non-numerical. We can associate a random variable with coin tossing only through the assignment of numbers to these outcomes, as would be the case in a wager where a head results in winnings of $1 and a tail in loss of $1. In that case, winnings, rather than the side showing, would be the random variable, with possible values of $1 and −$1. As we shall see in the next section, an expected value for the random variable can be obtained by an averaging procedure. Thus, we can determine an average level of winnings from the coin toss. But there is no way to average the head and the tail, which are non-numerical.

The Probability Distribution

The concept of a random variable is fundamental in applying probability theory to decision making. The relation between a random variable's values and their probabilities is summarized by the *probability distribution.*

Each possible random-variable value corresponds to a particular

---

* Since there are 38 equally likely slots, the probability of getting 7 is 1/38. To be a fair gamble, the payoff should be 37 to 1. The house does not pay on 0 or 00, giving it an edge and a built-in source of long-run profits.

composite event in the underlying sample space. We may use the procedures of Chapter 2 to find the probabilities for each possible value. For example, consider again the winnings from a roulette gamble. For the single-number better, winnings equal to $35 occur whenever the event "the ball drops into the slot of the number played" does. Likewise, winnings equal to −$1 (that is, losing $1) occur when the complementary event "some other slot receives the ball" occurs. There are 37 out of 38 equally likely possibilities for this second event. Thus, the probabilities of our random-variable values are equal to the probabilities of the corresponding events. In this instance,

$$P[\text{winnings} = \$35] = 1/38$$
$$P[\text{winnings} = -\$1] = 37/38$$

Notice that the above probabilities sum to one, which follows from the fact that possible random-variable values correspond directly to events that are *collectively exhaustive and mutually exclusive.* In roulette, the wager is either won or lost.

Many probability distributions can be expressed in terms of a table like Table 3-1 for the rate of return to be achieved from operating a new piece of equipment. Notice that the probabilities sum to 1. When there are too many possibilities to list conveniently in a table, we can use an algebraic expression to describe a probability distribution.

Table 3-1
PROBABILITY DISTRIBUTION OF THE RATE OF RETURN

Possible Rate of Return	Probability
10%	.05
11	.10
12	.15
13	.17
14	.12
15	.08
16	.09
17	.06
18	.05
19	.05
20	.04
21	.04
Total	1.00

EXPECTED VALUE 3-2

In making business decisions under uncertainty each possible choice ordinarily leads to a different random variable with its own probability distribution. Thus, in comparing alternative budget decisions, a company president may be faced with a variety of choices, each having a somewhat different rate of return probability distribution similar to the one in Table 3-1. It is hard to compare several tables. To facilitate the choice, each probability distribution is often summarized by a single "average" value. These summary numbers can then help to rank the various alternatives.

Such an average may be computed directly from the probability distribution. The resulting figure is called the *expected value* of the random variable. It is found by multiplying every possible value by its probability and summing all the products; the expected value is thus a weighted average, with the probabilities serving as weights. Table 3-2 shows the expected-value calculation for the number of dots obtained in tossing a six-sided die cube.

Table 3-2
EXPECTED-VALUE CALCULATION FOR THE NUMBER OF DOTS IN A DIE TOSS

Number of Dots	*Probability*	*Number × Probability*
1	1/6	1/6
2	1/6	2/6
3	1/6	3/6
4	1/6	4/6
5	1/6	5/6
6	1/6	6/6
	1	21/6 = 3.5
	Expected value = 3.5 dots	

The Meaning of Expected Value

The expected value has many uses. In a gambling game it tells us what our long-run average losses per play will be. Sophisticated gamblers know that slot machines have poor payoffs in relation to the actual odds and that the average loss per play will be less in roulette or dice games. In the early 1960s Edward Thorp, a mathematician, caused quite a stir when he demonstrated that various betting strategies in playing the card game blackjack would result in positive expected winnings.*

We can illustrate the meaning of expected value by considering again the roulette example. The expected winnings from betting $1 on 7 are calculated as follows:

Winnings	Probability	Winnings × Probability
+$35	1/38	+$35/38
−$ 1	37/38	−$37/38
		−$ 2/38 = −$.053

The expected winnings from a single gamble is a loss of 5.3 cents. This means that the gambler who keeps making $1 bets indefinitely will lose an average of 5.3 cents from each. Of course, an individual gamble will show either a gain of $35 or a loss of $1. But—again, on the average—the gambler will get $35 in only 1 out of 38 gambles, while losing $1 in 37 out of 38.

Notice that in both illustrations the expected values of the random variables are not themselves outcomes of the uncertain situation. It is impossible for 3.5 dots to show; the outcome must be a whole number (1, 2, 3, 4, 5, or 6). The roulette player will always be dealing in whole dollars. In either case, the expected value is an average result only. Although it is possible in some random experiments, there is no reason why the expected outcome should be a possible result in a single circumstance.

As any decision involving uncertain outcomes is viewed as a gambling situation, we may use expected value to help us choose among alternative courses of action. But unlike a dice game, practical decisions in business often involve nonrepeatable situations, such as the sales response to an advertising budget. In such cases there is only one opportunity to "play." Here uncertainty must be measured in terms of subjective probabilities. An expected value may still be calculated, but in these situations it represents an average of the decision-maker's *convictions* about the outcomes. We may illustrate this by calculating in Table 3-3 the expected rate of return for the budget decision discussed earlier.

* See Edward Thorp, *Beat the Dealer,* 2nd ed. (New York: Random House, 1966). Unlike other gambling games, blackjack allows for bets to be placed when odds are in the player's favor, because the card deck may not be reshuffled after each stage of play. By significantly raising their bets at these times players will on the average make a profit.

Table 3-3
EXPECTED-VALUE CALCULATION FOR THE RATE OF RETURN

Possible Rate of Return	Probability	Rate × Probability
10%	.05	.50%
11	.10	1.10
12	.15	1.80
13	.17	2.21
14	.12	1.68
15	.08	1.20
16	.09	1.44
17	.06	1.02
18	.05	.90
19	.05	.95
20	.04	.80
21	.04	.84
	1.00	14.44%

Expected rate of return = 14.44%

What does 14.44% obtained as the expected rate of return mean? In this circumstance the future conditions that give rise to a particular percentage return are nonrepeatable, so that the given probabilities really express the decision-maker's convictions that the respective percentages will result. Thus, the expected value calculated from these subjective probabilities expresses the decision-maker's "average conviction" as to what the return will be.

Variance of a Random Variable

The expected value measures the *central tendency* of a probability distribution. Often a measure of *dispersion or variability* is desired as well. This second type of measure summarizes the degree to which the possible random-variable values differ among themselves. For this purpose we use the *variance*, which expresses the average of squared deviations of the individual values from their expected value or mean. This is analogous to the variance encountered in statistics. For illustration, the variance for the number of dots obtained from a die toss is calculated in Table 3-4.

Because the variance expresses dispersion in terms of original units squared (squared dots for a die), its square root is often used instead to measure dispersion. The resulting value is called the *standard deviation*.

Table 3-4
VARIANCE CALCULATION FOR THE NUMBER OF DOTS IN A DIE TOSS

Number of Dots	Deviation: Number − 3.5	(Number − 3.5)²	Probability	(Number − 3.5)² × Probability
1	−2.5	6.25	1/6	6.25/6
2	−1.5	2.25	1/6	2.25/6
3	− .5	.25	1/6	.25/6
4	.5	.25	1/6	.25/6
5	1.5	2.25	1/6	2.25/6
6	2.5	6.25	1/6	6.25/6
				17.50/6

Variance = 17.50/6 = 2.917

The standard deviation for the die toss outcome is

$$\sqrt{2.917} = 1.71 \text{ dots}$$

In evaluating choices among outcomes that are random variables, both the expected value or mean and the variance may prove useful. In investment decisions the variance is often used as a measure of risk. For example, in analyzing stock portfolios, each possible security combination may be portrayed in two dimensions: expected return and variance in returns.* The concept of variance is very important in decision making where sample information is used. Later in this chapter we will show how the normal distribution may be characterized in terms of two parameters, the mean and the variance (or standard deviation).

3-3 THE BINOMIAL DISTRIBUTION

In making decisions under uncertain conditions it is often necessary to use sample data. Many applications involve situations with only two complementary non-numerical outcomes. Consider these three examples: (1) When deciding to place a magazine advertisement, an advertiser must ultimately consider whether or not the reader will be persuaded enough to buy the product. (2) A politician retains a polling agency to find out whether or not he or she is preferred by a majority of

---

* See Harry M. Markowitz, *Portfolio Selection: Efficient Diversification of Investments* (New Haven: Yale University Press, 1959).

the voters. (3) A medical researcher wishes to determine if a new drug does or does not provide most patients with some degree of relief. In each case, the relevant answers to be sought are, respectively, the number of persons who will buy, the number of voters favoring the candidate, and how many patients will respond favorably to treatment. Because many people may be involved in all of the foregoing situations, any evidence used to find the answers is usually provided by a sample.

A person selected for the sample will provide one of two opposite responses: purchase the product or not, prefer the candidate or not, or respond to treatment or not. In sampling from such qualitative populations, the only numerical result ordinarily of interest is how many times or in what proportion a particular attribute occurs.

The *number* of persons providing the desired response (such as the number of readers who will buy the product) is the key issue in each of our illustrations. Knowing the probability distribution of this random variable should facilitate determining a course of action. For example, the medical researcher would be less prone to promote the drug if only a few sample patients responded favorably to treatment, for the probability of such an outcome would be small if the drug were truly effective.

We may expect each situation to have a different probability distribution. There is no reason except coincidence why the probability that 50 voters will prefer the candidate should be the same as the probability that 50 patients will respond favorably to the drug. Yet, similarities between these cases prove advantageous in finding their respective probability distributions; they have common characteristics that place them in the same family. Members of this family have a probability distribution referred to as a *binomial distribution*. The binomial distribution is epitomized by coin tossing and can be explained in terms of the following illustration.

Suppose that an evenly balanced coin is fairly tossed five times. This may be viewed as a five-stage experiment having the probability tree diagram in Figure 3-2, where the sample space is also listed. Our initial problem is to find the probability of obtaining exactly two heads. As each of the 32 outcomes is equally likely, the basic definition of probability allows us to proceed as follows. Count the number of elementary events including two heads, and then divide this result by the total number of equally likely events. The sample space contains 32 elementary events, 10 of which are two-head outcomes (see asterisks in Figure 3-2). Thus, we can determine that

$$P[\text{exactly two heads}] = 10/32$$

It is impracticable to list all possible outcomes unless only a few exist. For instance, if 10 tosses were to be considered, the analogous list

3-3   THE BINOMIAL DISTRIBUTION

would contain 1024 (2^{10}) entries. For even longer toss sequences, it would be necessary to use various short cuts and probability laws developed to ease computation. Before discussing a procedure to simplify finding such probabilities, it will be helpful to relate coin tossing to a similar class of situations.

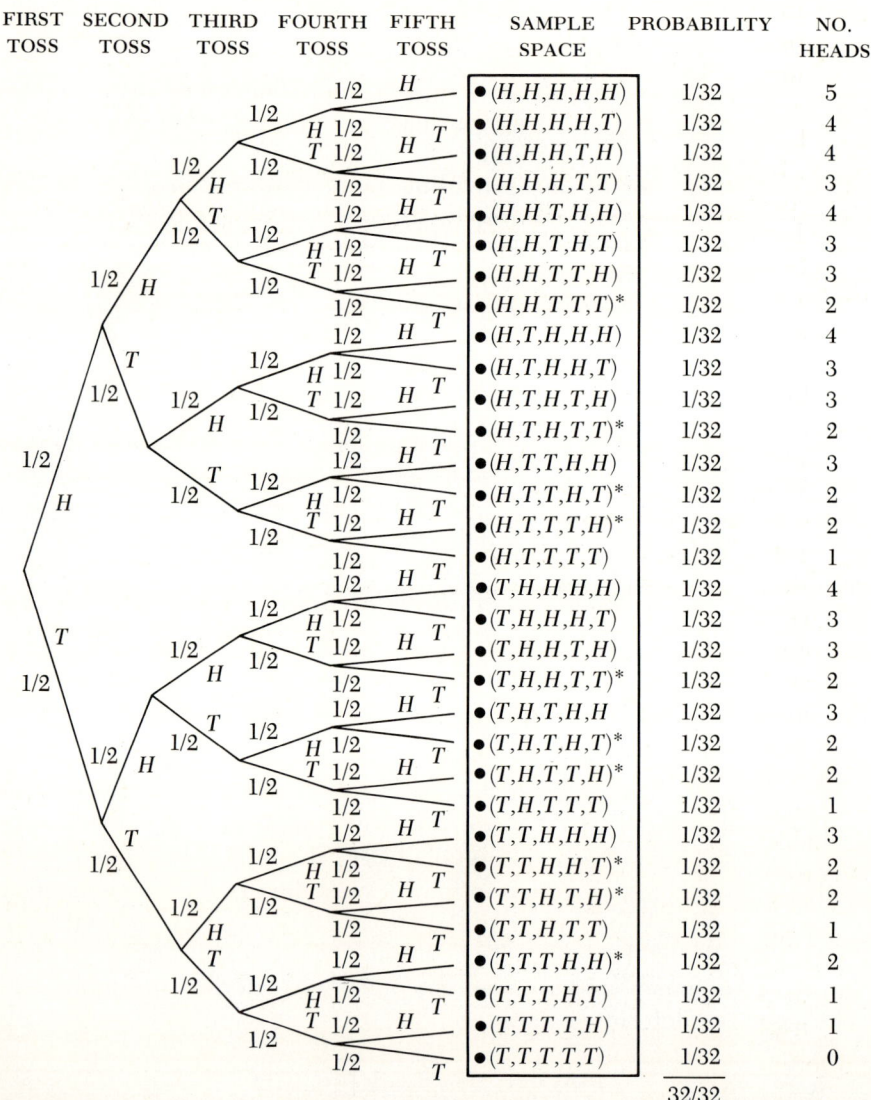

Figure 3-2
Probability tree diagram for five tosses of a fair coin.

The Bernoulli Process

A sequence of coin tosses is one example of a *Bernoulli process.** A great many situations fall into the same category. All involve a series of experiments (such as tosses of a coin) referred to as *trials. Each trial has only two possible complementary outcomes,* like head or tail. Usually one outcome is referred to as a *success* and the other as a *failure.* Success is a broad term that covers the kind of outcome for which we wish to find the probability that a particular number of the same outcomes will occur. In the preceding illustration, getting a head would be a success. (This designation is arbitrary; in another context, a head might be construed a failure.)

Other examples include: single childbirths, where each birth is a trial resulting in a boy or girl; canning a vegetable, where each trial is a full can that is slightly overweight or underweight (cans of precisely the correct weight are so improbable that we may ignore them); and keypunching numerical data, where each completed card is a trial which will either contain errors or be correct. In all cases, only two opposite trial outcomes are considered.

What further distinguishes these situations as Bernoulli processes is that *the success probability remains constant* from trial to trial. Thus, the probability of getting a head is the same, regardless of which toss is considered—and this must be the case for delivering a boy for any successive single birth in a maternity hospital, picking up an overweight can of vegetables, and getting a correctly punched card each time. (The last condition would not hold if the keypuncher tires over time, so that the probability could be higher that an earlier card would be correct than that a later card would be.)

A final characteristic of a Bernoulli process is that *successive trial outcomes must be independent events.* Like a fairly tossed coin, the probability of getting a success (head) must be independent of what occurred in previous trials (tosses). The births in a *single family* might violate this requirement if the parents use recent techniques to obtain a second child whose sex is the opposite of their first child. Or, a keypuncher's errors may occur in batches, due to fatigue, so that once an error is made it is more likely to be followed by another.

The results of sampling to determine response to advertising, voter preference, or favorable response to drug treatment may all be classified as Bernoulli processes. In order not to violate the requirements of independence and constant probability of success, we must sample with

---

* After Jacob Bernoulli, an eighteenth century mathematician.

replacement (see Chapter 2, page 40). This type of sampling allows each person the same chance of being selected each time, and perhaps of being chosen more than once. The probability of a trial success would in each case be the proportion of persons in the respective population who would provide the desired response.

The Binomial Formula

When the trial outcomes are the results of a Bernoulli process, the number of successes is a random variable having a binomial distribution. The following expression may then be used to find the probability values. It is referred to as the *binomial formula*

$$P[\text{successes} = r] = \frac{n!}{r!(n-r)!} P^r (1-P)^{n-r}$$

where n = Number of trials achieved

P = Trial success probability

$r = 0, 1, \ldots, n$

Here we use factorial notation by placing an exclamation point after the quantity. A 5 factorial is

$$5! = 5 \times 4 \times 3 \times 2 \times 1 = 120$$

and in general

$$n! = n \times (n-1) \times (n-2) \times \cdots \times 2 \times 1$$

with the following defined values

$$0! = 1$$
$$1! = 1$$

The above expression can be used to determine the probability found earlier for getting successes = 2 heads in $n = 5$ tosses of a fair coin. In this case, $P = P[\text{head}] = \frac{1}{2}$ and $1 - P = P[\text{tail}] = \frac{1}{2}$, so that

$$P[\text{successes} = 2] = \frac{5!}{2!(5-2)!} \left(\frac{1}{2}\right)^2 \left(1 - \frac{1}{2}\right)^{5-2} = \frac{5!}{2!3!} \left(\frac{1}{2}\right)^2 \left(\frac{1}{2}\right)^3$$

$$= 10 \left(\frac{1}{2}\right)^5 = \frac{10}{32}$$

The factorial terms in the above product provide the number of outcomes involving exactly 2 heads, which is equal to 10 and represents the number of combinations of 2 particular tosses that may result in heads out of a total of 5 tosses made. The product involving 1/2 represents the probability of getting any one of the 10 two-head sequences represented by the end positions on the probability tree diagram in Figure 3-2. Each of these positions is reached by traversing a particular path of 2 head and $5 - 2 = 3$ tail branches. The probability of doing this may be obtained by applying the multiplication law. Since a two-head result can happen in any one of 10 equally likely ways, the addition law of probability indicates that we add 10 of the identical terms together, or, more simply, multiply by 10.

The entire binomial distribution that corresponds to the number of heads resulting from $n = 5$ fair coin tosses is given in Table 3-5, where the probability values are found by applying the binomial formula for all possible r values.

Table 3-5
BINOMIAL DISTRIBUTION FOR THE NUMBER OF HEADS OBTAINED IN FIVE COIN TOSSES

Possible Number of Heads r	$P[heads = r]$	
0	$\frac{5!}{0!5!}\left(\frac{1}{2}\right)^0\left(\frac{1}{2}\right)^5 = \frac{1}{32} =$	.03125
1	$\frac{5!}{1!4!}\left(\frac{1}{2}\right)^1\left(\frac{1}{2}\right)^4 = \frac{5}{32} =$	.15625
2	$\frac{5!}{2!3!}\left(\frac{1}{2}\right)^2\left(\frac{1}{2}\right)^3 = \frac{10}{32} =$	.31250
3	$\frac{5!}{3!2!}\left(\frac{1}{2}\right)^3\left(\frac{1}{2}\right)^2 = \frac{10}{32} =$	.31250
4	$\frac{5!}{4!1!}\left(\frac{1}{2}\right)^4\left(\frac{1}{2}\right)^1 = \frac{5}{32} =$	.15625
5	$\frac{5!}{5!0!}\left(\frac{1}{2}\right)^5\left(\frac{1}{2}\right)^0 = \frac{1}{32} =$	.03125
	Total	1.00000

As we have already noted, different Bernoulli processes will have different probability values. But the number of successes from each process is a random variable belonging to the binomial distribution family. Note that the probabilities for all possible rs depend on the value of P. Different sizes for n will result in a larger or smaller number of possible rs and will also affect each probability value.

Cumulative Probabilities

Using the binomial formula to calculate probabilities can be quite a chore. Imagine the effort necessary to determine the probability for 17 successes in $n = 58$ trials when $P = .13$. Ordinarily, we may simply find the probabilities we need from a table. But most tables available provide *cumulative probabilities*.

To illustrate this concept, consider the binomial probabilities in Table 3-6 provided for the number of aircraft departure delays at a major airport. These have been computed for $n = 10$ departing flights on different dates. We assume that a Bernoulli process applies and that the probability that any particular flight is delayed is $P = .4$. The cumulative probabilities appear in column (3). The values in this column are obtained by adding all the preceding entries for column (2). Thus,

$$P[\text{successes} \leq 0] = P[\text{successes} = 0] = .0060$$

and

$$P[\text{successes} \leq 1] = P[\text{successes} = 0] + P[\text{successes} = 1]$$
$$= .0060 + .0404$$
$$= .0464$$

and

$$P[\text{successes} \leq 2] = P[\text{successes} = 0] + P[\text{successes} = 1]$$
$$+ P[\text{successes} = 2]$$
$$= .0060 + .0404 + .1209$$
$$= .1673$$

By $\leq$ we mean less than or equal to, so that successes ≤ 2 means either exactly 0, 1, or 2 successes. Table 3-6 is thus constructed cumulatively from the individual probability values, so that the values obtained constitute the *cumulative probability distribution* for the number of successes.

The individual probabilities are graphed as spikes in the top portion of Figure 3-3 (no spike appears for 10 successes, since the probability for this outcome is too low to show). The cumulative probability distribution is shown at the bottom. The cumulative probability value corresponding to any particular number is obtained from the *highest*

Table 3-6

CUMULATIVE PROBABILITY DISTRIBUTION FOR THE NUMBER OF AIRCRAFT DEPARTURE DELAYS

(1) Number of Successes (Delays) r	(2) $P[successes = r]$	(3) Cumulative Probabilities $P[successes \leq r]$
0	.0060	.0060
1	.0404	.0464
2	.1209	.1673
3	.2150	.3823
4	.2508	.6331
5	.2007	.8338
6	.1114	.9452
7	.0425	.9877
8	.0106	.9983
9	.0016	.9999
10	.0001	1.0000
	1.0000	

point on the "stairway" directly above. For instance, the cumulative probability for 5 or fewer delays is .8338, and not .6331, which belongs to the lower "step." Notice that the size of each step is the same as the height of the respective spike of the individual probability in the top graph. The underlying probability distribution may be obtained from the cumulative probability distribution by finding these step sizes. For example, to find the probability that there will be exactly 5 departure delays, we find the difference

$$P[successes = 5] = P[successes \leq 5] - P[successes \leq 4]$$
$$= .8338 - .6331 = .2007$$

Using Binomial Probability Tables

Appendix Table A provides cumulative binomial probability values computed for various sizes of n, with a separate tabulation for each of several Ps. It is possible to use this table to compute probabilities for the number of successes in a variety of situations. For illustration, assume that we are interested in finding probabilities regarding the number of $n = 100$ readers who will remember an aspirin advertisement

3-3 THE BINOMIAL DISTRIBUTION

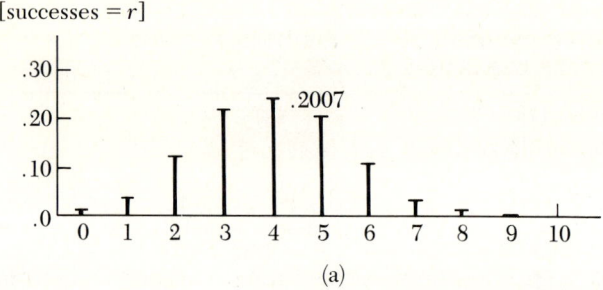

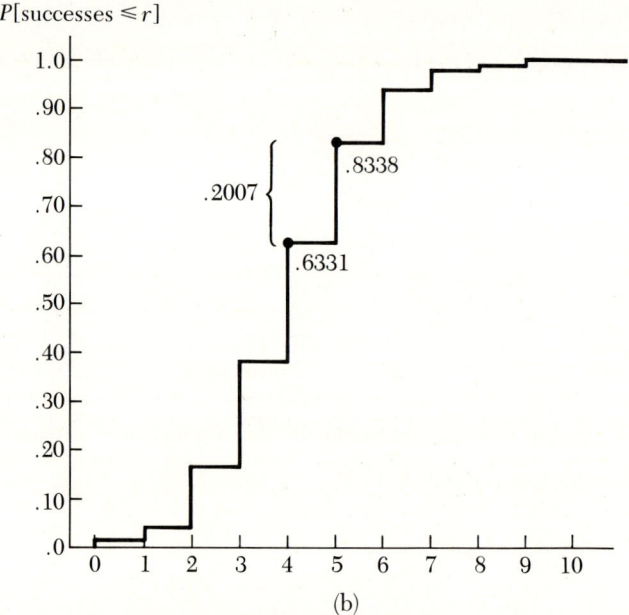

Figure 3-3

(a) Binomial probability mass function and (b) cumulative probability distribution function for the number of successes from a Bernoulli process with $n = 10$ and $P = .4$.

appearing on the back cover of *Time*. We will suppose that $P = .30$ is the underlying proportion of all readers who will remember the ad. We will use the portion of Appendix Table A that begins at $n = 100$.

(1) *To obtain a result less than or equal to a particular value:* The probability that 40 or fewer sample persons will remember the ad is a

74   PROBABILITY DISTRIBUTIONS AND EXPECTED VALUE

cumulative probability value that may be read directly from the table when $r = 40$ successes:

$$P[\text{successes} \leq 40] = .9875$$

(2) *To obtain a result exactly equal to a single value:* Recall that cumulative probabilities represent the sum of individual probability values and are portrayed graphically as a stairway (see Figure 3-3). A single-value probability may be obtained by determining the size of the step between two neighboring cumulative probabilities by finding the difference:

$$P[\text{successes} = r] = P[\text{successes} \leq r] - P[\text{successes} \leq r - 1]$$

For example, the probability that exactly $r = 32$ of the persons will remember the ad is

$$P[\text{successes} = 32] = P[\text{successes} \leq 32] - P[\text{successes} \leq 31]$$
$$= .7107 - .6331$$
$$= .0776$$

(3) *To obtain a result strictly less than some value:* In this case we need only observe that

$$P[\text{successes} < r] = P[\text{successes} \leq r - 1]$$

For example, the probability that fewer than $r = 30$ successes are achieved is the same as the probability that exactly $r - 1 = 29$ or less successes are obtained, or

$$P[\text{successes} < 30] = P[\text{successes} \leq 29] = .4623$$

(4) *To obtain a result greater than or equal to some value:* Here we use the fact that

$$P[\text{successes} \geq r] = 1 - P[\text{successes} < r] = 1 - P[\text{successes} \leq r - 1]$$

In finding the probability that at least $r = 20$ of the readers will remember, we look up the cumulative probability that $r - 1 = 19$ or less will remember and subtract this value from 1, or

$$P[\text{successes} \geq 20] = 1 - P[\text{successes} \leq 19]$$
$$= 1 - .0089 = .9911$$

3-3   THE BINOMIAL DISTRIBUTION

Note that a related problem involves a situation where the result must be *strictly greater than* some value. In such a case, we find the cumulative probability for r itself and subtract this from 1. For example, the probability that more than $r = 20$ people will remember the ad is 1 minus the complementary probability that 20 or fewer remember, or

$$P[\text{successes} > 20] = 1 - P[\text{successes} \leq 20]$$
$$= 1 - .0165 = .9835$$

(5) *To obtain a result that lies between two values:* Suppose we want to find the probability that the number of successes will lie somewhere between 25 and 35, inclusively; that is, we want to determine

$$P[25 \leq \text{successes} \leq 35]$$

In this case, we obtain the difference between two cumulative probabilities:

$$P[\text{successes} \leq 35] - P[\text{successes} \leq 24] = .8839 - .1136 = .7703$$

The underlying rationale is that the first term above represents all outcomes with 35 or fewer successes, but we do not want to include those outcomes with successes numbering 24 or fewer. By subtracting the second cumulative probability from the first, we account only for those outcomes that are between 25 and 35 rememberers.

(6) *To find probabilities when the trial success probability exceeds .5:* For brevity, our binomial probability table stops at $P = .5$. Suppose we wish to find probabilities for the number of successes when the trial success probability is bigger (say, .7). To do this, we can still use Appendix Table A by using r as the number of failures and P as the trial failure probability.

Consider a keypuncher who correctly punches cards 99 percent of the time. Suppose we want the probability that at least 95 percent of $n = 100$ cards have been punched correctly. Here a success represents a correct card and $P = .99$. We observe that more than 95 correct is the same as 5 or less incorrect (failures). Using $1 - .99 = .01$ for P, the trial failure probability, and using the portion of Table A where $n = 100$, we find

$$P[\text{failures} \leq 5] = .9995$$

This illustrates that for every success event there is a corresponding failure event with the same probability.

Mean and Variance of Binomial Distribution

The expected number of successes may be determined from probabilities obtained from the binomial formula or from the table for a particular n and P. But rather than multiplying these probabilities by the respective number of successes and summing the products, we can use a special feature of the binomial distribution that allows us to get the answer quickly. The following expression provides the expected number of successes:

$$\text{Expected successes} = nP$$

Thus, the expected number of aircraft delays when $n = 10$ and $P = .4$ is $10(.4) = 4$.

A similar expression applies for the variance and the standard deviation:

$$\text{Variance} = nP(1-P)$$

$$\text{Standard deviation} = \sqrt{nP(1-P)}$$

For the aircraft delay example, the variance is $10(.4)(1-.4) = 2.4$ and the standard deviation is $\sqrt{2.4} = 1.55$.

THE NORMAL DISTRIBUTION 3-4

The normal distribution plays a central role in sampling. It is used to describe frequency patterns for a great many phenomena, such as the physical characteristics of both things and people. It is often used to express the probability distribution for times needed to complete work tasks, such as a bank-teller's transaction, the installation of an automobile bumper, or the completion of a delivery route. The normal distribution is an extremely important tool for analyzing business decisions that contain a variety of uncertain variables.

The normal distribution applies to *continuous random variables*, such as times, weights, and diameters measured on a continuous scale. It is usually described in terms of a bell-shaped curve, as shown in Figure 3-4. Here x represents the possible values of the random variable, and the height represents the relative frequency at which the corresponding values occur. A particular normal distribution is specified by two parameters—the *mean* μ (Greek lower case *mu*) and the

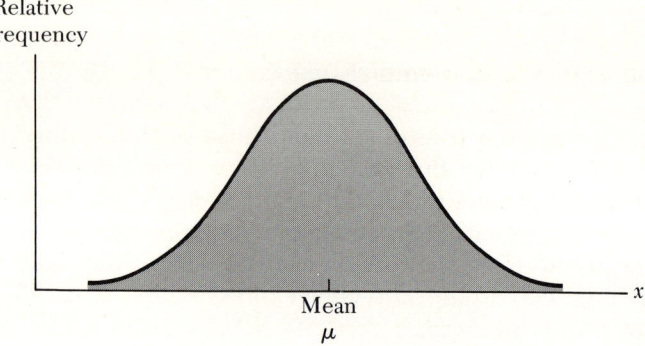

Figure 3-4
Frequency curve for the normal distribution.

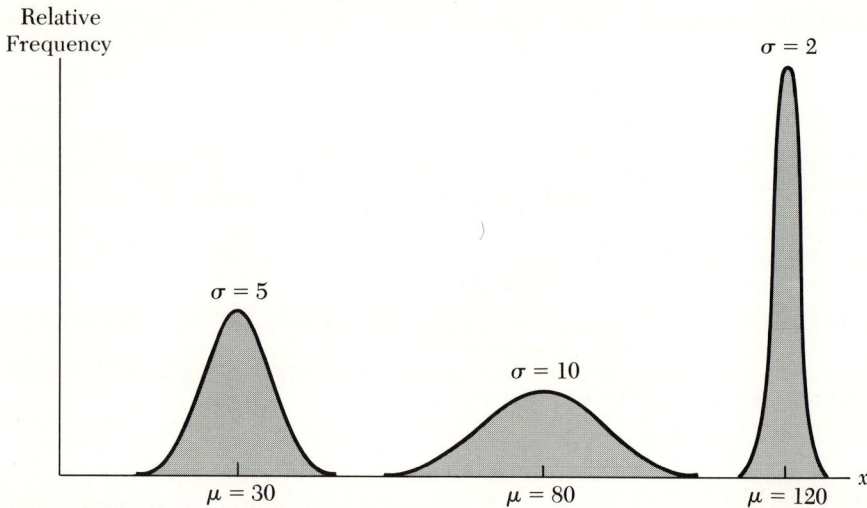

Figure 3-5
Three different normal distributions graphed on a common axis.

standard deviation σ (Greek lower case *sigma*).* The location or center of the corresponding normal curve is determined by the mean, while its shape is established by the standard deviation. Figure 3-5 shows the curves for three different normal distributions.

* Mathematically, this curve is called a *probability density function* and its height may be determined from

$$f(x) = \frac{1}{\sqrt{2\pi\sigma^2}} e^{-[(x-\mu)^2/2\sigma^2]}$$

where $\pi = 3.1416$ and e is the base of natural logarithms (2.7183).

Because the height of the normal curve above any point expresses relative frequency, or proportional occurrence, the total area beneath the curve is 1. We may find the probabilities for various values of a normally distributed random variable by determining *areas* under the applicable portions of its normal curve; these areas correspond to the proportion of times that the particular range of values would occur when identical conditions are repeated.

The areas beneath the normal curve are tied to the distance separating the points of interest from the mean. For example, the Stanford-Binet IQ test was designed so that the scores of persons taking it fall at a mean of $\mu = 100$ with a standard deviation of $\sigma = 16$. A feature of every normal curve is that about 68 percent of the values will fall within plus or minus one standard deviation from the mean. Thus, 68 percent of all persons should achieve IQ scores within the range $\mu \pm 1\sigma$ or 100 ± 16, that is, these persons should have IQs between 84 and 116. Likewise, about 95.5 percent of the values will be within $\mu \pm 2\sigma$, which for IQs would be $100 \pm 2(16)$, or between 68 and 132. Also, about 99.7 percent of all scores should fall within the interval $\mu \pm 3\sigma$, so that the IQs of practically all people lie between $(100 - 3(16)) = 52$ and $(100 + 3(16)) = 148$. Of course higher or lower scores are possible, but like geniuses the extremes are rare; theoretically, the tails of the normal curve never touch the axis, so that there is always some area, and hence probability, for any extreme set of values.

Finding Areas Under the Normal Curve

In order to obtain probability values for normally distributed random variables, we must first find the appropriate area lying under the normal curve. This can be accomplished by using Appendix Table B.

How would you find the desired areas for the time taken by a particular typesetter to compose 500 lines of standard type? Assume that the population of times is normally distributed, with a mean of $\mu = 150$ minutes and a standard deviation of $\sigma = 30$ minutes. The time for any given 500 lines, such as the next ones to be composed, represents a randomly chosen time from that population.

The probability that between 150 and 175 minutes will be required is represented by the shaded area under the normal curve in Figure 3-6. As we have seen, the area beneath the normal curve between the mean and a certain point depends only on the number of standard deviations separating the two points. We see that 175 minutes is equivalent to a .83 standard deviation from the mean. This figure is determined by observing that 175 minutes minus the mean of 150 minutes equals

25 minutes. Since the standard deviation is 30 minutes, 25 minutes is 25/30 or .83 of the standard deviation.

Appendix Table B has been constructed for the *standard normal curve*, which provides the area between the mean and a point above the mean some specified distance measured in standard deviations. Because the distance will vary with the situation, it is treated as a variable and denoted z. Sometimes the value of z is referred to as a *normal deviate*. The distance z that separates a possible normal random-variable value x from its mean may be determined from the following expression for the *normal deviate*:

$$z = \frac{x - \mu}{\sigma}$$

A negative value will be obtained for z when x is smaller than μ.

The first column of Table B lists values of z to a single decimal place. The second decimal place value is located at the head of one of the remaining 10 columns. The area under the curve between the mean and z standard deviations is found at the intersection of the correct row and column. For example, when $z = .83$, we find the area of .2967 by reading the entry in the .8 row and the .03 column. The area under the normal curve for a completion time between 150 and 175 minutes is thus .2967, which represents the probability that the next 500 lines of print will take this long to set.

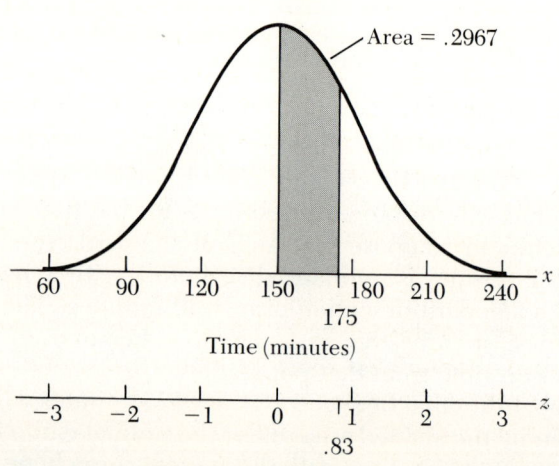

Figure 3-6
Determining the area under a normal curve.

Although Table B only provides areas between the mean and some point above it, it may be used to find areas in other common probability situations, such as those in Figure 3-7. Each of these is described below:

(a) *Area between mean and some point lying below it.* To find the probability that the completion time lies between 125 and 150 minutes, first we calculate the normal deviate

$$z = \frac{125 - 150}{30} = -.83$$

Here z is negative because 125 is a point lying below the mean. Since the normal curve is symmetrical about the mean, this area must be the same as it would be for a positive value of z of the same magnitude (in this case .2967, as before). It is therefore unnecessary to tabulate areas for negative values of z. The area between the mean and a point lying below it will equal the area between the mean and a point equally distant above it.

(b) *Area to the left of a value above the mean.* To find the probability that the type can be set in 185 minutes or less, we have to find the entire shaded area below 185. Here, we must consider the lower half of the normal curve separately. Since the entire normal curve area is 1, the area under the half to the left of 150 must be .5. The area between 150 and 185 is found from Table B, with $z = (185 - 150)/30 = 1.17$, to be .3790. The entire shaded portion is the sum of the two areas, or .5000 + .3790 = .8790.

(c) *Area in upper tail.* We find the probability that the number of minutes required exceeds 195 by first finding the area between the mean and 195. The normal deviate is $z = (195 - 150)/30 = 1.50$, for which Table B yields the area .4332. Since the area in the upper half of the normal curve is .5, our desired area is found by subtracting the unwanted portion, or .5000 − .4332 = .0668.

Because the total area under the normal curve is 1, we may use the upper tail area to calculate the area to the left of 195. This may be found by subtracting the upper tail area from 1, giving 1.0000 − .0668 = .9332 as the area to the left of 195 (or the probability that the time will be less than 195 minutes). Similarly, when the area to the left of a point is known, the area to its right can be found by subtracting this value from 1. For example, in (b) above, we found the area to the left of 185 to be .8790. Thus, the area to the right of 185 must be 1 − .8790 = .1210.

(d) *Area in lower tail.* We find the probability that 90 minutes or less will be taken to set the type by two steps similar to those in (c)

3-4   THE NORMAL DISTRIBUTION

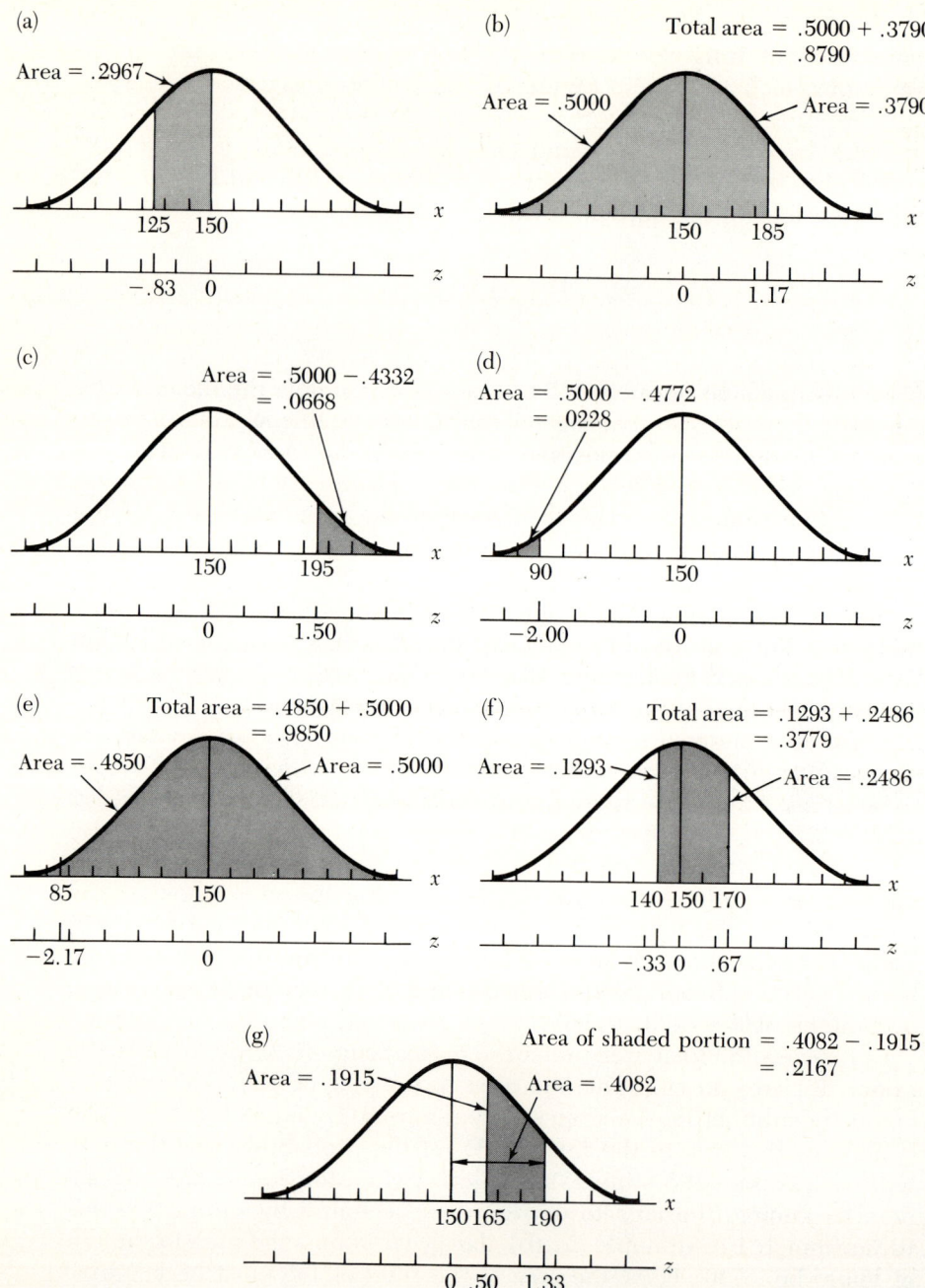

Figure 3-7
Various areas under normal curve. x = completion time, in minutes; z = standard deviations.

above. First the area between 90 and 150 is found. Using $z = (90 - 150)/30 = -2.00$, we obtain .4772 from Table B. We subtract this value from .5 and obtain $.5000 - .4772 = .0228$.

(e) *Area to the right of a value below the mean.* To find the probability that the completion time will be equal to or greater than 85 minutes, the area between 85 and the mean is added to the area to the right of the mean, which is .5. Here, we calculate $z = (85 - 150)/30 = -2.17$; from Table B, the area is .4850. Adding this to .5, we find the combined area to be $.5000 + .4850 = .9850$.

From this value, the area in the lower tail below 85 may be found by subtracting .9850 from 1: $1 - .9850 = .0150$.

(f) *Area under portion overlapping the mean.* In order to find the probability that the time taken will be between 140 and 170 minutes, we need only add the portion of the shaded area that lies below the mean to the one above it. The respective normal deviate values are calculated to be $z = (140 - 150)/30 = -.33$ and $z = (170 - 150)/30 = .67$. From Table B, the lower area is .1293 and the upper area is .2486; thus, the combined area is $.1293 + .2486 = .3779$.

Suppose we wish to find the probability that between 120 and 180 minutes will be taken. The normal deviates are $z = (120 - 150)/30 = -1$ and $z = (180 - 150)/30 = 1$. From Table B, the area is the same for both sides (.3413), and the combined area is $.3413 + .3413 = .6826$. Because z expresses the number of standard deviation units from the mean, we see that .6826 is a more precise value for the area between $\mu \pm 1\sigma$ than the value mentioned at the outset.

(g) *Area between two values lying above or below the mean.* To find the probability that the composition time lies between 165 and 190 minutes, we must first determine the areas between the mean and each of these two values. The respective normal deviates are therefore $z = (165 - 150)/30 = .50$ and $z = (190 - 150)/30 = 1.33$. From Table B, we see that the area between the mean and 190 is .4082, while the area between the mean and 165 is only .1915. Thus, the shaded area is found by subtracting the smaller area from the larger one: $.4082 - .1915 = .2167$.

A similar procedure could be applied for an area lying below the mean. It is also possible to find the value for a complementary situation — that the time will be either below 165 minutes or greater than 190 minutes — by subtracting the shaded area from 1, or: $1 - .2167 = .7833$.

The normal curve represents values lying on a continuous scale, such as height, weight, and time. There is zero probability that a specific value, such as 129.40 minutes, will occur (there is zero area under the normal curve covering a single point). Thus, in finding probabilities, it does not matter whether we use "strict" inequalities, such as the composition time is "less than" (<) 129.40 minutes, or ordinary inequalities, such as the time is "less than or equal to" (≤) 129.40 minutes. Using $z = (129.40 - 150)/30 = -.69$, we find the area to be the same in either case: $.5000 - .2549 = .2451$.

Standard Normal Random Variable

The area under any normal curve may be found by using the standard normal curve. This curve provides the probability distribution for the *standard normal random variable* Z. Here, our notation of using capital letters for random variables means that the lower case z represents a point on the scale of possible values for Z. Because z expresses distance in standard deviations above or below the mean, the center of the standard normal curve lies at zero, so that the expected value of Z is zero. Likewise the standard deviation of Z is 1.

In the type-composition time illustration, we in essence transformed the original random variable, which we denote by capital X, the time to complete 500 lines, into the standard normal random variable Z whenever we used Table B to find areas. Such a transformation may be accomplished physically by a procedure consisting of two parts: shifting the center of the curve and then stretching or contracting it. To shift the original curve so that its center lies above the point $x = 0$, subtract μ from each point on the x axis. Then the repositioned curve may be stretched or squeezed so that the scale on the horizontal axis matches the scale for the standard normal distribution. This may be accomplished by dividing all values of the random variable by its standard deviation. The transformed curve will have the same shape as the standard normal curve illustrated in Figure 3-8. The net effect will always be the same, no matter what the values of μ and σ are. The horizontal scale may be either expanded or contracted.

Fortunately, a physical transformation of the original random variable X into the standard normal random variable is unnecessary. Instead, we may algebraically manipulate X itself, according to the following expression, to make the *transformation of X into the standard normal variable*

$$Z = \frac{X - \mu}{\sigma}$$

EXAMPLE The Sunflower Vegetable Oil Company supplies its customers from barrels containing about 100 gallons apiece. The current stock of barrels fluctuates in carrying capacity, having a mean of $\mu = 100$ gallons with standard deviation $\sigma = .6$ gallon. Letting X represent the capacity of any particular barrel selected

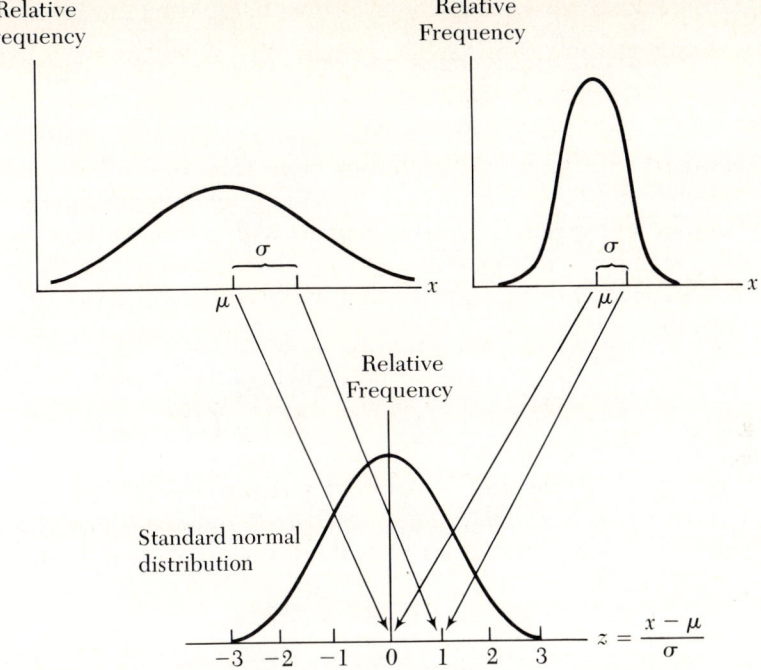

Figure 3-8
Illustration of the linear transformation of normal random variables into the standard normal distribution.

at random from those ready for shipment to a certain customer, we may determine the probability that the capacity is 99 gallons or less by transforming X into the standard normal random variable:

$$P[X \leq 99] = P\left[\frac{X-\mu}{\sigma} \leq \frac{99-100}{.6}\right]$$

Subtracting $\mu = 100$ from both sides of the original inequality and then dividing both sides by $\sigma = .6$ preserves the desired relationship. This change transforms X into the standard normal random variable Z and 99 into a normal deviate value -1.67, so that finding the original probability is equivalent to evaluating $P[Z \leq -1.67]$.

From Table B, the area under the standard normal curve between 0 and $z = 1.67$ is .4525. By the symmetry of the curve, this is also the area between $z = -1.67$ and 0. As we desire the lower tail area, we must subtract .4525 from .5, yielding our result

$$P[X \leq 99] = P[Z \leq -1.67] = .5000 - .4525 = .0475$$

From the above, we see that about 5 percent of all barrels shipped will be short 1 gallon or more from the billed amount of 100 gallons. To avoid possible ill-will, Sunflower management has decided to replace its present barrels with a more uniform variety having mean $\mu = 100$ gallons and standard deviation $\sigma = .25$ gallon. In this case, the probability that a chosen barrel has a 99-gallon capacity or less is

$$P[X \leq 99] = P\left[\frac{X-\mu}{\sigma} \leq \frac{99-100}{.25}\right] = P[Z \leq -4.0]$$

From Table B, the area between 0 and 4.0, and therefore between $z = -4.0$ and 0 is .49997. The new barrels then provide the following probability of being 1 gallon or more short of the billed amount:

$$P[X \leq 99] = P[Z \leq -4.0] = .5000 - .49997 = .00003$$

Less than 3 times out of 100,000, on the average, will such a barrel be chosen.

Suppose that σ was even smaller than the .25 used in the above example. z would then be so large in absolute value that Table B would not provide the area. Our table has to stop somewhere, for the tails of the normal curve extend indefinitely. In general, whenever z exceeds 4, the area between the mean and z is so very close to .5 that for practical purposes .5 would be used. The upper and lower tail areas would be so close to 0 as to be negligible.

The Normal Distribution and Sampling

In several applications of quantitative methods we use sample information to facilitate the final choice. Frequently the value of the *sample mean* is the pivotal factor in such decisions. It is therefore important to be able to compute probabilities for the possible values that the sample mean might take in a given situation. The normal distribution plays a crucial role in establishing these probabilities.

We use a special symbol $\overline{X}$ to represent the sample mean. It may be calculated from

$$\bar{X} = \frac{X_1 + X_2 + \cdots + X_n}{n}$$

The above expression indicates that $\bar{X}$ is the arithmetic average of the n sample observations taken from a population or universe. We presume that the sample is selected randomly. Because the actual value for $\bar{X}$ cannot be known until after the sample has been taken, until then the sample mean must be treated just like any other random variable. Its expected value is the mean μ of the population from which the sample comes. The standard deviation of that population σ partly determines the variability in the possible levels for $\bar{X}$.

A fundamental theorem of statistics, the *central limit theorem*, states that regardless of the population characteristics,* *probabilities for the value of $\bar{X}$ may be closely approximated from the normal curve when the sample size is large.* This normal curve has mean μ and standard deviation $\sigma_{\bar{X}} = \sigma/\sqrt{n}$, reflecting the fact that $\bar{X}$ should have less variability and cluster more tightly about its expected value μ than would any single randomly made observation. Thus, we may use the normal curve for a tremendous variety of analysis situations where samples are involved.

EXAMPLE The mean gasoline mileages of compact and intermediate cars of the same manufacturer are to be estimated by a consumer testing service. No assumption will be made regarding the distributions of the underlying populations, other than that the standard deviations are 2 miles per gallon (mpg) for the compacts and 4 mpg for the intermediates. The mileages of intermediate cars are thus a more disperse population. The applicable standard deviations for the sample means, when a sample size of $n = 100$ is used in each case, are given below:

For compacts: $\sigma_{\bar{X}} = \dfrac{2}{\sqrt{100}} = .2$

For intermediates: $\sigma_{\bar{X}} = \dfrac{4}{\sqrt{100}} = .4$

Figure 3-9 illustrates the normal curves obtained for the respective distributions of $\bar{X}$. The two curves are drawn on separate graphs to emphasize the fact that different means are involved, with compacts having the smaller standard deviation. The shaded areas provide the probabilities that each sample mean will lie within $\pm.5$ mpg of the respective unknown population means.

---

* There is one essential restriction of minor importance in business applications: the population variance must be finite.

3-4   THE NORMAL DISTRIBUTION

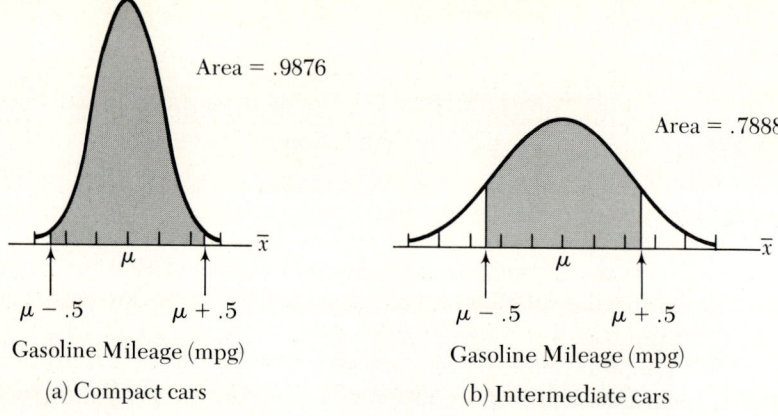

Figure 3-9
Sampling distributions for sample means taken from populations having different standard deviations.

These are

$$P[-.5 \leq \bar{X} - \mu \leq +.5] = P\left[\frac{-.5}{.2} \leq \frac{\bar{X}-\mu}{\sigma_{\bar{X}}} \leq \frac{+.5}{.2}\right]$$

$$= P[-2.5 \leq Z \leq +2.5]$$

$$= 2(.4938) = .9876 \text{ for compacts}$$

$$P[-.5 \leq \bar{X} - \mu \leq +.5] = P\left[\frac{-.5}{.4} \leq \frac{\bar{X}-\mu}{\sigma_{\bar{X}}} \leq \frac{+.5}{.4}\right]$$

$$= P[-1.25 \leq Z \leq +1.25]$$

$$= 2(.3944) = .7888 \text{ for intermediates}$$

A more reliable result is obtained for the compacts, whose normal curve for possible sample means provides a tighter clustering of $\bar{X}$ about μ. This is because the standard deviation of the sample mean is smaller for the compact cars.

3-5 POISSON AND EXPONENTIAL DISTRIBUTIONS

Two further probability distributions are very important in management science applications. One of these, the *Poisson distribution*, provides probabilities for the number of events that might occur over time. A related distribution, the *exponential distribution*, provides probabilities for the times between events. Both distributions are used extensively in queuing (waiting line) analyses, where the events of interest are customer *arrivals* to the service facility being evaluated. Because we will use the Poisson and exponential distributions primarily in conjunction with queuing analyses, a detailed discussion of these distributions will be reserved until Chapter 16.

PROBLEMS

3-1 From the following probability distributions for the receipts and expenses of a charity carnival, determine the probability distribution for the net proceeds (Receipts − Expenses). In doing this, assume that receipts and expenses are independent.

Receipts	*Probability*	*Expenses*	*Probability*
$30,000	1/3	$30,000	1/3
40,000	1/3	40,000	1/3
50,000	1/3	50,000	1/3
	1		1

3-2 A coin is tossed three times. Determine the probability distribution for the number of heads, using the binomial formula. Then calculate the expected number of heads.

3-3 Determine the probability distribution of the winnings achieved by a player placing a $1 bet on the red field in roulette. Then calculate the expected winnings and state verbally the meaning of your answer.

3-4 During the early 1950s, canasta was a popular card game. In canasta, points are assigned to cards in the following manner: red three = 100 points; joker = 50 points; ace or deuce = 20 points; eight through king = 10 points; black threes and four through seven = 5 points. A canasta deck is comprised of two ordinary decks of playing cards, each containing 52 cards and 2 jokers. For the first card dealt from a shuffled canasta deck, determine the probability distribution for its corresponding points.

3-5 Calculate the mean, the variance, and the standard deviation for the points of the first card dealt from the canasta deck in Problem 3–4, using your probability distribution from that problem.

3-6 An investor wishes to buy a stock to be held for one year in anticipation of capital gain. The choice has been narrowed down to High-Volatility Engineering and Stability Power. Both stocks currently sell for $100 per share and yield $5 dividends. The probability distributions for next year's price has been judgmentally assessed for each stock. These are given on the next page.

HIGH-VOLATILITY ENGINEERING		STABILITY POWER	
Price	Probability	Price	Probability
$ 25	.05	$ 95	.10
50	.07	100	.25
75	.10	105	.50
100	.05	110	.15
125	.10		1.00
150	.15		
175	.12		
200	.10		
225	.12		
250	.14		
	1.00		

    (a) Determine the expected prices for a share of each stock.
    (b) Should the investor select the stock with the highest expected value? Discuss.

3-7 Can each of the following situations be classified as a Bernoulli process? If not, state why.
    (a) Childbirths in a hospital, the relevant events being the sex of each newborn child.
    (b) The outcomes of successive rolls of a die, considering only the events odd or even.
    (c) A crooked gambler has rigged his roulette wheel so that whenever the player loses, a mechanism is released which gives him better odds; likewise, when a player wins, his chance of winning on the next spin is somewhat smaller than before. Consider the outcomes of successive spins.
    (d) The measuring mechanism that determines how much dye to squirt into paint being mixed to customer order occasionally violates the required tolerances. The mechanism is very reliable when it is new, but it continually wears with use, becoming less accurate with time. Consider the outcomes (within or not within tolerance) for successive mixings.
    (e) A machine produces items that are sometimes too heavy or too wide to be used. The events of interest express the quality of each successive item in terms of both weight and width.

3-8 An evenly balanced coin is fairly tossed seven times.
    (a) Use the binomial formula to determine the probabilities of obtaining: (1) exactly two heads; (2) exactly four heads; (3) no tails; (4) exactly three tails.
    (b) What do you notice about your answers to (2) and (4)? Why is this so?

3-9 n parts are randomly chosen from a production process which yields 5 percent defectives. How many defectives are expected when (a) $n = 5$? (b) $n = 10$? (c) $n = 100$?

3-10 Using the probability values in Table 3-5, construct the cumulative probability distribution for the number of heads.

3-11 A fair coin is tossed 20 times in succession. Using Appendix Table A, determine the probability that the number of heads obtained is
(a) Less than or equal to 8. (b) Equal to 10.
(c) Less than 15. (d) Greater than or equal to 12.
(e) Greater than 13. (f) Between 8 and 14, inclusively.

3-12 The chief engineer in a chemical plant has established a policy that five sample vials be drawn from the final stage of a chemical process at random times over a four-hour period. If one or more vials (20 percent or more) have impurities, all the settling tanks are cleaned. Find the probability that the tanks must be cleaned when
(a) The process is so clean that the probability of a dirty vial is $P = .01$.
(b) Same as (a), but with $P = .05$.
(c) Same as (a), but with $P = .20$.
(d) Same as (a), but with $P = .50$.
(*Hint:* Use the fact that $P[\text{at least one dirty vial}] = 1 - P[\text{no dirty vials}]$.)

3-13 A production process produces defective parts at rate of .05. If a random sample of five items is chosen, what is the probability that at least 80 percent of the sample will be defective?

3-14 A lopsided coin provides a 60 percent chance of a head on each toss. If the coin is tossed 20 times, find the probability that the number of heads obtained is
(a) Less than or equal to 8.
(b) Equal to 9.
(c) Less than 15.
(d) Greater than or equal to 12.
(e) Greater than 13.
(f) Between 8 and 14, inclusively.

3-15 A student marks an examination consisting of 50 true-or-false questions by tossing a coin. Assuming that half the correct answers should be marked true, find the probability that the student will pass the examination by marking at least 60 percent of the answers correctly.

3-16 The measurement errors for the height of a weather satellite above a ground station are normally distributed with a mean of zero and a standard deviation of one mile. These errors will be negative if the measured altitude is too low and positive if the altitude is too high. Find the probability that for the next orbit the error will be

(a) Between zero and +1.55 miles.
(b) Between −2.45 and zero miles.
(c) +.75 miles or less.
(d) Greater than +.75 miles.
(e) −1.25 miles or less.
(f) Greater than −1.25 miles.
(g) Between +.10 and +.60 miles.
(h) Between +1 and +2 miles.

3-17 The lifetime of a particular model of a stereo cartridge is normally distributed with a mean of $\mu = 1000$ hours and a standard deviation of $\sigma = 100$ hours. Find the probability that one of these cartridges will last
(a) Between 1000 and 1150 hours.
(b) Between 950 and 1000 hours.
(c) 930 hours or less.
(d) More than 1250 hours.
(e) 870 hours or less.
(f) Longer than 780 hours.
(g) Between 700 and 1200 hours.
(h) Between 750 and 850 hours.

3-18 The quality-control manager shuts down an automatic lathe for corrective maintenance whenever a sample of parts it produces has an average diameter either greater than 2.01 inches or smaller than 1.99 inches. The lathe is designed to produce parts with a mean diameter of 2.00 inches, and the sample averages have a standard deviation of .005 inches. Using the normal distribution:
(a) What is the probability that the quality-control manager will stop the process when the lathe is operating as designed, with $\mu = 2.00$ inches?
(b) Suppose a part within the lathe wears out, and it begins to produce parts that on the average are too wide, with $\mu = 2.02$ inches. What is the probability that the lathe will continue to operate?
(c) Suppose that an adjustment error causes the lathe to produce parts that on the average are too narrow, so that $\mu = 1.99$ inches. What is the probability that the lathe will be stopped?

3-19 The city public health department closes down a certain beach when the concentration of *E. coli* bacteria, present in raw sewage, becomes too high. Assume that on a particular day the contamination-level index is normally distributed, with a mean of $\mu = 160$ and a standard deviation of $\sigma = 20$ for each liter of water. A sample of $n = 25$ liters is taken, and the mean index value $\bar{X}$ is found.
(a) Calculate $\sigma_{\bar{X}}$.
Determine the probability that $\bar{X}$ will
(b) Lie between 150 and 160.
(c) Exceed 148.
(d) Fall at or below 153.
(e) Lie between 165 and 170.
(f) Fall above 162.

3-20 A large bus transportation company wishes to estimate the mean

mileage that can be obtained on a new type of radial tire. Due to operating methods, a tire may be used on several buses during its useful life. A separate mileage log must therefore be kept on each tire in the sample. Since this procedure is costly, only $n = 100$ tires are to be used. In a previous study on another tire type, a standard deviation of $\sigma = 2000$ miles was determined. It is assumed that the same figure will apply with the new tires.
(a) What is the probability that the sample mean will be within 500 miles of the population mean?
(b) The maintenance superintendent has stated that the new tires may have greater mileage variability than the ordinary ones. Assuming that the standard deviation is changed to $\sigma = 4000$ miles, find the probability that the sample mean differs from the population mean by no more than 500 miles.
(c) Comparing your answers to parts (a) and (b), what may you conclude about the effect of increased population variability on the reliability of the sample mean as an estimator?
(d) Suppose that a sample of size $n = 200$ tires is used instead. Using a standard deviation of $\sigma = 2000$ miles, find the probability that the sample mean differs from the population mean by no more than 500 miles.
(e) Comparing your answers to parts (a) and (d), what may you conclude about the effect of increased sample size on the reliability of the sample mean as an estimator?

3-21 In order to make a decision regarding the optimal number of toll booths to open during various times of the week, the operations manager of a port authority has ordered an extensive study. One unanticipated finding is that the mean time to collect a toll decreases as the traffic becomes heavier. For example, on late Friday afternoon, the collection times were found to have a mean of $\mu = 10$ seconds with a standard deviation of $\sigma = 2$ seconds. On slower Wednesday mornings, the mean was $\mu = 12$ seconds and the standard deviation was $\sigma = 3$ seconds. A consistency check is now to be made to determine whether the season of the year affects efficiency. Random samples of $n = 25$ cars are taken on Wednesday mornings and Friday afternoons. Assuming that the above results are true population parameters, answer the following:
(a) What is the probability that the Wednesday sample mean will differ by more than 1 second from the assumed mean?
(b) What is the same probability for Friday?
(c) Why do the probabilities found in (a) and (b) differ?

Four

Forecasting

Forecasting the future is a fundamental aspect of business decision making. Future sales is the most important variable in business forecasts. Unit sales establish levels for most business activities—from purchasing and production to marketing—and knowledge about sales is a prerequisite to the budgetary and planning process.

A variety of quantitative techniques have been developed to forecast future values. The underlying models can be classified into three broad categories:

(1) *Forecasting Using Past Data.* The historical patterns of a variable are identified and projected into the future. These patterns are obtained through extrapolation from time-series data.

(2) *Forecasting Using Causal Models.* A relationship is found between the unknown variable and one or more other known variables. The values of the known variables are then used to predict the value of the variable of interest.

(3) *Forecasting Using Judgment.* Quantitative representations are used to express judgments in terms of subjective probabilities. These methods can incorporate the forecaster's actual "batting average" and may provide a way to express collective judgments.

This chapter surveys the forecasting methods commonly used in each of these three categories.

4-1 FORECASTING USING PAST DATA: TIME-SERIES ANALYSIS

This type of forecasting transforms past experiences into forecasts of future events. Thus, a government economist who wishes to predict future tax revenues can forecast future personal income by projecting from the trend indicated by the levels of personal income in previous years. Or an electric company that wishes to project its generating capacity 5, 10, or 20 years into the future may forecast that the demand for power will grow at a similar rate to the rate that prevailed during the previous decade. Or a department store buyer can rely on past experience to decide what purchases to make and in what quantities. In each case, values of the variable being predicted are available for several past periods of time. Such data are called *time-series data,* and a statistical procedure that employs such values is called a *time-series analysis.*

A time series is best described in terms of a graph like the one shown in Figure 4-1, in which the gross national product (GNP) of the United States is plotted against time for the period from 1929 to 1974. The graph shows that GNP has grown over the years, but that this growth has been erratic—faster in some years than in others. Wide swings are evident in the graph: The GNP declines during the Great Depression of the 1930s and then rises rapidly with the advent of World War II. One goal of time-series analysis is to identify the swings and fluctuations of a time series and then to sort them into various categories by the arithmetic manipulation of the numerical values obtained.

Several models can be used to characterize time series. The classical model used by economists provides the clearest explanation of the four components of time-series variation and how they relate to each other:

(1) Secular trend (T_t)
(2) Cyclical movement (C_t)
(3) Seasonal fluctuation (S_t)
(4) Irregular variation (I_t)

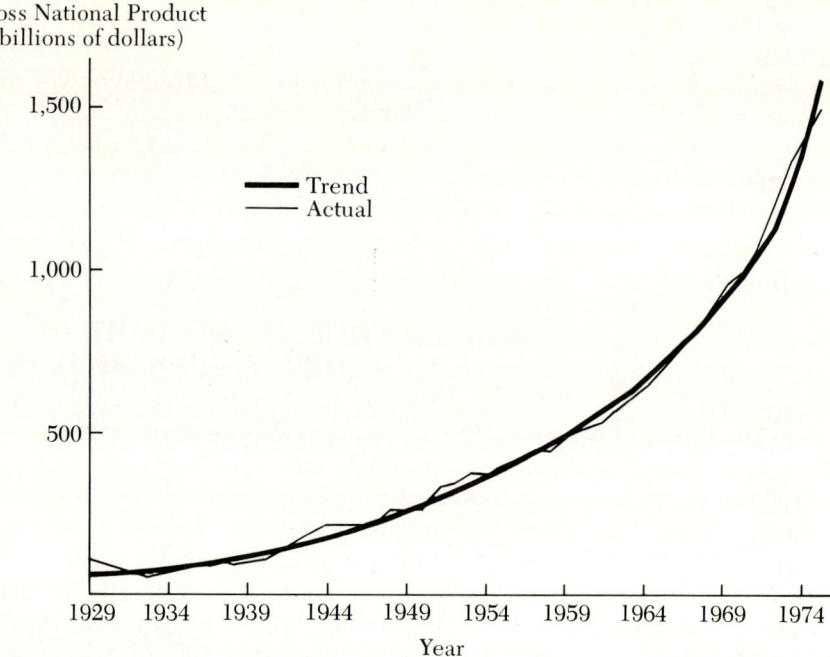

Figure 4-1
U.S. Gross National Product, 1929–1974.
(SOURCE: *Economic Report of the President,* 1970, 1976).

These components can be related to the forecast variable by mathematical equations. The forecast variable is denoted by the symbol Y_t, where the subscript t refers to a period of time. Examples of Y_t are annual sales, passenger miles flown by domestic airlines, and acre-feet of water supplied to a city.

Secular trend is defined as the long-range general movement in Y_t over an extended period of time. In this chapter, we will develop methods for isolating trend from other variational components in a time series. *Cyclical movement* in time-series data is characterized by wide swings—usually a year or more in duration—upward or downward from the secular trend. Cyclical movements are temporary in nature and are typified by alternating periods of economic expansion and contraction or recession. *Seasonal fluctuation* is a generally recurring upward and downward pattern of movement in Y_t, usually on an annual basis. A classic example of seasonal fluctuation is the household consumption of fossil fuels, such as oils, coal, or natural gas. *Irregular variations* are characterized by events that are completely unpredictable. These variations are among the most perplexing ones encountered in time series and are sometimes referred to as *random factors*.

The Classical Time-Series Model

The classical time-series model originally used by economists combines the four components of time-series variation in the equation

$$Y_t = T_t \times C_t \times S_t \times I_t$$

This equation states that factors associated with each of these components can be multiplied together to provide the value of the dependent variable.

This model can be explained by means of a hypothetical time series—the sales Y_t of stereo speakers by the Speak E-Z Company. To construct this time series, we will begin with the trend component T_t, shown in Figure 4-2 as a straight line relating sales to time period. Each successive quarter raises the level of sales by .2 million. Thus, initial sales of 1 million units have grown by the summer of 1978 (10 periods later) to $1 + .2(10) = 3$ million units.

Now let's consider the influence of cyclical movement on the series

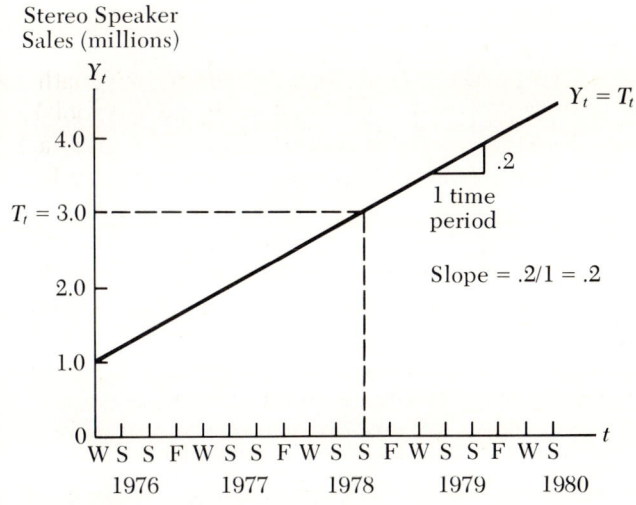

Figure 4-2
Trend line for Speak E-Z sales.

4-1 FORECASTING USING PAST DATA: TIME-SERIES ANALYSIS

that produces sales temporarily above the trend in good years or below it in lean years. For convenience, we express the cyclical effect as a proportion of trend, as shown in Figure 4-3(a). The average value of C_t

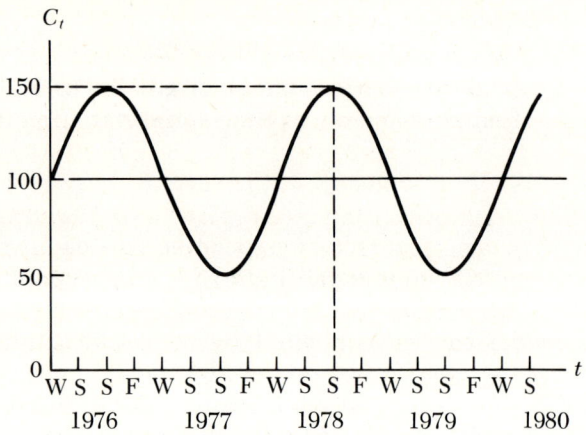

(a) C_t = Component of cyclical movement in stereo speaker sales (percentage of trend)

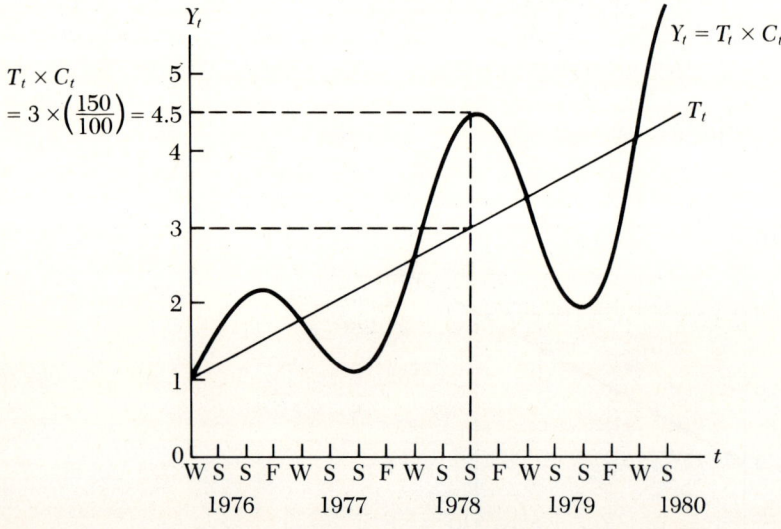

(b) Stereo speaker sales (billions of dollars)

Figure 4-3
Cyclical movement component of Speak E-Z sales and time series, showing only trend and cyclical components.

throughout an entire cycle is considered to be 100 percent. In the summer of 1978, the value of C_t is 150 percent, indicating that sales are 50 percent above the trend during that quarter. The time series for speaker sales with this added component is graphed in Figure 4-3(b), where the curve for C_t has been superimposed on the trend line.

We can follow the same procedure in dealing with seasonal fluctuations in stereo speaker sales, which can be viewed as short-term swings about the longer term sales level indicated by the combined trend and cyclical components. Sales will lie above this level during the busy season and below it during slack times. Thus, we can consider S_t to be a proportion of the long-term sales level established by T_t and C_t, which again can be conveniently expressed as a percentage.

The values of S_t, referred to as *seasonal indexes*, are shown in Figure 4-4. For the summer of 1978, the seasonal index is $S_t = 60$ percent, indicating that sales were only 60 percent of "normal" during this period. The time series obtained by superimposing the seasonal fluctuations on longer term sales is shown in Figure 4-5.

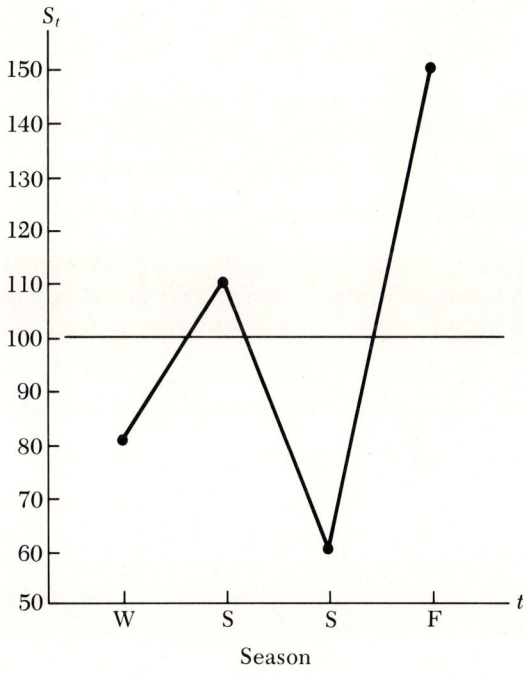

Figure 4-4

Seasonal fluctuations of Speak E-Z sales. S_t = seasonal index of fluctuation about the long-term sales level, expressed as a percentage of $T_t \times C_t$.

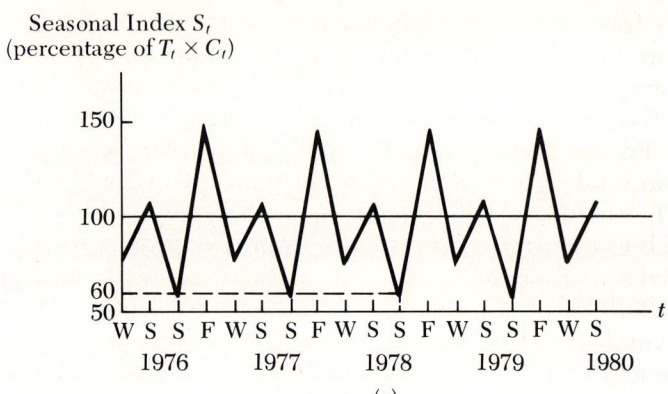

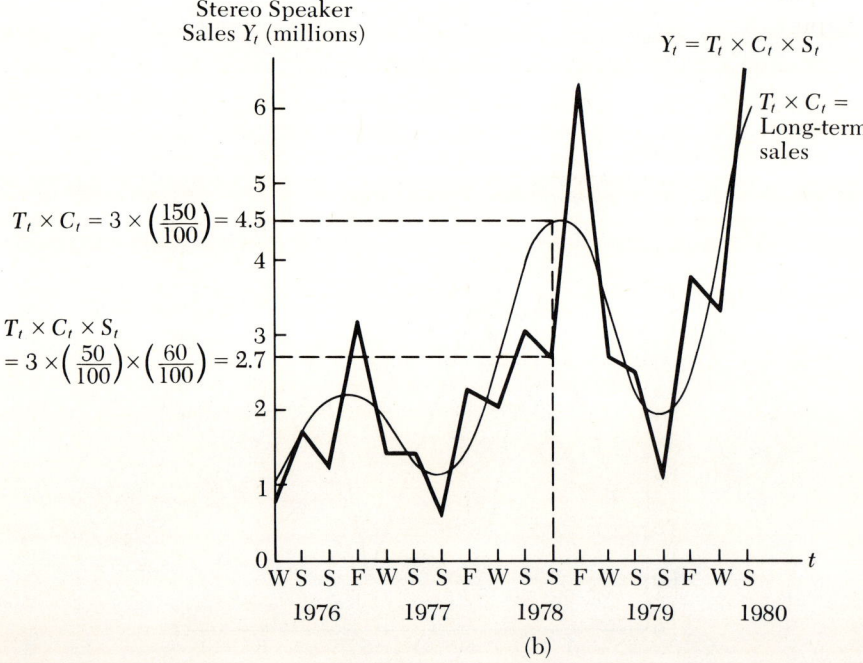

Figure 4-5
(a) Seasonal index component of Speak E-Z sales and (b) time series showing only trend, cyclical, and seasonal components.

We must still consider the irregular component of variation in speaker sales. As in the case of C_t and S_t, this variation is represented by a percentage I_t. Viewing all irregular movement as short term in nature, we can consider I_t to be the last factor—the one that raises or lowers sales from the level established by the regular pattern of systematic factors that we have already considered. The values used to construct the graph for I_t (shown in Figure 4-6) have been obtained randomly, so that the long-run average value of I_t is 100 percent.

For the summer of 1978, I_t is 97 percent of "normal." These irregular variations can be superimposed on the curve we obtained previously for T_t, C_t, and S_t to provide a complete hypothetical time series for Speak E-Z's sales. The variational influence of each component is summarized in Figure 4-7, where the final time series is obtained.

This illustration has shown us how a hypothetical time series can be synthesized from the assumed characteristics of the four components. In actual applications, however, we may not know anything about T_t, C_t, S_t, or I_t. Usually, we begin with the raw time-series data and reverse the procedure, shifting the data to sort out and identify the components. We will discuss some examples of this technique in this chapter.

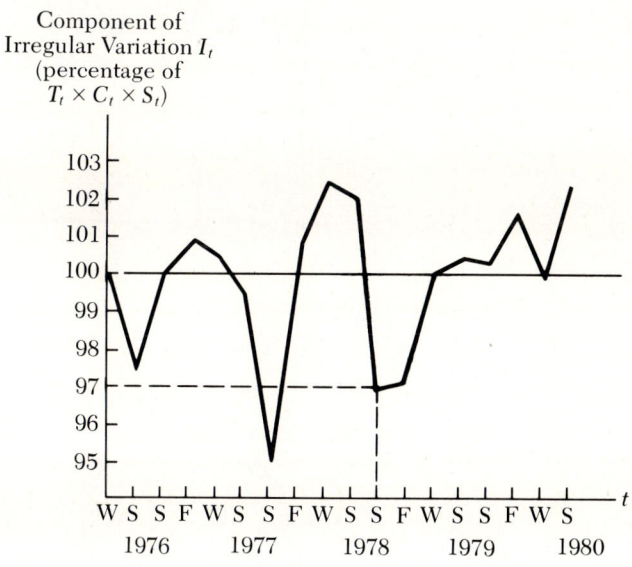

Figure 4-6
Component of irregular fluctuation in Speak E-Z sales.

4-1 FORECASTING USING PAST DATA: TIME-SERIES ANALYSIS

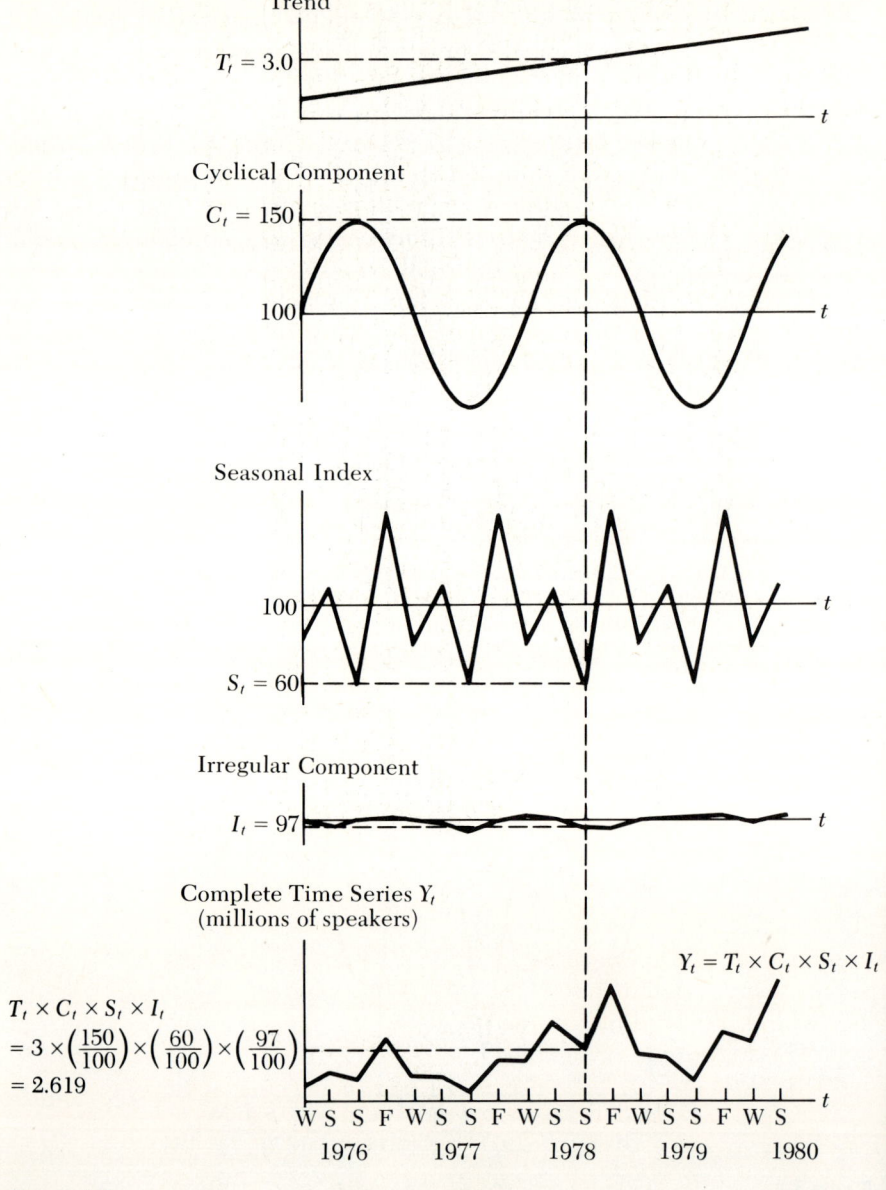

Figure 4-7
The construction of a complete time series for Speak E-Z sales, using individual components.

FORECASTING TREND USING REGRESSION 4-2

The secular trend component I_t of a time series may be the most valuable variable in making forecasts. Trend analysis focuses on finding the appropriate trend line or curve that provides the best fit to the historical scatter of Y_t over time.

Determining Trend Using Least Squares

As an example, we will consider the unit sales of Blitz Beer. Each year's sales are plotted as a point on the *scatter diagram* in Figure 4-8. The heavy line, representing trend, was constructed to minimize the sum of the squared deviations. These deviations are represented by the vertical segments connecting each point to the trend line.

The trend line is found by the *method of least squares*, according to the *regression equation*

$$\hat{Y} = a + bX$$

Here, $\hat{Y}$ represents the computed value of the *dependent variable* (the variable being forecast) of the time series, and X represents the *independent variable* (the time period). We use X instead of t, because it is simpler to express time relative to a base period.

The *regression coefficients* a and b are obtained from the equations

$$b = \frac{n\Sigma XY - (\Sigma X)(\Sigma Y)}{n\Sigma X^2 - (\Sigma X)^2}$$

$$a = \bar{Y} - b\bar{X}$$

where $\bar{Y}$ and $\bar{X}$ are the respective mean values. The individual X and Y values represent the time-series *raw data*. These data appear in Table 4-1, where the preliminary least-squares calculations are made.

The regression coefficients are calculated as

$$b = \frac{10(3{,}701.2) - 45(795.6)}{10(285) - 45^2} = 1.47$$

$$\bar{X} = 45/10 = 4.5 \quad \text{and} \quad \bar{Y} = 795.6/10 = 79.56$$

$$a = 79.56 - 1.47(4.5) = 72.95$$

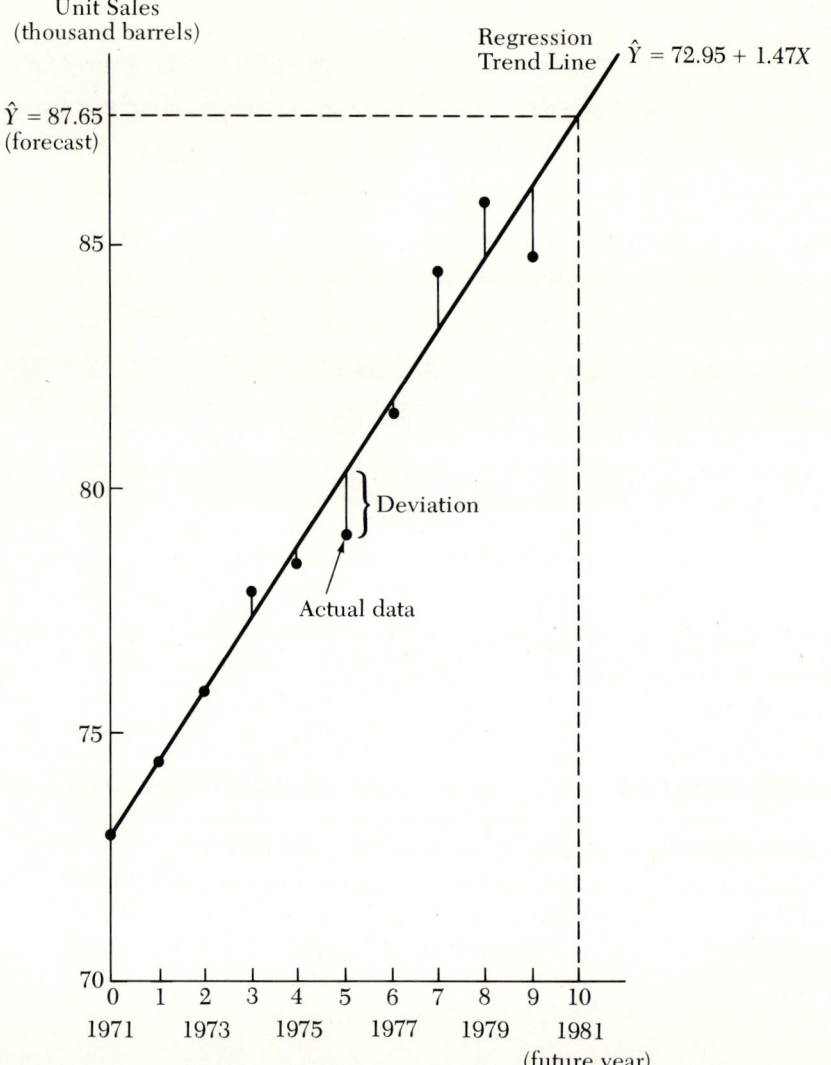

Figure 4-8
Least-squares regression line for trend in unit sales of Blitz Beer.

The regression equation for the trend line in Blitz Beer sales (in thousands of barrels) is therefore

$$\hat{Y} = 72.95 + 1.47X \qquad (X = 0 \text{ for } 1971)$$

This equation indicates that for 1971 the trend value is sales of 72.95

Table 4-1
COMPUTATIONS FOR FITTING LEAST-SQUARES TREND LINE TO BLITZ BEER SALES

Year	Year in Transformed Units X	Unit Sales (thousands of barrels) Y	XY	X²
1971	0	72.9	0	0
1972	1	74.4	74.4	1
1973	2	75.9	151.8	4
1974	3	77.9	233.7	9
1975	4	78.6	314.4	16
1976	5	79.1	395.5	25
1977	6	81.7	490.2	36
1978	7	84.4	590.8	49
1979	8	85.9	687.2	64
1980	9	84.8	763.2	81
	45 = ΣX	795.6 = ΣY	3,701.2 = ΣXY	285 = ΣX^2

thousand barrels and that Y_t increases by 1.47 thousand barrels per year. Because the calendar years have been transformed, it is important to indicate the base year: $X = 0$ for 1971.

Forecasting Trend

We can forecast Blitz Beer sales for 1981 on the basis of the trend line. To do this, we must use $X = 10$, because this year is $X = 1981 - 1971 = 10$ periods beyond the base year. From the trend equation, we can project that 1981 Blitz Beer sales will be

$$\hat{Y} = 72.95 + 1.47(10) = 87.65 \text{ thousand barrels}$$

The estimate of 87.65 is an *extrapolation*. Its validity depends on the assumption that the growth pattern of beer sales in the ensuing year will be similar to the pattern in the past.

The Trend Curve

A straight line provides a poor fit to the data for many time series, because it assumes that Y_t increases or decreases by a constant amount each year. In most time series, Y_t can change at either an increasing or a decreasing rate. Figure 4-9 shows the time series for domestic airline

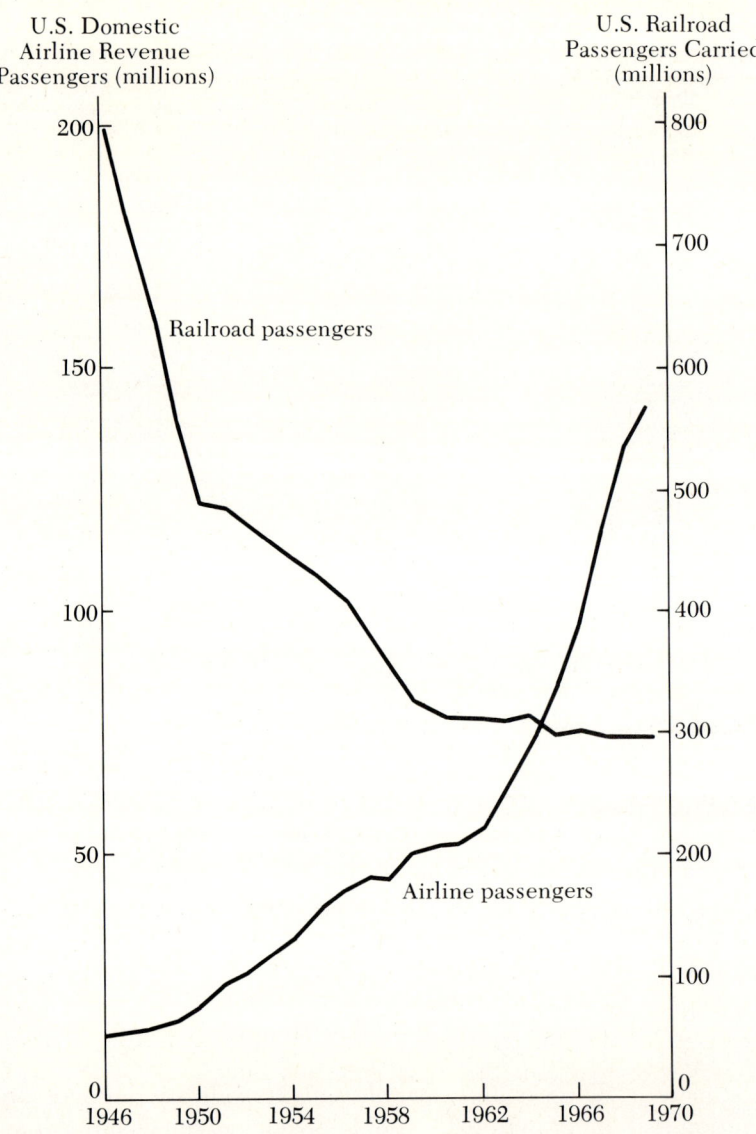

Figure 4-9
Domestic airline and railroad passenger data, 1946–1970. (SOURCE: *Moody's Transportation Manual,* 1970).

revenue passengers from 1946 to 1970. Here, the number of passengers has increased at an increasing rate over time—in contrast to the number of domestic railroad passengers carried, also shown, which exhibits a decreasing trend at a seemingly decreasing rate.

Part of the decline in rail passengers carried can be explained by a

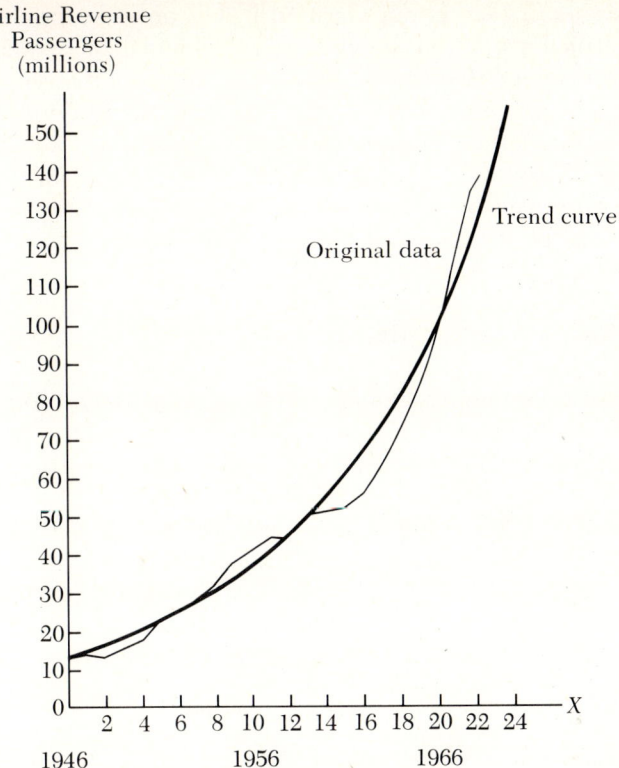

Figure 4-10
Trend curve and original data for domestic airline passengers.

preference for airplane travel and by wider use of the automobile. Few passenger trains run over long distances in the United States, and the railroads have declined to such a degree that the government now runs most rail passenger service. The fact that the number of railroad passengers carried leveled off at about 300 million in 1970 may be attributed to the growing significance of commuters, who now comprise a high proportion of rail passengers. A trend curve and the original time series for domestic airline passengers are shown in Figure 4-10. Detailed discussions of procedures for finding trend curves can be found in some of the selected references listed at the back of the book.

FORECASTING USING SEASONAL INDEXES   4-3

In this section, we will examine a procedure for isolating seasonal fluctuations in time-series data. Identifying seasonal patterns is a necessary first step in short-range planning. The management of a firm whose business drops in May is not alarmed if it is only the beginning of an annual seasonal trough. Likewise, government economists recognize that the Consumer Price Index will rise or fall in certain months solely due to the influence of seasonal factors, such as changing varieties of produce on the market. To monitor the performance of a business or an economy, it is useful to "deseasonalize" time-series data to determine whether a current drop or rise is greater than normal. A technique for doing this will be described at the end of this section.

Ratio-to-Moving-Average Method

The ratio-to-moving-average method is widely used to isolate seasonal fluctuations. This approach is the reverse of the sequence we followed in constructing the Speak E-Z time series earlier. Beginning with the actual time series, the trend and cyclical elements are isolated together in what is referred to as a "smoothed" time series. The isolation of the long-term elements is accomplished by means of *four-quarter moving averages*.

In the context of the classical time-series model, the ratio-to-moving-average method is summarized by the expression

$$\frac{Y_t}{\text{Moving average}} = \frac{T_t \times C_t \times S_t \times I_t}{T_t \times C_t} = S_t \times I_t$$

The moving average provides both trend and cycle, so that $T_t \times C_t$ is obtained for each time period. Dividing Y_t by the moving average is therefore equivalent to canceling the $T_t \times C_t$ terms from the multiplicative model, so that only the seasonal and irregular components, expressed by $S_t \times I_t$, remain.

To illustrate this procedure, data for average weekly freight-car loadings are provided in Table 4-2. The original data are listed in column (2), and the moving totals for four successive quarters appear in column (3). For 1968, the quarterly figures are 508.0, 565.7, 549.7, and 543.7 thousands of carloads. The total of these four quarters is 2,167.1, which represents all of the carloading figures for 1968. This is not an annual total, however, because the original data are weekly averages. The entries in column (3) are positioned in the table to fall *between* the quarters. These numbers must be adjusted to arrive at a true value for each quarter.

To illustrate this procedure, we will consider the first two entries, 2,167.1 and 2,166.4, from column (3). Their sum, 4,333.5, represents two overlapping years of carloadings and appears in column (4) in the row for the summer quarter of 1968. Because three quarters have been counted twice, the value 4,333.5 represents a total of eight quarterly figures. The four-quarter moving average for Summer 1968 is obtained by dividing the sum 4,333.5 by 8. This yields 541.7, which is entered in column (5), where four-quarter moving averages have been similarly obtained for the remaining quarters.

The four-quarter moving averages from column (5) of Table 4-2 are graphed in Figure 4-11 along with the original time-series data. Note that two quarters at the beginning and end of the series are "lost." If

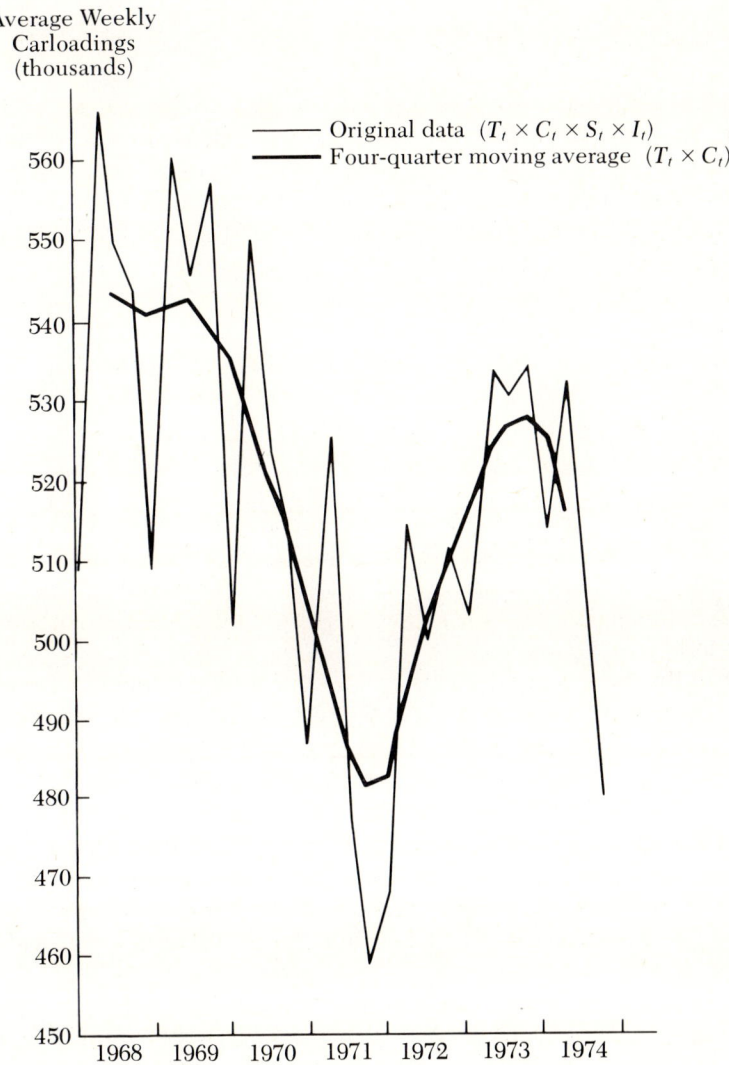

Figure 4-11
Four-quarter moving averages and original data for average weekly carloadings.

4-3   FORECASTING USING SEASONAL INDEXES

Table 4-2
RATIO-TO-MOVING-AVERAGE AND DESEASONALIZATION CALCULATIONS FOR AVERAGE WEEKLY CARLOADINGS

(1) Quarter	(2) Average Weekly Carloadings (thousands)	(3) Four-Quarter Moving Total	(4) Sum of Two Successive Four-Quarter Totals	(5) Four-Quarter Moving Average $[(4) \div 8]$	(6) Original Data as a Percentage of Moving Average $[(2) \div (5)] \times 100$	(7) Seasonal Index	(8) Deseasonalized Data $[(2) \div (7)] \times 100$
1968							
Winter	508.0					96.11	528.7
Spring	565.7					103.66	545.7
Summer	549.7	2,167.1	4,333.5	541.7	101.48	100.25	548.3
Fall	543.7	2,166.4	4,328.8	541.1	100.48	99.98	543.8
		2,162.4					
1969							
Winter	507.3	2,158.0	4,320.4	540.1	93.93	96.11	527.8
Spring	561.7	2,171.3	4,329.3	541.2	103.79	103.66	541.9
Summer	545.3	2,162.7	4,334.0	541.8	100.65	100.25	543.9
Fall	557.0	2,151.3	4,314.0	539.3	103.28	99.98	557.1
1970							
Winter	498.7	2,129.7	4,281.0	535.1	93.20	96.11	518.9
Spring	550.3	2,086.0	4,215.7	527.0	104.42	103.66	530.9
Summer	523.7	2,073.0	4,159.0	519.9	100.73	100.25	522.4
Fall	513.3	2,048.7	4,121.7	515.2	99.63	99.98	513.4
1971							
Winter	485.7	2,002.0	4,050.7	506.3	95.93	96.11	505.4
Spring	526.0	1,946.0	3,948.0	493.5	106.59	103.66	507.4
Summer	477.0	1,928.3	3,874.3	484.3	98.49	100.25	475.8
Fall	457.3	1,916.0	3,844.3	480.5	95.17	99.98	457.4

1972						
Winter	468.0	1,939.3	3,855.3	481.9	97.12	96.11	486.9
Spring	513.7	1,993.3	3,932.6	491.6	104.50	103.66	495.6
Summer	500.3	2,028.0	4,021.3	502.7	99.52	100.25	499.1
Fall	511.3	2,047.6	4,075.6	509.5	100.35	99.98	511.4
1973						
Winter	502.7	2,077.3	4,124.9	515.6	97.50	96.11	523.0
Spring	533.3	2,100.3	4,177.6	522.2	102.13	103.66	514.5
Summer	530.0	2,109.3	4,209.6	526.2	100.72	100.25	528.7
Fall	534.3	2,108.3	4,217.6	527.2	101.35	99.98	534.4
1974						
Winter	511.7	2,085.3	4,193.6	524.2	97.62	96.11	532.4
Spring	532.3	2,030.7	4,116.0	514.5	103.46	103.66	513.5
Summer	507.0					100.25	505.7
Fall	479.7					99.98	479.8

SOURCE OF DATA: *Moody's Transportation Manual*, 1975.

the series curve provided by the moving averages (the heavier line segments in the graph) represents only the trend and cyclical elements, the fluctuations in the original data about this curve illustrate the seasonal and irregular components. The combination $S_t \times I_t$ can be obtained by dividing the original data by the corresponding four-quarter moving average. For Summer 1968, the actual average weekly carloading value is 549.7 thousand. Dividing this number by the corresponding moving average of 541.7 and multiplying by 100 gives us the *percentage of moving average*

$$\frac{549.7}{541.7} \times 100 = 101.48$$

The percentages of moving averages for the remaining quarters, provided in column (6) of Table 4-2, are plotted in Figure 4-12. Note the repetitive nature of the oscillations, which are more or less regular from one time period to the next. The overall pattern is not precisely the same for all years, however, due to the irregular variation I_t. The remaining step in the ratio-to-moving-average method is to isolate a seasonal index completely by removing the irregular component.

The classical model assumes that short-term random influences will either increase or decrease the value of Y_t from its expected level for a

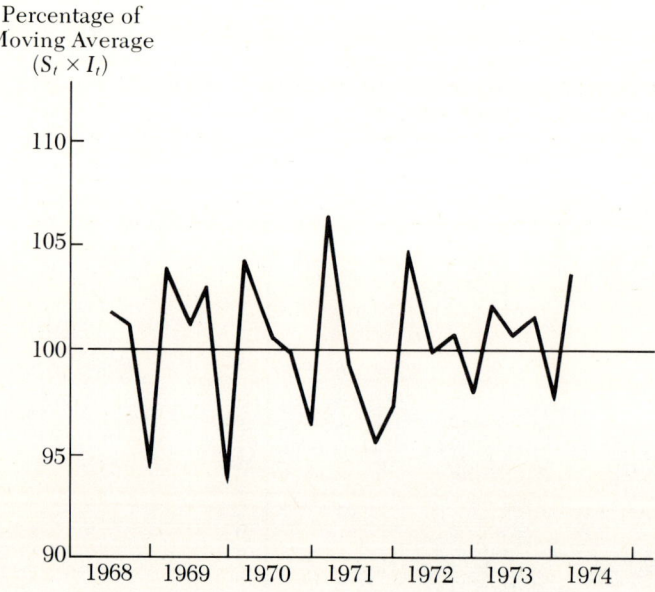

Figure 4-12
Original average weekly carloading data as percentage of four-quarter moving average.

particular quarter. If the summer quarters for several different years are considered, the irregular fluctuations will have a positive effect in some years and a negative influence in others. For the duration of the time series, we can assume that the average effect of random factors will be 0.

We can isolate S_t by averaging the $S_t \times I_t$ values for the same season. This is illustrated in Table 4-3, where the percentage of moving average values from column (6) of Table 4-2 are grouped into the four seasonal categories. Note that the values for winter range from a low of 93.20 for 1970 to a high of 97.62 for 1974. The median will be used to represent the true seasonal factor. For winter, this value is 96.53, which is found by averaging the two middle-sized values:

$$\frac{95.93 + 97.12}{2} = 96.53$$

(For an odd number of years, the median is simply the middle-sized value itself.)

The successive medians for the remaining groups are 104.11, 100.69, and 100.42. From these medians, a seasonal index can be obtained for each quarter. The sum of the medians is 401.75. A further adjustment (multiplying each median by 400/401.75) is necessary for the seasonal indexes to sum to 400. For instance, the seasonal index for the winter quarter is 96.53(400/401.75) = 96.11.

Table 4-3
CALCULATION OF SEASONAL INDEXES FROM THE PERCENTAGE OF MOVING-AVERAGE VALUES FOR CARLOADING DATA IN TABLE 4-2

Year		QUARTER			
		Winter	Spring	Summer	Fall
1968				101.48	100.48
1969		93.93	103.79	100.65	103.28
1970		93.20	104.42	100.73	99.63
1971		95.93	106.59	98.49	95.17
1972		97.12	104.50	99.52	100.35
1973		97.50	102.13	100.72	101.35
1974		97.62	103.46		
	Median	96.53	104.11	100.69	100.42
Sum of medians = 401.75					
Seasonal index = $\frac{400}{401.75} \times$ median					
	=	96.11	103.66	100.25	99.98

4-3 FORECASTING USING SEASONAL INDEXES

Monthly Data

Because a quarter is too long a time period to provide an accurate seasonal index for many businesses, fluctuations are often predicted on the basis of a 12-month seasonal cycle instead. The general procedures illustrated for quarterly data can also be applied to monthly figures. First, 12-month moving totals are obtained and centered by finding the sum of two successive totals. The 12-month moving average is determined by dividing the centered totals by 24 (the number of monthly figures included). The percentage of moving average is then found by dividing the original monthly data by the respective moving averages. Seasonal indexes are obtained by grouping all the percentages for the same month in each year together to obtain 12 groups. The median of each monthly group is then calculated, and the sum of the medians is determined. Finally, these medians are adjusted so that their sum is 1,200 (12 months per year × 100 percent).

Deseasonalized Data

The ratio-to-moving-average method isolates the seasonal indexes. The seasonal indexes can be used to deseasonalize the original time-series data, which is often an asset in analyzing long-term movement in a time series. A deseasonalized series is sometimes used in place of smoothed data to identify cyclical activity and can help to determine whether a turning point has been reached. For example, inflation may be expressed in terms of the Consumer Price Index (CPI), which is computed by the U.S. Bureau of Labor Statistics and measures the percentage change in current prices beyond a base period. Government economists base current monetary and fiscal policies on the level of the CPI, after the seasonal influence has been removed. Thus, a slower increase in the deseasonalized CPI may indicate that the peak in an inflationary period has been reached. Monthly deseasonalized CPI values may also be converted on an annual basis. Thus, an increase of .5 percent over the previous month's value would be multiplied by 12 to provide an annual rate of inflation of 6 percent.

Seasonal fluctuations are removed by dividing the original time-series data points by the corresponding seasonal indexes. In terms of the classical model, this is expressed symbolically as

$$\text{Deseasonalized value} = \frac{Y_t}{\text{Seasonal index}} = \frac{T_t \times C_t \times S_t \times I_t}{S_t}$$
$$= T_t \times C_t \times I_t$$

Dividing Y_t by the seasonal index removes the S_t component from the series, leaving only the trend, cyclical, and irregular components, $T_t \times C_t \times I_t$. The seasonal indexes—the values corresponding to the respective quarter in each year—are entered in column (7) of Table 4-2. The original data values in column (2) are then divided by the seasonal index in column (7) and multiplied by 100. The resulting values are deseasonalized and shown in column (8). For instance, the actual average number of weekly carloadings for Winter 1968 is 508.0 thousand, and the seasonal index is 96.11. Thus, for this time period

$$\text{Deseasonalized value} = \frac{508.0}{96.11} \times 100 = 528.7 \text{ (thousand)}$$

Making the Forecast

Seasonal indexes are useful in making short-term forecasts. First, a trend over the annual period is determined, and then seasonal adjustments are made for each period within the year. For example, suppose the managers of a department store who wish to forecast monthly sales for the next calendar year determine the following trend equation:

$$\hat{Y} = 1{,}025{,}000 + 50{,}000X$$

where X is in months and $X = 0$ for January 15 of next year. Calculations of the monthly forecasts of department store sales are provided in Table 4-4. The 12 monthly seasonal indexes appear in column (3), and the

Table 4-4
CALCULATIONS OF THE MONTHLY FORECASTS OF DEPARTMENT STORE SALES

(1)	(2)	(3)	(4)	(5)
			Monthly Sales	Monthly Sales
		Seasonal	Trend Level	Forecast
Month	X	Index	$\hat{Y}$	[(3) × (4)] ÷ 100
Jan.	0	56.7	$1,025,000	581,175
Feb.	1	64.5	1,075,000	693,375
Mar.	2	62.1	1,125,000	698,625
Apr.	3	99.9	1,175,000	1,173,825
May	4	83.6	1,225,000	1,024,100
Jun.	5	67.4	1,275,000	859,350
Jul.	6	58.2	1,325,000	771,150
Aug.	7	100.1	1,375,000	1,376,375
Sep.	8	110.6	1,425,000	1,576,050
Oct.	9	137.7	1,475,000	2,031,075
Nov.	10	167.3	1,525,000	2,551,325
Dec.	11	191.9	1,575,000	3,022,425
		1,200.0		

monthly sales trend levels are calculated in column (4) from the managers' trend equation. For January, the trend value of $1,025,000 is multiplied by 56.7 percent to obtain the forecast sales of $581,175. The sales forecasts for all 12 months are listed in column (5).

4-4 IDENTIFYING CYCLES

Cyclical movement is the most troublesome systematic component of time-series data to analyze. Unlike seasonal fluctuation, which is repetitious and fairly regular from year to year, longer term oscillations, or *cycles*, tend to be erratic. Seasonal influences are predictable and occur periodically. It is virtually certain, for example, that a department store will achieve greater sales in the fall quarter than in any other period within a particular year. With cyclical variation, the peak may occur at any point within a calendar year, and the cycle's duration may vary from one to several years. Cyclical activity usually varies in both intensity and distance from peak to successive peak, making the task of forecasting a cycle formidable—if not impossible.

Identifying past cycles in time-series data is difficult in itself. One problem is that it is normally impossible to achieve a true separation of trend and cyclical movement using the statistical tools available. Determining a trend curve is largely a matter of judgment. For instance, other methods in addition to the least-squares method may be used to fit the data to a regression line. The number of time periods to be included and the particular procedure to be used are matters of individual choice. Different trend forecasts will result from the various techniques used. Procedures for identifying cycles are described in the bibliography in the back of the book.

4-5 EXPONENTIAL SMOOTHING

Exponential smoothing is a popular forecasting procedure because it provides two basic advantages: It simplifies forecasting calculations, and its data-storage requirements are small. Exponential smoothing produces self-correcting forecasts with built-in adjustments that increase or decrease in the opposite direction of earlier errors, much like a thermostat.

Single-Parameter Exponential Smoothing

The basic exponential smoothing procedure provides the next period's forecast directly from the current period's actual and forecast values. This is summarized by the expression

$$F_{t+1} = \alpha Y_t + (1 - \alpha) F_t$$

where t is the current time period, F_{t+1} and F_t are the forecast values for the next period and the current period, respectively, and Y_t is the current actual value. α (the lower-case Greek letter alpha) is the *smoothing constant*—a chosen value lying between 0 and 1.

To illustrate, we will suppose that the period 10 (October) actual sales of Blitz Beer were $Y_{10} = 5{,}240$ barrels and that $F_{10} = 5{,}061.6$ had been forecast earlier for this period. Using a smoothing constant of $\alpha = .20$, the forecast for period 11 (November) sales can be calculated as

$$F_{11} = .20(5{,}240) + (1 - .20)(5{,}061.6) = 5{,}097.3$$

Elementary exponential smoothing is extremely simple, because only one number—last period's forecast—must be saved. But, in essence, the entire time series is embodied in that forecast. If we express F_t in terms of the preceding actual Y_{t-1} and forecast F_{t-1} values, then the equivalent expression for next period's forecast is

$$F_{t+1} = \alpha Y_t + \alpha(1 - \alpha) Y_{t-1} + (1 - \alpha)^2 F_{t-1}$$

Continuing this for several earlier periods shows us that all preceding Ys are reflected in the current forecast. The name for this procedure is derived from the successive weights α, $\alpha(1 - \alpha)$, $\alpha(1 - \alpha)^2$, $\alpha(1 - \alpha)^3$, ..., which *decrease exponentially*. Thus, the more current the actual value of the time series is, the greater its weight is. Progressively less forecasting weight is assigned to older Ys, and the oldest Ys are eventually wiped out. The forecasting procedure can be modified at any time by changing the value of α.

Table 4-5 provides the actual and forecast Blitz Beer sales for 20 periods when $\alpha = .20$. There, the actual sales figure for period 1 has been used for the initial forecast for period 2. (Eventually, the same Fs will be achieved in later time periods, regardless of the initial value.) The errors in this procedure are determined by subtracting the forecasts from their respective actual values. α should be set at a level that minimizes these errors. Often several trial periods are used to "tune" the

Table 4-5

FORECAST OF BLITZ BEER SALES BY SINGLE-PARAMETER EXPONENTIAL SMOOTHING ($\alpha = .20$)

Period t	Actual Sales Y_t	Forecast F_t	Error $Y_t - F_t$
1	4,890	—	—
2	4,910	4,890.0	20.0
3	4,970	4,894.0	76.0
4	5,010	4,909.2	101.8
5	5,060	4,929.4	130.6
6	5,100	4,955.5	144.5
7	5,050	4,984.4	75.6
8	5,170	4,997.5	172.5
9	5,180	5,032.0	148.0
10	5,240	5,061.6	178.4
11	5,220	5,097.3	122.7
12	5,280	5,121.8	158.2
13	5,330	5,153.5	176.5
14	5,380	5,188.8	191.2
15	5,440	5,227.0	173.0
16	5,460	5,269.6	190.4
17	5,520	5,307.7	192.3
18	5,490	5,350.2	139.8
19	5,550	5,378.1	171.9
20	5,600	5,412.5	187.5

smoothing constant to past data. Large αs assign more weight to current values, whereas small αs emphasize past data. By trial-and-error, an optimal level can be found for α that minimizes *variability* in forecasting errors.

Two-Parameter Exponential Smoothing

Note that the forecast Blitz Beer sales are smaller than (lag behind) the actual sales. Whenever there is a pronounced upward trend in actual data (here, increasing sales), forecasts resulting from the single-parameter exponential smoothing procedure are consistently low.

Two-parameter exponential smoothing eliminates such a lag by explicitly accounting for trend—by using a second smoothing constant for trend itself. A total of three equations are employed:

$$V_t = \alpha Y_t + (1 - \alpha)(V_{t-1} + b_{t-1}) \quad \text{(smooth the data)}$$
$$b_t = \gamma(V_t - V_{t-1}) + (1 - \gamma)b_{t-1} \quad \text{(smooth the trend)}$$
$$F_{t+1} = V_t + b_t \quad \text{(forecast)}$$

Here, V_t represents the smoothed value for period t. The difference between the current and the prior smoothed values provides the current trend: $V_t - V_{t-1}$. The *trend-smoothing constant* γ (the lower-case Greek letter gamma) is used in the second equation to obtain smoothed trend values. The last equation provides the forecast.

Table 4-6 lists the forecasts of Blitz Beer sales using $\alpha = .20$ and $\gamma = .30$. (The initial values of $V_2 = 4{,}890$ and $b_2 = 20$ were obtained from the actual sales for periods 1 and 2.) As an illustration, to forecast period 8 sales, first we obtain the smoothed data value for period 7:

$$V_7 = .20Y_7 + (1 - .20)(V_6 + b_6)$$
$$= .20(5{,}050) + .80(5{,}045 + 35.7)$$
$$= 5{,}075$$

Then we compute the smoothed trend value for period 7:

$$b_7 = .30(V_7 - V_6) + (1 - .30)b_6$$
$$= .30(5{,}075 - 5{,}045) + .70(35.7)$$
$$= 34.0$$

Table 4-6
FORECAST OF BLITZ BEER SALES BY TWO-PARAMETER EXPONENTIAL SMOOTHING ($\alpha = .20$ and $\gamma = .30$)

Period t	Actual Sales Y_t	Smoothed Data V_t	Smoothed Trend b_t	Forecast F_t	Error $Y_t - F_t$
1	4,890	—	—	—	—
2	4,910	4,890	20.0	—	—
3	4,970	4,922	23.6	4,910.0	60.0
4	5,010	4,958	27.3	4,945.6	64.4
5	5,060	5,000	31.7	4,985.3	74.7
6	5,100	5,045	35.7	5,031.7	68.3
7	5,050	5,075	34.0	5,080.7	−30.7
8	5,170	5,121	37.6	5,109.0	61.0
9	5,180	5,163	38.9	5,158.6	22.4
10	5,240	5,210	41.2	5,201.9	39.1
11	5,220	5,245	39.3	5,251.2	−31.2
12	5,280	5,283	38.9	5,284.3	− 4.3
13	5,330	5,324	39.5	5,321.9	9.1
14	5,380	5,367	40.6	5,363.5	16.5
15	5,440	5,414	42.5	5,407.6	32.4
16	5,460	5,457	42.7	5,456.5	3.5
17	5,520	5,504	43.9	5,499.7	20.3
18	5,490	5,536	40.3	5,547.9	−57.9
19	5,550	5,571	38.7	5,576.3	−26.3
20	5,600	5,608	38.2	5,609.7	− 9.7

which indicates sales were increasing at a rate of 34.0 barrels per period at that time. The forecast for period 8 is the sum of the preceding period's smoothed data value and trend:

$$F_8 = V_7 + b_7 = 5{,}075 + 34.0 = 5{,}109.0$$

The forecasts that result from this procedure are close to the actual sales values. The current trend itself is readjusted for each period to coincide with the latest growth in the raw data.

Further Exponential Smoothing Procedures

A wide variety of exponential smoothing procedures can be used. One adjusts the smoothing constant α itself from period to period. Others consider nonlinear relationships between values. A somewhat more complicated procedure than the one just described involves three parameters and provides *seasonal smoothing* in addition to trend smoothing.

4-6 FORECASTING USING CAUSAL MODELS: REGRESSION ANALYSIS

Thus far, we have discussed forecasting procedures that are based only on extrapolations from time-series data. Therefore, until this point, our conclusions have been somewhat tenuous. Such forecasts—especially long-range ones—can be severely in error, because they are based on historical patterns that will not necessarily continue in the future. Often the cause for such patterns cannot even be identified.

More satisfactory forecasts can sometimes be achieved by using a causal model that explains the dependent variable in terms of the level of one or more predictor variables (rather than simply in terms of a period of time). Ideal predictors *lead* (have values that are determined in advance of) the main variable. Thus, a student's success at college might be predicted from his or her high-school grade point average. Predictions of future growth in GNP might be based on today's prices, level of employment, and plant capacities. Or a product's sales forecast might be determined from its current share of the market and planned advertising expenditures.

Simple Regression

When one predictor variable is used, forecasts are obtained from a regression line. This procedure is referred to as *simple* regression analysis. To illustrate, we will forecast the monthly sales Y of Deuce Hardware Store outlets using floorspace X as the independent variable. Table 4-7 provides the pertinent data from a sample of 10 stores.

The regression coefficients are

$$b = \frac{n\Sigma XY - (\Sigma X)(\Sigma Y)}{n\Sigma X^2 - (\Sigma X)^2} = \frac{10(48,690) - 191(2,270)}{10(594,832) - (2,270)^2} = .067$$

$$\overline{X} = 2,270/10 = 227 \quad \text{and} \quad \overline{Y} = 191/10 = 19.1$$

$$a = \overline{Y} - b\overline{X} = 19.1 - .067(227) = 3.9$$

Thus, the regression equation is

$$\hat{Y} = 3.9 + .067X$$

This equation can be used to forecast the monthly sales of a new store of a particular size. For instance, the forecast of monthly sales for a store with $X = 300$ square yards of floorspace is

$$\hat{Y} = 3.9 + .067(300) = 24.00, \text{ or } \$24,000$$

Table 4-7
DEUCE HARDWARE STORE SALES AND FLOORSPACE DATA, WITH REGRESSION CALCULATIONS

Store	Monthly Sales (thousands of dollars) Y	Floorspace (square yards) X	XY	X²
1	20	305	6,100	93,025
2	15	130	1,950	16,900
3	17	189	3,213	35,721
4	9	175	1,575	30,625
5	16	101	1,616	10,201
6	27	269	7,263	72,361
7	35	421	14,735	177,241
8	7	195	1,365	38,025
9	22	282	6,204	79,524
10	23	203	4,669	41,209
	191 = ΣY	2,270 = ΣX	48,690 = ΣXY	594,832 =ΣX²

Multiple Regression

We will now expand the method of least squares so that it can be applied to *multiple regression analysis*, which includes several independent predictor variables. Multiple regression often improves forecasting accuracy.

The essential advantage of considering two or more independent variables is that it permits us to make greater use of the information that is available. For example, a regression line that expresses a new store's sales in terms of the population of the city it serves should yield a poorer sales forecast than an equation that also considers median income, number of nearby competitors, and the local unemployment rate. A plant manager should be able to predict the cost of processing a new order more precisely if, in addition to the size of the order, he considers the total volume of orders, the current manpower level, or the production capacity of available equipment. A marketing manager ought to gauge the sales response to a magazine advertisement more accurately by considering, in addition to the magazine's circulation, the demographical features of its readers, such as median age, median income, or proportion of urban readers.

Linear multiple regression analysis involves two or more independent variables. In the case of two independent variables, denoted by X_1 and X_2, the *estimated multiple regression equation* is

$$Y = a + b_1 X_1 + b_2 X_2$$

Here, two independent variables and one dependent variable, or a total of three variables, are considered. The sample data will consist of three values for each sample unit observed, so that a scatter pattern of these observations will be three dimensional.

To explain how multiple regression data can be portrayed in three dimensions, we will draw an analogy using the walls and floor of a room. Letting a corner of the room represent the case when all three variables have values of zero, we can denote the data points by suspending marbles in space at various distances from the floor and the two walls. A marble's height above the floor can represent the value of Y for that observation. Its distance from the wall on the left then measures the observed value of X_1, and its distance from the wall on the right expresses the observed value of X_2. Figure 4-13 is a pictorial representation of a three-dimensional scatter for a hypothetical set of data.

The regression equation corresponds to a plane. This plane must be slated in such a way that it provides the best least-squares fit to the

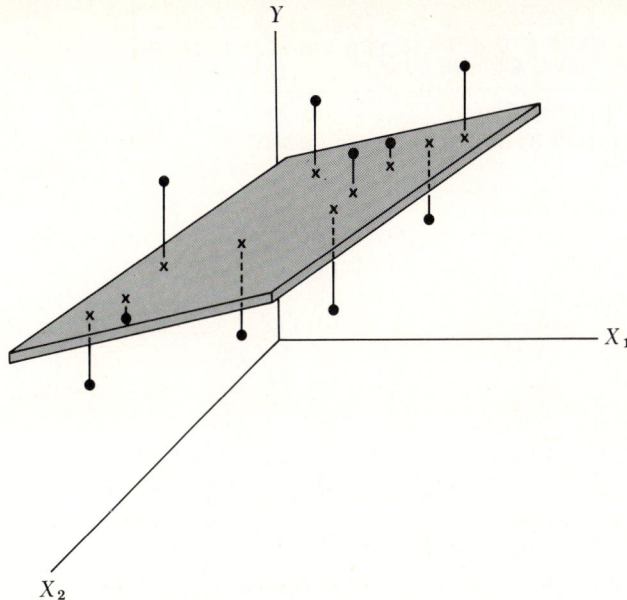

Figure 4-13
A multiple regression plane for multiple regression, using three variables.

sample data. The three-dimensional surface that results is referred to as the *regression plane*. Slanting this plane can be compared to determining how to position a pane of glass through the suspended marbles so that its incline approximates the incline of the pattern of scatter.

The coefficients of the estimated regression plane can be determined by solving a set of three equations in three unknowns. These are referred to as the *normal equations*:

$$\sum Y = na + b_1 \sum X_1 + b_2 \sum X_2$$
$$\sum X_1 Y = a \sum X_1 + b_1 \sum X_1^2 + b_2 \sum X_1 X_2$$
$$\sum X_2 Y = a \sum X_2 + b_1 \sum X_1 X_2 + b_2 \sum X_2^2$$

We find a, b_1, and b_2 by calculating the required sums from the data for the various combinations of Y, X_1 and X_2 and then substituting these values into the normal equations, which are solved simultaneously. To illustrate, we will consider our Deuce Hardware Store example again. In addition to floorspace (now denoted by X_1), Table 4-8 includes a new independent variable, daily advertising expenditures, denoted by X_2.

Table 4-8
DEUCE HARDWARE STORE DATA FOR SALES, FLOORSPACE, AND DAILY ADVERTISING EXPENDITURE

Store	Monthly Sales (thousands of dollars) Y	Floorspace (square yards) X_1	Daily Advertising Expenditure (dollars) X_2
1	20	305	35
2	15	130	98
3	17	189	83
4	9	175	76
5	16	101	93
6	27	269	77
7	35	421	44
8	7	195	57
9	22	282	31
10	23	203	92

The intermediate calculations required to solve the regression equation appear in Table 4-9, where the columns contain the individual variable values and the squared and product terms. We obtain the following normal equations:

$$191 = 10a + 2{,}270b_1 + 686b_2$$
$$48{,}690 = 2{,}270a + 594{,}832b_1 + 139{,}565b_2$$
$$12{,}569 = 686a + 139{,}565b_1 + 52{,}682b_2$$

Solving these equations simultaneously for the unknowns a, b_1, b_2, we obtain

$$a = -23.074$$
$$b_1 = .1148$$
$$b_2 = .2349$$

The values of a, b_1, and b_2 provide the estimated multiple regression equation

$$\hat{Y} = -23.074 + .1148X_1 + .2349X_2$$

which can be used to forecast the sales of a particular store. Suppose a new store is to be built that will have 250 square yards of floorspace and spend $75 in daily advertising, so that $X_1 = 250$ and $X_2 = 75$. The forecast sales level is

$$\hat{Y} = -23.074 + .1148(250) + .2349(75) = 23.244, \text{ or } \$23{,}244$$

Table 4-9
INTERMEDIATE CALCULATIONS FOR OBTAINING REGRESSION COEFFICIENTS

Y	X_1	X_2	X_1Y	X_2Y	X_1X_2	X_1^2	X_2^2
20	305	35	6,100	700	10,675	93,025	1,225
15	130	98	1,950	1,470	12,740	16,900	9,604
17	189	83	3,213	1,411	15,687	35,721	6,889
9	175	76	1,575	684	13,300	30,625	5,776
16	101	93	1,616	1,488	9,393	10,201	8,649
27	269	77	7,263	2,079	20,713	72,361	5,929
35	421	44	14,735	1,540	18,524	177,241	1,936
7	195	57	1,365	399	11,115	38,025	3,249
22	282	31	6,204	682	8,742	79,524	961
23	203	92	4,669	2,116	18,676	41,209	8,464
191	2,270	686	48,690	12,569	139,565	594,832	52,682
$=\Sigma Y$	$=\Sigma X_1$	$=\Sigma X_2$	$=\Sigma X_1 Y$	$=\Sigma X_2 Y$	$=\Sigma X_1 X_2$	$=\Sigma X_1^2$	$=\Sigma X_2^2$

Comparison of Simple and Multiple Regression

Table 4-10 shows the Deuce Hardware sales forecasts made by applying both simple and multiple regression to the actual data. Note that multiple regression provides greater accuracy, because the forecasting errors tend to be smaller when this procedure is used. Including the second predictor variable (daily advertising expenditures) allows us to "explain" more variation in sales Y.

It is not obvious whether or not including more variables generally reduces forecasting error. In some cases, adding independent variables

Table 4-10
COMPARISON OF FORECASTING ERRORS USING SIMPLE AND MULTIPLE REGRESSION

ACTUAL DATA			SIMPLE REGRESSION		MULTIPLE REGRESSION	
			Forecast	Error	Forecast	Error
Y	X_1	X_2	$\hat{Y}$	$Y - \hat{Y}$	$\hat{Y}$	$Y - \hat{Y}$
20	305	35	24.3	− 4.3	20.2	− .2
15	130	98	12.6	2.4	14.9	.1
17	189	83	16.6	.4	18.1	−1.1
9	175	76	15.6	− 6.6	14.9	−5.9
16	101	93	10.7	5.3	10.4	5.6
27	269	77	21.9	5.1	25.9	1.1
35	421	44	32.1	2.9	35.6	− .6
7	195	57	17.0	−10.0	12.7	−5.7
22	282	31	22.8	− .8	16.6	5.4
23	203	92	17.5	5.5	21.8	1.2

can even confuse the analysis. Independent variables must be chosen with care and must have some rational basis for affecting Y.

Further Considerations

We have barely scratched the surface of regression analysis. For example, we have entirely avoided an examination of nonlinear relationships. Forecasts made from the regression line or plane can be qualified in a statistical sense by means of confidence intervals. The procedures involved, however, are based on a formidable thicket of theoretical assumptions that are too complex to discuss here. Regression analysis is often accompanied by *correlation analysis,* where the major concern is how strongly the variables are related. Advanced techniques, such as stepwise multiple regression, help determine not only the regression equation but also the particular predictor variables that are best to include. An area of statistics and economics called *econometrics* considers causal models in great depth and wide breadth. References dealing with this topic are provided in the Bibliography.

4-7 FORECASTING USING JUDGMENT

The third major forecasting technique is based on judgment. In a sense, all forecasting involves some judgment, even when data are extensively analyzed. In this section, we will learn how to use judgment to make forecasts even when no data at all is available.

Until now, all of the forecasting methods we have discussed involve *point forecasts;* that is, they provide future predictions in the form of specific numerical values. Such forecasts are almost certain to be in error: The actual data will inevitably differ in some way from the forecasts (at best, the forecasts will be slightly above or below the actual values). It may therefore be more realistic to predict a *range of values.* An even better method might be to include future uncertainty by treating it as a random variable with a *probability distribution.* Here, two procedures will be presented that involve subjective probability distributions.

Judgmental Probability Distribution: Interview Method

This procedure can be applied to any variable that has a large number of possible values, such as product demand.

A natural and fairly simple way to obtain a probability distribution judgmentally is to use cumulative probabilities. By posing a series of

50-50 gambles, it is quite simple for a decision maker to determine a random variable's cumulative probability distribution judgmentally. Each response provides a point that can be plotted on a graph; a smoothed curve is then drawn through the points. This curve completely specifies the underlying probability distribution. The following example illustrates how this procedure works.

The president of a food-manufacturing concern uses judgment to determine the probability distribution of the demand for a new snack product. A staff analyst obtains answers to a series of questions. The interview proceeds as follows:*

- Q. What do you think the largest and smallest possible levels of demand are?
- A. Certainly demand will exceed 500,000 units. But I would set an upper limit of 3 million units. I don't think that we could sell more than this amount under the most favorable circumstances.
- Q. Okay, we have determined the range of possible demand. Now I want you to tell me what level of demand divides the possibilities into two equally likely ranges. For example, do you think demand will be just as likely to fall above 2,000,000 as below 2,000,000?
- A. No. I'd rather pick 1,500,000 units as the 50-50 point.
- Q. Very good. Now let's consider the demand levels below 1,500,000. If demand were to fall somewhere between 500,000 and 1,500,000 units, do you think it would lie above or below 1,000,000?
- A. Above. I would say that a demand of 1,250,000 units would be a realistic dividing point.
- Q. We will use that amount as our 50-50 point. Let's do the same thing for the upper range of demand.
- A. If I were to pick a number, I would choose 2,000,000 units. I feel that demand is just as likely to fall in the 1.5 to 2 million range as it is to fall in the 2 to 3 million range.
- Q. Excellent. We're making good progress. Now, to get a finer fix on the points obtained so far, I want you to tell me whether you think demand is just as likely to fall between 1.25 and 2 million units as it is to fall outside that range.
- A. Inside. I suppose this means I'm being inconsistent.
- Q. Yes, it does. Let's remedy this. Do you think that we ought to raise the 1,250,000 dividing point or lower the 2 million unit figure?

---

* This procedure was inspired by that of Howard Raiffa in his book *Decision Analysis: Introductory Lectures on Choices Under Uncertainty* (Reading, Mass.: Addison-Wesley, 1968).

A. Lower the 2 million figure to 1.9 million.
Q. Let's check to see if this disturbs our other estimates. Do you think that 1,500,000 splits demand over the range from 1,250,000 to 1,900,000 into two equally likely regions?
A. Yes, I am satisfied that it does.
Q. Just a few more questions. If demand is above 1,900,000, what level splits this demand range into two equally likely regions?
A. I'd say 2,200,000.
Q. Good. Now if demand is between 2,200,000 and 3,000,000, where would you split this demand range?
A. My guess would be that 2,450,000 units would be the 50-50 point.
Q. What if demand is below 1,250,000?
A. Try 1,100,000 units.
Q. And when demand is between 500,000 and 1,100,000 units?
A. I think demand is far more likely to be close to the higher figure. I would bet on 950,000 units.

The information obtained from this interview is provided in Table 4-11. The initial decision to divide demand at 1,500,000 units makes this level the 50 percent point or median. Since the chance that demand will be below 1,500,000 has been judged to be .5, we will refer to this as the .5 fractile. This means that the probability is .5 that the actual demand will be 1,500,000 units *or less*. Our decision maker has chosen to divide the range from 500,000 to 1,500,000 units at a demand level of 1,250,000. Believing that the chance demand will fall in this range is .5, the president estimates that the chance that demand will be at or below 1,250,000 units will be .5(.5) = .25. We therefore refer to 1,250,000 units as the .25 fractile. Again, this establishes a .25 probability that demand will be less than or equal to 1,250,000.

Table 4-11

A FOOD MANUFACTURER'S JUDGMENTAL ASSESSMENT OF FRACTILES FOR THE DEMAND OF A NEW SNACK PRODUCT

Fractile	Amount
0	500,000
.0625	950,000
.125	1,100,000
.25	1,250,000
.50	1,500,000
.75	1,900,000
.875	2,200,000
.9375	2,450,000
1.000	3,000,000

Likewise, the median of the range from 1,500,000 to 3,000,000 units is 1,900,000, which becomes the .75 fractile, since the probability is $.5 + .5(.5) = .75$ that demand will fall somewhere below 1,900,000 units. The analyst has determined the median of each region by working outward from the 50-percent point previously found. Thus, the .125 fractile of 1,100,000 units is the median demand for possible levels below the .25 fractile (1,250,000 units), which had to be determined first. The median of the demands above 1,900,000 units is the .875 fractile, 2,200,000 units. Similarly, the median of the demands below 1,100,000 is the .0625 fractile, 950,000 units, and the median demand level beyond 2,200,000 is the .9375 fractile, 2,450,000 units.

The fractiles and the corresponding demands are plotted as points in the graph in Figure 4-14, where the vertical axis represents the cumulative probability of demand. The curve smoothed through these plotted points serves as an approximation of the cumulative probability distribution of the first-year demand for the new snack product. The curve is S-shaped: The slope first increases and then decreases as de-

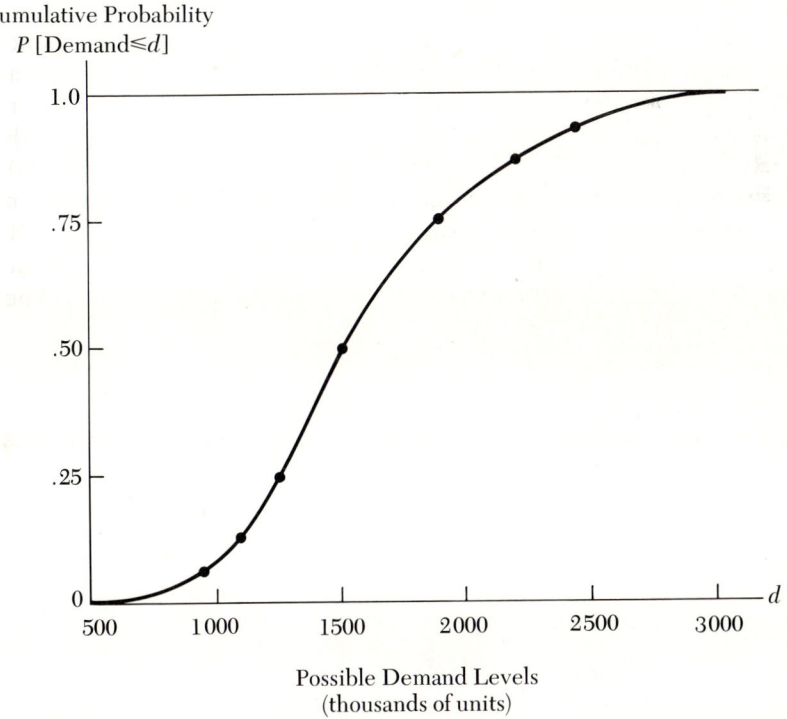

Figure 4-14
The cumulative probability distribution function obtained for a new snack product using judgmental assessments.

mand levels become higher. The slope changes most rapidly for large and small demands, so that more points plotted in these regions provide greater accuracy. This is why the decision maker worked outward from the median in assessing the demand fractiles.

This example illustrates how a detailed measurement of judgment can be obtained by posing a few 50-50 gambles. As a rule of thumb, the seven fractile values in Table 4-11, ranging from .0625 to .9375, are adequate for this purpose. Little is to be gained by obtaining additional fractiles: Further gambles might result in a lumpy curve and would probably not alter the basic S shape anyway. Besides, there is no reason to "gild the lily" nor to try the decision maker's patience. A curve obtained using this method provides about as accurate a measurement of judgment as is humanly possible.

It is difficult to use the cumulative S curve directly in decision analysis, where expected values must be determined. Expected-value calculations are ordinarily made from a table listing the possible variable values and their probabilities. Table 4-12 shows how the demand probabilities have been obtained by reading values from the cumulative probability distribution curve in Figure 4-14.

Table 4-12
DEMAND PROBABILITIES FOR INTERVALS AND APPROXIMATE EXPECTED DEMAND CALCULATION

(1) Demand Interval (thousands)	(2) Interval Midpoint (thousands)	(3) Probability for Demands at or Below Upper Limit (obtained from curve)	(4) Probability for Demand Interval	(5) Demand Probability (2) × (4)
500–750	625	.02	.02	12.50
750–1,000	875	.08	.06	52.50
1,000–1,250	1,125	.25	.17	191.25
1,250–1,500	1,375	.50	.25	343.75
1,500–1,750	1,625	.68	.18	292.50
1,750–2,000	1,875	.80	.12	225.00
2,000–2,250	2,125	.89	.09	191.25
2,250–2,500	2,375	.95	.06	142.50
2,500–2,750	2,625	.98	.03	78.75
2,750–3,000	2,875	1.00	.02	57.50

Approximate expected demand = 1,587.50

Finding a Probability Distribution from Actual/Forecast Ratios

The interview method is most suitable for use on a one-time basis when uncertain circumstances are involved that may never be encountered again. When judgmental forecasts of a single value are made more often, they provide a history that can be used to determine the underlying probability distribution.

We will illustrate this procedure with an example involving weekly sales forecasts for Blitz Beer made by the company's sales manager. The relevant data over a 10-month period are provided in Table 4-13. We will assume that the forecasts have been made solely from judgment. The actual sales values are divided by the respective forecast sales figures to provide *actual/forecast ratios*.

Table 4-13
BLITZ BEER WEEKLY SALES (IN BARRELS) SHOWING JUDGMENT FORECASTS AND ACTUAL/FORECAST RATIOS

Actual	*Forecast*	*Actual/Forecast*
1,133	1,200	.94
1,422	1,150	1.24
1,288	1,300	.99
1,317	1,370	.96
1,080	1,410	.77
1,344	1,580	.85
1,506	1,650	.91
1,752	1,650	1.06
1,924	1,750	1.10
1,783	2,000	.89

Actual sales of Blitz Beer for the first week were 1,133 barrels. The manager had forecast 1,200 barrels. Thus,

$$\frac{\text{Actual sales}}{\text{Forecast sales}} = \frac{1,133}{1,200} = .94 \quad \text{(actual/forecast ratio)}$$

The sales manager's forecasting record is summarized in the cumulative probability graph in Figure 4-15. To plot this, the actual/forecast ratios are arranged in increasing value. There are 10 ratios, so each ratio is assigned a probability of 1/10. Thus, a .10 step in cumulative probability occurs at each value. A smoothed curve is then drawn freehand through the resulting cumulative probability stairway. This curve can be combined with the sales manager's next forecast to obtain the cumulative probability distribution of beer sales for that week. The cumulative probability graph in Figure 4-15 provides the probability distribution when the sales forecast is 1,900 barrels. There, the horizonal axis has been found by multiplying the actual/forecast ratios by 1,900.

4-7 FORECASTING USING JUDGMENT

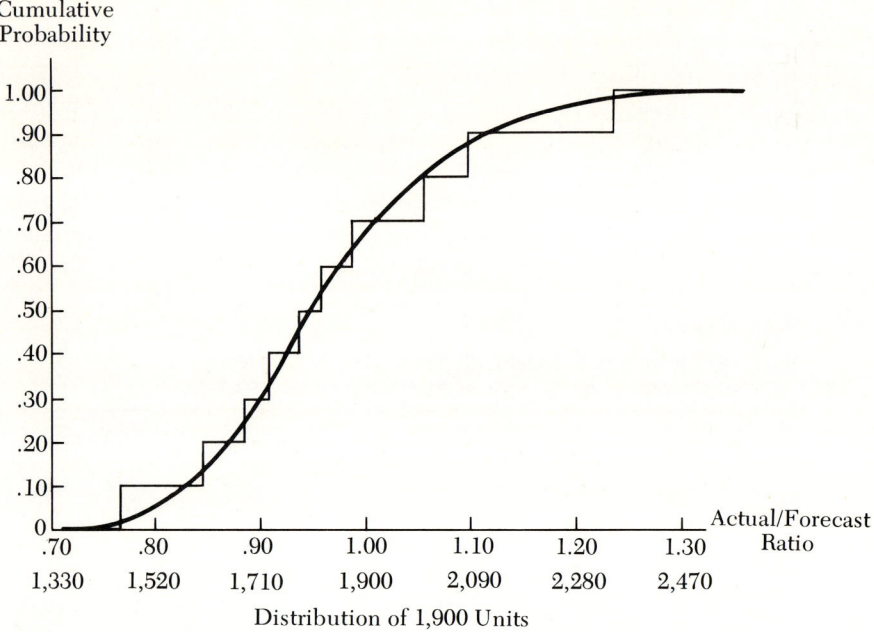

Figure 4-15
Subjective probability distribution of Blitz Beer sales based on actual/forecast ratios.

Delphi Forecasting and Other Methods

In one popular prediction procedure called *Delphi forecasting,* individual judgments regarding future events are combined to express a collective opinion. Delphi forecasting has been successfully employed in predicting technological breakthroughs and scientific advancements. It has also been used to forecast long-range sales and profits.

Another judgmental application, *scenario projection,* is often used in government and military planning. Here, detailed circumstances are used as stage settings to provide background for a future analysis that simulates reality. *Industrial and world dynamics* operate in the same vein. In these procedures, mathematical models are employed to make long-range predictions and to simulate future conditions.

There are many other types of forecasting methods too numerous to discuss here. More detailed discussions of forecasting methods can be found in some of the references in the Bibliography at the end of this book.

PROBLEMS

4-1 The Variety Galore Store wishes to forecast its sales for the next calendar year. The following components have been determined by its accountant:

Quarter t	Trend T_t	Cyclical Component C_t	Seasonal Index S_t
Winter	$100,000	90	80
Spring	110,000	110	70
Summer	121,000	100	100
Fall	133,100	90	150

Use the multiplicative time-series model to determine the forecasts of sales Y_t for each quarter.

4-2 The sales data for Humpty Dumpty Toys, Inc., have been analyzed, and the trend, cyclical, seasonal, and irregular components have been determined for operations during the preceding four quarters. Supply the missing values in the following table, assuming that the time-series components are multiplicative.

Quarter t	Trend T_t	Cyclical Component (percentage) C_t	Seasonal Index (percentage) S_t	Irregular Component (percentage) I_t	Sales Y_t
Winter	$1,000,000	107	50	101	
Spring	1,100,000	105	70		$ 820,000
Summer	1,200,000	105		98	987,840
Fall	1,300,000		200	97	2,622,880

4-3 The following annual sales have been recorded for a large retailing corporation:

Year	Sales (in millions)	Year	Sales (in millions)
1969	$18	1975	$ 82
1970	28	1976	89
1971	26	1977	108
1972	43	1978	121
1973	55	1979	155
1974	54		

(a) Plot these time-series data on graph paper.
(b) Would a straight line provide a suitable summary of the trend in sales? Explain.

4-4 The following amounts of annual electricity usage (in million kilowatt-hours) have been recorded for a region served by a certain utility company:

Year	Consumption	Year	Consumption
1970	205	1975	241
1971	206	1976	267
1972	223	1977	268
1973	234	1978	277
1974	231	1979	290

(a) Plot these time-series data on graph paper.
(b) Using the method of least squares, determine the equation for the estimated regression line $\hat{Y} = a + bX$, with X in years and $X = 0$ in 1970. Draw this line on your graph.
(c) What is the forecast consumption for 1980?

4-5 The following percentages of moving average values have been obtained for a dairy's ice cream sales.

	Quarter			
Year	Winter	Spring	Summer	Fall
1973			156	111
1974	49	92	137	109
1975	53	93	148	108
1976	52	91	162	104
1977	51	89	153	110
1978	51	90	151	112
1979	48	88		

Determine the seasonal index for each quarter.

4-6 The following quarterly sales data (in millions of dollars) were recorded for a certain men's clothing chain:

	1975	1976	1977	1978	1979
Winter	3.9	7.8	12.9	13.9	13.5
Spring	6.1	10.6	15.2	14.4	18.2
Summer	4.3	6.9	10.3	10.2	14.2
Fall	10.8	13.5	18.7	17.3	20.7

(a) Plot these time-series data on graph paper.
(b) Determine the four-quarter moving averages.
(c) Calculate the percentage of moving-average values and use them to determine the seasonal indexes.
(d) Deseasonalize the original sales data and plot them on your graph.

4-7 In arranging for short-term credit with its bank, the Make-Wave Corporation must project its cash needs on a monthly basis. To help management do this, seasonal indexes are to be developed from the following historical data pertaining to cash requirements (in hundreds of thousands of dollars):

	1975	1976	1977	1978	1979
Jan.	2.7	2.9	3.5	2.5	4.2
Feb.	5.4	6.4	7.3	8.1	9.6
Mar.	9.3	10.1	11.3	7.9	12.4
Apr.	2.4	4.1	3.8	5.2	6.2
May	6.1	7.8	8.1	9.2	8.7
Jun.	7.3	7.4	6.9	8.1	8.3
Jul.	6.5	5.5	6.5	7.6	6.6
Aug.	9.7	9.6	8.9	9.3	9.8
Sep.	13.4	13.5	14.3	15.8	16.3
Oct.	10.6	10.7	11.5	12.6	13.4
Nov.	5.1	4.8	6.5	7.2	6.9
Dec.	3.4	2.8	3.9	4.1	6.1

(a) Using 12-month moving averages, determine the seasonal index for each month by means of the ratio-to-moving-average method.

(b) Make-Wave's cash needs for the coming year are forecast to be $1,000,000 per month on the average. Using the seasonal indexes calculated in (a), estimate the cash requirements for each month.

4-8 Use one-parameter exponential smoothing with $\alpha = .40$ to forecast sales levels from the actual data given in Table 4-5 (page 118).

4-9 Repeat Problem 4-8 with $\alpha = .50$.

4-10 Use two-parameter exponential smoothing, with $\alpha = .30$ and $\gamma = .20$, to forecast sales levels from the actual data given in Table 4-6 (page 119).

4-11 A statistician for the Civil Aeronautics Board wishes to determine an equation that relates destination distance to freight charge for a standard-sized crate. From a random sample of ten freight invoices, he obtains the following results:

Distance (in hundreds of miles)	Charge (to nearest dollar)
14	68
23	105
9	40
17	79
10	81
22	95
5	31
12	72
6	45
16	93

(a) Plot a scatter diagram for these data.

(b) Using the method of least squares, determine the equation for the estimated regression line. Then plot the regression line on the scatter diagram.

4-12 A stereo-cartridge manufacturer wishes to conduct a regression analysis to estimate the average cartridge lifetime (in hours) at various record tracking forces X (in grams). He has obtained the following regression equation for a sample of $n = 100$ cartridges that were played at various tracking forces until they were worn out: $\hat{Y} = 1{,}300 - 200X$. Find the forecast lifetimes when (a) $X = 1$ gram; (b) $X = 2$ grams; and (c) $X = 3$ grams.

4-13 Restaurant sales predictions are to be made from a regression equation based on total floor space and number of employees. The following data have been obtained for a sample of $n = 5$ restaurants:

Sales (thousands of dollars) Y	Floor Space (thousands of square feet) X_1	Number of Employees X_2
20	10	15
15	5	8
10	10	12
5	3	7
10	2	10

Calculate the multiple regression equation for these data.

4-14 Suppose that a college admissions director relies on high school GPA X_1 and IQ score X_2 to predict college GPA Y. Using the regression equation

$$\hat{Y} = .5 + .8X_1 + .003X_2$$

forecast the college GPA for each of the following students:

	(a)	(b)	(c)	(d)
High School GPA	2.9	3.0	2.7	3.5
IQ Score	123	118	105	136

4-15 A record manufacturer uses special machines to press recording grooves onto blank disks from a die. Each die lasts for about 1,000 pressings. Due to the time constraints inherent in the record business, it is sometimes necessary to use several pressing machines simultaneously. Because each machine requires an expensive die disk and many production runs are completed before the useful lifetime of each die disk is achieved, this increases production costs. For $n = 100$ production runs, the total manufacturing cost Y (in thousands of dollars) has been determined for the number of pressings made X_1 (in thousands) and the number of die disks required X_2. The following regression equation applies:

$$\hat{Y} = 1.082 + 1.2X_1 + .553X_2$$

Forecast the cost $\hat{Y}$ of each of the following production runs:

Run	Number of Pressings (thousands)	Number of Die Disks
(a)	15	5
(b)	20	3
(c)	15	4
(d)	100	10

4-16 Using the cumulative probability distribution function given in Figure 4-16, determine the following probabilities:

(a) $P[D > 500]$ (b) $P[D \leq 150]$
(c) $P[D \geq 300]$ (d) $P[200 \leq D \leq 800]$

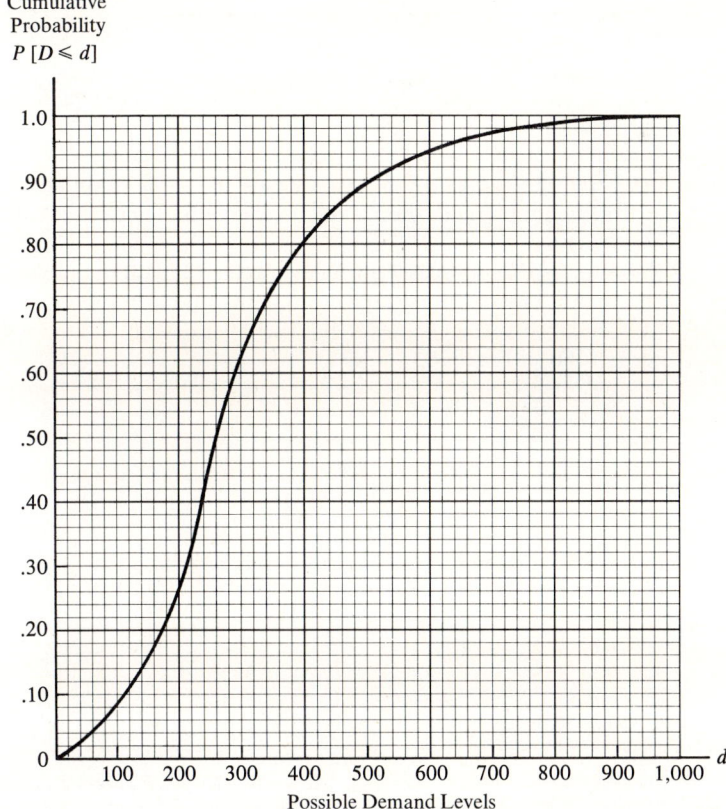

Figure 4-16

4-17 Using the cumulative probability distribution graph in Figure 4-16, determine the following fractiles: (a) .10; (b) .50; (c) .125; (d) .75; (e) .37.

4-18 Envision your income during the first full calendar year after graduation. Establish your own subjective probability distribution of the adjusted gross income figure that you will report to the IRS. (If applicable, include your spouse's earnings, interest, dividends, etc.) If your graph has an unusual shape, try to eliminate any inconsistencies or to identify the nonhomogeneous factors (pregnancy, unemployment, divorce, etc.) that might explain the variations in its shape. Remember, you are the expert about yourself.

4-19 Using the cumulative probability distribution graph in Figure 4-16, construct the probability distribution of demand using five intervals in increments of 200.

4-20 A sports writer has forecast Rod Carew's seasonal batting average for a 10-year period. The following values apply:

Actual	Forecast	Actual	Forecast
.273	.250	.350	.278
.332	.315	.364	.340
.366	.320	.359	.355
.307	.365	.331	.360
.318	.330	.388	.373

(a) Compute the actual/forecast ratios. Plot the cumulative probability graph and then sketch a smoothed curve through the stairway.

(b) Suppose the forecast batting average is .350 for the next baseball season. Read your graph to find the sports writer's subjective probability that Carew's batting average falls (1) ≤ .300; (2) ≤ .360; (3) ≤ .375.

Five

Basic Concepts of Decision Making

The central focus of this book is using quantitative methods in decision making. This chapter considers the structural properties of decisions in general. We make a basic distinction between decision making under certain conditions, where no elements are left to chance, and decision making under uncertainty, where one or more random factors affect a choice's outcome. By considering common features shared by all decisions, we set the stage for discussions relating to decision situations with particular applications and more detailed quantitative methods.

5-1 CERTAINTY AND UNCERTAINTY IN DECISION MAKING

The least complex applications of quantitative methods are found in *decision making under certainty*. Perhaps the simplest decision of this sort is selecting what clothes to wear; although the possible combinations of various items of attire may be numerous, we all manage to quickly make our choices with little bother. But not all decisions are this easy—remember your childhood and how hard it was to choose candy bars. Nor are all decisions under certainty as trivial; we shall see some sophisticated managerial problems with an unlimited number of alternatives.

When the outcomes are only partly determined by the decision-maker's choice, so that the result is affected also by random factors, a decision takes on added complexity. We must somehow cope with the unpredictability resulting from our choices. To set the stage in structuring a decision under uncertainty, consider the choice of whether to carry an umbrella or some other rain protection throughout the day. Here we are faced with two alternatives: carrying an ungainly item that can, in the event of rain, help to defer a cleaning bill or a cough, versus challenging the elements with hands free, hoping not to be caught in the rain. Lack of human skill at accurate weather prediction causes us to be uncertain whether it will rain. Yet faced with the daily needs of life we must make our decision in spite of our uncertainty. This illustrates a common *decision under uncertainty:* a choice of action must be made even though its outcome is unknown and determined by chance.*

In this chapter we present a framework within which we may explain how and why particular choices are made. Our decisions in coping with weather illustrate the essential features of all decisions under uncertainty. We choose the umbrella when the chance of rain seems uncomfortably high, whereas we do without it when rain is unlikely. But two people occasionally make different choices. Is there a correct decision? If so, how do we explain that two persons do not always make the same choice? We can begin to answer these questions by identifying several key elements common to all such decisions and then structuring them in a convenient form for analysis.

5-2 ELEMENTS OF DECISIONS

Every decision problem under certainty exhibits two elements: *acts* and *outcomes.* The decision-maker's choices are the acts. For example, in choosing among three television programs in the 9 PM time slot, each candidate represents a potential act. The outcomes may be

---

* This class of decisions has often been divided into categories—decision making under *risk*, where outcome probabilities are known, and under *uncertainty*, where these probabilities are unknown. We make no such distinction and assume that probabilities may always be found somehow—either objectively through long-run frequency, or subjectively.

characterized in terms of the enjoyment we might derive from each of the various programs.

Should the decision be made under uncertainty, a third element exists. This involves *events*. Continuing with the rain uncertainty illustration, the acts are "carry an umbrella" and "leave the umbrella home." All decisions involve selection of an act. But the outcomes resulting from each act are uncertain, because *an outcome is determined partly by choice and partly by chance*. For the act "carry an umbrella" there are two possible outcomes: (1) unnecessarily carting rain paraphernalia and (2) weathering a shower fully protected. The other act, "leave the umbrella at home," has either of the outcomes: (1) getting unnecessarily wet and (2) remaining dry and unencumbered. Again, whether the first or second happens depends only on the occurrence of rain. The outcome for any particular chosen act is dependent on which *event*, rain or no rain, occurs.

Decision Table

To facilitate analysis, a decision problem may be summarized by a *decision table*, which indicates the relationship between pairs of decision elements. The decision table for the umbrella illustration is provided in Table 5-1. Each row corresponds to an event; each column corresponds to an act. The outcomes appear as entries in the body of the table. Each event-act combination has a specific outcome, reflecting the fact that it is the interplay between act and event that determines the ultimate result.

Table 5-1
DECISION TABLE FOR THE UMBRELLA DECISION

	ACTS	
EVENTS	*Carry Umbrella*	*Leave Umbrella Home*
Rain	Stay dry	Get wet
No rain	Carry unnecessary burden	Be dry and free

The acts included in the decision table are only those the decision maker wishes to consider. In the above illustration, staying home is another possible act, which we exclude because it is not contemplated. The acts are mutually exclusive and collectively exhaustive, so that exactly one will be chosen. The events are also mutually exclusive and collectively exhaustive. A more elaborate decision structure might consider events for various amounts or durations of rain; then each amount or duration event considered would have two outcomes, one for each of the two acts.

Decision Tree Diagram

Another convenient method of representation is a *decision tree diagram* like that shown in Figure 5-1. This portrayal proves especially convenient for decision problems with choices that must be made at different times over an extended duration. It is similar to the probability tree diagrams used previously. The choice of acts is shown as a fork with a separate branch for each act. The events are also represented by branches in separate forks. Because decision tree diagrams can be quite elaborate, we must distinguish act forks from event forks; to do so we use squares for act-fork nodes and circles for event-fork nodes. A basic guideline for constructing such a diagram is that the flow should be chronological from left to right. The acts are shown on the initial fork,

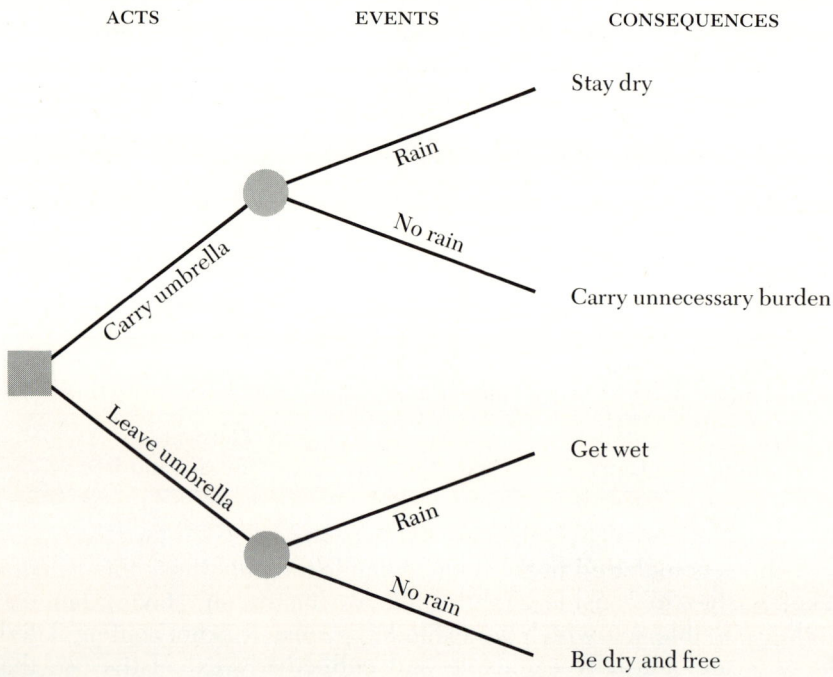

Figure 5-1
Decision tree diagram for the umbrella illustration.

because the decision must be made *before* it is known whether or not there will be rain. The events are thus shown as branches in the second-stage forks. The outcome resulting from an event-act combination is shown as the end position of the corresponding path from the base of the tree.

5-3 RANKING THE ALTERNATIVES AND THE PAYOFF TABLE

In this chapter we shall concern ourselves with how the choice of act should be determined. Everyone who has faced the problem of coping with rain has managed to make an umbrella decision. But we wish to analyze the decision-making process in order that better decisions can be made. In doing this, we focus on two measures: one for *uncertainty* and one for the comparative worth or *payoff* of the outcomes to the decision maker. These two key elements are interwoven into the fabric of quantitative analysis.

For now we will consider examples with outcomes that have obvious associated numerical values as payoffs. These payoffs may be dollars, expressing profits, costs, or assets, or some other numerical value. Every outcome, that is, every event-act combination, will have a payoff value. Since the payoffs actually received after having chosen a particular act are conditional on whichever event happens, they are sometimes referred to as *conditional values*. These values may be conveniently arranged in a *payoff table*, as indicated in Table 5-2 for the gambling decision. This arrangement is also called a *conditional value table*. The decision is to choose one of two acts, either to gamble or to not gamble. Regardless of the choice made, a coin will be tossed with two possible events: head or tail. The possible outcomes correspond to the four event-act combinations. A wager of $1 will be made if the decision maker gambles; viewing net winnings as a payoff measure, $1 represents the result if a head occurs when the act to gamble is chosen.

Table 5-2

PAYOFF TABLE FOR THE DECISION WHETHER OR NOT TO GAMBLE

EVENTS	ACTS	
	Gamble	*Don't Gamble*
Head	$1	$0
Tail	−$1	$0

Likewise, the payoff is −$1 when a tail results. If the player chooses to not gamble, there is no wager, so the payoff will be the same regardless of the coin toss results: $0, in either case.

Objectives and Payoff Values

In determining payoffs to be assigned to outcomes we shall assume that the decision maker wishes to select a course of action that will bring him closest to some objective. We shall suppose that each decision outcome may somehow be ranked in terms of how close it brings the decision maker to his goal. If the decision maker selects as a payoff some measure expressing the degree of goal attainment, then the payoff table will provide a meaningful basis for comparison, thus enhancing the decision-maker's ability to make a good choice.

For example, if a business decision-maker's goal is to achieve a high level of profits, then a natural payoff for each outcome would be its profit. But profit is a valid measure for a limited set of objectives. It is by no means the top concern of all business managers. The founder of a successful corporation may have a goal of maintaining personal control, possibly consciously keeping profits low to avoid having the firm look too attractive to another merger-minded entrepreneur.

Viewed in a more general context, decision making may have many different kinds of goals, each requiring a distinct payoff measure. Consider the following illustrations.

When the United States made its World War II decision to develop the atomic bomb, three different technologies could have been pursued. Had the goal been to select the technology that minimized cost, then only the one believed least costly would have been chosen. Instead, the goal was to develop an operational bomb before the Germans did; thus, the overriding objective was a quick attainment of nuclear-weapon capability. The course of action chosen was to develop all three technologies simultaneously: the most expensive alternative, but also the fastest. *Time savings* was the payoff measure used.

In selecting alternative designs for manned spacecraft, NASA has demonstrated the importance of safety. Thus, *system reliability* is a more valid measure to use for payoff than time or cost would be. The latter were extremely important in the race to the moon, but they served more as constraints on the number of alternative system designs, rather than as measures of goal attainment, especially following the Apollo disaster in 1967.

In designing defensive military systems, the objective is to maximize survivability in the face of a host of enemy threats. A commonly used payoff for ranking alternatives is the *probability of damage* resulting from an attack. Here too, although time and cost are important, they are often secondary considerations.

Decision makers with different goals may select unlike measures for payoffs when they each consider the same set of alternatives. As the following example shows, the best choice for each may be a different course of action.

EXAMPLE Charles Snyder, Herman Brown, and Sylvia Gold want to choose from among three routes from Los Angeles to San Francisco. The routes are: (1) Interstate No. 5, which is a freeway nearly all the way and has a high minimum speed limit; (2) State Highways 118 and 33, which are fairly direct and have no minimum speed limit; and (3) State Highway 1, which winds along the Pacific coast and is slow and long but very beautiful. Mr. Snyder is a salesman who travels to San Francisco regularly; his goal is to reach his destination as quickly as possible. Mr. Brown is an economy "nut"; he wants to reach San Francisco as cheaply as possible. Ms. Gold is on vacation and loves to drive on hilly, winding, scenic roads; she wishes to select the route yielding the greatest driving pleasure.

Table 5-3 provides the payoffs that each person would assign to the three routes. Mr. Snyder uses time savings, in comparison to the slowest route, as his payoff measure. Thus, he chooses Interstate 5, which yields the greatest payoff of 4 hours. Mr. Brown likes to drive at a moderate speed that provides maximum gasoline mileage, while taking as short a route as possible. His payoff measure is gasoline savings (based on the amount of gasoline re-

Table 5-3
PAYOFFS FOR THE ALTERNATIVE ROUTES RELEVANT TO THE GOALS OF THREE DECISION MAKERS

ALTERNATIVE ROUTE	PAYOFF MEASURES		
	MR. SNYDER *Time Savings (hours)*	MR. BROWN *Fuel Savings (gallons)*	MS. GOLD Enjoyment *(subjective rating)*
Interstate 5	4	3	1
Highways 118 & 33	3	7	3
Highway 1	0	0	10

quired on the most expensive route), so that he chooses the back roads, State Highways 118 and 33, where he saves 7 gallons. Ms. Gold has rated the routes in terms of points of interest, type of scenery, and number of hills and curves. This rating serves as her payoff measure, so that for her the best route is scenic State Highway 1, which rates 10.

We may conclude that *the selection of a payoff measure should be made so that the payoff will rank outcomes by the degree to which they attain a decision-maker's goals.* It is the goal that dictates which measures are valid. A disturbing feature of many decision problems is that there may be no obvious payoff measure with which to rank consequences, when their effects are subjective. We will directly confront this problem by means of utility theory, discussed in detail in Chapter 9. Utilities are values that correspond to a decision-maker's preferences for the outcomes.

As a detailed example of a business decision under uncertainty, we consider a hypothetical toy manufacturer who must choose among four prototype designs for Tippi-Toes, a dancing ballerina doll that does pirouettes and bourrées. Each prototype represents a different technology for the moving parts, all powered by small electric motors using batteries. One is a complete arrangement of gears and levers. The second is similar, using springs instead of levers. Another works on the principle of weights and pulleys. The movement of the fourth design is controlled pneumatically through a system of valves that open and close at the command of a small solid-state computer housed in the head cavity. The dolls are identical in all functional aspects.

Tippi-Toes will be sold through distributors, who will be charged an average price of $10. The choice of movement design will depend solely on comparative contributions to profits. Gears and levers will provide the lowest tooling and setup costs, $100,000, but the highest per unit variable cost, $5. Spring action will have slightly higher fixed cost, $160,000, with somewhat lower variable costs, $4 per unit. A computer-controlled pneumatic movement will involve the highest fixed cost, $500,000, and the lowest per unit variable costs, $2. The weights and pulleys will have a fixed cost of $300,000 and variable costs of $3. All other costs are classified as overhead and are identical for each movement type. The demand for Tippi-Toes is uncertain, but management feels that one of the following events will occur:

> Light demand (25,000 units)
> Moderate demand (100,000 units)
> Heavy demand (150,000 units)

Table 5-4 is constructed with payoffs expressed in terms of total contribution to profit and overhead. Our payoffs represent the contributions for the various event-act combinations. For example, if 25,000 dolls are sold and the gears and levers movement is chosen, the total contribution to profit and overhead is computed as follows:

$$\text{Revenue} - \text{Total variable costs} - \text{Fixed costs}$$
$$= \$10(25{,}000) - \$5(25{,}000) - \$100{,}000 = \$25{,}000$$

The payoff entries in Table 5-4 are calculated in this manner.

Table 5-4
PAYOFF TABLE FOR THE TIPPI-TOES DECISION

EVENTS	ACTS (CHOICE OF MOVEMENT)			
	Gears and Levers	Spring Action	Weights and Pulleys	Pneumatic
Light demand	$ 25,000	−$ 10,000	−$125,000	−$300,000
Moderate demand	400,000	440,000	400,000	300,000
Heavy demand	650,000	740,000	750,000	700,000

In this example, the toy manufacturer has considered only three possible levels of demand. This will simplify our analysis. Demand need not be precisely 25,000 or 100,000 units. The problem could be analyzed for several hundred thousand possible levels of demand, say from 0 to 500,000 dolls. The techniques we will develop can be applied to a more detailed probability distribution. Because of the computational requirements, an approximate probability distribution might consider demand to the nearest 100, 1000, or 10,000 units. A continuous distribution having nice mathematical properties might also be used as an approximation to the discrete demand distribution.

Our example has only four alternatives. In the practical business decision-making environment, the number of possible alternatives can be large. For instance, the decision regarding what mix of toys to sell could easily involve trillions of alternatives. *The decision analysis need only include every alternative that the decision maker wishes to consider.* This includes "doing nothing" when there is no compelling reason for choosing one of the alternatives. The search for attractive alternatives is essential to good decision making. However, decision analysis cannot tell us what should and should not be considered, even though it can be useful in guiding our selection.

Reducing the Number of Alternatives:
Inadmissible Acts

Regardless of the process we ultimately select for making a choice, an initial screening may be made to determine if there are any acts that will never be chosen. To illustrate this, consider the payoffs in Table 5-4. An interesting feature is exhibited by the payoffs of two acts: the weights and pulleys, and the pneumatic. No matter which demand event occurs, the weights and pulleys act leads to a greater payoff. For instance, if a light demand occurs, the payoff for weights and pulleys is $-$125,000, which is more favorable than the $-$300,000 payoff from the pneumatic movement; a similar finding results by comparing these two acts for the other possible demand events. Thus the weights and pulleys movement will always be a superior choice to the pneumatic one. We say that the first act *dominates* the second one. An act dominates another one whenever it achieves a better or equal payoff, regardless of which events occur, and when it is strictly better for one or more events.

In general, whenever an act is dominated by another one, it is inadmissible. We see that the pneumatic movement is an *inadmissible act*. The toy-manufacturer's decision can be simplified by eliminating that movement from further consideration. Removing the pneumatic act leaves us with the modified payoff table in Table 5-5.

Table 5-5
MODIFIED PAYOFF TABLE FOR THE TIPPI-TOES DECISION

EVENTS	ACTS (CHOICE OF MOVEMENT)		
	Gears and Levers	*Spring Action*	*Weights and Pulleys*
Light demand	$ 25,000	−$ 10,000	−$125,000
Moderate demand	400,000	440,000	400,000
Heavy demand	650,000	740,000	750,000

A simple way to find whether an act is inadmissible is to see if every entry in its column is less than or equal to all corresponding entries in some other column. It is easily verified that this is not true for the entries in Table 5-5, so the remaining movement acts must remain. They may be called *admissible acts*.

EXPECTED PAYOFF 5-4

How does one choose an act? When there is no uncertainty, the answer is straightforward: select the act that yields the highest payoff (although finding this particular optimal act can be a very difficult task when the alternatives are many). But with uncertain events, the act having the greatest payoff for one event may have a lower payoff than a competing act when some other event occurs. In the next chapter we consider several criteria that may be used. For the present, we use expected value as the basis for decision making.

**Maximizing Expected Payoff:
Bayes Decision Rule**

Suppose that our toy manufacturer accepts the following probabilities for the Tippi-Toes demand:

Light demand	.10
Moderate demand	.70
Heavy demand	.20
	1.00

If we treat the payoff values for each act as separate random variables, where the above probability values apply in each case, we can calculate the expected payoff for each act as shown in Table 5-6. We find that the spring-action movement results in the maximum expected payoff of $455,000. Thus, using maximum expected payoff as a decision-making criterion, our toy manufacturer would select the spring-action movement for the Tippi-Toes doll.

Table 5-6

CALCULATION OF EXPECTED PAYOFFS FOR THE TIPPI-TOES DECISION

DEMAND EVENT	PROBA-BILITY	GEARS AND LEVERS		SPRING ACTION		WEIGHTS AND PULLEYS	
		Payoff	Payoff × Probability	Payoff	Payoff × Probability	Payoff	Payoff × Probability
Light	.10	$ 25,000	$ 2,500	−$ 10,000	−$ 1,000	−$125,000	−$ 12,500
Moderate	.70	400,000	280,000	440,000	308,000	400,000	280,000
Heavy	.20	650,000	130,000	740,000	148,000	750,000	150,000
		Expected payoffs	$412,500		$455,000		$417,500

The criterion of selecting the maximum expected payoff act is sometimes referred to as the *Bayes decision rule*. This criterion is named after Thomas Bayes, whom we associate with using empirical evidence for revising prior probabilities, because maximization of expected payoff is a suitable rule to use when decision making involves such experimental information.

The criterion of maximum expected payoff makes full use of information about the chances of the various payoffs. But, as we shall see, it is not a perfect device and can lead to a choice which is not truly the most desirable one. But we shall see also that it is a suitable basis for decision making under uncertainty when the payoff values are themselves selected with great care.

5-5 DECISION TREE ANALYSIS

So far we have encountered decisions under uncertainty that may be portrayed in terms of a payoff table. But some problems are too complex to be represented in that fashion. Difficulties arise when the same events do not apply for all acts. For example, a contractor might need to choose between seeking a construction job for a dam or for an airport. Not having sufficient resources to bid on both, the contractor must choose just one. Regardless of the job chosen, there is some probability (which may differ for the two projects) of winning the job bid on. Separate sets of events and probabilities are required for each set.

Often, decisions must be made at two or more points in time, with uncertain events occurring between decisions. Sometimes such problems may be analyzed in terms of a payoff table. But usually the earlier choice of act has bearing on the type, quantity, and probabilities of any later events. This makes it cumbersome at best to attempt to force the decision into the limited confines of the rectangular arrangement of a payoff table.

But the decision tree diagram may also be used to portray a decision problem. The tree representation allows us to meaningfully arrange the elements of a complex decision without the restrictions of the tabular format. It has further advantages in that it serves as a marvelous management communication tool because the tree makes every course of action and all possible outcomes easy to see.

To emphasize the need for a more general decision structure, consider again the toy manufacturer's decision evaluated earlier with a payoff table. We purposely kept that decision uncomplicated. There is merit in doing so, for some excluded factors may be unimportant. But there are also dangers from oversimplification that can lead to a less than optimal choice.

For instance, we eliminated the computer-controlled pneumatic doll-movement act, because it was dominated by weights and pulleys. But a computer-controlled movement might be adapted to an entire line of mechanical toys, thereby making the movements of all such toys cheaper than otherwise. A decision to do this can be made only at a later point in time, and then only if this particular movement is used. But such attractive alternatives have a value to the decision maker and ought to be reflected in the formulation of the decision structure.

Other factors might also be considered. For instance, the amount of advertising to use could be incorporated into the decision analysis. This would affect the total doll sales, and a decision to use more advertising may possibly make the choice of another doll movement more attractive than the choice made previously.

Our problem also assumed that the respective doll movements were equally attractive to the buyer. This need not be the case. In a society of rapidly expanding technology, the computer-controlled doll may be sold at a premium. Its sales might be increased if it is advertised as the "first doll with a genuine brain." A legitimate act would be to include different promotional appeals for each type of doll movement. Any differences in the sales potentials might be reflected by the event probabilities, which need not be the same for each act.

We recognize that the outcome of a decision about marketing a new product is not determined wholly by the simple interaction of a product-choice act with a consumer-demand event. The initial choice is simply the first in what can be a rather long, complicated chain of decisions to be made where intervening uncertain events must be encountered. For instance, later decisions must be made about the product's distribution, its intended market, its level of advertising, its method of production, its production schedule, and so forth. Each of these decisions will be influenced by uncertainties.

The ultimate outcome of such an involved decision may not be determined for years. During this period, new decisions must be made continually. Decision tree analysis accounts for this and also allows for the continual updating of the informational data base as a finer gauging of future uncertainties becomes possible. We illustrate decision tree analysis with a detailed discussion of a hypothetical situation.

The president of Ponderosa Record Company, a small independent recording studio, has just signed a contract with a four-person group, the Fluid Mechanics, whom he heard at a recent music festival. The contract covers a single long-playing record and may be extended at the company's option for two years. Tapes have been cut, and Ponderosa must decide whether or not to market the recording. If they market the record, the pressing run must be decided. Its size will depend on whether a choice is made to test market the record or to immediately place it on a national market. If test marketing is to be done, then a

5000-record run will be made and promoted regionally; this may result in a later decision to distribute nationally an additional 45,000 records, for which a second pressing run must be made. If immediate national marketing is chosen, a pressing run of 50,000 records will be made. Regardless of the test marketing results, the president may decide to enter the national market or decide not to.

It is the nature of Ponderosa's business that a record is either a complete success or failure in its market. A successful recording sells all records pressed, while a failure's sales are practically nil. Success in a regional market does not guarantee success nationally, but it is a fairly reliable predictor.

The Decision Tree Diagram

The structure of the Ponderosa decision problem is provided by the decision tree diagram in Figure 5-2. Notice that decisions are to be made at two different points in time or stages. The immediate choice requires selecting one of three acts: test market, market nationally, or abort the recording. These acts are shown as branches on an initial fork at node a. Suppose that test marketing is chosen. Then the result to be achieved in the marketplace is uncertain. This is reflected by an event fork at node b, the branches representing success and failure. Regardless of which event occurs, a new decision is required: to market nationally or to abort. These acts occur at a later stage, and their choice is shown as a pair of act forks, one each corresponding to the two different conditions under which this decision may be made: at node c when the test marketing is a success and at node d when it results in a failure. If national marketing is chosen, the success or failure of the recording still remains unknown, and the possible events are reflected on the decision tree as branches on the terminal event forks at nodes e and f. If the immediate choice at decision point a is instead to market nationally, the remaining uncertainty is reflected by an event fork of identical form at node g. The path leading to g contains two "dummy" branches, a diagrammatical convenience to allow event and act forks of similar form to appear at the same stage of the decision process. This also allows all paths to terminate at a common stage. If the abort act is selected at decision point a, then there are no further acts or events.

Every path leading from the base of the decision tree leads to a terminal position corresponding to an outcome of the decision. Each possible combination of acts and events, or path, has a distinct outcome. For instance, O_1 represents the following sequence of events and acts: test market, success, market nationally, success.

A first step in analyzing the decision problem is to obtain a payoff for each outcome.

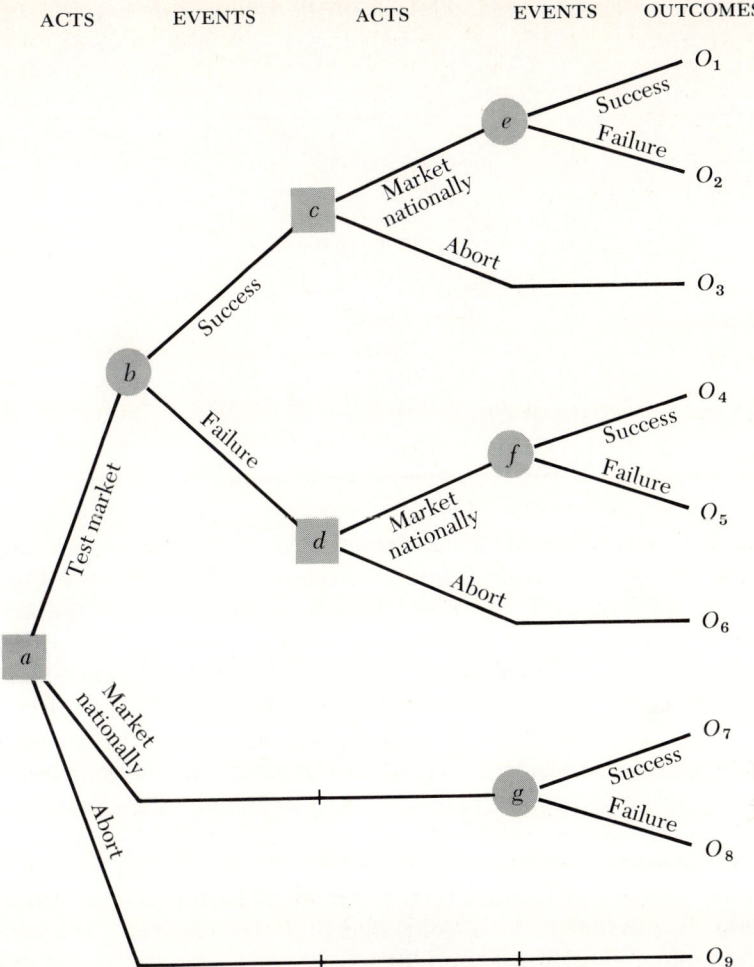

Figure 5-2
Decision tree diagram for the Ponderosa decision.

Determining the Payoffs

The terms of the contract with the Fluid Mechanics call for a $5000 payment if records are produced. Ponderosa arranges with a record manufacturer to make its pressings. Each pressing run has a $5000 fixed charge plus $.75 for each record. The record jackets, handling, and distribution cost an additional $.25 per record. The total variable cost per record is, thus, $1.00. Using these figures, we may calculate the immediate cash effect of each act in the initial fork at decision

5-5   DECISION TREE ANALYSIS   153

point *a* of the decision tree. These will be referred to as *partial cash flows*.

Act	Partial Cash Flow	
Test market	−$ 5,000	(for fee)
	− 5,000	(fixed cost of pressing)
	− 5,000	(variable costs of 5000 records
	Total −$15,000	@ $1.00)
Market nationally	−$ 5,000	(for fee)
	− 5,000	(fixed cost of pressing)
	− 50,000	(variable costs of 50,000 records
	Total −$60,000	@ $1.00)
Abort	$0	

The negative cash flows indicate expenditures. We show each partial cash flow on the respective branches from decision point *a* of the decision tree in Figure 5-3. In a similar manner, we determine the partial cash flows for the acts in the forks at decision points *c* and *d*: −$50,000 for marketing nationally ($5000 fixed pressing charge plus $1.00 each in variable costs for 45,000 records) and $0 for abort.

Ponderosa receives $2 for each record sold through retail outlets. Since the events, success and failure, represent respective sales of all and no records, the partial cash flows may be obtained by multiplying the number of records sold by $2. The partial cash flows for the events of the fork at node *b* are therefore +$10,000 (for 5000 records sold) and $0 (for no sales). Also, the amounts for events at nodes *e* and *f* are +$90,000 (for 45,000 records sold) and $0, while for the events from node *g* we obtain +$100,000 and $0.

The payoff for each outcome may be obtained by adding the partial cash flows on the branches of the path leading to its terminal position. Thus for O_1 we add the partial cash flows: −$15,000, +$10,000, −$50,000, and +$90,000. The payoff is thus +$35,000. The payoffs are calculated similarly for each outcome and are shown at the respective terminal positions in Figure 5-3.

Assigning Event Probabilities

Our decision maker wishes to choose that act which yields the maximum expected payoff. Before such a choice can be determined, probability values must be assigned to the events in the decision

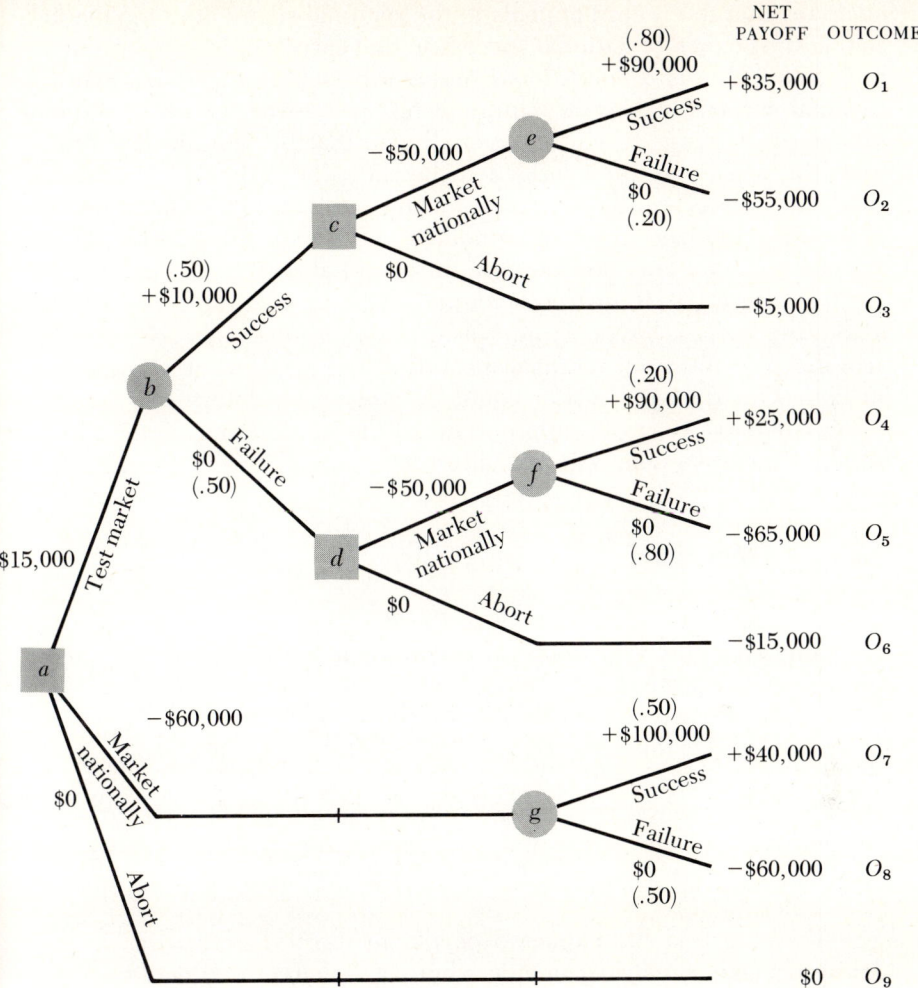

Figure 5-3
The Ponderosa decision tree diagram showing partial cash flows and probabilities on branches with net cash flow payoffs at end positions.

structure. Suppose that Ponderosa's president believes that the chance of successfully test marketing the recording is .50, so that the probability of failure is its complement (1 − .50), or also .50. These values are placed in parentheses along the branches at node b in Figure 5-3. In assigning probability values to the success and failure events for national marketing, our decision maker is faced with three distinctly different situations. If there should be no test marketing, the chance of national success is judged to be .50. Successful test marketing dem-

5-5 DECISION TREE ANALYSIS

onstrates that the record appeals to the regional segment of the market, so that the chance of national success in that case is judged to be a much higher .80; this is a *conditional* probability, where the given event is regional success. Likewise, failure at test marketing would be a likely precursor of things to come nationally, so that the conditional probability of success is then judged to be .20. The following probability values are placed on the branches for the events in the remaining forks of the decision tree diagram: at node e, .80 for success, .20 for failure; at node f, .20 for success, .80 for failure; and at node g, .50 for success, .50 for failure. (It is just coincidental that the probability of national marketing success given failure of test marketing equals .20, which is also the probability of national marketing failure after a test marketing success. Our decision maker could possibly have determined another value, such as .10, to be appropriate as the conditional probability of national success given regional failure.)

Backward Induction

We are now ready to analyze the decision problem posed in the foregoing example. Our decision maker wishes to select an immediate act at decision point a. The first act we evaluate is test marketing. What is the expected payoff for this act? Referring to Figure 5-3, we see that six outcomes, O_1 through O_6, may result from this choice. How can we translate the corresponding payoffs into an expected value? This is not possible without first specifying the intervening acts at nodes c and d that will be chosen. In general, *it is impossible to evaluate an immediate act without first considering all later decisions that result from this choice.*

Thus, to find the expected payoff for the test marketing act, our decision maker must first decide whether to market nationally or abort if (1) test marketing has proven successful or (2) test marketing has failed. This illustrates an essential feature of analyzing multistage decisions: *evaluations must be made in reverse of their natural chronological sequence.* Before deciding whether to test market, our decision maker must first decide what to do if the test marketing is a success or if it is a failure. The procedure for making such evaluations is called *backward induction.*

Let us make this point clearer by describing how this is done for our problem. For simplicity, the Ponderosa president's decision tree diagram is redrawn in Figure 5-4 with the partial cash flows left off.

Consider the act fork at decision point c. If Ponderosa's president chooses to market nationally, then he is faced with the event fork at node e. With probability .80, marketing nationally will be a success, in which case a net payoff of +$35,000 is achieved; failure has a .20 probability and leads to a net payoff of −$55,000. The expected payoff may be determined for this event fork as follows:

$$.8(\$35,000) + .2(-\$55,000) = +\$17,000$$

The amount +$17,000 is entered on the decision tree at node *e*, since

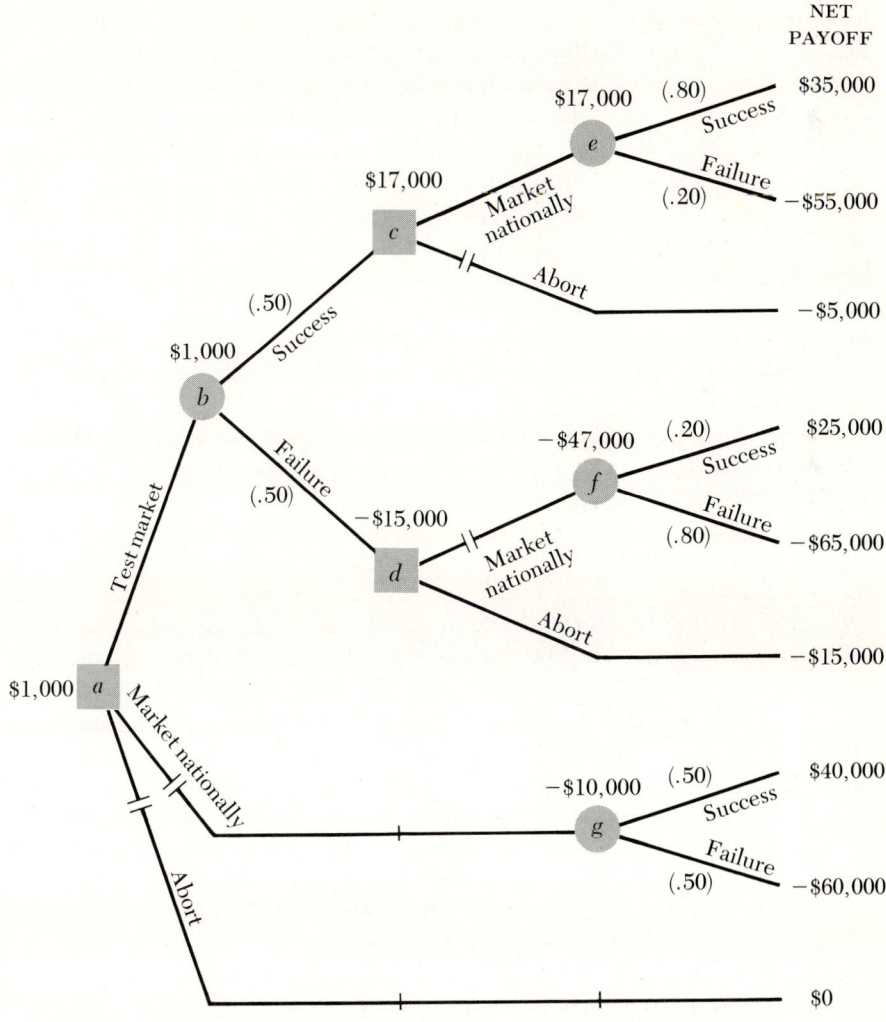

Figure 5-4
The Ponderosa decision tree diagram showing backward induction analysis.

this is the expected payoff from the act to market nationally. For convenience we place the expected payoff for a sequence of acts and events above the applicable node.

The act abort, at decision point c, leads to a certain payoff of $-\$5000$. Since the expected payoff of the act to market nationally is larger, $+\$17,000$, the latter act should be chosen over aborting. We may reflect this future choice by "pruning" from the tree the branch corresponding to abort; this act merits no further consideration, since on reaching decision point c, the president would choose instead to market nationally. Thus, if the decision maker were to have decided originally to test market and then this turned out to be successful, he would choose to market nationally. We thus assign $+\$17,000$ as the expected payoff resulting from making the best choice at decision point c. We bring back the amount $+\$17,000$ to be entered onto the diagram above the node at c.

As a rule of thumb in performing backward induction, ultimately all but one act will be eliminated at each decision point (except in the case of ties), so that all but branches leading to the greatest expected payoff will be pruned. Only the *best single payoff* from the later stage is brought backward to the preceding decision point (square). *Branch pruning takes place in act forks only, never in event forks.* Event forks, instead, always involve an expected value calculation, so that an average payoff is always brought backward from the later stage to one of these preceding nodes (circles).

The available choices when test marketing results in failure may be handled in the same way. First we calculate the expected payoff at node f arising from the act to market nationally:

$$.2(+\$25,000) + .8(-\$65,000) = -\$47,000$$

We place this figure on the diagram above node f. Since the act to abort leads to a payoff of $-\$15,000$, which is larger than $-\$47,000$, the branch for the act to market nationally is pruned from the tree. The best choice when the test marketing fails is to abort. We therefore bring back and enter the amount $-\$15,000$ onto the diagram above the node at decision point d.

In a similar fashion, the expected payoff of the event fork at node g, when the initial choice is to market nationally, is determined as follows:

$$.5(+\$40,000) + .5(-\$60,000) = -\$10,000$$

We are still unable to compare all the acts in the initial-act fork, but we do notice that abort is superior to the act to market nationally, so that the branch of the latter is pruned from the tree. Our decision maker must now compare the test market and abort acts at decision point a. We see that the expected payoff from the act to test market is still to be determined. This is the expected payoff for the event fork at node b, which has two event branches. The branch corresponding to success leads to a portion of the tree with an expected payoff of $17,000. The other branch leads to a later choice whose expected payoff we have evaluated at −$15,000. We may calculate the expected payoff at node b using these two amounts:

$$.5(+\$17,000) + .5(-\$15,000) = +\$1000$$

We enter the amount +$1000 on the diagram above node b.

We can now compare the test marketing act at decision point a to aborting. We see that test marketing's expected payoff is higher: +$1000 versus $0 for aborting. Thus our decision maker would choose to test market, leading to an expected payoff of $1000; this amount is brought back and placed above node a. The branch corresponding to abort is pruned. Our backward induction is complete.

A decision has been indicated. Our decision maker should choose to test market the Fluid Mechanic's record. Then if the test marketing is successful, he must market nationally; if it is not, he ought to abort the recording. This result is illustrated in Figure 5-4 by the unpruned branches remaining in the decision tree. Because the consequences of immediate acts could not be determined until later decisions were resolved, the decision was analyzed using backward induction.

Additional Remarks

The later-stage choices are not irrevocable, and this analysis does not preclude a later change of the decision-maker's mind. New information may be received before the future decision at c, for instance, indicating a need to revise the chance of national success downward. If there is bad publicity by one of the Fluid Mechanics, for example, the expected payoff from national marketing might be smaller than that obtained by aborting. The possible changing conditions do not invalidate the original backward induction analysis. *The choice to test market is the best decision that can be made with the currently available information.* Although test marketing was chosen primarily on the strength of expected payoffs following the initial acts, we assume during our analysis that there is no reason to suspect an adverse personal public reaction to the Fluid Mechanics. If there were grounds for expecting such an event, an additional event fork should have been included in the decision tree.

The decision tree structure is suitable for analyzing decisions extending over a long time period. It indicates the best course of action for the current decision. But as time progresses, some uncertainties may be reduced and new ones might arise. Previously identified future optimal acts may turn out to be obviously poor choices, and brand new candidates may be determined. The relevant portion of the decision tree can be updated and revised prior to each new immediate decision. But each such decision is analyzed in the same general manner, using the best information available at the time a choice has to be made.

Although a decision tree is analyzed by moving backward in time, the analysis is really forward-looking. It indicates the optimal course of action to take when reaching future decision points. The dollar amounts brought backward to each branching-point node represent the best payoff the decision maker can expect to achieve if at a later time he should arrive at that position. Regardless of what events have occurred, the course of action optimal for the future choices is indicated by the original analysis (provided the basic structure and information used has not changed, like the bad publicity possibility indicated above).

PROBLEMS

5-1 A young bachelor is deciding whether to spend his Christmas vacation at a ski resort or surfing in Hawaii. He must commit himself to one of these alternatives in the early fall, since reservations have to be made months in advance. He really enjoys skiing more than surfing. Unfortunately he cannot be certain about December snow conditions; should there be poor snow, his ski trip will be ruined. The Hawaii trip would be a sure thing. But if he must go there when the snow is good elsewhere, his trip will be somewhat spoiled by regrets that he did not arrange to ski.
(a) Construct his decision table.
(b) Draw his decision tree diagram.

5-2 Ted Jones, the founder of a computer-programming services firm, wishes to arrange expansion into the manufacture of peripheral equipment. Funds must be raised to build and operate the necessary facilities. Three alternatives are available: (1) issue additional common stock, (2) sell bonds, and (3) issue nonvoting preferred stock. A common stock issue will provide a strong financial base for future expansion through borrowing, but will considerably reduce Mr. Jones' percentage of ownership and control from its current 100 percent. New common stock will also cause future earnings to be divided into smaller amounts per share. Bonds will allow existing shareholders to take all the benefits of new earnings, but will also result in greater risk of forced liquidation if the new venture proves unsuccessful. Preferred stockholders have no claims on the firm's assets, but will drastically reduce the rate of earnings participation by existing common stockholders. Table 5-7 summarizes the forecast financial status of the firm if the manufacturing venture is successful.

For each of the following goals, suggest an appropriate payoff measure. Then use it to identify the best and worst alternative choices for financing, in terms of the degree to which the *single* goal is met. Indicate any ties.

(a) Maintain a high percentage of control by Jones family.
(b) Maximize earnings of Jones family shares.
(c) Maximize availability of short-term credit.
(d) Maximize potential for cash dividends to Jones family.

Table 5-7

	ALTERNATIVES FOR FINANCING		
POSSIBLE PAYOFF MEASURE	Additional Common Stock	Bonds	Preferred Stock
1. Earnings after taxes and preferred dividends	$5,000,000	$3,500,000	$4,000,000
2. Common shares outstanding	1,000,000	500,000	500,000
3. Earnings per common share	$5.00	$7.00	$8.00
4. Jones' percentage of common ownership	50	100	100
5. Emergency line of credit	$1,000,000	$400,000	$500,000
6. Earnings available for common dividends	$5,000,000	$2,000,000	$4,000,000
7. Maximum possible dividends per share of common stock	$5.00	$4.00	$8.00

5-3 Consider the following payoff table.

			ACTS	
EVENTS	PROBABILITY	A_1	A_2	A_3
E_1	.3	$10,000	$20,000	$ 5,000
E_2	.5	5,000	−10,000	10,000
E_3	.2	15,000	10,000	10,000

Compute the expected payoffs for each act. According to the Bayes decision rule, which act should be chosen?

5-4 Recompute the expected payoffs for the Tippi-Toes decision in Table 5-5 assuming that the demand event probabilities are now:

Light demand	.20
Moderate demand	.50
Heavy demand	.30

According to the Bayes decision rule, which act should the toy manufacturer choose?

5-5 An appliance manufacturer wishes to select one of three feasible prototype designs for a new high-intensity fluorescent lamp. Lamp A will cost $100,000 for tooling plus $20 each for labor, parts, and materials. The fixed and variable costs for the other two candidates are $50,000 and $35 for B and $200,000 and $10 for C. The lamp will sell for $50. There are three possible equally likely levels of unit sales for the lamp, which are independent of the design chosen: E_1, 4000; E_2, 8000; and E_3, 12,000. For the design decision, profit will be used as the payoff.
(a) Construct the payoff table.
(b) Construct the decision tree diagram.
(c) Compute the expected payoff for each act. If the manufacturer wishes to maximize expected payoff, which act would be chosen?

5-6 Identify any inadmissible acts in the following payoff table.

EVENTS	ACTS				
	A_1	A_2	A_3	A_4	A_5
E_1	3	4	4	5	1
E_2	6	2	1	4	2
E_3	1	8	8	7	3

5-7 For the decision tree diagram in Figure 5-5, perform backward induction analysis to determine the maximum expected payoff strategy. The event probabilities and payoffs are shown on the tree.

5-8 Suppose that the president of Ponderosa Record Company uses the following probability values to analyze his decision.

$P[\text{national marketing success}|\text{test marketing success}] = .9$
$P[\text{national marketing failure}|\text{test marketing failure}] = .6$
$P[\text{national marketing success}] = .7$
$P[\text{test marketing success}] = .75$

Repeat the decision tree analysis used in the chapter to determine the optimal strategy. Assume that all payoffs remain unchanged.

5-9 The manager of an oil company's data-processing operations personally interviews applicants for jobs as keypunchers. Persons hired with no previous experience are placed in a one-month training program on a trial basis. Satisfactory employees are retained, while the others are let go. Most of the persons let go in the past have been found lacking in aptitude. The manager is contemplating contracting for the testing services of a personnel agency, which for a $100 fee per applicant will administer a battery of aptitude tests. She has developed the decision tree in Figure 5-6 to help her make her hiring decisions. The event probabilities are indicated on the corresponding branches of the tree. As a payoff measure she has chosen per employee net recoverable training expenses. For trainees retained, all expenses except testing fees are recoverable; they also contribute an additional salary savings of $1000 over hiring already experienced personnel. For trainees not retained, neither the $500-training costs nor the testing fee are recoverable. Perform backward induction to determine what strategy or course of action will maximize expected payoff.

5-10 The president of Hercules Helicopter Corporation must decide whether to propose to design and perhaps later to build a new all-purpose junglecopter for the Army. If Hercules submits a proposal, two results are possible: (1) it may win an R & D contract, or (2) it may lose to a competitor. If Hercules wins the contract, the following choice will still have to be made: either (a) invest in personnel and facilities with the hope of winning a follow-on production con-

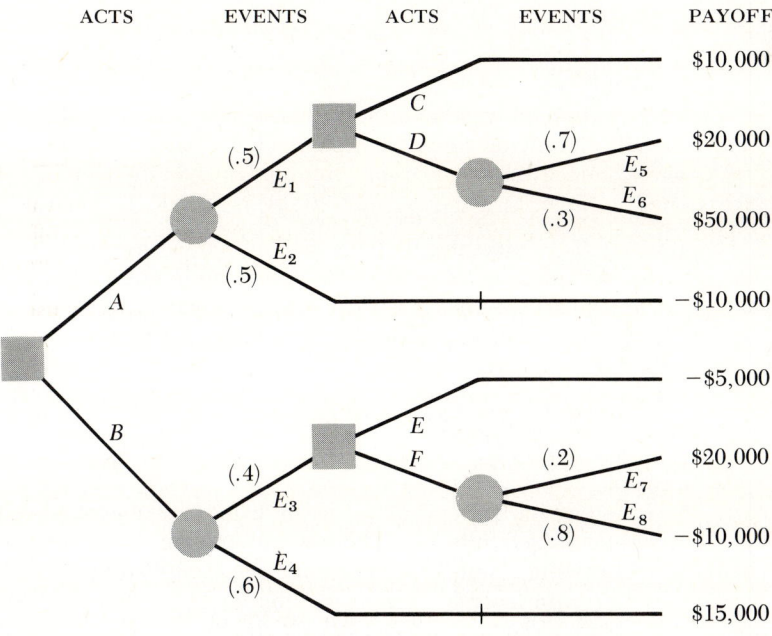

Figure 5-5

CHAPTER 5 PROBLEMS

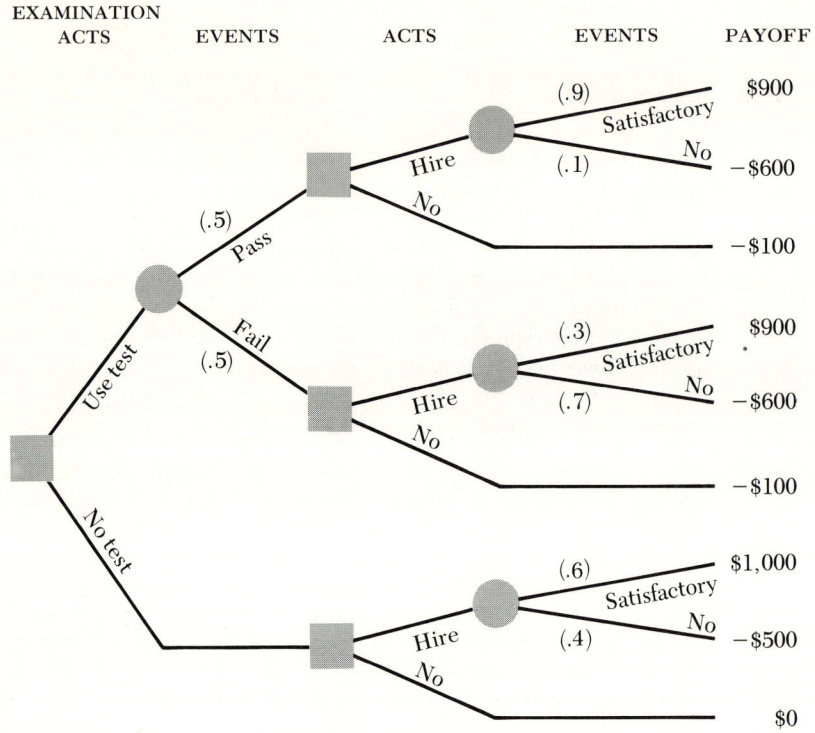

Figure 5-6

tract, or (b) not invest. In either case (a) or (b), Hercules may win or lose the follow-on production contract, but additional investment would increase its chances of winning. Diagram the Hercules decision problem.

5-11 Buzzy-B Toys must decide the course of action for a new whistling yo-yo. An initial decision must be made whether or not to market it at all or to first conduct a test marketing program. After test marketing has been done, a decision must be made whether to abandon or nationally distribute the yo-yo.

A national success will increase profits by $500,000, and a failure will reduce them by $100,000, while abandoning the product will not change profits. The test marketing will cost Buzzy-B a further $10,000.

If no test marketing is done, the probability of a national success has been judged to be .45. The assumed probability for a favorable test marketing result is .50. The conditional probability of national success given favorable test marketing is .80 and that for national success given unfavorable test results is .10.

Construct the decision tree diagram and perform backward induction to determine the optimal course of action using net change in profits as the payoff.

5-12 A product manager for a soap manufacturer wants to determine whether or not to market a new toothpaste. In addition to these choices, the manager can order a consumer testing program for $50,000. The present value of all future profits for a successful toothpaste is $1,000,000, whereas failure of the brand would result in a net loss of $500,000. Not marketing it would not change profits. The manager has judged that the toothpaste would have a 50-50 chance of success without testing. Customer testing will be either favorable (40 percent chance) or unfavorable. Given a favorable test result, the chance of product success is judged to be 80 percent. But for an unfavorable test result, the toothpaste's success probability has been judged to be only 30 percent.

Construct the product manager's decision tree diagram. Perform backward induction to determine which course of action provides the greatest expected profit.

5-13 A government official wishes to decide the best way to control crop damage from the gypsy moth. Three methods for attacking the pest are: (1) spray with DDT; (2) use a scent to lure and trap males, so that those that remain must compete for mating with a much larger number of males that have been sterilized in a laboratory and then released; and (3) spray with juvenile hormone, which prevents the larvae from developing into adults.

The net improvement in current and future crop losses using DDT is zero, for it is assumed that DDT will never completely eradicate the moth.

The scent-lure program has probability .5 of leaving a low number of native males, with a .5 chance of a high number. Once the scent-lure results are known, a later choice must then be made either to switch back to DDT or to release sterile males. The cost of the scent lures is $5 million and that for sterile males is an additional $5 million. But if this two-phase program is successful, the present and future crop savings will be $30 million. If scent lures leave the remaining native male population small, there is a 90-percent chance of success using sterile males, otherwise there is only a 10-percent chance of success with sterile males. A failure results in zero crop savings.

The juvenile hormone must be synthesized at a cost of $3 million. There is only a .20 probability that the resulting product will work. If it does, the crop savings would be $50 million, as the gypsy moth would become extinct. If not, crop savings would be zero.

Construct a decision tree diagram for the official's decision. Using crop savings minus cost as the payoff measure, determine the maximum expected payoff course of action.

Six

Elements of Decision Theory

Modern analysis of decision making under uncertainty has its roots in the area of study called *statistical decision theory*. Although most major developments in this field have occurred during the last fifty years, many early contributions were made more than two hundred years ago by the same pioneer mathematicians who formulated the theory of probability. In addition to probability, decision theory contains elements of statistics, economics and psychology.

A primary focus of statistical decision theory is establishing systematic means for choosing an act. This is accomplished largely through the payoff table introduced in the preceding chapter. Various *decision-making criteria* may be employed in selecting the best act. The payoff measure itself is a key element in selecting rules for decision making, and decision theory considers a variety of these.

We begin our discussion of decision theory with some of the well-known criteria used in selecting a best act. Then we describe opportunity loss, a payoff measure that provides the basis for explaining the worth of *information* that may be obtained regarding uncertain events. Indeed, we use the adjective *statistical* because sampling is a rich source of such information.

For various reasons, we shall see that the Bayes decision rule, which chooses the act having the best expected payoff, is the favored criterion. Decision theoretical concepts largely expand on this rule, since only it makes use of all the information at the disposal of the decision maker. When the proper payoff measure is used, the Bayes decision rule always leads to the most desirable choice. The device making this possible is the utility payoff, which measures a decision-maker's preference; utility theory is a special field within the broader context of decision theory.

This chapter surveys decision theory. In later chapters we will consider special topics. Chapter 7 discusses how experimental information may be systematically incorporated into decision making. In Chapter 8, which is more statistical in nature, specific probability distribution structures are melded with decision-making concepts. Chapter 9 describes utility theory and provides the practical details for obtaining and using utility values. This tropical grouping concludes in Chapter 10 with a discussion of game theory, which helps to explain interactive decision making, where two or more persons independently determine outcomes.

DECISION CRITERIA 6-1

Maximin Payoff

No decision-making theory could be complete without considering various rules that might be used in selecting the most desirable act. We will begin with the simplest criterion: *maximin payoff*. This procedure guarantees that the decision maker can do no worse than achieve the best of the poorest outcomes possible. As an illustration, we will use the payoff table of Table 6-1, which presents the toy-manufacturer's choice of doll movement for the Tippi-Toes doll discussed in Chapter 5. As our measure of payoff, we will use contribution to profit.

Suppose that our toy manufacturer wishes to make his choice of act so as to ensure a favorable outcome no matter what happens. This may be accomplished by taking a pessimistic viewpoint, determining the worst outcome for each act, regardless of event. For the gears and levers act the lowest possible payoff is $25,000 when light demand occurs. The

Table 6-1
PAYOFF TABLE FOR THE TIPPI-TOES DECISION

EVENTS	ACTS (CHOICE OF MOVEMENT)		
	Gears and Levers	*Spring Action*	*Weights and Pulleys*
Light demand	$ 25,000	−$ 10,000	−$125,000
Moderate demand	400,000	440,000	400,000
Heavy demand	650,000	740,000	750,000

lowest payoff for the spring-action movement is a negative amount, −$10,000, also obtained when demand is light. For the weights and pulleys movement it is −$125,000. By choosing the act that yields the largest of these payoffs, our decision maker can guarantee a minimum return that is the best of the worst. In this case, a gears and levers movement for the doll will guarantee the toy manufacturer a payoff of at least $25,000.

The gears and levers act is the act with the maximum of the minimum payoffs. This may be stated more concisely: gears and levers is the *maximin payoff act*. To show how this may be determined in general, we construct the payoff table in Table 6-2.

In most of the decision-making illustrations so far, we have used profit as the measure of payoff. As noted in Chapter 5, a variety of measures might be used in ranking outcomes. In business applications, *cost* is often used for this purpose when the goal is to minimize operational cost and when revenues are not subject to chance. We may apply the maximin payoff criterion to a situation involving costs by reversing our rule, selecting that act having the minimum of the maximum costs.

Table 6-2
DETERMINING MAXIMIN PAYOFF ACT FOR THE TIPPI-TOES DECISION

EVENTS	ACTS (CHOICE OF MOVEMENT)		
	Gears and Levers	*Spring Action*	*Weights and Pulleys*
Light demand	$ 25,000	−$ 10,000	−$125,000
Moderate demand	400,000	440,000	400,000
Heavy demand	650,000	740,000	750,000
Column minimums	25,000	− 10,000	− 125,000

Maximum of column minimums = $25,000
Maximin payoff act = Gears and levers

Comparable terminology for this rule would be *minimax cost*. But this criterion is identical to the previous one in the sense that cost may be viewed as negative profit, so that what gets minimized and maximized must be reversed; either way, the criteria lead to choosing the best of the worst. To avoid confusion we will always use maximin and minimax as adjectives that must be connected with a noun, such as profit, or cost.

How suitable is the maximin payoff criterion? This depends on the nature of the decision. Consider the decision problem in Table 6-3. Here we have a situation where the decision maker chooses A_1 over A_2.

Table 6-3
MAXIMIN PAYOFF DETERMINATION FOR A HYPOTHETICAL DECISION

EVENTS	ACTS	
	A_1	A_2
E_1	$0	−$1
E_2	1	10,000
Column minimums	0	−1
Maximum of column minimums = $0		
Maximin payoff act = A_1		

Most readers would agree with the author that A_2 would be a better choice if the chance of E_2 were high enough. The maximin decision maker is giving up an opportunity to gain $10,000 in order to avoid a possible loss of $1. To avoid losing $1, the decision maker is choosing an act that will guarantee at least the maintenance of the status quo. One can envision circumstances, however, where A_1 would be the best choice of act. Suppose that our decision maker has only $1 and must use this to pay a debt to a loan shark or lose his life. In this case the payoffs do not realistically represent the true value assigned them by the decision maker.

Consider another situation provided in Table 6-4. Here the maximin payoff act is A_1. This would be a good choice for a decision maker who could not tolerate a loss of $10,000, no matter how unlikely it was. Few people would risk losing their business by choosing an act leading to the possibility of bankruptcy unless the odds were extremely small. But an individual who could survive a loss of $10,000 would find A_2 superior if the probability of E_2 were substantially lower than E_1.

Our examples illustrate a key deficiency of maximin payoff: it is an extremely conservative decision criterion and can lead to some very

Table 6-4

PAYOFF TABLE FOR A HYPOTHETICAL DECISION

EVENTS	ACTS	
	A_1	A_2
E_1	$1	$10,000
E_2	−1	−10,000

bad decisions. Any alternative with slightly larger risks is passed over in favor of a comparatively risk-free alternative, which can be far less attractive. Taken to its ludicrous extreme, a maximin payoff policy would force any firm out of business. No inventories would be stocked, because there is always a possibility of unsold items. No new products would be introduced, because one can never be certain of their success. No credit would be granted, because one can always count on some customers not paying.

Another major deficiency of the maximin criterion exists if the likelihoods of the various events are known. Maximin payoff is mainly suited to decision problems whose probabilities are unknown and cannot be reasonably assessed. As our illustrations indicated, maximin payoff in extreme cases—the person hounded by loan sharks or the business that could go bankrupt—can lead to the best decision. But most of us, when faced with the same decision, would not choose the maximin payoff act because we attach different measures of worth to the outcomes. As we shall see later in this chapter, utility values may be used to explicitly measure the true relative worth of the various decision outcomes.

Maximum Likelihood Criterion

Another rule that has served as a model for decision-making behavior is the *maximum likelihood criterion*. Here the focus is on the most likely event, to the exclusion of all others. Table 6-5 illustrates this criterion for the toy-manufacturer's decision analyzed previously.

For this decision we see that a moderate demand has the highest probability of .7. The maximum likelihood criterion tells us to ignore the light and heavy demand events completely, in effect to assume that they will not occur. This rule then tells us to choose the best act assuming that a moderate demand will occur. In this example, the *maximum likelihood act* is to use the spring-action doll movement, which for a moderate demand provides the greatest profit of $440,000.

Table 6-5
DETERMINING MAXIMUM LIKELIHOOD ACT FOR THE TIPPI-TOES DECISION

DEMAND EVENTS	PROBA-BILITIES	ACTS (CHOICE OF MOVEMENT)		
		Gears and Levers	*Spring Action*	*Weights and Pulleys*
Light	.10	$ 25,000	−$ 10,000	−$125,000
Moderate	.70	400,000	440,000	400,000
Heavy	.20	650,000	740,000	750,000

Most likely event = Moderate demand
Maximum row payoff = 440,000
Maximum likelihood act = Spring action

How suitable is the maximum likelihood criterion for decision making? Using it, we don't explicitly consider the range of outcomes for the spring-action set—from a $10,000 loss if a light demand occurs to a $740,000 profit if it is heavy. We also ignore much of the rest of the possible outcomes, including the best (selecting weights and pulleys when demand is heavy, which yields a $750,000 profit) and the worst (again selecting weights and pulleys when demand is light, which leads to a $125,000 loss). In a sense, the maximum likelihood criterion would have us "play ostrich," ignoring much that might happen. If this is so, why is it discussed here?

We describe this criterion partly to be complete, but mainly because it seems so prevalent in the decision-making behavior of individuals and businesses. We may use it to explain certain anomalies that would otherwise be hard to rationalize. These quirks are epitomized by the so-called "hog cycle" in the raising and marketing of pigs, which relates to the more or less predictable two-year-long pork price movement from higher to lower levels and back again to high prices. Hog farmers have been blamed for this, since they expand their herds when prices are high, so that one year later the supply of mature hogs is excessive and prices are driven downward; then when prices are low, these same farmers reduce their herds, cutting the supply of marketable hogs, and the next year's prices consequently rise.

Why don't the farmers break this cycle? After all, it doesn't seem rational to be wrong consistently and pervasively in timing hog production. One explanation is that the hog farmers use the maximum likelihood criterion. In their minds, the most likely future market price is the current one—and we know that this has proven to be very poor judgment. Given that premise, the maximum likelihood act is to increase herd sizes when current prices are high and to decrease them when they are low. This peculiarity in human behavior extends to other decisions. The small investor has been accused of buying most heavily just as the stock market peaks and selling most strongly at the bottom. Even sophisticated corporate managers too often accentuate business cycles by investing excessively in plant and inventory just prior to recessions and retrenching prior to recovery. Such decision making is not unlike that of the hog farmers.

Criterion of Insufficient Reason

Another criterion that has been employed is *insufficient reason*. This may be used when a decision maker has no information about the chances of the events. In this case, no event may be regarded as more likely than another, and all events are assigned equal probability values. Since the events are collectively exhaustive and mutually exclusive, the probability of each must be

$$\frac{1}{\text{Number of events}}$$

Using these probabilities, one chooses the act with the maximum expected payoff.

A major criticism of this criterion is that there are few situations where some knowledge of the relative chances of events is not available. When it is available, the Bayes decision rule employing more realistic probabilities would be more valid.

Bayes Decision Rule Preferred

The foregoing three criteria have obvious inadequacies. *None of the three incorporates all information* available to the decision maker. Maximin payoff totally ignores probabilities for the events. Although this has been argued to be a strength when probabilities are not easily determined, there are few circumstances where judgment cannot be used in arriving at acceptable probability values.

The maximum likelihood criterion ignores all events but the most likely one, even if that event happens to be a lot less likely than the union of the rest. (For instance, among 20 events the most likely one may have a probability of .10, but there is a .90 probability that one of the other 19 events will occur.)

The criterion of insufficient reason essentially asks us to violate our judgments and "willy nilly" assume that all events are equally likely; this must be so even with such listed events as war and peace and boom and depression.

The Bayes decision rule has proven to be the central focus of statistical decision theory when all relevant evidence is used in determining a choice of action. It makes the greatest use of information. It alone allows us to extend decision theory to incorporate sampling or experimental information. Its major deficiency occurs when alternatives involve different magnitudes of risk. To illustrate the point, consider the decision structure in Table 6-6. Acts A_1 and A_2 are equally attractive under the criterion of maximum expected payoff, which is $500,000, the same amount for either act. Yet most decision makers would clearly prefer A_2, because it avoids the rather large risk of a million-dollar loss.

Table 6-6
PAYOFF TABLE FOR A HYPOTHETICAL DECISION

EVENTS	PROBABILITY	ACT A_1		ACT A_2	
		Payoff	Payoff × Probability	Payoff	Payoff × Probability
E_1	.5	−$1,000,000	−$ 500,000	$250,000	$125,000
E_2	.5	2,000,000	1,000,000	750,000	375,000
	Expected payoffs		$ 500,000		$500,000

The paradox here may be resolved not by choosing another criterion, but rather by reconsidering the values chosen for the payoffs. The theory of utility presented in Chapter 9 provides a way of setting the payoffs at values that express their true worth to the decision maker.

DECISION MAKING USING STRATEGIES 6-2

One important aspect of decision making is using information that might be helpful in making a choice. We may expand the concepts developed so far to accommodate such information. Business has numerous examples of these kinds of decision situations. In establishing an employment policy based on a screening test, an employer must use an applicant's score as the basis for hiring or rejecting that person; regardless of the score achieved, when hired, a person will ultimately perform satisfactorily or not. In receiving components for possible assembly into a final product, manufacturers generally use the information contained in a random sample before deciding to accept or reject a shipment; the ultimate quality of the entire shipment will be known only after this decision has been made. As a further example, consider the choice between adding a new product to the line or abandoning it. The results of a marketing research study might be used before deciding; the success or failure of the new product will only be known after it has been introduced.

All of the above situations are decisions with two points of uncertainty. The first of these is the kind of information obtained — the screening test score, the number of defective sample items, or the results of the survey. The second uncertainty concerns the ultimate outcome — the new employee's performance, the quality of the shipment, the new product's performance. Between these points in time a decision has to be made. The act chosen may depend on the particular event that occurred before.

It is possible to determine in advance the best acts to select for each informational event. The resulting decision rule is called a *strategy*. The ultimate decision requiring our analysis is the selection of the particular strategy. We will show how this is done by means of an illustration that contains sampling and inspection.

A cannery inspector monitors tests for mercury contamination levels before authorizing shipments of canned tuna. The procedure is to randomly select two crates of canned fish from a shipment and determine the parts per million of mercury. The number of these crates R exceeding government contamination guidelines is then determined. The inspector may then approve (A) or disapprove (D) the shipment. If approved, the shipment is sent to distributors who perform more detailed testing and determine whether the entire shipment's average mercury levels are excessive (E) or tolerable (T). An excessively contaminated shipment is returned to the cannery. If the company inspector originally refuses shipment, the production batch is sent to the rendering department to be converted into pet food. At this time, it is determined whether the entire shipment does indeed contain excessive average levels of mercury contamination.

The decision tree diagram for the inspector's decision is provided in Figure 6-1. Eight strategies, denoted symbolically by S_1 through S_8, are identified in Table 6-7. A strategy must specify which act, approve or disapprove, to choose for each possible test result. Thus, we see that strategy S_1 is a decision rule specifying that the shipment must be approved no matter what the number of excessively contaminated crates R happens to be. Strategy S_2 specifies approval if $R = 0$ or $R = 1$, but disapproval if $R = 2$. Eight strategies are possible because for each of the 3 events there are 2 choices and, thus, $2^3 = 8$ distinct decision rules.

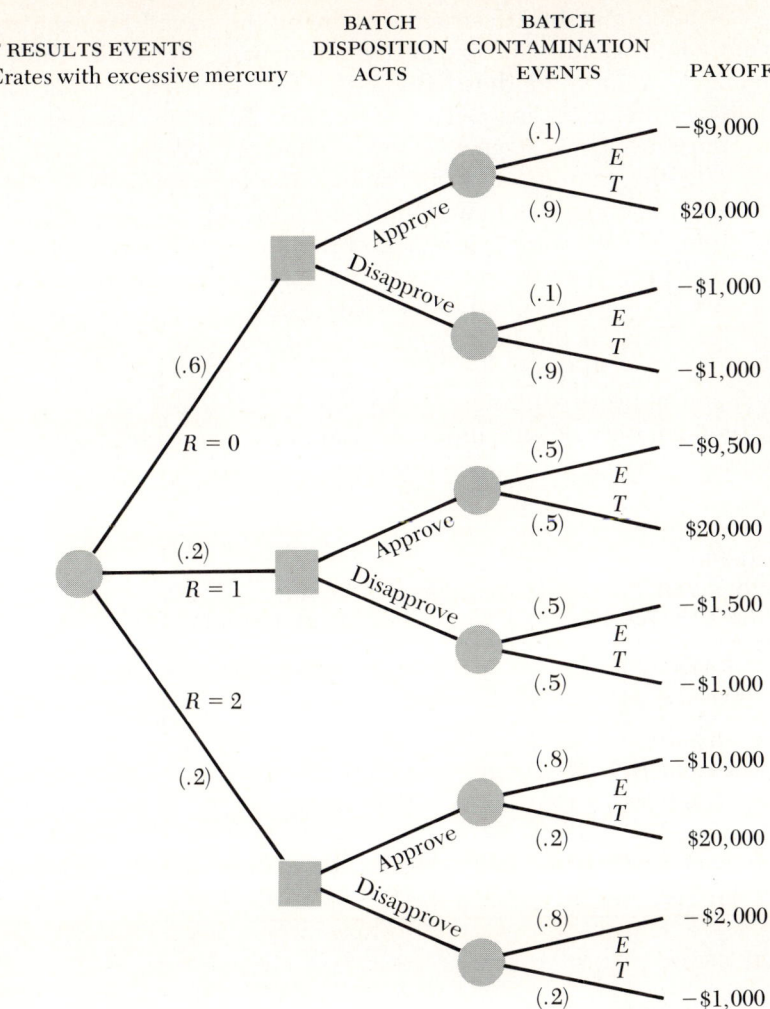

Figure 6-1
Decision tree diagram for the cannery inspector.

Table 6-7
STRATEGIES FOR THE CANNERY INSPECTOR'S DECISION

TEST RESULT EVENTS	STRATEGY							
	S_1	S_2	S_3	S_4	S_5	S_6	S_7	S_8
$R = 0$	A	A	A	D	A	D	D	D
$R = 1$	A	A	D	A	D	A	D	D
$R = 2$	A	D	A	A	D	D	A	D

6-2 DECISION MAKING USING STRATEGIES   175

A table may be constructed showing the payoff for each strategy-event combination. The payoff table obtained, shown in Table 6-8, is identical in form to those discussed for single-stage decisions, but strategies are used instead of acts. One difference is that there are uncertainties at two stages: (1) the number of excessively contaminated crates in the sample, and (2) whether the contamination level of the entire production batch will be found, on the average, excessive or tolerable. The six joint events are of the form $R = 0$ and E, $R = 2$ and T. The cell entry payoff values are the same as in the decision tree in Figure 6-1 and correspond to the joint event that occurs for the specified strategy. Thus, if the joint event $R = 2$ and E occurs when S_1 is used, the payoff is -10 thousand dollars, since this particular strategy has the inspector approve shipment whenever $R = 2$. If the inspector is using S_2, the same event will indicate disapproval, and because there is an excessive average batch-mercury-level, the payoff is -2 thousand dollars.

Table 6-8
PAYOFF TABLE FOR THE CANNERY INSPECTOR'S DECISION USING STRATEGIES (PAYOFFS IN THOUSANDS OF DOLLARS)

JOINT EVENTS	STRATEGY							
	S_1	S_2	S_3	S_4	S_5	S_6	S_7	S_8
$R = 0$ and E	-9	-9	-9	-1	-9	-1	-1	-1
$R = 0$ and T	20	20	20	-1	20	-1	-1	-1
$R = 1$ and E	-9.5	-9.5	-1.5	-9.5	-1.5	-9.5	-1.5	-1.5
$R = 1$ and T	20	20	-1	20	-1	20	-1	-1
$R = 2$ and E	-10	-2	-10	-10	-2	-2	-10	-2
$R = 2$ and T	20	-1	20	20	-1	-1	20	-1

This strategy-selection decision can be analyzed by applying any of the various criteria we have encountered earlier and treating each strategy in the same way as an act in a simpler decision structure. However, we will continue by maximizing expected payoff.

Extensive and Normal Form Analysis

This particular decision may be analyzed using the Bayes decision rule and maximizing expected payoff through either (1) backward induction on the decision tree or (2) direct computation from the values in the payoff table to find the strategy with the maximum expected payoff. *Both approaches will provide identical results.* When a decision tree is used, the procedure is called an *extensive form analysis.* Analysis performed on the payoff table is referred to as *normal form analysis.*

Figure 6-2 shows the extensive form analysis. The probability value determined for each event is shown on the corresponding branch.

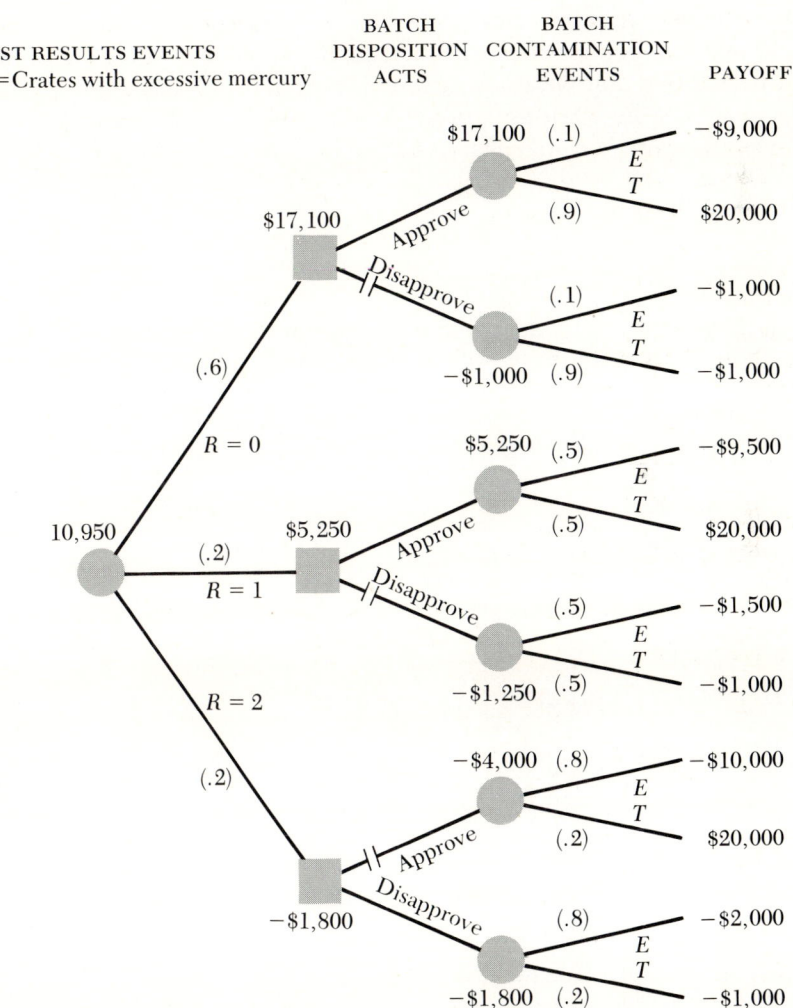

Figure 6-2
Extensive form analysis of the cannery inspector's problem, using the decision tree diagram.

Backward induction shows that the best procedure is to approve the shipment when $R = 0$ or $R = 1$ and to reject the shipment when $R = 2$; referring to Table 6-7, we see that this corresponds to strategy S_2.

The results of the normal form analysis are shown in Table 6-9. Strategy S_2 has the maximum expected payoff of 10.95 thousand dollars, which is the same as the result obtained in the extensive form analysis. Indeed, every strategy listed in Table 6-7 can be represented by a unique pruned tree, as shown in Figure 6-3. Fortunately, extensive form analysis requires that we prune the tree just once. In terms of computational efficiency, this makes decision tree analysis superior because fewer computations are required, and it is not even necessary to catalogue the various strategies. In backward induction, only the maximum expected payoffs need to be brought back to the earlier branching point.

Table 6-9
EXPECTED PAYOFF CALCULATIONS FOR THE CANNERY INSPECTOR'S DECISION USING STRATEGIES (PAYOFFS IN THOUSANDS OF DOLLARS)

(1) First-Stage Event Probability	(2) Second-Stage Event Probability	(3) Joint Probability (1) × (2)	(4) Payoff for S_2	(5) Payoff × Joint Probability (3) × (4)
$P[R=0] = .6$	$P[E\|R=0] = .1$	.06	− 9	− .54
$P[R=0] = .6$	$P[T\|R=0] = .9$	.54	20	10.80
$P[R=1] = .2$	$P[E\|R=1] = .5$	.10	− 9.5	− .95
$P[R=1] = .2$	$P[T\|R=1] = .5$	.10	20	2.00
$P[R=2] = .2$	$P[E\|R=2] = .8$	.16	− 2.0	− .32
$P[R=2] = .2$	$P[T\|R=2] = .2$	.04	− 1.0	− .04
			Expected payoff =	10.95

All strategies:	S_1	S_2	S_3	S_4	S_5	S_6	S_7	S_8
Expected payoff:	10.51	10.95	9.21	−.35	9.65	.09	−1.65	−1.21

Often extensive form analysis using a decision tree is the only approach possible, because the problem structure cannot be forced into the rectangular format of a payoff table. This is especially true of problems having two or more decision points, such as the Ponderosa Record Company example in Chapter 5 (see Figure 5-3 on page 155). Only problems with a symmetrical tree like that in Figure 6-2 can be analyzed either way in terms of expected payoff.

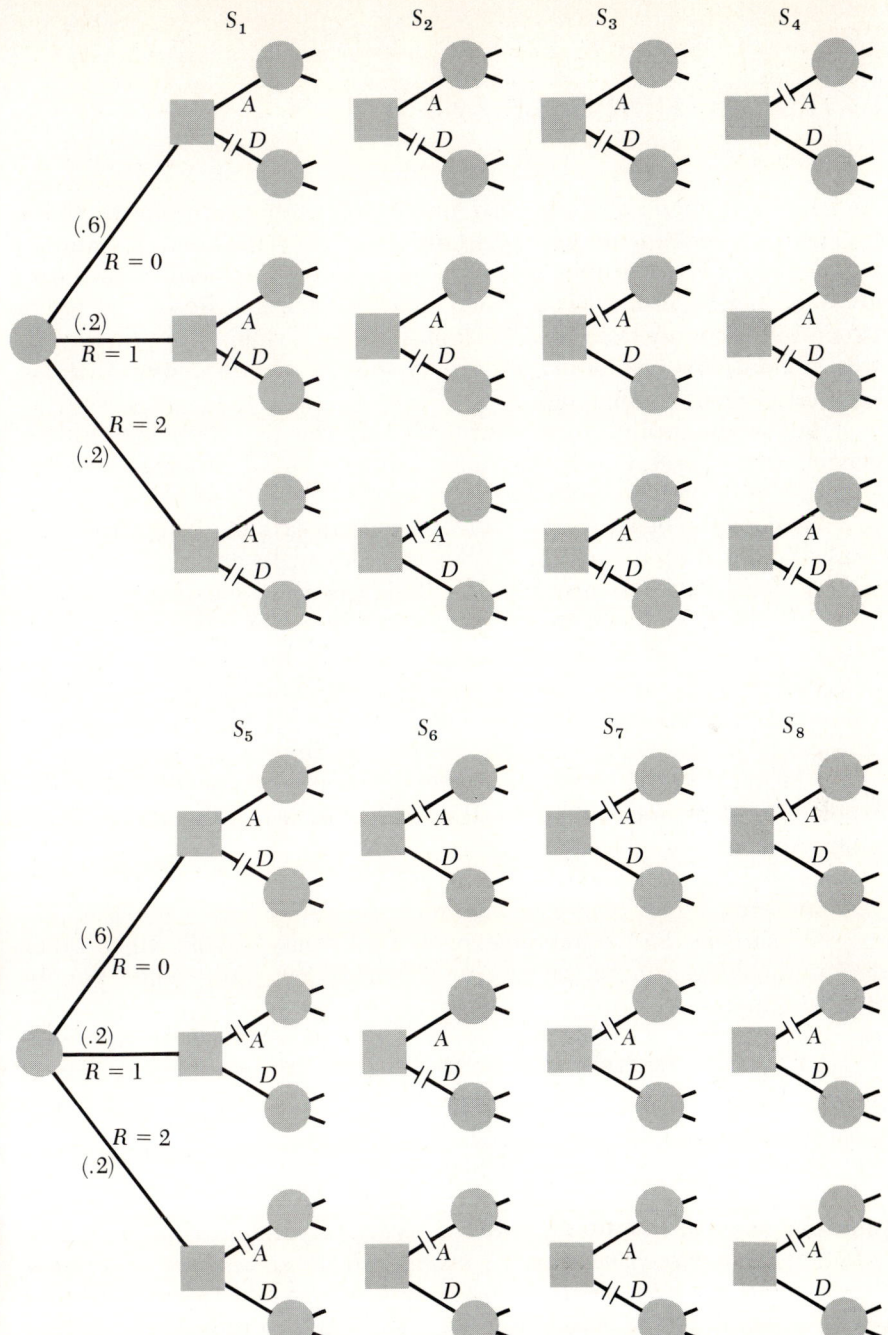

Figure 6-3
Pruned tree diagrams illustrating the eight strategies for the cannery inspector.

6-2 DECISION MAKING USING STRATEGIES

6-3 BAYES DECISION RULE AND UTILITY

We have made a strong case for using expected values as the basis for decision making under uncertainty. As we have seen, a criterion based on expected value uses all the available probability data and gives proper weight to every outcome; the other criteria use fewer structural elements from the decision. Expected value also provides us with a gauge for evaluating additional sources of information that can be used in decision making.

But when applied to monetary payoffs, the Bayes decision rule — maximizing expected profit and minimizing expected cost or loss — often leads to a less preferred choice.

Perhaps the best example of this occurs in casualty insurance decisions — where the choices are to buy a policy or to not buy one. Most persons have liability insurance for their cars, and most carry greater coverage than the legal minimum. It is well-known that the policy-owner's annual cost for that insurance exceeds the expected loss from an accident. (This is because insurance companies must charge more than what they expect to pay in claims, just to meet overhead and expenses.) But according to the Bayes decision rule, the best decision is not to insure — it has the greater expected monetary payoff (that is, the expected cost of not insuring is less than the cost of insurance). This contradicts the true preference of most people.

Similar breakdowns of the Bayes decision rule occur whenever a person prefers a less risky alternative to one that involves considerable risk but actually has a greater expected monetary payoff. Since other decision-making criteria have serious defects too, how should we objectively analyze decisions where great risks are involved?

Fortunately, *decision theory copes with attitude toward risk through an adjustment in the payoff values themselves.* This is accomplished by establishing for every outcome a true-worth index called a *utility* value. Thus, a decision may be analyzed using utilities instead of dollars or other standard payoff measures.

In Chapter 9 we will describe the theory of utility and its application in great detail. There is one very important principle established there: *when the Bayes decision rule is applied in a decision having utilities as payoffs, it always indicates the most preferred course of action.* This makes that rule the theoretically perfect criterion for decision making, no matter how complex the decision happens to be.

OPPORTUNITY LOSS AND EXPECTED VALUE OF PERFECT INFORMATION   6-4

Is it worthwhile to buy information that may help us choose the better act? Information is usually not free. Resources, for example, are required to take a sample or to administer a test. Here we attempt to place a value on such information. In doing this, we introduce the concept of opportunity loss.

Opportunity Loss

Suppose that we view each possible outcome in terms of a measure expressing the difference in payoff between the act chosen and the best that could have been achieved. Such a measure is referred to as an *opportunity loss*, which we define as follows:

> The *opportunity loss* for an outcome is the amount of payoff forgone by not selecting the act having the greatest payoff for the event that actually occurs.

Table 6-10 shows how the opportunity losses are obtained for the payoffs for the toy-manufacturer's doll-movement decision. The oppor-

Table 6-10
DETERMINATION OF OPPORTUNITY LOSSES FOR THE TIPPI-TOES DECISION

DEMAND EVENTS	PAYOFFS			ROW MAXIMUM
	Gears and Levers	*Spring Action*	*Weights and Pulleys*	
Light	$ 25,000	−$ 10,000	−$125,000	$ 25,000
Moderate	400,000	440,000	400,000	440,000
Heavy	650,000	740,000	750,000	750,000
	Row maximum − Payoff = Opportunity loss (thousands of dollars)			
Light	25 − 25 = 0	25 − (−10) = 35	25 − (−125) = 150	
Moderate	440 − 400 = 40	440 − 440 = 0	440 − 400 = 40	
Heavy	750 − 650 = 100	750 − 740 = 10	750 − 750 = 0	

tunity losses are calculated by first determining the best outcomes for each event, the maximum payoff in each row. The payoffs in each row are then subtracted from the row maximums.

The *opportunity loss table* is shown in Table 6-11. All opportunity loss values are non-negative, since they measure how much worse off the decision maker is by choosing an act other than the best for the occurring event. Let us consider the meaning of the values. For example, suppose that the gears and levers movement is chosen and a light demand occurs. The opportunity loss is zero, because, referring to Table 6-10, we see that no better payoff than $25,000 could have been achieved if another act had been chosen. But if gears and levers are used and a heavy demand occurs, the opportunity loss must then be $100,000. This is because that movement does not have the greatest payoff for a heavy demand; the weights and pulleys movement with a payoff of $750,000 does. Since for this event choosing gears and levers has a payoff of only $650,000, the payoff difference, $750,000 − $650,000 = $100,000, represents the additional payoff forgone. It should be emphasized that the $100,000-opportunity loss is not a loss in the accounting sense, for a net positive contribution of $650,000 to profits is obtained. Rather, the opportunity to achieve an additional $100,000 has been missed. We might say that the decision maker would have $100,000 in *regret* by not having chosen weights and pulleys instead of gears and levers, should demand prove to be heavy.

Table 6-11
OPPORTUNITY LOSS TABLE FOR THE TIPPI-TOES DECISION

	ACTS (CHOICE OF MOVEMENT)		
EVENTS	Gears and Levers	Spring Action	Weights and Pulleys
Light demand	$ 0	$35,000	$150,000
Moderate demand	40,000	0	40,000
Heavy demand	100,000	10,000	0

Bayes Decision Rule and Opportunity Loss

Since an opportunity loss is a numerical outcome, we can calculate the expected value of the opportunity losses for each act to be considered. Our goal is to select the act with the minimum expected opportunity loss. The expected opportunity loss for each act is calculated in Table 6-12 for the toy-manufacturer's decision. We see that the expected opportunity loss for the gears and levers movement is $48,000. Notice

Table 6-12
CALCULATION OF EXPECTED OPPORTUNITY LOSSES FOR THE TIPPI-TOES DECISION

DEMAND EVENT	PROBABILITY	GEARS AND LEVERS Loss	GEARS AND LEVERS Loss × Probability	SPRING ACTION Loss	SPRING ACTION Loss × Probability	WEIGHTS AND PULLEYS Loss	WEIGHTS AND PULLEYS Loss × Probability
Light	.10	$ 0	$ 0	$35,000	$3,500	$150,000	$15,000
Moderate	.70	40,000	28,000	0	0	40,000	28,000
Heavy	.20	100,000	20,000	10,000	2,000	0	0
Expected opportunity losses			$48,000		$5,500		$43,000

that the minimum expected opportunity loss is $5500 for the spring-action act. This act would be our decision-maker's choice under this criterion. The spring-action movement is the *minimum expected opportunity loss act*.

In Chapter 5 we saw that the spring-action movement was also the maximum expected payoff act and was thus the best choice according to the Bayes decision rule. Our new criterion leads to the same choice. It may be established mathematically that this will always be so. Since either criterion will always lead to the same choice, we can say that the *Bayes decision rule is to select the act having the maximum expected payoff or the minimum expected opportunity loss*.

Expected Value of Perfect Information

So far we have pictured our toy manufacturer selecting an act without benefit of any additional information beyond that acquired through experience with other toys. But it is possible to obtain better information about next season's demand through test marketing, from opinion and attitude surveys, or from inside information regarding competitors' plans. How much would the decision maker be willing to pay for additional information?

It will be helpful to consider the payoff that can be expected from improved information about the events. We will take the extreme case, where the decision maker can acquire *perfect information*. Using this information, the decision maker could guarantee selection of the act yielding the greatest payoff for whatever event actually occurs. Because we wish to investigate the worth of such information *before* it is obtained, we will determine the *expected payoff with perfect information*.

To calculate the expected payoff with perfect information, we determine the highest payoff for each event. This is illustrated for the doll-movement decision in Table 6-13. The maximum payoff for each demand level is determined by finding the largest payoff in each row. Thus for a light demand we find that choosing gears and levers gives the largest payoff, $25,000. If the perfect information indicated that light demand was certain to occur, our decision maker would choose that movement.

Table 6-13
CALCULATION OF EXPECTED PAYOFF WITH PERFECT INFORMATION FOR THE TIPPI-TOES DECISION

| DEMAND EVENT | PROBABILITY | ACT PAYOFFS | | | MAXIMUM PAYOFF FOR EVENT | MAXIMUM PAYOFF × PROBABILITY |
		Gears and Levers	*Spring Action*	*Weights and Pulleys*		
Light	.10	$ 25,000	–$ 10,000	–$125,000	$ 25,000	$ 2,500
Moderate	.70	400,000	440,000	400,000	440,000	308,000
Heavy	.20	650,000	740,000	750,000	750,000	150,000
				Expected payoff with perfect information =		$460,500

Similarly, $440,000 is the maximum payoff possible for moderate demand, and this amount can only be achieved if the spring-action movement is chosen. Likewise, $750,000 is the maximum possible payoff when a heavy demand occurs, corresponding to a choice of the weights and pulleys movement. The last column of Table 6-13 shows the products of the maximum payoffs and their respective event probabilities. Summing these, we obtain $460,500 as the expected payoff with perfect information. This figure represents the average payoff the toy manufacturer would experience if he were faced with the same situation repeatedly and always selected the act yielding the best payoff for the event indicated by the perfect information. Keep in mind that the $460,500 represents the payoff that will on the average be achieved, viewed from some point in time *before* the information has been made available. *After* the information has been obtained, exactly one of the payoffs, $25,000, $440,000, or $750,000, is bound to occur. When the information is actually obtained, the payoff is a known certainty.

We may now answer our question regarding the worth of perfect information to the decision maker. As we have seen, the Bayes decision rule leads to the choice of a particular act that maximizes the expected payoff without regard to any additional information. We shall refer to this value as the *expected payoff under uncertainty*. Since this is the best that our decision maker can do with no new information, and the expected payoff with perfect information is the average payoff that can be anticipated with the best possible knowledge, then the worth to him of perfect information is expressed by the difference in these two amounts. We call the resulting number the *expected value of perfect information*, which is conveniently represented by the abbreviation EVPI and may be expressed as

$$\text{EVPI} = \text{Expected payoff with perfect information} \\ - \text{Expected payoff under uncertainty}$$

For the toy-manufacturer's decision, we obtain the EVPI by subtracting the expected payoff under uncertainty of \$455,000 (calculated in Table 5-6 on page 149) from the \$460,500 expected payoff with perfect information:

$$\text{EVPI} = \$460,500 - \$455,000 = \$5500$$

In this case the EVPI represents the greatest amount of money the decision maker would be willing to pay in order to obtain perfect information about what the doll's demand will be. Stated differently, \$5500 is the increase in the decision-maker's expected payoff that can be attributed to perfect knowledge of demand. Neither the \$455,000 nor the \$460,500 has any meaning *after* the perfect information is obtained. Thus, the EVPI of \$5500 can only be interpreted *before* the perfect information has become known.

The expected value of perfect information is analogous to the expected claim from a hypothetical insurance policy that provides our decision maker with the difference between the payoff actually achieved and the best payoff that could have been achieved had the event that was to occur been known. Table 6-14 shows the calculation of the expected claim, which is the same figure, \$5500. Because the EVPI expresses how much worse off the decision maker is, on the average, by being uncertain which act will be best, it is sometimes called the *cost of uncertainty*.

Notice that the amount \$5500 is the same as the minimum expected opportunity loss calculated in Table 6-12 for the optimal choice of act under uncertainty (without perfect information). Note also that the hypothetical claim entries in column (5) of Table 6-14 are the same values as the individual opportunity losses for the spring-action movement. The expected value of these is \$5500, the EVPI. Thus we see that *the expected value of perfect information is equal to the expected opportunity loss for the optimal act.*

Table 6-14

EVPI CALCULATION USING A HYPOTHETICAL INSURANCE POLICY

(1) Demand Event	(2) Proba- bility	(3) Payoff for Optimal Act, Spring Action	(4) Greatest Payoff for Event	(5) Hypothetical Insurance Claim (4) − (3)	(6) Claim × Probability (2) × (5)
Light	.10	−$ 10,000	$ 25,000	$35,000	$3,500
Moderate	.70	440,000	440,000	0	0
Heavy	.20	740,000	750,000	10,000	2,000
		EVPI = Expected hypothetical insurance claim =			$5,500

Therefore we may calculate the expected value of perfect information by calculating the expected opportunity losses. The minimum of these is the EVPI. Table 6-15 summarizes the relationships among expected payoff, expected opportunity loss, and expected value of perfect information for the toy-manufacturer's decision. Notice that, for any act, the sum of the expected payoff and the expected opportunity loss is equal to the expected payoff with perfect information.

Table 6-15

RELATIONSHIPS AMONG EXPECTED PAYOFF, EXPECTED OPPORTUNITY LOSS, AND EVPI FOR THE TIPPI-TOES DECISION

	Gears and Levers	Spring Action	Weights and Pulleys
Expected payoffs	$412,500	$455,000	$417,500
Expected opportunity losses	48,000	5,500	43,000
Expected payoff with perfect information	$460,500	$460,500	$460,500
Expected value of perfect information (EVPI) = $5,500		↖Optimal act	

Since in practice perfect information is nonexistent in most real-world decision making, why do we care about the EVPI? Our answer is that it helps us to establish a limit on the worth of less-than-perfect information. For example, if a marketing-research study aimed at predicting demand costs $6000, which exceeds the EVPI by $500, then it should not be ordered—regardless of its quality. The concepts involving decision making with experimental information are investigated further in Chapter 7.

PROBLEMS

6-1 You have decided to participate in a gamble with the following monetary payoffs:

| | ACTS | |
EVENTS	Choose Red	Choose Black
Red occurs	$1	−$2
Black occurs	−1	100

(a) What is the maximin payoff act?
(b) Suppose that the probability of red is .99. Calculate the expected payoffs from each act. Which act is best under the Bayes decision rule? What act would you choose?
(c) Suppose the probability of red is .5. Calculate the expected payoffs for the acts. Which act has the maximum expected payoff? What act would you choose?
(d) In view of your answers to the above questions, what do you think of the maximin payoff decision criterion?

6-2 A decision maker must choose among three acts. His payoff table, along with the event probabilities, is provided below.

| | | ACTS | | |
EVENTS	PROBABILITY	A_1	A_2	A_3
E_1	.3	$10	$15	$20
E_2	.4	15	20	15
E_3	.3	25	15	15

(a) Which is the maximin payoff act?
(b) Which act is the maximum likelihood act?
(c) Calculate the expected payoffs. According to the Bayes decision rule, which act should be chosen?

6-3 A farmer intends to sign a contract to provide a cannery with his entire crop. He must choose one of the following five vegetables: corn, tomatoes, beets, asparagus, and cauliflower. His entire 1000 acres will be planted with the selected crop. The yield of each vegetable will be affected to various degrees by the weather. The following table indicates the approximate productivities for dry, moderate, and damp weather. It also lists the price per bushel that has been offered.

WEATHER TYPE	APPROXIMATE YIELD (BUSHELS PER ACRE)				
	Corn	Tomatoes	Beets	Aspara-gus	Cauli-flower
Dry	20	10	15	30	40
Moderate	35	20	20	25	40
Damp	40	10	30	20	40
Price/Bushel	$1.00	$2.00	$1.50	$1.00	$0.50

(a) Using approximate total cash receipts when the crop is sold as a payoff measure, construct the payoff table for this farmer's decision.
(b) Identify any inadmissible acts, and eliminate them from the payoff table.
(c) What is the maximin payoff act?
(d) Supposing that the following probability values have been assigned for the weather, calculate the expected payoff for each act and identify the act having the maximum expected payoff.

Weather	Probability
Dry	.3
Moderate	.5
Damp	.2

6-4 Using the payoff table below, construct an opportunity loss table.

	ACTS	
EVENTS	A_1	A_2
E_1	100	90
E_2	−50	20

6-5 Using the opportunity loss table below, determine which act yields the lowest expected opportunity loss.

		ACTS		
EVENTS	PROBABILITY	A_1	A_2	A_3
E_1	.4	10	0	20
E_2	.5	0	30	40
E_3	.1	50	5	0

6-6 For the payoff table on page 189, answer the following:
(a) What is the maximum expected payoff? To what act does this correspond?

ELEMENTS OF DECISION THEORY

(b) What is the expected payoff with perfect information?
(c) Using your answers from (a) and (b), calculate the expected value of perfect information.
(d) What is the minimum expected opportunity loss?
(e) What do you notice about your answers to (c) and (d)?

		ACTS		
EVENTS	PROBABILITY	A_1	A_2	A_3
E_1	1/3	10	20	30
E_2	1/3	40	-10	20
E_3	1/3	20	50	20

6-7 A newsdealer must decide how many copies of a particular magazine to stock in December. He will not stock less than the lowest possible demand nor more than the highest. Each magazine costs him $0.50 and sells for $1.00. At the end of the month, unsold magazines are thrown away. Three levels of demand are equally likely: 10, 11, and 12. If demand exceeds stock, sales will equal stock.
(a) Using December profit as his payoff, construct the newsdealer's payoff table.
(b) According to the maximin criterion, how many copies should he stock?
(c) Which number of copies will provide the greatest expected payoff?

6-8 A paper company is planning its capital-investment expenditures for new equipment. Two alternative machines are being considered for the manufacture of kraft paper used in cardboard boxes. Machine A costs $100,000 and produces paper at an operating cost of $10 per ton, including materials and labor. Machine B costs $500,000 and makes paper at an operating cost of $5 per ton. The company currently buys kraft paper for $20 per ton from another mill. Total kraft-paper requirements throughout the next five years is the major uncertainty affecting choice of machines. Management has chosen as its payoff measure total five-year savings over purchasing the paper from outside.
(a) How many tons of paper must be used before machine A has been "paid off"? How many for machine B?
(b) What is the number of tons that will yield equal savings from either machine?
(c) Suppose two levels of total production are judged equally likely: 50,000 tons and 100,000 tons. Construct the payoff table. Then determine the maximum expected payoff act.
(d) Construct the opportunity loss table for this decision. Then determine the minimum expected opportunity loss act.
(e) Was the same act chosen in (c) and (d)? Why was this so?

CHAPTER 6 PROBLEMS

6-9 An oil wildcatter must decide whether to drill on a candidate drilling site. His judgment leads him to the conclusion that there is a 50-50 chance of oil. Should he drill and strike oil, his profit would be $200,000. But if the well turns up dry, his net loss will be $100,000.
   (a) Using the Bayes decision rule, should the wildcatter drill or abandon the site?
   (b) What is the wildcatter's EVPI?
   (c) A seismologist offers to conduct a high-reliability seismic survey. The results could be used in helping the wildcatter make the decision. What is the most the wildcatter would consider paying for such seismic information?

6-10 A cannery manager classifies each truckload of apricots purchased under contract from local orchards as either underripe, ripe, or overripe. Then the manager must decide whether a particular truckload will be used for dried apricots (D) or for apricot preserves (P). A truckload of apricots used in preserves yields a profit of $6000 if the fruit has a high sugar content, but only $4000 if the sugar content is low (because costly extra sugar must be added). Regardless of sugar content, a truckload of dried apricots yields a profit of $5000. In either case, the actual sugar content can only be determined during final processing.

The probability for an underripe truckload is .3, for a ripe one it is .5, and for an overripe one it is .2. The following probabilities have been established for sugar content for given levels of ripeness:

	Underripe	Ripe	Overripe
Low sugar	.9	.4	.2
High sugar	.1	.6	.8
	1.0	1.0	1.0

   (a) Construct the manager's decision tree diagram and perform an extensive form analysis to determine the maximum expected payoff strategy for disposing of a truckload of apricots.
   (b) List the possible strategies for disposing of a truckload. Perform a normal form analysis to select the strategy yielding greatest expected profit.

Seven

Decision Making with Experimental Information

We usually associate the term "experiment" with a test or investigation. Experiments may be very elaborate, as in science where many years of effort and much expensive equipment are devoted to activities such as studying physical laws by observing solar eclipses. Or they may be very simple, such as asking a person questions in order to become better acquainted. No matter what their scope, all experiments have one feature in common: *they provide information*. This information may serve to realign uncertainty. Information obtained by observing a solar eclipse can support hypotheses regarding the effect of the sun's gravity on stellar light rays. A person's response to your questions can help you decide whether he or she is worth befriending. *An experiment can help us make better decisions under uncertainty.* Scientists can become more certain that the sun's gravity has an effect on light rays, and their observations can lead to finer choices for further experiments. The answers to our questions can convince us that an ugly person is really beautiful or that a physically beautiful person is vain and selfish.

Most experiments, however, are not conclusive. Any test can camouflage the truth. For instance, some potentially good employees will flunk well-designed employment screening tests, while some incompetents will pass them. Another good example is the oil wildcatter's seismic survey. Although not completely reliable, a seismic survey can deny the presence of oil in a field already producing oil and confirm the presence of oil under a site already proven to be dry. Still, such imperfect experiments can be of value. An unfavorable test result can increase the chance of rejecting a poor prospect—job applicant or drilling lease—and a favorable one can enhance the likelihood of selecting a good one.

In this chapter, we will incorporate experimentation into the framework of our decision-making analysis. The information obtained will affect the probabilities of those events that determine the consequences of each act. We can revise the probabilities of these events upward or downward depending on the evidence obtained. Thus a geologist will increase the subjective probability of oil on obtaining a favorable seismic survey analysis, but will lower it if the survey is unfavorable.

The seismic survey epitomizes experimental information in decision making. In business situations several other classic sources of such information are commonly employed. A marketing research study serves to realign uncertainty regarding the degree of success a new product will achieve in the marketplace. An aptitude test is often used to help predict a job applicant's future success or failure should he or she be hired—a decision involving considerable uncertainty. A sampling study is frequently employed in quality-control decisions to facilitate decisions relating to how satisfactorily items are produced or the amount of defective items arriving from a supplier.

In this chapter, we first investigate how to revise probabilities in accordance with experimental results. In doing this we will apply the probability concepts associated with Bayes' theorem discussed in Chapter 2. We meld this probability information with all the decision elements by means of a decision tree diagram. How much information is incorporated into the decision serves as a prelude to a more general analysis of the initial choice to experiment in the first place. For example: Would the oil wildcatter use a seismic survey if it cost $50,000? The concepts presented in this chapter are expanded in Chapter 8, where decision making based upon sampling experiments is considered in detail.

7-1 REVISING PROBABILITIES

In a typical situation, the decision maker has some kind of judgment about the uncertain events. This may be expressed as a set of *prior probabilities* regarding the occurrence of the respective events. On occasion, such judgment must be quantified in terms of subjective probabilities, since the events in question frequently arise from non-repeatable circumstances. At other times, the prior probabilities may be objective in nature. In accordance with the information obtained from the experiment, the event uncertainties are realigned to obtain *posterior probabilities*. Figure 7-1 shows the sequence of steps involved in this procedure, exactly the one originally proposed by Thomas Bayes.

As an illustration, we will use an oil wildcatter's decision whether to drill for oil at a leased site. He is contemplating hiring a geologist to conduct a detailed seismic survey of the area. For the present we are only concerned with the probability portion of this problem.

As a first step, the wildcatter must *exercise judgment* regarding the

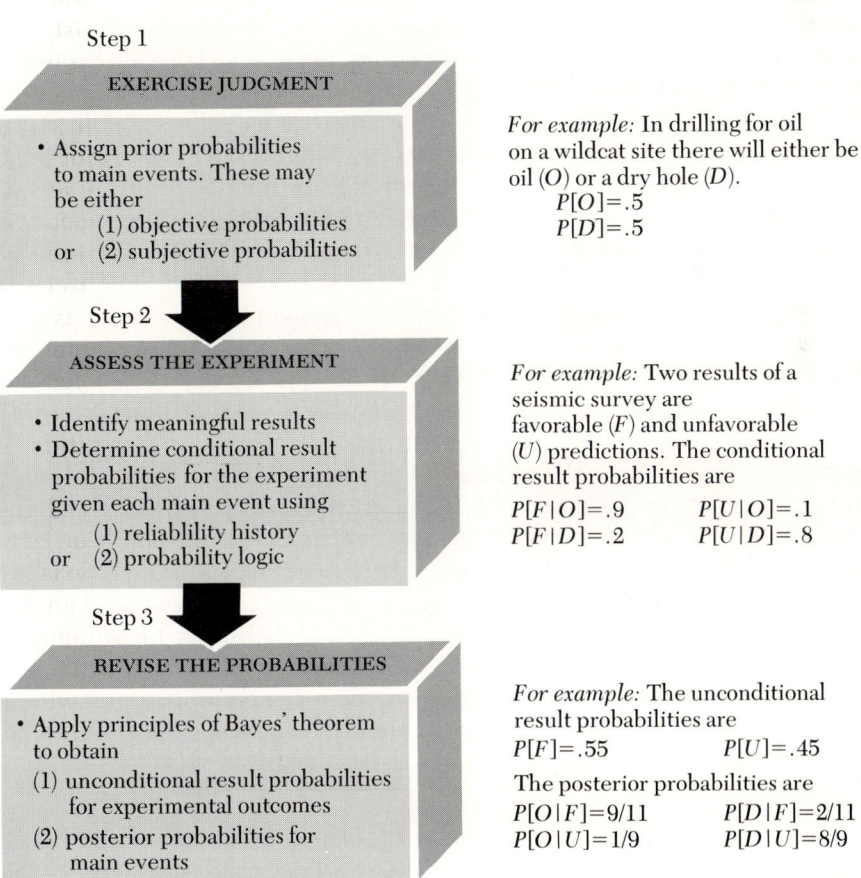

Figure 7-1
Steps in performing the probability portion of the decision analysis when experimental information is used.

7-1 REVISING PROBABILITIES

likelihood of striking oil. Since no two unproven drilling sites are very much alike, there is no historical frequency that can be used for this purpose. The wildcatter must therefore rely on a subjective probability value. Suppose that he believes there is a 50–50 chance of striking oil. Letting O represent oil and D stand for dry hole, the prior probabilities of the basic events are

$$P[O] = .5$$
$$P[D] = .5$$

As the next step, the wildcatter *assesses the experiment,* the seismic survey in this case. He starts by contemplating what results would be meaningful to him. Although the seismic output might be very complex and varied, for simplicity we suppose that the geologist's analysis will lead to only two meaningful results: a favorable (F) prediction for oil or an unfavorable one (U). It is necessary to obtain *conditional result probabilities* for the respective seismic outcomes given each possible basic event. Ordinarily, the conditional result probabilities for the experiment may be obtained objectively, either through estimation from historical frequencies or by applying the underlying logic of probability. Thus, we might refer to these values as "logical-historical" probabilities to help distinguish them from the several types encountered.

In the present example, the geologist has kept a "batting average" for the procedure. Historical records show that on 90 percent of known producing oil fields his prediction of oil has proven favorable. That is, 90 percent of similar seismic survey data have provided favorable oil predictions when indeed oil exists; in other words, the seismic survey method is 90 percent reliable in arriving at a favorable forecast when oil is actually present. (Of course, such a number should not be biased by the fact that the seismic survey result may have affected the earlier decisions to drill on those sites. A reliability figure is best obtained through a special study where the tester itself is tested; this might be done by taking special seismic measurements on already producing sites.) Through simulated readings on known dry holes, the geologist has also determined that the survey is only 80 percent reliable in making an unfavorable prediction when no oil is present. The appropriate conditional result probabilities are

$$P[F|O] = .90 \text{ and } P[U|O] = .10$$
$$P[F|D] = .20 \text{ and } P[U|D] = .80$$

The above probabilities are "historical" and in the nature of statistical estimates of the underlying values, since they are based on limited samples of drilling sites. (Notice that the conditional probability of a favorable result given oil is greater than that for an unfavorable prediction given dry; there is no reason why a test must be equally discerning in both directions.)

In other situations, conditional result probabilities for an informational experiment may be obtained more directly without using past history. This would be true, for example, in assessing a quality-control sample. The precise probability distribution for the sample result may be determined through logical deduction, based only on probability principles and the type of events that characterize the sampled population.

The final step toward incorporating experimental information into the probability portion of decision analysis is to *revise the probabilities.* This revision ordinarily results in two kinds of probability values, each applicable at a different stage of uncertainty. The *posterior probabilities* serve for the main events and the *unconditional result probabilities* for the experimental outcomes themselves. Although the underlying concepts of Bayes' theorem are used in arriving at these values, a somewhat more streamlined procedure, illustrated in Figure 7-2, proves more convenient when using decision trees to analyze a decision.

Using Probability Trees

We start with the probability tree diagram 7-2(a). This portrays the *actual chronology* of events. Here the first fork represents the events for the site status: oil or dry. The second stage is represented by a fork for the seismic survey results. This particular arrangement represents the sequence in which the events actually arise: first, nature determined (several million years ago) whether this site would cover an oil field; second, our present-day geologist conducts a seismic test. The actual chronology also adheres to the manner in which the probability data are initially obtained. The wildcatter has directly assessed the probabilities for the site status events; and the geologist has indicated the reliabilities for the survey. Thus, the values given earlier for the prior probabilities of oil and dry and the conditional result probabilities are placed on the corresponding branches in diagram (a).

Probability tree diagram 7-2(b) represents the *informational chronology.* This is the sequence in which the decision maker finds out which events occur. First the wildcatter obtains the result for the seismic survey, portrayed by the initial event fork. Then, if he chooses to drill, he ultimately determines whether or not the site covers an oil field. This

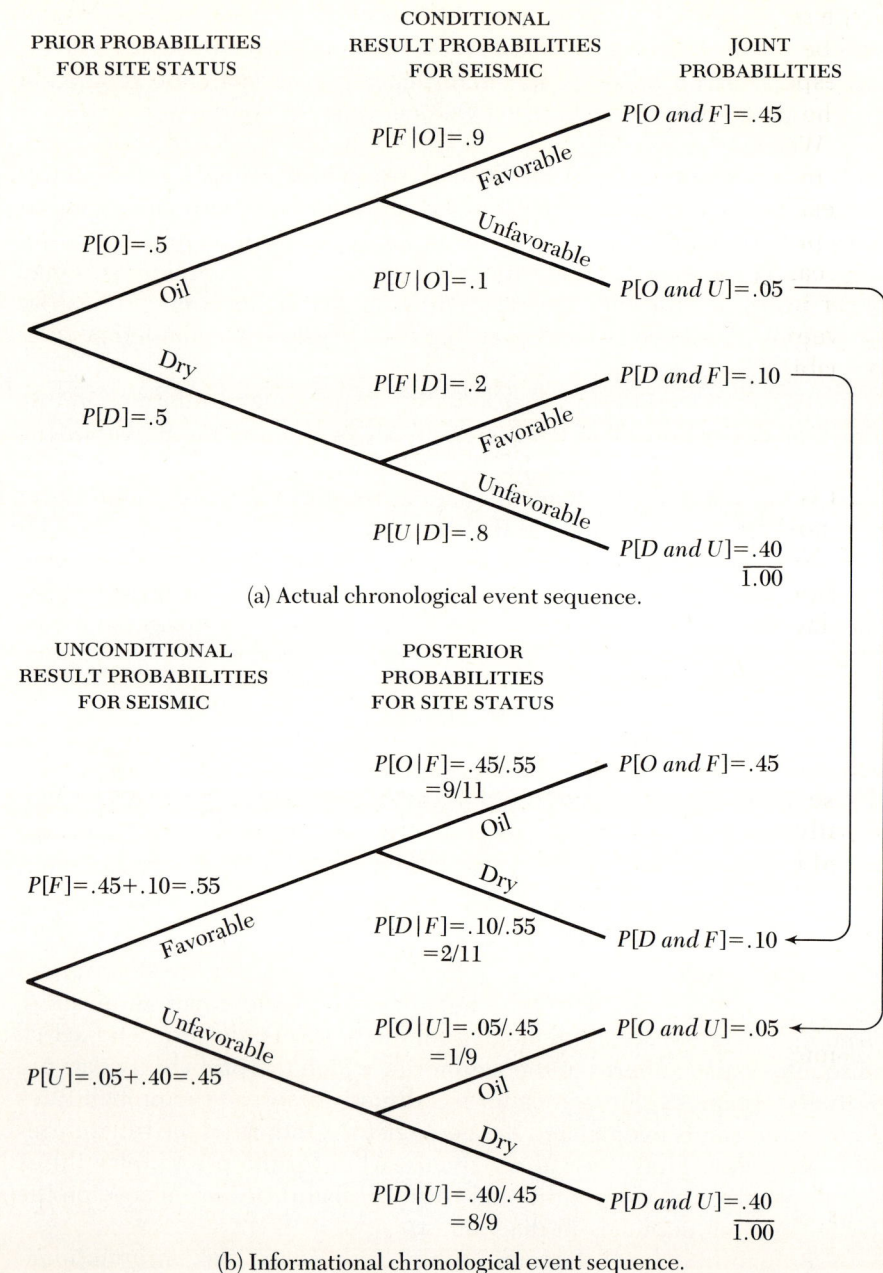

Figure 7-2
Probability tree diagrams showing event chronologies for drilling a wildcat well and using a seismic survey.

is the sequence of events as they would appear on a decision tree (which will be discussed later). But this particular chronology does not directly correspond to the initial probability data. Additional work is needed to get the probability values shown on tree diagram 7-2(b).

We start by multiplying together the branch probabilities on each path in tree diagram 7-2(a) to obtain the corresponding joint probability values. The same numbers apply regardless of chronology, so that the joint probabilities can be transferred to diagram (b). This must be done with care, since the in-between joint outcomes are not listed in the same order in (b) as in (a), because analogous paths (event sequences) differ between the diagrams. For example, in diagram (a) we obtain the joint probability of oil and an unfavorable seismic result

$$P[O \text{ and } U] = P[O] \times P[U|O] = .5 \times .1 = .05$$

This is the second joint probability in (a) and corresponds to the third end position in (b).

Next, we work entirely in diagram (b). First, we compute the unconditional result probabilities at the first stage. Here we use the addition law to obtain

$$P[F] = P[O \text{ and } F] + P[D \text{ and } F] = .45 + .10 = .55$$
$$P[U] = P[O \text{ and } U] + P[D \text{ and } U] = .05 + .40 = .45$$

These values are placed on the applicable branches at the first stage. Finally, the posterior probabilities for the second-stage events are computed using the basic property of conditional probability:

$$P[A|B] = \frac{P[A \text{ and } B]}{P[B]}$$

Thus, we determine the posterior probability for oil given a favorable seismic survey result:

$$P[O|F] = \frac{P[O \text{ and } F]}{P[F]} = \frac{.45}{.55} = \frac{9}{11}$$

This value is placed on the second-stage branch for oil preceded by the earlier branch for a favorable result. In a like manner, the other posterior probabilities shown in diagram (b) are each found by dividing the respective end-position joint probability by the probability on the preceding branch.

Revision of probabilities in the manner illustrated above is generally required whenever experimental information is used in decision making. This happens because we ordinarily get our probabilities in the reverse chronology from that needed to analyze the problem.

7-2 POSTERIOR ANALYSIS

Figure 7-3 shows the decision tree diagram illustrating the wildcatter's choices once the seismic results are known. Here we have assumed that: (1) the lease will be sold for $250,000 upon striking oil;

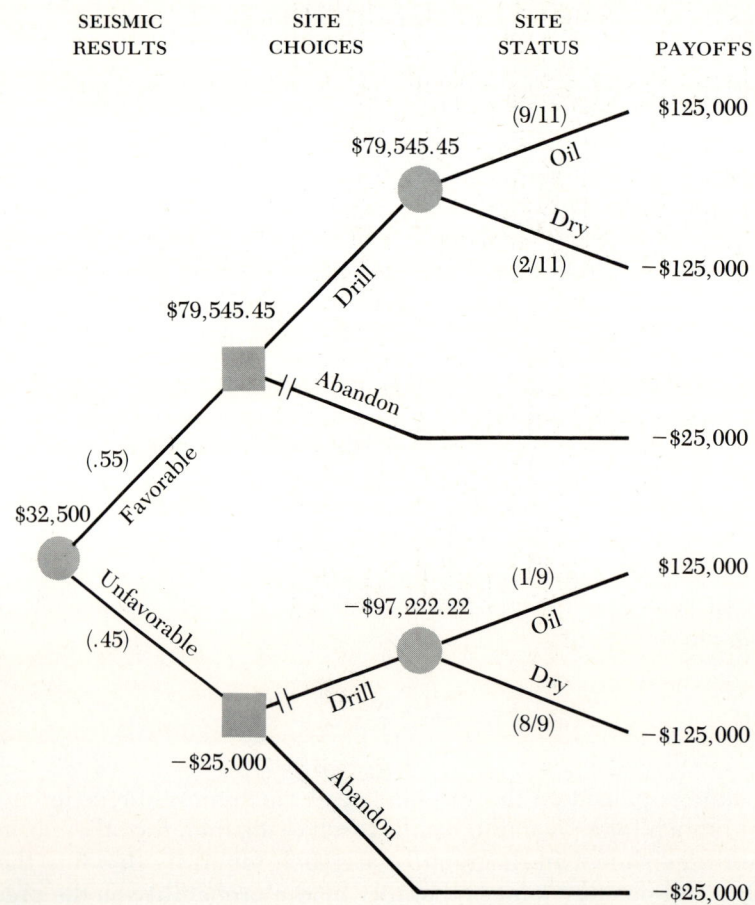

Figure 7-3
The wildcatter's decision tree diagram when seismic survey is taken.

(2) the cost of drilling is $100,000; and (3) the seismic survey will cost $25,000. We show the decision to drill or to abandon the lease as following the seismic survey result, since the wildcatter obviously would not decide before finding out the geologist's prediction. The revised probabilities found earlier for the informational chronology are used. Since the posterior probabilities for the site status events apply at the two decision points, using this decision tree as the basis for decision making is called *posterior analysis*.

Notice that there is no event fork following the act to abandon the lease, because the oil wildcatter will never find out if there is oil unless he drills for it. (The uncertainty still exists, nevertheless; it would do no harm to have event forks for oil versus dry at those points, but the payoff would be $-$25,000 in either case, and an identical conclusion would be reached.)

Performing the backward induction, we see that the wildcatter would prune the abandon branch and drill if a favorable seismic result were obtained and would do the opposite in the case of an unfavorable prediction. Even though drilling will lead to identical payoffs for either seismic result, the posterior probabilities of oil and dry are different for the favorable and unfavorable predictions. The expected payoff from drilling is $79,545.45 for the favorable seismic, but it is a negative value, $-$97,222.22, in the case of an unfavorable one. His expected payoff for the optimal strategy is $32,500. This number will be useful, as we shall see later, in determining whether the seismic survey should be used at all.

Obviously Non-Optimal Strategies

In the simpler decision structures, it may be convenient to streamline the decision tree diagram. For the wildcatter's problem, we can conclude that he would prune the same branches regardless of the numbers involved. Since he is paying $25,000 for the seismic survey and this experiment provides fairly reliable predictions, he should choose acts consistent with the information obtained. But the tree in Figure 7-3 allows for three other strategies: drill regardless of result (prune both abandon branches); abandon in either case (prune the two branches for drill); and do the opposite of what is predicted (prune the drill branch if the seismic is favorable and prune the abandon branch if it is unfavorable). The last strategy is ridiculous and would never be considered. The other two are inferior to drilling or to abandoning without benefit of seismic results, since in either case the $25,000 cost could be saved. Such inferior strategies are *obviously non-optimal strategies*.

Figure 7-4 shows how the wildcatter's decision tree diagram could

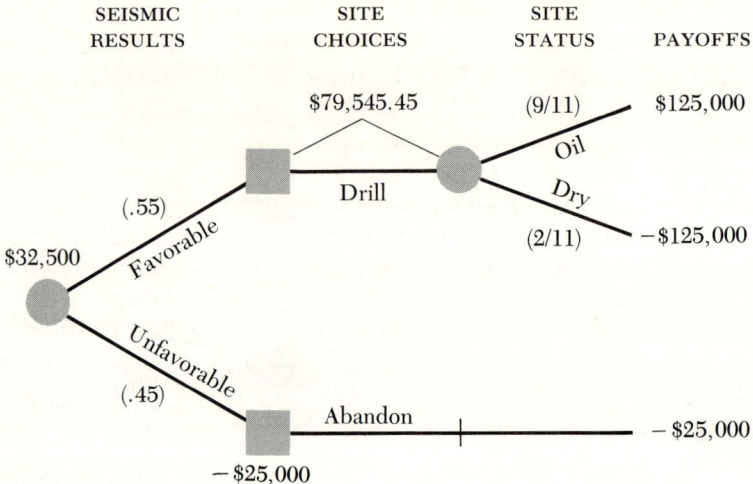

Figure 7-4
The simplified wildcatter's decision tree diagram with obviously non-optimal strategies left off.

have been drawn by excluding the obviously non-optimal strategies. This representation might help simplify an otherwise complex decision tree. However, for expository convenience, we will always use the complete tree structure presented earlier. When more than two acts or experimental results are involved, it is not easy to determine which strategies are obviously non-optimal.

7-3 DECISION TO EXPERIMENT: PREPOSTERIOR ANALYSIS

We have illustrated the use of experimental information and have described posterior analysis, which indicates what act to select for each experimental outcome. Now we will incorporate the additional choice of whether or not to obtain such information in the first place. Thus the decision is expanded to include an initial stage involving selection of acts concerning experimentation. The procedure that evaluates this expanded decision is sometimes referred to as *preposterior analysis*.

To illustrate how to incorporate the decision to use experimental information, we expand the oil wildcatter's decision. Figure 7-5 shows the decision structure. The added decision about whether or not to take the seismic is treated as an initial decision point, which is the initial act fork having branches for taking and for not taking the seismic. If the seismic is used, there follows an event fork relating to the seismic result to be achieved; here the unconditional result probabilities apply. These events are followed by the final decision to drill or to abandon. If the wildcatter drills, the last set of event forks represent the oil and dry events and the posterior probabilities apply. Should the initial decision be to not take the seismic, then the choice to drill or abandon must be made without any information, which is shown as the act fork at the bottom of the tree. In this case, drilling leads to a final event fork for the site status events. Here the prior probabilities originally obtained apply for oil and dry. The payoffs in this bottom portion of the tree are $25,000

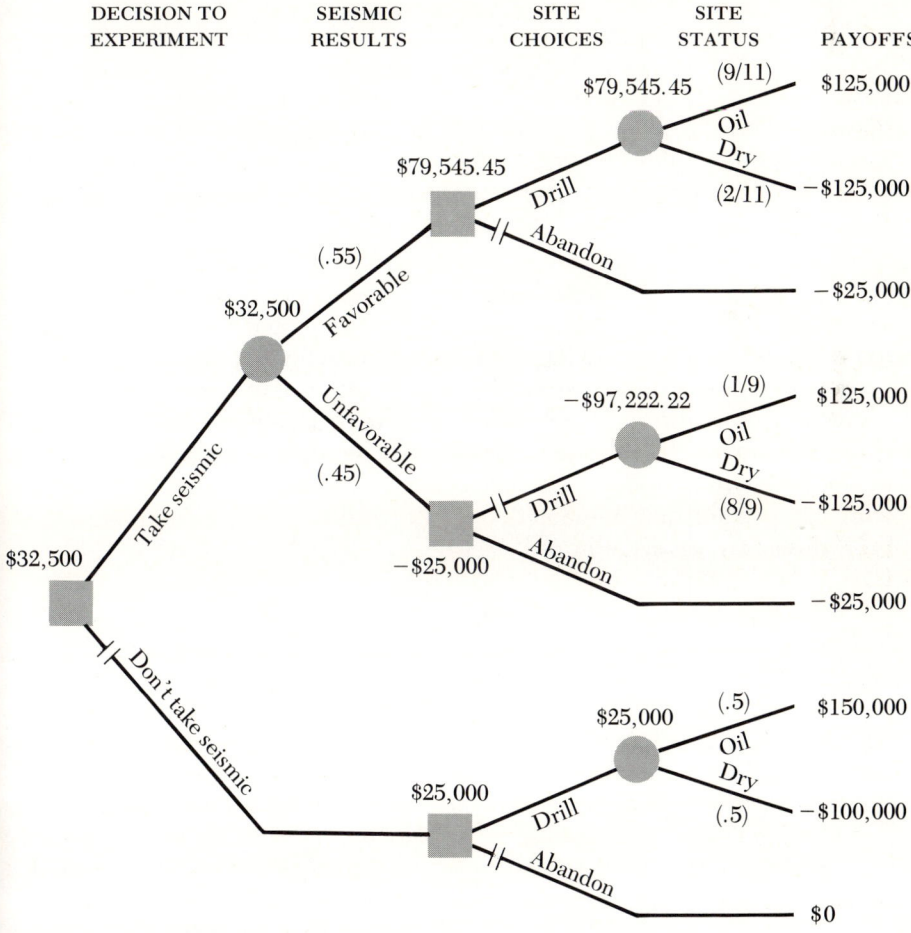

Figure 7-5
The wildcatter's decision tree diagram with the initial decision regarding seismic.

7-3   DECISION TO EXPERIMENT: PREPOSTERIOR ANALYSIS

greater than their counterparts directly above, since the cost of the seismic survey is saved.

We now have a two-stage decision problem to analyze. Performing backward induction on the top portion of Figure 7-5, we obtain the result found earlier: using the seismic yields an expected payoff of $32,500. We find that not using the survey leads to a smaller expected payoff of only $25,000. Thus, at the first decision point, the branch for don't take the seismic is pruned. The course of action maximizing expected payoff is: take the seismic survey; if it is favorable, drill, but if it is unfavorable, abandon.

Role of EVPI

In some situations the foregoing procedure may be considerably shortened. Recall that the expected value of perfect information, or EVPI, indicates the worth of the best possible or ideal information about the events in the main decision. Usually information obtained through experiments is far from perfect in its predictive powers. If such evidence would cost more than it can at best be worth, it should obviously not be obtained. In Table 7-1 the wildcatter's EVPI is calculated to be $50,000. (Here the prior probabilities are used, since the seismic survey does not apply.) Had the cost of the seismic survey been a higher figure, say $60,000, the oil wildcatter would be better off not bothering with it, regardless of how reliable its predictions would be. In effect, the seismic branch would be pruned from the tree, without any need to calculate posterior probabilities or to do any of the preposterior analysis described above. Of course, this shortcut applies only when the cost of the information exceeds the EVPI. Since the wildcatter had to spend only $25,000, which is smaller than the $50,000 EVPI, in this case the complete preposterior analysis was required.

Table 7-1
CALCULATION OF THE WILDCATTER'S EVPI

| EVENTS | PROBABILITY | PAYOFFS | | ROW MAXIMUM | ROW MAXIMUM × PROBABILITY |
		Drill	Abandon		
Oil	.5	$150,000	$0	$150,000	$75,000
Dry	.5	−100,000	0	0	0
	1.0				$75,000

Expected payoff with perfect information = $75,000
Expected payoff under uncertainty (drilling)
  = .5($150,000) + .5(−$100,000) = $25,000
EVPI = $75,000 − $25,000 = $50,000

PROBLEMS

7-1 For the probability tree diagram in Figure 7-6 showing the actual chronological sequence of events, determine the missing values for the end position joint probabilities. Then find the missing values for the informational chronology probability tree diagram in Figure 7-7.

7-2 The structure of a boat-builder's decision is provided in Figure 7-8.
  (a) List all strategies.
  (b) Perform an extensive form analysis using backward induction to determine the optimal strategy.

7-3 Referring to the above boat-builder's decision, suppose that $50,000 is saved by not conducting test marketing. Answer the following. (Assume that the payoffs in Figure 7-8 include the cost of test marketing.)
  (a) Expand the boat-builder's decision tree diagram to show an initial act fork for the decision whether to test market. Revise the monetary payoffs for those end positions resulting from not test marketing and assume that without test marketing the prior probability of high sales is .5.

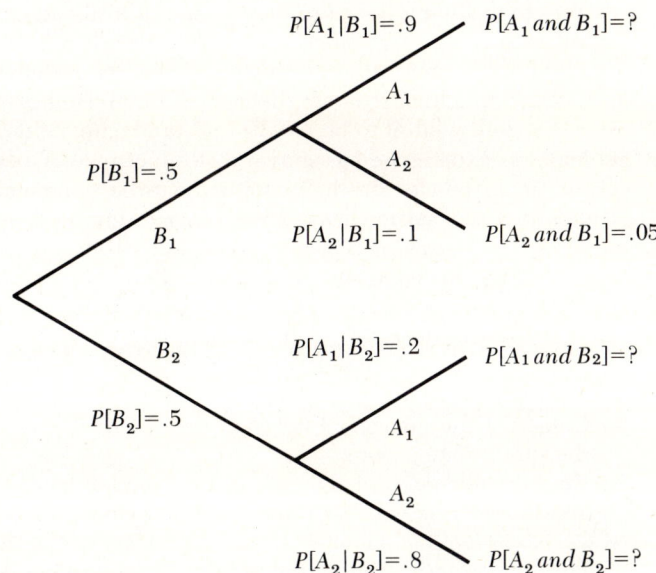

Figure 7-6

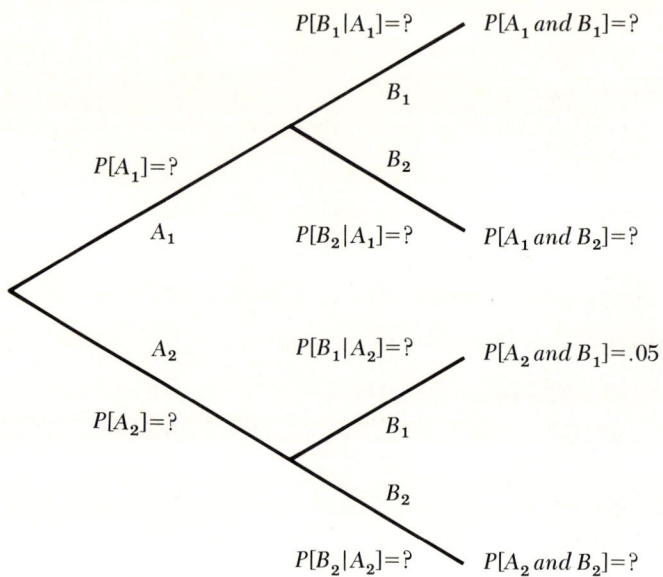

Figure 7-7

(b) Perform backward induction analysis to determine whether the builder would choose to test market.

7-4 The exploration manager for a small oil company must decide whether to drill on a parcel of leased land or to abandon the lease. To aid in making this choice he can first decide whether to pay $30,000 for a seismic survey, which will confirm or deny the presence of the anticlinal structure necessary for oil. He has judged his prior probability of oil to be .30. For oil-producing fields of similar geology, his experience has shown that the chance of a confirming seismic is .9; but for dry holes with about the same features, the probability that a seismic survey will deny oil has been established to be only .7. Drilling costs have been firmly established at $200,000. If oil is struck, his company plans to sell the lease for $500,000.

(a) What is the manager's EVPI for the basic decision, using profit as the payoff measure? Comparing this value to the cost of the seismic, can we conclude definitely that no seismic would be used?

(b) Construct the manager's decision tree diagram and determine the appropriate payoffs.

(c) Find the revised probabilities for the informational chronology and place these values on the corresponding branches of your decision tree diagram.

(d) Perform backward induction analysis to determine the course of action providing maximum expected profit.

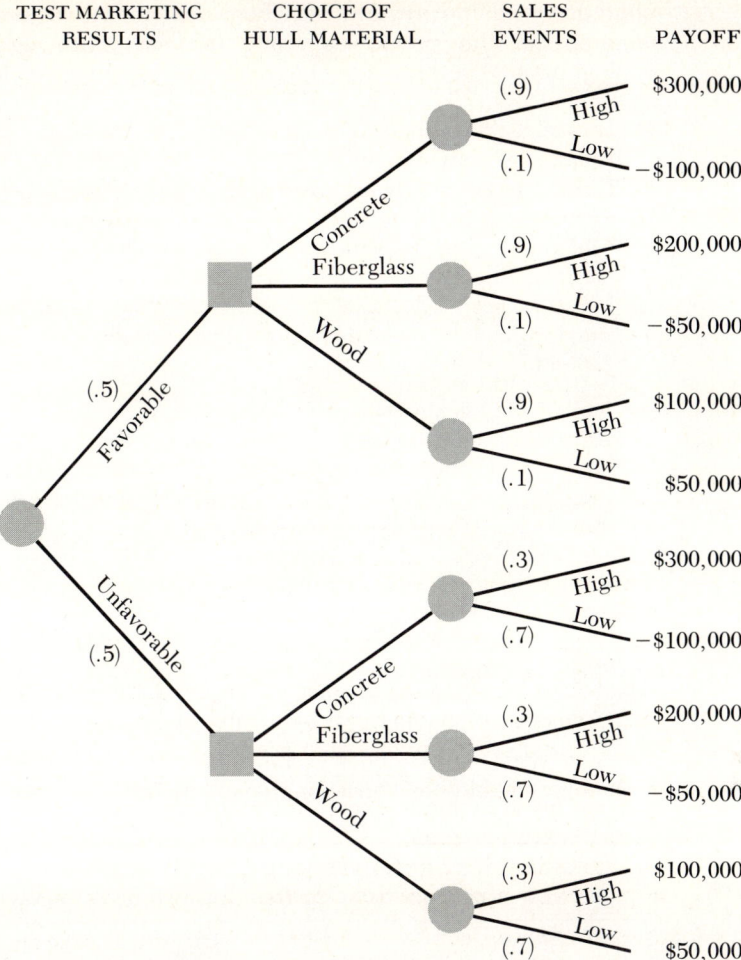

Figure 7-8

7-5 The following payoff table for marketing choices for a new film has been determined by the management of a motion picture studio.

Box Office Result Events	Distribute as "A" Feature	Sell to TV Network	Distribute as "B" Feature
Success	$5,000,000	$1,000,000	$3,000,000
Failure	−2,000,000	1,000,000	−1,000,000

The prior probability of a box office success has been judged to be .3. The studio plans a series of sneak previews. Historically, it has

CHAPTER 7 PROBLEMS 205

found that favorable previews have been obtained for 70 percent of all successful films previewed, while unfavorable previews have resulted from 80 percent of the box office failures subjected to such experimentation.

(a) Construct the probability tree diagrams for the actual and informational chronologies.
(b) Construct a table showing all possible strategies for management contingent upon the results of the sneak preview.
(c) Construct a tree diagram for the studio's decision, assuming that it will definitely use the sneak preview.
(d) Perform backward induction analysis. What is the optimal course of action? To which strategy in part (b) does this correspond?

7-6 The makers of Quicker Oats oatmeal have packaged this product in cylindrical containers for 50 years. The usual box had been believed inseparable from the product's image. But with consumer tastes changing, the new marketing vice-president wonders whether younger people regard the round box as old-fashioned and unappealing. The vice-president wishes to analyze the case for a rectangular box that will save significantly on transportation costs due to the elimination of dead space in the packing cartons. It is also believed that the change can actually expand Quicker Oats' market by uplifting the product's image. But previous study has shown that a small segment of the existing market buys the oatmeal primarily for the round box; these customers would be lost by the change. The following payoff table has been established for the present net worth of retaining the old box versus implementing the new one.

NATIONAL MARKET RESPONSE TO NEW BOX EVENTS	ACTS	
	Retain Old Box	Use New Box
W: Weak	$0	−$2,000,000
M: Moderate	0	0
S: Strong	0	3,000,000

As prior probabilities for new box response events, the marketing chief has judged the following values: $P[W] = .20$, $P[M] = .30$, $P[S] = .50$. A "barometer" city is chosen for six month's test marketing of the new box. Three outcomes are possible: sales decreased (D), unchanged (U), and increased (I). Historical experience with other products has established the following conditional result probabilities:

$$P[D|W] = .8 \quad P[D|M] = .2 \quad P[D|S] = 0$$
$$P[U|W] = .2 \quad P[U|M] = .4 \quad P[U|S] = .1$$
$$P[I|W] = 0 \quad P[I|M] = .4 \quad P[I|S] = .9$$

(a) Construct the probability tree diagrams for the actual and informational chronologies.
(b) Construct the Quicker Oats decision tree diagram, assuming that test marketing will be used.
(c) Perform backward induction. Then for each test outcome, indicate the maximum expected payoff act. What is the optimal strategy?

7-7 Lucky Jones must decide whether to participate in a card game offered by Inscrutable Smith. For the price of $5, Jones will draw a card from an ordinary deck of playing cards. If the card is a king,

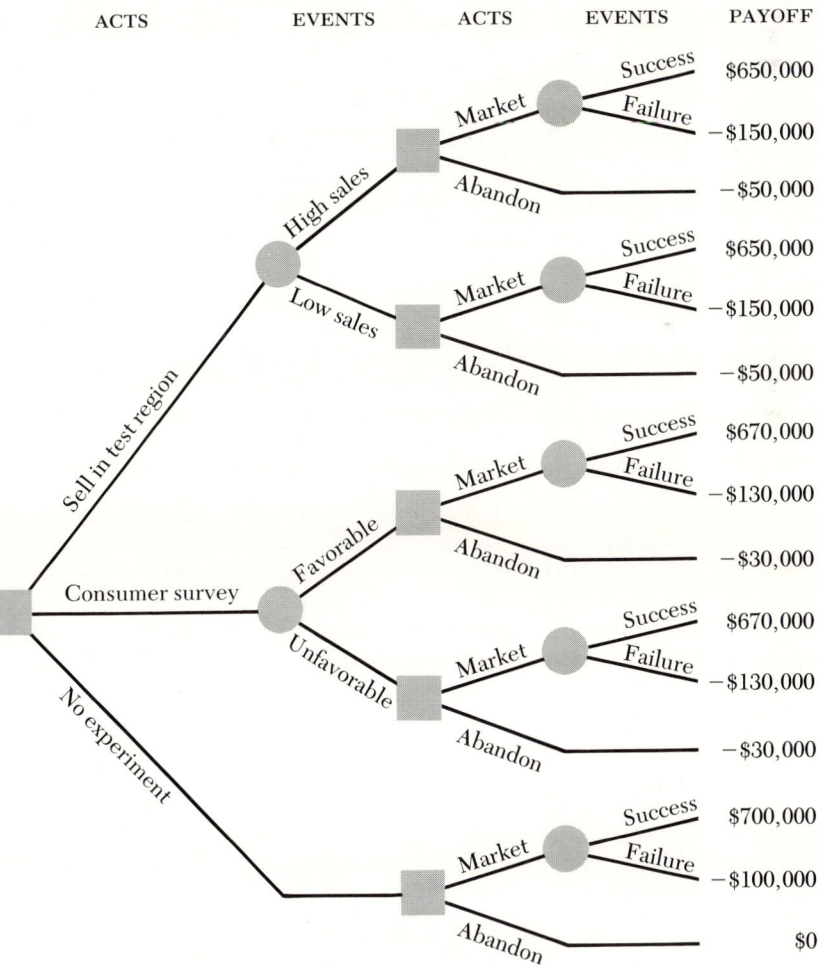

Figure 7-9

then Smith pays Jones $60 (so that Jones wins $55). But if it is not a king, Jones receives nothing for the $5. Smith, eager for action, thus offers Jones an additional enticement. For $3 Jones can draw a card without looking at it. Smith will then tell Jones whether or not the card is a face card. If Jones wishes to continue, for an additional payment of $5 the game will proceed as before.

(a) Construct a decision tree diagram showing the structure of Jones' decision.
(b) Determine the probabilities for the events and the total profit for end position.
(c) What course of action provides Jones with the greatest expected payoff?

7-8 The decision tree diagram in Figure 7-9 has been determined for a marketing manager deciding how to introduce a new product. She has determined a .40 prior probability for marketing success.

(a) From a consumer survey costing $30,000, she can obtain an 80% reliable indication of the product's impact in the marketplace. Thus, the probability of a favorable survey result given market success is .80, while that for an unfavorable result given market failure is .80. Find the posterior probabilities of the market events and the unconditional result probabilities for the survey events.
(b) For a sales program in a test region costing $50,000, the results are judged 95 percent reliable. Find the posterior and unconditional result probabilities.
(c) Using the information given in the statement of the problem and your answers to parts (a) and (b), perform backward induction to find the optimal course of action. (The payoffs in Figure 7-9 include the cost of experimenting.)

7-9 Your friend gives you a choice between two gambles involving the random selection of a coin from a box. The box contains two coins: one has two heads and one is ordinary. If you choose gamble A, he will pay you $2 if the coin is two-headed, but you must pay him $1 if the coin is the ordinary one. If you choose gamble B, he will toss the coin for the price of $1. Seeing the showing side, you may then decide to stop or continue. If you continue, the coin is then examined, and the same money amounts are exchanged as in gamble A.

(a) Construct a decision tree diagram for the choice between the two gambles. Evaluate each end position, using your profit as the payoff measure.
(b) Find the appropriate event branch probabilities.
(c) Perform backward induction to determine which gamble provides the maximum expected payoff.
(d) Formulate the optimal decision rule for gamble B, indicating whether you should stop or continue for each possible coin toss result.

Eight

Decision Making with the Normal Distribution

In Chapter 7, we considered the general problem of decision making with experimental information. We will now consider a decision commonly encountered in business situations when only *two acts* are involved and the experiment is to take a *random sample* from a population whose characteristics affect the ultimate payoffs. The decision-maker's choice depends on the particular sample result obtained. We will examine situations in which the uncertain events are levels of the population mean μ. As we will see, it can be advantageous to base the actual decision on the value of the sample mean $\bar{X}$.

A COMPUTER MEMORY DEVICE DECISION   8-1

To illustrate decision making with the sample mean, we consider the decision faced by a computer center about the kind of peripheral memory storage device to use in its computer system. The two proposed units are based on laser technology, and both will operate more efficiently than the current memory storage. One of the choices, based on photographic principles, uses special film for storing the data. The other alternative uses holography, a process by which a three-dimensional image is retrieved from a special wafer. A photographic memory unit costs less to lease than a holographic one, but it is slower and thus more costly to operate; their storage capacities and reliabilities are identical.

The annual savings achieved under either alternative depends on the daily volume of peripheral memory access. Although the actual number of bits stored or retrieved varies daily, the mean daily access level can be used to establish average annual access savings for each alternative. When this is added to the fixed lease cost, the resulting mean total annual savings serves as the payoff measure for this decision. This payoff depends on the mean daily gigabits (billion bits) accessed μ, which represents the average volume taken over all days.

The computer facility manager is uncertain about the value of μ, since past history regarding the density of peripheral memory traffic is incomplete. We treat the unknown μ as a random variable with a *continuous prior probability distribution*. For any given level of μ, we also use a *continuous conditional probability distribution* for the possible values of $\bar{X}$.

The particular distributions used in both cases are members of the *normal distribution* family. Although a variety of other prior distributions might be used for μ, we know from the central limit theorem (discussed in Chapter 3) that $\bar{X}$ tends to be normally distributed and that this is the only appropriate one to use.* Although different normal curves apply for μ and $\bar{X}$, it will be established that the true shape of the prior distribution for μ makes little difference.

8-2 DECISION STRUCTURE

The decision structure for using sample information when a normal distribution applies for μ is provided by the decision tree diagram in Figure 8-1. Here the initial choice of whether or not to use sample information is made. If no sample is taken, a memory unit must be selected with ultimate payoff based on the uncertain level of μ; in that case, the prior probability distribution for μ applies. If sampling is chosen, sample size must be selected, the sample data collected, and the sample mean calculated.

The manager believes that for an extra few hundred dollars per day he can determine the precise level of peripheral memory access on sample days by adding a special accounting program to the software system. Any sampling cost arises from the slower processing that results. A sample of $n = 9$ days is to be used for this purpose.

---

* The necessary conditions are that the population variance be finite and known and that the samples be large and independently selected.

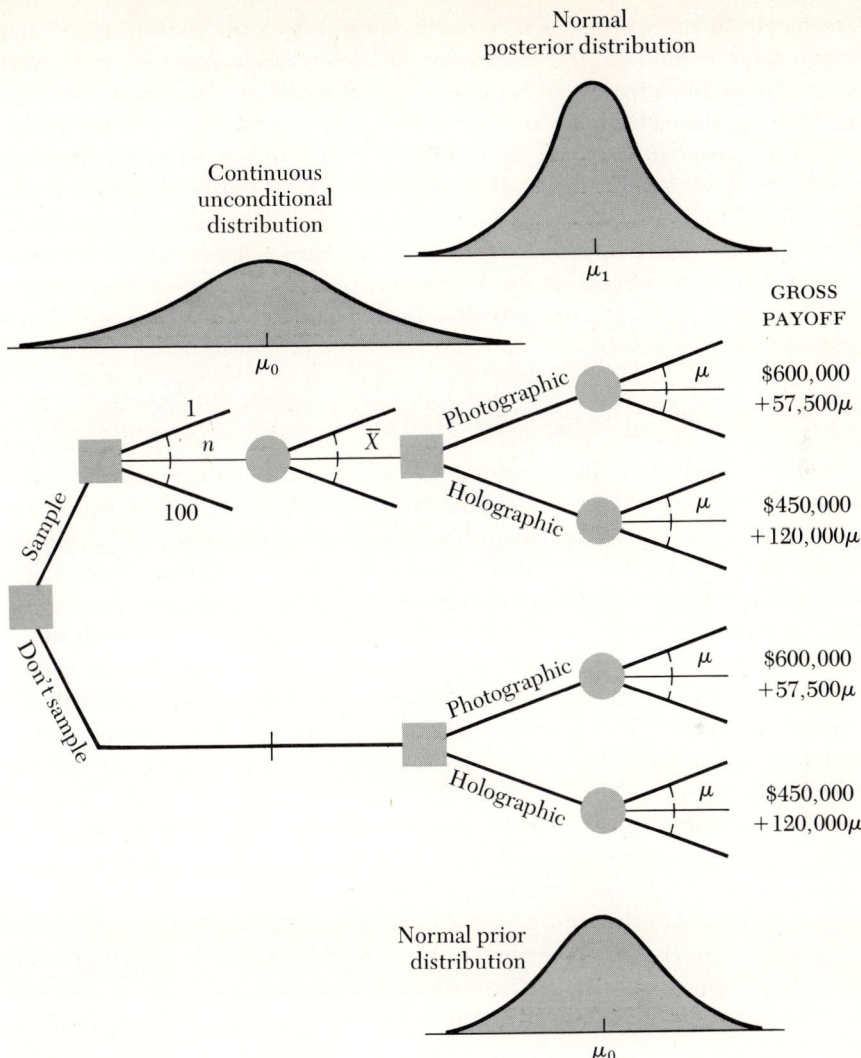

Figure 8-1
The structure of the computer memory device decision when a normal prior distribution applies for the population mean.

Since the sample data will be used to predict mean daily access level, it is appropriate to summarize the sampling results in terms of the sample mean memory access level, computed from

$$\overline{X} = \frac{X_1 + X_2 + \cdots + X_n}{n}$$

where X_1, X_2, etc., are the observed levels for individual sample days.

8-2 DECISION STRUCTURE

Based on the value achieved for $\bar{X}$, either the photographic or the holographic memory is chosen. The ultimate value experienced for μ determines the annual savings, expressed here as gross payoff (since the cost of the sample is not included). With sampling, the *posterior probability distribution for μ* applies.

The event forks for the values of $\bar{X}$ and μ have many branches, since each variable is continuous. In each case probability values can only be obtained by finding appropriate areas under the curves representing the unconditional distribution for $\bar{X}$ and the prior or posterior normal distributions for μ. The gross payoffs (annual savings) are expressed algebraically by

$$\text{Gross payoff} = \begin{cases} \$600{,}000 + \$\ 57{,}500\mu & \text{for photographic} \\ \$450{,}000 + \$120{,}000\mu & \text{for holographic} \end{cases}$$

The probability distributions provided in the upper portion of the decision tree represent the informational chronology. This event sequence is the reverse of how probability information is generally given. Figure 8-2 shows the probability trees for the two chronologies. The actual chronology in (a) begins with the value for μ (which must come first) followed by the event fork for $\bar{X}$. The normal prior distribution for μ is centered at a presumed value of the population mean denoted μ_0 (the subscript zero indicating initial value); the mean of the conditional normal distribution for $\bar{X}$ has uncertain center μ. The informational chronology in (b) provides two curves with different centers; the unconditional distribution for $\bar{X}$ has mean μ_0, whereas the posterior distribution for the population mean is centered at a *revised value μ_1*.

Since our probability distributions are continuous, it is not easy to get the revised versions needed for the decision tree. Also complicated is the backward induction required to determine the optimal decision rule, which specifies the action to take for each possible sample result. We must, therefore, depart from decision tree analysis and revert to normal form analysis, which itself must now be dressed in unfamiliar clothing.

8-3 DECISION MAKING USING OPPORTUNITY LOSSES

Up to this point we have been able to analyze decisions by maximizing expected payoff, a procedure we sometimes refer to as the Bayes decision rule. We have established that an equivalent criterion is to minimize expected opportunity loss. For two-action problems involving continuous probability distributions it is more convenient to focus on opportunity losses as the basis for decision making.

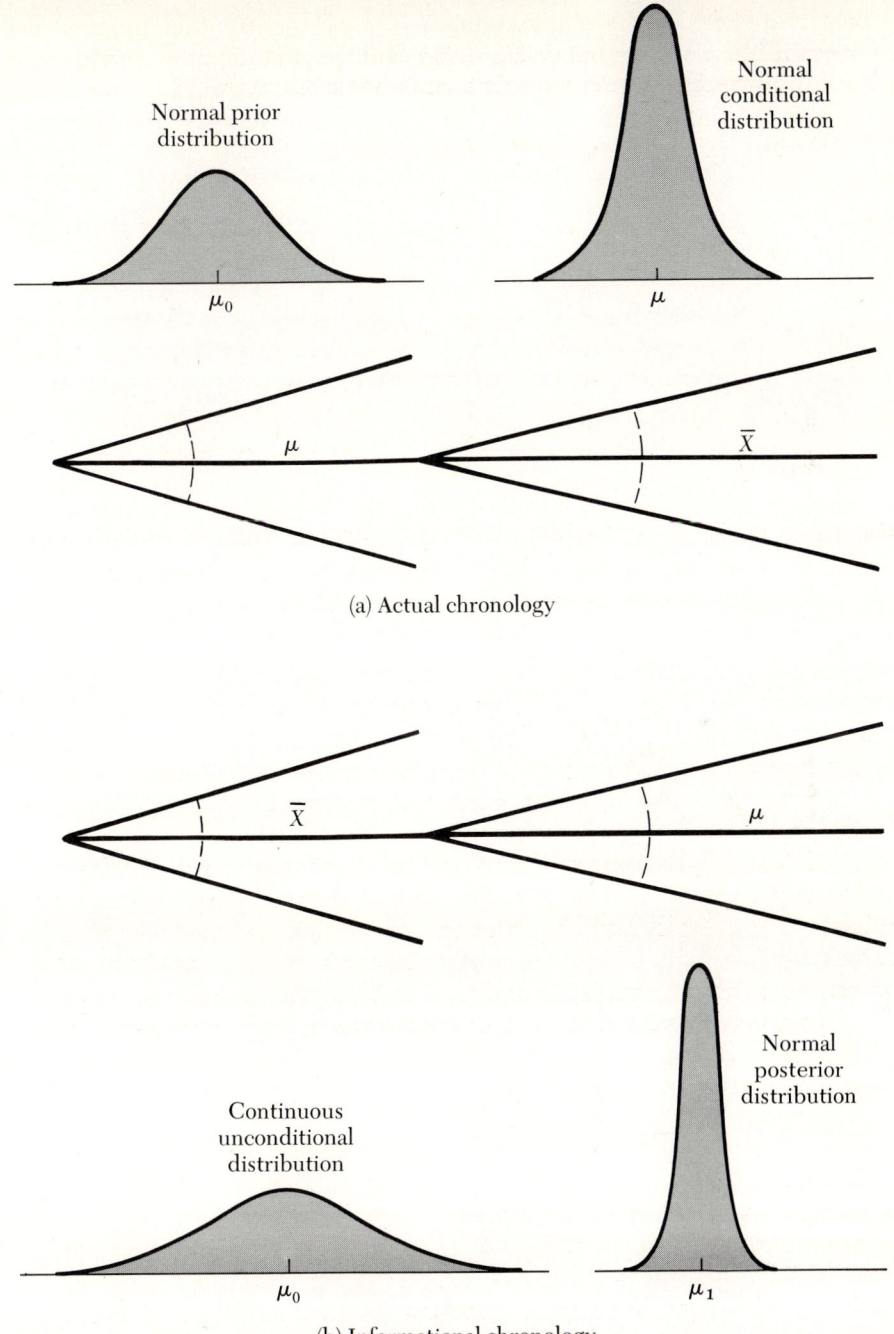

Figure 8-2
The representation of revising probabilities for the computer memory device decision.

8-3 DECISION MAKING USING OPPORTUNITY LOSSES

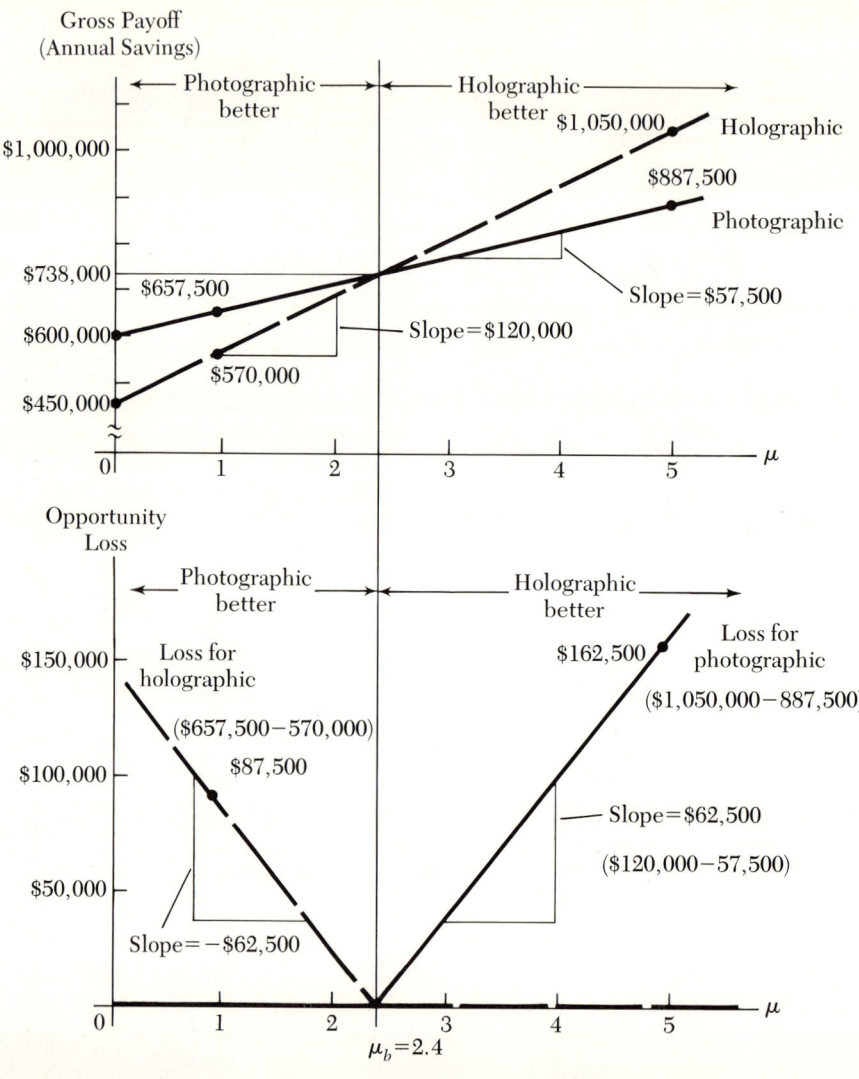

Figure 8-3
Payoff and opportunity loss graphs for the computer memory device decision.

Figure 8-3 shows the essential relationship for our peripheral memory storage illustration. The lines in the top graph represent gross payoff (annual savings) for the two memory units. The height of the respective lines at any level μ may be determined from the corresponding equations provided earlier. The slope of the photographic-unit payoff line is \$57,500, that for the steeper holographic-unit payoff line is

$120,000. The two lines cross at that value of μ where the gross payoff is identical under each act. This value is referred to as the *break-even mean* and is denoted as μ_b. The break-even mean is found by setting the two payoff expressions equal to each other and solving for μ_b:

$$\$600{,}000 + \$57{,}500\,\mu_b = \$450{,}000 + \$120{,}000\,\mu_b$$

so that

$$(\$120{,}000 - \$57{,}500)\,\mu_b = \$600{,}000 - \$450{,}000$$

$$\$62{,}500\,\mu_b = \$150{,}000$$

and

$$\mu_b = \$150{,}000/\$62{,}500 = 2.4 \text{ gigabits per day}$$

For μ less than $\mu_b = 2.4$, the photographic memory yields the greatest annual savings, whereas for means greater than μ_b the holographic unit is better. At $\mu = \mu_b$, the annual savings is \$738,000, identical under either alternative.

The bottom graph in Figure 8-3 represents the *opportunity losses* for the same alternatives. The photographic unit is the better choice when the true population mean lies below the break-even level μ_b. Thus, for all μs less than or equal to μ_b choosing the photographic unit results in zero opportunity loss, represented by the horizontal line segment to the left of μ_b. Should the true mean exceed the break-even level, the photographic unit's opportunity losses rise, as represented by the upwardly sloping line segment beginning at μ_b. The reverse holds for the holographic memory. For true population means beyond μ_b, the holographic alternative is better and its opportunity losses must be zero, as represented graphically by the dashed horizontal line segment to the right of μ_b. To the left of μ_b, the holographic unit's opportunity losses rise, as represented by the dashed line segment rising leftward from μ_b. The heights of points falling on the V-shaped portion represent the difference in savings between the best and worst acts at each level of μ. The "V" is symmetrical, and the two rising line segments have identical slopes (with opposite signs) of magnitude equal to the difference in the slopes of the two payoff lines: \$120,000 − \$57,500 = \$62,500.

8-4 PRIOR ANALYSIS WITHOUT SAMPLE INFORMATION

We assume in this chapter that μ is a random variable having prior probabilities obtainable from the normal curve. Recall from Chapter 3 that any particular normal curve may be specified entirely by its mean and standard deviation (or variance). We represent these parameters as μ_0 and σ_0, where the subscript zero indicates that these are the initial, prior values and are not based on sampling information. Here μ_0 is the expected value for the unknown population mean. It is the central value. We will refer to μ_0 as the *expected mean*. The standard deviation σ_0 summarizes the variability in possible levels of μ.

Minimum Expected Opportunity Loss Acts

We must base the values for μ_0 and σ_0 largely on judgment, because the computer center has no historical data relating directly to μ. In other applications, however, μ_0 and σ_0 might be obtained from previous experience. For example, μ might represent the mean ingredient yield in several successive batches of raw material used in chemical processing, and records might have been kept on what mean yields had been achieved.

When no sample is taken, the decision is an easy one. Figure 8-4 shows how we may relate the opportunity losses to the probabilities for μ. The normal curve for μ is superimposed on the respective opportunity loss graphs for the two acts. Figure 8-4 (a) shows a possible arrangement when the expected mean μ_0 lies below break-even level. Should μ_0 be less than μ_b, it is easy to see that the photographic unit's expected opportunity loss will be smaller than that of the holographic unit, since most of the area under the normal curve is concentrated in the range of μ where the opportunity loss is zero. (Remember, it is the *area* under the normal curve that provides probability.) The positive opportunity losses represented by the rising line segment occur for unlikely levels of μ covered by the upper tail of the normal curve. The rising portion of the line for the holographic memory unit, on the other hand, falls within the most likely range of μs, so the expected opportunity loss is greater for that act.

The reverse situation is shown in Figure 8-4 (b), where $\mu_0 > \mu_b$ and the holographic memory has the smaller expected opportunity loss.

From these graphs, we may conclude that *the optimal act having minimum expected opportunity loss is the one whose zero opportunity losses lie on the same side of the break-even level as the expected mean.* In our present example, the photographic memory is optimal if $\mu_0 < \mu_b$, whereas the holographic unit is optimal when $\mu_0 > \mu_b$. *Should the expected mean coincide with the break-even level, the two alternatives are equally attractive.*

Suppose that the computer-center manager determined that $\mu_0 = 2.5$ gigabits per day applies. Since this value is greater than $\mu_b = 2.4$ and is at a level where the holographic unit has zero opportunity loss, he would maximize expected savings and minimize expected opportunity loss by choosing that peripheral memory.

If no sample were to be taken, we could make our decision and end the chapter. But it may be better to take a sample before choosing the

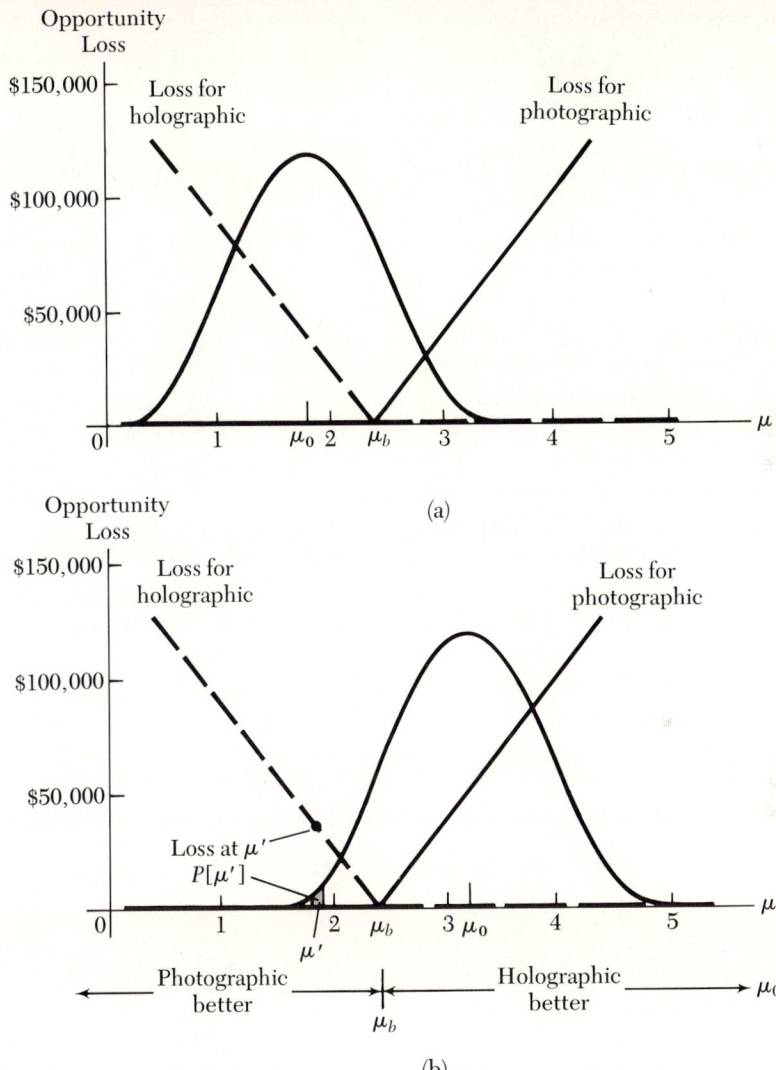

Figure 8-4
Normal curves and opportunity losses applicable when no sample is taken.

memory unit. Before deciding that, we must quantitatively measure the action of choosing a holographic unit right now—seemingly the best act. We must, therefore, determine the actual expected opportunity loss for this action. The resulting number would be the EVPI for the decision. (Recall that the expected value of perfect information is equal to the expected opportunity loss for the best act.)

8-4 PRIOR ANALYSIS WITHOUT SAMPLE INFORMATION

Determining the EVPI:
The Normal Loss Function

Unlike the situations encountered in earlier chapters, we have a continuous variable μ. Instead of a table of payoffs or losses for a few possible μs, we must confront an infinite number of μs. One way out of this dilemma would be to approximate the continuous distribution for μ by a table involving a few typical values, whose probabilities are obtained from the normal curve. We could then compute an approximate expected opportunity loss in the usual manner.

For instance, consider one possible mean μ' in Figure 8-4 (b). All possible values in an interval about μ' could be represented by this typical value, and the shaded area shown under the normal curve is the probability that any one of those values occurs. By considering several such intervals, the expected opportunity loss may be approximated by multiplying the respective areas by the loss for the typical value and summing the products. The more intervals used, the better this approximation would become. Fortunately, this has already been done for us.

The following expression may be used to compute the expected opportunity loss for the optimal act, that is, the expected value of perfect information:

$$\text{EVPI} = |\text{slope}|\ \sigma_0 L(D_0)$$

where $L(D_0)$ is the *normal loss function* provided in Appendix Table C. Three constants applicable to the particular problem are used: (1) the absolute value of the slope of the opportunity loss line; (2) the standard deviation of the prior probability distribution for μ; and (3) the *standardized distance*,

$$D_0 = \frac{|\mu_b - \mu_0|}{\sigma_0}$$

which expresses the separation between μ_b and μ_0 in standard deviation units (the numerator must always be positive, so absolute values are used).

Now, suppose that the computer-center manager has selected $\mu_0 = 2.5$ gigabits per day with $\sigma_0 = 1$ gigabit per day. We have established that the holographic unit is best for this μ_0. Referring to Figure 8-3, we see that the holographic loss line has slope $= -\$62{,}500$, so that $|\text{slope}| = \$62{,}500$. The standardized distance separating the expected mean from the break-even level is

$$D_0 = \frac{|\mu_b - \mu_0|}{\sigma_0} = \frac{|2.4 - 2.5|}{1} = .1$$

Referring to Appendix Table C, we find for $D_0 = .1$ that

$$L(D_0) = L(.1) = .3509$$

and the minimum expected opportunity loss for using the holographic memory is

$$\begin{aligned} \text{EVPI} &= \$62{,}500(1)L(.1) \\ &= \$62{,}500(1)(.3509) \\ &= \$21{,}931 \end{aligned}$$

The above figure tells us that a perfect prediction for μ is worth only $21,931. This sets an upper limit on what the decision maker would be willing to pay for less-than-perfect sample information.

As we have seen, the EVPI is a very useful number in deciding what and how much sample information to gather. We are now ready to consider this question.

8-5 POSTERIOR ANALYSIS FOR A GIVEN SAMPLE SIZE

Our analysis of the sampling decision begins with an arbitrarily chosen sample size n. Later we consider just how large n should be.

Recall that for a given sample size, the Bayes criterion leads to the choice of a decision rule indicating what act to take for each possible value of the sample mean $\bar{X}$. Such a rule takes the form

Choose Act 1 if $\bar{X} \leq C$

Choose Act 2 if $\bar{X} > C$

where C is the critical value that minimizes expected opportunity loss and maximizes expected gross payoff. When we are dealing with a normal prior distribution for μ, our procedure for finding C is less direct than before. We must first consider the characteristics of the posterior probability distribution for μ that corresponds to a given sample result.

Posterior Probability Distribution for μ

Let's summarize certain essential features of the problem being analyzed. A random sample of size n is *to be* selected from the population of daily peripheral memory access levels, and a replacement memory type will be chosen in accordance with the value achieved for the sample mean. The population itself has a frequency distribution of unspecified shape (it might be normal but need not be). This population has an uncertain mean μ, and we have a prior probability distribution for μ. Treating this unknown mean as a random variable, we assume that it has expected value μ_0 and standard deviation σ_0 and that its distribution is provided by the normal curve with these parameters.

The central limit theorem tells us that $\overline{X}$ has a probability distribution closely approximated by a normal curve when n is large. This curve is centered at μ and has standard deviation

$$\sigma_{\overline{X}} = \frac{\sigma_I}{\sqrt{n}}$$

where σ_I denotes the standard deviation of the population. The quantity σ_I summarizes variability in *individual* daily memory access levels (and is not to be confused with σ_0, which summarizes variability in the possible values for the *mean* daily access levels μ). Thus, there are two normal curves with different shapes and centers — one for μ and another for $\overline{X}$. The normal curve for $\overline{X}$ depends on the particular value that happens to be the true μ, and it therefore represents the conditional probability distribution for $\overline{X}$ given μ.

To get the posterior probability distribution for μ given the level for $\overline{X}$, we must apply the concepts of Bayes' theorem using the above two normal curves. The mathematics for doing this is beyond the scope of this book. But it may be established that *the posterior probability distribution for μ is also a normal distribution with mean μ_1 and standard deviation σ_1*. The values for these parameters are

$$\mu_1 = \frac{\mu_0(1/\sigma_0^2) + \overline{X}(1/\sigma_{\overline{X}}^2)}{1/\sigma_0^2 + 1/\sigma_{\overline{X}}^2}$$

$$\sigma_1^2 = \sigma_0^2 \frac{\sigma_{\overline{X}}^2}{\sigma_0^2 + \sigma_{\overline{X}}^2}$$

with

$$1/\sigma_1^2 = 1/\sigma_0^2 + 1/\sigma_{\overline{X}}^2$$

The rationale for the above results may be explained in terms of the information contained in the prior distribution and the sample. If the informational content of a finding is summarized by the reciprocal of the variance, then the third expression above tells us that

Posterior information = Prior information + Sample information where $1/\sigma_1^2$, $1/\sigma_0^2$, and $1/\sigma_{\bar{X}}^2$ measure the informational content of the posterior distribution, prior distribution, and sample, respectively. Thus, we may view μ_1 as the weighted average of μ_0 and $\bar{X}$, where the weights are simply the proportion of the posterior information derived prior to sampling and from sampling, respectively.

To illustrate these concepts, we return to our memory device decision where we had $\mu_0 = 2.5$ gigabits per day and $\sigma_0 = 1$. Suppose that a sample of $n = 25$ days will be monitored by a special program and that the daily access levels will be determined precisely. From these, the sample mean might be computed to be a value such as $\bar{X} = 2.65$ gigabits per day. Let us suppose that by examining the records of a similar facility the manager had determined that $\sigma_I = 3$ gigabits per day applied to his center. Then

$$\sigma_{\bar{X}} = \frac{3}{\sqrt{25}} = .6$$

Using these values, we have

$$1/\sigma_0^2 = 1/(1)^2 = 1$$
$$1/\sigma_{\bar{X}}^2 = 1/(.6)^2 = 2.78$$

and

$$\mu_1 = \frac{2.5(1) + 2.65(2.78)}{1 + 2.78} = 2.61$$

$$\sigma_1^2 = (1)^2 \frac{(.6)^2}{(1)^2 + (.6)^2} = .265$$

$$\sigma_1 = \sqrt{.265} = .51$$

The new expected mean of $\mu_1 = 2.61$ lies between the prior value of $\mu_0 = 2.5$ and the sample mean $\bar{X} = 2.65$. It lies closer to $\bar{X}$ than to μ_0, reflecting the fact that the informational content of sampling in this situation is greater than that available prior to sampling, $(1/\sigma_{\bar{X}}^2 = 2.78$ versus $1/\sigma_0^2 = 1)$; thus greater weight has been given to the sample mean.

The quantity of posterior information is

$$1/\sigma_1^2 = 1/.265 = 3.77$$

which exceeds the informational content for sampling and that prior to sampling as well. Notice that the new standard deviation $\sigma_1 = .51$ is smaller than either σ_0 or $\sigma_{\bar{X}}$. This must always be so since the posterior information exceeds the informational content of both the prior distribution and the sample.

Figure 8-5 helps to explain the process involved. The population (non-normal) of individual daily access levels is provided at the top. Although the standard deviation in individual daily levels is presumed to be $\sigma_I = 3$, the population center is unknown. This unknown mean μ is the entire focus of our analysis. The sample mean of n random daily observations $\overline{X}$ will be computed. Since its value is presently unknown, statistical theory tells us that the tall solid normal curve (Figure 8-5) provides probabilities for $\overline{X}$; this curve is a conditional one, since it is presumed to be centered at μ_0, the prior expected mean. The second, flatter solid normal curve represents prior probabilities for the value of the unknown μ, and it too is centered at μ_0.

When actually computed, the sample mean value might fall anywhere in the vicinity of μ_0. Depending on the location of the sample mean, the appropriate posterior normal curve for μ (represented here by the dashed curve centered at μ_1) is obtained. The center of the posterior normal curve will always lie between μ_0 and the computed $\overline{X}$.

Finding the Critical Value

We may now return to our earlier problem of finding the appropriate decision rule to use in the posterior analysis. This involves selecting that critical value C where the expected opportunity loss is minimized according to the rule

Select photographic unit if $\overline{X} \leq C$

Select holographic unit if $\overline{X} > C$

The best choice for C is the point of demarcation between those possible levels for $\overline{X}$ where the photographic unit is the better choice and those where the holographic one is better; that is, it is the level for $\overline{X}$ where the expected opportunity losses are identical under either act.

Earlier, we established that both acts are equally attractive when the expected mean equals the break-even level. After sampling, the posterior expected mean applies, so that the point of demarcation must be that $\overline{X}$ providing a posterior expected mean where

$$\mu_1 = \mu_b$$

Thus we may substitute C for $\overline{X}$ in the earlier expression for μ_1 and set

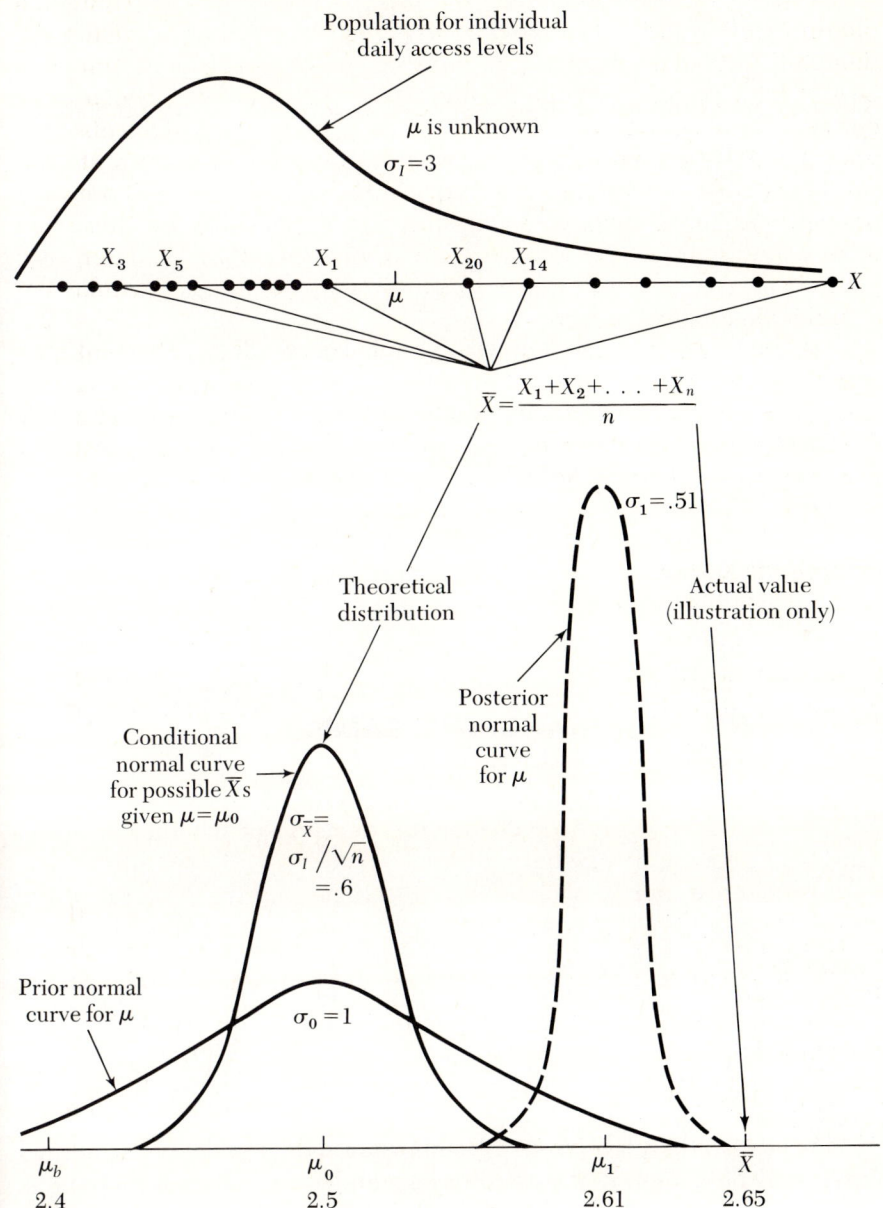

Figure 8-5
Distributions involved in posterior analysis with sampling (not drawn to scale).

8-5 POSTERIOR ANALYSIS FOR A GIVEN SAMPLE SIZE

the whole thing equal to μ_b. Solving for C we obtain

$$C = \frac{\mu_b[1/\sigma_0^2 + 1/\sigma_{\bar{X}}^2] - \mu_0(1/\sigma_0^2)}{1/\sigma_{\bar{X}}^2}$$

Then, substituting $\mu_b = 2.4$, $\sigma_0 = 1$, $\sigma_{\bar{X}} = .6$, and $\mu_0 = 2.5$ into the above, we have

$$C = \frac{2.4[1/(1)^2 + 1/(.6)^2] - 2.5[1/(1)^2]}{1/(.6)^2}$$

$$= 2.36$$

The optimal decision rule for a sample of size $n = 25$ is

Select photographic unit if $\bar{X} \leq 2.36$

Select holographic unit if $\bar{X} > 2.36$

Thus, if it is decided to sample with $n = 25$ and $\bar{X}$ turns out to be larger than $C = 2.36$, say $\bar{X} = 2.65$, the holographic memory should be chosen; but if a smaller mean is found, such as $\bar{X} = 2.2$, the photographic unit would be optimal.

8-6 DECISIONS REGARDING THE SAMPLE: PREPOSTERIOR ANALYSIS

We are now ready to consider the decision of whether or not to sample at all, and, if so, what n to use.

In a sense, our previous discussion regarding the posterior probability distribution of μ is misleading. *The final normal curve for μ depends on the actual computed value for the sample mean.* Since we have not yet decided whether to sample at all (nor how many sample observations to take), we cannot use some future value of $\bar{X}$ to make a present decision about the sampling procedure itself. Until we know the actual $\bar{X}$ exactly, we do not know the center of the posterior distribution for μ.

We must, therefore, treat μ_1 itself as a random variable. Its normal curve will be centered at μ_0 and has a standard deviation denoted σ_{μ_1}. Although the underlying concepts are beyond the scope of this book, it has been established that

$$\sigma_{\mu_1}^2 = \sigma_0^2 \frac{\sigma_0^2}{\sigma_0^2 + \sigma_{\bar{X}}^2}$$

Although the expressions are superficially similar, keep in mind that σ_1 and σ_{μ_1} are different values and represent different variabilities. The first applies to the posterior distribution found after we know $\bar{X}$; the latter applies before the actual sample result is obtained and pertains to the variability in the yet-to-be determined center of the posterior distribution. In using the above expression, remember that σ_0 must be specified in advance and $\sigma_{\bar{X}}$ may be calculated before sampling, using the known value for σ_I and the sample size n:

$$\sigma_{\bar{X}} = \frac{\sigma_I}{\sqrt{n}}$$

Expected Value of Sample Information

Recall that the EVPI expresses the worth of perfect information. A similar measure expresses the worth of sample information:

EVSI = Expected value of sample information

Analogous to the EVPI, the EVSI indicates the overall improvement in expected payoff that results when the main decision is made in accordance with sample evidence. The EVSI is based on our expectations about the center of the posterior distribution for μ and, in particular, on the value of σ_{μ_1}. Since the standard deviation for μ_1 depends on $\sigma_{\bar{X}}$, which itself depends on the still-to-be decided n, the EVSI will depend partly on the value eventually chosen for n. In keeping with our earlier notation, we will represent this dependence by using the expression EVSI(n) to represent the expected value of sample information.

The expected value of sample information may be found in a fashion similar to that used in finding the earlier EVPI (when no sample applies). All that changes from the EVPI calculation are the constants used. Here,

$$\text{EVSI}(n) = |\text{slope}| \; \sigma_{\mu_1} L(D_E)$$

where

$$D_E = \frac{|\mu_b - \mu_0|}{\sigma_{\mu_1}}$$

expressing the distance between μ_0 (the expected value for μ_1) and the break-even level in standard deviation units.

For the peripheral memory storage illustration, we have been using $\mu_b = 2.4$, $\mu_0 = 2.5$, $|\text{slope}| = \$62{,}500$, and for $n = 25$, $\sigma_{\bar{X}} = .6$. The variance of μ_1 is

$$\sigma_{\mu_1}^2 = (1)^2 \frac{(1)^2}{(1)^2 + (.6)^2} = .74$$

so that the standard deviation is

$$\sigma_{\mu_1} = \sqrt{.74} = .86$$

The standardized distance is

$$D_E = \frac{|2.4 - 2.5|}{.86} = .12$$

so that, from Appendix Table C,

$$L(D_E) = L(.12) = .3418$$

and

$$\text{EVSI}(n) = \$62,500(.86).3418 = \$18,372$$

The result EVSI(25) = $18,372 tells us the true worth of a sample of $n = 25$ to the decision maker. As long as the sampling cost is less than this figure, the computer center manager would be better off with, rather than without, that sample information. As we have already seen, he would use a decision rule for $\overline{X}$ having critical value $C = 2.36$ to determine the act to choose.

The Decision to Sample

Suppose that the computer center manager may determine the precise access level on each sample day at a cost of $100 per day. Then for a sample size of $n = 25$, the cost of sampling is $2500. Since this amount is smaller than EVSI(25), *the manager should definitely use a sample of some size* rather than decide with no information at all. The remaining question is: How large should n be?

Determining the Optimal Sample Size

We may answer this question by finding the *expected net gain of sampling* for various sample sizes. This is computed from

$$\text{ENGS}(n) = \text{EVSI}(n) - \text{Cost}(n)$$

The optimal sample size is the one having the greatest value for ENGS(n). By trial and error, trying various ns, we can determine the sample size to use. Table 8-1 shows the ENGS(n) values for a few sample sizes. Notice that the expected net gain rises until $n = 30$, after which it falls. Thus $n = 30$, which has ENGS(30) = $16,052, is the optimal sample size.

Table 8-1
EXPECTED NET GAIN OF SAMPLING COMPUTED
FOR SEVERAL SAMPLE SIZES

n	$\sigma_{\bar{X}} = 3/\sqrt{n}$	σ_{μ_1}	D_E	$L(D_E)$	EVSI(n)	Cost(n)	ENGS(n)
10	.95	.73	.14	.3328	$15,184	$1000	$14,184
25	.60	.86	.12	.3418	18,372	2500	15,872
29	.56	.87	.11	.3464	18,836	2900	15,936
30	.55	.88	.11	.3464	19,052	3000	16,052
31	.54	.88	.11	.3464	19,052	3100	15,952
35	.51	.89	.11	.3464	19,269	3500	15,769
40	.47	.90	.11	.3464	19,485	4000	15,485

The Optimal Decision Rule

We have now determined the optimal course of action for the computer-center manager. He should choose to sample, since this has a positive expected net gain. Furthermore, a sample size of $n = 30$ provides the greatest expected net gain of sampling. The manager should, therefore, use a sample of 30 days and determine the precise memory access levels for these computing $\bar{X}$.

The standard deviation for $\bar{X}$ is

$$\sigma_{\bar{X}} = \frac{\sigma_I}{\sqrt{n}} = \frac{3}{\sqrt{30}} = .55$$

and, by using the appropriate constants for this problem, the critical value for $\bar{X}$ is computed to be

$$C = \frac{2.4[1/(1)^2 + 1/(.55)^2] - 2.5[1/(1)^2]}{1/(.55)^2}$$

$$= 2.37$$

8-7 A SUMMARY OF THE PROCEDURES

Before concluding, it should be helpful if we tie together the concepts and procedures of this chapter. This is best explained by considering the various time frames involved, shown in Figure 8-6, where decision making with the normal curve is separated into four stages.

We begin with *prior analysis*, where the prior distribution for the unknown μ is obtained, generally through judgment. During this stage, payoffs are determined as linear functions of μ; this leads directly to a break-even analysis. The main decision might be made in this stage by comparing the mean μ_0 of the prior distribution to the break-even level μ_b. Whether or not we stop at this stage depends on how worthwhile any further information about μ happens to be. This is roughly gauged by the EVPI, and further investigation should be made only if the EVPI is great enough to warrant the extra bother of evaluating sample information. (Clearly an EVPI of only $10 wouldn't be enough to justify any further analysis, and even an EVPI of $100 is likely to be greater than the cost of a modest sampling study.)

If further information should be pursued, then the *preposterior analysis* stage comes next. Here, the question is mainly one of whether or not to sample, and if so, what size n of a sample should be taken. The evaluation is computationally lengthy and involves calculations of various EVSIs and sampling costs for several ns, so that the size having the greatest expected net gain of sampling can be determined.

The next stage involves *posterior analysis*. Here the decision rule is established, the sample collected, and the actual sample mean $\overline{X}$ is calculated. Depending on the value obtained for $\overline{X}$, the choice of action for the main decision is indicated.

An *optional* fourth stage completes the procedure. Here the *future analysis* is concerned with the posterior distribution for μ. *This distribution is not needed in making the main decision*, although it can serve as the starting point for future decisions involving μ. (This fact is not obvious from our earlier discussions, where we had to investigate the characteristics of the posterior distribution for μ to explain the procedures involved in posterior and preposterior analysis.)

Most students of this material suffer from a mild form of "symbol shock." And for good reasons! We have five different standard deviations and an equal number of means. Furthermore, $\overline{X}$ and μ_1 appear as subscripts to other symbols. Unfortunately, this Greek alphabet soup is unavoidable. It may help to mention a few of the pitfalls encountered in applying the various analyses.

(1) Try not to confuse σ_1 with σ_{μ_1}. The former expresses variability

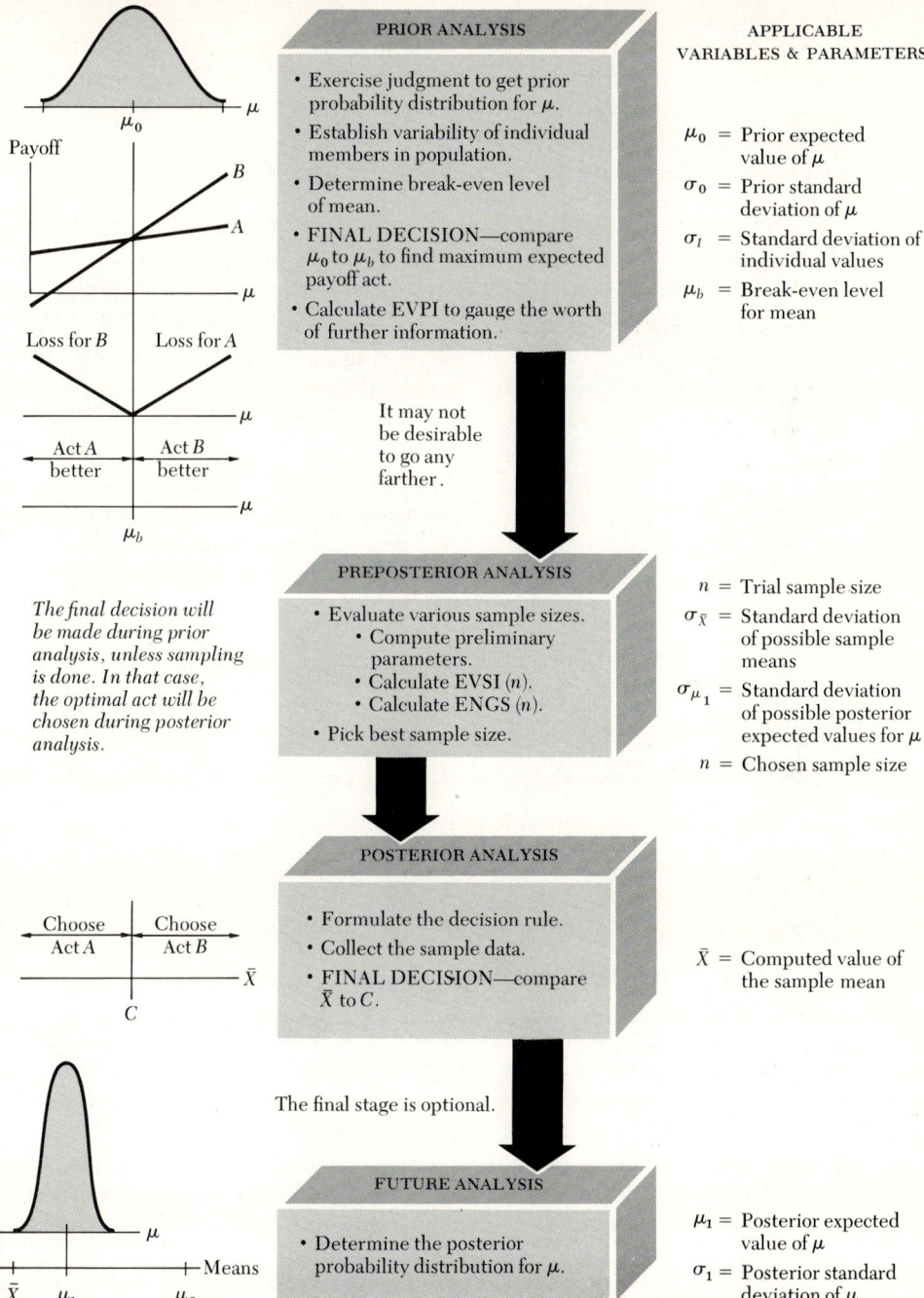

Figure 8-6
A summary of how the concepts and procedures relate for decision making with the normal distribution.

8-7 A SUMMARY OF THE PROCEDURES

in μ after everything is done and is generally not even calculated except for future analysis. More essential is σ_{μ_1}, which expresses variability in the center μ_1 of the posterior distribution and is only used during preposterior analysis, when μ_1 is uncertain. (After sampling, μ_1 can be calculated and is certain, so that there is no variability.) To make matters worse, σ_1^2 and $\sigma_{\mu_1}^2$ are calculated from similar-looking expressions. Make sure you use the right one.

(2) Remember that some expressions involve the standard deviation σ and others the variance σ^2. Be sure to take the square root of the variance to get the corresponding standard deviation when needed, and to square the latter to get the variance.

(3) Prior analysis involves comparing μ_b and μ_0, whereas posterior analysis compares $\overline{X}$ to C. Only one of these comparisons is ultimately used in making the main decision.

(4) Do not confuse σ_0 with σ_I. The former expresses variability in μ itself and gauges how close to μ_0 we judge that μ might lie. The other standard deviation pertains to individual population values. Ordinarily σ_0 and σ_I are of unequal value. (In a decision involving human heights, σ_0 might be $\frac{1}{4}$ in., reflecting our lack of precision in predicting the population mean. And σ_I could be $2\frac{1}{2}$ in., expressing variability from person to person.)

(5) Keep in mind that μ remains unknown. There will be no population census, and its value will be uncertain throughout the entire analysis. On the other hand, μ_0 and μ_1 are the expected values for μ, applying at the beginning and end of the analysis, respectively. The value of μ_0 is known throughout, while μ_1 is itself uncertain throughout most of the analysis and can only be calculated after everything else. Also, the value of $\overline{X}$ is uncertain until after the sample has been collected.

8-8 CONCLUDING REMARKS

The special difficulties in dealing with several different normal curves have forced us to depart from the usual decision tree analysis that has been the central theme throughout this book. If we approximated the various continuous probability distributions by discrete tables (using typical values for μ and $\overline{X}$), we could apply the methods of Chapter 7 to reach conclusions nearly identical to those achieved using the procedures of this chapter. But it proves more convenient to focus on opportunity losses and to use the normal form analysis when the prior distribution for μ can be represented by the normal curve and the sample observations themselves range over a continuous scale (so that probabilities for $\overline{X}$ are represented by another normal curve).

What if the prior distribution for μ is not a normal curve? After all, there may be no compelling reason why some other type of distribution cannot apply. An amazing fact, established by Robert Schlaifer, who originally proposed the procedures in this chapter,* is that *for practically any other type of prior distribution, the posterior probability distribution for μ will still be very near a normal curve.* Thus, it really matters little what form applies to the prior distribution for μ.

Another nice feature of the present approach for decision making with sample information is that it is simpler than applying the earlier decision tree analysis with approximate probability distributions, which would involve a tremendous number of computations that are unnecessary here. The present procedure entirely avoids the problem of finding the unconditional result probabilities for $\bar{X}$. The nature of the opportunity loss lines permits us to evaluate the two-action problem through a break-even analysis that considers only the central value for μ and the nature of its prior probability distribution.

There are limitations, however. For instance, we cannot use the procedures presented here when the payoffs cannot be graphed as straight lines nor when more than two basic actions are contemplated. We have presented a special-purpose tool that applies only to limited situations. Fortunately, a great deal of practical business decision-making applications fall into this category.

PROBLEMS

8-1 In each of the following situations the prior distribution for the population mean is represented by the normal curve. Below the break-even level for the mean, alternative A is more profitable; beyond the break-even level alternative B is better. In each case: (1) indicate which act is better and (2) calculate the EVPI.

	(a)	(b)	(c)	(d)
Mean:	50	100	60	40
Standard deviation:	10	10	20	10
Break-even level:	55	90	62	38
Slope:	$1000	$5000	$5000	$10,000

8-2 Sonic Phonics specializes in stereo headphones. It is considering adding a new stereo helmet receiver for motor cyclists, but the

---

* Much of the material in his two books, *Probability and Statistics for Business Decisions* (New York: McGraw-Hill, 1959) and *Introduction to Statistics for Business Decisions* (New York: McGraw-Hill, 1961), carefully develops the concepts of this chapter.

owner is uncertain about the mean annual sales volume per outlet in the retail chain it supplies. He believes that the mean is normally distributed with mean 60 and a standard deviation of 10 helmets per store. Altogether there are 100 stores involved. The helmet will have a product lifetime of about one year, after which the novelty will wear off. Production costs are $50,000 for set up, and each helmet will have a variable cost of $30 and will be sold to the retail stores for $40.

(a) Assuming that total increase in profit is to be maximized, determine an expression for the payoff, in terms of the mean number of helmets sold per store, for making and not making the helmet. What is the break-even level?

(b) Should Sonic Phonics make the helmet?

(c) Calculate the EVPI.

8-3 The marketing manager of Blitz Beer must determine whether or not to sponser Blitz Day with the Gotham City Hellcats. She is uncertain what the effect of the promotion will be in terms of mean increase in daily sales volume that would result during the 100-day baseball season. The cost of sponsership is $10,000 and each can of Blitz has a marginal cost of 20 cents and sells for 40 cents.

(a) Assuming that change in profit is to be maximized, express the payoff function for the two alternatives in terms of the mean daily increase in cans sold.

(b) Suppose that Blitz Day will result in a mean increase judged to be normally distributed with a mean of 600 and a standard deviation of 50 cans per day. Should the brewer sponsor the event?

(c) What is the expected value of perfect information? Do you think it is worthwhile to obtain further information? Can a sample from the underlying population even be helpful in this decision? Explain.

8-4 Consider the illustration described in the chapter for choosing between photographic and holographic peripheral memory storage units. Suppose that the following annual savings payoff function applies instead, where the access portion depends on the unknown mean access level of μ gigabits per day.

$$\text{Payoff} = \begin{cases} \$500{,}000 + \$\ 65{,}000\mu & \text{for photographic} \\ \$330{,}000 + \$150{,}000\mu & \text{for holographic} \end{cases}$$

(a) Find the break-even level for the population mean.

(b) Which unit maximizes annual savings when the prior expected mean is $\mu_0 = 2.5$ gigabits per day?

8-5 Problem 8-4 continued. Suppose that the prior probability distribution for the population mean access level has expected value 2.3 gigabits per day and standard deviation of 2, and that the population of individual daily access levels has a standard deviation of 2 gigabits per day.

(a) Calculate the EVPI.
(b) Suppose that a random sample of $n=16$ days is chosen. Find the optimal value of C that maximizes expected annual savings.
(c) Suppose that the sample mean turns out to be 1.75 gigabits per day. Determine the mean and standard deviation of the posterior probability distribution for μ. What memory would be chosen?
(d) Using your results from (c), find the probability that the mean daily access level lies above the break-even level.

8-6 Problem 8-4 continued. No sample has been decided on, but the cost of each daily observation is now $500. Using the constants provided earlier, calculate the expected net gain of sampling for the indicated sample sizes.
(a) 4.
(b) 9.
(c) 100.
(d) Which one of the above sample sizes is the best one? Formulate the optimal decision for the sample mean that corresponds.

8-7 A decision is to be made between Act 1 and Act 2. Act 1 will be chosen if $\bar{X} \leq C$. The applicable constants are $\mu_0 = 5$, $\sigma_0 = 2$, $\sigma_I = 24$, and $\mu_b = 4.5$. Each sample observation costs $.50, while the absolute value for the slope of the opportunity loss lines is $200.
(a) Determine the EVPI applicable when no sample is to be taken.
(b) Calculate the EVSI for: (1) $n=4$; (2) $n=9$; (3) $n=25$; (4) $n=100$.
(c) Calculate the ENGS(n) for your results from (b). Which of the sample sizes listed above is the best one to use?
(d) Suppose a sample size of $n=100$ is used. Formulate the optimal decision rule. What act should be chosen if (1) $\bar{X} = 3.6$? (2) $\bar{X} = 3.9$?

8-8 The first stage of a chemical process yields a mean of μ grams of active ingredient for every liter of raw material processed. Because of variations in the raw material and control settings, the true population mean for any particular batch is unknown until processing is complete. The plant superintendent believes that μ is normally distributed with mean 30 g and standard deviation 2 g. The amount of variation in individual liters within a batch is summarized by a standard deviation of 6 g.

The plant superintendent will use the active ingredient in one of two final-stage processes: high-pressure or low-pressure. Each provides an identical final product. The ultimate profit for each alternative is partly determined by μ. The following apply:

$$\text{Payoff} = \begin{cases} \$10{,}000 + \$300\mu & \text{for high-pressure processing} \\ \$13{,}100 + \$200\mu & \text{for low-pressure processing} \end{cases}$$

(a) Determine the break-even level for μ. Which process, high- or low-pressure, yields the greater expected profit?

(b) Calculate the value for the slope of the opportunity loss lines and the superintendent's EVPI.

8-9 Problem 8-8 continued. For a cost of $1 per liter, the superintendent can determine the actual yield of active ingredient per liter.
   (a) Calculate the expected value of sample information for: (1) $n = 4$; (2) $n = 9$; (3) $n = 16$.
   (b) Calculate ENGS(n) for the above sample sizes. Which of them is the best to use?
   (c) Determine the optimal decision rule for the sample size found in (b). Which process should be used if: (1) $\bar{X} = 30$ g? (2) $\bar{X} = 32$ g? (3) $\bar{X} = 33$ g?

Nine

Decision Making with Utility

The goal of this chapter is to broaden the scope of decision theory through the introduction of a new payoff measure. As we have seen, a good payoff measure should rank all possible outcomes in terms of how well they meet the decision-maker's goals. This is often an easy task when there is no uncertainty. But the presence of uncertainty may severely complicate the issue in decision situations with extreme outcomes as possibilities. Such decisions contain elements of *risk*. Because people usually have different attitudes about risk, two persons faced with identical decisions might actually prefer different courses of action.

The crucial role of attitude in any decision may be illustrated by the divergent behavior of different persons faced with the same decision. The umbrella situation nicely demonstrates this point. *How can we explain why everyone does not carry an umbrella when we do?* To a certain extent we can say that not all individuals are equally adept at selecting and exercising appropriate decision criteria. This is but one possible explanation. With much justification, however, we can conclude that the difference in behavior may also be explained by differing attitudes toward the consequences. Getting wet may be fun to some people, but to others it is viewed as an invitation to pneumonia and possibly the first step into a premature grave. Some persons think it chic to carry rain paraphernalia when it's not raining; others would as soon lug around a ball and chain. Even if we can find two persons with identical attitudes toward the decision consequences, we will find that occasionally they make opposite decisions. Such a difference can be explained if they do not have identical judgments regarding the chance of rain. One person may rely on the Weather Service radio broadcasts as a source of information, judging its subjective probabilities to be adequate. Another person may instead depend on his lumbago pains as a fairly reliable measure of the probability of rain.

In this chapter, we discuss utility as an alternative expression of payoff reflective of a person's attitudes. We begin by discussing the rationale for buying insurance. We then present a brief historical discussion of utility and provide the underlying assumptions of a theory of utility. Finally, we introduce a procedure whereby utility values can be determined. The utility function so obtained provides a basis for our discussion of some basic attitudes toward risk.

9-1 ATTITUDES, PREFERENCES, AND UTILITY

Chapter 6 presented various procedures and criteria that aid the decision maker to choose in the presence of uncertainty. In all cases, a payoff value for each outcome is required in order to analyze the decision. As we have seen, not all outcomes have an obvious numerical payoff. In this section, we indicate how payoffs may be determined in such cases. Later in this chapter, we develop methodology to allow valid quantification of such consequences as reduced share of market, loss of corporate control, and antitrust suits. Even when numerical outcomes can be naturally determined, we have noted that it may be unrealistic to select the act with the maximum expected payoff. In some cases, an extremely risky act fares better under the Bayes decision rule than one obviously preferred. As noted in Chapter 6, this difficulty is not the fault of the Bayes criterion, but rather is caused by payoff values that do not reflect their true worth to the decision maker.

Decision to Buy Insurance

The inadequacy of using such obvious measures as dollar costs or profits for payoffs may be vividly illustrated by evaluating an individual's decision whether or not to buy casualty insurance.

Table 9-1
PAYOFF TABLE FOR THE DECISION TO BUY FIRE INSURANCE

		ACTS			
		BUY POLICY		NO POLICY	
EVENTS	PROBABILITY	Payoff	Payoff × Probability	Payoff	Payoff × Probability
Fire	.002	−$100	−$ .20	−$40,000	−$80.00
No fire	.998	− 100	− 99.80	0	0
		Expected payoffs	−$100.00		−$80.00

EXAMPLE Spiro Pyrophobis wishes to decide whether to buy a fire insurance policy for his home. For simplicity there are only two relevant events, fire and no fire. Our decision-maker's payoffs will be expressed in terms of his out-of-pocket costs, which we shall represent by negative numbers. Our question is: Will the Bayes decision rule lead to the choice of act actually preferred?

In answering this question, we will use the hypothetical payoff table provided in Table 9-1. Here we have greatly simplified the decision by considering just one kind of coverage to be supplied by a single company. The acts are to buy or not buy an annual policy with a $100 premium charge. Should there be a fire, we assume his home and all its contents, valued at $40,000, will be completely destroyed; partial damage is impossible. We also assume that the company will reimburse our homeowner fully for all fire losses. In addition, we suppose that the home and its contents are fully owned and, if destroyed, will be replaced at identical cost by our hapless decision maker.

For homes in the category of Mr. Pyrophobis', the insurance company actuaries have established that historically 2 out of every 1000 such homes burn down each year. The probability of such a fire has, therefore, been set at $2/1000 = .002$ for Mr. Pyrophobis. Thus, the complementary event, no fire, has probability $1 - .002 = .998$. Using these probability values, we calculate the expected payoffs for each act in Table 9-1. The maximum expected payoff is −$80, which corresponds to the act buy no policy and is larger than the −$100 payoff from buying fire insurance.

In the example just given, the *Bayes decision rule indicates that it is optimal to buy no insurance*. Yet most persons faced with this decision do choose to buy insurance. Loss of a home, which for many persons comprises the major portion of a lifetime's savings, is a dreadful prospect. The expenditure of an annual premium, although not exactly appealing, buys a feeling of security that seems to outweigh the difference between the expected payoffs. Furthermore, insurance policy premiums are intentionally set at a price higher than the expected cost of potential claims (or equivalently, the policyholder's expected dollar loss); they must be, if the insurance company is to pay wages and achieve profits. Thus the buying of insurance may be looked on as an unfair gamble, where the payout is not in the buyer's favor. An individual can expect to pay more in insurance premiums than he will collect in claims.* Most persons feel blessed at not having to file a claim.

The Bayes decision rule selects the less preferred act. Does this mean that it is an invalid criterion? Rather than attempt to provide an immediate no as the answer, let us consider the payoffs used. The true worth of the outcomes is not reflected by the dollar payoffs. A policyholder is willing to pay more than the expected dollar loss for "peace of mind." We can say that the policyholder derives greater "utility" from having insurance. If dollar losses are valued on a scale of true worth or *utility*, then each additional dollar loss will make our decision maker feel disproportionately worse off. Thus a 10 percent reduction in wealth may be more than twice as bad as a 5 percent reduction. The same would ordinarily be true for gains in dollar wealth; the second increase may not raise the sense of well being as much as the first one. In the parlance of economics, *the policyholder's marginal utility for money is decreasing.* Each successive dollar brings a smaller increase in utility; each additional dollar loss reduces utility by a greater amount than before.

Thus, we may question the validity of using dollars as our payoff measure. Instead, we might find it fruitful to use an outcome's worth or utility as the payoff.

9-2 NUMERICAL UTILITY VALUES

We seek to find numbers that express the true worth of the payoffs corresponding to decision consequences. We have referred to such numbers as utilities. Much investigation has been made of the true worth of monetary payoffs. The early eighteenth-century mathematician Daniel Bernoulli pioneered in efforts to develop a measure of utility. He proposed that *the true worth of one's wealth is the logarithm of the amount of money.* Thus a graphical relationship between utility and money would have the basic shape of the curve in Figure 9-1. Note that this curve has a slope which, although always positive, decreases as the amount of money increases, reflecting the assumption of decreasing marginal utility for money.

* Life insurance, ordinarily a form of savings, is excluded.

Saint Petersburg Paradox

A gambling game called the Saint Petersburg Paradox led Bernoulli to his conclusion. In the game, a balanced coin is fairly tossed until the first head appears. The gambler's winnings are based upon the number of tosses made before the game ends. If a head appears on the first toss, the player wins $2. If not, the "kitty" is doubled to $4—the reward if a head appears on the second toss. If a tail occurs, the kitty is doubled again. The pot keeps doubling at every coin toss. The winnings achieved is $2 raised to the power of the number of tosses until and including the first head. It will be most interesting if you pause to think what amount you would be willing to pay for the privilege of playing this game.

The probability that $n + 1$ tosses occur before payment is the probability that there is a run of n tails and that the $(n + 1)$st toss is a head: $(1/2)^{n+1}$. The payoff for $n + 1$ tosses is 2^{n+1}. We may therefore calculate the player's expected receipts from the sum

$$\$2(1/2) + \$2^2(1/2)^2 + \$2^3(1/2)^3 + \cdots = \$1 + \$1 + \$1 + \cdots = \$\infty$$

Since the number of 1s in this sum is unlimited, the *expected receipts from a play of this game are infinite!* How much were you willing to pay to play? Whatever amount you chose, it must have been a finite amount, and thus less than the expected receipts. Thus the expected payoff from this gamble is also infinite, no matter what price is paid to play.

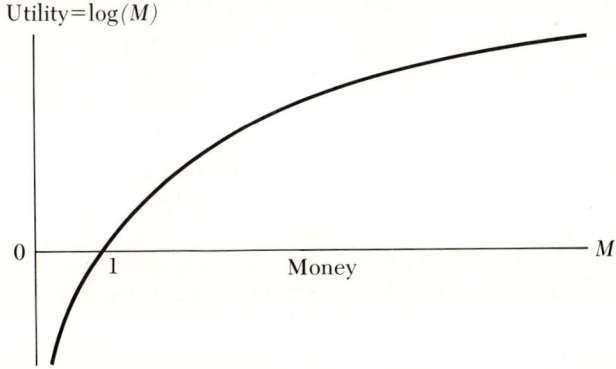

Figure 9-1
The utility function for money assumed by Bernoulli.

Few people are willing to pay more than $10 to play the game. Even at this price, a player would come out ahead in only 1 out of 8 games, on the average. At $500, you would show a profit in an average of only 1 out of 256 gambles. The natural reticence of players to pay very much for this gamble led Bernoulli to his conclusion about the utility for money. In general, we say that a person has *decreasing marginal utility for money* if he prefers not to participate in a gamble where the expected receipts exceed the price to play.

Validity of Logarithmic Values

Other early mathematicians, through different paths of reasoning, arrived at conclusions similar to Bernoulli's: that the marginal utility for money is decreasing. They proposed other utility curves with the same basic shape. A major fault of these early works is that they do not account for individual differences in the assignment of worth. More modern treatment of utility in the abstract sense was advanced by Von Neumann and Morgenstern in their book *Theory of Games and Economic Behavior*. There they proposed that a utility curve can be tailored for any individual, provided certain assumptions about the individual's preferences hold. These assumptions allow several valid basic utility-curve shapes, including curves similar to Bernoulli's. We shall investigate some of these later in the chapter.

Outcomes Without a Natural Payoff Measure

So far, we have concentrated on examples where the outcomes have a natural numerical payoff measure, such as dollars profit, gasoline gallons saved, or time. But we have noted decisions with outcomes for which there are no such numbers. As decision makers, we ought to be able to assess the relative worths of such outcomes.

For most decisions, it is possible to determine preferences—but we do not propose that this task is always easy. Indeed, value judgments may be the most difficult step in analyzing a decision. Consider the young student choosing one of several top universities, the child selecting a candy bar, the bachelor contemplating losing his freedom by getting married, the tired corporate founder pondering merger and retirement versus retaining control and delegating operating responsibility to his son-in-law, or the innocent person choosing between pleading guilty to manslaughter or facing a trial for murder. If we assume the capability to rank the consequences in order of preference, we can extend the notion of utility so that numerical payoffs can be made for the most intangible outcomes.

UTILITY THEORY 9-3

The fundamental proposition of the modern treatment of utility is that it is possible to obtain a numerical expression of one's preferences. For a set of outcomes ranked by preference, we can assign utility values that convey these preferences. The largest utility number is assigned to the most preferred outcome, the next largest to the second most preferred, and so forth. Suppose, for instance, that in contemplating a menu you prefer New York steak to baked halibut. Were you to assign utility values to these entrees in accordance with your preferences, then if the utility of steak is 5, that is, $u(\text{steak}) = 5$, $u(\text{halibut})$ must be some number smaller than 5.

Before describing how specific utility numbers can be obtained, we shall first discuss some of the assumptions underlying the theory of utility.

Assumptions of Utility Theory

Various assumptions have been made about the determination of utilities.* These have one feature in common: that the values obtained pertain only to a *single individual* who behaves *consistently* in accordance with his or her own tastes.

The first assumption of utility theory is that a person can determine for any pair of outcomes O_1 and O_2 whether he or she prefers O_1 to O_2, O_2 to O_1, or regards both equally. This assumption is particularly nice when we consider monetary values, for then we can assume that more money is always better than less. But as we have seen, a preference ranking can be very difficult when qualitative alternatives are considered. Can a person always determine a preference or establish indifference between outcomes? If not, then utilities cannot be found for these outcomes.

The second assumption is that if A is preferred to B and B is preferred to C, then A must be preferred to C. This property has been called *transitivity* and reflects an individual's consistency. Again, when we are dealing with monetary figures for outcomes, we can usually assume transitivity.

---

* Those discussed in this book are simplifications of the original axioms postulated by Von Neumann and Morgenstern.

Before discussing the assumptions of utility any further, we will introduce gambles between outcomes so that uncertainty may be incorporated into the determination of utility.

Gambles and Expected Utility

We are presently concerned with making choices under uncertainty. Thus the payoffs for decision acts are unknown. Each act may, therefore, be viewed as a *gamble* with uncertain rewards. To evaluate such decisions, we must extend the concept of utility to gambles.

Recall that the Bayes decision rule involves comparisons between the expected payoffs of acts or strategies, so that the "optimal" choice has the maximum expected payoff. But the major difficulty with this criterion, as we have seen, is that the indicated course of action can be less attractive than some other. For example, the Bayes decision rule tells us not to buy fire insurance under circumstances when most persons would believe insurance most desirable. We wish to overcome this obstacle by using utilities in place of ordinary dollar payoffs. Thus, we require that the expected utility payoffs provide a valid means for comparing actions so that the candidate action having the greatest expected utility is actually preferred to the alternative actions. Thus, buying fire insurance should have greater expected utility than not buying.

But we can go one step further. Suppose that the most preferred action has the greatest expected utility, the next most preferred the next greatest, and so forth. If this is so, then expected utility would express preference ranking, and *expected utility values would themselves be utilities*. Each would express the worth of a *gamble* between outcomes and would be obtained by averaging the utility values of the outcomes, using their respective probabilities as weights. This may be stated more precisely as a property of utility theory:

In any gamble between outcome A and outcome B, with probabilities q for A and $1 - q$ for B,

$$u(\text{gamble}) = qu(A) + (1 - q)u(B)$$

Thus the utility of a gamble between two outcomes equals the expected utility of the gamble. When acts having uncertain outcomes are viewed as gambles, an act's utility equals the expected utility of its outcomes. *With utilities as payoffs, the Bayes decision rule would indicate that the act having maximum expected utility is optimal,* so that this criterion would always select the most preferred act or strategy.

Determining Expected Utilities

To see how this works, suppose that our homeowner in the example values the dollar changes in his assets according to the following utility function:

$$u(M) = \sqrt{M + 40{,}000} - 200$$

where M expresses the change in cash position associated with each outcome.

Table 9-2
DETERMINATION OF UTILITIES FOR OUTCOMES OF THE FIRE INSURANCE DECISION AND CALCULATION OF EXPECTED UTILITIES

(1) Event	(2) Probability	(3) Cash Change M	(4) Utility $\sqrt{M + 40{,}000} - 200$	(5) Utility × Probability
		BUY INSURANCE		
Fire	.002	−$100	−.25	−.0005
No fire	.998	− 100	−.25	−.2495
			Expected utility =	−.2500
		DON'T BUY INSURANCE		
Fire	.002	−$40,000	−200	−.40
No fire	.998	0	0	0
			Expected utility =	−.40

Table 9-2 shows the utility calculations and the expected utility calculations for the acts buy insurance and don't buy insurance. For instance, when no insurance is bought and there is a fire, there is a loss, so that $M = -\$40{,}000$, a negative change in cash position. The utility for this outcome is obtained by the calculation

$$u(-\$40{,}000) = \sqrt{-40{,}000 + 40{,}000} - 200$$
$$= \sqrt{0} - 200 = -200$$

The utilities for the other outcomes are calculated in a similar manner; $u(0) = 0$, while $u(-\$100) = -.25$.

Each act is a gamble. Buying insurance is a gamble having two identical outcomes in terms of dollar expenditure, −$100, since the same amount applies whether or not there is a fire. Buying no insurance is a gamble with cash outlays of −$40,000 if there is a fire and $0 if there is no fire. The utilities of the respective acts are thus the expected utilities of the corresponding gambles. Therefore, we see from Table 9-2 that the expected utilities are −.25 for buying insurance and −.4 for not buying insurance. Since buying insurance has the higher utility, it must be preferred by the decision maker; stated differently, the act to buy insurance has the maximum expected utility payoff, so the Bayes decision rule indicates that it is the optimal choice.

We see that when we use utilities as payoff values, the "proper" result is obtained with the Bayes decision rule. We may not, however, conclude that with utilities as payoffs this criterion will always lead to a decision to buy insurance. The choice depends on the relation between the chance of fire and the insurance policy's price. Suppose, for example, that the price of a policy is raised to $200, so that the utility of the dollar payoffs for buying insurance is

$$u(-\$200) = \sqrt{-200 + 40{,}000} - 200$$
$$= \sqrt{39{,}800} - 200 = -.50$$

The expected utility for buying insurance is −.50, so that if the probability of fire remains the same as before, the act don't buy insurance would have utility −.4, which is greater than −.50, so that don't buy insurance is the preferred act. This is the opposite of the choice made above. The insurance has become too expensive to be attractive.

Many persons facing the same circumstances would buy insurance even if the premium were raised to $1000 or more. *Their tastes would be different and this would be reflected by different utility values for each outcome.* The price of a policy may partly explain why there is a prevalence of coverage against fire while there is a paucity of protection against natural disasters, such as earthquakes, tornados, or floods. One reason why people do not generally buy such insurance policies might be explained by the high premium required by insurance companies for such coverage (if it is offered at all) in relation to the probabilities (which are difficult to obtain actuarily for such rare phenomena).

Further Assumptions of Utility Theory

The third assumption of utility theory is that of *continuity*. This says there is some gamble having the best and worst outcomes as rewards that the individual regards as equally preferable to some middling or in-between outcome. To illustrate continuity, consider the following example.

EXAMPLE Homer Briant has a small hardware store in a declining neighborhood. He is contemplating a move. Because he is still young and has no special skills, he will not consider leaving the hardware business. A move cannot be guaranteed to be successful, since relocating will involve maximum stretching of his lines of credit, and there will be no time for a gradual buildup of business. Moving will, therefore, bring either an improvement over his present business or disaster. Thus, he will be faced with one of the following outcomes:

Least preferred O_1: imminent bankruptcy (if move is a failure)
O_2: decreasing sales (if he stays)
Most preferred O_3: increasing sales (if move is a success)

Whether a move will be a success depends largely on luck or chance. Our assumption of continuity presumes that there is some probability value q of a successful move that will make Mr. Briant indifferent between staying and moving. Figure 9-2 shows a decision tree diagram for his decision. The fork at node b represents a gamble between O_3 and O_1 resulting from the act to move. Continuity may be justified by observing that if the value of q is near 1, so that a move will almost certainly be a success, Mr. Briant would prefer the gamble of moving to staying. But if q is close to 0, making bankruptcy a near certainty, he will prefer to stay in his present location. Thus, there must be a value of q somewhere between 0

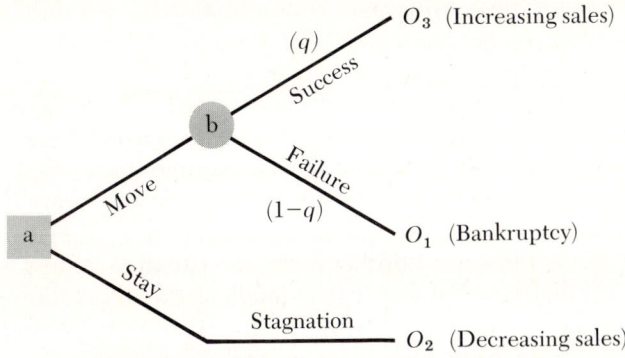

Figure 9-2
Mr. Briant's decision tree diagram for possible business relocation.

and 1 beyond which his preference will pass from O_2 to the gamble; this value of q makes the gamble equally preferable to O_2.

Continuity is a very crucial assumption of utility theory, yet it may be hard to accept, especially if the outcomes include the ultimate one, death.

Suppose that you are allowed to participate in a far-fetched lottery where the price is $100 if you win and death if you lose. Is there any probability of winning for which you would be indifferent between the status quo and playing? A natural response is that this is not a very meaningful gamble. All right then, let us recast the situation. Suppose that you are informed by a reliable source that you can drive your car one mile down the road where a man is passing out hundred-dollar bills, one to a person. There are no gimmicks and there will be no inconvenience from a mob of people. Would you go? If your answer is yes, then consider your chances of getting killed in an automobile accident on your journey. For the past several years, approximately 50,000 persons have been killed from such accidents in the United States annually. Thus, although quite small, the probability of your rather untimely death occurring while collecting your $100 prize is not zero. Going to get your $100 is a gamble with death as a possibility, and you prefer the gamble to the status quo. Suppose now that we increase the chance of death. To reach the man you must cross a condemned bridge. Would you still go? Probably not, as the chance of death would be significantly higher. Somewhere between these two cases is a probability for safely getting your $100, with a complementary probability of death, for which you would be indifferent between the status quo and the gamble.

A fourth assumption of utility allows us to revise a gamble by *substituting* one outcome for another regarded equally well. The premise is that the person will be indifferent between the original and revised gambles. The substitutability assumption may be illustrated by means of the following example.

EXAMPLE A husband and wife cannot agree how to spend Saturday night. In desperation they agree to a gamble where the toss of a coin will determine the kind of entertainment they will select. If a head occurs, they will spend the evening at the opera (her preference), and if a tail, they will go to a basketball game. Suppose that the wife changes her mind and wants instead to go to a dance. The husband dislikes dancing just as much as the opera. He would then be indifferent between tossing for the opera or basketball and a revised gamble between dancing and basketball. This will hold regardless of the odds, providing the chance of going to the basketball game remains the same for the original and revised gambles.

The principle of substitutability also holds if we treat a gamble as an outcome. For any outcome we may substitute an *equivalent gamble*, one regarded equally as well as the outcome the gamble replaces, having as rewards two other outcomes. For example, suppose that the wife instead insists on a movie, where she wants to see a romance story, while he feels that to be compensated for being dragged to a movie, they should see an adventure film. Suppose that the husband is indifferent between an opera or a coin toss determining which of the two movies will be seen. The second coin toss is an equivalent gamble to the opera outcome. Thus the husband should be indifferent between the single- and two-stage gambles in Figure 9-3.

The final assumption of utility theory concerns any pair of gambles with identical outcomes. The gamble that has the greater probability for the more desirable outcome must be preferred. Thus, the preference for gambles between the same two outcomes increases with the probability of attaining the better outcome. That this is plausible should be apparent. Suppose you are offered the proposition that when a coin is tossed it pays you $100 if a head occurs and nothing for a tail. The probability of winning $100 is 1/2. It should be obvious that this gamble would be

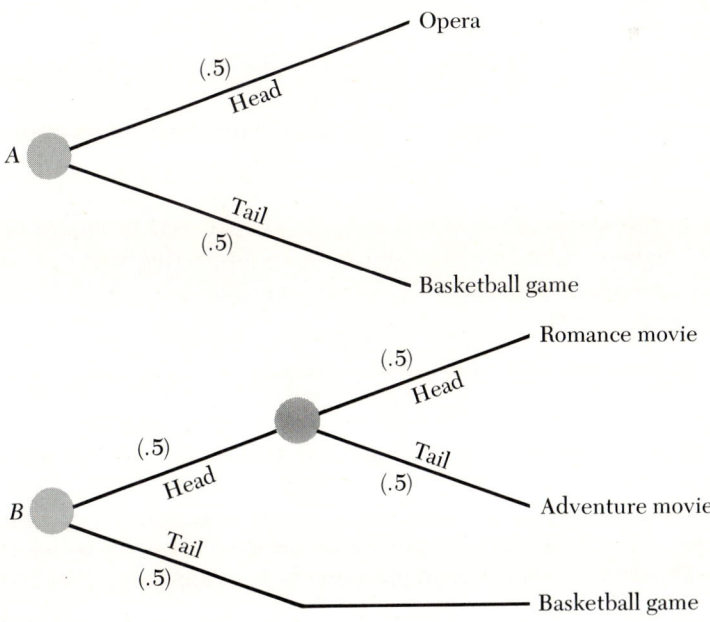

Figure 9-3
An illustration of the assumption of substitutability. The gamble at A is regarded equally as well as the two-stage gamble at B.

decidedly inferior to one where the outcomes are the same but where the probability of winning is greater than 1/2.

9-4 DETERMINING UTILITY VALUES

We are now ready to show how utility values may be assigned to outcomes. Figure 9-4 outlines the procedure for doing this. The numbers are obtained by using a series of gambles between a pair of outcomes.

The process begins with a preference ranking of all outcomes to be considered. The most preferred and least preferred outcomes are determined, and then a gamble between these is used to establish the individual's utilities. We call this a *reference lottery*. It has two events: win, corresponding to achieving the best outcome, and lose, for attaining the worst outcome. Such a gamble is purely *hypothetical* and only provides a framework for assessing utility. The events win and lose do not relate to any events in the actual decision structure and are used to divorce the reference lottery from similar but real gambles. *The probability of winning the hypothetical reference lottery is a variable*, changed according to the attitudes of the decision maker and denoted q.

The initial assignment of utility values for the best and worst outcomes is *completely arbitrary*, so that any numbers may be used. It does not matter what values are chosen; different values for these arbitrary utilities will result in different utility scales. This is just like temperature, where two different and quite arbitrary values are used to define the Fahrenheit and Celsius scales. The choices of 32° Fahrenheit and 0° Celsius for the freezing point of water, with 212°F and 100°C for the boiling point, have resulted in quite different values in the two scales for any particular temperature.

Once the extreme utility values are set, the decision maker then may use the reference lottery to obtain utilities for intermediate outcomes. This is accomplished by varying the win probability q until the decision maker establishes a value of q that serves as a *point of indifference* between achieving that outcome for certain or letting the reward be determined by the reference lottery. That particular value of q makes the reference lottery a gamble equivalent to the intermediate outcome so evaluated. As we have seen, the assumption of continuity makes this possible. We may again add meaning to this procedure by considering the similarities with temperature. The decision-maker's subjective evaluation is analogous to designing a thermometer. A thermometer is designed by determining a core diameter such that a substance such as mercury can rise to various levels in its tubular cavity. For each level of

(1) All outcomes are ranked. A convenient designation is to let a subscript denote the order of preference:

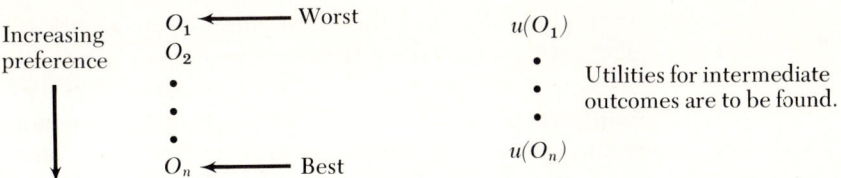

(2) Utilities for best and worst outcomes are arbitrarily assigned:

$u(O_1)$
$\vdots$
$u(O_n)$

Utilities for intermediate outcomes are to be found.

(3) A reference lottery is formulated. This is a gamble having rewards O_n if won and O_1 if lost. The probability of winning the reference lottery q is treated as a variable, to be changed at the will of the decision maker. The reference lottery is strictly hypothetical.

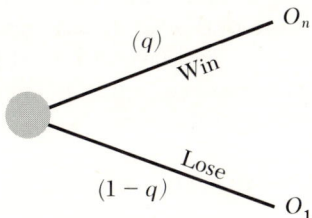

(4) For each intermediate outcome, the decision maker establishes a value of q making him indifferent between the outcome itself and the reference lottery. Thus for outcome O_k a win probability q_k is determined which results in a reference lottery regarded equally as well as O_k.

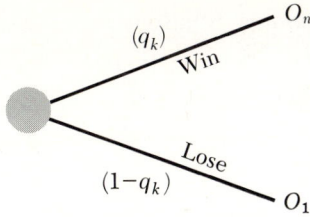

(5) The utility of O_k may be determined. It is equal to the expected utility for the reference lottery with win probability q_k.

$$u(O_k) = q_k u(O_n) + (1 - q_k) u(O_1)$$

Figure 9-4
The procedure for establishing utility values for a set of outcomes.

9-4 DETERMINING UTILITY VALUES

heat, there corresponds a height to which the mercury must rise. With the Celsius scale the 100-degree mark corresponds to the mercury's height when the thermometer is inserted into boiling water. Various levels of heat between freezing and boiling points of water corresponds to marks at prescribed heights above the thermometer's zero mark, allowing heat to be relatively measured in degrees. In an analogous manner, the values of q established to make the decision maker indifferent between respective intermediate outcomes and the reference lottery serve to relatively measure his or her preferences. The indifference values of q are like the markings on a thermometer, where the different outcome preferences are analogous to different levels of heat. These values of q are established through introspection, and they have nothing to do with the actual chance of winning, just as the design of a thermometer is not related to tomorrow's temperature.

Once an indifference value of q has been established for an outcome, its utility value may be determined. This is accomplished by calculating the expected value of the reference lottery with that value of q. Letting O_1 and O_n represent the least and most preferred outcomes, we may then find the utility of an outcome O_k of intermediate preference from

$$u(O_k) = q_k u(O_n) + (1 - q_k) u(O_1)$$

Here q_k is the value of q making the decision maker *indifferent* between the certain achievement of O_k and taking his chances with the reference lottery. The utility value $u(O_k)$ is analogous to a numerical degree value placed beside a marking on a thermometer.

To show how this works we continue with the illustration of Homer Briant contemplating relocation of his small business. He has ranked his preferences for the outcomes of bankruptcy (O_1), decreasing sales (O_2), and increasing sales (O_3). The reference lottery is shown in Figure 9-5.

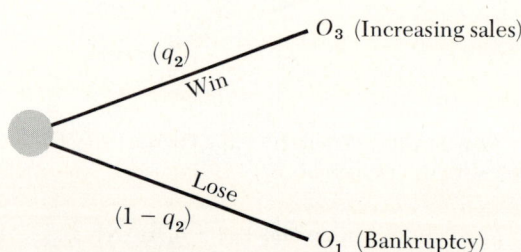

Figure 9-5
The reference lottery for Mr. Briant's decision.

Suppose that the utility values of the extreme outcomes are arbitrarily set at 10 and −5:

$$u(O_3) = 10$$
$$u(O_1) = -5$$

Suppose now that Mr. Briant contemplates the reference lottery in terms of 100 marbles in a box, some labeled W for win and the rest labeled L for lose; a marble will be selected at random, and if it has a W, then he will be guaranteed outcome O_3, increasing sales, but if it is marked with an L, he will go bankrupt with certainty, achieving outcome O_1. He is then asked what number of W marbles he would require before he would be indifferent between facing declining sales, outcome O_2, or taking his chances with the lottery. After considerable thought, Mr. Briant replies that 75 W marbles would make him regard O_2 and the reference lottery equally well. Thus he establishes a reference lottery win probability q_2 that makes it an equivalent gamble to outcome O_2:

$$q_2 = 75/100 = .75$$

From the preceding expression this probability may be used to calculate the utility of declining sales:

$$u(O_2) = q_2 u(O_3) + (1 - q_2) u(O_1)$$
$$= .75(10) + .25(-5)$$
$$= 6.25$$

Attitude Versus Judgment

It must be emphasized that the value $q_2 = .75$ is merely a device used to establish indifference. *The probability selected for winning the lottery has nothing to do with the chance that the most favorable outcome will occur.* In setting $q_2 = .75$, the decision maker is expressing his *attitude* toward one outcome in terms of the rewards of a hypothetical gamble. This value was obtained by looking inward in an attempt to balance his tastes and aspirations between remaining in a declining business or gambling to improve it. He is assumed capable of switching roles from this kind of introspection to that of dispassionate *judgment* when asked later what he believes his actual chance is that moving his business will be a success. To arrive at the probability of success, our decision maker must use his experience and knowledge of such factors as the history of failures by relocated businesses, prevailing economic conditions, and possible competitor reactions.

Suppose that Mr. Briant judges his chance of success after moving to be 1/2. We may now analyze his decision problem by applying the Bayes decision rule with utilities as payoffs. The decision tree diagram is shown in Figure 9-6. The expected utility payoff for the event fork at b is 2.5, which is the utility achieved by moving. Since this value is smaller than the 6.25 utility achieved by remaining in his present location, Homer Briant should not move. Thus we prune the branch corresponding to the act to move and bring the 6.25 utility payoff back to node a.

Utility and the Bayes Decision Rule

This example illustrates why the Bayes decision rule is valid when utility payoffs are used. The basic property (page 242) states that the utility of a gamble is the expected value of the utilities assigned to its rewards. Since any act with uncertain outcomes may be viewed as a gamble, the act providing the greatest utility, and hence the one that must be preferred, is the one with the maximum expected utility payoff. The Bayes decision rule can therefore be viewed as just an extension of utility theory, the criterion serving only to translate one's preferences into a choice of act. Thus Homer Briant decides to stay put because, of the two acts, this provides the greatest utility — which can only be the

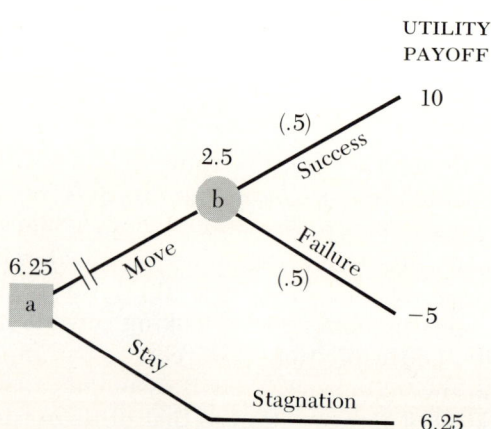

Figure 9-6
Mr. Briant's decision tree diagram showing backward induction analysis with utility payoffs.

case, our theory states, if remaining in the present location is the preferred act. *In arriving at a choice, both the decision-maker's attitudes toward the consequences and his judgment regarding the chances of the events are considered and integrated.* The choice indicated by the Bayes criterion is optimal because it is preferred above all others.

Had some other success probability, say .90, been determined, Mr. Briant would relocate, since doing so would have the highest utility: $.9(10) + .1(-5) = 8.5$. This might be the case, for example, if he learned that his major would-be competitor's business was to be taken over by his incompetent son. Changing the probability of events reflects only the decision-maker's judgment regarding factors influencing their occurrence. Only the expected utilities of uncertain *acts* can be affected by revision of event probabilities. Regardless of the chance of relocation's success, the decision-maker's utilities for the ultimate *outcomes* must remain unchanged. Only a change of taste or attitude can justify revision of these. This might be caused by a death in his family or brought about by a change in personal finances.

THE UTILITY FOR MONEY AND ATTITUDES TOWARD RISK 9-5

Applying the Utility Function in Decision Analysis

The reference lottery may be used to construct a utility function for money. For this purpose we select as the best outcome some amount of money no smaller than the greatest possible payoff. The worst outcome is likewise no larger than the lowest payoff. Monetary outcomes offer some special advantages. The amounts can be measured on a continuous scale, so that the utility function itself will be continuous. This suggests that it may be determined by finding an appropriate smoothed curve relating money values to their utilities. To do this, only a few key dollar amounts and some knowledge of the curve's general shape need be evaluated. The curve obtained by fitting the points so obtained may then serve as an approximation to the utility function.

Such a curve is shown in Figure 9-7 for the Ponderosa Record Company decision of Chapter 5. This utility curve has been derived according to the procedures just described by applying a reference lottery and using a few key monetary amounts as the outcomes. The reference lottery used is between the amounts +$100,000 (for win) and −$75,000 (for lose), which for ease of evaluation are more extreme than

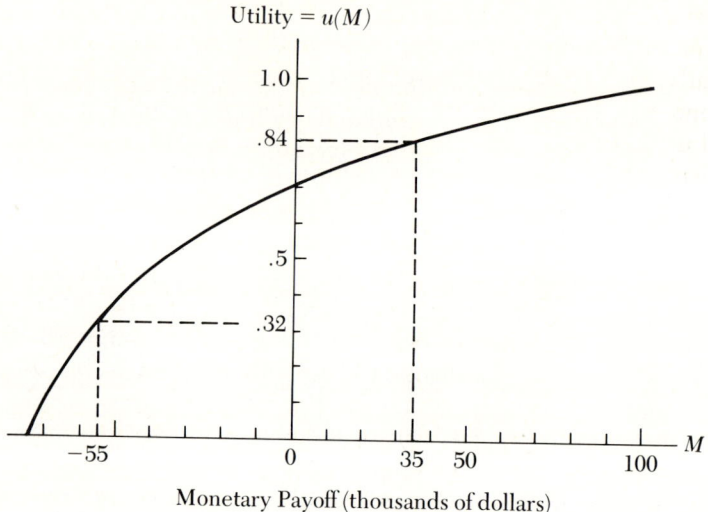

Figure 9-7

The utility function for the president of the Ponderosa Record Company.

any possible payoff. Arbitrary utility values of $u(+\$100{,}000) = 1$ and $u(-\$75{,}000) = 0$ were set for simplicity.

In practice, a utility function is empirically found by personally interviewing the decision maker. It will ordinarily be described graphically rather than by a mathematical equation, with utilities read directly from the curve.

We may use the utility curve in Figure 9-7 to analyze the Ponderosa president's decision problem. The original decision tree diagram is reconstructed in Figure 9-8. The utilities corresponding to each monetary payoff have been obtained from the utility curve. For instance, we find the utilities for the monetary payoffs \$35,000 and −\$55,000 to be .84 and .32, respectively. The backward induction may be performed using utilities instead of dollars. The analysis proceeds in the same fashion as in Chapter 5.

We begin by determining the expected utility for a terminal event fork of the tree. The expected utility of the event fork at branching point e is calculated:

$$.8(.84) + .2(.32) = .736$$

The value .736 is entered above node e and represents the expected utility of the act to market nationally in the fork at c. The choice of acts at decision point c can now be determined. Aborting leads to an outcome utility of .69, which is lower than the .736 expected utility of marketing nationally, so that the abort branch is pruned, and .736 is brought back to be entered above node c. The rest of the backward induction is conducted using utilities instead of dollars, in the usual manner.

Using utilities, we thus find that the optimal choice is to abort. The

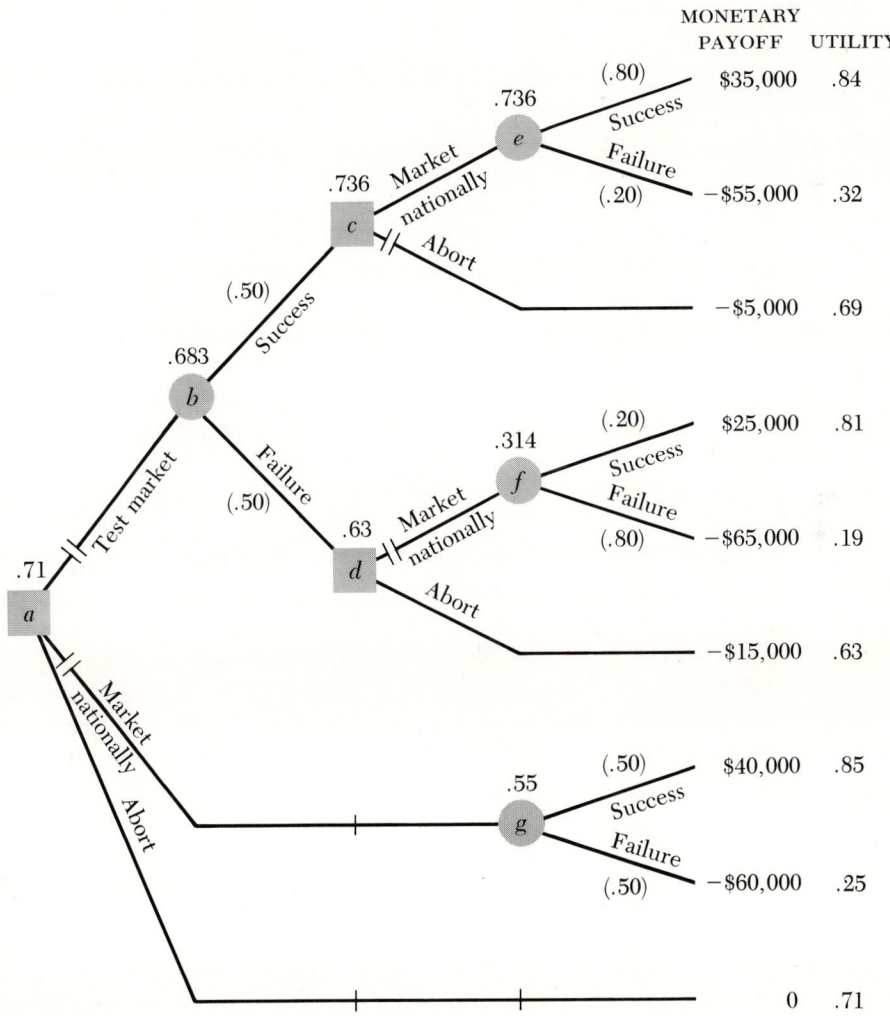

Figure 9-8
The Ponderosa decision tree diagram showing backward induction analysis with utility payoffs.

9-5   THE UTILITY FOR MONEY AND ATTITUDES TOWARD RISK

two alternatives that involve marketing the record are too risky to the president of Ponderosa. Recall that a different conclusion was reached in Chapter 5, where expected monetary values were used. But since utility values express the true worth of monetary outcomes, our latest solution is the valid one to use.

Attitudes Toward Risk
and the Shape of the Utility Curve

The utility function for money may be used as a basis for describing a person's attitudes toward risk. Three basic attitudes have been characterized. The polar cases are the *risk averse* individual, who takes only favorable gambles, and the *risk seeker*, who will pay a premium for the privilege of participating in a gamble. Between these extremes lies the *risk neutral* individual, who assigns the face value of money as its true worth. The utility functions for each basic attitude are shown in Figure 9-9. Each function has a different shape, corresponding to the decision-maker's fundamental outlook. All three utility functions show that utility increases as monetary gain rises. This reflects the underlying assumption of utility theory that utility increases with preference, which is combined with an additional assumption that more money will always increase one's well being, so that the outcomes having greater payoff are more preferred. (This may not be a strictly true assumption, but except for eccentrics, most persons behave in a manner supporting it.)

Throughout most of his or her life, a typical person is risk averse. Such an individual buys plenty of casualty insurance. He or she is typified by a disdain for actions involving high risks — the chance of a large monetary loss. Only a gamble that will yield an expectation of a considerable payoff will be attractive. A risk averse person's marginal utility for money diminishes as the monetary gain becomes larger. Thus the utility curve of the risk averter [Figure 9-9(a)] has decreasing slope as the amounts become larger. Such a curve is *concave* when viewed from below.

The risk seeker's behavior is the opposite. Many of us are risk seekers at some stages of our lives. This attitude is epitomized by the "high roller" whose behavior seems reckless. This person is motivated by the possibility of achieving the maximum reward in any gamble. The risk seeker will prefer *some* gambles having a negative expected monetary payoff to the status quo. The greater the maximum reward, the wider is the risk seeker's divergence from the risk averter's behavior. The risk seeker is typically self-insured, believing that the risk is superior to forgoing money spent on premiums. The risk seeker's marginal utility for

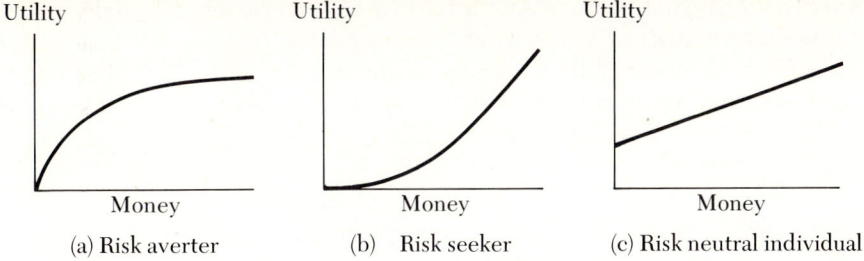

Figure 9-9
A graphical portrayal of utility functions for basic attitudes toward risk.

money is increasing; each additional dollar brings a disproportionately greater sense of well being. Thus the risk seeker's utility curve, shown in Figure 9-9(b), has increasing slope as the monetary gain becomes greater. This curve is *convex* when viewed from below.

Our third characterization of attitude toward risk is that of risk neutrality. A risk neutral individual is one who prizes money at its face value. The utility function for such an individual is thus a straight line, as shown in Figure 9-9(c). His or her utility for a gamble equals the utility of the expected monetary payoff. Such an individual buys no casualty insurance, since the premium charge is greater than the expected loss. Risk neutral behavior is epitomized by individuals with enormous wealth. Decisions of large corporations are often based on the Bayes decision rule applied directly to monetary payoffs, reflecting that increments in dollar assets are valued at their face amount.

Generally, risk neutrality holds true only over a limited range of money values. Many large firms, for example, do not carry casualty insurance. But nearly all giant corporations will insure against extremely large losses; for example, airlines buy hijacking insurance. The same holds true for individuals. Many risk averse persons are risk neutral when the stakes are small. The player in office World Series pools falls into this category; losses are hardly noticeable and winnings allow for indulging in some luxury. (Small gambles may add spice to a person's life—they are a form of entertainment; thus a person might play poker with more skillful persons, where the expected payoff would be negative, just for the fun of it.) That people are risk neutral for small risks is illustrated by their car insurance purchases. Many generally risk averse people have deductible comprehensive coverage on automobile policies, and when their car gets old, usually only the liability coverage is kept. Again this is reflective of risk neutrality over a limited range of monetary outcomes. This does not contradict the curve shapes in Figures

9-9(a) and (b), for throughout a narrow monetary interval each curve can be approximated by a straight-line segment.

Many persons will exhibit both risk averse and risk seeking attitudes depending on the range of monetary values considered. Consider an entrepreneur starting his own business. Here the risks are definitely huge—a lifetime's savings, plenty of hard work, burnt career bridges, a heavy burden of debt, and a significant chance of bankruptcy. A person embarking upon the hard road of self-employment may often be viewed as a risk seeker. He is motivated primarily by the rewards, monetary and otherwise, of being his own boss. Let us take his development to the point where his business is becoming established and he is viewed by his peers as a future pillar of the community. His attitude toward risk will have evolved to a point where he may now be characterized as risk averse. He is much more conservative (there is now something to conserve). Hardly any deal would be imaginable where he would be willing to risk everything he owns to further his wealth.

We can conceive that an individual's attitudes will switch back and forth between risk seeking and risk aversion over time. Usually a risk seeker has some definite goal or *aspiration level,* which a specific level of money will allow him to achieve. A young man needing enough money to buy his first motorcycle might be willing to participate in an unfair gamble if winning would provide sufficient cash for a down payment. The young professional may speculate in volatile stocks until he or she earns enough money to make a down payment on a fancy home. For such risk-seeking people, losing is not much worse than the status quo. But once the goal is achieved, the risk seeker's outlook changes, and with sated appetite he becomes a risk averter, until some new goal enters his horizon.

A utility curve for such an individual is shown in Figure 9-10. The horizontal axis is total wealth, as measured in monetary units, rather than changes in current cash position. Here the utility function is convex until an aspiration level is reached. Until that goal is achieved, the person is risk seeking. Upon reaching his goal the individual becomes a conservative risk averter until more wealth permits germination of a newer, higher order goal. Then the cycle begins all over again with risk seeking, followed by another spell of risk aversion.

Such a curve portrays behavior over a long period of time and is only an idealization of a long-run utility function. A great many factors can cause an individual's attitudes to change over time, and it may not be possible to obtain meaningful measures of the influence of remote goals. Generally a utility curve's validity is very short-lived and will change with factors such as age, life style, family size, and total wealth. To be successfully employed, the utility function ought to be updated prior to each decision.

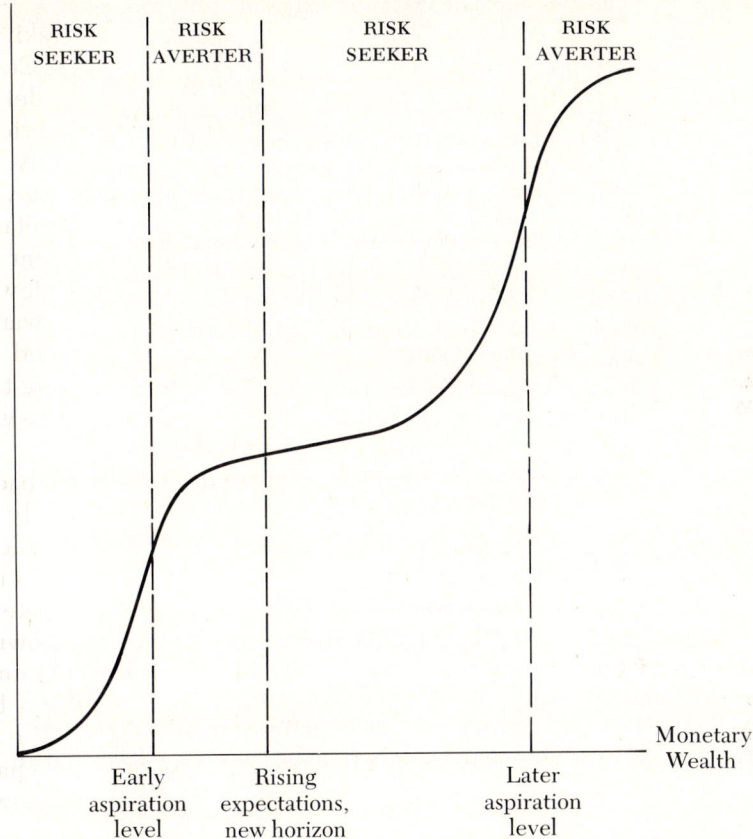

Figure 9-10
A graphical portrayal of evolving utility function for an individual over a long time period.

PROBLEMS

9-1 Suppose that you are offered a gamble by Ms. I. M. Honest, a representative of a foundation studying human behavior. A fair coin is to be tossed. If a head occurs, you will receive $10,000 from Ms. Honest. But if the result is a tail, you must pay her foundation $5000. If you do *not* have $5000, a loan will be arranged, which must be repaid over a five-year period at $150 per month and can be deferred until you have graduated from school.
(a) Calculate your expected profit from participating in this gamble.

(b) Would you be willing to accept Ms. Honest's offer? Does your answer indicate that your marginal utility for money is decreasing?

9-2 Mr. Smith has offered you a deal similar to that of Ms. Honest in Problem 9-1. If a head occurs, he will hand you $1.00. But if the result is a tail, you must pay Mr. Smith $0.50.
(a) Calculate your expected profit by participating in this gamble.
(b) Would you be willing to accept Mr. Smith's offer?

9-3 Suppose a homeowner with a house valued at $40,000 was offered tornado insurance for an annual premium charge of $500. Suppose that there are just two mutually exclusive outcomes, complete damage or none from a tornado, and that the probability of damage from a tornado is .0001.
(a) Construct the homeowner's payoff table for a decision whether to buy tornado insurance.
(b) Calculate the decision-maker's expected monetary payoff for each act. Which has the maximum expected payoff?
(c) Suppose the homeowner decides not to buy tornado insurance. Does this contradict decreasing marginal utility for money? Explain.

9-4 A contractor must determine whether to buy or rent equipment required to do a job up for bid. Because of lead-time requirements in getting the equipment, he must decide before knowing whether the contract is won. If he buys, a contract would result in $120,000 profit, net of equipment resale returns; but should he lose the job, then the equipment will have to be sold at a $40,000 loss. By renting, his profit from the contract, if he wins it, will be only $50,000, but there will be no loss of money if the job is not won. His chances of winning are 50-50. The contractor's utility function is $u(M) = \sqrt{M + 40,000}$.
(a) Construct the contractor's payoff table using profit as the measure.
(b) Calculate the expected profit payoff for each act. According to the Bayes decision rule, what act should he select?
(c) Construct the contractor's payoff table when utilities are used for payoffs.
(d) Calculate the expected utility payoff for each act. Which act provides the maximum expected utility?
(e) Which act should the decision maker choose? Explain.

9-5 Another decision maker has as her utility function for monetary gains, $u(M) = \sqrt{M + 10,000}$. The size of a certain monetary gain that would make her indifferent between two more extreme amounts must have utility equal to the gamble's expected utility, u_g.
(a) Show that she would be indifferent between zero gain and a 50-50 gamble between $30,000 and $-$10,000.

(b) What amount of certain monetary gain would make her indifferent between it and a 50-50 gamble with rewards $80,000 or $-$7500? Use the fact that $M = (u(M))^2 - 10,000$.

(c) What is the most she would be willing to pay as the annual premium for an insurance policy covering theft of her coin collection, valued at $10,000, if the chance of a theft sometime during the year were .1? If the probability were .01? If the probability were .001?

9-6 Consider the following outcomes that you may achieve; no rights are transferable.
- 100 new records of your choice
- A grade of C on the next examination covering utility
- A year's assignment to Timbuktu, Mali
- Confinement to an airport during a three-day storm
- A month of free telephone calls to anywhere

(a) Rank these in ascending order of preference, designating them O_1, O_2, O_3, O_4, and O_5.

(b) Let the utilities be $u(O_1) = 0$ for the worst outcome and $u(O_5) = 100$ for the best. Consider a box containing 1000 marbles, some labeled Win, the remainder labeled Lose. If a Win marble is selected at random from the box, you will achieve O_5. If a Lose marble is chosen, you attain O_1. Determine how many marbles of each type would make you indifferent between gambling or achieving O_2. Determine the same for O_3 and O_4.

(c) The corresponding probabilities q_k of winning may be determined by dividing the respective number of Win marbles by 1000. Use these to calculate $u(O_2)$, $u(O_3)$, and $u(O_4)$.

9-7 Suppose that Alvin Black's attitude toward risk is generally averse. For each of the following 50-50 gambling propositions indicate whether he (1) would be willing, (2) might desire, or (3) would be unwilling to participate. Explain the reasons for your choices.
(a) $10,000 versus $0.
(b) $10,000 versus $-$1000.
(c) $15,000 versus $-$10,000.
(d) $500 versus $-$600.
(e) $20,000 versus $10,000.

9-8 Lucille Brown is risk neutral. Would she buy comprehensive coverage on her automobile if she agreed with company actuaries regarding the probability distribution of future claim sizes? Explain.

9-9 Victor White is a risk seeker. Does this necessarily imply that he will never buy casualty insurance? Explain.

9-10 Suppose that the record maker discussed has a utility function for money $u(M) = [(M + 65,000)/10,000]^2$.
(a) Redraw Figure 9-8 and calculate the utility for each end position.

(b) Perform backward induction analysis using the new utilities you have calculated. Which strategy is optimal?

(c) On a piece of graph paper plot the utilities calculated in part (a) as a function of monetary payoffs M. Sketch a curve through the points. Of what attitude toward risk is the shape of your curve indicative?

9-11 J. P. Tidewasser has just undergone the first traumatic phase of determining his utility function for a range of money values. By his response to a series of gambles, it has been established that he is indifferent between the 50-50 gambles listed below and receiving the certain amounts of money shown on the right.

Rewards of Gamble		Equivalent Amount
+$30,000	−$10,000	$ 0
+ 30,000	0	+ 10,000
0	− 10,000	− 7,000
+ 10,000	− 7,000	− 1,000

(a) If he sets $u(\$30,000) = 1$ and $u(-\$10,000) = 0$, then determine what his utility should be for $0.
(b) Calculate his utilities for +$10,000 and −$7,000.
(c) Calculate his utility for +$1,000. Do you notice any inconsistencies between this and previous answers?

9-12 Hoopla Hoops is a retail boutique catering to current crazes. The owner must decide whether or not to stock a batch of Water Wheelies. Each item costs $2.00 and sells for $4.00. Unsold items cannot be returned to the supplier, who sells them in batches of 500. The following probability distribution is assumed to apply for the demand to be experienced for Water Wheelies:

Demand	Probability
100	.05
200	.10
300	.15
400	.20
500	.20
600	.15
700	.10
800	.05
	1.00

By demand we mean the potential for sales. No more than what is demanded may be sold; but if demand exceeds on-hand inventory, then not all of it can be fulfilled.

(a) Calculate the expected demand. If you assume that the expected demand were actually to occur, what profit corresponds to this amount? Using the utility curve in Figure 9-11, determine the utility value that corresponds.

(b) Calculate the expected profit from stocking 500 Water Wheelies. Does this differ from the amount found in part (a)? Explain this. Also, determine the utility value for the expected profit.

(c) Calculate the expected utility for stocking 500 Water Wheelies. (First, calculate the profit for each level of possible demand; then find the utility of each; finally, apply the probability weights.) Which act, stocking or not stocking Water Wheelies, provides the greatest expected utility?

(d) Compare your utility values from (a), (b), and (c). Do these differ? Explain. Which one applies?

9-13 Suppose that a person faced with the decision structure provided in Figure 5-5 (p. 163) has the utility function shown in Figure 9-12. Answer the following:

(a) Redraw the decision tree diagram of Figure 5-5, entering the appropriate probability values on the corresponding branches.

(b) For each end position's monetary payoff value determine the decision-maker's approximate utility values from the curve in Figure 9-12.

(c) Perform backward induction analysis using utilities as payoffs. Which strategy is optimal?

9-14 Consider the plight of the decision maker in Problem 5-9 (p. 162). She must interview dozens of candidates annually for keypunching jobs. Losses of her recoverable training expenses can therefore be significant. Suppose that she has constructed the utility function shown in Figure 9-11. Answer the following:

(a) Redraw Figure 5-6.

(b) For each end position's monetary payoff value determine the decision-maker's approximate utility values from the curve in Figure 9-11.

(c) Perform backward induction analysis using utilities as payoffs. Which strategy is optimal?

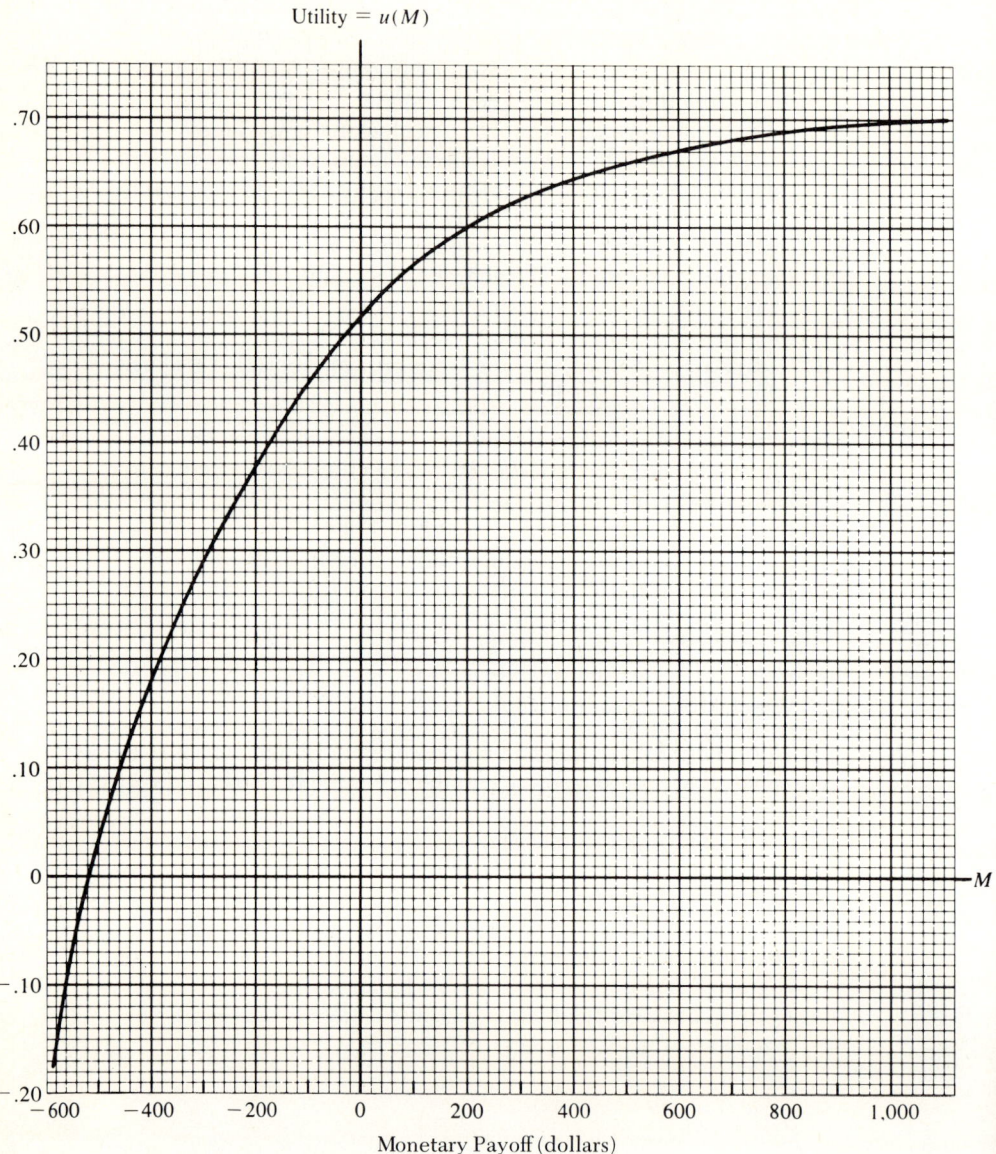

Figure 9-11

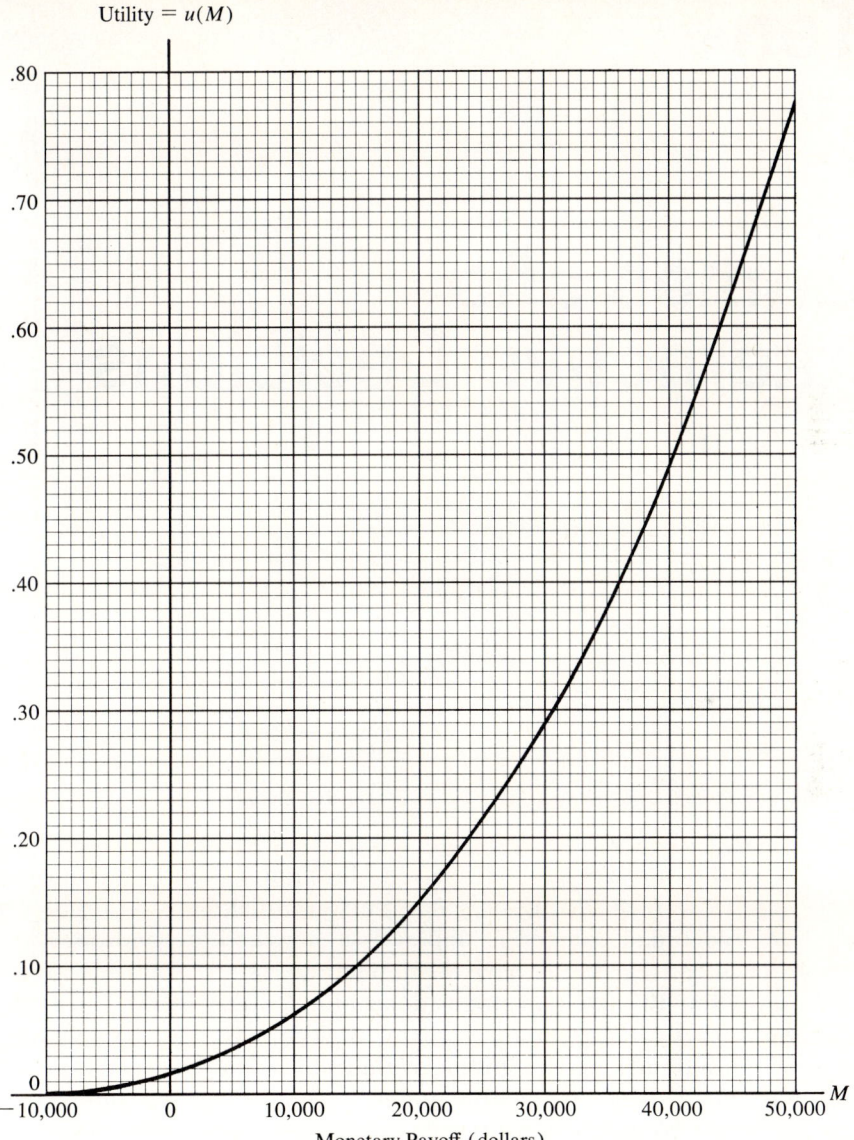

Figure 9-12

Ten

Games and Interactive Decisions

So far we have discussed decision-making situations in which choices are made by only one person. Such decision problems fall into two broad categories depending on whether conditions are certain or uncertain. As we have seen, when decisions are made under uncertainty the ultimate outcome is determined jointly by the particular act chosen and by whatever uncertain event occurs. Uncertain events are generated randomly and might be called *nature's choices*. We might therefore view decision making under uncertainty as an interactive process with two participants, the decision maker and nature.

10-1 INTERACTIVE DECISION MAKING AND GAME THEORY

This chapter is concerned with *interactive decision making* involving more than one person. Outcomes are thus determined by whatever combination of actions results from the independent choices of several individual decision makers. Many important business decisions involve interaction between two or more participants. Interaction often occurs in the pricing of products, where a firm's ultimate sales are determined not only by the levels it selects but also by the prices its competitors set. The interaction between several decision makers is also felt in operational issues. Television provides a good example. In recent years, networks have found program success to be largely dependent upon what the competition presents in the same time slot; the outcomes of one network's programming decisions have therefore been increasingly influenced by the corresponding decisions made by other networks. Even financial planning involves interactive decision making. The success of a business tax strategy depends in large measure on the position taken by the Internal Revenue Service regarding the expenses that may be disallowed.

When two or more persons collectively determine the outcomes, decision-making analysis takes on added complexity. Good decision making requires not only evaluation of personal alternatives, but also investigation of the opponent's or competitor's possible choices. A certain amount of second-guessing and role playing is required. Interactive decision making is much like a parlor game, such as chess, *Monopoly*, or bridge. In establishing a winning strategy, successful players must empathize with their opponents' positions and try to anticipate their actions. The need to consider the other person's goals and choices distinguishes interactive decision making from ordinary decisions under uncertainty, in which the only opponent is nature, who chooses randomly. In the latter situations, it is obviously pointless for us to rationalize why nature will choose a particular event or how the occurrence of that event might be influenced by our actions. (We exclude decisions made about how to influence the environment or weather.)

Within the past 40 years an analytical framework for interactive decision making based on investigations of game situations has been developed. This effort was pioneered by John von Neumann and Oskar Morgenstern, culminating in 1947 with their book *Theory of Games and Economic Behavior*. As an area of academic study, *game theory* has provided a series of mathematical models that are quite useful in explaining interactive decision-making concepts. But as a practical tool, game theory is severely limited in scope. As we shall see, the situations that may be analyzed by game theory must be extremely simple. For instance, most parlor games, such as chess, have not yet been thoroughly analyzed mathematically and might never be; even computerized systems cannot beat a competent human in chess, much less Bobby Fisher. And chess is orders of magnitude less complex than many interactive decisions encountered in business. Although in certain special situations game-theoretical principles can be used directly to make optimal decisions, the primary value of game theory is the conceptual framework it provides in explaining interactive decision making.

The simplest game to analyze involves two players who must each make exactly one choice from his or her own set of alternatives. The game's outcome depends only on the particular pair of acts selected. Each player receives a numerical payoff depending on the outcome they collectively determine.

Example from the Battle of the Bismarck Sea

A vivid illustration of such a game situation may be taken from the Battle of the Bismarck Sea during World War II.

> In the critical stages of the struggle for New Guinea, intelligence reports indicated that the Japanese would move a troop and supply convoy from the port of Rabaul at the eastern tip of New Britain to Lae, which lies just west of New Britain on New Guinea. It could travel either north of New Britain, where poor visibility was almost certain, or south of the island, where the weather would be clear; in either case, the trip would take three days. General Kenney had the choice of concentrating the bulk of his reconnaissance aircraft on one route or the other. Once sighted, the convoy could be bombed until its arrival at Lae. In days of bombing time, Kenney's staff estimated the following outcomes for the various choices:*

TABLE 10-1

KENNEY'S STRATEGIES	JAPANESE STRATEGIES	
	Northern Route	*Southern Route*
Northern Route	2	2
Southern Route	1	3

Which routes should the two opponents have chosen? By going north, the Japanese commander could have been no worse off than if he instead took the southern route; the northern route also provided the best of the worst possible exposures to bombing. General Kenney's choice was also clear; by concentrating his forces in the north, he could guarantee having two full bombing days. As it turned out, both commanders selected the northern alternatives. As we shall see, their choices were consistent with the principles of game theory.

* This example was developed by O. G. Haywood, Jr., and the above quote is taken from R. Duncan Luce and Howard Raiffa, *Games and Decisions* (New York: Wiley, 1958), pp. 64–65.

TWO-PERSON ZERO-SUM GAMES 10-2

Another detailed example will be helpful to clarify the principles of game theory. Consider the case of Ms. Gray and Mr. Flannel, two bored rail commuters who while-away the mind-numbing hours by playing several games of Color-Bland daily. To play this game each player writes a color on a slip of paper. Patriotically, each participant may choose red, white, or blue. Depending on the colors chosen, varying numbers of pennies will be exchanged. The payoff amounts used by Gray and Flannel are determined before playing each game of Color-Bland by a formula based on how many cars of the respective colors are seen by each person between stations (Ms. Gray looks out the left side and Mr. Flannel uses the right). Between Dullstone and Blahsburg, Table 10-2 was constructed; the amounts shown are what Ms. Gray receives from Mr. Flannel (a negative figure represents a payment to Flannel).

Table 10-2

MS. GRAY'S COLOR-BLAND PAYOFF TABLE (AMOUNTS IN CENTS)

		MR. FLANNEL'S ACTS		
		Red	White	Blue
MS. GRAY'S ACTS	Red	−3	2	5
	White	−2	1	6
	Blue	−3	−3	−7

Color-Bland is the simplest type of game encountered. The gain of one player is matched by a corresponding loss to the opponent. Mr. Flannel's payoff table would involve identical amounts to Ms. Gray's with the signs reversed. For instance, if both players select red, Ms. Gray's payoff is −3 and Mr. Flannel's is +3, because she then pays him 3 cents; if both choose white, Mr. Flannel pays Ms. Gray 1 cent, so her payoff is +1 and his is −1. Since the payoffs for either player provide all the essential information, only one player's payoff table is required to evaluate the decisions. By convention, the payoff table for the player listed at the left is used for this purpose. Regardless of outcome, Mr. Flannel's payoff will always be the negative of Ms. Gray's, so that the two players' respective payoffs sum to zero. For this reason, Color-Bland is referred to as a *two-person zero-sum game.*

Analyzing the Decision: Minimax Principle

We now consider the respective acts that Ms. Gray and Mr. Flannel should choose. Our clue as to how these choices should be made may be taken from the Bismark Sea example, where the opposing commanders each selected that act whose worst outcome was best. Such a decision-making criterion is referred to as the *minimax principle,* and for two-person zero-sum games it always leads to the most preferred choices for both players.

Returning to the Color-Bland game, consider Mr. Flannel's choices. His losses or payments to Ms. Gray are represented in Table 10-3 by the quantities in the respective *column* for each of his color-choice acts. Wanting to minimize his long-run losses from playing the game, we may assume that Mr. Flannel wants to keep his payments to Ms. Gray as small as possible. He should therefore focus on the *circled* numbers; these are the *column maximums* that represent the greatest payments he might have to make to Ms. Gray. The smallest of these losses is −2, occurring when Mr. Flannel chooses red and Ms. Gray picks white; regardless of what Ms. Gray selects, by choosing red Flannel can do no worse than lose minus two cents (receive 2¢). Mr. Flannel's red choice

Table 10-3

MS. GRAY'S COLOR-BLAND PAYOFF TABLE

		MR. FLANNEL'S ACTS			
		Red	White	Blue	Row minimum
MS. GRAY'S ACTS	Red	☐−3☐	⊙2⊙	5	−3
	White	⊙−2⊙	1	⊙6⊙	−2 ←Maximin payoff
	Blue	−3	−3	☐−7☐	−7
Column maximum		−2 ↑ Minimax loss	2	6	

is called his *minimax loss act* since its column has the minimum of the maximum possible payments to his opponent.

The possible payoffs to Ms. Gray for each of her color choice acts are provided in the corresponding *rows*. We may assume that she views the game similarly and wants to have her receipts from Flannel as large as possible. Since the payoffs given in Table 10-3 are what she receives, she is concerned with the *boxed* quantities, which represent the *row minimums*. She can do no worse than receive one of these values, and the best of them occurs for her choice of white; this is a payoff of -2 occurring when Mr. Flannel chooses red. We refer to her choice of white as Ms. Gray's *maximin payoff act* because its row contains the maximum of her minimum possible payoffs from her opponent.

Had the payoffs been originally given from Mr. Flannel's point of view, then all the signs in Table 10-3 would have been reversed and the numbers would represent payments to him. A choice of white by Ms. Gray would then be the act with the smallest of her greatest possible payments to Mr. Flannel, so that her white would also be her minimax loss act. Because one player's loss is always another player's gain, a feature of zero-sum games is that *one player's minimax loss act must be identical to that same person's maximin payoff act*. Thus, Mr. Flannel's choice of red is the same act that maximizes his own minimum potential gains.

For this particular Color-Bland game, Ms. Gray should choose white and Mr. Flannel ought to select red. Both participants would thereby be acting in accordance with the minimax principle of keeping their maximum losses to the other player as small as possible. It is easy to argue why no other criterion should be used for this game.

By choosing his minimax loss act (red), Mr. Flannel guarantees himself a gain of at least two cents (loss of $-2¢$) regardless of the color picked by Ms. Gray. There is no advantage for him to choose another color such as blue with a potentially larger gain of seven cents (loss of $-7¢$) when Ms. Gray also chooses blue; that amount cannot be guaranteed since Ms. Gray could reverse the take by picking red or white. Similarly, Ms. Gray can guarantee herself a payoff of at least $-2¢$ by choosing her maximin payoff act (white). Mr. Flannel can make her outcome worse if she chooses any other color. In following the minimax principle, neither player can sabotage the plans of the opponent without doing himself unnecessary harm.

Saddle Points and Value of Game

Notice in Table 10-3 that the quantity -2 in the white row and red column is both boxed and circled. It is both the minimum of the column maximums and the maximum of the row minimums. We refer to this value as a *saddle point*, since it is the minimum value in its row and the maximum quantity in its column. Games having saddle points exhibit special features.

Even if the game is played repeatedly, no participant can advantageously deviate for very long from the minimax principle. Each player will always choose the same act, the one that provides minimax loss to the other player and, at the same time, maximin payoff to himself. The two acts so obtained are referred to as the *equilibrium act-pair*. As long as either player stays with one of these acts, it is of no advantage for the other player to choose any other act.

When a saddle point is present, it is easy to find the *value of the game*. This quantity is the payoff amount in the saddle point position. For the foregoing Color-Bland game we have

$$\text{Value of the game} = -2 \text{ cents} \quad (\text{to Gray})$$

The game's value is always expressed from the point of view of the participant whose receipts appear in the payoff table (and whose acts are listed on the left). In this example, the value to Ms. Gray is minus two cents, since that would be her payoff when both players use the minimax criterion.

Other Features in Two-Person Zero-Sum Games

The examples considered so far involve competitive situations in which each player has the same kind and number of acts to choose from. This need not be so. One player can have more acts, as in the game with the payoffs shown in Table 10-4. There player A has only three possible choices, while player B has five. Also, opponents may have different types of acts. In Color-Bland, one player might pick green, yellow, or orange, while the other selects red, white, or blue. In some competitive

Table 10-4

A PAYOFF TABLE FOR A GAME INVOLVING MORE CHOICES FOR ONE PLAYER

		B_1	B_2	B_3	B_4	B_5
	A_1	1	2	4	5	0
PLAYER A'S ACTS	A_2	3	3	4	5	4
	A_3	4	③	5	5	6

PLAYER B'S ACTS

situations, opponent's alternatives are not remotely similar. For example, a firm in a regulated industry may be considering alternative *price levels* for a particular product, while at the same time government officials are selecting *allowable rates of return* on invested capital. The company's future financial position obviously depends on its pricing choice and the rate of return selected by the government. Although it would be hard to put such a situation into a game framework, analogous disparities in types of player choices exist in simple games too.

The game in Table 10-4 exhibits a saddle point, when player A chooses act A_3 and player B selects act B_2. This same game has another saddle point (and we leave it as an exercise for you to find). When a game has several saddle points, the corresponding payoff quantities must all be identical, and each one equals the value of the game.

More perplexing are games *without a saddle point*. We next consider how such a game should be played.

MIXED STRATEGIES IN GAMES WITHOUT A SADDLE POINT 10-3

Suppose that the bored commuters continue their contest from Blahsburg to Gotham City, and that en route their car counts result in the new game of Color-Bland summarized in Table 10-5. This game does

Table 10-5

MS. GRAY'S NEW PAYOFF TABLE

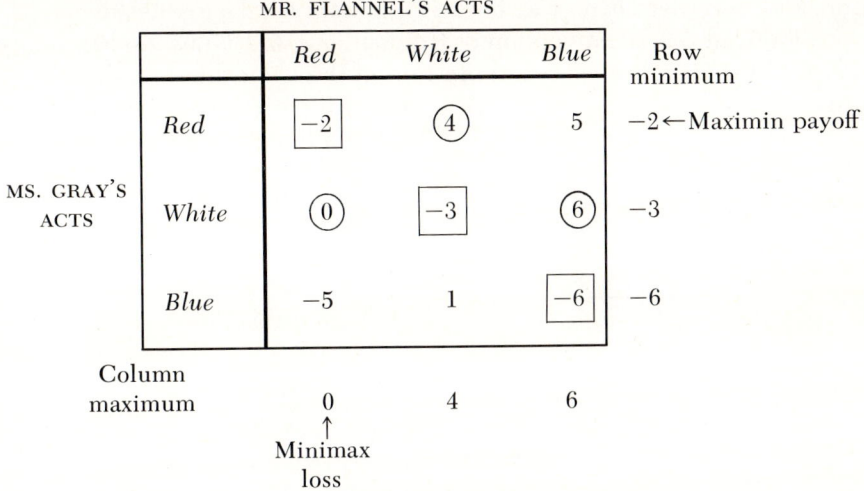

not have a saddle point, since no payoff is both largest in its column and smallest in its row. Ms. Gray's maximin act is to choose red, and Mr. Flannel's minimax loss act is also to pick red.

Would they each apply the minimax criterion? Consider first Ms. Gray, who thinking that Mr. Flannel will pick red, might plausibly choose to play white instead, thereby achieving for herself the better payoff of zero. Guessing she will do this, Flannel would switch to white, giving Gray a worse payoff. But Gray, knowing what Flannel is guessing, can choose to pick red to his white, dramatically improving her outcome. But Flannel is no dummy, for he knows that she knows what he should be guessing, and he would pick red versus her red. Knowing all of this, Gray should pick white instead of red, and the second-guessing begins all over again.

There is no single act that one player can choose to guarantee either one the best of the worst outcomes. Since this game does not have a saddle point, there is no equilibrium act-pair.

The Mixed Strategy

Game theory seeks to remove all the players' guesswork by indicating an optimal course of action for each. When there is a saddle point a player can base his choice of act upon the predictability of his opponent. In games without saddle points, paradoxically, the guesswork can be eliminated only by *removing* all elements of predictability. And the only way for a player to confuse an opponent is to not know himself what act he will choose. This can be accomplished if each player selects his or her act randomly. Even if such a game is played the same way repeatedly, random selection of acts will provide no pattern for prediction, and thus there is no way for the opponent to take undue advantage.

Thus, in the latest version of Color-Bland, Ms. Gray and Mr. Flannel might each roll a six-sided die to find the color they should select. For instance, Ms. Gray might choose red if the die toss results in a one or two, white if a three or four, and blue if a five or six. Since each die has six equally likely faces, each potential color act would have probability one-third, so that the following decision rule applies for Ms. Gray.

Ms. Gray Chooses Act	*With Probability*
Red	$P_R = 1/3$
White	$P_W = 1/3$
Blue	$P_B = 1/3$

Such a rule is referred to as a *mixed strategy*, because any one of several acts might be chosen.

For games with a saddle point each player will choose just one act. When a single act is selected, it is sometimes referred to as a *pure strategy* (and is a special case of the mixed strategy where that act has probability one and all others probability zero).

Similarly, Mr. Flannel might apply his rule so that he picks red if his die results in the one face, white if it shows two through five, and blue if it comes up six. His mixed strategy would be

Mr. Flannel Chooses Act	With Probability
Red	$Q_R = 1/6$
White	$Q_W = 4/6$
Blue	$Q_B = 1/6$

Notice that Mr. Flannel's probabilities can differ from Ms. Gray's. By convention we will use subscripted Ps to denote the probabilities for that player whose payoffs appear directly in the payoff table (and whose acts are listed on the left): subscripted Qs represent the probabilities for the other player. The symbols are necessary because each player must select an optimal mixed strategy and, thus, the Ps and Qs must be treated as variables.

Because we now have uncertainty present, each player must evaluate his or her strategy in terms of expected payoff or expected loss. The calculations for obtaining Ms. Gray's expected payoff are shown in Table 10-6.

First, the original amounts in each payoff table row are multiplied by the probability that Ms. Gray will choose the act in that row. The products are then summed one column at a time, so that the resulting subtotals provide Ms. Gray's expected payoffs *given* Mr. Flannel's color choice. Those calculations provide

Mr. Flannel's choice:	Red	White	Blue
Ms. Gray's expected payoff:	−7/3¢	2/3¢	5/3¢

Since Mr. Flannel's acts are also chosen randomly, the final step is to multiply each subtotal by Mr. Flannel's corresponding probability Q for that color-choice act and then to sum the resulting products. Under these initial strategies, Ms. Gray's expected payoff is 1/3¢. This means that after repeatedly playing this version of Color-Bland, Ms. Gray would expect to achieve an average payoff of one-third of a cent.

Table 10-6

**MS. GRAY'S EXPECTED PAYOFF CALCULATIONS
WHEN BOTH PLAYERS USE INITIAL MIXED STRATEGIES**

MS. GRAY'S ACTS	PROBABILITIES	$P \times$ Payoff MR. FLANNEL'S ACTS		
		Red	White	Blue
Red	$P_R = 1/3$	−2/3	4/3	5/3
White	$P_W = 1/3$	0	−3/3	6/3
Blue	$P_B = 1/3$	−5/3	1/3	−6/3
	Subtotals	−7/3	2/3	5/3
Mr. Flannel's Probabilities		$Q_R = 1/6$	$Q_W = 4/6$	$Q_B = 1/6$
	$Q \times$ Subtotal	−7/18	8/18	5/18
		Expected payoff $= -7/18 + 8/18 + 5/18$ $= 6/18 = 1/3$		

The above amount is deceptive, since it reflects Ms. Gray's expected winnings only if Mr. Flannel plays the above mixed strategy. However, he can dramatically worsen her situation by simply changing his strategy. For instance, if Mr. Flannel makes a certain choice of red, her expected payoff would be −7/3¢ (worse by nearly 3¢). As we have seen with the earlier games, a player should assume the worst from an opponent. Ms. Gray might improve her situation by changing strategies. What is her best mixed strategy? We may suppose that *Ms. Gray's goal is to maximize her expected payoff, regardless of the strategy Mr. Flannel chooses.* The *minimax theorem,* proved by von Neumann, tells us that it is possible for Ms. Gray to achieve this goal. An identical conclusion applies as well to Mr. Flannel, who may minimize his maximum expected loss (payment) to Ms. Gray through judicious selection of his own strategy — again, regardless of how Ms. Gray plays the game.

Before showing how the players may find their optimal strategies, we will introduce a shortcut that permits us to simplify considerably the required mathematics.

Elimination of Inadmissible Acts

In Chapter 5, we first showed how some acts in a decision problem can be eliminated at the outset before any further analysis is required. The decision structure is thereby simplified because a smaller number of acts can be considered. We have called these *inadmissible acts*, since they would never be chosen. We may extend this concept to games. Should a player have an act inferior to another act regardless of the choice his opponent might make, then that act is inadmissible.

Consider the latest Color-Bland game. For convenience, the payoffs are repeated in Table 10-7. It is easy to see that Ms. Gray would never choose blue, as that act provides smaller payoffs than red does for each of Mr. Flannel's color choices. Ms. Gray's red act *dominates* her blue one, making blue inadmissible. Thus, Ms. Gray would never choose blue under any circumstance, and its row may therefore be crossed out of the payoff table. Likewise, consider Mr. Flannel's blue color-choice act. Ignoring the last row, we see that his blue provides greater payoffs to Ms. Gray than either red or white do, no matter what action she takes. Mr. Flannel's red and white both dominate his blue, which is thus inadmissible. The blue column can be crossed out. The remaining rows and columns are all admissible, so that the reduced payoff table must be analyzed further.

Table 10-7

MS. GRAY'S PAYOFF TABLE WITH INADMISSIBLE ACTS ELIMINATED

		MR. FLANNEL'S ACTS		
		Red	White	Blue
MS. GRAY'S ACTS	Red	−2	4	5
	White	0	−3	6
	Blue	−5	1	−6	Inadmissible

Inadmissible

Notice that the blue column does not become inadmissible until the blue row gets eliminated, because the −6 in the blue-blue position is smaller than the blue-white payoff of 1 and the blue-red payoff of −5, making blue a better choice for Mr. Flannel than red or white should Ms. Gray actually make a blunder by picking blue. Thus, we see that whenever a row is crossed out, all columns must be evaluated again, or vice versa, before stopping.

In games with saddle points, successive elimination of inadmissible acts crosses out all rows and columns except those representing equilibrium act-pairs. In some games it is possible for an entry to be both the minimum value in its row and the maximum value in its column

10-3 MIXED STRATEGIES IN GAMES WITHOUT A SADDLE POINT

and yet lie in the row or column of an inadmissible act. Although such an entry is technically a saddle point, it cannot correspond to an equilibrium act-pair. In games with several saddle points there may be ties (but not necessarily so) for equilibrium act-pairs. Before determining the latter, *be sure to check all saddle points to see if any lie in inadmissible rows or columns.*

10-4 OPTIMAL MIXED STRATEGIES FOR ZERO-SUM GAMES

We are left with the 2×2 game in Table 10-8, where each player has just two acts to choose from. We must now find act probabilities for each player. To simplify things, we observe that all Ps and all Qs must sum to 1, and that P_B and Q_B are now zero. It follows that

$$P_W = 1 - P_R$$
$$Q_W = 1 - Q_R$$

so that only two quantities, P_R and Q_R, are unknown

Table 10-8

MS. GRAY'S PAYOFFS FOR COLOR-BLAND REDUCED TO A 2 × 2 GAME

		MR. FLANNEL'S ACTS	
		Q_R	$1 - Q_R$
		Red	White
MS. GRAY'S ACTS — P_R	Red	-2	4
$1 - P_R$	White	0	-3

We begin by evaluating Ms. Gray's possible strategies. Here expected payoff depends on the color Mr. Flannel picks and may be calculated for any value of P_R using the payoffs in the applicable column of the payoff table. These may be expressed as

$$-2P_R + 0(1 - P_R) = -2P_R \quad \text{(if Flannel picks red)}$$
$$4P_R - 3(1 - P_R) = -3 + 7P_R \quad \text{(if Flannel picks white)}$$

Graphical Solution

The procedure and rationale for finding the players' respective optimal mixed strategies may easily be explained by means of a graph. Figure 10-1 shows how Ms. Gray's expected payoffs vary with each possible level for P_R, which can range from zero to one.

Consider first the case in which Mr. Flannel picks red, so that only the first column of the payoff table applies. If Ms. Gray used $P_R = 0$, she will be certain to choose white, and her expected payoff of 0 is obtained from the bottom cell in the red column of Table 10-8; this provides the point on the origin in the graph. At the other extreme, she might use $P_R = 1$, in which case her expected payoff is -2, appearing in the top cell

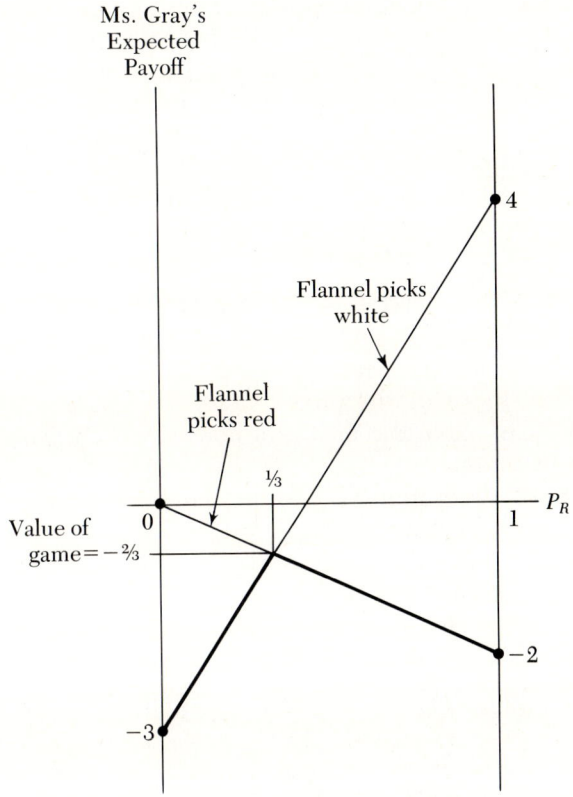

Figure 10-1
A graphical representation to explain Ms. Gray's optimal mixed strategy.

10-4 OPTIMAL MIXED STRATEGIES FOR ZERO-SUM GAMES

in the red column of her payoff table; this corresponds to a second point, at the bottom of the graph on the right side. The straight line connecting these two points provides her expected payoffs for all levels of P_R between 0 and 1, assuming that Mr. Flannel chooses red.

Should Mr. Flannel instead choose white, then the expected payoffs of -3 when $P_R = 0$ and 4 when $P_R = 1$ appear in the white column of the payoff table. The line connecting the two corresponding points on the graph provides Ms. Gray's expected payoff for all levels of P_R between 0 and 1.

What value should Ms. Gray choose for P_R? Remember that she wants to guarantee herself the largest expected payoff regardless of what her opponent does. Thus we must consider how Mr. Flannel would behave were he to know Ms. Gray's P_R value. Notice that the two expected payoff lines in Figure 10-1 cross at $P_R = 1/3$. Suppose Ms. Gray picks a smaller red probability, such as 1/4. Knowing this, Mr. Flannel would choose white, as that act provides Ms. Gray with the lower expected payoff line. On the other hand, if she uses a P_R value greater than 1/3, such as 2/3, then Mr. Flannel will choose to play red, which corresponds in that case to the lowest line. Mr. Flannel can effectively limit Ms. Gray's expected payoffs to those points on the heavy line segments meeting at $P_R = 1/3$. There she receives her greatest expected payoff, where the lines cross. Using $P_R = 1/3$ she will receive the same expected payoff regardless of the act Mr. Flannel chooses:

$$-2P_R = -2(1/3) = -2/3 \quad \text{(if Flannel picks red)}$$
$$-3 + 7P_R = -3 + 7(1/3) = -2/3 \quad \text{(if Flannel picks white)}$$

Unfortunately for Ms. Gray, this particular Color-Bland game is not in her favor. But by using the mixed strategy with $P_R = 1/3$ and $P_W = 1 - P_R = 2/3$ she can make the best of a poor situation. This then is her optimal mixed strategy.

We must still determine Mr. Flannel's optimal mixed strategy. This is tantamount to finding his best level for Q_R. Using the applicable rows of the payoff table, we may express Mr. Flannel's expected payoffs in terms of this unknown quantity by

$$-2Q_R + 4(1 - Q_R) = 4 - 6Q_R \quad \text{(if Gray picks red)}$$
$$0Q_R - 3(1 - Q_R) = -3 + 3Q_R \quad \text{(if Gray picks white)}$$

Figure 10-2 shows the graph that corresponds with separate lines plotted (as before) for each of Ms. Gray's possible color choices. Mr. Flannel wants to minimize Ms. Gray's expected payoff (his expected loss). By knowing his level for Q_R, she can effectively limit the game's outcome

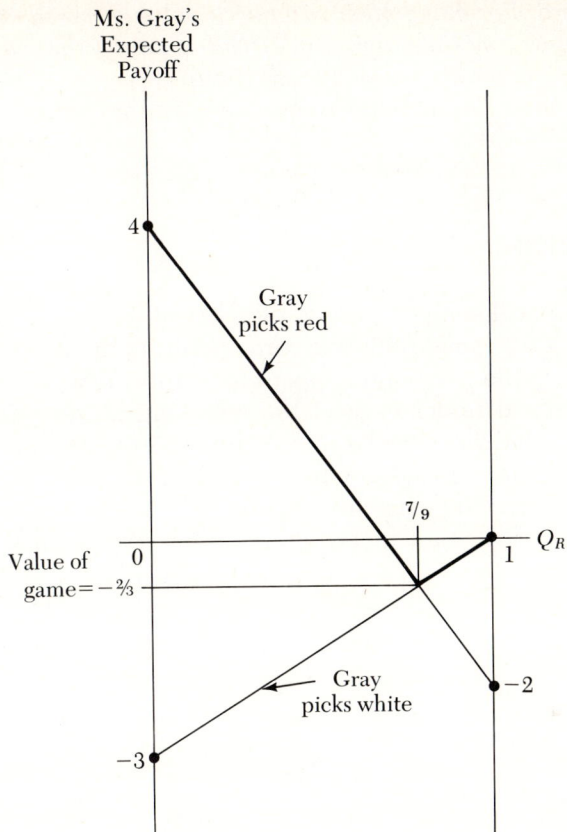

Figure 10-2
A graphical representation to explain Mr. Flannel's optimal mixed strategy.

to the amounts on the heavy line segments. The minimum expected payoff that Mr. Flannel can guarantee occurs when $Q_R = 7/9$, where the two lines cross.

Mr. Flannel's optimal mixed strategy is to use $Q_R = 7/9$ and $Q_W = 1 - Q_R = 2/9$, which leads to the same expected payoff regardless of Ms. Gray's choice:

$$4 - 6(7/9) = -2/3 \quad \text{(if Gray picks red)}$$
$$-3 + 3(7/9) = -2/3 \quad \text{(if Gray picks white)}$$

Notice that by following this strategy, Mr. Flannel guarantees a minimum expected payoff equal to Ms. Gray's maximum expected payoff.

This illustrates how we may assign a value to the present version

10-4 OPTIMAL MIXED STRATEGIES FOR ZERO-SUM GAMES

of Color-Bland. *For any zero-sum game involving mixed strategies, the value of the game is the maximum expected payoff that can be guaranteed, and this amount is also the minimum expected loss that can be assured.* For the present Color-Bland game we have the

$$\text{Value of the game} = -2/3 \text{ cents}$$

Algebraic Solution

The graphical analysis provides the key for finding a player's mixed strategy in a 2 × 2 game. It always corresponds to the point at which the two lines cross. And that point happens to be the one where the expected payoff is identical under each of the opposing player's acts. We may algebraically solve the game by setting the two expected value equations equal to each other and solving for the unknown probability.

For Ms. Gray, the expected payoffs are $-2P_R$ (if Flannel picks red) and $-3 + 7P_R$ (if Flannel picks white). Thus, the optimal level for P_R occurs when

$$-2P_R = -3 + 7P_R$$
$$-9P_R = -3$$

and, thus,

$$P_R = 3/9 = 1/3$$

As before, $P_W = 1 - P_R = 2/3$, and the value of the game is $-2/3$.

For Mr. Flannel, we have expected payoffs of $4 - 6Q_R$ (if Gray picks red) and $-3 + 3Q_R$ (if Gray picks white), so that Q_R must satisfy

$$4 - 6Q_R = -3 + 3Q_R$$
$$-9Q_R = -7$$

and thus,

$$Q_R = 7/9$$

and $Q_W = 1 - Q_R = 2/9$, as before.

Solving 3 × 2 and Larger Games

The above procedures may be applied to games in which one of the players has more than two acts from which to choose. An algebraic solution to such a game is more complex than that of the 2 × 2 game. However, we may easily extend the graphical method to find the optimal mixed strategies for each player as long as one of the players has only two acts.

As a change of pace we will consider an illustration of a conflict situation in which one party's gain is the other's loss. Union and management bargaining over a labor contract provides a good example of such a conflict, where each side can adopt a variety of stances and ploys. We will consider the case of a star baseball player who is seeking a salary increase from the owner of the Gotham City Robins. He is considering one of the three negotiating approaches shown in Table 10-9, which also shows the assumed percentage salary increases. These payoffs are partly determined by the stance chosen by the owner.

Investigation of the payoff table does not show a saddle point, so mixed strategies must be determined. Since no inadmissible acts can be found, we must find three probabilities, P_1, P_2, and P_3, for the baseball star's acts and two, Q_1 and Q_2, for the owner's choices.

We consider first the owner's problem, since he has only two acts. He has only one variable Q_1, since the probability for his second act may be found from this: $Q_2 = 1 - Q_1$. He wants to pick a level for Q_1 that keeps the star's expected percentage increase as small as possible. The graph in Figure 10-3 shows the expected payoff lines for each of the ballplayer's choices, with the heavy segments indicating the largest levels he can achieve for various Q_1 levels. The lowest point on these line segments occurs at the intersection of the S_2 and S_3 lines, which corresponds to the Q_1 level the owner should use.

To find Q_1, we first determine the expected payoff expressions assuming that one of these acts will be chosen by the ballplayer. Using only those payoffs in the S_2 and S_3 rows of Table 10-9, we find that the

Table 10-9
BASEBALL STAR'S PERCENTAGE SALARY INCREASE BARGAINING

			OWNER'S ACTS	
			Q_1	$Q_2 = 1 - Q_1$
			O_1 Benevolent	O_2 Stingy
	P_1	S_1 Go fishing	30	10
BASEBALL STAR'S ACTS	P_2	S_2 Firm stand	25	15
	P_3	S_3 Hat in hand	10	25

10-4 OPTIMAL MIXED STRATEGIES FOR ZERO-SUM GAMES

following expressions apply:

$$25Q_1 + 15(1 - Q_1) = 15 + 10Q_1 \quad \text{(if ballplayer picks } S_2\text{)}$$
$$10Q_1 + 25(1 - Q_1) = 25 - 15Q_1 \quad \text{(if ballplayer picks } S_3\text{)}$$

Since the above expressions represent the equations for the S_2 and S_3 lines in the graph, the Q_1 value where the lines intersect is found by setting the equations equal to each other and solving for the unknown value:

$$15 + 10Q_1 = 25 - 15Q_1$$
$$25Q_1 = 10$$
$$Q_1 = 10/25 = .4$$

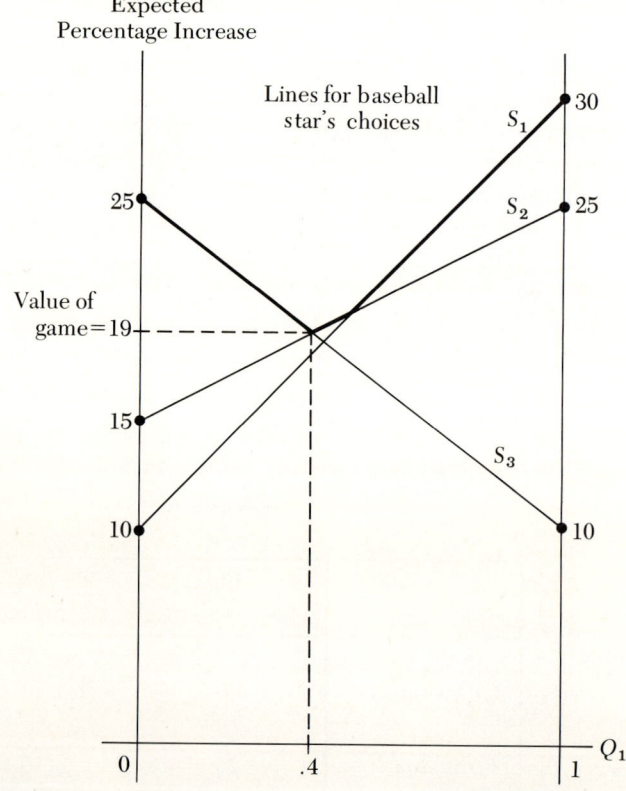

Figure 10-3
A graphical representation to find the baseball team owner's optimal mixed strategy.

The value of the game may be found by substituting $Q_1 = .4$ into either of the above expected payoff expressions. Using the one for S_2 we have

$$\text{Value of the game} = 15 + 10(.4)$$
$$= 19 \text{ percent}$$

Thus the owner of the Robins can guarantee a minimum expected salary increase of 19 percent to his star by following a mixed strategy assigning probability $Q_1 = .4$ to being benevolent (O_1) and $Q_2 = 1 - Q_1 = .6$ to acting stingy (O_2).

We have yet to establish the ballplayer's mixed strategy. Figure 10-3 shows that he would never choose S_1, since the owner could then guarantee a lower expected payoff when using $Q_1 = .4$. Thus, the player must consider a mixed strategy between S_2 and S_3 only and set $P_1 = 0$. This means that $P_2 + P_3 = 1$, and thus $P_3 = 1 - P_2$. Using the S_2 and S_3 rows of the payoff table, we may determine the ballplayer's expected payoffs for each of the owner's possible acts:

$$25P_2 + 10P_3 = 25P_2 + 10(1 - P_2)$$
$$= 10 + 15P_2 \quad \text{(if owner picks } O_1\text{)}$$

and

$$15P_2 + 25P_3 = 15P_2 + 25(1 - P_2)$$
$$= 25 - 10P_2 \quad \text{(if owner picks } O_2\text{)}$$

Setting the above expressions equal to each other, we solve for the unknown P_2:

$$10 + 15P_2 = 25 - 10P_2$$
$$25P_2 = 15$$
$$P_2 = 15/25 = .6$$

The ballplayer's optimal mixed strategy is thus not to go fishing by choosing S_1 ($P_1 = 0$), to take a firm stand (S_2) with probability $P_2 = .6$, and to plead with "hat in hand" (S_3) with probability $P_3 = 1 - P_2 = .4$. To verify this, we compute his expected payoff using either of the above expressions to see if his expected percentage increase is identical to the minimum expected value found earlier for the owner's strategy. Plugging

$P_2 = .6$ into the first one, we have

$$10 + 15(.6) = 19 \text{ percent}$$

which is identical to the value of the game established earlier.

When both players of a game have more than two acts, then a more involved procedure must be used to find the mixed strategies. It is based upon linear programming principles and will be described later in this chapter.

10-5 NON-ZERO-SUM AND OTHER GAMES

The two-person zero-sum game is easiest to analyze. A wide variety of other games have been studied. Unlike two-person zero-sum games, these more complex situations often have no pat solutions acceptable to all players.

Two-Person Non-Zero-Sum Games

A two-person non-zero-sum game occurs when one player's gain need not equal the other player's loss. This might be the case in games similar to those described earlier in this chapter when the particular payoff measure itself does not reflect the true worth of an outcome. For example, in playing Color-Bland Ms. Gray may derive much greater satisfaction by beating Mr. Flannel than the payoffs indicate, while losing a little bit can be just as terrible as losing a lot. Analogous feelings may apply to Mr. Flannel as well. A player's ego needs from playing a simple parlor game might be the dominant factor in its evaluation. Rather than simple points or monetary values, personal utility values would better serve to rank outcomes in such cases.

The essential feature exhibited by non-zero-sum games is not how the true payoff values themselves are determined, but rather that for at least one act-pair the respective payoffs achieved by the two players do not sum to zero. This feature can severely complicate the analysis.

The Prisoner's Dilemma

A classical example of a non-zero-sum game is provided by the following "prisoner's dilemma."

> Two suspects are taken into custody and separated. The district attorney is certain that they are guilty of a specific crime, but he does not have

adequate evidence to convict them at a trial. He points out to each prisoner that each has two alternatives: to confess to the crime the police are sure they have done, or not to confess. If they both do not confess, then the district attorney states he will book them on some very minor trumped-up charge, such as petty larceny and illegal possession of a weapon, and they will both receive minor punishment; if they both confess they will be prosecuted, but he will recommend less than the most severe sentence; but if one confesses and the other does not, then the confessor will receive lenient treatment for turning state's evidence whereas the latter will get "the book" slapped at him.*

Table 10-10
OUTCOMES FOR THE PRISONER'S DILEMMA GAME

		PRISONER B'S ACTS	
		Not Confess	Confess
PRISONER A'S ACTS	Not Confess	1 year each	10 years for A and 3 months for B
	Confess	3 months for A and 10 years for B	8 years each

The outcomes in Table 10-10 might apply. Regardless of the numerical utility payoff values assigned to the various outcomes, the essential feature is that when one suspect confesses and the other doesn't, materially different payoffs result. Consider just the outcomes for prisoner A:

	B Doesn't Confess	B Confesses
A Doesn't Confess	1 year	10 years
A Confesses	3 months	8 years

It is easy to see that confessing achieves superior results for A than not confessing does—regardless of what B does. Not confessing is therefore an inadmissible act, and rationally it should not be picked. A similar conclusion applies to prisoner B.

* R. Duncan Luce and Howard Raiffa, *Games and Decisions* (New York: Wiley, 1958), p. 95.

Thus if both prisoners behave rationally, they will each confess, receiving 8 year sentences as their reward. The paradox here is that *if both prisoners behave irrationally instead, each will be significantly better off.* If both don't confess, each will then receive light sentences of one year each.

The joint confessions serve as an equilibrium act-pair, just as in zero-sum games. As long as the prisoners are not allowed to cooperate, confessing is the minimax loss act for both suspects. If they were allowed to *cooperate* and enter a binding agreement, then it would clearly be in their best interests for both to not confess, each prisoner receiving the one-year sentence.

Similar interactive decision-making situations are sometimes encountered in business. For instance, two small firms, each dominant in a separate region, might consider whether or not to market in the other's territory. As long as neither firm invades the other's region, both firms will continue to earn satisfactory profits. Should one begin a surprise invasion into the other's territory, when the second company has not also planned to expand, the latter firm might be eliminated. If both firms try to expand simultaneously, each may survive—but at a lower level of profits than before. If the companies are not allowed to cooperate, the only rational outcome is for both firms to engage in the damaging expansion—just like joint confessions in the prisoner's dilemma. Clearly, if allowed to cooperate, both would choose to maintain the status quo.

Unlike the simpler zero-sum games, where it is never advantageous for a player to disclose his or her planned action, different solutions may arise in non-zero-sum games when disclosure and cooperation is allowed than when the game is strictly competitive. A variety of special situations arise in the study of non-zero-sum games. The prisoner's dilemma provides us with just one example. With varying degrees of success, these other forms have been analyzed. In general, the non-zero-sum game is much more difficult to solve, and even when solutions are obtained they are often not completely satisfactory.

Games with Several Players

So far in this chapter, we have considered games involving only two persons. When three or more participants are involved, situations may be too complex to arrive at satisfactory solutions. The variety added by a third or fourth person is staggering. For instance, it allows two or more players to gang up on the others, and collusions and partnerships of varying kinds and degrees are possible. Worse than the two-person non-zero-sum game, multiplayer games are even less amenable to solution.

CONCLUDING REMARKS 10-6

Game theory, as we have seen, serves primarily as a model for explaining interactive decision making. In simpler situations, it may even be used to determine the best course of action. Its applicability to real-world problems is, thus, quite limited. Even when it might apply, the practicality of its results have been criticized. It is hard to imagine a board chairman or an army general letting his final choice be determined by the role of dice. Nor should we expect two bored commuters to really solve a linear program just so that they can determine probabilities to three decimal places for choosing a color to play—all of this to win a few pennies.

But some successful and meaningful results can sometimes be achieved by exercising game theoretical principles. Interactive decision making is horrendously complex, and game theory can sometimes provide good approximations for analyzing an otherwise intractable problem. For instance, the prisoner's dilemma problem can help to explain oligopolistic behavior and has also served to explain farmers' crop-planting decisions. Another such approximation is provided by the mixed strategy. Although game theory presumes that one player knows the other's acts and outcomes precisely, this is rarely true in the real world; paradoxically, this fact makes the notion of mixed strategies more relevant. You do not have to literally toss dice in order to give your actions that element of unpredictability sought by a formal mixed strategy.

The analysis of games serves as a microcosm for all quantitative methods, which to varying degrees share its strengths and imperfections. Nearly all mathematical models developed to solve practical problems are imperfect approximations to reality. And even the simplest models may help to organize problem evaluation and to cull out the myriads of poor solutions. At the very minimum, game theory provides us with a point of departure for investigating the most difficult type of decision making, and, as such, it is a very valuable management-science tool.

PROBLEMS

10-1 Find the saddle point (or points) in each of the following two-person zero-sum games.

(a)

	B_1	B_2
A_1	3	-1
A_2	4	3

(b)

	B_1	B_2	B_3
A_1	4	4	10
A_2	2	3	1
A_3	6	5	7

(c)

	B_1	B_2
A_1	0	8
A_2	0	6
A_3	-2	4

(d)

	B_1	B_2	B_3
A_1	5	3	3
A_2	6	2	4

10-2 Find the inadmissible acts in the following game.

	B_1	B_2	B_3	B_4	B_5
A_1	3	2	4	3	4
A_2	2	3	3	2	3
A_3	2	3	-5	4	1
A_4	3	0	4	3	5

10-3 For the following game determine the minimax course of action for player X and for player Y. What is the value of the game?

	Y_1	Y_2
X_1	2	0
X_2	3	2

10-4 Consider the following game (payoffs are profits to player A). P is the probability that player A chooses act A_1 and Q is the probability that player B chooses act B_1.

		Q	$1-Q$
		B_1	B_2
P	A_1	5	-4
$1-P$	A_2	-4	3

(a) Construct a graph that locates the optimal P that player A should use regardless of the action B takes.
(b) Algebraically determine the optimal P for player A. Then find the value of the game.
(c) Find the optimal mixed strategy for player B.
(d) Find player A's expected payoff from using the P found in (b) if player B uses $Q = 1/5$ instead of applying his or her optimal mixed strategy. Is this different from the value of the game found in (b)? Explain.
(e) Find player A's expected payoff when B uses the Q found in (c) and A uses $P = 1/4$. Is this different from the value of the game found in (b)? Explain.
(f) Find player A's expected payoff when B uses the Q given in part (d) and A uses $P = 1/4$. Is this different than the value of the game found in (b)? Explain.

10-5 Consider the following game.

	B_1	B_2	B_3
A_1	2	7	4
A_2	5	1	5
A_3	3	4	4

(a) Eliminate any inadmissible acts.
(b) Determine the optimal mixed strategy for player B.
(c) What act would player A never choose?
(d) Find player A's optimal mixed strategy and the value of the game.

10-6 Compass Point is a game played by two people. Each player has a small wheel with a pointer that must be set at north, east, south, or west. One player is designated as northeast-adjacent and receives 2 points if two adjacent compass points (for example, north and west) are chosen. The other is the southwest-opposite, who receives 4 points when two opposite directions get picked (north-south, east-west). Should the same direction be picked by both players, then 5 points are awarded to that player whose designation includes that direction (that is, 5 points to the northeast-adjacent player if both choose north or both pick east).
(a) Construct the payoff table representing points awarded to the northeast-adjacent player.
(b) Eliminate any inadmissible acts.
(c) Does this game have an equilibrium act-pair?
(d) Find the best course of action for each player and the value of the game.

10-7 The Amalgamated Coffin Workers of Transylvania are negotiating with Dracula Enterprises over how many new converts must be housed in the coming year. The union desires to make as few coffins as possible, whereas Dracula wants to maxmize the number of coffins. The following payoff table represents the number of coffins expected to be made for the various combinations of union and management acts.

		UNION'S ACTS		
		Tranquil	*Strike*	*Wooden Stake Sabotage*
	Tranquil	15	8	10
DRACULA'S ACTS	*Lock-in*	10	12	15
	Bite Union Leaders	10	10	15

Find the optimal course of action for the participants and the value of the game.

10-8 The tennis coaches for Old Ivy College and Slippery Rock University must each determine which of their leading men and women players should be paired in a mixed-doubles match. Although the two schools have never had men and women playing together before, a record has been kept of the number of sets won in previous all-male and all-female matches. Both coaches feel that the difference in past sets won represents the relative advantage or disadvantage of a player against a particular opponent. The following tables represent the net number of sets won by the Old Ivy player.

		SLIPPERY ROCK WOMEN	
		Ann	Belva
OLD IVY WOMEN	Cheryl	5	−3
	Sandra	−4	2

		SLIPPERY ROCK MEN	
		Harry	Larry
OLD IVY MEN	Fred	−3	8
	Ted	0	4

(a) Assuming that the relative advantage to a particular mixed-doubles team over its opponent may be expressed by adding the respective historical net winnings of the corresponding all-male and all-female matches, determine the net advantages to Old Ivy for each possible combination of mixed-doubles teams.
(b) Suppose that each coach must determine who will play before finding out who the opponents will be. Assuming that the net advantages for each possible team combination expresses the payoff for a zero-sum game, eliminate the inadmissible teams.
(c) Using the reduced payoff table from part (b), determine the minimax action for each coach. Which school has the advantage? How many sets does it equal?

10-9 Avery's is a small chain of neighborhood department stores located in a suburban county. C. P. Blomberg is a similar establishment situated in an adjacent county. Both have enough financial strength to expand, and the only viable manner in which this might be carried out is for each to open stores in the other's county. The tables on the next page provide the anticipated average profit levels over the next 5 years for the various courses of action.

AVERY'S PROFITS

	Blomberg Doesn't Expand	Blomberg Expands
Avery's Doesn't Expand	$300,000	−$100,000
Avery's Expands	500,000	100,000

BLOMBERG'S PROFITS

	Blomberg Doesn't Expand	Blomberg Expands
Avery's Doesn't Expand	$200,000	$400,000
Avery's Expands	−200,000	50,000

(a) Is this situation a zero-sum game? Explain.
(b) Find the equilibrium act-pair, if there is one.
(c) If the two chains are prohibited by state anti-trust laws from cooperating, what courses of action would the two stores take?
(d) If the two stores can cooperate, what would each prefer doing?

10-10 It is possible to treat single-person decision making under uncertainty as a game involving nature as a second participant, with the uncertain events being nature's choices. Consider the following payoff table regarding a new product, which may be produced in-house or whose patent may be sold to another manufacturer for a fixed fee plus a royalty on future sales.

ACTS	PRODUCT EVENTS	
	Success	Failure
Make	$100,000	−$50,000
Sell Patent	15,000	10,000

(a) Using the minimax principle of game theory, determine the manufacturer's optimal course of action. What payoff level corresponds?
(b) Suppose that the manufacturer judges a 50-50 chance for product success. According to the Bayes decision rule, which course of action should he or she take? What expected payoff corresponds?
(c) Using the probability information given in part (b), calculate the manufacturer's expected payoff for the action indicated in part (a).

(d) In view of your answers to the above, does the minimax principle maximize the manufacturer's expected payoff as it would in a two-person game? Explain.

10-11 The two opposing political parties are nominating candidates for governor in separate conventions held simultaneously. The following probabilities apply for the respective party winning the election for the indicated nominee pair.

Democratic Nominee	Republican Nominee	Probability for Democrat Winning	Probability for Republican Winning
Muck	Raker	.75	.25
Muck	Slinger	.25	.75
Mudd	Raker	.30	.70
Mudd	Slinger	.60	.40

We may assume that each party wishes to maximize its probability of winning the election.

(a) Subtracting the Republican's win probability from the Democrat's, the resulting difference can be used as the Democrat's payoff measure, so that a zero-sum game applies. Construct the payoff table.

(b) Applying the minimax criterion, what are the optimal actions for the two parties?

10-12 The zero-sum game is a special case of the *constant-sum game*, and the same principles may be used to analyze both games. For example, in playing Color-Bland against Ms. Gray, the chauvinistic chivalrous Mr. Flannel may give her a handicap by increasing each of her regular payoffs by 5 cents. Consider the following game without a handicap.

MR. FLANNEL'S ACTS

		Red	White	Blue
MS. GRAY'S ACTS	Red	−2	4	−3
	White	1	2	−4
	Blue	1	1	1

(a) Solve the above game to find the minimax courses of action for the two players. What is the value of the game?

(b) Construct Ms. Gray's payoff table with the 5-cent handicap included. Then solve the game. Are the optimal actions the same? Compare the value of the handicapped game to that found in part (a). What is the difference in these amounts?

Eleven

Inventory Decisions

Inventory control is one area in business decision making where quantitative methods have been very successful in achieving cost savings. A primary reason for this success story is that inventories comprise such a vast segment of economic activity. In the United States alone, hundreds of billions of dollars are presently invested in inventories at all levels of business, from manufacturer to consumer, and in all types of organizations from clubs to national governments at all levels. Because of the sheer size of inventory investments, even minor improvements in controlling inventories can bring about large savings.

Two phenomena have contributed to the improvements in controlling inventories. One has been the application of mathematical models and optimization techniques in achieving efficiencies. This chapter focuses on these quantitative methods. A second source of savings has been the development of the digital computer with improved information processing and retrieval capabilities. Managers within complex organizations now have immediate access to all kinds of information relevant to inventories which was once impossible to obtain quickly. The closing of this information gap has dramatically reduced the need for inventories. Many inventory systems are even automated to the extent that orders to replenish stock are issued by computer.

An inventory of physical goods may be required for a variety of reasons. The fundamental need, however, occurs whenever a disparity exists between the circumstances under which a good is demanded and the manner in which it becomes available. This disparity may be temporal, such as a seasonal item like corn, enough of which must be saved from a limited harvest period for an entire year. Or, the gap might be geographical, where a product such as photographic film is produced in a few plants and consumed all over the world; a minimum inventory level must be achieved just to keep the distribution "pipeline" full. Other justifications exist, such as price fluctuations in commodities; for example, an inventory of raw materials might be held by a manufacturer to take advantage of the lower prices that occur from time to time. In retail establishments inventories may be required merely for display purposes so that customers will be encouraged to buy what they see.

The central problem in any decision involving physical storage is finding an efficient *inventory policy*. A key element in establishing such a policy is determining how many items should be stocked periodically, and when replenishment should occur. It is convenient to refer to the number of items as the *order quantity* and to the level of inventory when the requisition is made as the *order point*. For example, a family might always purchase two gallons of milk (the order quantity) and repurchase milk only when all of it has been drunk (zero, the order point). Such a policy may be dictated by how long milk can remain fresh in the refrigerator and may also control the inventory order point for all food items purchased at the same time. An efficient inventory policy is one where various costs are balanced. In the case of family food, time and gasoline are spent in going to the supermarket; these costs may be high enough to discourage a policy of buying only one gallon of milk (which would require twice as many trips).

Our objective is to find optimal inventory policies. This chapter considers the basic structure of inventory decisions and presents some of the models applicable when all factors are certain. These serve to explain the essential concepts held in common with more advanced models. The chapter concludes with inventory decisions made under uncertainty.

11-1 FACTORS INFLUENCING INVENTORY POLICY

The usual long-run objective of an inventory policy is to maximize profits or to minimize costs. In the simpler situations encountered in this chapter, these two goals coincide. The desired end result is ordinarily achieved by minimizing average inventory cost over a short period such as one year. Our initial models will all be based on minimizing annual cost.

Inventory Cost Components

Various costs are considered in evaluating inventory systems. In typical business situations, these are

(1) Ordering and procurement costs for items stocked.
(2) Holding or carrying costs.
(3) Shortage costs.

Ordering and procurement costs represent all expenses incurred in ordering or manufacturing items and include not only the raw acquisition costs but the costs of transporting, collecting and sorting, and placing items in storage. Also included in this category are any managerial and clerical costs associated with placing an order. Often these costs vary with the size of the order, as, for example, when products are priced with quantity discounts. Such costs are of two kinds: a fixed portion occurring for each order independent of the number of items stocked; and a variable portion dependent on the number of items stocked. We will refer to the variable portion as procurement costs and to the fixed portion as the ordering costs.

Inventory holding costs are the expenses incurred during the storage of items. Included are physical costs, the most common being the operation of warehouse facilities. In addition are the costs of insurance and property taxes. Other cost components might be expenses arising from pilferage, spoilage, and obsolescence. A very important portion of holding costs is the opportunity cost of those funds invested in inventory which might profitably be used elsewhere. All such costs depend on *how many* items are stored and for *how long*. Frequently such costs run to 20 or 25 percent of the value of items held in inventory.

Inventory shortage costs occur whenever there is a demand for items not currently in stock. For those items ordinarily backordered, such as a new car having particular color and options, shortage costs may have only a fixed component—the extra paperwork and managerial expenses incurred in processing the order. For shortages of more mundane items, such as a particular brand of paint, an additional variable cost component that depends on the *duration* of the shortage must be considered. This cost is largely due to potential loss of customer goodwill that may be expected to rise in proportion to the length of delay; such a decline in goodwill might be reflected in loss of future business. In extreme cases, as with a convenience product such as cigarettes or a necessity such as gasoline, there is no backordering at all; under these circumstances a shortage causes a lost sale. The minimum cost of a lost sale is the marginal profit for the item, but it can be larger due to loss of goodwill.

In evaluating an inventory policy, some or all of the above costs might be considered. But it is very important that only *relevant costs* be used. These involve only those expenses somehow affected by inventory policies themselves. Certain legitimate accounting costs may therefore be ignored. For instance, the rent on a warehouse would not be included as a carrying cost if the same facility were to be used regardless of the number of items stocked. It would properly be considered an overhead item like the company president's salary. No proration of overhead items should be reflected in the inventory costs, unless these somehow differ from policy to policy. But certain nonaccounting costs, such as the opportunity cost of invested capital and loss of customer goodwill, are definitely relevant and should be incorporated into the evaluation.

Structure of Inventory System

Inventory systems can be extremely complex. Multi-echelon systems may involve a hierarchy of stocking points, each fulfilling different needs. For example, a product might be inventoried at the plant level, in regional distribution centers, in local warehouses, and on the retailer's shelves. Often it may be possible to fill a demand from more than one inventory point. For example, a buyer may acquire a Sears tire from either a retail store or through a catalogue order from a regional warehouse. Equally complex systems may arise in manufacturing, where raw-materials inventories are drawn down and processed into various semifinished states, with work-in-progress inventories arising at various stages of production. Traditional quantitative methods are severely limited in coping with these more complex inventory structures.

In this book we focus on the simplest inventory systems. Only one stocking point for an item is considered. All demands are filled from there. Such a system is the most universal one faced by a small retailer or wholesaler. The concepts developed through study of this simple system may be expanded to more complex situations.

Types of Inventory Items

Several hundred types of items can be stocked in even a modest inventory system, such as in a retail hardware store. In large department stores, hundreds of thousands of different items might be stocked.

Military supply systems might contain millions. The relationships between items can be complex. Some products are demanded singly, some in sets (like nuts with bolts). Some items may be substituted for others (8-penny or 12-penny nails for the 10-penny size; galvanized nails for the uncoated ones). The demand for one item may be correlated with another (like coats with pants). As a further complication, individual products compete for scarce storage space.

Any model that attempts to relate items exactly as they are in the real world will become hopelessly bogged down in detail when applied to even modest systems. Some simplification is necessary. Items may be categorized, like pounds of nails (representing all sizes and types). The author studied the inventory and distribution system for a thousand-product fertilizer and pesticide manufacturer by dividing the items into two categories: bulk and packaged. Even when the number of items is so reduced, difficulties may occur in treating the demands separately because of interdependencies. Further simplification may require that the demands be independent.

The simple models presented here involve a single product. Again, a thorough study of the simple case can better equip us to analyze the more complicated situations.

Nature of Demand and Supply

In typical business situations demands occur erratically. The demands for most items also occur discretely, that is, a few items at a time. In this chapter demands are assumed to occur continuously (as if each item were a cubic foot of natural gas fed into an always lit heater — either from a pilot light or by the main flame) and at the same rate over time (as if the gas heater was always on full flame). As long as demand is predictable, such a simplifying assumption makes little difference in the inventory costs or in the particular policy that minimizes cost.

But one element does matter. Demands typically occur randomly over time, so that the overall level is generally uncertain. Our discussion begins with those cases where the demand is certain and known in advance. These cases prepare us for the final discussion, where uncertainty in demand is explicitly considered.

How items are supplied is another important element in establishing inventory policies. Generally, this is handled in one of two ways. From the retailer's or wholesaler's point of view, the only question is how long does it take to fill an order. This is the *lead time* for receiving the units ordered. Like demand, lead time is often uncertain. In the present chapter, we will only consider constant lead times. This considerably simplifies the analysis and usually allows us to analyze a problem without bothering to explicitly consider lead time at all, as if replenishment of inventories were instantaneous.

The question of supply differs for the manufacturer who must produce items for later sale. Here replenishment cannot be treated instantaneously. Rather, items are added to inventory at a rate equal to the speed at which they are produced.

11-2 ECONOMIC ORDER QUANTITY MODEL

The simplest inventory model involves one type of item whose demand is known and constant and which is resupplied instantaneously. No backordering of items is allowed. The problem objective is to select an inventory policy — choose the order quantity (which in turn establishes the time when an order must be placed) — in such a way that the annual inventory cost is minimized.

The Mathematical Model

The following parameters are used in establishing a mathematical model for this problem.

k = Cost of placing an order

A = Annual number of items demanded

c = Unit cost of procuring an item

h = Annual cost per dollar value for holding items in inventory

T = Time between orders

The objective is to choose the number of items to order

$$Q = \text{Order quantity}$$

such that the total annual cost

Total annual cost = Ordering cost + Holding cost + Procurement cost

is minimized.

The features of this inventory system are illustrated in Figure 11-1, where the inventory level is plotted versus calendar time. This graph

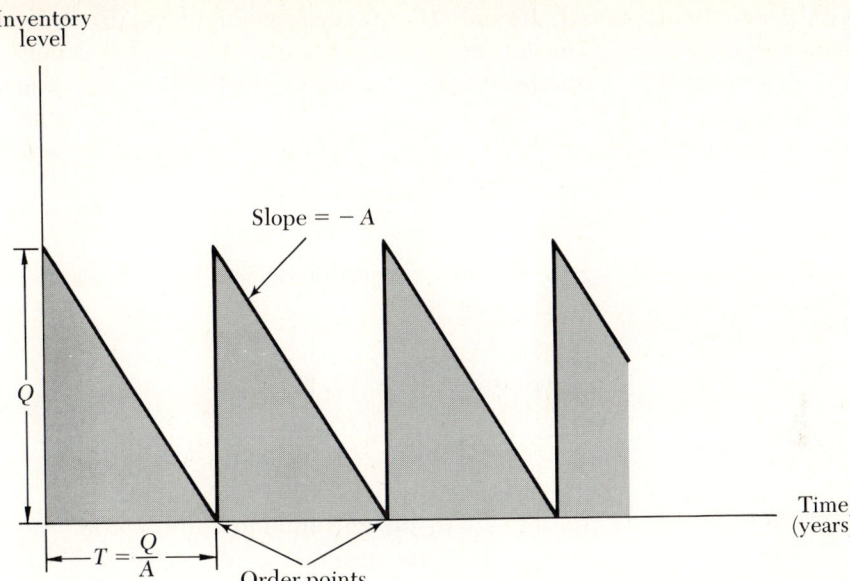

Figure 11-1
Graphical representation of inventory system for simple economic order quantity model.

will help explain development of the mathematical model. Q items are replenished periodically, at which time a new *inventory cycle* begins and an old one ends. Each cycle has a duration of T years (some fraction of one year), and this depends on the order quantity Q. The length of time is equal to the proportion of the annual demand consumed in one inventory cycle:

$$T = \frac{Q}{A}$$

The units are depleted at the rate of A units per year, so that the slanting line segments, each of slope $-A$, represent the level of inventory at any given point in time. The saw-tooth effect represents the sequence of inventory depletions and replenishments which constitute successive inventory cycles. Because it costs something to hold items in inventory, there is no advantage to restocking until the inventory is zero. Thus each inventory cycle may be pictured as a triangle of height Q and base T, with a new triangle beginning where the leg of the last one touches the time axis.

In finding a mathematical expression for the objective, we begin

11-2 ECONOMIC ORDER QUANTITY MODEL

with the first component, annual ordering cost, which depends on how many orders are placed each year. The number of annual orders depends on two things: (1) the annual number of items demanded A; and (2) the quantity ordered Q. It follows that

$$\text{Number of annual orders} = \frac{A}{Q}$$

Multiplying the above by the cost per order, we obtain the result for the annual ordering cost:

$$\text{Annual ordering cost} = \left(\frac{A}{Q}\right)k$$

The second cost component is the annual holding cost. It is based on the number of items placed in inventory and the duration they are held. Individually, some items will be sold immediately, while others will be held until the inventory is restocked. However, we need only be concerned with an average value. Since the inventory level in any cycle ranges from Q downward to zero, and because there is a constant rate of depletion, we have for any cycle:

$$\text{Average inventory} = \frac{Q}{2}$$

This same quantity applies from cycle to cycle, and thus represents the average inventory level throughout the entire operating life of the inventory system.

It is realistic to base the holding cost on the value of the items held. This is certainly true of the opportunity cost of the invested capital and applies for other costs such as insurance and property taxes as well. (Physical storage costs usually correlate highly with an item's value too.) Here we base an item's value on its procurement cost. The cost of holding an item in inventory for one year is thus the product of annual holding cost per dollar h and the procurement cost c:

$$\text{Annual holding cost of one item} = hc$$

We may now determine the annual holding cost for all the items involved by multiplying the above cost by the average inventory:

$$\text{Annual holding cost} = hc\left(\frac{Q}{2}\right)$$

There is another way of looking at this annual cost component that will prove useful in discussing later models. Consider the single-cycle holding cost. This may be related to the area of a triangle in Figure 11-1, which represents the average item time (product years) for one inventory cycle:

$$\text{Triangle area} = \frac{1}{2} \text{ base} \times \text{height}$$

$$= \frac{1}{2} TQ$$

$$= \frac{1}{2}\left(\frac{Q}{A}\right)Q = \frac{Q^2}{2A}$$

The holding cost for a single cycle is the product of hc and this area, $hc(Q^2/2A)$. Since there are A/Q inventory cycles in one year, the annual holding cost may be obtained by multiplying the single-cycle value by A/Q. Cancelling terms, we obtain the same expression given earlier for annual holding cost.

For the entire year, A units will be demanded, so that the annual cost of procuring items must be

$$\text{Annual procurement cost} = Ac$$

Adding together the three cost components, we find the total annual cost expression:

$$\text{Total annual cost} = \left(\frac{A}{Q}\right)k + hc\left(\frac{Q}{2}\right) + Ac$$

The objective is to select the value Q that minimizes the above cost.

However, we only need to consider relevant costs (which differ with inventory policies). We may ignore the last term for procurement cost Ac, since that expense will arise regardless of the value chosen for Q. Equivalently, the objective for our model is to

$$\text{Minimize } TC = \left(\frac{A}{Q}\right)k + hc\left(\frac{Q}{2}\right)$$

where TC is the total annual *relevant* cost.

Finding the Optimal Solution

The TC equation is a mathematical expression that we refer to as the *objective function*. The value of TC depends on the order quantity Q. The TC expression is plotted in Figure 11-2, where the vertical axis

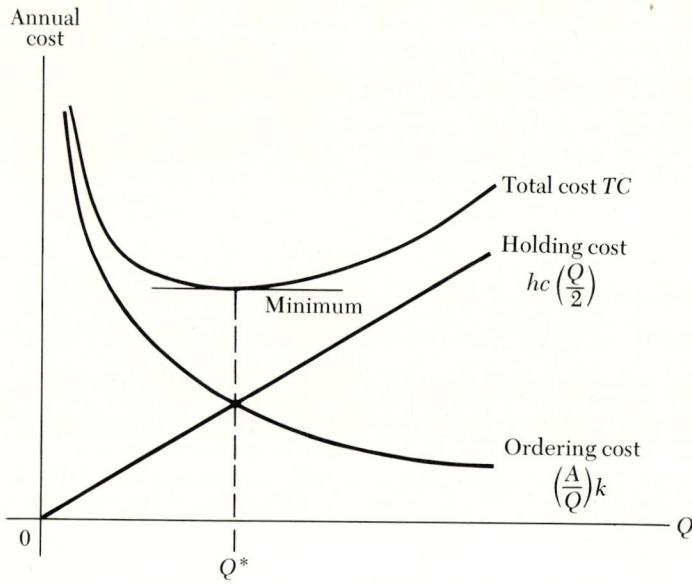

Figure 11-2
Graphical representation of inventory cost components.

provides annual cost and the horizontal axis represents the order quantity Q. The total annual relevant cost has two components: annual ordering cost and annual holding cost. Each of these components is also plotted in Figure 11-2. Since TC is the sum of ordering and holding costs, the height of the curve for TC at any level for Q is the sum of the respective heights of the curve for ordering cost and the line for holding cost.

The annual ordering-cost curve has the geometrical shape of a hyperbola. Recall that each order costs an amount k, regardless of how many items are requested each time. Thus, tiny levels for Q will involve a great number of orders throughout the year, and ordering costs will be huge. As Q becomes larger, fewer orders are involved, so the annual ordering cost declines as we move to the right on the curve. The annual holding cost plots as a straight line because this component is a constant multiple of the average inventory level. This line starts with zero holding cost at $Q = 0$, where no inventory is held. Each item is sold as demanded, so that the line rises with constant slope as Q increases. This is because progressively larger order quantities raise the average inventory level, making holding costs rise in proportion.

The *optimal solution* to the objective function occurs where total annual relevant cost is minimized. We denote the optimal order quantity by Q^*. This level corresponds to the minimum-cost point on the TC curve, where its slope is zero. The slope equation of a curve may be found using mathematical procedures. Once the equation for the slope has been found, it may be set equal to zero and algebraically solved to determine what order quantity corresponds.*

The equation for the optimal order quantity is

$$Q^* = \sqrt{\frac{2Ak}{hc}}$$

which is sometimes referred to as the *economic order quantity*.

The above equation is often referred to as the Wilson formula, in honor of the man who first proposed it. Once Q^* has been obtained, the corresponding reorder time is automatically determined to be

$$T^* = \frac{Q^*}{A}$$

and a complete optimal inventory policy is thereby obtained which tells how much should be ordered and when each order should be placed. The annual relevant cost of this policy may be determined by substituting the value of Q^* for Q in the expression for TC.

Referring again to Figure 11-2, we see that Q^* happens to be the order quantity where holding cost equals ordering cost. You may verify the Wilson formula by setting the respective component cost equations equal to each other and algebraically solving for Q. Study of the Q^* formula allows us to draw some interesting conclusions. The economic (optimal) order quantity increases with the square root of the annual demand A instead of being proportional to it. Also, it is inversely proportional to the square root of the unit procurement cost c, indicating that everything else equal, fewer expensive items should be ordered than would be the case for cheaper ones. This indicates that the various *parameters* k, A, c, and h really serve to determine the optimal inventory policy and that widely different results may be obtained for different levels for these constants.

* This is done by means of calculus. The first derivative of the objective function $TC(Q)$ is obtained and set equal to zero:

$$\frac{dTC(Q)}{dQ} = -\frac{A}{Q^2}k + \frac{hc}{2} = 0$$

Because $TC(Q)$ is convex from below, solving for Q the minimum cost occurs when

$$Q = \sqrt{\frac{2Ak}{hc}}$$

An Illustration

Suppose a liquor store sells 5200 cases of beer each year. For simplicity, we will assume that the beer is sold at a constant rate throughout the year. Each case has a net cost to the store of $2. The wholesale supplier charges $10 for each delivery, regardless of how many cases have been ordered; delivery always occurs the day after ordering. The owner's only working capital is tied up in inventory, and these funds have been borrowed from the local bank at 10-percent annual simple interest. In addition, the owner must pay a state franchise tax of 5 percent of the annual inventory value, while theft insurance amounts to another 5 percent. All other operating costs are either fixed in nature or do not depend on the amounts of beer ordered.

The owner wishes to evaluate his present procedure of ordering 100 cases each week and establish a better inventory policy that will minimize the annual costs of doing business in beer. The following constants apply:

$k = \$10$ per order

$A = 5200$ cases per year

$c = \$2$ per case

$h = \$.20$ per year per dollar value of beer held in inventory

The present policy of ordering every week involves an order quantity of

$$Q = \frac{5200}{52} = 100 \text{ cases}$$

The total relevant annual cost of this policy is

$$TC = \left(\frac{A}{Q}\right)k + hc\left(\frac{Q}{2}\right)$$
$$= \left(\frac{5200}{100}\right)10 + .20(2)\left(\frac{100}{2}\right)$$
$$= 520 + 20$$
$$= 540 \text{ dollars per year}$$

Notice that the annual ordering cost of $520 is much larger than the annual $20 holding cost. These two cost components should be the same for an optimal inventory policy.

To establish the optimal inventory policy, we first determine the economic order quantity from the Wilson formula:

$$Q^* = \sqrt{\frac{2Ak}{hc}}$$

$$= \sqrt{\frac{2(5200)10}{.20(2)}} = \sqrt{260,000}$$

$$= 509.9 \text{ or } 510 \text{ cases of beer}$$

The optimal time between orders is

$$T^* = \frac{510}{5200} = .098 \text{ years}$$

which may be converted to once every $365(.098) = 35.8$ or approximately 36 days. The optimal inventory policy is therefore to order 510 cases of beer every 36 days. The resulting total annual relevant cost is

$$TC = \left(\frac{5200}{510}\right)10 + .20(2)\left(\frac{510}{2}\right)$$

$$= 101.96 + 102.00$$

$$= 203.96 \text{ dollars per year}$$

(The two cost components differ by 4 cents because we rounded the value for Q^* to the nearest whole number.) We see that more than \$300 in annual beer costs alone can be saved by switching to the optimal policy.

To show how results depend so much on the parameter values, consider the store's inventory policy for fine domestic wine. Suppose that only 1000 cases of such wine are sold yearly at a net cost of \$20 each. The liquor store is located in San Francisco, and the owner who prides himself on the caliber of his product makes periodic trips through the Napa Valley to pick up orders at various wineries. He always rents a large truck and travels a fixed route; the cost is a flat \$100 per trip. The same holding costs apply as with beer. Thus,

$k = \$100$ per order

$A = 1000$ cases per year

$c = \$20$ per case

$h = \$.20$ per dollar value of wine held in inventory for one year

The optimal inventory policy (again, assuming known constant demand rate and predictable inventory-replenishment lead time) is

$$Q^* = \sqrt{\frac{2(1000)100}{.20(20)}} = \sqrt{50{,}000}$$

$$= 223.6 \text{ or } 224 \text{ cases of wine}$$

$$T^* = \frac{224}{1000} = .224 \text{ years (or approximately 82 days)}$$

The total annual relevant cost is

$$TC = \left(\frac{1000}{224}\right)100 + .20(20)\left(\frac{224}{2}\right)$$

$$= 894.43 \text{ dollars per year}$$

Notice how the wine result differs from the one for beer.

Applying the economic order quantity analysis to two different items is only valid under special conditions. Here, we must assume that beer and wine have independent demands. Furthermore, we assume that the storage capacity is sufficient to handle any contemplated quantities of each product. Should beer and wine compete for limited space or should there be a constraint on the amount of working capital that can be tied up in inventories, the products must be analyzed jointly and the mathematics can be quite complicated.

11-3 OPTIMAL INVENTORY POLICY WITH BACKORDERING

The simple model just described assumes that no backorders are possible. We will now consider items that may be sold even after the inventory has been exhausted. Such situations might apply when buying automobile tires, for example; a retailer may not have the exact size in current stock but might be willing to place a special order to satisfy customers. An inventory system that allows for backordering is summarized in Figure 11-3. As before, Q represents the order quantity. Since sales may be made up even after the on-hand inventory reaches zero level, it may be desirable to use part of each successive order to fill backordered items. The *order level* is represented by S; this quantity is the on-hand inventory position at the beginning of each inventory cycle. The optimal inventory policy must specify those values of both Q and S that minimize total annual cost.

Each inventory cycle is now represented by two phases. The initial

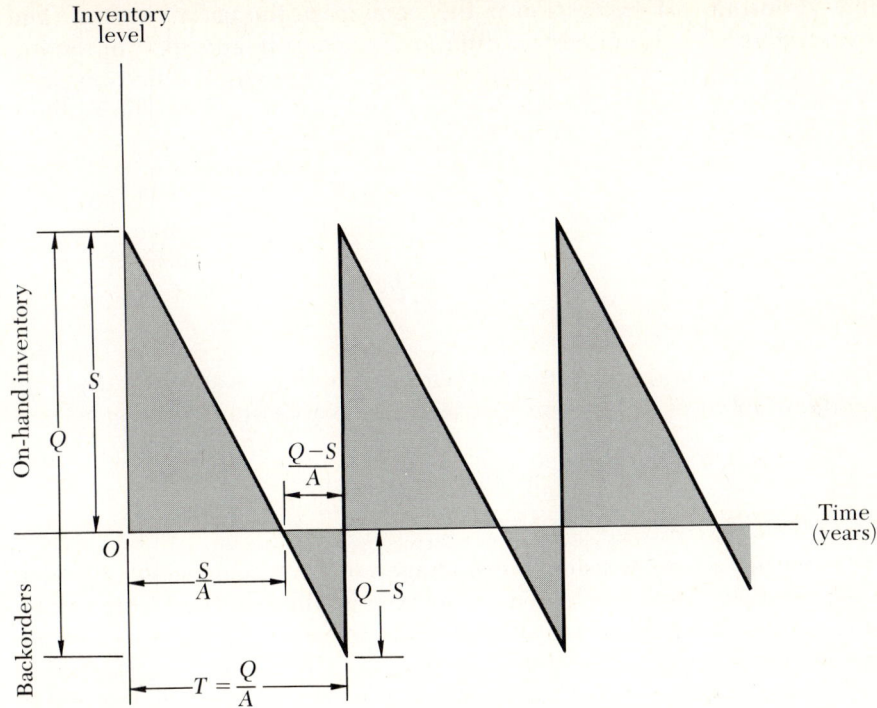

Figure 11-3
Graphical representation of inventory system when backordering is allowed.

phase occurs when all demands can be filled from current on-hand inventory. It is represented by the large triangles of height S; that quantity is the initial inventory level after filling those demands shorted in the previous cycle. The duration of the first phase is that fraction of one year that it takes to deplete S items from on-hand inventory: S/A. The second stage is represented by the smaller upside-down triangle; its height is $Q - S$, the number of items that are backordered, and its base is the duration of time taken for these backorders to accumulate: $(Q - S)/A$.

We now assume that a shortage cost applies, and that this, like holding cost, depends on how many items are short and the amount of time each shortage lasts. Such a penalty, represented by p, arises largely from loss of goodwill. (An additional fixed shortage penalty that depends only on the number of items short is sometimes used. For simplicity, that second penalty is not included here.)

In expressing total annual relevant cost, we now have

$$TC = \text{Ordering cost} + \text{Holding cost} + \text{Shortage cost}$$

The ordering cost expression is the same as in the earlier model. The expression for holding cost is different, since only a portion of the entire order is ever stored and this cost only applies in the first phase of the inventory cycle. The single-cycle cost is obtained by multiplying the area of the first triangle by hc:

$$hc \times \text{First area} = hc\left[\frac{1}{2}S\left(\frac{S}{A}\right)\right]$$

$$= \frac{hcS^2}{2A}$$

The above is then converted into annual holding cost by multiplying by the number of orders per year, A/Q, and cancelling terms:

$$\text{Annual holding cost} = \frac{hcS^2}{2Q}$$

To get the expression for shortage cost, we again consider what happens in a single cycle. The penalty p applies to the average item-time short. Multiplying p by the area of the second triangle, we obtain the single-cycle shortage cost:

$$p \times \text{Second area} = p\left(\frac{1}{2}\right)\left[\left(\frac{Q-S}{A}\right)(Q-S)\right]$$

$$= \frac{p(Q-S)^2}{2A}$$

As with the holding cost, multiplying the above by the annual number of inventory cycles A/Q, we have

$$\text{Annual shortage cost} = \frac{p(Q-S)^2}{2Q}$$

The total annual relevant cost may be expressed as

$$TC = \left(\frac{A}{Q}\right)k + \frac{hcS^2}{2Q} + \frac{p(Q-S)^2}{2Q}$$

The objective is to find values for Q and S that minimize TC. The following expressions may be used to calculate the optimal values:*

---

*It can be established that the function $TC(Q, S)$ is convex over the ranges considered. These equations are derived by taking the partial derivatives with respect to Q and S, setting these equal to zero, and solving them algebraically.

$$Q^* = \sqrt{\frac{2Ak}{hc}} \sqrt{\frac{p+hc}{p}}$$

$$S^* = \sqrt{\frac{2Ak}{hc}} \sqrt{\frac{p}{p+hc}}$$

and the time between orders is

$$T^* = \frac{Q^*}{A}$$

Consider the liquor store discussed earlier. Beer is a convenience product that cannot be backordered (customers will always buy it elsewhere rather than wait). However, the wine customers are connoisseurs who are willing to order out-of-stock items. The store owner, nevertheless, does incur some penalty when running short of wine.

Suppose that every day a customer waits for a favorite wine costs the store a penny per case; this means that the annual penalty is $p = \$3.65$ per case. Using the same constants as before ($k = \$100$, $A = 1{,}000$, $c = \$20$, and $h = \$.20$) we can establish the optimal inventory policy:

$$Q^* = \sqrt{\frac{2(1000)100}{.20(20)}} \sqrt{\frac{3.65 + .20(20)}{3.65}} = 324$$

$$S^* = \sqrt{\frac{2(1000)100}{.20(20)}} \sqrt{\frac{3.65}{3.65 + .20(20)}} = 154$$

and

$$T^* = \frac{324}{1000} = .324 \text{ years (or approximately 118 days)}$$

The optimal policy involves ordering 324 cases of wine every 118 days. Only 154 of these will be stored in inventory; the remaining $Q^* - S^* = 170$ cases will be used to satisfy outstanding backorders. The total annual relevant cost of this policy is

$$TC = \left(\frac{1000}{324}\right)100 + \frac{.20(20)(154)^2}{2(324)} + \frac{3.65(170)^2}{2(324)}$$

$$= 617.82 \text{ dollars per year}$$

Notice that the above value is smaller than the optimal cost of $894.43 found when no backordering was allowed. This is because fewer orders are placed under backordering and the average on-hand inventory level is lower. Although there are now shortage costs, these are lower than the combined cost reductions for ordering and holding items.

11-4 INVENTORY POLICY FOR LOST SALES

As we noted at the outset, some items, like convenience products, cannot be backordered. When a demand cannot be met from on-hand inventory, a sale is lost. It is possible to extend the model developed for backorders to handle this special case. However, a complete analysis of the lost sales case here is merely a mathematical exercise. If an inventory system is going to be operated at all, it may be shown that the basic economic order quantity model should be used, so that no shortages leading to lost sales should be allowed.

Remember, this chapter involves certain, constant demand and predictable lead time for resupply. We know that many successful retail establishments occasionally run out of items like cigarettes and do lose some sales because of this. But these businesses operate with uncertain demands; these stores would never run out of those convenience items if demand could be precisely predicted and lead times never varied.

11-5 FIXED PRODUCTION-RATE MODEL

The models presented so far involve instantaneous filling of orders. Identical results are obtained when there is a constant lead time, so that all items arrive at some future date fixed when the order is actually placed. We now consider a special case encountered by a manufacturer which may supply demanded items either from inventory or from current production. Since production itself requires some time, replenishment of inventory items is not instantaneous. We will assume that production, like demand, occurs at some known constant rate of B items per year. We will assume that no backorders are allowed and that the production rate exceeds the demand rate: $B > A$.

Figure 11-4 illustrates such an inventory system. Each inventory cycle consists of two phases, depending on whether or not production is occurring. The production phase is represented by the upward-sloping triangle on the left. Although the total amount produced is Q, a portion of the items produced is siphoned off to customers before they can be stored, so that the maximum inventory build-up is

$$\text{Maximum inventory} = Q\left(\frac{B-A}{B}\right)$$

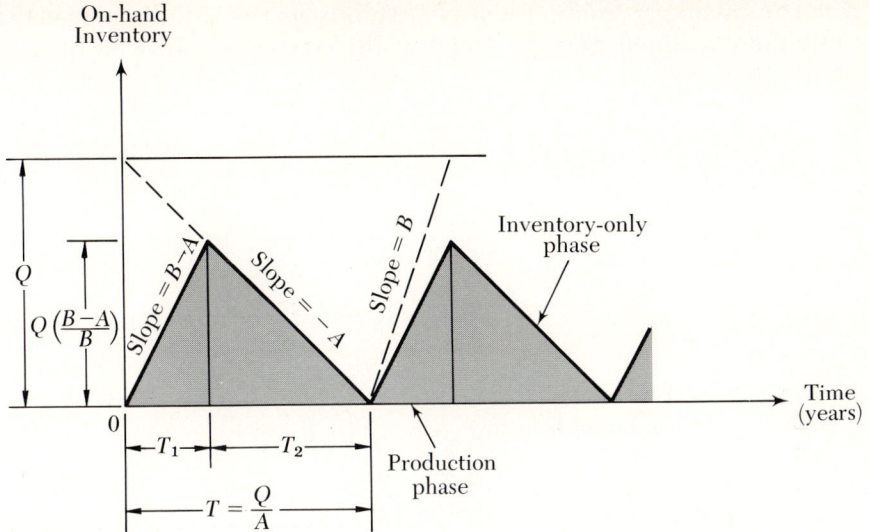

Figure 11-4
Production and inventory system when items are produced at a uniform rate.

at which point production stops. The net accumulation of on-hand inventory occurs at the rate of $B - A$ units; we will represent the duration of the production phase by T_1. The demand-only phase, represented by the downward sloping triangle, then starts. In this stage, all demand is filled from inventory until zero stock is reached; we represent the duration of this second phase by T_2. The respective phase durations are

$$T_1 = \frac{Q}{B}$$

$$T_2 = T - T_1 = \frac{Q}{A} - \frac{Q}{B}$$

$$= Q\left(\frac{B - A}{AB}\right)$$

In place of the usual ordering cost k, we instead use the fixed cost of making a production run. This quantity is referred to as a *set-up cost* or start-up cost. The annual set-up cost (like the ordering cost) is exactly the same as before.

$$\text{Annual set-up cost} = \left(\frac{A}{Q}\right)k$$

11-5 FIXED PRODUCTION-RATE MODEL

The inventory holding cost per cycle is hc times the average area under the combined triangle (which is the sum of the areas for the two smaller triangles):

$$hc\left[\frac{1}{2}T_1Q\left(\frac{B-A}{B}\right) + \frac{1}{2}T_2Q\left(\frac{B-A}{B}\right)\right] = hc\left[\frac{Q^2(B-A)}{2B^2} + \frac{Q^2(B-A)^2}{2AB^2}\right]$$

$$= hc\frac{Q^2}{2A}\left(\frac{B-A}{B}\right)$$

Multiplying the above by the number of inventory cycles per year A/Q, we obtain

$$\text{Annual holding cost} = hc\left(\frac{Q}{2}\right)\left(\frac{B-A}{B}\right)$$

The annual relevant total cost is thus

$$TC = \left(\frac{A}{Q}\right)k + hc\left(\frac{Q}{2}\right)\left(\frac{B-A}{B}\right)$$

which is only slightly different from the first model described. The minimum-cost production (order) quantity may be called the *economic production quantity* and is found from

$$Q^* = \sqrt{\frac{2Ak}{hc}}\sqrt{\frac{B}{B-A}}$$

Consider a manufacturer whose product demand is $A = 100{,}000$ units per year. Assume that the product can be produced at the rate of $B = 200{,}000$ units per year. Each production run costs $k = \$5000$ to set up, and each item has a variable production cost of $c = \$10$. The annual cost of holding inventory is $h = \$.20$ (20 cents) per dollar value.

The optimal production run is of size

$$Q^* = \sqrt{\frac{2(100{,}000)5000}{.20(10)}}\sqrt{\frac{200{,}000}{200{,}000 - 100{,}000}}$$

$$= 31{,}623 \text{ items}$$

and each production run lasts

$$T_1^* = \frac{Q^*}{B} = \frac{31{,}623}{200{,}000} = .158 \text{ years (or approximately 58 days)}$$

while a new production run occurs every

$$T^* = \frac{Q^*}{A} = \frac{31{,}623}{100{,}000} = .316 \text{ years (or approximately 115 days)}$$

The total annual relevant cost of the above production plan is

$$TC = \left(\frac{100{,}000}{31{,}623}\right)5000 + .20(10)\left(\frac{31{,}623}{2}\right)\left(\frac{200{,}000 - 100{,}000}{200{,}000}\right)$$

$$= 15{,}811 + 15{,}812$$

$$= 31{,}623 \text{ dollars per year}$$

11-6 INVENTORY DECISIONS WITH UNCERTAIN FACTORS

Two major uncertain variables are encountered in inventory decisions. The most important variable is demand. The other variable is the lead time required when filling orders. Our model provides an (r,Q) policy, so that orders are triggered whenever the current inventory position falls below the *reorder point*, denoted by r. At that time, Q items are ordered.

Figure 11-5 portrays the behavior of an inventory system when de-

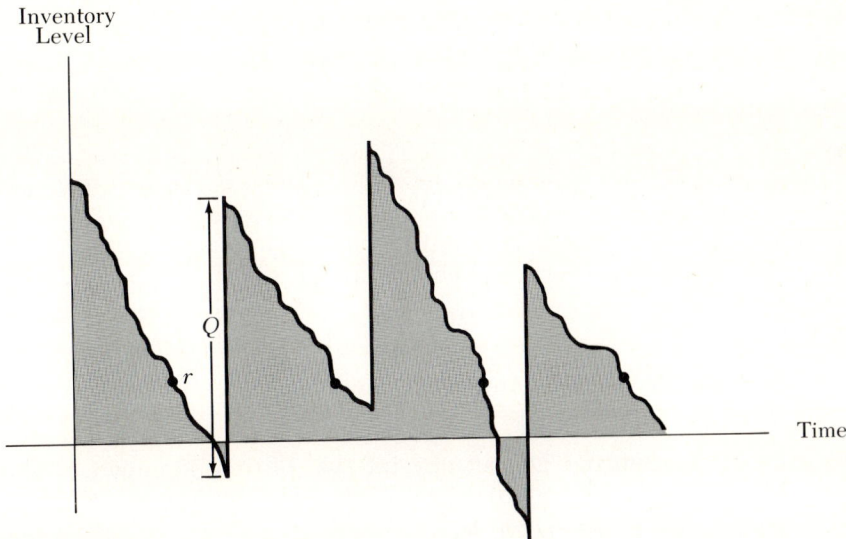

Figure 11-5
Behavior of inventory system over time using (r,Q) policy with uncertain demand and lead time.

mand and lead time are uncertain. Notice that the inventory depletion occurs erratically because of the varying intensity of demand. Orders are placed whenever the inventory position falls below r. But because of continued variations in demand and unpredictable lead times, shortages occur in some periods and not in others. Thus erratic behavior results in varying cycle durations and beginning inventory positions.

We present two simple continuous review models that may be used to find the optimal inventory policy in the multi-period case. Our models are only approximately correct, although they usually will provide solutions as good as more complex formulations. We consider only the case where *shorted items are backordered* and where no sales are lost due to shortages. (Although only a minor adjustment in these models is needed to handle the case of lost sales, a detailed discussion is beyond the scope of this book.)

EOQ Model for Uncertain Demand

Our objective is to minimize total annual relevant cost. Since demands and lead times are now uncertain, the quantity minimized must be an *expected cost*. This quantity is the sum of the following expected values:

(1) Annual ordering cost
(2) Annual holding cost
(3) Annual shortage cost

Although demand no longer is presumed to be certain, we will assume that the mean annual demand rate applies uniformly over time. We use the symbol

$$A = \text{Mean annual demand rate}$$

(Although the *mean* rate is constant, demands can vary from period to period.) If Q items are ordered each time, at a cost of k per order, it then follows that

$$\text{Expected annual ordering cost} = \left(\frac{A}{Q}\right)k$$

The actual demand D over any interval of time is uncertain and must be specified in terms of a probability distribution, as earlier in the chapter. Rather than some fixed calendar period like a day, week, or month, our model considers that level of demand occurring during the lead time for filling an order. For this purpose we use *the probability distribution of lead-time demand*:

Probability of d units demanded in lead time $= P_L[D = d]$

The above distribution reflects two uncertainties: that regarding the demands themselves and that surrounding the duration of the lead time. Our model focuses on the expected value for D:

$$\mu = \text{Mean lead-time demand}$$

Each inventory cycle begins when an order arrives. At this time, stock is depleted until it falls below the reorder point r (assumed to exceed μ), when a new order is placed. Continued depletion occurs until the order arrives. Any items short are then provided from the incoming shipment. The expected level of inventory just before the order arrives is $r - \mu$, so that the subsequent cycle begins with an expected inventory of $Q + r - \mu$ items. Because the mean rate of depletion is uniform, the average inventory level during a cycle must be the average of these quantities. Thus,

$$\text{Expected average cycle inventory} = \frac{1}{2}[(Q + r - \mu) + r - \mu]$$

$$= \frac{Q}{2} + r - \mu$$

As in the earlier EOQ models, we let h represent the annual cost per dollar value for holding items in inventory. It follows that

$$\text{Expected annual holding cost} = hc\left[\frac{Q}{2} + r - \mu\right]$$

The most complicated part of the model involves the shortage cost component. This depends on the number of items backordered each cycle, which because of the uncertain lead-time demand, is a random variable. Since items are only backordered when lead-time demand exceeds the reorder point r, we determine *the expected number of backorders per cycle*:

$$B(r) = \sum_{d>r} (d - r) P_L[D = d]$$

The expected number of cycles per year is A/Q, so that multiplying $B(r)$ by this and the penalty s for each item short, we obtain

$$\text{Expected annual shortage cost} = s\left(\frac{A}{Q}\right) B(r)$$

(We use s to represent the cost of each item short, regardless of how long it is backordered. Thus, this parameter differs from its counterpart in the earlier backordering model, where the penalty applied to the duration of the shortage. Since backordering occurs, no lost sales revenue is included in s.)

The total annual expected cost may be expressed as

$$TEC\ (r,Q) = \left(\frac{A}{Q}\right)k + hc\left[\frac{Q}{2} + r - \mu\right] + s\left(\frac{A}{Q}\right)B\ (r)$$

We wish to find the values Q and r that minimize the above expression.

A mathematical analysis provides the following procedure for finding the optimal levels of these variables:

(1) For a given order quantity Q, the optimal reorder point r is the *smallest* quantity having a cumulative lead-time demand probability such that

$$1 - \frac{hcQ}{sA} \leq P_L[D \leq r]$$

(2) For a given order point s, the optimal order quantity is found from

$$Q = \sqrt{\frac{2A[k + sB(r)]}{hc}}$$

To solve for either r or Q, the value of the other variable must be known. Before we can get started, a seed value must be obtained for one or the other. This then determines the level for the second variable, which can be used to refine the value of the other one. This procedure continues back and forth—using the last Q to get the next s and that s to get the next Q—until no values change.

A good starting value may be obtained using the Wilson formula for the economic order quantity when no backordering is allowed:

$$Q_1 = \sqrt{\frac{2Ak}{hc}}$$

The subscript 1 indicates that this is just the first try at the order quantity.

An Illustration

Suppose a stationery store stocks carbon typewriter ribbons. The demands and lead times are uncertain, but historical experience indicates that the lead-time demand distribution in Table 11-1 applies.

Table 11-1

LEAD-TIME DEMAND PROBABILITY DISTRIBUTION FOR THE TYPEWRITER RIBBONS

Possible Demand d	Probability $P_L[D=d]$	Demand × Probability	Cumulative Probability $P_L[D \le d]$
0	.01	0	.01
1	.07	.07	.08
2	.16	.32	.24
3	.20	.60	.44
4	.19	.76	.63
5	.16	.80	.79
6	.10	.60	.89
7	.06	.42	.95
8	.03	.24	.98
9	.01	.09	.99
10	.01	.10	1.00
		$\mu = 4.00$	

The mean annual demand is 1500 ribbons per year; the cost of placing an order is $5; each ribbon has a wholesale price of $1.50; the store finances its working capital through bank loans at a rate of 12% per annum; and the store incurs a penalty in future profits estimated to be 50 cents for each ribbon short and backordered. Thus, we have the following parameters:

$$A = 1500$$
$$k = \$5$$
$$c = \$1.5$$
$$h = \$.12$$
$$s = \$.5$$

and the mean lead-time demand is computed in Table 11-1 to be

$$\mu = 4$$

The starting value for the order quantity is

$$Q_1 = \sqrt{\frac{2(1500)5}{.12(1.5)}} = 289$$

Using the value $Q = 289$ in step number 1, we compute

$$1 - \frac{hcQ}{sA} = 1 - \frac{.12(1.5)289}{.5(1500)} = .93$$

The smallest cumulative probability greater than or equal to the above is determined from Table 11-1 to be

$$P_L[D \leq 7] = .95$$

so that the reorder point is $r = 7$ ribbons.

Using $r = 7$ in step 2, we must first evaluate the corresponding expected number of backorders per cycle, $B(r) = B(7)$. This quantity is computed as follows:

Demand d	Probability $P_L[D = d]$	Difference $d - r = d - 7$	Difference $\times$ Probability
8	.03	1	.03
9	.01	2	.02
10	.01	3	.03
			$B(7) = .08$

Substituting $B(7) = .08$ into the expression for Q, we have

$$Q = \sqrt{\frac{2(1500)[5 + .5(.08)]}{.12(1.5)}} = 290$$

Since this differs from the initial value for Q of 289, we must continue the procedure with a second *iteration*.

Returning to step 1, we use $Q = 290$ to recompute the order point. First we find

$$1 - \frac{hcQ}{sA} = 1 - \frac{.12(1.5)290}{.5(1500)} = .93$$

which is identical to the cumulative probability indicated for $r = 7$ found before. The reorder point does not change. Thus, the optimal (r, Q) policy involves

$$r = 7$$
$$Q = 290$$

so that $Q = 290$ ribbons should be ordered whenever the current inventory falls below $r = 7$. The total annual expected cost of this policy is

$$TEC = \left(\frac{1500}{290}\right)5 + .12(1.5)\left[\frac{290}{2} + 7 - 4\right] + .50\left(\frac{1500}{290}\right)(.08)$$

$$= 25.86 + 26.64 + .21$$

$$= 52.71 \text{ dollars}$$

Notice that the Wilson formula for the simple inventory model provides an order quantity of $Q_1 = 289$, which is very close to the final optimal solution of $Q = 290$. Although the starting and final values will not always be so close (this depends on the various parameter values and the lead-time demand distribution), this illustration shows that sometimes the naive inventory model works quite well—even though it assumes demand is certain and constant.

The expected inventory on-hand when an order arrives is called the *safety stock*. This is the difference between the reorder point and mean lead-time demand:

$$\text{Safety stock} = r - \mu$$

In the above illustration the safety stock is $7 - 4 = 3$ ribbons. On the average, with the optimal policy of (7,290), 3 ribbons will be on hand when any order arrives.

EOQ Model When Demand Is Normally Distributed

For large inventory systems involving many units or for one selling divisible quantities, such as gasoline, it is convenient to represent demand by a continuous probability distribution. The preceding model needs only slight modification to find the optimal (r, Q) policy when lead time is normally distributed.

The main change is the manner for computing the expected number of backorders per cycle $B(r)$. This is somewhat complicated because of the nature of continuous random variables. To illustrate the principles involved, consider Figure 11-6, where the normal curve for lead-time demand is superimposed on a graph relating number of items short to possible demands; the line rising at 45 degrees (with slope one) indicates that each unit demanded beyond the order point is a shortage and must be backordered.

Recall that it is the *area* under the normal curve which provides

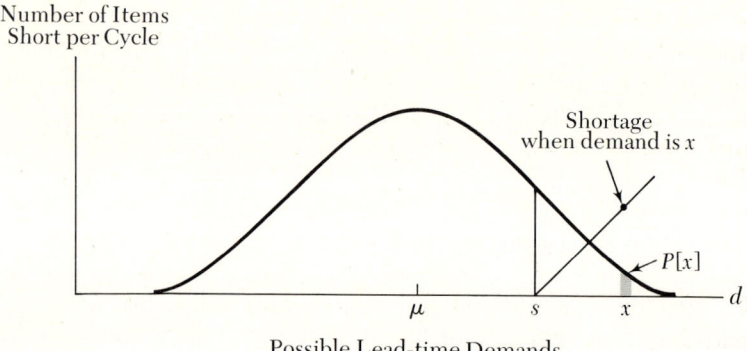

Figure 11-6
Graphical explanation of a normal loss function.

probability values. By dividing the area in the upper tail beyond s into small intervals, we may see how the desired expected value can be computed. If the area corresponding to each interval is multiplied by the shortage at a representative demand for that interval, as illustrated at point x, and summed, the resulting value approximates the expected number of backorders. Fortunately, it is not necessary to actually make the approximation, since a table has been constructed for this purpose. Thus we compute

$$B(r) = \sigma L\left(\frac{r-\mu}{\sigma}\right)$$

where μ = Mean lead-time demand

σ = Standard deviation in lead-time demand

L is the *normal loss function*, having values listed in Appendix Table C.*

An Illustration

We may illustrate this normal demand model with an example of how to find the optimal inventory policy for unleaded gasoline at an oil refinery. Because of varying crude-oil availability and other petroleum processing requirements, the starting time for processing a batch of unleaded gasoline is unpredictable. The lead time is the period from

---

* This function is ordinarily used in calculating expected opportunity losses, which accounts for its name. Those applications are discussed in Chapter 8.

when an order is issued until the final gasoline begins to flow into the holding tanks. We will assume that the demand occurring while this is happening is normally distributed with a mean of $\mu = 200{,}000$ gallons and a standard deviation of $\sigma = 20{,}000$ gallons. When the unleaded tank is empty, trucks scheduled to deliver that fuel are dispatched with other gasolines, and the unleaded customers receive their backordered requirements with a later special delivery.

The mean annual demand rate for unleaded fuel from this refinery is $A = 40$ million gallons per year. The fixed costs of a production run are $k = 1000$ dollars, and the wholesale value of this gasoline is 40 cents per gallon or $c = .40$ dollars. The annual opportunity cost of funds tied up in inventory is 20 cents per dollar value, or $h = .20$ dollars. From the refinery's point of view, the only cost for backordering fuel is the expense of the special delivery, which exceeds regular costs by a nickel per gallon, so that $s = .05$ dollars per gallon. (For simplicity we will assume that the production rate is so much greater than the inventory depletion rate that the savings in holding costs while simultaneously filling and emptying the holding tank are too small to matter.)

First Iteration. As the first step in finding the optimal order quantity, we determine a starting value

$$Q_1 = \sqrt{\frac{2(40{,}000{,}000)(1000)}{.20(.40)}} = 1{,}000{,}000 \text{ gallons}$$

We then use this for Q in calculating

$$1 - \frac{hcQ}{sA} = 1 - \frac{.20(.40)(1{,}000{,}000)}{.05(40{,}000{,}000)} = .96$$

The reorder point r is that possible lead-time demand with a cumulative probability *equal* to the above (since the distribution is continuous). This corresponds to a normal deviate z for the area under the standard normal curve. We choose that normal deviate having area between the mean and z closest to $.96 - .5 = .46$. Reading Appendix Table B in reverse, we have

$$z = 1.75$$

This means that the reorder point r lies z standard deviations above the mean lead-time demand. Thus,

$$r = \mu + z\sigma$$
$$= 200{,}000 + 1.75(20{,}000)$$
$$= 235{,}000 \text{ gallons}$$

The above figure is used to calculate Q again using step 2 on page 318. This requires computing the expected number of backorders in an inventory cycle $B(r)$. For $r = 235{,}000$ gallons this is

$$B(235{,}000) = (20{,}000) L\left(\frac{235{,}000 - 200{,}000}{20{,}000}\right)$$

$$= (20{,}000) L(1.75)$$

From Appendix Table C, we find that $L(1.75) = .01617$, so that

$$B(235{,}000) = (20{,}000)(.01617) = 323.4$$

Substituting the above and the other parameter values into the equation for Q, we determine an improved value for the order quantity:

$$Q = \sqrt{\frac{2(40{,}000{,}000)[1000 + .05(323.4)]}{.20(.40)}} = 1{,}008{,}050 \text{ gallons}$$

Since the above value differs from the starting value of $Q_1 = 1{,}000{,}000$, a further iteration is required.

Second Iteration. Returning to step 1, we use the above order quantity to calculate

$$1 - \frac{hcQ}{sA} = 1 - \frac{.20(.40)(1{,}008{,}050)}{.05(40{,}000{,}000)} = .9597$$

The nearest normal deviate corresponding to the above is $z = 1.75$, which is identical to the last one. *No further steps are required,* since r, and hence Q, will not change from before.

The optimal policy is

$$Q = 1{,}008{,}050 \text{ gallons}$$

$$r = 235{,}000 \text{ gallons}$$

11-7 ANALYTIC AND NUMERICAL SOLUTION METHODS

The EOQ (economic order quantity) models discussed in this chapter have been purposely kept simple. More complex models are available to handle situations where demand is certain. For instance, a second shortage penalty that does not depend upon the duration of a backorder is sometimes included in more general representations.

The models described here can be expanded to include several different types of items. These more advanced models consider constraints that might reflect limitations on storage space or the dollar investment in inventory. Slight extensions of the basic EOQ models also permit treatment of quantity discounts.

The procedures for analyzing inventory decisions are often quite complex. These may be divided into two categories. *Analytic methods* solve the model mathematically, giving precise answers that lead to truly optimal policies. All the procedures described so far are analytic methods. Unfortunately, we have seen that the problem situations for which a particular model applies are severely limited. Often, the representation of the inventory system itself must be simplified or slightly changed in order to make an existing model fit the situation. This might lead to decidedly inferior solutions in spite of their mathematical perfection.

To avoid the above pitfall, complex inventory systems are often evaluated by *numerical methods*. Strict optimization is not the goal; rather, a reasonably good policy is sought. A numerical solution may be obtained by an essentially "trial and error" process or by making suitable approximations. Two major types of numerical methods are employed. One of these embodies *heuristic procedures*, which might be called an "optimal-seeking" approach. Under such a scheme, a starting solution is obtained and successively improved through minor changes until further improvements are hard to find.

When uncertainty is present, *Monte Carlo simulation* is a very satisfactory numerical solution procedure. (Chapter 18 is devoted entirely to this topic.) Usually done with the assistance of a digital computer, simulation evaluates alternatives "on paper" through exhaustive trial operation. As applied to inventory decisions, various combinations of (r, Q) policies can be evaluated by playing each one out over a very long time frame, such as 100 years. The one yielding minimum average cost is then chosen for actual use. Simulation can be used to tackle very complicated problems too intractable to solve realistically any other way.

PROBLEMS

11-1 A department sells 1000 water beds per year. At a 100% mark-up, the beds sell for $80 each. It costs $200 to place an order with the supplier. The annual holding cost per dollar value of items held in inventory is $.25. Find the economic water-bed order size. How often should orders be placed?

11-2 Albers, Crumbly, and Itch sells mosquito repellents all over the world. Demand for the Malabug brand is 10,000 bottles per year. The African supplier charges AC&I $2 per bottle; the fixed cost of placing an order for Malabug is $100. AC&I targets a 15-percent annual rate-of-return on working-capital funds. The cost for physical storage of Malabug is fixed.
(a) Determine the optimal order quantity and inventory cycle duration for Malabug.
(b) How many orders should be placed each year?
(c) Find the total relevant annual inventory cost for Malabug.

11-3 A car-parts wholesaler supplies 20 batteries each weekday to various service stations. Batteries are purchased from the manufacturer in lots of 100 each for $1000 per lot. Multiple and fractional lots can be ordered at any time, and all orders are filled the next day. Each order placed with the manufacturer incurs a $50-handling charge plus a $200 per lot freight charge. The incremental cost is $.50 per year to store a battery in inventory. The wholesaler finances inventory investments by paying its holding company $1\frac{1}{2}$ percent monthly for borrowed funds.
(a) Determine the values for k, A, c, and h.
(b) How many batteries should be ordered, and how often, in order to minimize total annual inventory cost?

11-4 Suppose that the store in Problem 11-2 can backorder Malabug when it is out of stock. But since most customers are simply itching to go back packing and may have to delay their departure while waiting, there is a penalty of $10 per year in lost goodwill for every bottle short.
(a) Determine the optimal order quantity, inventory level, and time between orders. What proportion of the time is Malabug out of stock?
(b) Compute the total annual relevant cost for the inventory policy found above. Is this larger or smaller than your answer to Problem 11-2 (c)? Do you think the same conclusion would be reached if the annual shortage penalty were $1000 per bottle?

11-5 The headquarters office for a large conglomerate buys 1000 reams of stationery every two months at a cost of $5 each. Usage of paper is uniform and constant over time. The cost of placing an order with the supplier is $50. Assume that the present inventory policy is optimal, so that it minimizes annual stationery inventory cost. How many reams are demanded in one year? What is the annual holding cost per dollar value of items held in inventory implicit under the present policy?

11-6 Suppose that the office in the above problem finds that it costs $2 to hold a ream of paper in inventory for one year.
(a) What is the annual holding cost per dollar value of items held in inventory?

(b) Suppose that the policy of ordering 1000 reams every two months must be re-evaluated because shortages are now allowed. Using an annual penalty of $10 per ream short, determine the optimal order quantity and inventory level. How often should orders be placed?

11-7 The manufacturer of Snail Hail, a garden mollusk pesticide, distributes its product from a plant warehouse. The plant has the capacity for making 1000 tons per year at a variable cost of $100 per ton. However, only 200 tons of Snail Hail are sold annually. The cost of setting up a production run is $2000. The net cost for holding the highly volatile Snail Hail in inventory is $.40 per dollar value per year.
(a) Find the economic production quantity.
(b) How long is each inventory cycle?
(c) What is the duration of a production run for Snail Hail?

11-8 Ace Widgets Supply distributes two products, the Regular and the Deluxe, throughout the Midwest. The demands for the two items are independent; a total of 2000-Regular and 4000-Deluxe items are sold every year. The Regular items cost Ace $10 each; the Deluxe models cost twice as much. Ace's holding cost is $.25 annually for each dollar invested in inventory. Ordering costs are $100 per batch for each item, and the Regular version may be ordered only when a Deluxe order is placed, but Regulars can be ordered less often.
(a) Find the optimal order quantities for each item. What are the total annual relevant inventory costs in each case?
(b) Suppose that a maximum of $10,000 can be invested in inventory at any given time. Can the quantities found in part (a) still apply?
(c) Ace's warehouse can only store at most 1000 items. Can the quantities found in part (a) still apply?
(d) Suppose that the Regular and Deluxe models must be ordered at the same time and that each order costs $200. Treating combinations of one-Regular and two-Deluxe units as a single item, determine the economic order quantity and the corresponding total annual relevant cost. Would this procedure be less costly than the one in part (a)? Explain.

11-9 Mrs. Moo's is a self-sufficient dairy where all feed grasses are grown on the premises. To rejuvenate the grass and trigger growth, periodic fertilizing is necessary. The dairy herd eats full-grown grass at the rate of 5000 acres per year. Each fertilizing costs $100 to set up and requires $50 worth of chemicals per acre to create full growth. It takes a fertilized acre one-tenth of a year to reach maturity. There are 1000 acres of grassland at Mrs. Moo's. The dairy finances its chemical purchases through the local bank at 10-percent annual interest.

(a) Determine the number of acres Mrs. Moo's should fertilize with each application, how often fertilizing should take place, and how many applications must be made each year.
(b) Do you think the EOQ model is wholly satisfactory for this problem? Explain.

11-10 A large vending-machine operating company must establish a policy for periodically restocking its candy machines and at the same time collecting coins deposited by customers. The total labor cost to restock a machine is $7, most of which is due to travel time. Each machine can hold quite a lot of candy, so they need not be filled to capacity. All machines are identical, and each satisfies a demand of 5000 candy bars per year. Candy bars cost 10 cents each and are sold for a quarter. The firm's annual opportunity cost of working capital is 20 percent. A significant aspect in establishing a policy are all those quarters uselessly locked up in coin boxes — quicker retrieval of these funds translates directly into smaller working-capital requirements.
(a) What amounts apply for c and h? (You may assume that the same cost of working capital applies to the value of the candy and to the value of the coins. Also, the average candy-bar inventory is the same as the average inventory of quarters.)
(b) Determine the restocking quantity that minimizes total annual cost. How often should the machines be restocked?

11-11 Sylvester's Bootery caters to a clientele that cannot obtain the more difficult sizes of shoes anywhere else. An optimal policy is sought for stocking size $8\frac{1}{2}$ EEE men's wingtip shoes. These cost Sylvester $20-a-pair. The manufacturer charges a flat $10 for each size and style special ordered, regardless of quantity. When out of stock, all customers will backorder this shoe; but they will ordinarily reheel and resole their present shoes while waiting, so Sylvester loses some amount of future profits, which he judges to be $5 for each pair shorted. He finances his inventory with a 10-percent annual interest bank loan. The following lead-time demand probabilities apply.

Demand	Probability
5	.1
6	.2
7	.3
8	.2
9	.1
10	.1

Sylvester sells an average of 100 size $8\frac{1}{2}$ EEE wingtip pairs each year.
(a) Determine the mean lead-time demand.

(b) Find the optimal levels for the order quantity, order point, and order level.
(c) What is the safety stock level?
(d) Determine the expected annual inventory cost for this particular store.

11-12 Sylvester in the above problem experiences the same costs for size 10 AA shoes, which are rarer, involving an average of only 50 sales per year. The following lead-time demand distribution applies.

Demand	Probability
8	.05
9	.13
10	.21
11	.36
12	.11
13	.07
14	.04
15	.03

For this shoe, answer (a)–(d) given above.

11-13 Suppose that the oil refinery discussed in the chapter experiences identical costs for its leaded regular gasoline, which has a mean annual demand of 100 million gallons and a normally distributed lead-time demand of 500,000 gallons with a standard deviation of 100,000 gallons.

Determine the optimal order quantity, order point, and order level.

Twelve

Linear Programming: An Introduction

This chapter considers what is perhaps the most successful quantitative procedure currently used in helping to make business decisions. Referred to as *linear programming,* this collection of tools has a wide variety of applications. It is used by oil companies to determine the best mixture of ingredients for blending gasoline. It has successfully served in developing optimal schedules for transportation, production, and construction. And it has been applied in such diverse areas as finance and advertising. Without doubt, linear programming has had the widest impact of all modern quantitative methods. Annual cost savings attributable to it alone have been estimated to be billions of dollars.

What is linear programming? The word programming, here, is not to be confused with the written instructions to a computer called computer programs. In the present context, we speak of programming as a form of planning. This involves the economic allocation of scarce resources so that all basic requirements are met. Thus, *programming establishes a plan that efficiently applies all factors toward achieving the desired objective.* For example, such a program plan will tell a refinery manager the precise number of gallons of various petroleum distillates to use in blending a batch of gasoline with a certain octane rating; the plan furthermore achieves this in such a way that costs are minimized and the ultimate automobile exhaust meets environmental pollution limits.

By linear programming we mean that the ultimate plan is obtained through a mathematical procedure involving *linear relationships.* That is, the entire problem can be expressed in terms of straight lines, planes, or analogous geometrical figures. There can be no curved surfaces in any graphical representation of the problem. The mathematical model expressing the problem relates all requirements and management's goals by means of algebraic expressions representing straight lines.

Although this book is restricted to linear situations, similar allocation models and procedures exist for more general relationships. Under the umbrella of mathematical programming are included integer, quadratic, convex, and stochastic programming; each approach is similar to linear programming but involves mathematics beyond the scope of this text.

A PROBLEM ILLUSTRATION 12-1

The Redwood Furniture Company manufactures tables and chairs as part of its line of patio furniture. Table 12-1 shows the resources consumed and the unit profits for each product. For simplicity, it is assumed that only two resources are consumed in manufacturing the patio furniture: wood, of which there are 300 board feet in inventory, and labor, 110 hours of which are available. The owner wishes to determine how many

Table 12-1
DATA FOR THE REDWOOD FURNITURE PROBLEM

RESOURCE	UNIT REQUIREMENTS		AMOUNT AVAILABLE
	Table	*Chair*	
Wood (board feet)	30	20	300
Labor (hours)	5	10	110
Unit profit	$6	$8	

tables and chairs should be made in order to maximize total patio furniture profit.

Linear programming is not essential to establishing such a production plan. After all, it is a recent technique widely used only for the last 30 years, while people have made furniture for several thousand years. Without any knowledge of linear programming, the owner might decide to make as many chairs as possible, since these are the most profitable items. Altogether there is enough labor for exactly 11 chairs, and the owner's profit would be $88. But this plan would leave 80 board feet of wood unused. Might the owner be better off making some tables and fewer chairs? If so, how many of each? Which brings us back to the start. Linear programming will tell the owner of Redwood Furniture the exact number of tables and chairs that will *maximize profit*.

12-2 FORMULATING THE LINEAR PROGRAM

We begin by treating the number of tables and the number of chairs as unknown quantities, or *variables*. We then will express the problem algebraically, using the following symbols:

$$X_T = \text{Number of tables made}$$
$$X_C = \text{Number of chairs made}$$

Our usual convention will be to represent a problem's essential variables in terms of X, with subscripts taken directly from the variable's description. Thus, using X_T (X sub T) to represent the number of tables, where T is the first letter in the word table, eases our task in abstracting the problem into a *mathematical model*. On occasions we will use letters other than X and numbers to represent subscripts.

Each resource places limitations on the values of X_T and X_C. In the case of wood, any production plan must meet the requirement that

$$\text{Wood for tables} + \text{Wood for chairs} \leq \text{Available wood}$$

The above *constraint* says that the wood used cannot exceed the amount available. Note that this constraint does not require that every single foot of wood be used, only that we may not use more than there is. This is why we use the symbol $\leq$, which means "less than or equal to." It would be less flexible, and hence less desirable, to be unduly restrictive by forcing the use of all wood, which is what using $=$ in the above constraint would indicate.

The wood constraint is referred to as an *inequality*. It is convenient to express it in terms of the table and chair quantity variables in the following equivalent form:

$$30X_T + 20X_C \leq 300 \quad \text{(wood)}$$

The first term on the left side $30X_T$ expresses the total amount of wood to be used in the manufacture of tables and is found by multiplying the 30 board feet of wood required for each table by the number of tables X_T. Similarly, since each chair requires 20 board feet, $20X_C$ represents the total amount of wood that will be used in chairs.

An analogous constraint pertains to the labor resource:

$$5X_T + 10X_C \leq 110 \quad \text{(labor)}$$

As before, this simply says that the total quantity of labor expended on either tables or chairs cannot exceed the 110 units available. Together, the above constraint inequalities establish limits for the values of X_T and X_C.

The profit objective may also be stated algebraically. Representing total profit by P, we relate this to the variables by

$$P = 6X_T + 8X_C$$

since total profit consists of the profit derived from tables at $6 each plus that from chairs at $8 each. Thus, $6X_T$ is the profit earned by making and selling tables, while $8X_C$ is the corresponding amount from making chairs. Remember that the owner wants to achieve the greatest possible profit. That is, he wishes to maximize P. We may incorporate this objective directly into the mathematical model by writing the profit equation as

$$\text{Maximize} \quad P = 6X_T + 8X_C \quad \text{(objective)}$$

In this form, the above profit expression provides the *objective function*.

Before proceeding, we note that there are two fundamental types of objective functions, depending upon the goal. Instead of maximizing profit, in some problems we want to minimize cost. In such situations the objective function would take the form minimize C with C representing the unknown cost variable.

We are now ready to incorporate all of the above into a single mathematical model. This is simply a prescription of exactly what is to be done within the resource limitations. The model itself, referred to as a *linear program*, is

Letting X_T = Number of tables made

X_C = Number of chairs made

Maximize $\quad P = 6X_T + 8X_C \quad$ (objective)

Subject to $\quad 30X_T + 20X_C \leq 300 \quad$ (wood)

$\quad 5X_T + 10X_C \leq 110 \quad$ (labor)

where $\quad X_T, X_C \geq 0 \quad$ (non-negativity)

The above linear program identifies the variables and specifies the objective, subject to those constraints that limit what may be done.

The linear program includes further limitations not previously encountered. The *non-negativity conditions* state that the variables cannot assume negative values. Although a negative quantity of tables or chairs makes no sense at all, without these prescriptions it would be mathematically possible to get a solution such as $X_T = -10, X_C = 16$, with a profit of $68. Obviously this solution is impossible because it implies the absurdity of disassembling 10 tables, retrieving all the wood and labor used to fabricate them, with both the resources "saved" going into more chairs than could have been made with the original wood and labor!

12-3 THE GRAPHICAL SOLUTION METHOD

A linear program is only a mathematical *formulation*. It merely sets up the problem. We still don't have an answer to the question: How many tables and chairs should be made? The answer is provided by the *solution* to the linear program.

Several different approaches or *algorithms* might be used in solving this problem. In this book we will consider a variety of algorithms for solving linear programs. For simple problems, the easiest procedure is the *graphical method*.

We begin by constructing a graph. This graph represents the linear program in two dimensions, one for the number of tables X_T and the other for the number of chairs X_C. We start with a piece of graph paper, using a ruler to make a heavy horizontal line for the X_T axis and then a vertical one for the X_C axis as in Figure 12-1. For convenience, we place tick marks every five squares along the respective axes, labeling these in increments of 5, starting at zero in each case. Any point in this two-dimensional space corresponds to a production quantity combination, or plan, for tables and chairs.

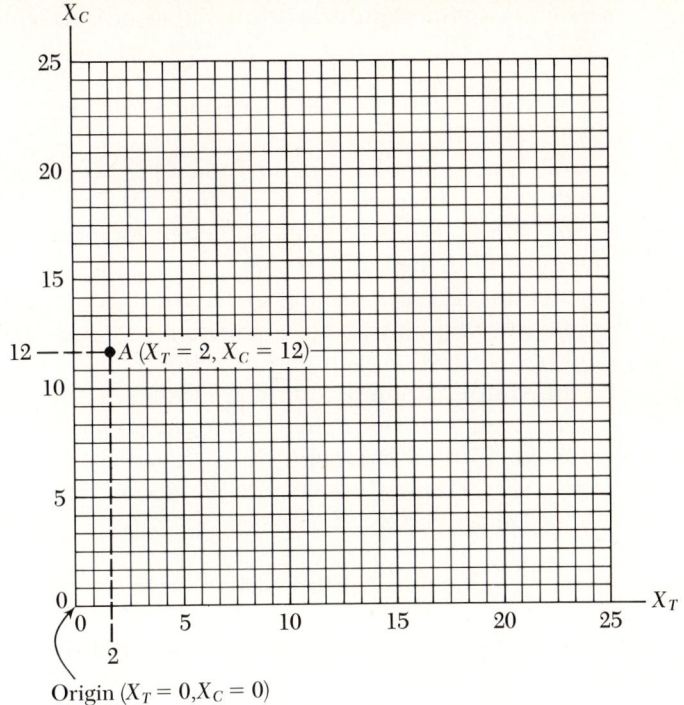

Figure 12-1
Linear programming axes constructed with graph paper.

The *origin* is the point where the two axes cross and can be represented in terms of its coordinates along the respective axes: ($X_T = 0$, $X_C = 0$). Point A has coordinates ($X_T = 2$, $X_C = 12$), representing its distance of 2 units along the X_T axis and its height of 12 units along the X_C axis. This same point represents a production plan for 2 tables and 12 chairs.

Plotting Constraint Lines

Our next step is to plot the constraints on the graph. We begin with the wood constraint

$$30X_T + 20X_C \le 300 \quad \text{(wood)}$$

Temporarily, we consider the special case where the left side (wood

12-3 THE GRAPHICAL SOLUTION METHOD

used) is precisely equal to the right side (available wood), which gives us the wood *equation*

$$30X_T + 20X_C = 300 \qquad \text{(wood)}$$

When plotted on our graph, the above expression will provide a line. It is therefore referred to as the wood *constraint line*. All points falling on this line represent combinations of table and chair quantities that consume exactly the amount of available wood.

In constructing this line, we use the geometrical principle that any line can be defined by two points. These may then be connected by positioning a straight-edge beside each and drawing the connecting line.

Generally, the simplest points to find are the ones where the line cuts the respective axes. Consider first the X_T axis. The intersection point is called the *horizontal intercept*. Since it will have no vertical height, it will have $X_C = 0$ for one coordinate. Plugging this value for X_C into the wood equation we have

$$30X_T + 20(0) = 300$$

Since 20 times zero is zero, we may ignore the second term on the left, so that we have

$$30X_T = 300$$

Dividing both sides by 30 we obtain

$$X_T = 300/30 = 10$$

Thus, the remaining coordinate for the horizontal intercept is $X_T = 10$. In a similar way, we obtain the *vertical intercept* by setting $X_T = 0$ and solving the wood equation for X_C:

$$30(0) + 20X_C = 300$$

$$X_C = 300/20 = 15$$

We then plot these intercepts in Figure 12-2 and draw the wood constraint line to connect them. (For clarity, the grid squares have been omitted.)

The wood constraint line represents all possible production plans where the entire 300 board feet of available wood is consumed. This is true for the vertical intercept ($X_T = 0$, $X_C = 15$), which corresponds to 0 tables and 15 chairs, and for the horizontal intercept ($X_T = 10$, $X_C = 0$), where 10 tables and 0 chairs are made. For any other point on this line,

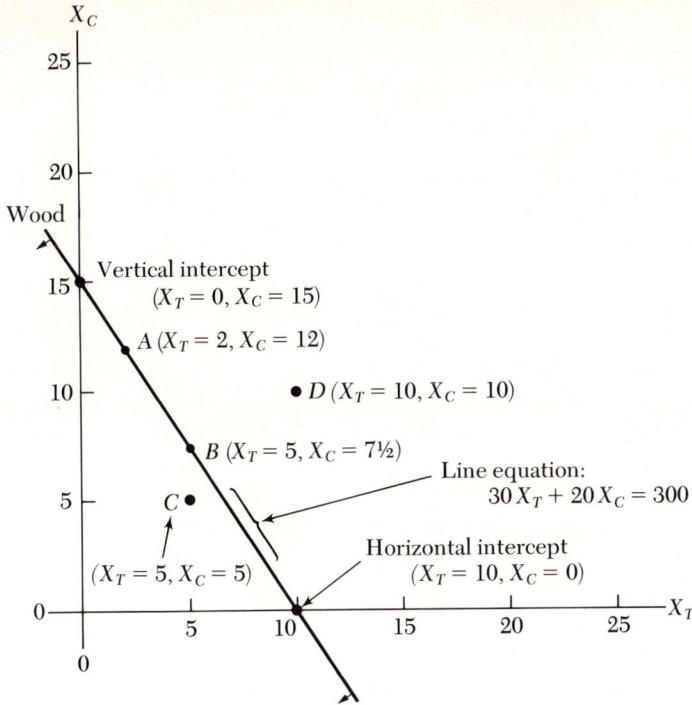

Figure 12-2
Plotting the wood constraint line for the Redwood Furniture problem.

such as point A ($X_T = 2$, $X_C = 12$) or point B ($X_T = 5$, $X_C = 7\frac{1}{2}$), exactly 300 board feet of wood are used. Note that it is possible in linear programming to have fractional quantities; they need not be whole numbers.

Finding the Valid Side of the Constraint Line

Of course, the original wood constraint does not force us to use all the available wood. We must reconsider the temporarily forgotten ≤. Actually, an inequality relationship like the one for wood may be incorporated in the graph. Any inequality allows all points falling on one side or the other of the constraint line to be valid. The question is: Which is the valid side?

A very simple check is to evaluate a point not on the line itself. If that point satisfies the constraint, then all points on the same side will; if not, then all points on the other side of the line are the valid ones.

12-3 THE GRAPHICAL SOLUTION METHOD

The simplest point to evaluate is the origin. If ($X_T = 0$, $X_C = 0$) satisfies the original wood constraint, then every point on the same side of the wood line will also satisfy it. To check this, we plug the origin's coordinates into the original wood inequality

$$30(0) + 20(0) \leq 300$$

and obtain

$$0 \leq 300$$

which is a true statement. Thus, we know that the origin is valid, and therefore all points lying on the same side, below and left of the line, apply. We indicate the valid side with small arrows, as shown on Figure 12-2.

(Keep in mind that for this particular constraint and situation, the origin happens to be valid. In a different situation, the origin may not satisfy the constraint, and the side of the line opposite to it would be the valid one.)

To show that other points on the same side of the wood line satisfy the constraint, we may consider point C ($X_T=5$, $X_C=5$). This production plan consumes $30(5) + 20(5) = 250$ board feet of wood, which is indeed less than the available 300. Point C is a valid one. Point D ($X_T = 10$, $X_C = 10$), which lies above the wood line, is *infeasible,* since it would consume more, $30(10) + 20(10) = 500$, than the original 300 board feet of wood.

The Feasible Solution Region

The entire procedure outlined above must be duplicated for the labor constraint. The labor equation (again ignoring the $\leq$) is

$$5X_T + 10X_C = 110 \quad \text{(labor)}$$

and the horizontal intercept is $X_T = 110/5 = 22$, while the vertical intercept is $X_C = 110/10 = 11$. The labor line is plotted in the same graph with the wood line in Figure 12-3. The valid side of the labor line lies toward the origin (doing nothing meets the labor constraint).

Any workable production plan must simultaneously satisfy the wood and labor constraints. Any such plan is called a *feasible solution.* The feasible solutions correspond to those points that lie on the valid sides of both constraint lines, within the shaded area in Figure 12-3, called the *feasible solution region.* Since the non-negativity conditions

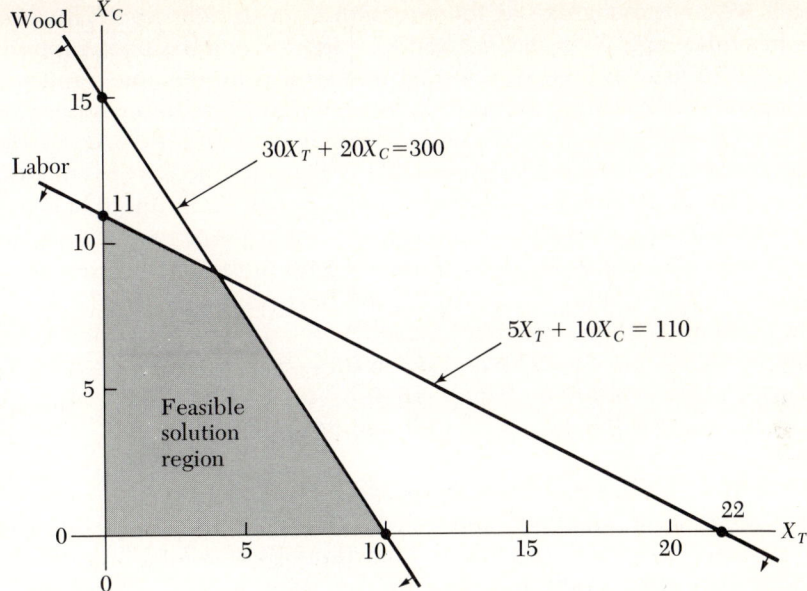

Figure 12-3
A complete graph of the Redwood Furniture problem constraints, showing the feasible solution region.

disallow negative levels for either X_T or X_C, the feasible solution region is bounded not only by the two constraint lines but also by the axes.

The Most Attractive Corner

Redwood Furniture Company could produce that number of tables and chairs corresponding to any point in the feasible region; all of them are possible. However, the owner's objective is to maximize total profit as expressed by the equation

$$P = 6X_T + 8X_C$$

To complete the graphical method, we must incorporate profit in the graph.

Because P itself is unknown we must try out various values for profit on our graph. If we consider $P = 48$ dollars, the objective function may be written as

$$48 = 6X_T + 8X_C$$

which we may recognize as the equation for a straight line. This *profit line* has intercepts $X_T = 48/6 = 8$ and $X_C = 48/8 = 6$ and has been plotted in Figure 12-4 as a dashed line to distinguish it from the constraint lines found earlier. Of course, we could plot a similar line for any other value for P, such as 47, 49, or 53. We chose $P = 48$ because it is evenly divisible by both the unit profits. This made the $P = 48$ profit line easy to construct.

Consider all the points falling on the $P = 48$ profit line that also lie inside the feasible solution region. Every such point corresponds to a production plan yielding profit of exactly $48. But the basic question is: Can we do better, and if so, what is the best profit possible? Let's see what happens with a larger profit, such as $P = 72$ (again, a value evenly divisible by $6 and $8). The corresponding profit line has been plotted as a second dashed line in Figure 12-4. Notice that the $P = 72$ profit lies above the one for $P = 48$. All feasible points on the former will yield the larger profit of $72.

Notice that the two lines are *parallel*. This feature applies for any linear program and for any value of P. This property of parallel profit lines is all that we need to find the maximum profit. Together, the two profit lines on our graph indicate the *direction of increasing profit*, as indicated by the large arrow in Figure 12-4.

Now we can put it all together. We don't yet know the maximum P. But we do know that as larger possible values for P are tried we can plot

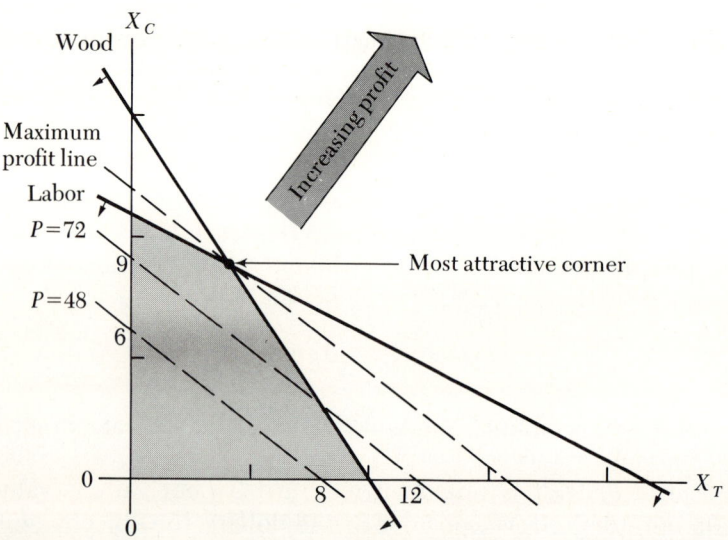

Figure 12-4
Finding the direction of increasing profit and the most attractive corner for the Redwood Furniture problem.

340 LINEAR PROGRAMMING: AN INTRODUCTION

profit lines that will be parallel to the first two and also lie above them. But there is a limit on how large P can become, because we are only interested in a profit that can be achieved by a feasible production plan. By positioning a straight-edge parallel to the original two profit lines in Figure 12-4 and sliding it in the direction of increasing profit, we can see through a visual inspection of the graph that the highest allowable P line must just touch the corner of the feasible solution region where the wood and labor lines intersect. Any higher P line will lie outside the feasible solution region. We refer to this last point as the *most attractive corner*. A third P line has been drawn passing through this corner; this is the maximum profit line. We must now determine which value of P applies to it.

Finding the Optimal Solution

The most attractive corner provides us with the production plan yielding the maximum possible profit. We refer to this plan as the *optimal solution*. Mathematically, the most attractive corner has coordinates determined by simultaneously solving the two equations in two unknowns:

$$30X_T + 20X_C = 300 \quad \text{(wood)}$$
$$5X_T + 10X_C = 110 \quad \text{(labor)}$$

The simplest procedure is to use the method of elimination. We do this by subtracting a multiple of one equation from the other in such a way that one of the variables has a zero coefficient in the resulting equation difference; this leaves only one unknown, whose value can then be directly found. We may eliminate X_C from the equation difference if we subtract 2 times the labor equation from the wood equation:

$$\begin{array}{r} 30X_T + 20X_C = 300 \quad \text{(wood)} \\ -2(5X_T + 10X_C = 110) \quad \text{(labor)} \\ \hline 20X_T + 0X_C = 80 \end{array}$$

Thus,

$$X_T = 80/20 = 4 \text{ tables}$$

Substituting this value into either of the constraint equations we may solve for the value of X_C. Using the wood equation, we have

$$30(4) + 20X_C = 300$$
$$20X_C = 300 - 30(4) = 300 - 120 = 180$$

so that

$$X_C = 180/20 = 9 \text{ chairs}$$

The optimal solution to the Redwood Furniture linear program is thus

$$X_T = 4 \text{ tables}$$
$$X_C = 9 \text{ chairs}$$

and the profit thereby obtained is calculated by substituting these numbers into the objective function:

$$P = 6(4) + 8(9) = 96 \text{ dollars}$$

Figure 12-5 shows the profit line that corresponds to $P = 96$. Notice that this line touches the most attractive corner, confirming our earlier conclusion that the profit line going through this point will have the maximum profit.

At this point, a logical observation is: Wouldn't it be simpler to read the coordinates of the most attractive corner and directly get the

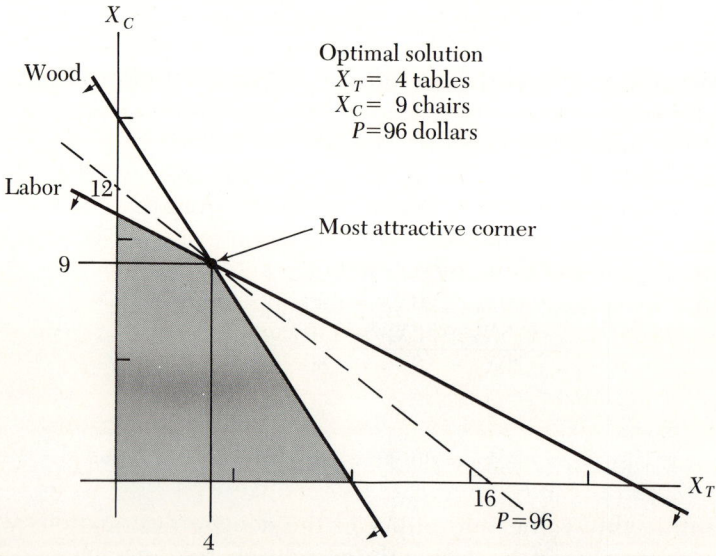

Figure 12-5
The optimal solution for the Redwood Furniture problem.

optimal solution? Just reading the graph would save us a lot of algebra. *For this problem*, that has certainly proven to be true. But what would happen if the true optimal solution had been $X_T = 4\frac{1}{32}$ and $X_C = 8\frac{15}{16}$? The thickness of the pencil lead used in drawing the lines would not allow us to read the graph accurately enough to obtain the answer given by the algebraic solution. The purpose of the graph is to tell us *by visual inspection* where the most attractive corner lies. Even a graph quickly sketched by hand, without graph paper, may suffice for this purpose. But only by then solving algebraically can we be sure to find the precise optimal solution.

SUMMARY OF PROCEDURE 12-4

The steps taken in solving linear programs can now be summarized.

(1) *Formulate the linear program.* A proper formulation begins with a definition of the variables which clearly tells how the symbols apply. The rest is algebraic. First, the objective function (maximize P or minimize C) is stated by an equation. This is followed by the expressions for the constraints. No formulation is complete without a final statement of non-negativity conditions, when they apply.

(2) *Construct a graph and plot the constraint lines.* Ordinarily, this involves finding two points to connect. The points are usually the horizontal and vertical intercepts found from each constraint equation. But for certain constraints, as we shall see, a different pair of points must be found in drawing these lines.

(3) *Determine the valid side for each inequality constraint.* The simplest approach is to see whether the origin (the point of "doing nothing") satisfies the constraint by plugging its coordinates (0, 0) into the inequality. If so, then all points on the origin's side of the line are valid, and the rest are infeasible; if not, the valid points lie on the side opposite the origin. The *two exceptions* to this rule of thumb will be discussed shortly.

(4) *Identify the feasible solution region.* This will be a collection of points on the graph valid for all constraints collectively. These points correspond to feasible plans. Ordinarily the feasible solution region is a contiguous area lying in the positive quadrant, since the non-negativity conditions preclude negative variable values.

(5) *Plot two objective function lines, determining the direction of improvement.* In the case of a profit maximization goal, two P lines will tell us the direction of increasing P. Two lines are needed because the

direction is not always predictable with a single line. The two P lines do not have to intersect the feasible solution region in order to find the direction of increasing P. When the goal is to minimize cost, two C lines will be plotted; here the direction of improvement is one of decreasing C.

(6) *Find the most attractive corner by visual inspection.* This corner will be the last point in the feasible solution region touched by that P or C line formed by sliding a straight-edge in the direction of improvement while holding it parallel to the original two objective lines.

(7) *Determine the optimal solution by algebraically finding the coordinates of the most attractive corner.* Often the optimal solution is represented by the intersection of two constraint lines. However, it might also be the coordinates of a corner point formed by the horizontal or vertical intercept of one constraint equation; in that case, the algebra has already been done, and the optimal solution may be read directly from the coordinates shown on the graph, with no error. *A common mistake of beginning linear programming students is to assume that the most attractive corner must be where the two constraint lines cross.* Were this so, we would never need to construct a graph. Furthermore, there can be three or more constraint lines (as there might have been in the furniture problem had machine time been included as a third resource); only the graph can indicate which intersection is the most attractive corner.

(8) *Determine the objective function value for the optimal solution.* This is found by substituting the optimal variable values into the P or C equation. No solution is complete unless the maximum value of P or the minimum value of C is stated.

12-5 COST MINIMIZATION: A FEED-MIX PROBLEM

Consider a simplification of a problem that might be faced by a seed packager. Determine the number of pounds of two types of seeds that should be used in formulating the wheat portion of a wild bird seed mixture batch. Table 12-2 shows the nutritional content of two seed types, buckwheat and sunflower wheat, along with the minimum required pounds of fat and protein. In addition, there is a roughage content maximum limit of 1500 pounds. Unlimited quantities of either seed type may be purchased at the costs indicated. The packager's goal is to minimize the total cost of satisfying the nutritional requirements.

Table 12-2
DATA FOR THE FEED-MIX PROBLEM

NUTRITIONAL ITEM	PROPORTIONAL CONTENT		TOTAL REQUIREMENT
	Buckwheat	Sunflower Wheat	
Fat	.04	.06	≥ 480 lb
Protein	.12	.10	≥ 1200
Roughage	.10	.15	≤ 1500
Cost per pound	$.18	$.10	

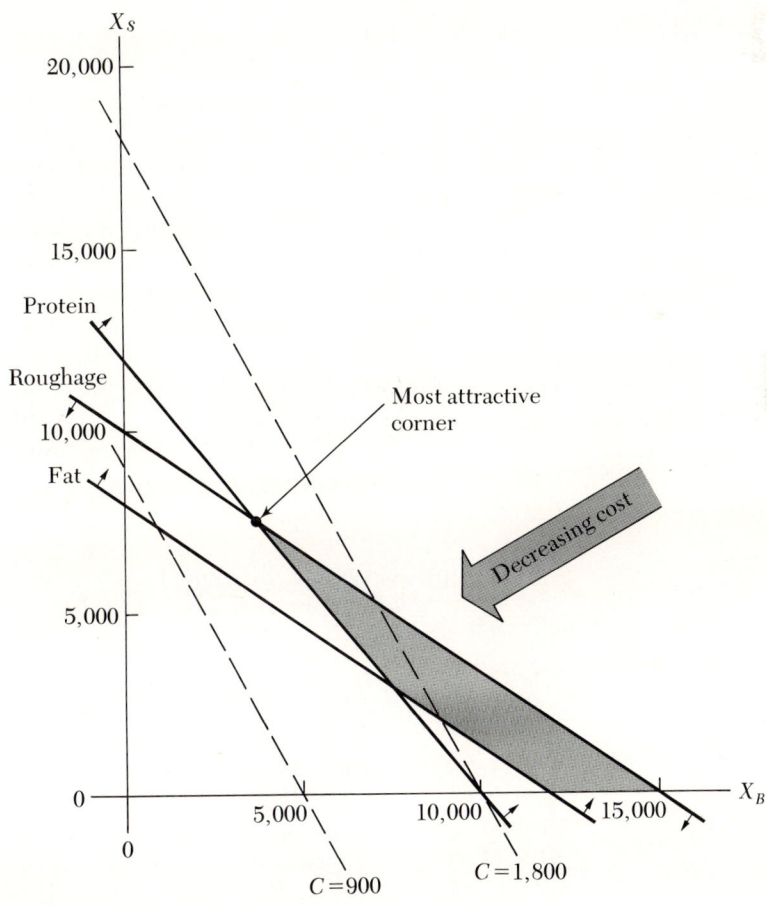

Figure 12-6
The graphical solution for the feed-mix problem.

12-5   COST MINIMIZATION: A FEED-MIX PROBLEM

The linear program for this problem may be formulated as follows:

Letting X_B = Pounds of buckwheat in mixture

X_S = Pounds of sunflower wheat in mixture

Minimize $C = .18X_B + .10X_S$

Subject to

$.04X_B + .06X_S \geq 480$ (fat)

$.12X_B + .10X_S \geq 1200$ (protein)

$.10X_B + .15X_S \leq 1500$ (roughage)

where $X_B, X_S \geq 0$

The fat and protein constraints are represented by $\geq$ (greater than or equal to) inequalities because minimum quantities of each have been established, and the total pounds of fat or protein (provided on the left sides) must be at least as large as these. The roughage constraint is a $\leq$ inequality, since total mixture roughage (represented on the left side) cannot exceed 1500 pounds.

Figure 12-6 shows the graphical representation of the problem. Notice that the valid sides for the fat and protein constraints lie opposite the origin (zero pounds of both seed types will satisfy neither constraint). Cost lines for $C = 1800$ and $C = 900$ dollars have been plotted. (Even though the $C = 900$ cost line lies outside the feasible solution region, the direction of decreasing cost is readily determined.) The most attractive corner occurs at the intersection of the protein and roughage lines.

Solving the protein and roughage equations simultaneously, we may determine the optimal solution:

$$\begin{array}{rl} .12X_B + .10X_S = 1200 & \text{(protein)} \\ -\frac{2}{3}(.10X_B + .15X_S = 1500) & \text{(roughage)} \\ \hline .0533X_B + 0X_S = 200 & \end{array}$$

$$X_B = 200/.0533 = 3752.345 \text{ lb}$$

Plugging the value for X_B into the protein equation, we find the value of X_S

$$.12(3752.345) + .10X_S = 1200$$

$$.10X_S = 1200 - .12(3752.345) = 1200 - 450.281 = 749.719$$

$$X_S = 749.719/.10 = 7497.19 \text{ lb}$$

The optimal solution (rounded) is

$$X_B = 3752.35 \text{ lb}$$
$$X_S = 7497.19 \text{ lb}$$

and the minimum cost is

$$C = .18(3752.35) + .10(7497.19) = 1425.14 \text{ dollars}$$

SPECIAL PROBLEMS IN CONSTRUCTING LINES   12-6

Earlier we indicated that most constraint lines may be constructed by connecting the horizontal and vertical intercepts. Even though we generally restrict solutions to the positive quadrant, there is no reason why one of these intercepts cannot be negative. Consider the line

$$-5X_1 + 3X_2 = 15$$

which is graphed as line A in Figure 12-7. Notice that the horizontal

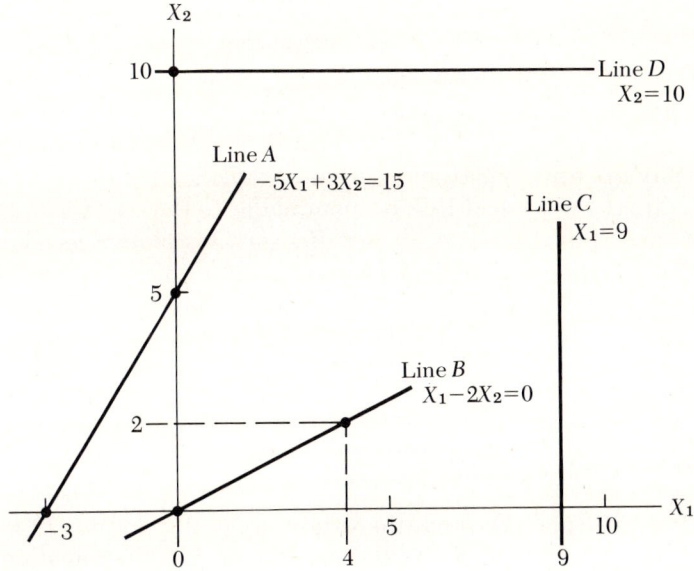

Figure 12-7
Examples of special types of lines.

intercept is

$$X_1 = 15/(-5) = -3$$

Line B in Figure 12-7 has equation

$$X_1 - 2X_2 = 0$$

which has both its vertical and horizontal intercepts at the origin. The intercept method yields a single point. A second point must be found. The choice of either coordinate of this second point is arbitrary. We can try $X_2 = 2$ and plug this value into the equation, getting the other coordinate:

$$X_1 - 2(2) = 0$$
$$X_1 = 0 - [-2(2)] = 0 - (-4) = 4$$

Connecting the origin with the point $(X_1 = 4, X_2 = 2)$, we have the required line.

A third type of line only has one intercept. Such lines are either horizontal or vertical. They have equations of the form

$$X_1 = 9 \quad \text{(line } C\text{)}$$
$$X_2 = 10 \quad \text{(line } D\text{)}$$

where only one variable appears in the equation. For $X_1 = 9$, the value of X_1 is restricted to be exactly 9, regardless of the value of X_2, which may be any quantity whatsoever. Figure 12-7 shows this relationship in terms of line C, a vertical line perpendicular to the X_1 axis and parallel to the X_2 axis. For the equation $X_2 = 10$, line D is plotted as a horizontal line perpendicular to the X_2 axis at height 10 units. Indeed, the axes themselves may be represented in terms of the equations $X_2 = 0$ (for the horizontal) and $X_1 = 0$ (for the vertical).

12-7 MIXTURE CONSTRAINTS

A line that goes through the origin generally applies to a special type of restriction called a *mixture constraint*. Such a constraint arises in manufacturing applications when some products must be made in a fixed ratio to others. The Redwood Furniture Company example may be slightly modified to incorporate a mixture constraint.

Ordinarily, tables and chairs are sold in sets, usually four chairs with each table. However, there is an occasional need for extra chairs. Thus, Redwood might desire to make at least four chairs for every table, which means that the number of chairs must be at least as large as the number of tables times four. That is, a further mixture constraint of the form

$$4 \times \text{Number of tables} \leq \text{Number of chairs}$$

could be added to the problem. Expressed in terms of the earlier variable symbols, this constraint says

$$4X_T \leq X_C \quad \text{(mixture)}$$

For convenience, all variables are usually collected on the left side of the inequality. Subtracting X_C from both sides, we obtain

$$4X_T - X_C \leq 0 \quad \text{(mixture)}$$

Temporarily ignoring the $<$ portion, we see that the mixture constraint line has equation

$$4X_T - X_C = 0 \quad \text{(mixture)}$$

which is the expression for a line going through the origin.

The graph for the expanded Redwood Furniture problem is provided in Figure 12-8. (The original wood and labor constraints have been plotted again.) The mixture constraint line was found by connecting the origin with the point $(X_T = 3, X_C = 12)$, since when there are 3 tables there must be four times as many, or 12 chairs.

Finding the valid side of the mixture constraint line is a bit tricky. Since the line goes through the origin, we cannot use the origin for this purpose. Rather we must evaluate some point lying off the line. Any such point will do; we choose $(X_T = 10, X_C = 15)$. Substituting these coordinates into the mixture inequality, we have

$$4(10) - 15 \leq 0$$

$$25 \leq 0$$

which is certainly not true. Thus, the side of the mixture line lying opposite this point applies.

The feasible solution region obtained by including the mixture constraint is smaller than before. (Additional constraints will ordinarily reduce the possible solutions. Why?) Visual inspection indicates that

12-7 MIXTURE CONSTRAINTS

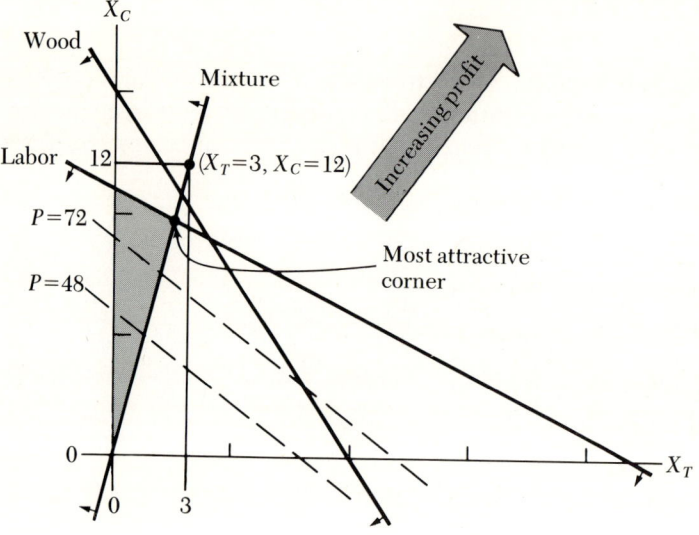

Figure 12-8

The graphical solution of the amended Redwood Furniture problem having a mixture constraint.

the most attractive corner for this new linear program lies at the intersection of the mixture and labor lines. Simultaneous solution of these provides the optimal solution

$$X_T = 22/9 = 2\tfrac{4}{9} \text{ tables}$$
$$X_C = 88/9 = 9\tfrac{7}{9} \text{ chairs}$$
$$P = 836/9 = 92\tfrac{8}{9} \text{ dollars}$$

(Remember that linear programming may produce fractional solutions. We may view the extra 4/9 table and 7/9 chair as work-in-progress inventory items.)

One interesting feature of the above solution is that there is leftover wood. The total amount of wood consumed is

$$30(22/9) + 20(88/9) = 268\tfrac{8}{9}$$

leaving $300 - 268\tfrac{8}{9} = 31\tfrac{1}{9}$ board feet of wood in inventory. Such unused resource is called *slack*. In the next chapter we will use the concept of slack extensively.

EQUALITY CONSTRAINTS 12-8

So far, all constraints encountered have been expressed as inequalities. As we have seen, inequalities produce valid points that lie to one side of a bisected plane. Under some circumstances, constraints may take the form of a strict equality. These are called *equality constraints*. For example, suppose that Redwood sold all tables and chairs in sets only and that *exactly* four chairs were required for each table. The basic constraint would have no < in it and would directly be expressed by the equation for the line

$$4X_T - X_C = 0 \quad \text{(revised mixture)}$$

Figure 12-9 shows the graph of this further amended linear program. Notice that *there is no valid side to the mixture line.* Valid points must

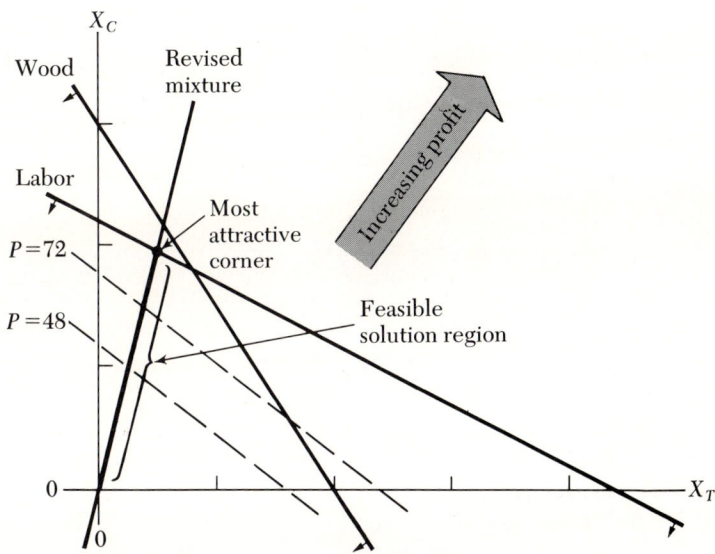

Figure 12-9
The graphical solution of the amended Redwood Furniture problem having an equality mixture constraint.

lie exactly on the line. The feasible solution region consists of that *line segment* of the mixture constraint that also satisfies the remaining resource constraints. Generally, where there is one equality constraint the feasible points will lie on a line segment. There are no other basic changes in the linear programming steps.

Should there be more than one equality constraint, things get ridiculously easy. Suppose that Redwood had to make exactly 2 tables because just this number could be sold. In this case, we would have the following *demand constraint:*

$$X_T = 2 \quad \text{(demand)}$$

Figure 12-10 shows the graph for this more restricted linear program. The demand constraint plots as a vertical line intersecting the X_T axis at 2. Notice that *the feasible solution region consists of a single point;* this is where the two equality constraints intersect. The most attractive corner is the same point! In this case, the optimal solution is $X_T = 2$ tables and $X_C = 8$ chairs, with profit $P = 76$ dollars.

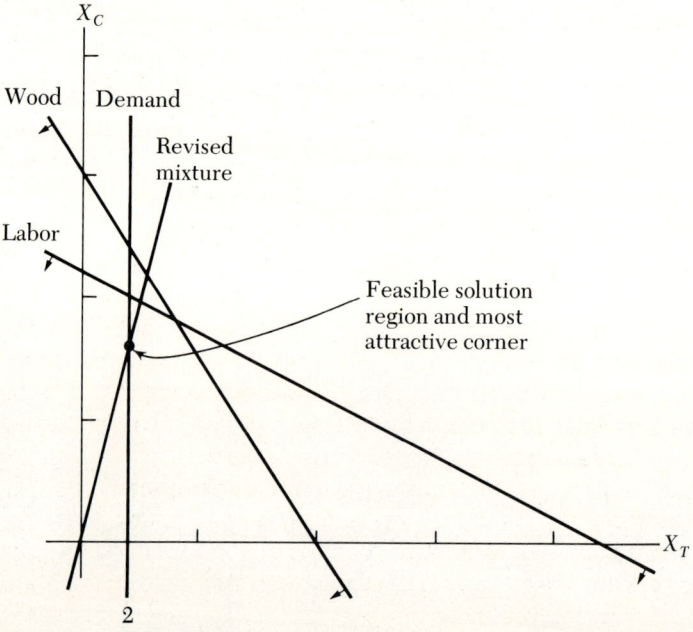

Figure 12-10
The graphical solution of the amended Redwood Furniture problem having two equality constraints.

MULTIPLE OPTIMAL SOLUTIONS   12-9

So far, we have seen linear programs with unique optimal solutions corresponding to the most attractive corner. Although the solution to a linear program generally consists of a corner point to the feasible solution region, more than one corner can be equally most attractive. As an example, consider the following linear program.

$$\begin{aligned}
\text{Maximize} \quad & P = 10X_1 + 12X_2 \\
\text{Subject to} \quad & 5X_1 + 6X_2 \leq 60 \quad \text{(resource } A\text{)} \\
& 8X_1 + 4X_2 \leq 72 \quad \text{(resource } B\text{)} \\
& 3X_1 + 5X_2 \leq 45 \quad \text{(resource } C\text{)} \\
\text{where} \quad & X_1, X_2 \geq 0
\end{aligned}$$

The above problem is graphed in Figure 12-11. Visual inspection indicates that two candidates exist for the most attractive corner: the intersection of the A and C lines at point (1) or the intersection A and B at point (2). To resolve the potential ambiguity, we must see which point is the last one touched by the highest P line. An eyeball analysis is not precise enough, since by sliding a straight-edge in the direction of increasing P, it is impossible to tell between the two corner points. We may simultaneously solve the respective equation pairs for both points, choosing the one with the greatest P. Doing this, we obtain

(1)	(2)
$X_1 = 4\frac{2}{7}$	$X_1 = 6\frac{6}{7}$
$X_2 = 6\frac{3}{7}$	$X_2 = 4\frac{2}{7}$
$P = 120$	$P = 120$

which both yield the same profit. This means that both points are equally attractive, and we therefore have *two most attractive corners*. Thus, both of the above solutions are optimal and the maximum profit is $P = 120$.

Why did we get two most attractive corners? The answer is that *the objective function line is parallel to one of the constraint lines.* Thus, the maximum P line must coincide with that constraint. You may verify this visually in Figure 12-11, where the $P = 30$ and $P = 60$ profit

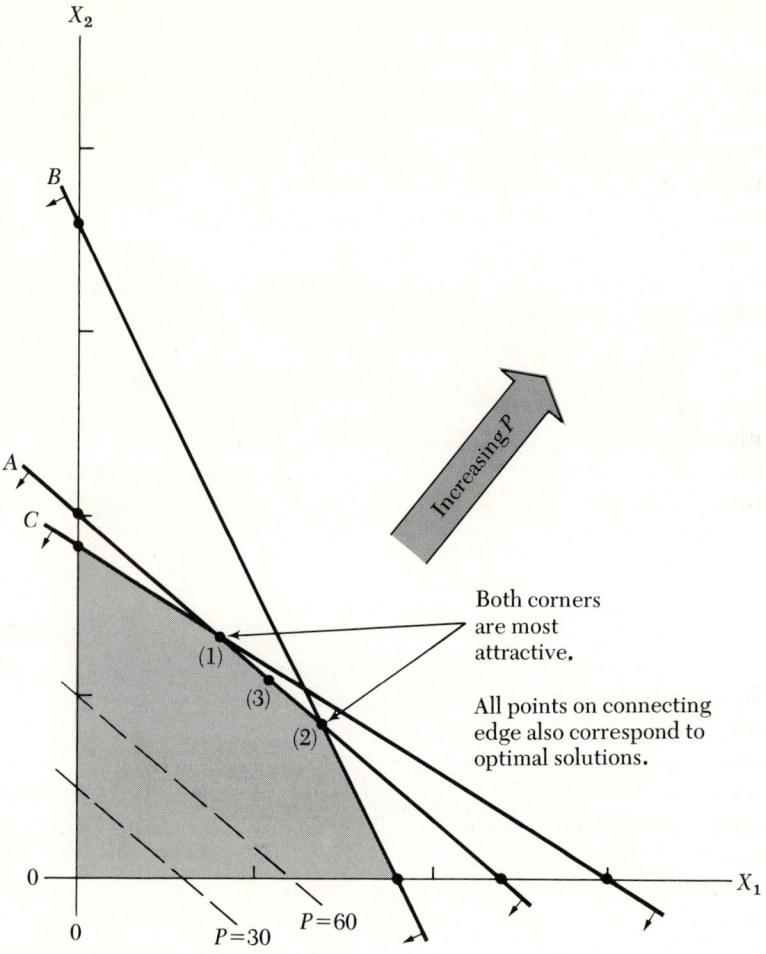

Figure 12-11
The graphical solution to the problem having multiple optimal solutions.

lines are parallel to the resource A constraint line. It is possible to prove mathematically that all P lines are parallel to that line by comparing their equations

$$P = 10X_1 + 12X_2 \quad \text{(objective)}$$
$$5X_1 + 6X_2 = 60 \quad \text{(resource } A\text{)}$$

Notice that the coefficients of the variables have a constant ratio to respective coefficients in the other equation. Looking at the X_1 terms, we have a 10 and a 5, so that the ratio is 10/5 = 2; this same ratio applies for X_2: 12/6 = 2. Thus, the coefficients in the P equation are exactly *twice* the value of those in the resource A equation. Whenever two equations have coefficients such that all of them are the same multiple of their counterparts in the other equation, the two lines must be parallel.

Whenever more than one corner provides the optimal solution, all points on the connecting edge will also correspond to optimal solutions. For example, consider point (3) midway on the optimal edge in Figure 12-11, with coordinates ($X_1 = 5\frac{4}{7}$, $X_2 = 5\frac{5}{14}$). This solution also has the maximum profit

$$P = 10(5\tfrac{4}{7}) + 12(5\tfrac{5}{14}) = 120$$

Any other point on the *most attractive edge* will also represent an optimal solution that has $P = 120$ as the profit. This reflects the fact that the maximum P line must coincide with this edge.

CONCLUDING REMARKS 12-10

In this chapter we have considered the essential features of linear programming. But we have only scratched the surface. By nature, the graphical solution procedure is limited to problems of only two variables, since our graphs can only represent two dimensions. It would be possible for us to extend this analysis to three variables, using three-dimensional graphs, but doing so would be cumbersome. When four or more variables are involved, entirely different algorithms must be used. In the next chapter, we will consider the most general solution procedure, the *simplex method*. In later chapters more efficient special-purpose algorithms will be described.

PROBLEMS

12-1 Using X_1 for the horizontal axis and X_2 for the vertical, plot the following lines on a graph.

(a) $X_1 + X_2 = 5$ (b) $2X_1 + 3X_2 = 18$
(c) $-3X_1 + 6X_2 = 24$ (d) $X_1 = 12$
(e) $X_2 = 9$ (f) $X_1 - 2X_2 = 0$

12-2 Solve each of the following equation pairs simultaneously.

(a) $X_1 + X_2 = 10$ (b) $2X_1 + 3X_2 = 6$
     $X_1 - X_2 = 5$ $X_2 = 1$
(c) $8X_1 + 7X_2 = 10$ (d) $4X_1 + 4X_2 = 12$
     $4X_1 + 5X_2 = 8$ $5X_1 + 3X_2 = 6$

12-3 Determine the optimal solution for the linear program

$$\begin{aligned} \text{Maximize} \quad & P = 5X_A + 6X_B \\ \text{Subject to} \quad & 3X_A + 2X_B \leq 12 \quad \text{(resource } W) \\ & 2X_A + 3X_B \leq 12 \quad \text{(resource } Y) \\ \text{where} \quad & X_A, X_B \geq 0 \end{aligned}$$

12-4 Determine the optimal solution to the linear program

$$\begin{aligned} \text{Minimize} \quad & C = .5X_A + .3X_B \\ \text{Subject to} \quad & X_A + 2X_B \geq 10 \quad \text{(restriction } Y) \\ & 2X_A + X_B \geq 8 \quad \text{(restriction } Z) \\ \text{where} \quad & X_A, X_B \geq 0 \end{aligned}$$

12-5 Determine the optimal solution to the linear program

$$\begin{aligned} \text{Maximize} \quad & P = 2X_1 - 3X_2 \\ \text{Subject to} \quad & 4X_1 + 5X_2 \leq 40 \quad \text{(resource } A) \\ & 2X_1 + 6X_2 \leq 24 \quad \text{(resource } B) \\ & 3X_1 - 3X_2 \geq 6 \quad \text{(mixture)} \\ & X_1 \geq 4 \quad \text{(demand)} \\ \text{where} \quad & X_1, X_2 \geq 0 \end{aligned}$$

12-6 Consider the following linear program.

$$\begin{aligned} \text{Maximize} \quad & P = 2X_1 + 4X_2 \\ \text{Subject to} \quad & 4X_1 + 8X_2 \leq 48 \\ & 8X_1 + 4X_2 \geq 48 \\ & X_2 \leq 5 \\ \text{where} \quad & X_1, X_2 \geq 0 \end{aligned}$$

(a) Plot the above constraints on a graph. Then determine the feasible solution region and plot two profit lines. Indicate the direction of increasing profit.
(b) How many attractive corners are there? Find the optimal solution corresponding to each one you find.
(c) Plot point ($X_1 = 8$, $X_2 = 2$) on your graph. What profit level corresponds? What may you conclude about this point?

12-7 Not all linear programs can be solved. Consider the following problem.

$$\begin{aligned} \text{Maximize} \quad & P = 2X_1 \\ \text{Subject to} \quad & X_1 + X_2 \leq 5 \\ & X_2 \geq 6 \\ \text{where} \quad & X_1, X_2 \geq 0 \end{aligned}$$

This problem is *infeasible*. Attempt to solve it graphically and briefly state any difficulties you encounter.

12-8 Ace Widgets makes two models of its ubiquitous product: regular and deluxe. Both models are assembled from an identical frame. The regular model differs from the deluxe only in terms of the finish work, which takes 5 hours of labor on the regular version, but 8 hours on the deluxe model. In planning the current month's production, Ace's foreman finds that only 12 frames and 80 hours of finishing labor are available. The supply of all other required materials and labor is unlimited. Any number of widgets can be sold at a profit: $10 for the regular model and $15 for the deluxe version. The foreman wants to produce quantities of the two models that will maximize company profit.
(a) Formulate the foreman's problem as a linear program.
(b) Solve the linear program graphically.

12-9 The marketing manager of Hops Brewery has an advertising budget of $100,000. He must determine how much to spend on television spots and magazine ads. Each spot is expected to increase sales by 30,000 cans, whereas each magazine ad will account for 100,000 cans in sales. Hops' gross profit on sales is 10 cents per can. One television spot costs $2000; each magazine ad requires an expenditure of $5000. To have a balanced marketing program, the advertising budget must involve no more than $70,000 in magazine ads nor $50,000 in television spots.
(a) Determine the net increase in operating profits for each television spot and magazine ad.
(b) Assuming that Hops management wishes to maximize net increase in beer profit, formulate the marketing manager's decision as a linear program.
(c) Solve the linear program graphically.

12-10 Mildred's Tool and Die Shop has an order to provide 10 experimental bits to a pneumatic drill company. The bits may either be shaped through forging or machined. Both procedures involve a final milling stage; the forged bits require more milling because they are not as smooth to begin with. In either case, only one bit at a time can be shaped under either process, and the order must be filled within two working days. The following table summarizes the restrictions.

PROCESS	HOURS PER ITEM		TOTAL HOURS AVAILABLE
	Forged	*Machined*	
Forging	3	—	15
Machining	—	2	16
Milling	2	4/3	16
Unit profit	$12	$9	

Assuming that the proprietor, Ms. Mildred Riveter, wishes to maximize profit, formulate a linear program specifying the number of bits to be made under each process in order to maximize total profit. Then solve this problem graphically.

12-11 Cee's Candy Company mixes its Rainbow Box from two basic confection types, chocolates and pastels. In order to meet its packaging requirements and to reflect changing ingredient costs, the company runs a linear program periodically to determine the number of pounds of each type of candy to put into the mix. The costs and requirements for a one pound box are provided below.

ITEM	PROPORTION OF CANDY WEIGHT		MINIMUM MIX REQUIREMENT
	Chocolates	*Pastels*	
Nuts	.15	.05	.10 lb
Soft centers	.50	1.00	.60
Hard centers	.50	0.00	.20
Total weight	1.00	1.00	1.00
Cost per pound	$1.20	$.80	

Formulate Cee's linear program, and then solve it graphically to determine the optimal weight for each candy type going into a one-pound mix.

12-12 *A Transportation Problem.* Druids' Drayage hauls rock from two quarries to three tombstone masons. The manager, H. Priest, wishes to minimize total shipping costs in such a way that every quarry operates precisely at full capacity and each mason receives exactly the number of stones he demands. The following unit shipping cost and quantity requirement data apply for tombstones.

FROM QUARRY	TO MASON			QUARRY CAPACITY
	Cedrick	*Dunstan*	*Eldred*	
Abinger	10/	15/	8/	100
Barnesly	12	9	10	200
Mason demand	50	150	100	300

A linear program can be used to establish a shipping schedule that indicates how many tombstones should be supplied from each quarry to the various masons. A quarry can service any number of masons, and any mason can receive shipments from one or more quarries.

Formulate this problem as a linear program. *Do not attempt to solve it.*

12-13 *An Assignment Problem.* Conformity Systems has three employees, a clerk, a typist, and a stenographer. Each person will be assigned exactly one of the following tasks: filing, bookkeeping, or report preparation. The manager wishes to assign workers to jobs so that total cost is minimized. The costs for each possible person-job assignment are provided below.

PERSON	Filing	JOB Bookkeeping	Report
Clerk	$20	$25	$35
Typist	25	20	30
Stenographer	30	25	25

Treating each possible single person to single job assignment as a separate variable, formulate this problem as a linear program. *Do not attempt to solve it.*

12-14 *An Oil-Refining Problem.* Shale–Bituminous Processors use gasification and pressurization to make low-sulfur and high-sulfur crude oil. The two processes require different mixtures of coal and shale solids. A batch under the gasification process requires an input of one ton of coal and two tons of shale to yield 100 gallons of low-sulfur crude and 200 gallons of high-sulfur crude. Under pressurization, each batch requires two tons of coal and one ton of shale to provide 150 gallons of low-sulfur crude and 100 gallons of high-sulfur crude.

The refinery manager wishes to determine how many batches to run under the various conversion processes in order to maximize the total profit in supplying an order for 10,000 gallons of low-sulfur and 5000 gallons of high-sulfur crudes. Available tonnages for filling this order are 100 of coal and 150 of shale. The costs of the solids per ton are $20 for coal and $25 for shale. The processor receives $.50 per gallon for low-sulfur crude and $.30 for high-sulfur crude.
(a) Suppose that 10 batches are run under gasification and 20 with pressurization. Determine how many
 (1) tons of coal are used.
 (2) tons of shale are used.
 (3) gallons of low-sulfur crude are made.
 (4) gallons of high-sulfur crude are made.
(b) Determine the profit per batch run under each process.
(c) Formulate the processor's problem as a linear program. *Do not attempt to solve it.*

12-15 *A Diet Problem.* Backpackers' Budget Shoppe is concocting a package to sell under the label of Hiker's Daily Dried Gruel. Designed only with nutrition and ease of preparation in mind, the food must meet the nutritional requirements provided on page 360.

NUTRIENT	NUTRITIONAL VALUE OF INGREDIENT PER KILOGRAM					MINIMUM REQUIRE- MENT
	Corn Meal	Beans	Spinach	Peanuts	Milk	
Calories	4,000	3,000	250	2,000	2,000	4,000
Protein	100	200	25	100	100	100 g
Iron	12	100	30	8	2	12 g
Vitamin A	4,000	1,000	50,000	5,000	13,000	5,000 units
Thiamine	2	6	1.5	1.5	1	2 mg
Riboflavin	1	5	3	1	6	3 mg
Niacin	12	25	8	80	3	20 mg
Ascorbic Acid	0	0	500	0	15	100 mg
Cost per kilogram	$.50	$.75	$1.25	$.75	$1.50	

Formulate a linear program that determines the minimum cost ingredient weights that satisfy the above requirements. *Do not attempt to solve the linear program.*

Thirteen

The Simplex Method in Linear Programming

We are now ready to tackle linear programs that are impossible to solve by the graphical method because they have too many variables to plot on a two-dimensional graph. An algebraic procedure, the *simplex method,* works on all linear programs—regardless of the number of variables. This technique, aided by a high-speed digital computer, can solve problems with thousands of variables and ten times that number of constraints. Indeed, without the simplex method, linear programming would be little more than a mathematical curiosity that could describe problems algebraically but not solve any with more than two or three variables.

The word simplex was *not* formed by adding the ubiquitous suffix -*ex* to the word simple (as in Kleenex and Memorex). Rather it is a legitimate term in the language of mathematics representing the simplest object in an n-dimensional space connecting $n + 1$ points. In one dimension, a simplex is a line segment connecting two points. In two dimensions it is a triangle formed by joining three points. A three-dimensional simplex is a four-sided pyramid having just four corners. Such geometrical objects, extended to higher dimensions, are used to explain how and why the simplex *method* works. Although the procedure itself is quite simple to master, the mathematical arguments justifying it are fairly complex.

Even though its underlying concepts are geometrical, the simplex algorithm itself is fundamentally an algebraic procedure. George B. Dantzig developed it after World War II, and he and other mathematicians have since extended and expanded it in a variety of ways. Like the graphical method, the simplex algorithm finds the most attractive corner of the feasible solution region, thereby solving the linear program. Ordinarily, the region itself exists in a higher dimensional space that can be imagined but not pictured. An underlying theoretical concept is that *any problem having a solution at all must have an optimal solution corresponding to a corner point.*

This means that we need only evaluate corner points. Although finding and evaluating corners would seem to be child's play, remember that they are not pictured, so we cannot see them. Furthermore, the number of corners associated with even a moderately large linear program can be huge; for example, solving a ten-product planning problem with ten resource constraints would involve nearly 200,000 corners. The biggest, fastest computer could not, in our lifetimes, evaluate all trillion trillions of corners in a problem just ten times that size. A second feature of the simplex method incorporates an efficient search through the formidable thicket of corners in order to rapidly find the most attractive one. Based on *economic analysis,* the searching procedure is so good that in the 10-product case mentioned above, only about 20 corners are evaluated.

In conclusion, the simplex method embodies geometry, but it uses algebra combined with economic principles to solve linear programs efficiently. Simplex is really an odyssey in n-dimensional space where you visit a few corner points on a multifaceted "gem stone" you can't see; each time you stop, you do a little analysis to find where to stop next; the journey ends at the most attractive corner.

Table 13-1
DATA FOR THE REDWOOD FURNITURE PROBLEM

RESOURCE	UNIT REQUIREMENTS		AMOUNT AVAILABLE
	Table	*Chair*	
Wood (board feet)	30	20	300
Labor (hours)	5	10	110
Unit profit	$6	$8	

BASIC CONCEPTS 13-1

To introduce the simplex method, we continue with the original Redwood Furniture problem, using the data repeated in Table 13-1. As before, X_T and X_C represent the number of tables and chairs; the linear program is

$$\begin{aligned}
\text{Maximize} \quad & P = 6X_T + 8X_C && \text{(objective)} \\
\text{Subject to} \quad & 30X_T + 20X_C \leq 300 && \text{(wood)} \\
& 5X_T + 10X_C \leq 110 && \text{(labor)} \\
\text{where} \quad & X_T, X_C \geq 0
\end{aligned}$$

Slack Variables

We will now solve this problem algebraically. Our first step is to acknowledge the existence of slack, which represents unused resources. We define the following *slack variables:*

$$X_W = \text{Amount of unused wood}$$
$$X_L = \text{Amount of unused labor}$$

(The original problem variables X_T and X_C are sometimes called *main variables* to distinguish them from the slacks.) Each slack variable is incorporated into the original constraints. In the case of wood, we may equivalently express the constraint as

Wood used in tables or chairs + Unused wood = Available wood

By adding the quantities of wood on the left side, this constraint now says: "what you use plus what you don't use must equal what you start with." The meaning of the constraint is the same as before. Stated algebraically, our revised wood constraint says

$$30X_T + 20X_C + X_W = 300 \quad \text{(wood)}$$

which is equivalent to the original expression. Adding the slack variable converts an inequality into an equality. The X_W term bridges the gap, taking up the slack between the less than (<) and the equals (=).

In the same way, we convert the labor constraint into an equality:

$$5X_T + 10X_C + X_L = 110 \quad \text{(labor)}$$

Notice that unused wood X_W appears only in the wood constraint equation, unused labor X_L only in the labor constraint equation.

Slack variables have a two-fold purpose. First, and most important, adding them allows us to convert inequalities into equalities and thereby put the linear program in a form amenable to algebraic solution. It is mathematically easier to analyze equalities than inequalities. Second, slack variables permit a more comprehensive economic interpretation of a solution than would otherwise be possible.

Expressing the Linear Program in Terms of Slacks

Incorporating the slack variables into the entire linear program formulation, we have

$$\text{Maximize} \quad P = 6X_T + 8X_C + 0X_W + 0X_L \quad \text{(objective)}$$
$$\text{Subject to} \quad 30X_T + 20X_C + 1X_W + 0X_L = 300 \quad \text{(wood)}$$
$$5X_T + 10X_C + 0X_W + 1X_L = 110 \quad \text{(labor)}$$
$$\text{where} \quad X_T, X_C, X_W, X_L \geq 0$$

X_W and X_L appear in the objective equation with coefficient zero reflecting the fact that unused resources contribute nothing to profit (or to cost); they remain as assets in inventory. The non-negativity conditions apply to X_W and X_L as well as to X_T and X_C. Slack variables cannot be negative (if they were, it would mean that more resource than originally available could be consumed, which removes the limitation of the original constraint).

For later convenience, X_W and X_L appear in their respective constraints with coefficient 1. We have also placed X_L with zero coefficient in the wood constraint, while X_W similarly appears in the labor constraint; this in no way distorts the original relationships, since a term appearing with zero coefficient is mathematically equivalent to being absent. This arrangement merely makes it easier to keep track of the problem.

Algebraic Solution

The feasible solution region to the new problem cannot be graphed, for we now have four variables and our problem is four-dimensional.

We have an algebraic system with 2 constraint equations and 4 unknowns:

$$30X_T + 20X_C + 1X_W + 0X_L = 300$$
$$5X_T + 10X_C + 0X_W + 1X_L = 110$$

We know how to solve 2 equations for 2 unknowns; we did this in Chapter 12 to find the coordinates for the most attractive corner. But here *we have more unknowns than equations*. How do we find the solution?

Let's take a slight detour. Consider the problem of finding values for x and y that satisfy the equation

$$2x + 4y = 12$$

Here we must solve 1 equation for 2 unknowns. You may recognize that this equation represents a line in the xy plane; you can even graph it. But, here we are faced with a dilemma essentially the same as that in the above linear program.

What's the answer? The line itself is the answer! Yes, but what are the x and y values? An infinite number of pairs of x and y values satisfy the equation, each pair being the coordinates of some point on the line.

To find any one solution, you must fix the value of x or y and then solve for the other. For example,

$$\text{set } x = 3$$

Then we have

$$2(3) + 4y = 12$$
$$4y = 12 - 2(3) = 12 - 6 = 6$$

and

$$y = \tfrac{6}{4} = 1\tfrac{1}{2}$$

Thus $(x = 3, y = 1\tfrac{1}{2})$ is one answer. For any other arbitrary value for x, we can get a different unique y. Likewise, for any arbitrary y, we can find a unique x. These ambiguous solutions are the best we can do.

Continuing with our detour, consider the equations

$$2x + 4y + 3z = 12$$
$$3x + 2y + 1z = 6$$

Again, we have more unknowns than equations. In a three-dimensional graph, each equation represents a plane and the solution is the intersection of the planes (imagine two sheets of paper held at different angles and crossing). The solution is a line again! As before, we can only get numerical values for x, y, and z which satisfy both equations by arbitrarily setting the value of one variable and then solving for the others. For example,

$$\text{set } y = 1$$

Then we have

$$2x + 4(1) + 3z = 12 \quad \text{or} \quad 2x + 3z = 8$$
$$3x + 2(1) + 1z = 6 \quad \text{or} \quad 3x + 1z = 4$$

and, solving for x and z, we get

$$x = \tfrac{4}{7}$$
$$y = 1$$
$$z = 2\tfrac{2}{7}$$

From our detour, we may draw the following conclusion: *Whenever the variables exceed the equations, the extra variables must be arbitrarily set at some value.*

The Variable Mix

Returning to the Redwood Furniture problem, we must do the same thing. We have two more variables than equations. These extra variables must be fixed at some value before proceeding algebraically. Part of our problem is deciding which variables are the extra arbitrarily valued ones and which are "free" to be solved for algebraically. A further question is: What arbitrary values should be used?

We will refer to the variables that must be solved for algebraically as the *variable mix*. As we have seen, their values can only be found after the others have been fixed at some arbitrary level; the fixed-valued variables are identified as not being in the variable mix. Table 13-2 shows all the possible combinations of variable-mix and non-mix variables for the Redwood Furniture problem. In each of the six cases, two complementary pairs of variables are involved.

We have noted that an essential feature of simplex is to evaluate corner points only. *Such a corner point is the algebraic solution to the constraint equations when the non-mix variables have been arbitrarily*

Table 13-2
POSSIBLE VARIABLE-MIX COMBINATIONS AND THEIR ALGEBRAIC SOLUTIONS

Corner Point	Variable Mix (Free Variables)	Non-Mix Variables (Arbitrarily Set at Zero)	Algebraic Solution				
			X_T	X_C	X_W	X_L	P
A	$X_W X_L$	$X_T X_C$	0	0	300	110	$ 0
B	$X_W X_C$	$X_T X_L$	0	11	80	0	$88
C	$X_L X_T$	$X_C X_W$	10	0	0	60	$60
D	$X_T X_C$	$X_W X_L$	4	9	0	0	$96
E	$X_L X_C$	$X_W X_T$	0	15	0	−40	infeasible
F	$X_W X_T$	$X_L X_C$	22	0	−360	0	infeasible

set at zero. This fact considerably simplifies finding solutions and allows us to greatly streamline the overall simplex method.

Each of the six cases in Table 13-2 involves a different corner point to the Redwood Furniture problem. All of these are shown in the graph in Figure 13-1. The first four of these are solved on page 368.

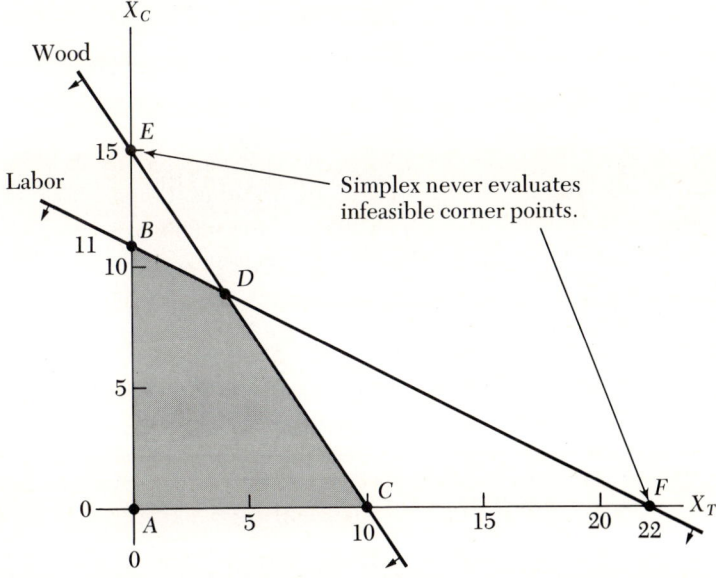

Figure 13-1
Corner points possible for the Redwood Furniture problem.

Corner point A:

(set $X_T = 0$, $X_C = 0$)

$$30(0) + 20(0) + 1X_W + 0X_L = 300$$
$$5(0) + 10(0) + 0X_W + 1X_L = 110$$

Getting: $\quad 1X_W = 300$

$\quad 1X_L = 110$

Solution: $\quad X_T = 0$, $X_C = 0$, $X_W = 300$, $X_L = 110$

Profit: $\quad P = 6(0) + 8(0) + 0(300) + 0(110) = 0$

Corner point B:

(set $X_T = 0$, $X_L = 0$)

$$30(0) + 20X_C + 1X_W + 0(0) = 300$$
$$5(0) + 10X_C + 0X_W + 1(0) = 110$$

Getting: $\quad 20X_C + X_W = 300$

$\quad 10X_C = 110$

Solution: $\quad X_T = 0$, $X_C = 11$, $X_W = 80$, $X_L = 0$

Profit: $\quad P = 6(0) + 8(11) + 0(80) + 0(0) = 88$

Corner point C:

(set $X_C = 0$, $X_W = 0$)

$$30X_T + 20(0) + 1(0) + 0X_L = 300$$
$$5X_T + 10(0) + 0(0) + 1X_L = 110$$

Getting: $\quad 30X_T = 300$

$\quad 5X_T + 1X_L = 110$

Solution: $\quad X_T = 10$, $X_C = 0$, $X_W = 0$, $X_L = 60$

Profit: $\quad P = 6(10) + 8(0) + 0(0) + 0(60) = 60$

Corner point D:

(set $X_W = 0$, $X_L = 0$)

$$30X_T + 20X_C + 1(0) + 0(0) = 300$$
$$5X_T + 10X_C + 0(0) + 1(0) = 110$$

Getting: $\quad 30X_T + 20X_C = 300$

$\quad 5X_T + 10X_C = 110$

Solution: $X_T = 4$, $X_C = 9$, $X_W = 0$, $X_L = 0$

Profit: $P = 6(4) + 8(9) + 0(0) + 0(0) = 96$

Only points A, B, C, and D are feasible; point E is infeasible because it violates the labor constraint (the algebraic solution leads to a negative quantity for X_L), and point F is likewise infeasible because it violates the wood constraint.

Before proceeding, let's put our current situation into its proper context. We are only illustrating the concepts of the simplex method. We have not yet described the algorithm's steps. Furthermore, it is never necessary to do all this work on a simple problem we have already solved graphically. Resolving the Redwood Furniture problem just makes it easier for us to understand what is happening. Ordinarily, *simplex will only be used when there are too many main variables in the original inequality formulation to be portrayed on a graph.* Keep in mind also that if we include slack variables, our present problem is four-dimensional, and we cannot construct a graph that directly incorporates slacks. In Figure 13-1, points on the constraint line represent zero slack for the particular resource; a feasible point off the line has positive slack in an amount that cannot be directly read from the graph.

Before describing the simplex algorithm in detail, a few more points will be helpful. Suppose we can identify all the corner points in a linear program (like we did in Table 13-2). Then why can't we simply evaluate all the feasible ones algebraically and pick the one having the largest P? In our example, the most attractive corner is point D, where profit is $96. After all, no picture is needed to list all combinations of variable mixes, and we know that each must correspond to a particular corner.

There are two reasons why we do not do the above. First, as we noted earlier, the number of corners can be astronomical for even a moderately sized problem. Even if we want to, it may be impossible to consider them all. Second, each corner-point evaluation involves a lot of algebra. For a 10-constraint linear program, each corner-point solution requires solving 10 equations in 10 unknowns—a horrendous task without some simplifying procedure. Simplex takes care of both difficulties.

THE SIMPLEX METHOD 13-2

Simplex ordinarily begins at the corner represented by "doing nothing," where only slacks are in the variable mix. It then moves us to the neighboring corner point which improves this solution at the greatest rate. It continues to move us progressively from neighboring corner to neighboring corner making the greatest possible improvement on each successive move. When no more improvements can be determined, the most attractive corner has been found. As we have noted, this method usually results in evaluating only a tiny fraction of all the corner points in a linear program; a huge number of them are simply skipped. It also saves a substantial percentage of our previous work, so that the task of algebraically solving for the unknowns at a corner can be reduced to a few simple arithmetic steps.

The Simplex Tableau

For convenience, we again express the latest Redwood Furniture linear program:

Maximize $\quad P = 6X_T + 8X_C + 0X_W + 0X_L \quad$ (objective)

Subject to $\quad 30X_T + 20X_C + 1X_W + 0X_L = 300 \quad$ (wood)

$\quad\quad\quad\quad\quad 5X_T + 10X_C + 0X_W + 1X_L = 110 \quad$ (labor)

where $\quad\quad\quad\quad X_T, X_C, X_W, X_L \geq 0 \quad$ (non-negativity)

Table 13-3

A SIMPLEX TABLEAU FOR THE REDWOOD FURNITURE PROBLEM

UNIT PROFIT	6	8	0	0	
Var. Mix	X_T	X_C	X_W	X_L	Sol.
X_W	30	20	1	0	300
X_L	5	10	0	1	110

All this information may be incorporated into Table 13-3, referred to as a *simplex tableau*. Along the top of the central portion of the tableau we list the problem variables in their original order of appearance in the formulated equations. In the top margin we list the corresponding per unit profits from the objective equation. The first row in the body of the table consists of the coefficients in the first constraint equation in their original order of appearance; the numbers in the second row are likewise copied from the second constraint. In essence, these two rows provide information that is identical to that in the original equations; *they are streamlined and equivalent versions of the original equations.*

The variable mix column lists the slack variables X_W and X_L; we will solve for these. All variables not listed there are in the non-mix category and are assumed to be arbitrarily fixed at zero; thus, X_T and X_C are presently set at zero. The solution column lists the values of the variable mix; here we have $X_W = 300$ and $X_L = 110$—all available wood and labor are unused. This is precisely what would be left of the original equations after zeroing out X_T and X_C:

$$30(0) + 20(0) + 1X_W + 0X_L = 300 \text{ or } X_W = 300$$

$$5(0) + 10(0) + 0X_W + 1X_L = 110 \text{ or } X_L = 110$$

The first rows of the simplex tableau simultaneously provide two things.

(1) Each row is written in a new form that preserves the original constraints.
(2) The rows indicate the variable mix for the corner point being evaluated. The variable mix values appear in the solution column; all non-mix variables have zero value.

The values in the central portion of the table represent the original constraint coefficients and are sometimes referred to as *exchange coefficients*, because they indicate how many units of the variable listed on the left must be given up to accommodate a unit increase in the variable listed at the top. Thus, the value 30 in the X_W row and X_T column indicates that 30 board feet of unused wood may be exchanged for one table. We see also that exactly 20 units of wood must be traded to get one chair. Similarly, to get one table we must give up 5 hours of unused labor, while one chair requires 10 hours. These figures are the same as those used at the outset in Table 13-1. The exchange coefficients are 0 or 1 for the mix variables and are not very meaningful; they say, for example, that 1 board foot of unused wood may be traded for 1 more board foot and that no unused wood is required to accommodate more unused labor.

There is more to the simplex tableau, which is expanded in Table 13-4. In the left margin we list the per unit profits for the mix variables. For slack variables X_W and X_L these are zeros. Below the heavy rule are two special rows. Here is where economic data are compiled that tell us which corner point is evaluated next. Values in the *sacrifice row* tell us what we lose in per unit profit by making a change. The *improvement row* indicates the per unit change in profit by making that same change.

To compute the sacrifice row entry under each column, the following computation is made:

Unit sacrifice = Unit profit column × Exchange coefficient column

Table 13-4

AN EXPANDED SIMPLEX TABLEAU

UNIT PROFIT		6	8	0	0		
	Var. Mix	X_T	X_C	X_W	X_L	Sol.	
0	X_W	30	20	1	0	300	← Exchange coefficients
0	X_L	5	10	0	1	110	
	Sac.	0	0	0	0	0 ←	Current P
	Imp.	6	8	0	0	—	

Such a calculation is done for all rows and then accumulated as a product sum. More precisely, the above calculation is a *vector product*, where the terms in each column constitute *vectors*. For example, under X_T we have

$$\frac{Profit\ Column \times X_T\ Column}{\begin{array}{l} 0 \times 30 = 0 \\ 0 \times\ \ 5 = \underline{0} \\ \text{Sacrifice for } X_T = 0 \end{array}}$$

The first product, 0 times 30, is the unit profit of unused wood multiplied by the amount needed to make one table; it is the reduction in unused wood profit needed to make one table. The other term is likewise the unused labor profit given up to make that table. Together, these constitute the profit given up by the solution mix variables to accommodate a unit increase in tables.

The above computation is also made for the solution column. The entry obtained is the current value of the objective function. For the tableau in Table 13-4, $P = 0$.

Since the profit column for the current variable mix consists of zeros, all the sacrifice terms result in product sums equal to zero. This seems obvious now, for we give up nothing in profit to make tables or chairs if the unused resource has no profit to begin with. But this concept will prove crucial later.

The entries in the improvement row are found by subtracting each sacrifice term from the corresponding unit profit listed at the top of the tableau:

$$\text{Unit improvement} = \text{Unit profit} - \text{Unit sacrifice}$$

In the present tableau, all the improvement terms are identical to the profits, since all the sacrifices are zero.

Summary of the Simplex Method

Before proceeding with the simplex algorithm, it will be helpful if we list the required steps.

(1) Formulate the linear program. Add slack variables to the problem, eliminating any inequality constraints. Construct the initial simplex tableau, using slack variables in the starting variable mix.

(2) Find the sacrifice and improvement rows.

(3) *Entry Criterion.* Find the currently non-mix variable that on increase from zero will improve the objective at the greatest rate. Break any ties arbitrarily. This variable is the *entering variable.* Mark the top of its column with an arrow pointing down. If no improvement can be found, the optimal solution is represented by the present tableau.

(4) *Exit Criterion.* Using the current tableau's exchange coefficient values from the column of the entering variable, calculate the following *exchange ratio* for each row:

$$\frac{\text{Solution value}}{\text{Exchange coefficient}}$$

Ignoring ratios with zero or negative denominators, find the smallest *non-negative* exchange ratio;* the mix variable for the row of this ratio is the *exiting variable.* Again ties are broken arbitrarily. Mark this variable's row with an arrow pointing left.

(5) Construct a new simplex tableau, replacing the variable mix label of the exiting variable with that of the entering variable; all other variable mix labels remain the same. Also, change the unit profit (unit cost) column value to correspond to the newly entered mix variable. Then recompute the variable mix row values, getting a brand new set of exchange coefficients. (This procedure is illustrated with the Redwood Furniture example.)

(6) Go back to step 2.

So far in our example, we have completed steps 1 and 2. We now must determine the *entering variable.* This is done through an economic analysis, by applying the *entry criterion* of step 3. In our profit maximization problem we accomplish this by finding the largest positive value in

---

* A zero divisor results in an infinitely large ratio (and is treated as such, even when the numerator is zero too). If all divisors are zero or negative, the problem is *unbounded,* a special case discussed on page 399.

TABLE 13-5

SIMPLEX TABLEAU SHOWING ENTERING AND EXITING VARIABLES AND PIVOT ELEMENT

UNIT PROFIT		6	8	0	0		
	Var. Mix	X_T	X_C	X_W	X_L	Sol.	Exchange ratios:
0	X_W	30	20 ↓	1	0	300	$300/20 = 15$
0	X_L ←	5	(10)	0	1	110	$110/10 = 11$*
	Sac.	0	0	0	0	0	*Smallest non-negative ratio
	Imp.	6	8	0	0	—	

Greatest per unit improvement

the unit improvement row. Referring to Table 13-5, we see that 8 is the largest per unit improvement, occurring under the X_C column. This means that we can improve the current solution by $8 per unit for each chair made. Increasing the value of the X_C variable from zero (remember, X_C is a non-mix variable and all such variables equal zero) to some positive quantity is the best change to make. (Another change, increasing tables, has a smaller unit improvement of only $6.) Thus X_C is the entering variable. We indicate this on the simplex tableau by a small arrow pointing downward.

In step 4 we find the *exiting variable*. As their names imply, one variable will enter the mix and replace another, which exits from the variable mix and assumes non-mix status. Such an exchange of variables is referred to as a *pivot operation*. Simplex involves a sequence of such pivots. In each case, the pivot identifies the next corner point to be evaluated. The current variable mix differs by only one variable from the subsequent one created by the pivot. The two corresponding corners are often called *neighbors*.

At this point we want to increase our entering variable X_C as much as possible from zero. Dividing the solution value by the corresponding exchange coefficient in the X_C column, we get

$$300/20 = 15 \quad \text{for the } X_W \text{ row}$$
$$110/10 = 11 \quad \text{for the } X_L \text{ row}$$

These *exchange ratios* tell us how many chairs we can make by trading all the current level for the respective mix variable. By trading away unused wood, of which we currently have 300 board feet, we can get 15

THE SIMPLEX METHOD IN LINEAR PROGRAMMING

chairs because one chair can be exchanged at the rate of 20 board feet. Likewise, by trading away all 110 hours of unused labor at an exchange rate of 10 hours per chair we can get 11 chairs.

The *exit criterion* requires that we find the smallest ratio, here 11; this value limits the chairs that can result from the exchange. It is impossible to make more than 11 chairs, for we use all available labor at that quantity. The exiting variable is thus X_L. X_C will replace X_L in the variable mix. X_W will remain in the mix, since we run out of labor before wood and there will still be some unused wood once the exchange is made. We indicate that unused labor exits the variable mix by placing a small arrow pointing toward the X_L in Table 13-5.

The circled value in the X_C column and the X_L row is called the *pivot element*. This value is used at the beginning in evaluating the new corner point represented by trading X_C for X_L. The evaluation is achieved by means of a *new* simplex tableau.

Constructing the New Simplex Tableau

We must find a new simplex tableau that provides the solution values for the new corner point. Each mix-variable row must also represent an equation, and together these equations must preserve the underlying constraint relationships. Let's deal with the equations. We started with

$$30X_T + 20X_C + 1X_W + 0X_L = 300 \quad \text{(old } X_W \text{ row)}$$
$$5X_T + 10X_C + 0X_W + 1X_L = 110 \quad \text{(old } X_L \text{ row)}$$

—Set at zero

Since X_C is to replace X_L, we want to transform the second equation so that X_C will have coefficient 1. Dividing both sides of the second equation by 10

$$\left(\frac{5}{10}\right)X_T + \left(\frac{10}{10}\right)X_C + \left(\frac{0}{10}\right)X_W + \left(\frac{1}{10}\right)X_L = \frac{110}{10}$$

provides us with the equivalent expression

$$\frac{1}{2}X_T + 1X_C + 0X_W + \frac{1}{10}X_L = 11 \quad \text{(new } X_C \text{ row)}$$

that we shall refer to as the new X_C row. If X_T and X_L are set at zero value, this equation directly provides the solution: $X_C = 11$.

Consider now the two equations

$$30X_T + 20X_C + 1X_W + 0X_L = 300 \quad \text{(old } X_W \text{ row)}$$
$$\tfrac{1}{2}X_T + 1X_C + 0X_W + \tfrac{1}{10}X_L = 11 \quad \text{(new } X_C \text{ row)}$$

The variable X_C can be eliminated from the first one, and X_C will then appear in only one of the equations. If we do that, then $X_C = 11$ is a solution value satisfying both equations. Subtracting 20 times the second equation from the first, we have

$$\begin{aligned}
30X_T + 20X_C + 1X_W + 0X_L &= 300 \\
-20\bigl(\tfrac{1}{2}X_T + 1X_C + 0X_W + \tfrac{1}{10}X_L &= 11\bigr) \\
\hline
20X_T + 0X_C + 1X_W - 2X_L &= 80 \quad \text{(new } X_W \text{ row)}
\end{aligned}$$

The equation for this difference may be referred to as the new X_W row, since it provides the solution $X_W = 80$ when the non-mix variables are set at zero ($X_T = 0$, $X_L = 0$). This reflects the fact that when 11 chairs are made, each requiring 20 board feet of wood, exactly $300 - 11(20) = 80$ board feet remain unused.

Our two new equations are

$$20X_T + 0X_C + 1X_W - 2X_L = 80 \quad \text{(new } X_W \text{ row)}$$
$$\tfrac{1}{2}X_T + 1X_C + 0X_W + \tfrac{1}{10}X_L = 11 \quad \text{(new } X_C \text{ row)}$$

$$\underbrace{}_{\text{Set at zero}}$$

Since each equation was obtained by dividing both sides of an original equation by a constant or by subtracting equal amounts from both sides, the two new equations preserve the problem constraints.

The beauty of the simplex method is that we don't have to do all the above work to get the new equations. We can work directly from the previous tableau to get the values for the new one. *The procedure may be summarized as follows:*

(a) Divide all values in the row of the exiting variable by the pivot element. (Such calculations are easily done in your head.) Place your answers in the *same position* in the new tableau. Label this row with the symbol of the newly entered variable.

(b) To get each of the remaining rows, find the value in that row which is also in the pivot element column in the old tableau. Then multiply the first number in the new row found in step (a) by this quantity and *subtract* that product from the old value in the first position; the result is the first term in the new row—place it there. Continue this process for all positions in the row, including the solution position. Do this for all remaining rows until the tableau is complete. The variable mix labels on these rows will be the same as before.

(c) Place the appropriate unit profits (costs) for the mix variables in the left margin.

The above procedure results in the second tableau provided in Table 13-6 for the Redwood Furniture problem. Every term in the new X_C row is found by dividing the respective old X_L row value by 10 (the pivot element). The new X_W row values were found by successively subtracting from the old X_W row the product: 20 (the old-X_W row value in the pivot element column) times the new X_C row value for that column position. Notice that the new tableau is exactly what we would get by transferring the coefficients from the equations on page 376. Notice also that this procedure yields *column* values for each mix variable that has a *one* where the variable's row and column intersect and a *zero* everywhere else; this feature ensures that the underlying equations provide solution values when the non-mix variables are zeroed out.

Table 13-6
GETTING THE NEW SIMPLEX TABLEAU

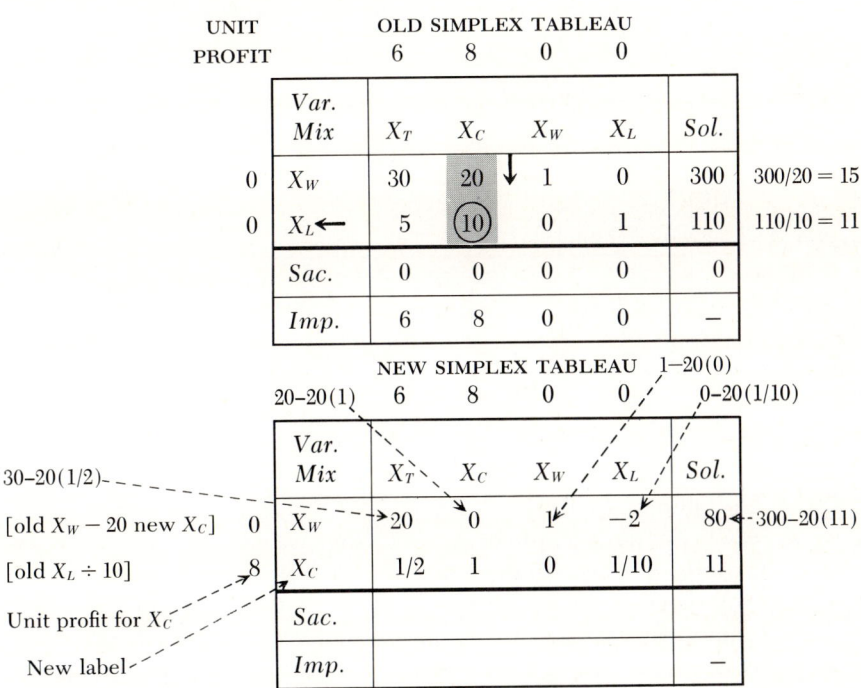

13-2   THE SIMPLEX METHOD

Finding the Optimal Solution

This completes the final simplex step for the Redwood Furniture problem. The procedure now sends us back to step 2, where we begin all over again with the new tableau and variable mix. We begin a new *iteration*. Each iteration repeats the earlier ones, using new values.

We must again find the unit sacrifice and improvement values. These are shown in Table 13-7. Before we show the calculations used to get them, let's assess the exchange coefficients in the X_T column. The value in the X_W row is 20, which indicates that we must give up a net of 20 board feet of unused wood to make one table—not the 30 board feet specified in the original problem statement. Where are the missing 10 board feet? The second number in that column, 1/2, tells us that we must also relinquish half a chair to get one table. This happens because some labor, all now spent on chairs, must be diverted to that table. From that half chair we get back 5 hours of labor and also the missing 10 board feet of wood.

Table 13-7

FINAL VERSION OF THE SECOND SIMPLEX TABLEAU

UNIT PROFIT		6	8	0	0		
	Var. Mix	X_T	X_C	X_W	X_L	Sol.	
0	X_W	20	0	1	−2	80	
8	X_C	1/2	1	0	1/10	11	
	Sac.	4	8	0	8/10	88	←--Current P
	Imp.	2	0	0	−8/10	—	

The exchange coefficients in the X_L column tell a similar story. To increase X_L by one unit—that is, to increase unused labor by one hour—we must trade back $-2X_W$. In other words, if one hour of labor is *taken away* (which is what increasing unused resource means) we must give up −2 board feet of unused wood, that is, we get back +2 board feet of unused wood (so that we use 2 feet less than before). The net changes in unused resources correspond to the requirements for a fraction of a chair, 1/10 to be exact, that must be relinquished if X_L is increased by one hour (remember, it takes 10 hours to make a whole chair). This is why the second exchange coefficient, in the X_C row, is 1/10.

The per unit sacrifice for X_T is thus:

$$\begin{array}{c} \text{Unit} \\ \text{profit} \end{array} \times \begin{array}{c} \text{Exchange} \\ \text{coefficient} \end{array}$$

$$0 \times 20 = 0$$
$$\underline{8 \times 1/2 = 4}$$
$$\text{Sacrifice for } X_T = 4$$

This represents the $4 profit forgone by giving up the 1/2 chair needed to accommodate 1 table. The per unit sacrifices for X_C and X_W are $8 and $0. For X_L, we get

$$\begin{array}{c} \text{Unit} \\ \text{profit} \end{array} \times \begin{array}{c} \text{Exchange} \\ \text{coefficient} \end{array}$$

$$0 \times -2 = 0$$
$$\underline{8 \times 1/10 = 8/10}$$
$$\text{Sacrifice for } X_L = 8/10$$

which is the $8/10 profit (one-tenth of eight dollars) lost by giving up the 1/10 of a chair that cannot be made if we increase unused labor by 1 hour. The value computed in the solution column is

$$0 \times 80 = 0$$
$$\underline{8 \times 11 = 88}$$
$$88$$

which is the $88 profit represented by the current variable mix solution.

The solution for the new variable mix may be read directly from Table 13-7:

$$X_T = 0,\ X_C = 11,\ X_W = 80,\ X_L = 0;\ P = 88$$

(X_T and X_L, not in the mix, must be zero.) Figure 13-2 summarizes our current situation. We are now at a second corner to the feasible solution region that must be further evaluated. For this purpose we must determine the possible per unit profit improvements from increasing one or the other non-mix variables.

The values in the per unit improvement row of the latest simplex tableau, shown again as the top tableau in Table 13-8, are found by subtracting the sacrifice values from the profits listed on the top margin. We see that only one value is positive, the 2 under X_T. This indicates that increasing X_T will result in a net increase in profits of $2 per unit. We do not get the full profit of $6 on each table because for every table

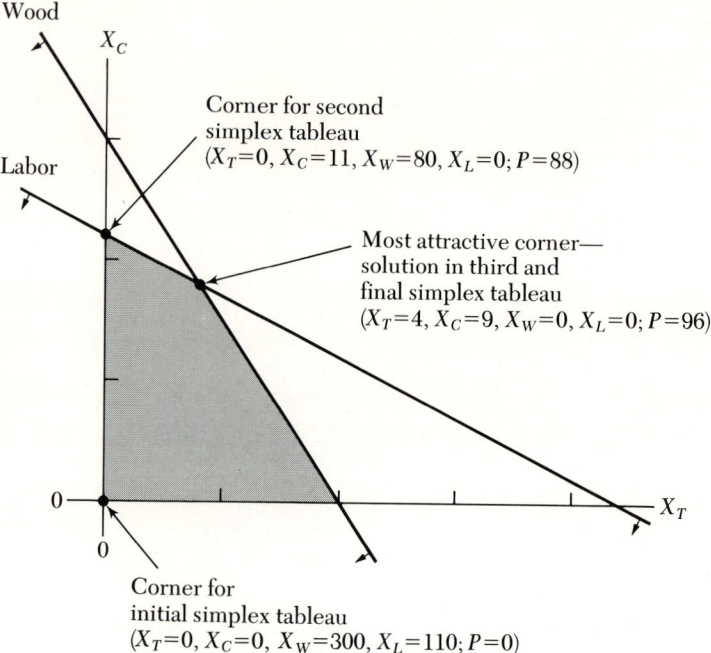

Figure 13-2
Graphical illustration of successive corners evaluated in simplex.

made, we must "steal" back resources that could be used to make half a chair, losing $4 of chair profit; thus we get only $6 − $4 = $2 profit per table.

Our entering variable is X_T. Applying the exit criterion, we see that the smallest exchange ratio applies to X_W, which limits table production the most (we run out of unused wood before giving back all chairs); this exchange will result in 4 tables and no unused wood. Thus the exiting variable is X_W. The present pivot element occurs where the X_W row and X_T column intersect and has value 20.

The new (third) simplex tableau is found by transforming the last one and is provided at the bottom of Table 13-8. This provides the solution

$$X_T = 4, \; X_C = 9, \; X_W = 0, \; X_L = 0; \; P = 96$$

which we know (from our earlier graphical analysis in Chapter 12) to be optimal. Simplex tells us that this must be the stopping point, since

Table 13-8
GOING FROM THE SECOND TO THIRD TABLEAU

	UNIT PROFIT		6	8	0	0		
		Var. Mix	X_T	X_C	X_W	X_L	Sol.	Exchange ratios:
	0	$X_W \leftarrow$	(20) ↓	0	1	−2	80	80/20 = 4*
	8	X_C	1/2	1	0	1/10	11	11/(1/2) = 22
		Sac.	4	8	0	8/10	88	* Smallest non-negative ratio
		Imp.	2	0	0	−8/10	−	
[old X_W ÷ 20]	6	X_T	1	0	1/20	−1/10	4	
[old X_C − 1/2 new X_T]	8	X_C	0	1	−1/40	3/20	9	
		Sac.	6	8	1/10	6/10	96	
		Imp.	0	0	−1/10	−6/10	−	

None of these is positive; no further improvement is possible.

none of the per unit improvement row values is positive. No further improvement is possible.

COMPUTATIONAL ASPECTS OF SIMPLEX 13-3

The only real thinking involved in solving a problem with linear programming occurs during the formulation phase. Once the initial tableau has been satisfactorily completed, the rest is just arithmetic. These simplex calculations can require a substantial amount of time. They are particularly onerous when getting the new tableau's exchange coefficients, since fractions such as 5/3, 2/17, and 23/31 often occur. It may be helpful to keep computations in fractional form throughout the process to avoid errors due to rounding. Side calculations on scratch paper, with the help of a calculator, will be helpful.

For example, suppose that we must subtract 4/7 times 6/21 from 5; we would make the calculation

$$5 - \left(\frac{4}{7}\right)\left(\frac{6}{21}\right) = 5 - \frac{24}{147}$$

and convert the difference to one in fractions having the same denominator:

$$5\left(\frac{147}{147}\right) - \frac{24}{147} = \frac{735 - 24}{147} = \frac{711}{147}$$

We can then attempt to reduce the resulting fraction to a form with the lowest common denominator, dividing 711 by factors comprising the denominator: 21, 7, and 3—to see if a whole number results. In this case, 711/3 = 237 exactly, so we can get 237/49 as a more elementary fraction; although this is equal to 4 and 41/49, it is preferable to enter the basic fraction 237/49 in the new tableau.

It is very easy to make arithmetic mistakes when doing simplex computations by hand. Unfortunately just one mistake can cascade throughout, ruining everything that follows. Checks can be made to catch obvious errors:

(a) The solution-column values may never be negative; if one value is negative, an error was made somewhere—no further steps should be made until it has been corrected.

(b) The mix-variable columns should contain a single 1 in the proper row, with zeros elsewhere, including the improvement row.

(c) The new P or C should be at least as good as the earlier one; if it isn't, an error was made.

(d) If any set of solution values violates the original problem's constraints, then again an error has been made.

Hand computation is not only error-prone but is also quite time consuming. A good arithmetician might spend a day or two solving a 10-row, 20-column simplex problem by hand; the same person would require more than a week to find the answer to a problem having twice as many rows and columns.

The computational difficulties in simplex would preclude the use of linear programming in many applications were it not for high-speed digital computers. The computer eliminates the errors so inevitable in hand calculations. It is also much faster. Today it is routine to use a computer in solving problems with thousands of variables and constraints. Rarely in business is a linear program completely solved by hand. In modern linear programming applications, the human element can be concentrated on the conceptual areas of problem formulation.

Computer programs are widely available for use in solving linear programs. It is no longer even necessary to write one from scratch. Most college computer centers and time-sharing systems have library programs that can solve large problems. Computer advisors should be able to explain how to arrange the input data and to interpret the computer printouts. Thus, any linear programming problem requiring more than nominal hand calculations can best be solved with the assistance of a computer.

SHORTCUTS IN CONSTRUCTING TABLEAUS 13-4

A variety of shortcuts exist for making simplex computations. The following rules of thumb always apply.

(1) In getting the new tableau from the old one, only the columns of the non-mix and exiting variables ever change. The columns of those mix variables remaining in that state can therefore be copied directly into the new tableau.

(2) To simplify calculations, wherever a zero is found in the pivot *column*, that *row* in the body of the tableau is repeated in the next tableau without change; wherever a zero is found in the pivot *row*, that *column* in the body of the tableau is repeated in the next one without change.

(3) The column of the newly entered mix variable will contain zeros everywhere, except that a 1 appears in the same position as the pivot element in the preceding tableau and the per unit profit or cost for this variable appears in the sacrifice row.

(4) Unless further analysis is to be performed, the column for an artificial variable may be eliminated after it exits from the variable mix.

SPECIAL SIMPLEX CONSIDERATIONS 13-5

We have described the simplex algorithm in detail. The same steps are taken regardless of the number of variables or constraints involved. But we must consider several further aspects before our discussion is complete.

As with the graphical technique, simplex may be applied to either profit maximization or cost minimization problems. Only a slight modification in procedure is required when minimizing C. Instead of profit, we use costs. As we shall see in the next chapter, we must reinterpret the improvement row to coincide with the different objective. This will cause a minor change in applying the entry criterion.

A major problem arises in simplex whenever a constraint is an equality (=) or takes the greater than or equal to form ($\geq$). Chapter 14 shows how to deal with these situations.

PROBLEMS

13-1 Consider the following simplex tableau:

UNIT PROFIT		5	7	9	7	8	
	Var. Mix	X_1	X_2	X_3	X_4	X_5	Sol.
9	X_3	-2	0	1	2	1	6
7	X_2	3	1	0	-3	2	3
	Sac.						
	Imp.						—

(a) Find the sacrifice and improvement row values.
(b) Find the entering variable and the exiting variable and identify the pivot element.

13-2 Consider the following simplex tableau:

UNIT PROFIT		5	3	4	5	0	
	Var. Mix	X_1	X_2	X_3	X_4	X_5	Sol.
5	X_4	-2	0	0	1	0	1.5
4	X_3	1	0	1	0	-1	2.5
3	X_2	3	1	0	0	2	3.0
	Sac.	3	3	4	5	2	26.5
	Imp.	2	0	0	0	-2	—

The entering variable is X_1 and the exiting variable is X_2. Determine the next simplex tableau.

13-3 For the linear program

Maximize $\quad P = 100X_1 + 200X_2 + 150X_3$
Subject to $\quad 5X_1 + 20X_2 + 30X_3 \leq 60 \quad$ (resource A)
$\qquad\qquad\;\; 10X_1 + 20X_2 + 50X_3 \leq 100 \quad$ (resource B)
where $\qquad\quad X_1, X_2, X_3 \geq 0$

the following final simplex tableau applies, where X_A and X_B are the slack variables for the first and second constraints, respectively.

UNIT PROFIT		100	200	150	0	0	
	Var. Mix	X_1	X_2	X_3	X_A	X_B	Sol.
100	X_1	1	0	4	−1/5	1/5	8
200	X_2	0	1	1/2	1/10	−1/20	1
	Sac.	100	200	500	0	10	1000
	Imp.	0	0	−350	0	−10	−

From this tableau, determine the optimal values for all five variables and the maximum possible profit.

13-4 Consider the linear program

Maximize $\quad P = 2X_1 + 3X_2$
Subject to $\quad 3X_1 + 2X_2 \leq 6 \quad$ (resource A)
$\qquad\qquad\quad X_1 \qquad\quad \leq 5 \quad$ (resource B)
$\qquad\qquad\qquad\quad X_2 \leq 4 \quad$ (resource C)
where $\qquad X_1, X_2 \geq 0$

(a) Solve this problem graphically.
(b) Reformulate the above problem in equation form suitable for simplex.
(c) Re-solve the problem using the simplex procedure.

13-5 Consider again Ace Widgets' problem of deciding how many regular and deluxe models to produce. The regular model requires 5 hours of finishing labor and 1 frame. The deluxe version needs 8 hours and 1 frame. Only 12 frames and 80 hours of labor are available. The unit profits are $10 for the regular model and $15 for the deluxe version.
(a) Formulate the linear program. Then solve it graphically.
(b) Reformulate the problem in an equation form that is suitable for the simplex method.
(c) Re-solve the problem using the simplex procedure.

13-6 For the Piney Woods Furniture Company, which makes tables (T), chairs (C), and bookcases (B), the following linear program applies.

Maximize $\quad P = 20X_T + 15X_C + 15X_B$
Subject to $\quad 10X_T + 3X_C + 10X_B \leq 100 \quad$ (wood)
$\qquad\qquad\quad 5X_T + 5X_C + 5X_B \leq 60 \quad$ (labor)
where $\qquad X_T, X_C, X_B \geq 0$

Apply the simplex method to determine how many of each item should be made.

CHAPTER 13 PROBLEMS

13-7 Sammy Love sells candied apples on the street corner. He has three types: butterscotch, cinnamon, and peppermint. In making today's batch, Sammy is limited only by the amounts of sugar and gelatin, since all other ingredients are in good supply. Each butterscotch apple requires 1 cup of sugar, while cinnamon and peppermint apples each need 1/2 cup of sugar. Cinnamon apples require 2 ounces of gelatin, peppermint apples use 1 ounce, and butterscotch apples need none. Only 200 cups of sugar are available, and Sammy has just 100 ounces of gelatin.

Sammy makes a profit of 10¢ on each butterscotch apple, 15¢ on each cinnamon, and 20¢ on each peppermint. He always sells his entire stock.

(a) Formulate Sammy's linear program.
(b) Identify any slack variables required to solve this problem using the simplex method.
(c) Apply the simplex method to determine how many candied apples of each type Sammy should make.

Fourteen

Additional Simplex Method Considerations

The applications of the simplex method described in Chapter 13 were limited to profit maximization problems with constraints of the ≤ form. We are now ready to consider more general problems with constraints involving ≥ or = relations. These applications require new auxiliary variables that play an analogous role to the slack variable we have already encountered. By including cost minimization, this chapter also expands the scope of the problems that can be solved using the simplex method. The chapter concludes with a discussion of special difficulties encountered in linear programming.

14-1 SURPLUS AND ARTIFICIAL VARIABLES: THE BIG-M METHOD

Suppose that we slightly modify the original Redwood Furniture problem by including a third product, benches, the quantity of which is represented by the variable X_B. This increases the number of dimensions for the problem beyond our capability to draw a simple graph, making the simplex method the essential procedure. Suppose that each bench requires 25 board feet of wood and 7 hours of labor and will be sold for a profit of $7. To further complicate the problem, we will assume that at least 2 benches must be made to satisfy outstanding orders; this creates a third "demand" constraint. The basic linear program is

$$\text{Maximize} \quad P = 6X_T + 8X_C + 7X_B \quad \text{(objective)}$$
$$\text{Subject to} \quad 30X_T + 20X_C + 25X_B \le 300 \quad \text{(wood)}$$
$$5X_T + 10X_C + 7X_B \le 110 \quad \text{(labor)}$$
$$X_B \ge 2 \quad \text{(demand)}$$
$$\text{where} \quad X_T, X_C, X_B \ge 0$$

The new demand constraint must be converted into an equality. This presents a special problem because the inequality points to the right. Since the value on the left can be larger than the minimum requirement of 2 benches, we can express any extra quantity beyond 2 as surplus benches. Thus, the constraint may be equivalently stated as

$$\text{Number of benches} - \text{Surplus benches} = 2$$

Or, if we let X_D represent the surplus benches beyond the demand requirement, this constraint becomes

$$X_B - X_D = 2 \quad \text{(demand)}$$

We refer to X_D as a *surplus variable*. Analogous to slack variables, surplus variables allow us to express linear programs in the equation form required by simplex. They also have economic meaning. As with any simplex variable, X_D must be non-negative (a negative surplus has no meaning here).

Our demand constraint has one further inadequacy. When zeroing out X_B, we are left with $0 - X_D = 2$, or $X_D = -2$; X_D would start as a negative value, which is disallowed. Thus, our demand constraint cannot serve, in its present form, as a starting simplex row, and X_D cannot be one of the *initial* mix variables. In fact, *surplus variables can never be in the initial variable mix*.

To get simplex started we introduce the *artificial variable*, a quantity that has no meaningful economic interpretation. It is merely a temporary expedient. We generally use the letter a, with an appropriate subscript, to identify this type of variable. In our problem, a_D will represent the artificial variable. This is added to the left side of the demand constraint equation, providing

$$X_B - X_D + a_D = 2 \quad \text{(demand)}$$

The above expression in no way distorts the underlying production requirement as long as a_D *ultimately assumes a value of zero*. To guarantee that $a_D = 0$ (so that it is not in the final variable mix), we must make it very unprofitable to do otherwise. We give it a very large negative per unit profit. For this purpose we use the letter M (for mammoth) to represent a huge number and assign a per unit profit of $-M$ to a_D.

Using X_W and X_L as before, and noting that surplus variables, like slacks, contribute nothing to profit (or cost), we obtain the expanded linear program in a form suitable for beginning the simplex:

Maximize

$$P = 6X_T + 8X_C + 7X_B + 0X_W + 0X_L + 0X_D - Ma_D \quad \text{(objective)}$$

Subject to

$$30X_T + 20X_C + 25X_B + 1X_W + 0X_L + 0X_D + 0a_D = 300 \quad \text{(wood)}$$
$$5X_T + 10X_C + 7X_B + 0X_W + 1X_L + 0X_D + 0a_D = 110 \quad \text{(labor)}$$
$$0X_T + 0X_C + 1X_B + 0X_W + 0X_L - 1X_D + 1a_D = 2 \quad \text{(demand)}$$

where $\quad X_T, X_C, X_B, X_W, X_L, X_D, a_D \geq 0$

As before, we list all variables in all equations; those not originally there appear with coefficients of zero.

The initial simplex tableau is provided in Table 14-1. The variable mix consists of the slack variables and the artificial variable. Notice

Table 14-1
INITIAL SIMPLEX TABLEAU FOR THE EXPANDED FURNITURE PROBLEM

UNIT PROFIT		6	8	7	0	0	0	$-M$		
	Var. Mix	X_T	X_C	X_B	X_W	X_L	X_D	a_D	Sol.	
0	X_W	30	20	25	1	0	0	0	300	300/25 = 12
0	X_L	5	10	7	0	1	0	0	110	110/7 = 15.71
$-M$	a_D	0	0	1	0	0	-1	1	2	2/1 = 2*
	Sac.	0	0	$-M$	0	0	M	$-M$	$-2M$	
	Imp.	6	8	$7+M$	0	0	$-M$	0	—	

14-1 SURPLUS AND ARTIFICIAL VARIABLES: THE BIG-M METHOD

Table 14-2

TABLEAUS FOR REMAINING ITERATIONS OF EXPANDED FURNITURE PROBLEM

	UNIT PROFIT		6	8	7	0	0	0	−M		
		Var. Mix	X_T	X_C	X_B	X_W	X_L	X_D	a_D	Sol.	
[old X_W −25 new X_B]	0	X_W	30	20 ↓	0	1	0	25	−25	250	250/20 = 12.5
[old X_L −7 new X_B]	0	X_L ←	5	(10)	0	0	1	7	−7	96	96/10 = 9.6*
[old a_D ÷ 1]	7	X_B	0	0	1	0	0	−1	1	2	2/0 = ∞
		Sac.	0	0	7	0	0	−7	7	14	
		Imp.	6	8	0	0	0	7	−M−7	—	
[old X_W −20 new X_C]	0	X_W ←	(20) ↓	0	0	1	−2	11	−11	58	58/20 = 2.9*
[old X_L ÷ 10]	8	X_C	1/2	1	0	0	1/10	7/10	−7/10	9.6	9.6/(1/2) = 19.2
[old X_B −0 new X_C]	7	X_B	0	0	1	0	0	−1	1	2	2/0 = ∞
		Sac.	4	8	7	0	.8	−1.4	1.4	90.8	
		Imp.	2	0	0	0	−.8	1.4	−M−1.4	—	
[old X_W ÷ 20]	6	X_T ←	1	0	0	1/20	−1/10	(11/20) ↓	−11/20	2.9	2.9/(11/20) = 5.27
[old X_C −(1/2) new X_T]	8	X_C	0	1	0	−1/40	3/20	17/40	−17/40	8.15	8.15/(17/40) = 19.18
[old X_B −0 new X_T]	7	X_B	0	0	1	0	0	−1	1	2	2/−1 = −2
		Sac.	6	8	7	.1	.6	−.3	.3	96.6	
		Imp.	0	0	0	−.1	−.6	.3	−M−.3	—	
[old X_T ÷ 11/20]	0	X_D	20/11	0	0	1/11	−2/11	1	−1	58/11	
[old X_C −(17/40) new X_D]	8	X_C	−17/22	1	0	−7/110	5/22	0	0	65/11	
[old X_B −(−1) new X_D]	7	X_B	20/11	0	1	1/11	−2/11	0	0	80/11	
		Sac.	72/11	8	7	7/55	6/11	0	0	1080/11	
		Imp.	−6/11	0	0	−7/55	−6/11	0	−M	—	

that the columns of these variables contain a 1 in their row and zeros elsewhere. The initial solution is $X_T = X_C = X_B = X_D = 0$, $X_W = 300$, $X_L = 110$, $a_D = 2$, and $P = -2M$ (a very poor profit indeed). Notice also that the sacrifice and improvement rows contain M terms.

The entering variable is X_B, since it has the largest profit improvement, at $7 + M$ dollars per unit. The exit criterion indicates that at most $2X_B$ can be traded in the variable mix for a_D, the exiting variable. The remaining iterations of the simplex method are shown in Table 14-2.

The optimal solution obtained from the final simplex tableau is

$X_T = 0$ $\qquad X_W = 0$

$X_C = 65/11$ $\qquad X_L = 0$

$X_B = 80/11$ $\qquad X_D = 58/11$

$P = 1080/11 = 98.18$ dollars

Notice that when benches are included in the product line it is no longer most profitable to make tables. We see also that the surplus variable has value greater than zero, indicating that $X_D = X_B - 2 = 58/11$ benches should be produced beyond the minimum level of 2. Finally, notice that the artificial variable is not in the final variable mix and has value zero; since a_D has no economic meaning, we ordinarily do not include it when reporting the optimal solution.

As a general rule, *a separate artificial variable should be used for every greater than constraint, each of which must also have its own surplus variable*. The mix variable in the initial simplex tableau must always be that artificial variable introduced into the constraint equation for that row. An artificial variable must also ordinarily be used when there is an *equality constraint* in the first formulation, as might be the case were Redwood Furniture forced to make *exactly* 1 table for every 4 chairs. Since such a constraint begins with an = expression, neither a surplus nor a slack variable is needed; but an artificial variable is required to get simplex started.

COST MINIMIZATION PROBLEMS 14-2

Simplex can be applied to solve cost minimization problems. All steps are the same as when maximizing P. The only major difference occurs in the entry criterion. Since the per unit improvement row consists of net changes in cost, *negative values* in that row indicate the improvement; the entering variable is thus the one having the largest (in absolute terms) negative entry in that row.

Table 14-3

LABELING REQUIREMENTS AND COST DATA FOR THE PERSIAN SAUSAGE PROBLEM

LABEL CATEGORY	PERCENTAGE OF WEIGHT			REQUIRED PERCENTAGE
	Beef	*Chicken*	*Lamb*	
Fat	20	15	25	$\leq 24\%$
Protein	20	15	15	$\geq 12\%$
Water and other	60	70	60	$\leq 64\%$
Percentage of total weight	any	any	$\geq 30\%$	
Cost per pound	\$1.00	\$.50	\$.70	

Suppose that a meat packer must determine the quantities of ingredients that should be used in making one hundred pounds of Persian sausage. Table 14-3 shows the package labeling requirements.

We will assume that spices and casings add an insignificant amount to the total sausage weight and that unlimited quantities of the main ingredients are available at the indicated costs. The total ingredient weight must equal 100 pounds. If we represent the number of pounds of beef by X_B, chicken by X_C, and lamb by X_L, the following linear program formulation applies:

$$\text{Minimize} \quad C = 1X_B + .5X_C + .7X_L \quad \text{(objective)}$$

Subject to
$$.20X_B + .15X_C + .25X_L \leq 24 \quad \text{(fat)}$$
$$.20X_B + .15X_C + .15X_L \geq 12 \quad \text{(protein)}$$
$$.60X_B + .70X_C + .60X_L \leq 64 \quad \text{(water)}$$
$$1X_L \geq 30 \quad \text{(ingredient)}$$
$$1X_B + 1X_C + 1X_L = 100 \quad \text{(total weight)}$$

where
$$X_B, X_C, X_L \geq 0 \quad \text{(non-negativity)}$$

Inspection of the above indicates that we must include two slack variables for the fat and water constraints, and two surplus variables for the protein and ingredient constraints. We denote these, respectively, as X_F, X_W, X_P, and X_I. Since they involve surplus variables, the protein and ingredient constraints must include the artificial variables a_P and a_I. Finally, we include an artificial variable, a_T for the equality constraint for total weight.

The pre-simplex formulation of the linear program is

Minimize

$$C = 1X_B + .5X_C + .7X_L + 0X_F + 0X_P + 0X_W + 0X_I + Ma_P + Ma_I + Ma_T$$

Subject to

$$.20X_B + .15X_C + .25X_L + 1X_F + 0X_P + 0X_W + 0X_I + 0a_P + 0a_I + 0a_T = 24$$
$$.20X_B + .15X_C + .15X_L + 0X_F - 1X_P + 0X_W + 0X_I + 1a_P + 0a_I + 0a_T = 12$$
$$.60X_B + .70X_C + .60X_L + 0X_F + 0X_P + 1X_W + 0X_I + 0a_P + 0a_I + 0a_T = 64$$
$$0X_B + 0X_C + 1X_L + 0X_F + 0X_P + 0X_W - 1X_I + 0a_P + 1a_I + 0a_T = 30$$
$$1X_B + 1X_C + 1X_L + 0X_F + 0X_P + 0X_W + 0X_I + 0a_P + 0a_I + 1a_T = 100$$

where   all variables ≥ 0

Handling these artificial variables differs in one way from those in handling the profit maximizing case. In the objective, a_P, a_I, and a_T have unit costs of *plus M*, making them terribly costly (and insuring that they leave the variable mix early).

The initial simplex tableau is provided in Table 14-4. From the improvement row, we see that X_L must be the entering variable, since the entry from its column is $.7 - 2.15M$, which in absolute terms exceeds the other negative entries of $1 - 1.2M$ and $.5 - 1.15M$. In determining this look first at the M terms; the biggest absolute value of the negative ones corresponds to the entering variable. For example, consider the follow-

Table 14-4
THE INITIAL SIMPLEX TABLEAU FOR THE PERSIAN SAUSAGE PROBLEM

UNIT COST		1	.5	.7	0	0	0	0	M	M	M	
	Var. Mix	X_B	X_C	X_L	X_F	X_P	X_W	X_I	a_P	a_I	a_T	Sol.
0	X_F	.20	.15	.25 ↓	1	0	0	0	0	0	0	24
M	a_P	.20	.15	.15	0	−1	0	0	1	0	0	12
0	X_W	.60	.70	.60	0	0	1	0	0	0	0	64
M	a_I ←	0	0	①	0	0	0	−1	0	1	0	30
M	a_T	1	1	1	0	0	0	0	0	0	1	100
	Sac.	1.2M	1.15M	2.15M	0	−M	0	−M	M	M	M	142M
	Imp.	1 −1.2M	.5 −1.15M	.7 −2.15M	0	M	0	M	0	0	0	—

14-2   COST MINIMIZATION PROBLEMS

ing two sets of hypothetical improvement values (the numbers in parentheses represent the case when $M = 1{,}000{,}000$):

	Set 1		Set 2	
$(4{,}997{,}000)$	$-3{,}000 + 5M$		$50{,}000 - 1M$	$(-950{,}000)$
$(-999{,}998)$	$2 - 1M$		$20{,}000 - 1M$	$(-980{,}000)$
$(-1{,}009{,}950)$	$50 - 1.01M$	← choices →	$2{,}000 - 1M$	$(-998{,}000)$
$(-499{,}980)$	$20 - .5M$		$5{,}000 - 1M$	$(-995{,}000)$

In set 1 we choose the third value, since it has the largest absolute value among the negative coefficients of M. Should more than one negative

Table 14-5
THE REMAINING ITERATIONS FOR THE PERSIAN SAUSAGE PROBLEM

UNIT COST		1	.5	.7	0	0	0	0	M	M	M	
	Var. Mix	X_B	X_C	X_L	X_F	X_P	X_W	X_I	a_P	a_I	a_T	Sol.
0	X_F	.20 ↓	.15	0	1	0	0	.25	0	−.25	0	16.5
M	a_P ←	(.20)	.15	0	0	−1	0	.15	1	−.15	0	7.5
0	X_W	.60	.70	0	0	0	1	.60	0	−.60	0	46
.7	X_L	0	0	1	0	0	0	−1	0	1	0	30
M	a_T	1	1	0	0	0	0	1	0	−1	1	70
	Sac.	1.2M	1.15M	.7	0	−M	0	−.7 +1.15M	M	.7 −1.15M	M	21 +77.5M
	Imp.	1 −1.2M	.5 −1.15M	0	0	M	0	.7 −1.15M	0	−.7 +2.15M	0	—
0	X_F	0	0	0	1	1 ↓	0	.10	−1	−.10	0	9
1	X_B	1	.75	0	0	−5	0	.75	5	−.75	0	37.5
0	X_W	0	.25	0	0	3	1	.15	−3	−.15	0	23.5
.7	X_L	0	0	1	0	0	0	−1	0	1	0	30
M	a_T ←	0	.25	0	0	(5)	0	.25	−5	−.25	1	32.5
	Sac.	1	.75 +.25M	.7	0	−5 +5M	0	.05 +.25M	5 −5M	−.05 −.25M	M	58.5 +32.5M
	Imp.	0	−.25 −.25M	0	0	5 −5M	0	−.05 −.25M	−5 +6M	.05 +1.25M	0	—

coefficient have the same largest absolute value, then choose the one having the lowest constant value (or, the largest absolute negative, if there are negative ones); thus in set 2 we choose the third entry.

The exit criterion does not change in cost minimization. We determine the ratios, selecting the smallest non-negative one, which establishes a_I as the exiting variable.

The remainder of the simplex procedure is provided in Table 14-5.

Table 14-5 (continued)

UNIT COST		1	.5	.7	0	0	0	0	M	M	M	
	Var. Mix	X_B	X_C	X_L	X_F	X_P	X_W	X_I	a_P	a_I	a_T	Sol.
0	X_F	0	−.05 ↓	0	1	0	0	.05	0	−.05	−.2	2.5
1	X_B	1	1	0	0	0	0	1	0	−1	1	70
0	X_W ←	0	(.10)	0	0	0	1	0	0	0	−.6	4
.7	X_L	0	0	1	0	0	0	−1	0	1	0	30
0	X_P	0	.05	0	0	1	0	.05	−1	−.05	.2	6.5
	Sac.	1	1	.7	0	0	0	.3	0	−.3	1	91
	Imp.	0	−.5	0	0	0	0	−.3	M	.3+M	−1+M	—
0	X_F	0	0	0	1	0	.5	.05 ↓	0	−.05	−.5	4.5
1	X_B ←	1	0	0	0	0	−10	(1)	0	−1	7	30
.5	X_C	0	1	0	0	0	10	0	0	0	−6	40
.7	X_L	0	0	1	0	0	0	−1	0	1	0	30
0	X_P	0	0	0	0	1	−.5	.05	−1	−.05	.5	4.5
	Sac.	1	.5	.7	0	0	−5	.3	0	−.3	4	71
	Imp.	0	0	0	0	0	5	−.3	M	.3+M	−4+M	—
0	X_F	−.05	0	0	1	0	1	0	0	0	−.85	3
0	X_I	1	0	0	0	0	−10	1	0	−1	7	30
.5	X_C	0	1	0	0	0	10	0	0	0	−6	40
.7	X_L	1	0	1	0	0	−10	0	0	0	7	60
0	X_P	−.05	0	0	0	1	0	0	−1	0	.15	3
	Sac.	.7	.5	.7	0	0	−2	0	0	0	1.9	62
	Imp.	.3	0	0	0	0	2	0	M	M	−1.9+M	—

The optimal solution is

$$X_B = 0 \qquad X_F = 3$$
$$X_C = 40 \qquad X_I = 30$$
$$X_L = 60 \qquad X_P = 3$$
$$X_W = 0$$

$$C = 62 \text{ dollars}$$

Thus, no beef should be used in the Persian sausage, while the main ingredients consist of 40 pounds of chicken and 60 pounds of lamb; there will be 3 pounds less fat than the maximum allowable, while the same weight of extra protein beyond the minimum level will result; also, 30 pounds of lamb beyond the minimum 30 are included.

14-3 SUMMARY OF SIMPLEX FORMULATION REQUIREMENTS

As we have seen, under various conditions the simplex procedure requires slack, surplus, or artificial variables in addition to the main problem variables. A summary of the simplex formulation requirements is provided in Table 14-6.

Table 14-6
SUMMARY OF SIMPLEX FORMULATION REQUIREMENTS

Type of Constraint	Constraint Relationship	Extra Variables Needed for Simplex	Objective Coefficient		Initial Variable Mix
			Max. P	Min. C	
Resource or maximum requirement	≤	Slack (added)	0	0	Yes
		No artificial	—	—	—
Demand or minimum requirement	≥	Surplus (subtracted)	0	0	No
		Artificial (added)	$-M$	$+M$	Yes
Mixture or exact requirement	=	No slack/surplus	—	—	—
		Artificial (added)	$-M$	$+M$	Yes

SPECIAL PROBLEMS IN LINEAR PROGRAMMING   14-4

So far we have substantially covered the simplex method. Only a few special problem areas remain to be discussed. First we consider two types of problems that have no practical solutions. We then describe what to do when there may be several optimal solutions (most attractive corners). Finally, we consider two technical difficulties inherent in the simplex procedure.

Infeasible Problems

We have been fortunate so far to encounter only problems that have solutions. It is possible, however, for constraints to be so restrictive that no solution exists. We call such a case an *infeasible problem*. Consider the following linear program:

$$\begin{aligned}
\text{Maximize} \quad & P = 6X_1 + 4X_2 \\
\text{Subject to} \quad & X_1 + X_2 \leq 5 \\
& X_2 \geq 8 \\
\text{where} \quad & X_1, X_2 \geq 0
\end{aligned}$$

This problem is graphed in Figure 14-1. Notice that there is no feasible solution region, since the constraints are mutually incompatible.

It is not so easy to see that a problem is infeasible when several variables and constraints are involved. Fortunately, the simplex method can determine for us whether or not a problem is feasible to begin with. Table 14-7 shows the simplex tableaus for this problem using S_1 as the slack in the first constraint, S_2 as the surplus for the second, and a as the artificial variable. The final tableau includes the artificial in the variable mix, with value $a = 3$. We know that this makes no economic sense. *If one or more artificial variables remain in the final variable mix, the linear program must be infeasible.*

Ordinarily, an infeasible problem signifies that a mistake was made in the initial formulation. The remedy is to check the constraint expressions to see that they properly reflect the problem. For example, one number may have been miscopied or given the wrong sign; or, perhaps a $\leq$ should really be a $\geq$. Once the mistake has been remedied, the corrected linear program may then be solved again. More perplexing is when the formulation properly reflects the problem, which itself represents contradictory requirements. Unless the impasse is resolved, the

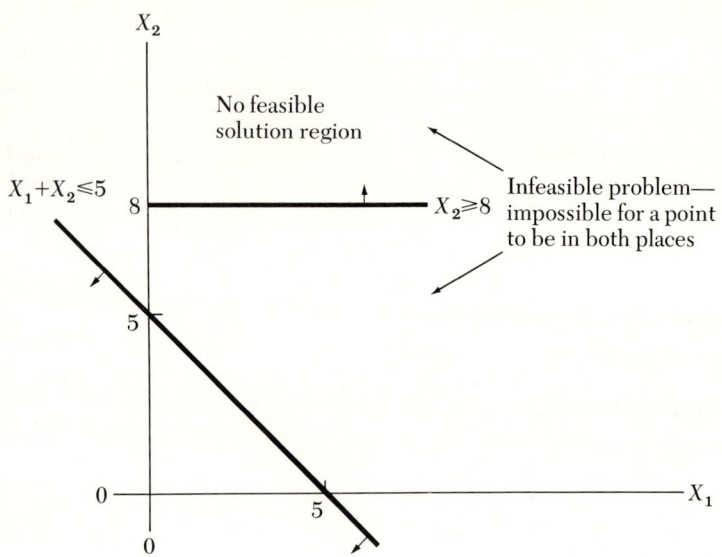

Figure 14-1
Graph for the infeasible problem.

Table 14-7
SIMPLEX TABLEAUS FOR THE INFEASIBLE PROBLEM

UNIT PROFIT		6	4	0	0	$-M$	
	Var. Mix	X_1	X_2	S_1	S_2	a	Sol.
0	$S_1 \leftarrow$	1	①↓	1	0	0	5
$-M$	a	0	1	0	-1	1	8
	Sac.	0	$-M$	0	M	$-M$	$5 - 8M$
	Imp.	6	$4 + M$	0	$-M$	0	—
4	X_2	1	1	1	0	0	5
$-M$	a	-1	0	-1	-1	1	3
	Sac.	$4 + M$	4	$4 + M$	M	$-M$	$20 - 3M$
	Imp.	$2 - M$	0	$-4 - M$	$-M$	0	—

398 ADDITIONAL SIMPLEX METHOD CONSIDERATIONS

decision maker will never be able to solve the problem. (No kind of answer, not even a poor one, is possible for an infeasible problem.)

Unbounded Problems

Another class of linear programs yields ridiculous solutions that place no effective limit on one or more variables; thus any level of profit is possible, even trillions of dollars or more. Such a linear program is *unbounded*. As an example, consider

$$\begin{aligned} \text{Maximize} \quad & P = 3X_1 + 6X_2 \\ \text{Subject to} \quad & 3X_1 + 4X_2 \geq 12 \\ & -2X_1 + X_2 \leq 4 \\ \text{where} \quad & X_1, X_2 \geq 0 \end{aligned}$$

This linear program's graph in Figure 14-2 shows that the feasible solu-

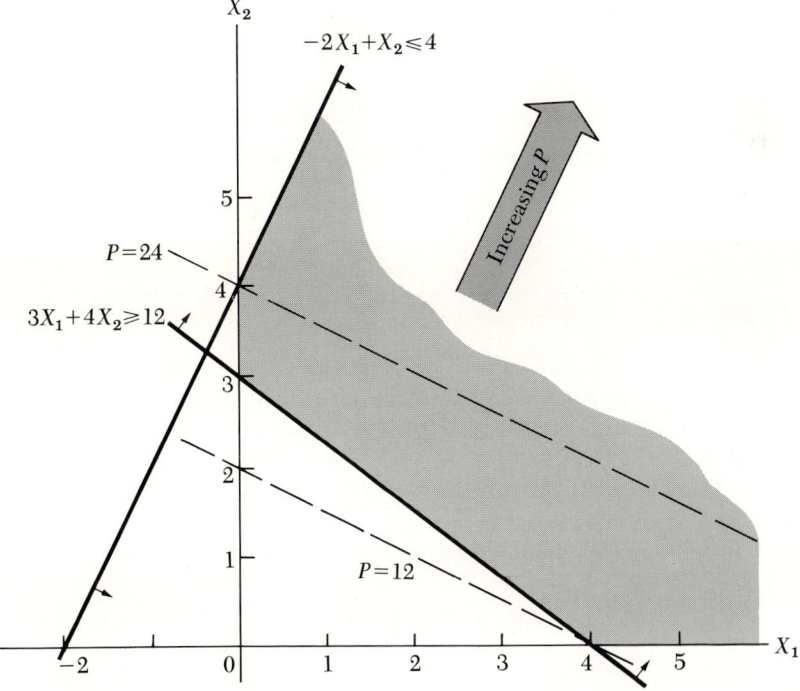

Figure 14-2
Graph for the unbounded problem.

tion region lies open and gets wider in the direction of increasing P. There is no most attractive corner, and P can be as large as you want it to be. No matter how large a P is chosen, lines for larger Ps can be drawn through the feasible solution region. In essence, P can be infinite.

As with infeasible problems, simplex can identify the unbounded problem for us. Table 14-8 shows the simplex iterations for this example, using S_1 and a as the surplus and artificial variables for the first constraint and S_2 as the slack variable for the second. Notice that in the third tableau no exiting variable can be found, because no entry in the X_1 column is positive. In essence, there is no limit on the quantity X_1; it can replace either X_2 or S_1 in the variable mix at any level desired.

Whenever the exit criterion fails, the linear program is unbounded. *We find a problem unbounded whenever none of the values in the entering variable's column is positive.*

Table 14-8
SIMPLEX TABLEAUS FOR THE UNBOUNDED PROBLEM

UNIT PROFIT			3	6	0	0	$-M$	
		Var. Mix	X_1	X_2	S_1	S_2	a	Sol.
$-M$		$a \leftarrow$	3	④	-1	0	1	12
0		S_2	-2	1	0	1	0	4
		Sac.	$-3M$	$-4M$	M	0	$-M$	$-12M$
		Imp.	$3 + 3M$	$6 + 4M$	$-M$	0	0	—
6		X_2	.75	1	$-.25$	0	.25	3
0		$S_2 \leftarrow$	-2.75	0	㉕	1	$-.25$	1
		Sac.	4.5	6	-1.5	0	1.5	18
		Imp.	-1.5	0	1.5	0	$-M - 1.5$	—
6		X_2	-2	1	0	1	0	4
0		S_1	-11	0	1	4	-1	4
		Sac.	-12	6	0	6	0	24
		Imp.	15	0	0	-6	$-M$	—

There is no exiting variable.

In the real world no economic situations are literally unbounded. Thus, when a linear program turns up unbounded, some essential restriction (plant capacity, initial inventory level, etc.) has been left out of the formulation. Once the missing constraint is found, the properly formulated linear program should have a realistic answer.

Ties for Optimal Solution

In Chapter 12, we saw that whenever a most attractive corner lies on an edge parallel to the objective function, there is another corner equally good at the opposite end; all points on this edge correspond to optimal solutions.

In higher dimensional problems encountered with simplex, similar ties for the most attractive corner apply. The simplex procedure can be used to evaluate every most attractive corner, finding all tying optimal solutions. Such ties occur when the objective function coefficients have a constant ratio to the respective coefficients in the expression for one constraint or another one that might result when two or more constraint equations are combined. Under some circumstances, there can be more than two most attractive corners, and thus a multitude of ties might occur; but ordinarily, there will be no ties at all.

Suppose that the Persian sausage problem must be slightly changed because beef sells for 70 cents per pound instead of a dollar. Table 14-9 shows in the top position the corresponding final simplex tableau. (For simplicity, the artificial variable columns have been left off.) The first tableau provides the optimal solution

$$X_B = 0 \qquad X_F = 3$$
$$X_C = 40 \qquad X_P = 3$$
$$X_L = 60 \qquad X_W = 0$$
$$X_I = 30$$
$$C = 62 \text{ dollars}$$

(which is identical to the one found earlier). Notice that *a zero improvement* exists for one of the non-mix variables X_B. This indicates that if some beef were used, so that X_B were a mix variable, there would be no change in total cost; in effect, a simplex pivot treating X_B as the entering variable would produce a new solution also having a cost of 62 dollars. In other words, a tie exists for optimal solution.

Suppose we carry out one more iteration, treating X_B (beef) as the entering variable. We see that X_I (surplus ingredient lamb) exits, and the

Table 14-9

A FURTHER SIMPLEX ITERATION TO FIND THE TYING OPTIMAL SOLUTION TO THE PERSIAN SAUSAGE PROBLEM

UNIT COST		.7	.5	.7	0	0	0	0	
	Var. Mix	X_B	X_C	X_L	X_F	X_P	X_W	X_I	Sol.
0	X_F	−.05↓	0	0	1	0	1	0	3
0	X_I ←	①	0	0	0	0	−10	1	30
.5	X_C	0	1	0	0	0	10	0	40
.7	X_L	1	0	1	0	0	−10	0	60
0	X_P	−.05	0	0	0	1	0	0	3
	Sac.	.7	.5	.7	0	0	−2	0	62
	Imp.	0	0	0	0	0	2	0	—
0	X_F	0	0	0	1	0	.5	.05	4.5
.7	X_B	1	0	0	0	0	−10	1	30
.5	X_C	0	1	0	0	0	10	0	40
.7	X_L	0	0	1	0	0	0	−1	30
0	X_P	0	0	0	0	1	−.5	.05	4.5
	Sac.	.7	.5	.7	0	0	−2	0	62
	Imp.	0	0	0	0	0	2	0	—

solution is provided by the second tableau, where

$$X_B = 30 \quad X_F = 4.5$$
$$X_C = 40 \quad X_P = 4.5$$
$$X_L = 30 \quad X_W = 0$$
$$X_I = 0$$
$$C = 62 \text{ dollars}$$

This solution ties for optimum with the first one. In general, *a tie for optimal solution exists whenever a non-mix variable has zero per unit improvement in the final simplex tableau.* This is true regardless of whether that variable is a main, slack, or surplus. The tying solution can be found by a further simplex pivot treating that variable as the entering one. (This feature is also present in the second tableau for X_I, which tells us that we could then enter X_I; finding that X_B exits, this brings us back to where we started. The process is reversible.) Once an optimal solution has been found, it is a simple matter to successively do further pivots to find all the tying solutions.

We have found two optimal corner-point solutions. Any feasible linear combination of these (point on the connecting edge) will also be optimal. When a fixed percentage of all the values of one corner is added to the complementary percentage of the other corner's values, such a combination results. For example, Table 14-10 shows the optimal edge point when 40 percent of the first corner is combined with 60 percent of the second.

Table 14-10
FINDING AN OPTIMAL SOLUTION LYING ON AN EDGE

VARIABLE	VALUES FOR TYING OPTIMAL CORNER		OPTIMAL EDGE POINT (40% First, 60% Second)
	First	Second	
X_B	0	30	$0 + 18 = 18$
X_C	40	40	$16 + 24 = 40$
X_L	60	30	$24 + 18 = 42$
X_F	3	4.5	$1.2 + 2.7 = 3.9$
X_P	3	4.5	$1.2 + 2.7 = 3.9$
X_W	0	0	$0 + 0 = 0$
X_I	30	0	$12 + 0 = 12$
C	62	62	62

Degeneracy and Redundant Constraints

Some linear programs have constraints which collectively make one or more of them *redundant*. Ordinarily, no problem is caused by including a redundant constraint in the problem, although the simplex computations can be shortened if obviously redundant constraints can be eliminated beforehand. For example, the second constraint provided below is less restrictive than the first one and is not needed:

$$2X_1 + 3X_2 \leq 6$$

$$2X_1 + 3X_2 \leq 7$$

Often it is difficult to determine in advance whether a redundancy exists. Under some circumstances, this may lead to a situation where simplex yields a *tie for exiting variable*. Our simplex rules say that any tie (whether for entering or exiting variable) may be broken arbitrarily. But when this happens during the exit phase, we end up with a new tableau having a value zero in the solution column, indicating that the variable for that row could just as well lie outside the variable mix; in effect, a redundancy is present somewhere in the problem.

Whenever there is a zero in the solution column, the linear program is said to be *degenerate*. Ordinarily, this is of no practical consequence whatsoever. But on very rare occasions, degeneracy may cause the simplex procedure to *cycle* indefinitely, repeating an identical sequence of pivots and never reaching a conclusion. Should this ever happen the remedy is simple: go back to the tableau where the tie occurred, select the other variable as the exiting one, and proceed from there.

Variables Unrestricted As to Sign

Simplex requires that every variable be non-negative. Certain real problems, however, have variables that can be either positive or negative. For example, a security investment problem might represent the number of shares of a particular stock by either a long position (a positive quantity), a short position (a negative quantity), or no shares (zero). Oil refining provides another example. Some by-products can be created in one stage and consumed in a later one, in varying amounts in either case; thus, the net amount of the by-product resulting could be either positive (more is created than is consumed) or negative (more is consumed than is made). In both applications *the sign of the variable is unrestricted*.

Simplex still requires non-negativity, even when applied to such a problem. One nice way to accommodate this demand is to represent the unrestricted variable by the difference between two different non-negative ones. For example,

	Investment	*Refining*
Unrestricted:	X_P = Position in stock	X_B = Net change in byproduct
New non-negative variables:	X_L = Shares held long X_S = Shares shorted	X_C = By-product created X_U = By-product used
	$X_P = X_L - X_S$	$X_B = X_C - X_U$

The difference $X_L - X_S$ or $X_C - X_U$ can be substituted everywhere X_P or X_B appears, and the respective linear programs will contain only nonnegative variables. Should the answer to the investment problem provide $X_L = 0$, $X_S = 100$, then $X_P = 0 - 100 = -100$; likewise, with $X_C = 10{,}000$, $X_U = 11{,}000$ for the refining solution, then $X_B = 10{,}000 - 11{,}000 = -1000$.

PROBLEMS

14-1 Consider the linear program

$$\text{Maximize} \quad P = 5X_1 + 6X_2$$
$$\text{Subject to} \quad 3X_1 + 4X_2 \leq 12 \quad \text{(resource)}$$
$$2X_1 + 6X_2 \geq 12 \quad \text{(mixture)}$$
$$\text{where} \quad X_1, X_2 \geq 0$$

(a) Solve this problem graphically.
(b) Reformulate the above problem in equation form suitable for simplex.
(c) Re-solve the problem using the simplex procedure.

14-2 Consider the linear program

$$\text{Maximize} \quad P = 2X_1 - 3X_2$$
$$\text{Subject to} \quad 4X_1 + 5X_2 \leq 40 \quad \text{(resource A)}$$
$$2X_1 - 6X_2 \leq 24 \quad \text{(resource B)}$$
$$3X_1 - 3X_2 \geq 6 \quad \text{(mixture)}$$
$$X_1 \geq 4 \quad \text{(demand)}$$
$$\text{where} \quad X_1, X_2 \geq 0$$

(a) Solve this problem graphically.
(b) Reformulate the above problem in equation form suitable for simplex.
(c) Re-solve the problem using the simplex procedure.

14-3 Consider the linear program

$$\text{Minimize} \quad C = .5X_A + .3X_B$$
$$\text{Subject to} \quad X_A + 2X_B \geq 10 \quad \text{(restriction Y)}$$
$$2X_A + X_B \geq 8 \quad \text{(restriction Z)}$$
$$\text{where} \quad X_A, X_B \geq 0$$

(a) Solve this problem graphically.
(b) Reformulate the above problem in equation form suitable for simplex.
(c) Re-solve the problem using the simplex procedure.

14-4 For each of the following linear programs, an intermediate or final simplex tableau is presented. For each, state whether the simplex procedure indicates (1) an optimal solution, (2) an unbounded problem, (3) an infeasible problem, (4) that further steps are required (in which case, find the entering and exiting variables), or (5) that a tie exists for optimal solution and the final tableau provides just one of these.

(a) Maximize $P = 14X_1 + 18X_2 + 16X_3 + 80X_4$
Subject to
$4\frac{1}{2}X_1 + 8\frac{1}{2}X_2 + 6X_3 + 20X_4 \leq 6000$ (resource A)
$X_1 + X_2 + 4X_3 + 40X_4 \leq 4000$ (resource B)
where all $Xs \geq 0$

UNIT PROFIT		14	18	16	80	0	0	
	Var. Mix	X_1	X_2	X_3	X_4	X_A	X_B	Sol.
14	X_1	1	2	1	0	1/4	−1/8	1,000
80	X_4	0	−1/40	3/40	1	−1/160	9/320	75
	Sac.	14	26	20	80	3	1/2	20,000
	Imp.	0	−8	−4	0	−3	−1/2	—

(b) Maximize $P = 2X_1 + 2X_2$
Subject to
$X_1 + X_2 \geq 3$ (limitation)
$X_1 + X_2 \leq 2$ (resource)
where $X_1, X_2 \geq 0$

UNIT PROFIT		2	2	0	0	−M	
	Var. Mix	X_1	X_2	X_L	X_R	a	Sol.
−M	a	0	0	−1	−1	1	1
2	X_1	1	1	0	1	0	2
	Sac.	2	2	M	$M+2$	$-M$	$4-M$
	Imp.	0	0	$-M$	$-M-2$	0	—

(c) Maximize $P = X_1 + X_2$
Subject to
$2X_1 + 2X_2 \leq 4$ (resource A)
$X_1 \leq 3$ (resource B)
where $X_1, X_2 \geq 0$

UNIT PROFIT		1	1	0	0	
	Var. Mix	X_1	X_2	X_A	X_B	Sol.
1	X_2	1	1	1/2	0	2
0	X_B	1	0	0	1	3
	Sac.	1	1	1/2	0	2
	Imp.	0	0	−1/2	0	—

(d) Maximize $\quad P = 5X_1 + 6X_2$
  Subject to $\quad -4X_1 + 2X_2 \leq 12 \quad$ (resource A)
        $-4X_1 + 3X_2 \leq 12 \quad$ (resource B)
  where $\quad\quad\quad X_1, X_2 \geq 0$

UNIT PROFIT		5	6	0	0	
	Var. Mix	X_1	X_2	X_A	X_B	Sol.
0	X_A	−4/3	0	1	−2/3	4
6	X_2	−4/3	1	0	1/3	4
	Sac.	−8	6	0	2	24
	Imp.	13	0	0	−2	—

(e) Minimize $\quad C = 40X_1 + 60X_2$
  Subject to $\quad 3X_1 + 3X_2 \geq 3 \quad$ (restriction A)
       $2X_1 + 3X_2 \geq 4 \quad$ (restriction B)
  where $\quad\quad\quad X_1, X_2 \geq 0$

UNIT COST		40	60	0	0	M	M	
	Var. Mix	X_1	X_2	X_A	X_B	a_A	a_B	Sol.
60	X_2	2/3	1	−1/3	0	1/3	0	1
M	a_B	1	0	1	−1	−1	1	1
	Sac.	40+M	60	−20+M	−M	20−M	M	60+M
	Imp.	−M	0	20−M	M	−20+2M	0	—

14-5 Grubby Stakes Mining Company is establishing a production plan for the current week at its Bonstock Lode, which has three main veins of varying characteristics. The net yields per ton for each of the veins is provided below.

	Eastern	Northern	Tom's Lucky
Gold	.2 oz	.3 oz	.4 oz
Silver	30 oz	20 oz	30 oz
Copper	50 lb	20 lb	25 lb

Gold presently sells for $150 per ounce, silver brings $5, and copper sells for $2 per pound. Eastern is the most accessible vein, involving 1 man-hour per ton of ore; Northern and Tom's Lucky veins are more remote and require 2 man-hours per ton. Only 300 man-hours are available altogether, and all labor costs are fixed. At least 100 tons must be removed from Northern this week so it can be re-shored next week; there are no tonnage limitations for the other tunnels. The company must also yield at least 5000 pounds of copper to meet contractual commitments.

Formulate Grubby's linear program to determine how many tons to mine from each vein in order to maximize total revenue. Then use simplex to find the optimal solution.

14-6 The owner of Real Reels, a fishing equipment manufacturing company, wishes to determine how many quarter-page ads to place in general-circulation men's magazines. His choice has been narrowed down to three monthlies: *Playboy*, *True*, and *Esquire*. This is to be done in such a way that total "exposure" to significant buyers of expensive fishing gear is maximized. Prior study has provided the percentage of readers in this category for each magazine. Exposure in any particular magazine is the number of ads placed times the number of significant buyers. The following data apply:

	Playboy	True	Esquire
Readers	10 million	6 million	4 million
Significant buyers	10%	15%	7%
Cost per ad	$10,000	$5000	$6000

Real has budgeted at most $100,000 to pay for the ads. The owner has already determined that *True* should have no more than five ads and that *Playboy* and *Esquire* must each have at least two ads.

Formulate Real's problem as a linear program. Then use the simplex method to solve it. How many ads should be placed in each magazine?

14-7 The Flying Chef supplies in-flight dinners to airlines. On a particular run, the passengers are given their choice among beef, chicken, or fish entrees. The owner must decide how many meals of each type to prepare in order to minimize total cost. Historically, it has been found that 55 percent of all passengers prefer beef, 30 percent chicken, and 15 percent fish. However, to compensate for varying tastes from flight to flight, the number of meals provided must be as great as the above percentages of total passengers. On the current flight there are 200 passengers and 300 meals must be provided. Airline policy states that on any given flight, at least half the extra meals on any flight must be beef. Costs are \$2 for each beef entree, \$1.50 for chicken, and \$1 for fish.

Formulate the above as a linear program. Then solve the problem using simplex. How many meals of each type should be provided?

14-8 For the linear program

$$\text{Maximize} \quad P = 6X_1 + 10X_2 + 2X_3$$
$$\begin{aligned}
\text{Subject to} \quad & 2X_1 + 4X_2 + 3X_3 \le 40 \quad \text{(resource A)} \\
& X_1 + X_2 \le 10 \quad \text{(resource B)} \\
& 2X_2 + X_3 \le 12 \quad \text{(resource C)}
\end{aligned}$$
$$\text{where} \quad X_1, X_2, X_3 \ge 0$$

the slack variables are X_A, X_B, and X_C. The final simplex tableau is provided below:

UNIT PROFIT		6	10	2	0	0	0	
	Var. Mix	X_1	X_2	X_3	X_A	X_B	X_C	Sol.
0	X_A	0	0	2	1	−2	−1	8
6	X_1	1	0	−1/2	0	1	−1/2	4
10	X_2	0	1	1/2	0	0	1/2	6
	Sac.	6	10	2	0	6	2	84
	Imp.	0	0	0	0	−6	−2	—

A tie exists for optimal solution.
(a) Identify the variable values for the solution. Then determine the tying optimal solution and give the variable values that correspond.
(b) Determine the optimal edge-point solution lying halfway between the two tying optimal corner points.

14-9 For the following linear program

$$\text{Maximize} \quad P = 5X_1 + 2X_2 + 10X_3$$
$$\begin{aligned}
\text{Subject to} \quad & X_1 - X_3 \le 10 \quad \text{(resource A)} \\
& X_2 - X_3 \ge 10 \quad \text{(limitation B)}
\end{aligned}$$
$$\text{where} \quad X_1, X_2, X_3 \ge 0$$

the extra variables are X_A (slack), X_B (surplus), and a (artificial).

Consider the intermediate simplex tableau provided below:

UNIT PROFIT		5	2	10	0	0	−M	
	Var. Mix	X_1	X_2	X_3	X_A	X_B	a	Sol.
5	X_1	1	0	−1	1	0	0	10
2	X_2	0	1	−1	0	−1	1	10
	Sac.	5	2	−7	5	−2	2	70
	Imp.	0	0	3	−5	2	−M−2	—

(a) Find the entering variable. Then determine the exiting variable. Do you notice anything unusual? Indicate your finding.

(b) The following constraint was missing from the earlier formulation:

$$X_1 + X_2 + X_3 \leq 10 \quad \text{(resource } C\text{)}$$

Solve the new problem from the beginning using simplex.

14-10 For the linear program

Maximize $\quad P = 20X_1 + 10X_2 + 2X_3$
Subject to $\quad 2X_1 + X_2 + X_3 \leq 9 \quad$ (resource A)
$\qquad\qquad\quad X_1 + X_2 \geq 10 \quad$ (limitation B)
where $\qquad\quad X_1, X_2, X_3 \geq 0$

the extra variables are X_A (slack), X_B (surplus), and a (artificial). The following final simplex tableau is obtained:

UNIT PROFIT		20	10	2	0	0	−M	
	Var. Mix	X_1	X_2	X_3	X_A	X_B	a	Sol.
20	X_2	2	1	1	1	0	0	9
−M	a	−1	0	−1	−1	−1	1	1
	Sac.	40+M	10	20+M	20+M	M	−M	180−M
	Imp.	−20−M	0	−18−M	−20−M	−M	0	—

(a) What feature of the problem does the solution obtained from the above tableau indicate?

(b) Suppose this is corrected by changing the limitation level for B from 10 to 4. Using simplex, start from the beginning to find the optimal solution for this revised problem.

Fifteen

The Transportation Problem

One of the most important and successful applications of quantitative analysis in solving business problems has occurred in the physical distribution of products. Great cost savings have been achieved through efficient routing of freight from supply points to required destinations. This chapter considers the *transportation problem,* which serves as the framework for analyzing such decisions. In its basic form, the transportation problem has a goal of minimizing the total cost of shipping goods from plants to warehouse distribution centers in such a way that each warehouse's needs are met and that every factory operates within its capacity.

Ordinarily, such a problem may be conveniently expressed mathematically in terms of a linear program. We have seen that all linear programs, including the transportation problem, may be solved by means of the simplex algorithm. But the simplex procedure is a general one, and its universality has built-in limitations. The special structure of the transportation problem has certain features that permit us to solve it by using a faster, more streamlined algorithm than simplex. In studying the transportation problem, we thereby gain a new insight into quantitative analysis: *judicious choice of the solution procedure itself can result in savings.* Put differently, this chapter illustrates "another way to skin a cat" that is better for certain kinds of cats. It is important to know that alternative procedures exist or can be developed for solving a variety of problems.

As our basic illustration, we will consider the operations of a sporting goods company that makes skis in three plants throughout the world. The plants supply four company-owned warehouses that distribute directly to ski shops. Depending on which mode is cheaper, the product is air-freighted or trucked from the factories to the warehouses. Table 15-1 shows the various point-to-point shipping costs for

Table 15-1
THE SHIPPING COSTS PER PAIR OF SKIS

FROM PLANTS	TO WAREHOUSES			
	Frankfurt	*New York*	*Phoenix*	*Yokohama*
Juarez	$19	$ 7	$ 3	$21
Seoul	15	21	18	6
Tel Aviv	11	14	15	22

a pair of skis. The monthly capacities of the plants, in terms of the number of pairs that can be made, are

Plant	Capacity
Juarez	100
Seoul	300
Tel Aviv	200
Total	600

and the warehouse demand requirements for next month are

Warehouse	Demand
Frankfurt	150
New York	100
Phoenix	200
Yokohama	150
Total	600

15-1 FORMULATING THE TRANSPORTATION PROBLEM

How many pairs of skis should be shipped from each plant to the various warehouses? This will result in a shipping schedule as shown in Table 15-2. The numbers of ski pairs sent over each route are unknown and are represented as variables by the letter X with appropriate subscripts. In general, we adopt the convention

$$X_{ij} = \text{Quantity shipped from plant } i \text{ to warehouse } j$$

where each possible i or j may be represented by a number $(1, 2, 3, 4, \ldots)$ or a letter abbreviation $(A, B, C, D, \ldots)$ corresponding to how the respective plant or warehouse is identified.

Table 15-2
THE SHIPMENT SCHEDULE FOR NEXT MONTH

FROM PLANTS	TO WAREHOUSES				Plant Capacity
	F	N	P	Y	
J	X_{JF}	X_{JN}	X_{JP}	X_{JY}	100
S	X_{SF}	X_{SN}	X_{SP}	X_{SY}	300
T	X_{TF}	X_{TN}	X_{TP}	X_{TY}	200
Warehouse demand	150	100	200	150	600

The Xs are to be chosen so that total shipping cost is minimized. Over each route, the total cost is the ski-pair freight charge times the quantity shipped. For Juarez to Frankfurt, this cost would be $19X_{JF}$. Summing like values from all routes, the problem objective is to

$$\begin{aligned}\text{Minimize} \quad C = \;& 19X_{JF} + 7X_{JN} + 3X_{JP} + 21X_{JY} \\ & + 15X_{SF} + 21X_{SN} + 18X_{SP} + 6X_{SY} \\ & + 11X_{TF} + 14X_{TN} + 15X_{TP} + 22X_{TY}\end{aligned}$$

It is convenient to represent the respective unit shipping costs by the symbol c_{ij}, so that for Tel Aviv to Frankfurt we have $c_{TF} = 11$ and the cost from Seoul to Yokohama is $c_{SY} = 6$. Our objective function may then be stated more concisely as

$$\text{Minimize} \quad C = \sum_i \sum_j c_{ij} X_{ij}$$

where Σ is the *summation sign* (Greek capital sigma). We use two summation signs, since for each row in the freight schedule, we first sum the products for each warehouse from a given plant and then total these sums for all plants.

The transportation problem involves two kinds of constraints. One set applies to the plants and specifies that *the total number of units shipped from each plant must equal the plant's capacity*. Letting P_i represent the capacity of plant i, we may express these constraints as

$$\sum_j X_{ij} = P_i \quad \text{(plant } i \text{ capacity)}$$

for all plants

Referring to Table 15-2, we see that the above constraints tell us that the sum of the variables in each row must *precisely equal* the capacity of the plant for that row; in effect, the sum of all shipments out of the ith plant, to whatever destinations, must equal P_i. In our example, $P_J = 100$ pairs for Juarez, $P_S = 300$ for Seoul, and $P_T = 200$ pairs for Tel Aviv. The problem has three plant capacity constraints:

$$X_{JF} + X_{JN} + X_{JP} + X_{JY} = 100 \quad \text{(Juarez capacity)}$$
$$X_{SF} + X_{SN} + X_{SP} + X_{SY} = 300 \quad \text{(Seoul capacity)}$$
$$X_{TF} + X_{TN} + X_{TP} + X_{TY} = 200 \quad \text{(Tel Aviv capacity)}$$

Analogously, another set of constraints must be met for every warehouse, so that *the total number of units shipped into each warehouse must equal the warehouse's demand*. If W_j denotes the demand of warehouse j, these constraints take the form

$$\sum_i X_{ij} = W_j \quad \text{(warehouse } j \text{ demand)}$$

for all warehouses

The above constraints indicate that the sum of the variables in each column must exactly equal the demand of the warehouse for that column. The quantities received, regardless of their origins, must sum to the warehouse demand. From Table 15-2 we see that $W_F = 150$, $W_N = 100$, $W_P = 200$, and $W_Y = 150$ for the Frankfurt, New York, Phoenix, and Yokohama warehouses, respectively. For our problem, the four warehouse demand constraints are expressed explicitly as

$$X_{JF} + X_{SF} + X_{TF} = 150 \quad \text{(Frankfurt demand)}$$
$$X_{JN} + X_{SN} + X_{TN} = 100 \quad \text{(New York demand)}$$
$$X_{JP} + X_{SP} + X_{TP} = 200 \quad \text{(Phoenix demand)}$$
$$X_{JY} + X_{SY} + X_{TY} = 150 \quad \text{(Yokohama demand)}$$

The number of constraints is dictated by the number of plants (or rows in the shipping schedule) and the number of warehouses (or columns in the shipping schedule). Altogether, every transportation problem must have exactly the following number of constraints of equality form:

Number of constraints = Number of rows + Number of columns

As we can see, each X is represented exactly once in the capacity constraints and once again in the demand constraints. This can happen if and only if the total quantity shipped is exactly equal to the total quantity received, which together with the individual constraints establishes the condition

$$\sum_i P_i = \sum_j W_j$$

or, that *total plant capacity must equal total warehouse demand*. In our example, the capacities add to 600, which is also the sum of the demands:

$$600 = 100 + 300 + 200 = 150 + 100 + 200 + 150$$

As we shall see later, this fact plays an important role in solving a transportation problem.

You may ask "Why must each plant produce exactly at its capacity and each warehouse receive precisely its demand? Isn't that unrealistic?" In response to the first question, these requirements are needed to solve the problem by the most efficient means. To the second question, our answer is "Of course." But, as we shall see later, it will always be possible through various tricks to formulate any transportation problem in the above manner, even when true demands and capacities are not in exact balance.

15-1 FORMULATING THE TRANSPORTATION PROBLEM

As with all linear programs, we must include the non-negativity conditions. It makes no sense at all to have minus 20 skis shipped from Juarez to Phoenix; this implies a return of 20 skis to the factory, and this would actually involve roundtrip costs of twice the $\$3 \times 20 = \$60$ one-way freight charge, not a freight cost of $\$3 \times (-20) = -\$60$ as the negative quantity implies. (Returns are not explicitly considered by the transportation problem anyway; we may view such costs as part of overhead, which we usually ignore.)

15-2 GETTING STARTED: NORTHWEST CORNER RULE

The transportation problem is solved in an iterative fashion, proceeding much like simplex does from solution to solution. We begin with an initial solution satisfying all constraints. A convenient procedure for getting started is the *northwest corner rule*.* We start with a blank shipping schedule, shown in Table 15-3. Each plant-warehouse route is represented by a cell. For convenience, the unit shipping costs are placed in the upper right-hand corners of each cell. The central portion of the cell is reserved for the quantity to be shipped.

The northwest corner rule begins in the cell in the upper left-hand corner, which on a map would be called the northwest corner. We put the largest possible quantity in that cell which satisfies the capacity and demand constraints. This means we look in the row and column margins for the smallest demand or capacity applicable and then write this number in the northwest corner cell. Further cell allocations are made by moving down or to the right in the direction of leftover demand or capacity, with maximum feasible quantities inserted at each step. We stop when the southeast corner has been allocated. The cell-to-cell movement in this procedure is analogous to the movement of chess pieces. Only horizontal and vertical movements, like those of the "rook," are allowed; no diagonal "bishop" moves are permitted.

Table 15-4 shows the northwest corner solution for the ski-distribution problem. Our beginning corner receives an allocation of 100 pairs to be shipped from Juarez to Frankfurt. This value is the largest possible amount that can go over that route, since Juarez's capacity is 100 pairs; although Frankfurt must receive 150 pairs, we cannot ship more from Juarez than it can make. This leaves an unfilled demand of $150 - 100 = 50$ pairs for Frankfurt, so our next cell for skis shipped from Seoul to Frank-

---

* More efficient starting procedures, such as Vogel's and Russell's approximation methods, exist. These are too complex for this book. For a detailed discussion, see F. S. Hillier, and G. J. Lieberman, *Introduction to Operations Research*, vol. 2, Holden-Day, 1974, Chapter 3.

Table 15-3
A BLANK SHIPMENT SCHEDULE

From \ To	F	N	P	Y	Capacity
J	19	7	3	21	100
S	15	21	18	6	300
T	11	14	15	22	200
Demand	150	100	200	150	600

furt lies directly below. The largest possible allocation to that cell is 50 pairs, since the gap in Frankfurt's demand is exhausted before this warehouse takes up Seoul's capacity. This leaves us with unused capacity for Seoul in the amount of $300 - 50 = 250$ pairs. We move to the cell at the right, where we must allocate a shipment from Seoul to New York. There we fill New York's total demand of 100; this leaves us with $300 - 50 - 100 = 150$ pairs under capacity at Seoul, so we move again to the right. There we allocate 150 pairs from Seoul to Phoenix; this does not exhaust that

Table 15-4
THE SHIPMENT SCHEDULE FOUND BY THE NORTHWEST CORNER RULE

From \ To	F	N	P	Y	Capacity
J	19 (100)	7	3	21	100
S	15 (50) →	21 (100) →	18 (150)	6	300
T	11	14	15 (50) →	22 (150)	200
Demand	150	100	200	150	600

15-2 GETTING STARTED: NORTHWEST CORNER RULE

warehouse's demand, leaving 200 − 150 = 50 pairs short in Phoenix. Moving down, we pick up 50 from Tel Aviv to take care of Phoenix, and then moving to the right, we allocate the rest of Tel Aviv's capacity as a 150-pair shipment to Yokohama. At this point, all constraints are satisfied.

The solution in Table 15-4 serves as the starting feasible solution. The cell entries are the values for the corresponding problem variables; empty cells correspond to zero quantities. The total cost of this shipment schedule is computed below to be $C = 11{,}500$ dollars.

Quantity	Unit Cost	Route Cost
$X_{JF} = 100$	$c_{JF} = 19$	$19 \times 100 = 1{,}900$
$X_{SF} = 50$	$c_{SF} = 15$	$15 \times 50 = 750$
$X_{SN} = 100$	$c_{SN} = 21$	$21 \times 100 = 2{,}100$
$X_{SP} = 150$	$c_{SP} = 18$	$18 \times 150 = 2{,}700$
$X_{TP} = 50$	$c_{TP} = 15$	$15 \times 50 = 750$
$X_{TY} = 150$	$c_{TY} = 22$	$22 \times 150 = 3{,}300$
		$C = 11{,}500$

15-3 SOLVING THE PROBLEM: THE TRANSPORTATION METHOD

We have just begun to solve this problem. Our next task is to search for improvements. One approach would be trial and error, reallocating cell values until it becomes hard to find improvements. Not only would that be inefficient, but there is no guarantee that the optimal solution would be found—and we would probably give up in frustration, not knowing if more improvements were possible. Instead, we will be systematic.

The Simplex Analogy

Let us recall some important features of simplex that apply equally well here. First, we know that any feasible bounded problem has at least one optimal solution that is a corner point. You may remember that a corner point can be defined as the solution to the underlying constraints when all so-called non-mix variables are fixed arbitrarily at zero. The free variables are called mix variables. Exactly the same principles apply with the transportation problem, which after all is just a special kind of linear program. Our mix variables for any shipment-schedule solution correspond to the non-empty cells (those having a circled value), while the empty cells represent the non-mix variables.

The northwest corner rule provides us with a corner-point solution (we refer to a corner in the higher dimensional space, not to the cell at the bottom left, etc., of the shipment-schedule table). As with simplex, we seek a neighboring corner to evaluate next. It is the one that improves cost at the greatest rate. And, as with simplex, we reach this corner by means of a pivot procedure, one in which the status of the cells is exchanged, a currently non-empty one going empty while a presently empty cell receives a quantity allocation. The new non-empty cell can be referred to as the *entering cell*, while the one it replaces is the *exiting cell*. Such a trade will result in a cheaper shipment schedule. Continuing in this manner, we will reach a most attractive corner that cannot be improved on and will have found the optimal solution.

Finding the Entering Cell: Row and Column Numbers

The entering cell is found through economic analysis, as in simplex. In the transportation problem, we evaluate every empty cell by determining the per unit cost improvement associated with allocating one unit into it. Our procedure for doing this may seem roundabout at first, but it is really quite efficient.

We begin by assigning special values to each row and column of the current shipping schedule. The *row numbers* are represented by the symbol r_i and the *column numbers* by k_j. These values are calculated so that the following relationship holds.

$$\text{for non-empty cells:} \qquad c_{ij} = r_i + k_j$$

To get started, *we begin by assigning zero as the row number for the first row*. The pattern of the non-empty cells and their unit costs then dictate the values of the remaining row and column numbers. These are found algebraically by solving a sequence of equations, each with one unknown.

Returning to our example, consider the present solution, shown in Table 15-5. The row and column numbers are written outside the shipment schedule in the respective margins. The letters indicate the *sequence* in which these were obtained. The proper sequence is extremely important when computing the *r*s and *k*s. Our general rule in finding the row and column numbers is to work from the last number found until all non-empty cells in the present row or column have their two numbers. Then we move to the row or column of the newest number(s) and do the

Table 15-5

ROW AND COLUMN NUMBERS FOR THE INITIAL SOLUTION

From \ To	F	N	P	Y	Capacity		
J	19 ⟨100⟩	7	3	21	100	$r_J = 0$	(a)
S	15 ⟨50⟩	21 ⟨100⟩	18 ⟨150⟩	6	300	$r_S = -4$	(c)
T	11	14	15 ⟨50⟩	22 ⟨150⟩	200	$r_T = -7$	(f)
Demand	150	100	200	150	600		

$k_F = 19$ (b) $k_N = 25$ (d) $k_P = 22$ (e) $k_Y = 29$ (g)

same thing. We always use the newest r in getting the next k, and vice versa. We stop when there is a full set of row and column numbers. A detailed explanation of how these were obtained is provided below.

(a) The first row is where we begin. It always receives a zero row number. Thus, $r_J = 0$.

(b) Looking at row J, we see that there is one non-empty cell JF that does not yet have a column number. For this cell,

$$c_{JF} = r_J + k_F$$

must hold. We know that $c_{JF} = 19$, and we have just found $r_J = 0$. Plugging these numbers into the above, we get

$$19 = 0 + k_F$$

and we find that $k_F = 19$.

(c) There are no other non-empty cells in row J. We now look in column F for non-empty cells that do not have a row number. SF does not. We know that

$$c_{SF} = r_S + k_F$$

Plugging $c_{SF} = 15$ and $k_F = 19$ into the above, we get

$$15 = r_S + 19$$

which yields

$$r_S = 15 - 19 = -4$$

(d) There are no more non-empty cells in column F. Searching row S, we see that cell SN has no column number. Plugging $c_{SN} = 21$ and $r_S = -4$ into

$$c_{SN} = r_S + k_N$$

we get

$$21 = -4 + k_N$$

and, thus, $k_N = 21 - (-4) = 25$. There are no more non-empty cells in column N, so we don't use it further. We are not finished, however, with row S.

(e) There remains non-empty cell SP in row S without its column number. Substituting $c_{SP} = 18$ and $r_S = -4$ into

$$c_{SP} = r_S + k_P$$

we find

$$18 = r_S + k_P$$

and, thus, $k_P = 18 - (-4) = 22$.

(f) We see that column P has non-empty cell TP without its row number. Plugging $c_{TP} = 15$ and $k_P = 22$ into

$$c_{TP} = r_T + k_P$$

we get

$$15 = r_T + 22$$

and thus, $r_T = 15 - 22 = -7$.

(g) There remains one non-empty cell, TY, in row T that has no column number. Substituting $c_{TY} = 22$ and $r_T = -7$ into

$$c_{TY} = r_T + k_Y$$

we get

$$22 = -7 + k_Y$$

and $k_Y = 22 - (-7) = 29$.

15-3   SOLVING THE PROBLEM: THE TRANSPORTATION METHOD

All rows and columns have their numbers.

With practice, the above computations can be made very rapidly in your head without ever having to use scratch paper.

The rs and ks obtained by the above procedure are used with the present freight schedule to find the entering cell. To do this we calculate the following difference *for the empty cells:*

$$c_{ij} - r_i - k_j$$

The above indicates the per unit cost *improvement* that can be achieved by raising the shipment allocation in the corresponding cell from its present level of zero. *The empty cell having the greatest absolute negative difference is the entering cell.*

Table 15-6 shows how the entering cell is found for our illustration. There we have found the differences which have been entered onto the schedule at the lower left-hand corners of each empty cell. For example, in cell JN we have the difference

$$c_{JN} - r_J - k_N = 7 - 0 - 25 = -18$$

Table 15-6

IMPROVEMENT VALUES AND CLOSED-LOOP PATH FOR THE INITIAL SOLUTION

From \ To	F	N	P	Y	Capacity	
J	19; (100) (−)	7; −18	3; (+) −19	21; −8	100	$r_J = 0$
S	15; (50) (+)	21; (100)	18; (150) (−)	6; −19	300	$r_S = -4$
T	11; −1	14; −4	15; (50)	22; (150)	200	$r_T = -7$
Demand	150	100	200	150	600	
	$k_F = 19$	$k_N = 25$	$k_P = 22$	$k_Y = 29$		

This tells us that raising the allocation to that cell will reduce costs by $18 for each pair of skis. The other differences are calculated in the same fashion.

We see that cells *JP* and *SY* tie for the greatest cost improvement at $19 per pair. We will break this tie arbitrarily, choosing *JP* as the entering cell. We must next see just how much we can allocate that cell.

Finding the New Solution: The Closed-Loop Path

We begin by placing a (+) in cell *JP* to indicate that its allocation (the shipment from Juarez to Phoenix) will be increased from zero quantity. Whatever change we make must be *balanced*, so that the new quantities in row *J* and column *P* sum to the respective capacity of 100 for Juarez and demand of 200 for Phoenix. Thus, we must reduce cell *JF* by the amount of the change; we place a (−) there to reflect this reduction. But if cell *JF* gets reduced, there must be a compensating change in column *F*. Our rule is: *there can be only one increasing and one decreasing cell in any row or column. Except for the entering cell all changes must involve non-empty cells.* Thus cell *SF* gets a (+), since it is the only non-empty cell in column *F*. This leaves us in row *S*, where a compensating (−) change must be made. We readily see that cell *SN* must be skipped because it is the only non-empty cell in its column. Instead, we place the (−) in cell *SP*, where we stop since all changes now balance.

Connecting the pluses and minuses with line segments, we see that they provide a *closed-loop path*. This path highlights the changes involved in reallocating the shipments. *For any entering cell, the closed-loop path is unique.* Its corners are alternating (+) and (−) cells, and only the entering cell is empty; *only the corner cells on the path will be changed.* (Those cells that a line segment passes over are not involved.) In finding the closed-loop path, we may proceed either clockwise or counter-clockwise, starting up, down, right, or left (but never moving diagonally). We proceed, turning at each new (+) or (−), until our path closes. Should we end with an impass, reaching a cell where we cannot turn (because all other cells in its column or row are empty), then we backtrack to the last turning point and go the other way or instead go forward to another non-empty cell in the same row or column.

The closed-loop path verifies that, indeed, we will save $19 by allocating into cell *JP*. Tracing its trajectory counter-clockwise, we have

Change: (+)   (−)   (+)   (−)

Cell: JP   JF   SF   SP

Each unit shifted along this path will result in a cost increase for the

(+) cells and a cost reduction for the (−) cells, so that the net unit cost change is, indeed,

$$3 - 19 + 15 - 18 = -19$$

The fact that we got -19 using rs and ks is not coincidental. (The $c_{ij} - r_i - k_j$ differences are analogous to the entries in simplex's per unit improvement row.)

We must now make our change in the shipment schedule. The shift in quantities will occur only for cells at the corners of the closed-loop path. *The amount shifted is equal to the smallest quantity in the losing cells.* The smallest (−) quantity is selected because all affected cells will change by plus or minus the same amount, and the resulting quantities cannot be negative. The smallest losing-cell shipment quantity occurs in JF, where 100 pairs can be taken away. Cell JF is the exiting cell.

Table 15-7 shows the new shipment schedule resulting from the allocation. The total cost savings are

$$100 \times 19 = 1900 \text{ dollars}$$

so that total cost is now $C = 11{,}500 - 1900 = 9600$ dollars.

Table 15-7

THE SECOND SOLUTION TO THE TRANSPORTATION PROBLEM

$$C = 9600$$

From \ To	F	N	P	Y	Capacity	
J	19	7	3 (100)	21	100	$r_J = 0$ (a)
	19	1		11		
S	15 (150)	21 (100)	18 (50) (−)	6 (+) −19	300	$r_S = 15$ (c)
T	11	14	15 (50) (+)	22 (150) (−)	200	$r_T = 12$ (d)
	−1	−4				
Demand	150	100	200	150	600	
	$k_F = 0$ (e)	$k_N = 6$ (f)	$k_P = 3$ (b)	$k_Y = 10$ (g)		

Our example involves rectangular closed-loop paths. But *closed-loop paths may assume unusual shapes,* such as Ls, figure 8s, or even loops inside of loops.

Further Iterations to Find the Optimal Solution

We now begin again with new row and column numbers. Notice that except for $r_J = 0$, those in Table 15-7 are all different than before. This is because the set of non-empty cells has changed. Furthermore, the sequence in which the numbers are obtained is different as well. There are no shortcuts; the *r*s and *k*s must be recomputed from scratch for each new shipping schedule.

Next, we find the differences for empty cells. We see that cell SY enters where costs are reduced by $19 per unit (coincidentally the same amount as before). The closed-loop path is indicated in Table 15-7, and the smallest quantity in the losing cells is 50 pairs.

Table 15-8 shows the next shipping schedule, where total cost has

Table 15-8
THE THIRD SOLUTION TO THE TRANSPORTATION PROBLEM

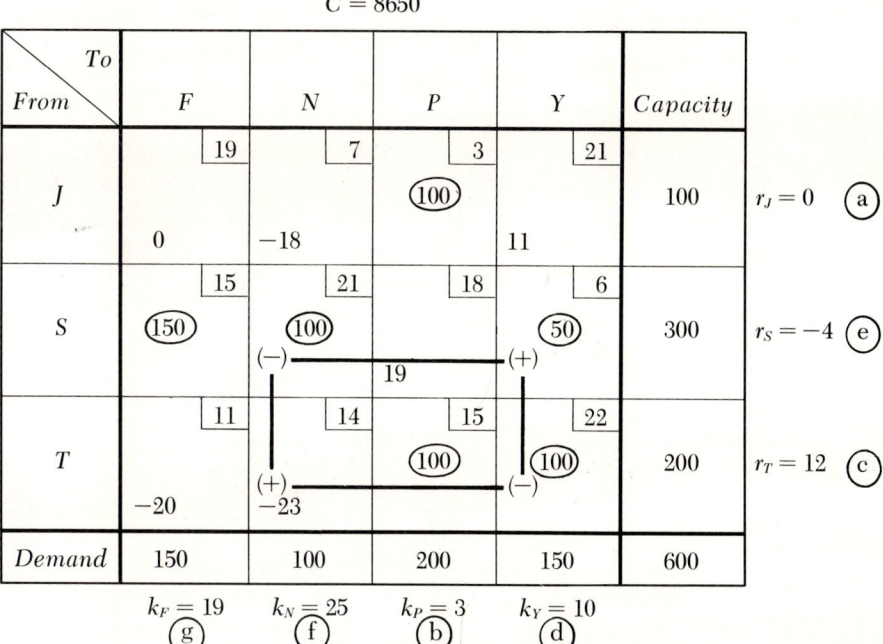

15-3 SOLVING THE PROBLEM: THE TRANSPORTATION METHOD

been reduced by 19 × 50 = 950 dollars, down to $C = 8650$ dollars. Recomputing the row and column numbers and finding the empty-cell differences, we see that cell *TN* is the entering cell. Increasing its allocation will save $23 per unit.

The smallest quantity in the losing cells is 100 pairs, which happens to be the same for cells *SN* and *TY*. Whenever such a tie exists for exiting cell, more than one cell will go to zero. This presents a problem not encountered so far. Before we proceed, a few more observations must be made regarding the nature of our solution procedure.

The Required Number of Non-Empty Cells

In our illustration there have always been exactly six non-empty cells. All the successive changes made in revising the shipment schedules guarantee this; this number is one less than the number of rows and columns. In general,

Number of non-empty cells = Number of rows + Number of columns − 1

The reason for the above is fundamental linear-programming solution procedure. To have a corner-point solution, there must be as many mix variables (here, non-empty cells) as there are non-redundant constraints in the linear program formulation.

Every transportation problem has as many constraints as there are rows and columns in the shipping schedule. However, together these constraints are redundant. This is because when the constraints are combined with the underlying condition that total capacity equal total demand, any one constraint can be eliminated without affecting the problem solution. Our illustration has three plant capacity requirements (rows) and four warehouse demand limitations (columns), or seven constraints in all. But total capacity and demand must be 600; were we to leave out the Yokohama demand constraint, for example, the other six constraints combined with this condition would still ensure that the Yokohama warehouse will get its required 150 pairs of skis. Only six constraints are non-redundant. This is why the number of non-empty cells is one less than the number of rows and columns.

With less than the necessary number of non-empty cells, it would be impossible to get a unique set of row and column numbers and, in some cases, to form closed-loop paths. (Too many non-empty cells cause similar problems.) This does not mean that our example cannot have a solution with only five non-zero cells, but it does mean that a total of six cells must be treated as non-empty.

Ties for Exiting Cell

Whenever there is a tie for exiting cell, both cells will lose all their allocation, going to zero value. To meet the required number of non-empty cells, exactly one of these tying cells must thereafter be treated as non-empty. Referring to Table 15-8, we see that both cell SN and cell TY will go to zero by reallocating 100 units along the closed-loop path. Either cell SN or cell TY must, however, continue to be treated as if it were non-empty. It does not matter which cell we choose, since in linear programming we can almost always break ties arbitrarily.

Table 15-9 shows the new shipping schedule. The cost savings are $23 \times 100 = 2300$ dollars and the new total cost is $C = 8650 - 2300 = 6350$ dollars. We use the circled zero in cell TY and treat it as non-empty, even though the shipment quantity is zero.

We see that by increasing the allocation into cell TF, $20 per unit can be saved. However, one of the losing cells is TY, which involves

Table 15-9
THE FOURTH SOLUTION TO THE TRANSPORTATION PROBLEM

$C = 6350$

From \ To	F	N	P	Y	Capacity		
J	19 0	7 5	3 (100)	21 11	100	$r_J = 0$	(a)
S	15 (−) (150)	21 23	18 19	6 (+) (150)	300	$r_S = -4$	(f)
T	11 (+) −20	14 (100)	15 (100)	22 (−) (0)	200	$r_T = 12$	(c)
Demand	150	100	200	150	600		
	$k_F = 19$ (g)	$k_N = 2$ (d)	$k_P = 3$ (b)	$k_Y = 10$ (e)			

15-3   SOLVING THE PROBLEM: THE TRANSPORTATION METHOD

zero quantity. We shift zero around the closed-loop path, giving us the new schedule in Table 15-10. This schedule has exactly the same cost as before, and the zero shipment quantity now appears in cell *TF*. Although no quantities have changed, the new pattern for the non-empty cells will provide an improvement.

Table 15-10
THE FIFTH SOLUTION TO THE TRANSPORTATION PROBLEM

$C = 6350$

From \ To	F	N	P	Y	Capacity	
J	19	7	3 ⟶ 100	21	100	$r_J = 0$ (a)
	20	5		31		
S	15 (−) 150	21	18 (+)	6 150	300	$r_S = 16$ (f)
		3	−1			
T	11 (0) (+)	14 100	15 100 (−)	22	200	$r_T = 12$ (c)
				20		
Demand	150	100	200	150	600	
	$k_F = -1$ (d)	$k_N = 2$ (e)	$k_P = 3$ (b)	$k_Y = -10$ (g)		

Determining the Optimal Solution

Cell *SP* in Table 15-10 provides a $1 cost improvement. The smallest quantity in the losing cells is 100 pairs. Reallocating this amount along the closed-loop path, we obtain the new shipping schedule in Table 15-11, where the cost saving is $1 \times 100 = 100$ and $C = 6350 - 100 = 6250$ dollars.

The schedule in Table 15-11 is optimal, since there are no empty cells yielding potential cost reductions, so that *further improvements are impossible*.

Table 15-11
THE FINAL SOLUTION TO THE TRANSPORTATION PROBLEM

$C = 6250$

From \ To	F	N	P	Y	Capacity	
J	19	7	3 ⓘ(100)	21	100	$r_J = 0$ (a)
	19	4		30		
S	15 (50)	21	18 (100)	6 (150)	300	$r_S = 15$ (c)
		3				
T	11 (100)	14 (100)	15	22	200	$r_T = 11$ (f)
			1	20		
Demand	150	100	200	150	600	
	$k_F = 0$ (d)	$k_N = 3$ (g)	$k_P = 3$ (b)	$k_Y = -9$ (e)		

15-4 DUMMY PLANTS AND WAREHOUSES

The ski-distribution example began with total demand and total capacity in balance. Ordinarily distribution situations are not perfectly balanced, there being excess system capacity or more demand than can possibly be filled. In such cases, the shipment schedule must include an additional plant or warehouse which takes up the slack. We refer to these fictional distribution points as *dummy plants or warehouses*.

Consider the following example, where there are two plants and three warehouses:

Plant Capacities		Warehouse Demands	
A	500	W	250
B	300	X	400
	800	Y	300
			950

Total demand is for 950 units, which exceeds the total capacity of 800 by

Table 15-12

THE OPTIMAL SHIPMENT SCHEDULE FOR THE PROBLEM REQUIRING A DUMMY PLANT

From \ To	W	X	Y	Capacity
A	2 ⟨250⟩	4 ⟨250⟩	6	500
B	3	3	1 ⟨300⟩	300
Dummy	0	0 ⟨150⟩	0 ⟨0⟩	150
Demand	250	400	300	950

150 units. The shortage in total capacity is made up by including a dummy plant having a 150-unit capacity. Table 15-12 shows the optimal shipping schedule for this expanded problem. All shipments from the dummy plant have zero cost, since they represent product not made and not sent. Notice that 150 units from the dummy plant are allocated to warehouse X. This means that warehouse X is shorted 150 units; in effect, X is the most costly warehouse to service, so it receives less than desired.

Consider the following example:

Plant Capacities		Warehouse Demands	
A	300	W	200
B	400	X	350
C	200	Y	250
	900		800

Here the total plant capacity of 900 units exceeds total demand for 800 by 100 units. The surplus capacity is handled by including a dummy warehouse with demand equal to the difference of 100. Table 15-13 provides the optimal solution to this problem. We use zero unit-shipping costs to the dummy warehouse, reflecting the fact that allocations to those cells represent product not made and not sent. We see that 50 units are allocated to the dummy warehouse from plant A and from plant B.

Table 15-13

THE OPTIMAL SHIPMENT SCHEDULE FOR THE PROBLEM REQUIRING A DUMMY WAREHOUSE

From \ To	W	X	Y	Dummy	Capacity
A	13	14	10 (250)	0 (50)	300
B	12	8 (350)	11	0 (50)	400
C	6 (200)	10	13	0	200
Demand	200	350	250	100	900

These amounts represent the unused surplus capacity in these plants; in terms of distribution costs, these plants are less efficient than plant C, which operates at full capacity.

SPECIAL PROBLEMS GETTING STARTED   15-5

The northwest corner rule is used to find a starting solution to the transportation problem. Recall that its allocations progress rightward and downward, always to an adjacent cell, and that diagonal jumps are not allowed. In certain problem situations, the northwest corner rule leads us to a point where no further movement is possible. This difficulty is easily remedied by slight modification of the rule.

Consider the shipping schedule in Table 15-14. Applying the northwest corner rule, we place 100 units in cell AW; then moving in the direction of surplus capacity, we allocate 150 units to cell AX. This exhausts the capacity of plant A, and the remaining 50 units of warehouse X demand get filled from plant B. At this point, an impass is reached—no further allocation can be made in row B or column X, and no horizontal or vertical movement is possible. We might bend our rule and move diagonally to cell CY, continuing from there. But by doing so, we would end up with one less non-empty cell than the transportation problem requires.

Table 15-14

AN IMPASSE IN GETTING STARTED USING THE NORTHWEST CORNER RULE

From \ To	W	X	Y	Z	Capacity
A	(100) →	(150)			250
B		(50) → no surplus capacity			50
C		no unfilled demand			150
D					50
E					400
F					100
Demand	100	200	300	400	1000

To avoid that pitfall, we will move to the cell at the right or below anyway. *The direction we choose is arbitrary.* Suppose we move down to cell *CX*. There we place a zero-quantity allocation. Cell *CX* will be treated as non-empty even though no shipment will be scheduled from plant *C* to warehouse *X*. We then proceed as before. Table 15-15 shows the completed shipment schedule. Although this problem has only one, two or more circled zeros may be required in some problems.

In proceeding to solve the problem, one of three things can happen to cell *CX:* (1) it will not be a turning point on the closed-loop path, remaining at zero quantity; (2) it will be a gaining cell, receiving allocation and joining the ranks of the other non-empty cells as a full-fledged member; or (3) it will be a losing cell, so that the zero will move to a presently empty cell location.

Should some starting procedure other than the northwest corner rule be used, special care must be taken to ensure that the proper number of cells be treated thereafter as non-empty. Often the "more efficient" methods yield fewer non-empty cells than required in the later iterations. Remember that there must always be exactly one less non-empty cell than the number of rows and columns. If there are fewer than this number of shipment-quantity allocations, then enough circled zeros must be placed to fill this requirement. With some starting methods it isn't obvious that one or more circled zeros are even needed. To compound the problem, such methods do not indicate where the needed circled zeros should be located. If an improper pattern of non-empty cells results, the rs and ks cannot all be found and closed-loop paths cannot be formed for some cells. A certain amount of trial and error placement may be needed before a workable starting solution is obtained. Fortunately, these difficulties are avoided entirely by the northwest corner rule.

Table 15-15
A NORTHWEST-CORNER STARTING SOLUTION
INVOLVING A ZERO SHIPMENT QUANTITY

From \ To	W	X	Y	Z	Capacity
A	(100)	(150)			250
B		(50)			50
C		(0)	(150)		150
D			(50)		50
E			(100)	(300)	400
F				(100)	100
Demand	100	200	300	400	1000

15-6 OTHER APPLICATIONS OF THE TRANSPORTATION PROBLEM

The scope of the transportation problem can be expanded to consider production costs as well as freight charges. For example, suppose that the three plants in the ski-distribution illustration all operated at different unit costs, say $60 for Juarez, $50 for Seoul, and $65 for Tel Aviv. Such cost differentials are just as important in choosing which warehouses will be serviced by which plants as the physical distance separating the production and consumption centers. By adding 60 to the row J costs, 50 to row S, and 65 to row T, the transportation problem can be re-solved so that the entire scope of distribution cost, not merely freight costs, can be optimized. Indeed, any formulation not reflecting all cost differentials between plants is undesirable and generally leads to inferior solutions. (We will leave this revised problem as an exercise.)

The transportation problem receives its name because it was originally applied to determining shipment schedules in distribution systems. However, its basic source-destination structure makes it suitable for solving a variety of other types of problems that do not involve physical distribution. For example, this format can be used to establish a plant's production schedule for several time periods.

As an illustration, suppose that the Juarez ski plant can actually operate at as much as 150 percent of the stated capacity during the August–November period by placing its work force on overtime. Furthermore, we will assume that company policy is to use this plant exclusively to service the Phoenix warehouse. We will assume that Juarez can make up to 100 pairs of skis monthly using regular labor at a cost of $60 per pair; for an additional $20 each, Juarez can make 50 additional pairs of skis per month using overtime. Finally, we will assume that the factory can store extra skis for later distribution at a cost of $1 per month.

Suppose that the following demands occur at the Phoenix warehouse:

August	100 pairs
September	150
October	200
November	100
	550 pairs

Table 15-16 shows the optimal production schedule. There are eight "plants," each representing the month and type of production (R for regular, O for overtime). There are four "warehouses," one for each monthly demand, plus one dummy warehouse (since total capacity exceeds total demand).

In constructing Table 15-16, we left out the unit freight charge, since it is the same for all cells. Notice that it is impossible to satisfy an earlier demand from later production. For the sake of completeness, the cells for these situations appear in the table; such allocations are given a very large unit cost of M dollars. (Should a starting solution involve such a cell, it would exit early in the game.) Notice also that the dummy column has zero-unit costs.

The transportation problem can also be used when the objective is to maximize profit. The simplest procedure would be to use the *negative* of the per unit profits just like costs. The same procedures would then apply, and no rules would change.

Table 15-16
THE OPTIMAL SKI PRODUCTION SCHEDULE

From Month \ To Month	A	S	O	N	Dummy	Capacity
AR	60 (100)	61 (0)	62	63	0	100
AO	80	81 (50)	82	83	0 (0)	50
SR	M	60 (100)	61 (0)	62	0	100
SO	M	80	81 (50)	82	0	50
OR	M	M	60 (100)	61	0	100
OO	M	M	80 (50)	81	0	50
NR	M	M	M	60 (100)	0	100
NO	M	M	M	80 (0)	0 (50)	50
Demand	100	150	200	100	50	600

15-7 ADVANTAGES OF THE TRANSPORTATION METHOD

Earlier in this chapter we indicated that a transportation problem could be solved using the simplex method described in Chapter 14. But the special structure of the transportation problem allows us to use a more limited algorithm tailor-made for it. At this point, you have worked with simplex and have seen what is required. Each iteration involves much messy computation, and one mistake ruins everything! To really appreciate the transportation method, you have to work a few problems to see just how much easier and faster it is.

One main advantage of the transportation problem is that it involves the main variables only. There is no need to use artificial variables, as in simplex. After applying the northwest corner rule, we are where simplex would be after getting rid of the artificial variables, which would take that procedure a minimum of iterations (tableaus) equal to the number of rows plus columns minus 1.

Although both procedures involve iterations, each new table found with the transportation method is much easier to get than a new simplex tableau would be. The rs and ks can be found quickly by simple arithmetic done in the head, and the empty-cell differences can be computed as fast as they can be written down. The pivot step is much easier in the transportation problem; finding the closed-loop path takes longest. The most time-consuming step is copying a blank shipment schedule for each iteration. (And even that time can be saved by using a copier or carbon paper.)

A final advantage of the transportation method is that it is not nearly as error prone as simplex is. A quick tally will tell whether or not the shipment quantities sum to the respective row and column totals. A mistake in the rs and ks will only slow the process down. Such mistakes are not fatal, as they are in simplex.

15-8 CONCLUDING REMARKS

It is possible to streamline further the solution of transportation problems. One very good way is to find a better starting procedure than the northwest corner rule, which totally ignores costs.

We have indicated that the transportation method is more efficient than the general-purpose simplex algorithm. As a matter of fact, the transportation method illustrated in this chapter is itself a variant form of simplex and is based upon exactly the same concepts. The row and column numbers are really analogous to the dual variable values, while the $c_{ij} - r_i - k_j$ differences represent the values in the per unit improvement row of the simplex tableau (that would apply if instead the transportation problem were solved that way).

Some problem situations have such a special structure that a refinement on the transportation method itself provides an even more efficient solution procedure. A special-purpose linear-programming algorithm has been developed for solving *assignment problems*, such as determining how to assign 10 persons to 10 jobs in order to minimize the total cost of performing all tasks. Another group of algorithms, based upon the concepts of flows through *networks*, are often used in place of the transportation method to solve similar problems. Further discussion of these and other linear programming algorithms is beyond the scope of this book. Many of the references at the back of the book provide complete discussions of these procedures.

PROBLEMS

15-1 A distribution system has the following requirements:

Plant Capacities		Warehouse Demands	
A	100	U	150
B	150	V	200
C	300	W	200

with unit shipping costs

From \ To	U	V	W
A	$10	$7	$8
B	15	12	9
C	7	8	12

(a) Formulate the above transportation problem as a linear program.
(b) Determine the optimal solution using the transportation method.

15-2 Problem 15-1 continued. Suppose that a new plant D is opened having capacity 200 and costing $8 per unit to serve each warehouse. Use the transportation method to determine the shipping schedule that minimizes total transportation cost.

15-3 Problem 15-1 continued. Suppose that a new warehouse X is opened having demand 100 and costing $15 for each unit shipped into it, regardless of origin. Use the transportation method to determine the minimum-cost shipping schedule using the original plants.

15-4 Druids' Drayage hauls rock from two quarries to three tombstone masons. The manager, H. Priest, wishes to minimize total shipping costs in such a way that every quarry operates precisely at full capacity and each mason receives exactly the number of stones he demands. The following unit shipping cost and quantity requirement data apply for tombstones.

FROM QUARRY	TO MASON			QUARRY CAPACITY
	Cedrick	Dunstan	Eldred	
Abinger	10/	15/	8/	100
Barnesly	12	9	10	200
Mason demand	50	150	100	300

Use the transportation method to determine the optimal number of tombstones to be hauled from each quarry to the respective masons.

15-5 Consider the following intermediate tableau for a transportation problem.

To From	J	K	L	M	N	O	P	Capacity
A	2	10	8	8 (100)	5 (100)	6	7	200
B	21	15	14	24	7 (100)	14	9	100
C	10	8 (200)	8	14 (100)	10	9	9	300
D	10	11 (200)	11	10	14	16	10	200
E	3	3 (200)	2	8	1	4 (100)	5	300
F	9 (200)	11	12	8 (200)	9	8	7	400
G	12	11 (200)	10	11	13	10	11 (100)	300
H	10	8	12	17	10 (200)	12 (100)	10	300
Demand	200	400	400	300	300	300	200	2100

Find the row and column numbers. Then find the closed-loop path. (*Hint:* the closed-loop path is defined by the turning points only.) *Do not solve the problem further,* but only indicate the new solution by crossing out the numbers that have changed and by indicating the new shipment quantities for the revised cells.

15-6 Hans and Fritz, and their cousins Gert and Zelda, wish to divide their chores to minimize total combined working time (and thus to maximize their playing time). Each is faster at certain daily chores. The following times apply.

	Chase Hippos	Pen Ostriches	Retrieve the Captain's Pipe	Scare Cannibals
Fritz	15 min	30 min	10 min	15 min
Hans	10	20	15	10
Gert	20	15	15	20
Zelda	10	20	10	15

Each brat will get exactly one chore, and all chores must be done.

Solve this problem using the transportation method. (*Hint:* treat each child-to-chore possibility like a shipment variable that will be a zero or a one; the chore "demands" and the child "capacities" each equal one.)

15-7 A freight dispatcher must supply five stores from two warehouses with daily shipments. The following unit cost and quantity requirements apply:

From Warehouse \ To Store	J	K	L	M	N	Warehouse Loading Capacity
A	$5	$8	$6	$4	$13	1000
B	6	9	4	5	6	500
Store requirement	400	300	200	300	300	1500

In addition, store N is so far from warehouse A that it is possible to send only one truckload per day from A to N; furthermore, up to 100 units may be carried in one trip.

(a) Construct the shipping schedule for this problem and find the northwest corner solution. (*Hint:* the special constraint may be handled with an extra source and dummy destination, and certain cell allocations are impossible and must, therefore, be very costly.)

(b) Continue with the problem, finding the optimal shipping schedule.

15-8 Consider the problem discussed in the chapter for providing skis from the Juarez plant to the Phoenix warehouse. Suppose the following demands apply instead:

August	25 pairs
September	175
October	150
November	150

Suppose also that the regular production costs are now $50 per pair, and the overtime premium is changed to $25 per pair. Also, the storage cost is now $5 per pair of skis.

Solve this problem using the transportation method to determine the optimal plan for ski production at Juarez.

15-9 Love and Peace Leather Works creates products from exotic skins obtained by the owner on hunting trips. After each hunt, she cuts the skins into strips and makes purse straps, belts, plant hangers, and hat bands. These items are sold to The Skin Boutique at an agreed price. On the latest trip our hunter has obtained the following number of strips: 30 rattlesnakes, 100 crocodiles, 50 armadillos, and 20 Gila monsters. Each strip is of equal size and any one type can be used for each final product. The Skin Boutique will buy up to 50 purse straps, 100 belts, 50 plant hangers, and 100 hat bands—regardless of the material used in making them. The prices yield the following profits to Love and Peace:

SKIN	PRODUCT			
	Purse Strap	Belt	Plant Hanger	Hat Band
Rattlesnake	$ 5	$12	$ 5	$10
Crocodile	10	15	5	10
Armadillo	8	10	10	5
Gila monster	10	20	20	15

Solve this problem using the transportation method to determine how Love and Peace can maximize profit.

15-10 The transportation method may be used in making cash management decisions. Suppose that a company in a highly seasonal business has the following cash flows.

Month	Cash Receipts	Cash Expenditures	Accounts Payable
January	$10,000	$5,000	$5,000
February	15,000	10,000	5,000
March	35,000	20,000	5,000
April	10,000	10,000	10,000
	$70,000	$45,000	$25,000

Accounts payable are to be paid under terms of 2 percent (10 days) net, 30 days; this means that there will be a 2 percent savings if these are paid in the month due, with no savings if paid in the next month. Bank loans may be taken at the rate of 1 percent simple interest per month, while cash held from one month to a later month will be invested in certificates of deposit at the same rate. Thus, each cash dollar invested and later converted costs $-1¢$ for each month held; if it is instead used to pay a current receivable, its cost is $-2¢$. There is no cost for using current cash receipts to fill current cash expenditures. The cost of a dollar borrowed is $1¢$ for each month held including the current month. Accounts payable must be paid no later than one month after due. The funds for these may derive from cash or loans obtained in the current or earlier months, in which case the 2 percent savings applies. Or, the accounts payable can be met from funds received or borrowed in the next month (but no later), with no savings from the discount. Cash requirements cannot be met with funds obtained in later months. The company has a $20,000 line of credit for each month.

We assume that cash will be managed at minimum cost over the four months. Treating cash receipts and loans taken in any given month as separate sources, with the monthly cash expenditures and accounts payable as destinations, set up a schedule suitable for solving this problem with the transportation method. Then solve the problem to determine the optimal cash management plan.

Sixteen

Network Planning with PERT

Important applications of quantitative methods can be made in the area of *project management,* where a great deal of effort is aimed at a specific accomplishment. Such a program might be construction of a dam, development of a new aircraft, implementation of a new computer system, or introduction of a new product. All these examples require management oriented toward directing and coordinating the activities of disparate organizations and people. Each project is fraught with uncertainties and takes a great deal of time to complete.

16-1 THE IMPORTANCE OF TIME IN PLANNING

Often *time* is a paramount factor in selecting alternative ways of completing such projects. This is especially true in construction, where the builder must generally complete work by the date on which the user plans to take over the facilities. A new headquarters building for a corporation illustrates the importance of timely completion.

Suppose a company's present lease expires in June, and it is planning a move from New York to the new San Francisco tower in July. The move itself requires planning to keep disruptions in company functions at a minimum; also, hundreds of employees will be selling their homes, buying new ones, and packing to move. If the new building isn't ready for occupancy until October, either a temporary San Francisco headquarters has to be found or all moving plans must be delayed. In either case, much bother and expense will result. The builder must therefore be given every incentive to finish the job in June. Such incentive might involve a bonus of thousands of dollars per day for early completion, with a substantial penalty imposed for each day's delay.

The builder should therefore desire to finish the job as quickly as possible with every expectation of achieving an acceptable profit. This too requires a lot of planning. The efforts of dozens of subcontractors, who will be separately responsible for such components as air-conditioning, excavation, glasswork, and carpeting, will have to be coordinated. Because the sequence of work is not very flexible (for instance, the framework must be completed before plumbing or wiring can begin), this coordination can be achieved through judicious *scheduling of activities*. All subcontractors must adhere to the overall schedule, for a delay by any one of them might result in the entire project's being late.

One procedure generally used to establish schedules for large projects is the *Program Evaluation and Review Technique*, usually referred to by the acronym PERT. This procedure may also be referred to as the *Critical Path Method*, or CPM. In addition to helping establish schedules, PERT can serve as a management tool for controlling the progress of any large project when timely completion is important.

PERT was developed in the late 1950s, when it came into extensive use in military research and development. Its first important application was in the Polaris program for the first submarine-launched ballistic missiles. PERT has been credited with saving several months in completion time over what could have been expected with more traditional procedures. Since then, PERT and other project management tools have been adopted by the Defense Department for most large research and development efforts. PERT was also adopted by the construction industry, and to a lesser extent it has been successfully used in other types of industrial applications.

BASIC CONCEPTS OF PERT 16-2

PERT builds from basic groupings of work. Such tasks are called *activities*. In construction, an activity is usually a function, such as excavating or installing plumbing, that is the responsibility of a single subcontractor. In the development of an aircraft, designing the landing gear might be one activity; that same component might involve several more activities in successive stages: testing materials, establishing final specifications, fabricating test gears, ground testing, and flight testing. Regardless of how the activities are identified, they have one feature in common: *activities take time*. Usually activities also consume resources —labor, material or money.

The number of activities identified will vary with the scope of the project. There may be only a handful of them for building a house. The construction of a nuclear power plant or an oil refinery might involve several thousand activities. One ballistic missile development program involved more than 2000 activities at the top management level, where the Air Force established schedules and directly monitored the progress of contractors. Several major contractors were responsible for separate systems of the missile, such as propulsion or guidance. Each organization had its own activities to control, so that for internal PERT purposes each contractor monitored several thousand activities. Altogether, tens of thousands of activities were involved in the development of this particular missile.

PERT involves structuring the various project activities in such a way that schedules may be developed, alternative plans investigated, and the project's status continuously monitored. This is done using a graphical procedure.

The PERT Network

The central focus of any PERT procedure is a logical representation of the project activities. This is accomplished by means of a *PERT network* showing the interrelationships between the activities in a chronological fashion. Figure 16-1 provides the PERT network for constructing a small home. Each activity is represented by an *arrow*,* each connected with one another in such a way that the required sequence of activities is adhered to. Before a network can be constructed, all activities must be identified and the immediately preceding activities determined. This information is provided in Table 16-1 for the home construction illustration.

We see that the project starts with excavating, activity (a). The foundation (b) and outside plumbing (c) follow immediately. Both the framing (d) and the brickwork (h) are preceded by the foundation (b), which must be completed before these activities can begin. The basic principle underlying a PERT network is that certain activities must be

---

* CPM applications use a circle to represent an activity. Although graphically reversed, the basic concepts of either procedure are the same.

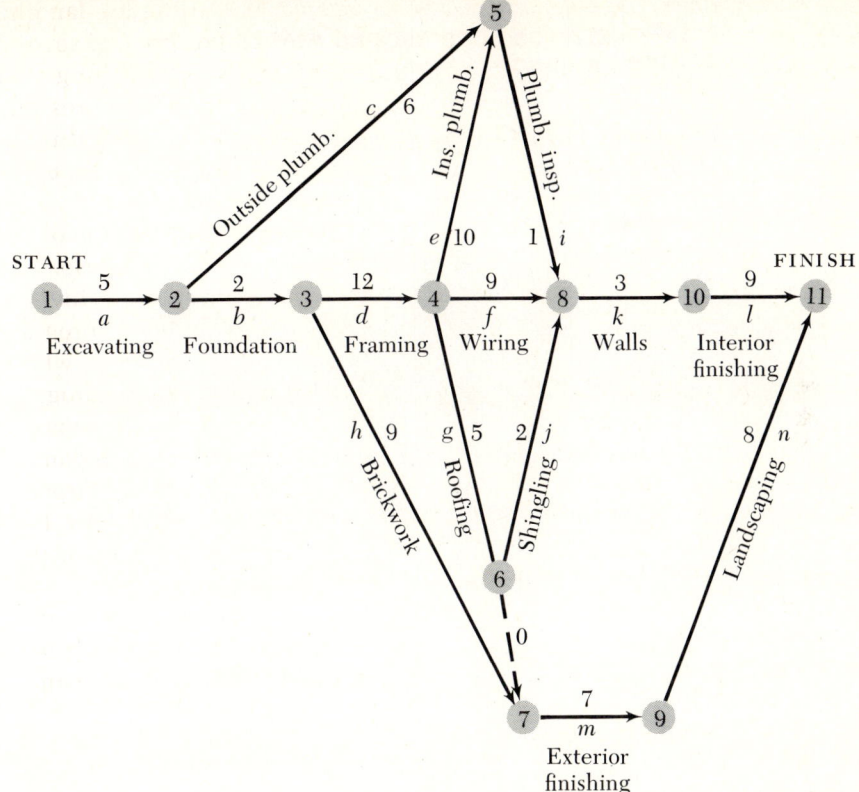

Figure 16-1
PERT network for building a home.

completed before others can begin, while some activities can be conducted simultaneously. The network must follow a basic chronological logic dictated by the characteristics of the project. In constructing a home, grading and excavation must be completed before the foundation can be poured. And the foundation must be present before the framework can be installed. The network in Figure 16-1 has purposely been kept simple (and some necessary details may be missing). It does not represent every house, only a particular one.

Notice that the arrows for the framing (d) and brickwork (h) activities begin at *circle* 3. This circle constitutes that *point in time* when the foundation (activity b) is completed. The PERT network for this project has eleven such points, called *events*. An event signals the completion or starting point of one or more activities. Although any arbitrary scheme can be used, the events in this illustration have been numbered so that each activity arrow begins with a lower numbered

16-2 BASIC CONCEPTS OF PERT   445

Table 16-1
BASIC DATA USED FOR CONSTRUCTING PERT NETWORK FOR BUILDING A HOME

Activity	Activity Immediately Preceding	Expected Completion Time
(a) Excavating	—	5 days
(b) Pour foundation	a	2
(c) Outside plumbing	a	6
(d) Framing	b	12
(e) Inside plumbing	d	10
(f) Wiring	d	9
(g) Roofing	d	5
(h) Brickwork	b	9
(i) Plumbing inspection	c, e	1
(j) Shingling	g	2
(k) Cover walls	f, i, j	3
(l) Interior finishing	k	9
(m) Exterior finishing	h, g	7
(n) Landscaping	m	8

event than the one where it ends. This scheme can be convenient when a PERT network is computerized, because each activity can then be defined by a beginning and terminating event pair. The events themselves consume neither time nor resources, and they serve mainly as *project milestones* and provide a logical "glue" for connecting the various activities.

The activities in any neighboring collection exhibit one of two basic relationships to each other. When activities must be completed in a strict sequence, they appear in a *series* as shown in Figure 16-2. For example, excavating (a), pouring the foundation (b), and framing (d) must be performed in that order. The activity sequence a-b-d must be represented by a succession of arrows, each following the other, indicating that an activity cannot begin until the preceding one has been completed. Such a sequence of activities forms a portion of a particular *path* through the network from start to finish. The sequence a-b-d-f-k-l is one of several such paths.

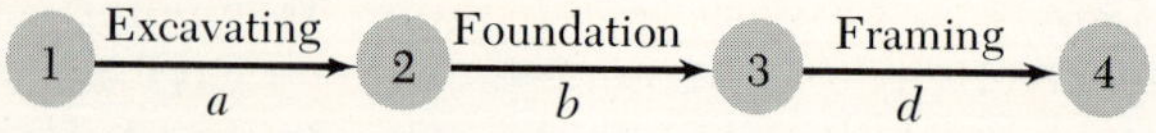

Figure 16-2
Activities in series.

NETWORK PLANNING WITH PERT

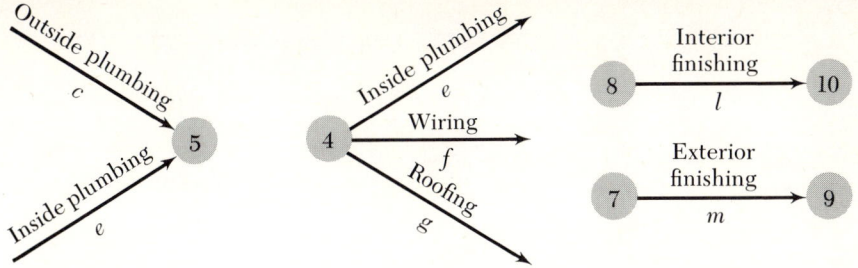

Figure 16-3
Activities in parallel.

Activities that may occur simultaneously can be stacked as shown in Figure 16-3. Any such arrangement involves *parallel* activities. Conceivably, plumbers, electricians, and roofers could all work on the house on the same day. Because parallel activities may have varying durations, it is not necessary for them to actually occur simultaneously, but we allow for that possibility in our PERT network. If for some reason electricians and plumbers cannot work together (perhaps because of cramped quarters), the present portrayal is unrealistic and the project network should be restructured to reflect a series arrangement between inside plumbing and wiring. *But activities should not be placed in series unless absolutely necessary.* Whenever two or more jobs may be done at the same time, this possibility should be reflected in the network—even if nobody ever thought of doing it that way before. This approach allows greater flexibility in planning and might actually help to shorten the project's duration.

Once the required activity sequence has been specified, the actual construction of the PERT network can begin. It is best to use a very large sheet of paper for this and to begin with a rough draft. It can then be copied and some events repositioned to keep the number of crossing arrows small. In some applications, the PERT network is drawn in successive revised versions, as new activities or interrelationships come to mind.

Computer routines have been written to aid in arriving at a final graphical display. It may be impractical to have any pictorial representation at all in very large projects. (If drawn, a PERT network with several thousand activities can completely cover the walls of a big room.) Such projects are usually processed entirely on a computer.

The arrow length and the duration of the corresponding activity are not related. In elaborate PERT systems, the network itself may be time-phased, so that *events* are positioned sequentially according to a master schedule (developed in an earlier PERT analysis) at distances from the

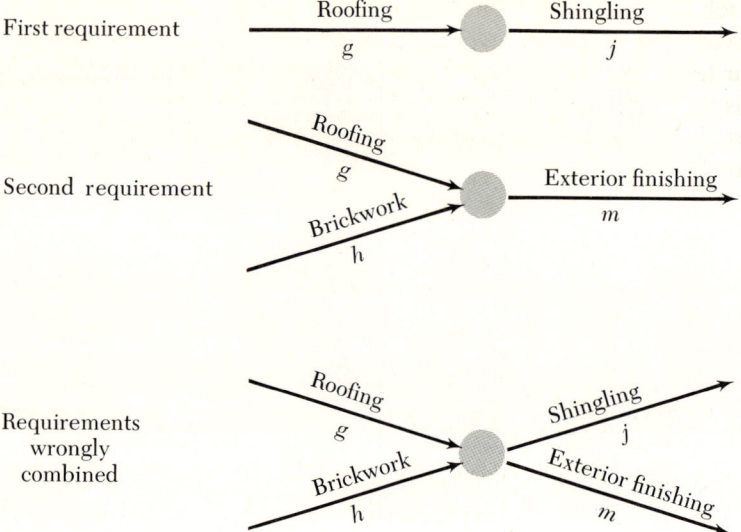

Figure 16-4
Incorrect network representation.

start of one week (or day or month) to an inch or some other fixed interval. Although such graphical niceties can be helpful when communicating with managers, they are not essential for successful application of PERT.

Dummy Activities

Notice the broken arrow in Figure 16-1 leading from event 6 to event 7. This is an example of a *dummy activity*. Such a portrayal is required to meet the underlying chronology of work without introducing spurious constraining relationships. The requirements in Table 16-1 indicate first that shingling (*j*) is preceded by roofing (*g*) and, second, that exterior finishing (*m*) is preceded by both the brickwork (*h*) and roofing (*g*). All of these constraints are met by the network arrangement shown in Figure 16-4.

However, the final portion of Figure 16-4 is incorrect, since it improperly indicates that shingling (*j*) cannot start until brickwork (*h*) is completed (see Figure 16-5):

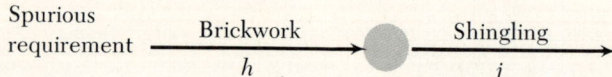

Figure 16-5
Spurious requirement induced by not having a dummy activity.

No such requirement exists, and there is no apparent reason why shingling cannot commence while the bricklayers are still working (this particular house doesn't have a fireplace protruding through the roof). This means that the entire X formed by the activities in the bottom portion of Figure 16-4 doesn't apply; only the first three of the portions shown in Figure 16-6 are correct.

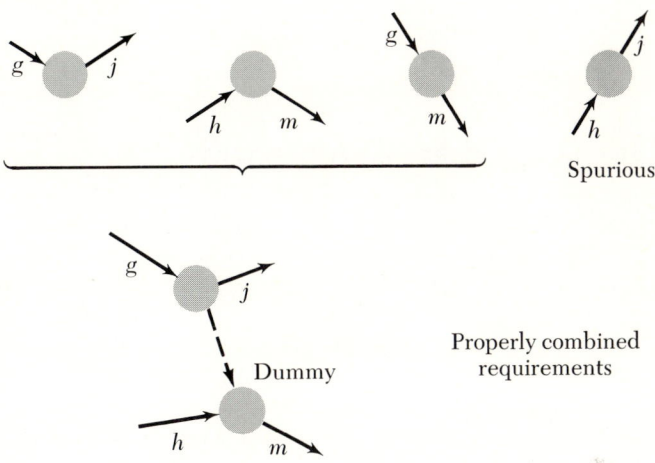

Figure 16-6
Correct network representation involving a dummy activity.

The graphical dilemma is solved by using two events in place of one and letting the precedence of activity g before activity m be represented by the broken arrow pointing downward. The resulting dummy activity explicitly disallows the spurious constraint indicated earlier. A dummy activity is necessary only to preserve the interactivity logic and consumes neither time nor resources.

Activity Completion Times

Ordinarily an activity's duration is uncertain. It is impossible to predict the exact number of working days it will take to frame a house, although reliable estimates accurate to plus or minus a few days can be made. Much less precision can be expected in estimating how long a research effort or a series of tests will take.

In its most general form, PERT treats activity completion times as random variables, each having a distinct probability distribution. To

16-2   BASIC CONCEPTS OF PERT

simplify further analysis, each variable is usually represented by a mean value, the *expected activity completion time*. The numbers appearing above the arrows in the PERT network in Figure 16-1 are the expected completion times for the various activities. For instance, framing (activity *d*) has a mean completion time of 12 days. After the job is done, the builder's records may show that it actually took 11.50 or 13.25 days to erect the frame. But before building begins the actual time is an unknown future value, and the expected time of 12 days is a convenient number to use in planning.

16-3   ANALYSIS OF THE PERT NETWORK

So far we have seen what a PERT network represents and how one may be constructed. We will soon see how it may be used in project planning and control. A major advantage in using PERT is that *the network provides a basis for establishing a compatible activity schedule permitting project completion in minimum time*. Additional PERT concepts will be discussed in describing the steps leading to a final schedule.

Keep in mind that much of the following discussion is essentially *deterministic*, since the expected activity times will be treated as if they were going to be the actual durations. Later in the chapter, we will investigate some of the implications of this approach.

Earliest Possible Event Times

PERT analysis begins by focusing on events. Recall that an event is simply a point in time representing either the completion of one or a group of parallel activities or the start of one or more activities. An event is thus a milestone to be reached by all activities directly preceding it before future ones can begin. For example, event 4 in the home-building network, redrawn for convenience in Figure 16-7, occurs when framing is just finished and must occur before either inside plumbing, wiring, or roofing can begin.

Our first steps are to find the *event times* when the respective events occur. If we want to schedule each activity so that it starts as soon as possible, the permissible starting time for a particular activity can be no later than the *earliest possible event time* for the event preceding it.

For convenience we use the letters *TE* to represent earliest possible event times that can be expected. We begin at the start of the

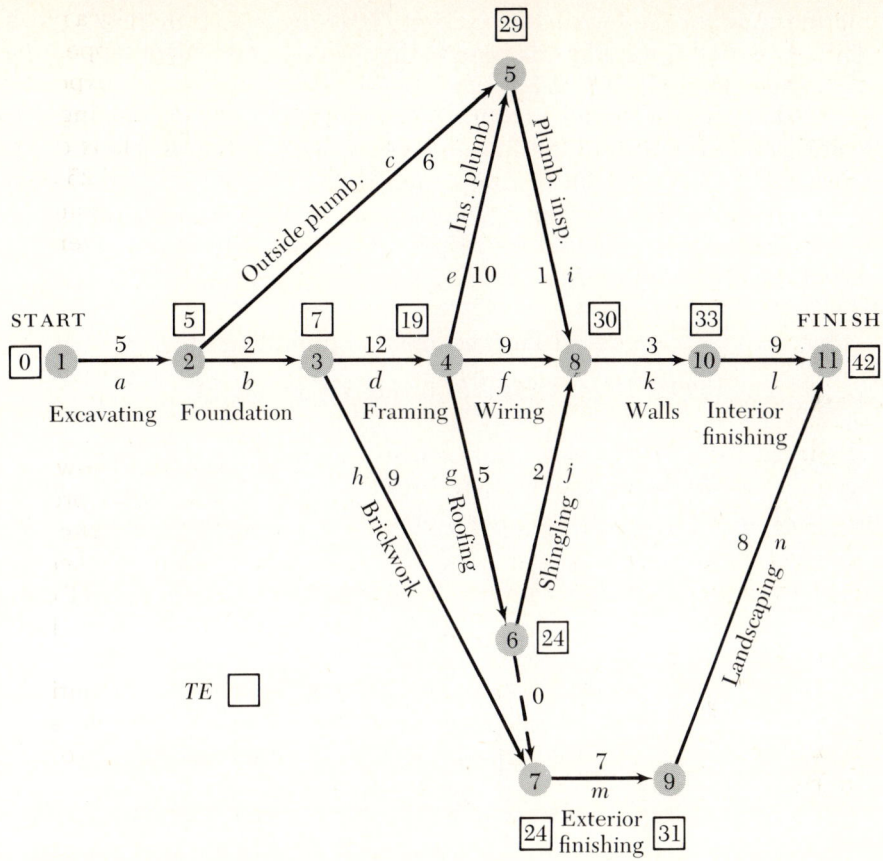

Figure 16-7
PERT network for building a home, showing the earliest possible event times (*TEs*).

project, designated as time zero (so that it can represent any calendar time desired, such as 8 AM on Wednesday, August 1, 1980). A *TE* value of 0 applies to event 1 in Figure 16-7. For ease of identification, each *TE* is placed in the *square* alongside its corresponding event. The *TE* for any event is based on the sum of a preceding *TE* plus the expected completion time for the activity that connects those two events. Figure 16-8 shows how to apply this principle.

Event 2 is connected to event 1 by excavating (activity *a*), which takes a mean of 5 days to complete. Thus, the *TE* for event 2 is $0 + 5 = 5$ days, and event 2 can be expected to occur at the *end* of the fifth working day into the project, at the earliest. Likewise, the *TE* for event 3 is obtained by adding the one found for event 2 to the two-day expected com-

16-3   ANALYSIS OF THE PERT NETWORK   451

pletion time for the foundation (activity *b*, connecting 2 to 3): $5 + 2 = 7$ days. At event 4, we add this time to the mean framing (activity *d*) time of 12 days, getting a *TE* of $7 + 12 = 19$ days.

When two or more activities terminate at a single event, that event cannot occur until all those activities are completed. Thus its *TE* equals that earliest point in time when the last activity is expected to be complete. Consider event 5, where both outside and inside plumbing (*c* and *e*) terminate; we find the respective expected number of working days for completion of these activities (at their earliest) to be

$$5 + 6 = 11 \text{ days for outside plumbing } (c)$$

$$19 + 10 = 29 \text{ days for inside plumbing } (e)$$

The largest sum of 29 days occurs for inside plumbing (*e*), which is expected to be the last of the two activities to be completed. Thus we must use a *TE* of 29 as the earliest possible time for event 5. In general, the

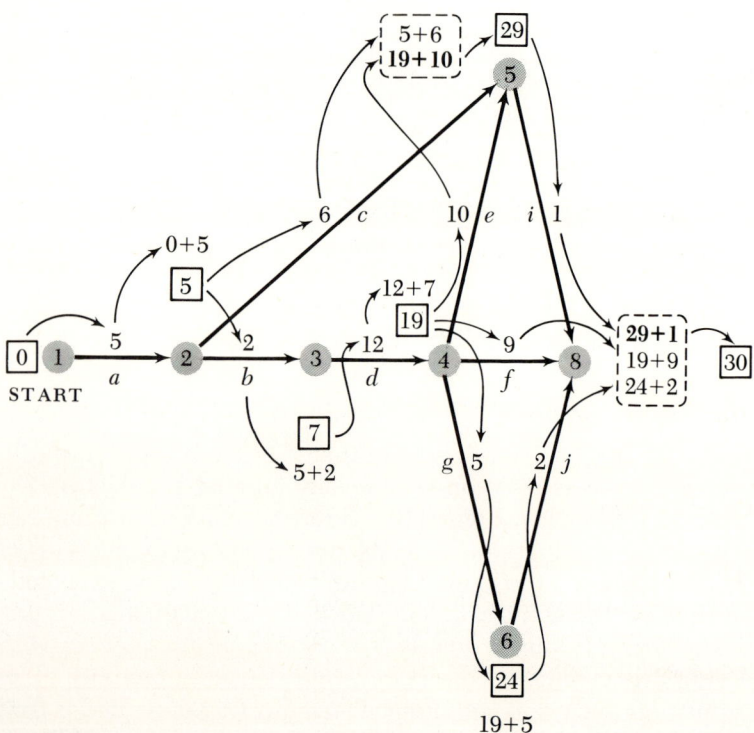

Figure 16-8
Illustration of how to find event *TE*s.

TE for an event must be the largest sum applicable to those activities terminating there.

Consider event 8, where three activities terminate. We find the sums:

$$29 + 1 = 30 \text{ days for plumbing inspection } (i)$$
$$19 + 9 = 28 \text{ days for wiring } (f)$$
$$24 + 2 = 26 \text{ days for shingling } (j)$$

As before, its TE must be the largest of the above, or 30.

TEs are found by making a *forward pass* through the network. They establish the earliest possible times expected for the respective events. By adding successive activity completion times together, we see that *an event's earliest possible time (TE) equals the longest duration of all activity paths leading to it from the start*. For instance, paths *a-c* and *a-b-d-e* lead to event 5; durations of these paths are

$$5 + 6 = 11 \text{ days for path } a\text{-}c$$
$$5 + 2 + 12 + 10 = 29 \text{ days for path } a\text{-}b\text{-}d\text{-}e$$

The longest duration path to event 5 takes 29 days, the same figure found for its TE. Likewise, event 8 has four paths leading to it; the durations of these paths are

$$5 + 6 + 1 = 12 \text{ days for path } a\text{-}c\text{-}i$$
$$5 + 2 + 12 + 10 + 1 = 30 \text{ days for path } a\text{-}b\text{-}d\text{-}e\text{-}i$$
$$5 + 2 + 12 + 9 = 28 \text{ days for path } a\text{-}b\text{-}d\text{-}f$$
$$5 + 2 + 12 + 5 + 2 = 26 \text{ days for path } a\text{-}b\text{-}d\text{-}g\text{-}j$$

with the longest duration of 30 days being the TE of event 8.

The Critical Path

The path with the longest total time through the PERT network from start to finish is called the *critical path*. This particular activity sequence is indicated in Figure 16-9 by the shaded arrows. For the home-construction project we have

$$\text{Critical path} = a\text{-}b\text{-}d\text{-}e\text{-}i\text{-}k\text{-}l$$

The above represents the succession of activities on the right.

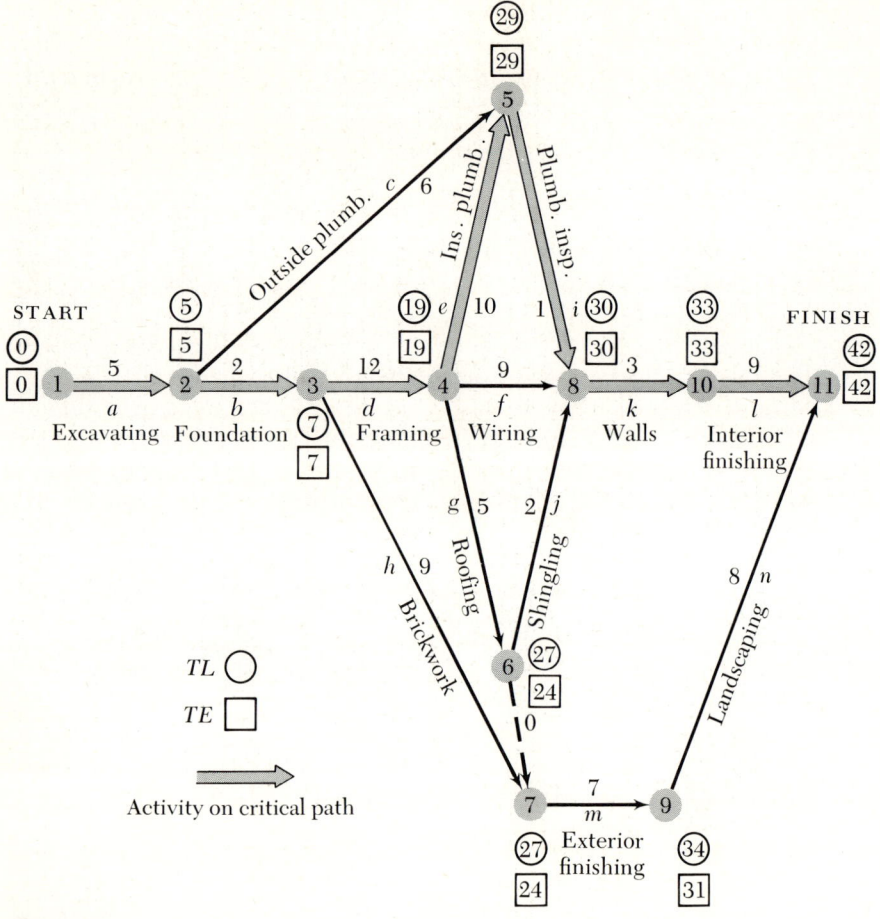

Figure 16-9
PERT network for building a home showing critical path, earliest possible event times *TE*s, and latest allowable event times *TL*s.

Activity Sequence	Expected Completion Time
START	
(a) Excavating	5 days
(b) Pour foundation	2
(d) Framing	12
(e) Inside plumbing	10
(i) Plumbing inspection	1
(k) Cover walls	3
(l) Interior finishing	9
FINISH Total	42 days

Because they comprise the critical path, the tasks in the preceding table are called *critical activities.*

The critical path has a duration equal to the *TE* of the last event in the project, which is event 11 in our example. That final milestone can happen no sooner than after 42 working days from the start. This is also the earliest time that all activities, and, hence, the project itself can be finished. Thus, *the duration of the critical path might serve as the expected completion time for the entire project.*

Although the critical path is *defined* by a particular activity sequence (the one taking longest time), it is *sometimes identified* in terms of an event sequence. In our illustration,

$$\text{Critical path} = 1\text{-}2\text{-}3\text{-}4\text{-}5\text{-}8\text{-}10\text{-}11$$
$$\phantom{\text{Critical path} = }\text{START} \qquad \text{FINISH}$$

A PERT network may have several activity sequences tying for longest. In such cases, each sequence would be a critical path. There is no reason why a project can't have several critical paths.

The critical path has many ramifications. Before investigating these further, two additional preliminary PERT procedures will be described.

Latest Allowable Event Times

The earliest event times are by themselves insufficient for establishing schedules because not all activities must start at the earliest opportunity. Many "harmless" noncritical activities can actually start later without delaying the entire project. A second set of numbers for the network events, called the *latest allowable event times,* serve to establish limits on the degree of possible scheduling flexibility.

The latest allowable event time is abbreviated by the letters *TL*. These times appear inside the *circles* beside the respective events in Figure 16-9. The *TL* value establishes the point in time when an event must occur before an automatic delay can be expected in everything that follows, including the project itself.

For example, consider event 9, following the exterior finishing (m); this milestone must occur before its latest allowable time of $TL = 34$ days, or else we cannot expect the project to be completed in the shortest possible duration of 42 working days. To see why this is so, suppose that event 9 doesn't occur until the end of the 36th working day; 8 more days are expected for landscaping, and the project would then be expected to take 44 days to complete.

The *TL*s are found in a similar fashion to the *TE*s, but they are com-

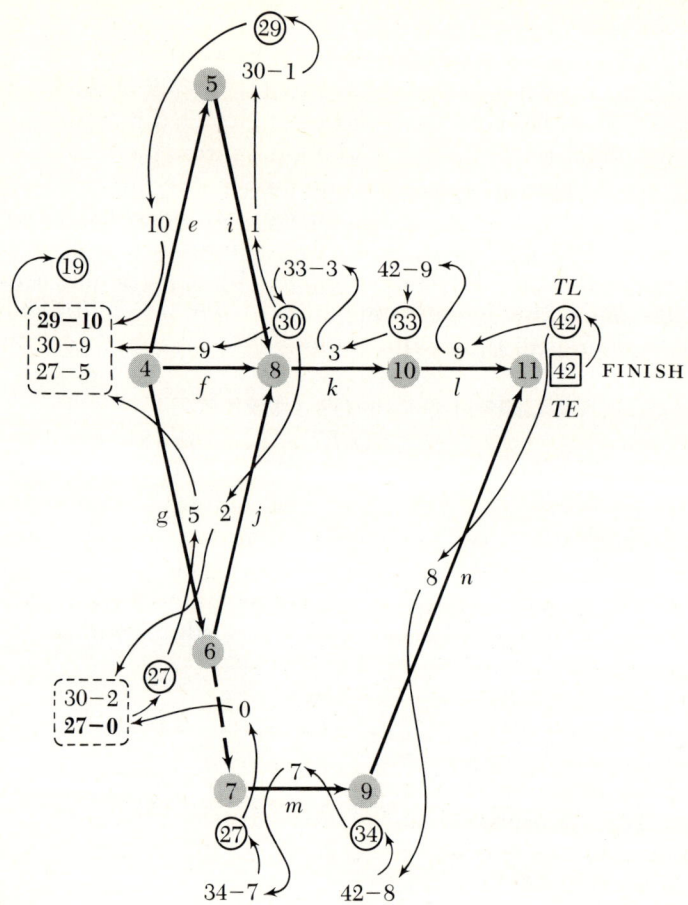

Figure 16-10
Illustration of how to find event *TL*s.

puted in a *backward pass* through the network, and expected activity completion times are *subtracted*. Figure 16-10 illustrates this procedure. We start at the project finish, assigning the same number for the *TL* of the last event as was obtained earlier for its *TE*. Thus, event 11 is assigned a latest allowable time of $TL = 42$ days. Subtracting the 9 days for completing interior finishing *(l)*, we obtain a *TL* of $42 - 9 = 33$ days for event 10. Repeating this step for event 8, we start with the *TL* just found and subtract the activity time of 3 for covering the walls *(k)*, the connecting activity, getting $33 - 3 = 30$ days, which is the *TL* for event 8.

No special problems exist until an event is encountered that is the beginning point for more than one activity, so that two or more arrows point away from it. For example, event 4 signals the starting point for three activities:

> (e) Inside plumbing, ending at event 5
>
> (f) Wiring, ending at event 8
>
> (g) Roofing, ending at event 6

To find the TL for event 4, we find the smallest difference between the TL for the terminating event and the activity time:

> $29 - 10 = 19$ days for inside plumbing (e)
>
> $30 - 9 = 21$ days for wiring (f)
>
> $27 - 5 = 22$ days for roofing (g)

Thus, the latest allowable time for event 4 is 19 days.

Similar to the TEs, each TL is related to an activity sequence: the longest duration path from the event to the project finish. The durations of these paths equal the sum of the applicable activity times and also the earliest *project* completion time minus the TL value. (In our example, the longest path leading from event 4 to the finish is expected to take $42 - 19 = 23$ days).

The significance of the TL values in project scheduling will be discussed later. We now consider the importance of that information gleaned from the TE and TL values together.

Event Slack Times: Finding the Critical Path

The TE value establishes the earliest possible time an event is expected to occur, and its TL is the latest allowable time for it to happen without expecting delays in the entire project. The difference between these quantities tells the project manager how much leeway exists in achieving such an event. We call this duration the *event slack time*, which may be computed from

$$\text{Event slack time} = TL - TE$$

As an example, consider event 9, which has a TL of 34 days and a TE of 31 days; its event slack time is $34 - 31 = 3$ days. In a similar manner, the slack times for the other home-construction events have been computed.

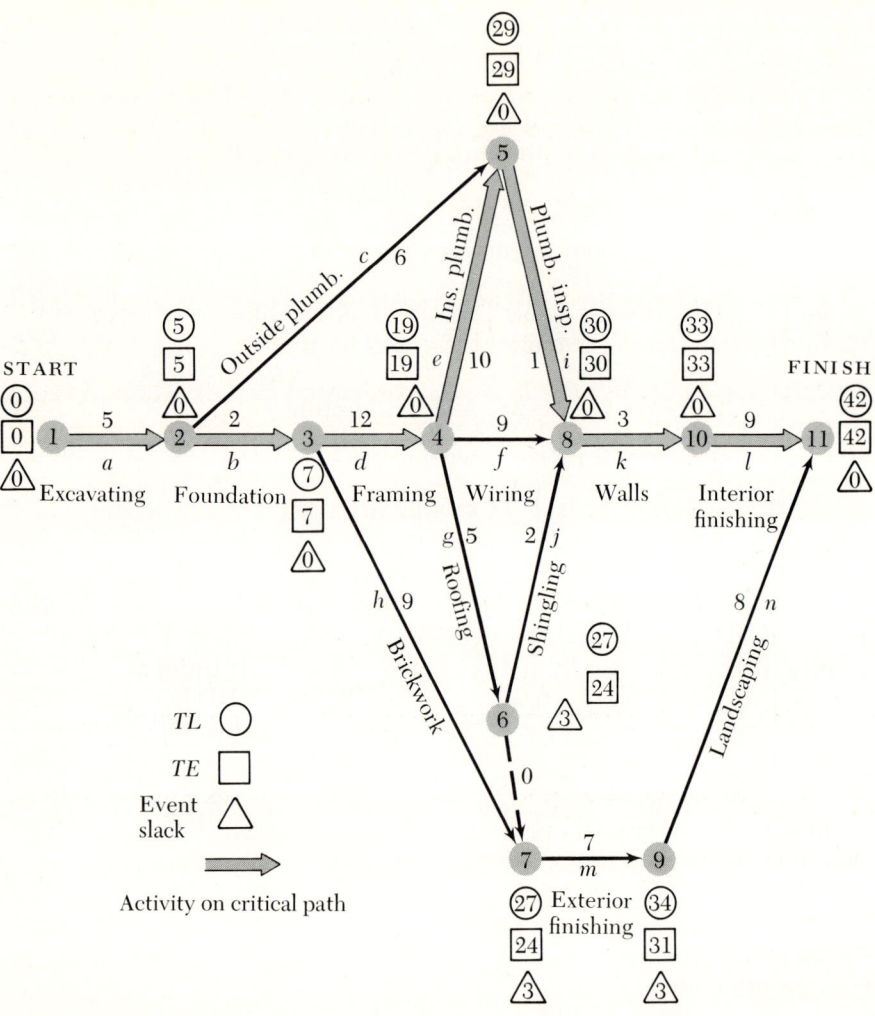

Figure 16-11
Complete PERT network for the home-building example.

These appear in the triangles beside the respective events in Figure 16-11.

The main advantage from knowing event slack times in PERT analysis is that they help to identify the critical path. Although the terminal event's *TE* tells us how long the critical path is, without some help it can be hard to identify exactly which acts comprise it. In a several-hundred activity network, there can be millions of distinct paths from start to finish, but perhaps only one critical path. It would be incredibly wasteful to locate it by trial and error.

Because it is the longest activity sequence from start to finish, it should be readily apparent that *all connecting events in the critical path must have zero slack times.* Thus, we may limit our search just to those paths connecting zero-slack events. In Figure 16-11, there are three such sequences:

$$1\text{-}2\text{-}5\text{-}8\text{-}10\text{-}11 \quad (\text{or, } a\text{-}c\text{-}i\text{-}k\text{-}l)$$
$$1\text{-}2\text{-}3\text{-}4\text{-}5\text{-}8\text{-}10\text{-}11 \quad (\text{or, } a\text{-}b\text{-}d\text{-}e\text{-}i\text{-}k\text{-}l)$$
$$1\text{-}2\text{-}3\text{-}4\text{-}8\text{-}10\text{-}11 \quad (\text{or, } a\text{-}b\text{-}d\text{-}f\text{-}k\text{-}l)$$

Two of these are not critical because their activity times do not sum to the project duration of 42 days, found earlier. The activity times in the first path sum to 24 days; in the last one they total only 40 days. The middle sequence describes the critical path identified in the network in Figure 16-11.

16-4 PLANNING AND CONTROL USING THE PERT NETWORK

The PERT network information in Figure 16-11 may be used to establish project schedules and to aid in controlling the activities so that delay-causing situations can be avoided.

Activity Scheduling

Recall that the earliest possible event time TE sets a lower limit on when succeeding activities may be expected to start. And the latest allowable event time TL indicates an upper limit on when preceding activities can end without expecting delays in the project. Thus, together the TE and TL values provide the basis for scheduling activities.

A schedule for an activity consists of a starting date and a completion date. The PERT network establishes limits for these dates. An activity may be expected to begin on any date between its *early starting time ES* and its *late starting time LS*. By adding the estimated activity completion time, these dates determine the *early finishing time EF* and the *late finishing time LF*.

An activity's early starting time is equal to the earliest possible time for the event immediately preceding it:

$$ES = TE \text{ for preceding event}$$

Adding the expected activity completion time, represented by the letter t, we may then compute the early finishing time for each activity as follows:

$$EF = ES + t$$

An activity's late finishing time equals the TL for the event where it ends:

$$LF = TL \text{ for succeeding event}$$

Subtracting the expected activity completion time, we calculate the late starting time

$$LS = LF - t$$

Table 16-2 shows these quantities for the home-construction project. Consider, for example, wiring (activity f). From Figure 16-11 we see that this activity is preceded by event 4 (with an earliest possible time of $TE = 19$) and succeeded by event 8 (with a latest allowable time of $TL = 30$). Thus, the early starting time for wiring is $ES = 19$ days from

Table 16-2
LIMITS FOR SCHEDULING ACTIVITIES

| | | | STARTING TIMES | | FINISHING TIMES | |
| | | | ES | LS | EF | LF |
ACTIVITY		t	Preceding TE	LF $-$ t	ES $+$ t	Succeeding TL
(a)	Excavating	5	0	0	5	5
(b)	Pour foundation	2	5	5	7	7
(c)	Outside plumbing	6	5	23	11	29
(d)	Framing	12	7	7	19	19
(e)	Inside plumbing	10	19	19	29	29
(f)	Wiring	9	19	21	28	30
(g)	Roofing	5	19	22	24	27
(h)	Brickwork	9	7	18	16	27
(i)	Plumbing inspection	1	29	29	30	30
(j)	Shingling	2	24	28	26	30
(k)	Cover walls	3	30	30	33	33
(l)	Interior finishing	9	33	33	42	42
(m)	Exterior finishing	7	24	27	31	34
(n)	Landscaping	8	31	34	39	42

project start. Adding the expected completion time of $t = 9$ days for this activity, the early finishing time for wiring is $EF = 19 + 9 = 28$ days from time zero. The late finishing time for wiring is $LF = 30$ days, and the late starting time is $LS = 30 - 9 = 21$ days.

In scheduling the project, the builder can start wiring anytime between the early starting time of $ES = 19$ and the late starting time of $LS = 21$. Thus, if the project is to start at 8 AM on Wednesday, August 1, 1980, wiring may be scheduled to begin sometime just after 19 working days, or at 8 AM on August 28 (the beginning of the 20th day) but not later than after 21 working days (8 AM on August 30). If the early starting time is chosen, wiring completion can be scheduled for any time between these two dates. But if a late starting time is chosen, wiring must be scheduled for completion exactly at the late finishing time (the end of the 30th working day, or 5 PM on September 11 — assuming that Labor Day is a working day).

Activity Slack Times

We have now identified points in time associated with the activities themselves. These points provide another set of measures useful for project planning. These values are the *activity slack times*, which like their event counterparts discussed earlier, indicate how much leeway exists in completing an activity before project delays can be expected. For any particular activity, this value is computed from the following difference between the late and early finishing times:

$$\text{Activity slack time} = LF - EF$$

(The same results can be obtained from the difference $LS - ES$.)

The activity slack times are computed for our example in Table 16-3. Notice that some activities have zero slack. *A critical path connects only zero-slack activities, and all such activities lie on at least one critical path.* Our example has only one critical path, *a-b-d-e-i-k-l*.

Although they are much alike, activity slack measures something different from event slack, and generally one set of values cannot be directly computed from the other.

Milestone Scheduling

Sometimes it is necessary to establish milestone schedules for project events rather than activities. When PERT is applied to military development programs, where the Defense Department specifies impor-

Table 16-3
ACTIVITY SLACK TIMES FOR HOME-BUILDING PROJECT

ACTIVITY	FINISHING TIME LF	EF	ACTIVITY SLACK TIME
(a) Excavating	5	5	0
(b) Pour foundation	7	7	0
(c) Outside plumbing	29	11	18
(d) Framing	19	19	0
(e) Inside plumbing	29	29	0
(f) Wiring	30	28	2
(g) Roofing	27	24	3
(h) Brickwork	27	16	11
(i) Plumbing inspection	30	30	0
(j) Shingling	30	26	4
(k) Cover walls	33	33	0
(l) Interior finishing	42	42	0
(m) Exterior finishing	34	31	3
(n) Landscaping	42	39	3

tant dates in contractual work statements, event scheduling is convenient. Although a PERT network may serve as the basis, the actual schedule times chosen are a matter for negotiation between the government agency and the contractor. To avoid potential delays in meeting these dates, the contractor must schedule each activity's finishing time to occur no later than the applicable milestone date for the succeeding event.

An example from a major weapon system project demonstrates how important PERT planning is in establishing milestone schedule dates. One contractor was responsible for designing and building hardware, which was then to be tested by another contractor. The second contractor was scheduled to provide the Air Force with its testing results on a certain date. But the first contractor's schedule called for delivery of the necessary hardware *after* the testing had to be performed. This obvious inconsistency in contractor schedules went unnoticed for several months, until a PERT network was developed and its critical path determined.

Managing with PERT

The above example illustrates an important feature of PERT: it can provide a structure for controlling the multitude of activities in a complex project. When separate organizations are responsible for work that must be done in small pieces over a long period of time at widely separated locations, good coordination of effort is a requisite for success. Strict adherence to mutually compatible schedules almost assures this. Although by no means a panacea, PERT accomplishes this function well.

Management through PERT doesn't stop with publication of schedules. Remember, the PERT analysis we have seen so far is based on a single set of numbers, the *expected* activity completion times. The actual amount of time required for a particular activity is really uncertain. Consider the framing of a house. Inclement weather, an accident on the job, poor workmanship, illness, or a variety of other circumstances might delay its completion. As we have seen in our home-construction example, this particular activity is critical, and a delay in framing will make the project late unless the lost time can be made up by speeding the completion of one or more later activities on the critical path.

If timely completion of the entire project is extremely important, the critical activities deserve special attention. This is an excellent application of the *management-by-exception principle.* Less attention need be paid to activities that are not on the critical path simply because small delays in completing these will not delay the entire project.

Again, we must emphasize that the expected activity completion times themselves are only estimated values. Should some activity not on the original critical list be unduly delayed, the critical path from that point in time onward might actually shift and make a new set of activities the critical ones. Special managerial attention might therefore be given to the critical and near-critical (low slack time) activities.

REPLANNING AND ADJUSTMENT WITH PERT 16-5

As indicated above, there is much more to PERT than setting schedules. If unusual delaying situations are encountered, PERT must somehow accommodate them. Also, our discussions so far have focused on time to the exclusion of resources that might be consumed in completing a project. This is natural, since PERT is essentially a time-minimizing procedure. But a project manager should also be concerned with minimizing the *cost* of the resources used.

The Time-Cost Tradeoff

The expected activity completion times used in the basic PERT analysis are predicated upon some assumed level of resource commitment. The dominant resource in most projects that use PERT is labor, and management has the greatest flexibility and control over this resource. For instance, it is possible to shorten an activity's completion time by concentrating more labor on it. This could be accomplished in framing a house simply by using a larger crew of carpenters than originally planned.

Ordinarily, shortening an activity can only be done by increasing its cost. For example, adding a third carpenter to the original two will be faster, but doing so will not necessarily increase overall crew output by 50 percent. This can only happen if a two-man crew is less than optimal (from a productivity point of view). Beyond the optimal crew size, the marginal productivity of each extra person is decreasing. Thus the total framing cost would be higher with three carpenters. Another way to get the job done faster is by working overtime. But any overtime wage premium would also raise the total cost of completing the task.

Figure 16-12 shows how project completion time and cost are related by a curve; each point on this *time-cost tradeoff curve* corresponds

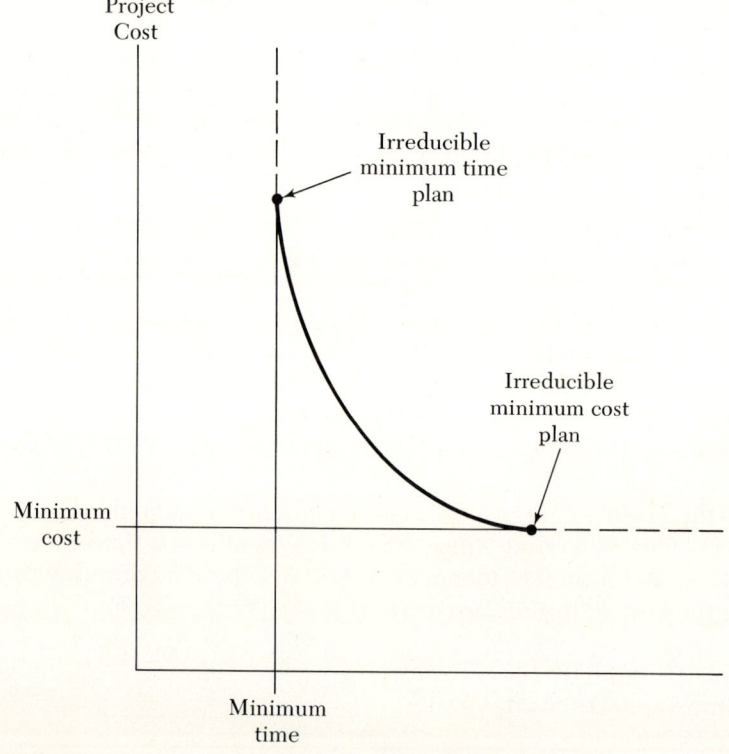

Figure 16-12
Time-cost tradeoff curve for a project.

to a possible project plan. Note the dilemma faced by a project manager: it is possible to reduce a project's duration only by increasing its cost, and its cost can be reduced only if the project is allowed to take longer. Furthermore, there are irreducible minimum plans with respect to time and cost. Only these plans and the ones lying between, represented by the solid portion of the time-cost tradeoff curve, will ever be considered.

Unless time savings can be expressed in terms of a dollar return, quantitative analysis cannot identify the best point on the curve, because minimizing time and minimizing cost are competing objectives.

Regular and Crash Activity Plans

A good activity manager should be aware not only of how long a particular task might take under varying working conditions, but also of how much these various working arrangements should cost. When quantified, such information can provide a graph like the one in Figure 16-13, where two planning extremes determine a time-cost tradeoff for an activity. The *activity crash plan* brings the expected activity completion time

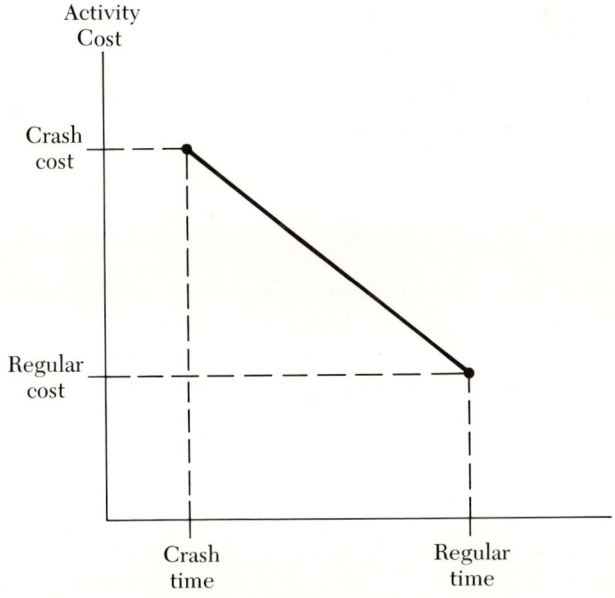

Figure 16-13
Time-cost tradeoff line for an activity.

16-5   REPLANNING AND ADJUSTMENT WITH PERT

to its irreducible minimum, regardless of cost. At the other extreme, the *activity regular plan* involves the most efficient working arrangement in terms of resource efficiency; it is the minimum-cost plan. Either of these plans, or one between them, might be chosen.

Table 16-4
REGULAR AND CRASH PROGRAMS FOR BUILDING A HOME

ACTIVITY	EXPECTED ACTIVITY TIMES		DIRECT COST		ADDED COST PER DAY REDUCED
	Regular	Crash	Regular	Crash	
(a) Excavating	5 days	4 days	$1,000	$1,300	$300 per day
(b) Pour foundation	2	2	500	500	—
(c) Outside plumbing	6	4	900	1,300	200
(d) Framing	12	8	2,400	2,800	100
(e) Inside plumbing	10	7	1,500	2,100	200
(f) Wiring	9	6	1,800	2,250	150
(g) Roofing	5	3	1,000	1,400	200
(h) Brickwork	9	7	1,800	2,150	175
(i) Plumbing inspection	1	1	50	50	—
(j) Shingling	2	2	400	400	—
(k) Cover walls	3	2	300	425	125
(l) Interior finishing	9	8	1,500	1,725	225
(m) Exterior finishing	7	5	1,200	1,650	225
(n) Landscaping	8	4	2,000	2,100	25
			$16,350	$20,150	

Table 16-4 shows how such data might look for our home-construction project. We see that excavating (activity a) is expected to take 5 days and cost $1000 in labor under the regular plan. On a crash basis larger equipment can be rented to reduce the completion time of excavating by one day to a crash time of 4 days with a total direct crash cost of $1300; the additional cost of shortening this activity's completion time is $300 per day reduced. Pouring the foundation (activity b) cannot be shortened. Next is outside plumbing (activity c) with an expected regular time of 6 days and a regular cost of $900. By having the plumbers work overtime, we can achieve an expected crash time of 4 days and a crash cost of $1300; the added cost comes from extra overtime pay, so that the crash program for outside plumbing costs $400 more and saves two days, and the daily cost of reducing that activity's completion time is $200. Altogether, the direct costs (nonmaterial) total $16,350 under the regular plans and $20,150 if all activities are crashed.

Constructing the Time-Cost Tradeoff Curve

The time-cost tradeoff curve can help the manager select a master plan for the project. To start, we consider the plan by which all activities are to be run on a regular basis, so that the first set of activity times in Table 16-4 apply. These times were used on the original PERT network, the final version of which is repeated in Figure 16-14. This plan has a completion time of 42 days and total direct costs of $16,350.

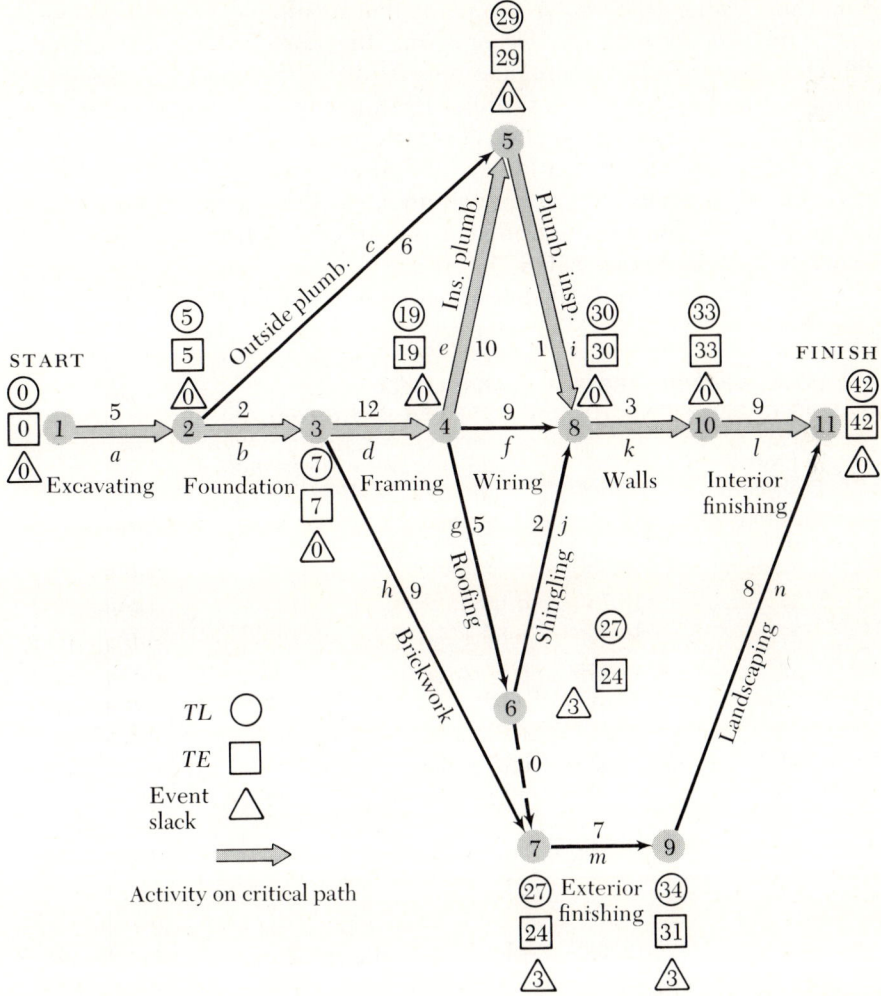

Figure 16-14
PERT network for the home-building example when all activities have regular expected completion times (Plan 1).

16-5   REPLANNING AND ADJUSTMENT WITH PERT

Since the duration of the project is dictated by the longest activity sequence through the PERT network, it can only be shortened by reducing the completion times of activities on the critical path. The initial plan has the critical path *a-b-d-e-i-k-l*. As long as the above path remains critical, any reduction in the expected completion time of one of the critical activities will reduce the project completion time by the same amount.

From the initial regular project plan, a succession of faster plans will be developed by crashing various activities in such a way that each new plan is the cheapest possible one for the indicated project completion time. Table 16-5 shows the plans that result.

The procedure starts by crashing the cheapest critical activity, which happens to be framing (activity *d*), since this increases the direct costs by the smallest amount (only $100 for each day saved). A maximum reduction of 4 days is possible. This faster plan yields a project completion time of 38 days with a larger total direct cost of $16,750.

The third plan is to crash activity *k* (walls), the next cheapest activity, at $125, for a reduction of 1 day in completion time. This plan takes 37 days and costs $16,875.

The cheapest critical activity remaining to be crashed is inside

Table 16-5
POTENTIAL HOME-BUILDING PROJECT PLANS, LISTED IN INCREASING ORDER OF ADDITIONAL COST PER DAY SAVED

Project Plan	Project Completion Time	Total Direct Cost	Last Activities Crashed	Additional Cost per Day Saved	Critical Paths
1	42 days	$16,350	none	—	*a-b-d-e-i-k-l*
2	38	16,750	*d* by 4 days	$100	*a-b-d-e-i-k-l*
3	37	16,875	*k* by 1 day	125	*a-b-d-e-i-k-l*
4	35	17,275	*e* by 2 days	200	*a-b-d-e-i-k-l*
					a-b-d-f-k-l
					a-b-d-g-m-n
5	34	17,525	*l* by 1 day	225	*a-b-d-e-i-k-l*
			n by 1 day	25	*a-b-d-f-k-l*
				250	*a-b-d-g-m-n*
6	33	17,825	*a* by 1 day	300	*a-b-d-e-i-k-l*
					a-b-d-f-k-l
					a-b-d-g-m-n
7	32	18,200	*e* by 1 day	200	*a-b-d-e-i-k-l*
			f by 1 day	150	*a-b-d-f-k-l*
			n by 1 day	25	*a-b-d-g-m-n*
				375	

plumbing (e), which costs $200 extra for each day's reduction. Although 3 days can be saved on inside plumbing itself by crashing it from 10 to 7 days, just 2 days of its reduced completion time will be felt by the project as a whole. Thus, the fourth plan incorporates a two-day reduction (a partial crash) in the expected completion time for activity e, to 8 days. This lowers the project time to 35 days, at a cost of $17,275. This plan, reflecting all the time changes made so far, has the PERT network in Figure 16-15. Notice that there are now three critical paths, each 35

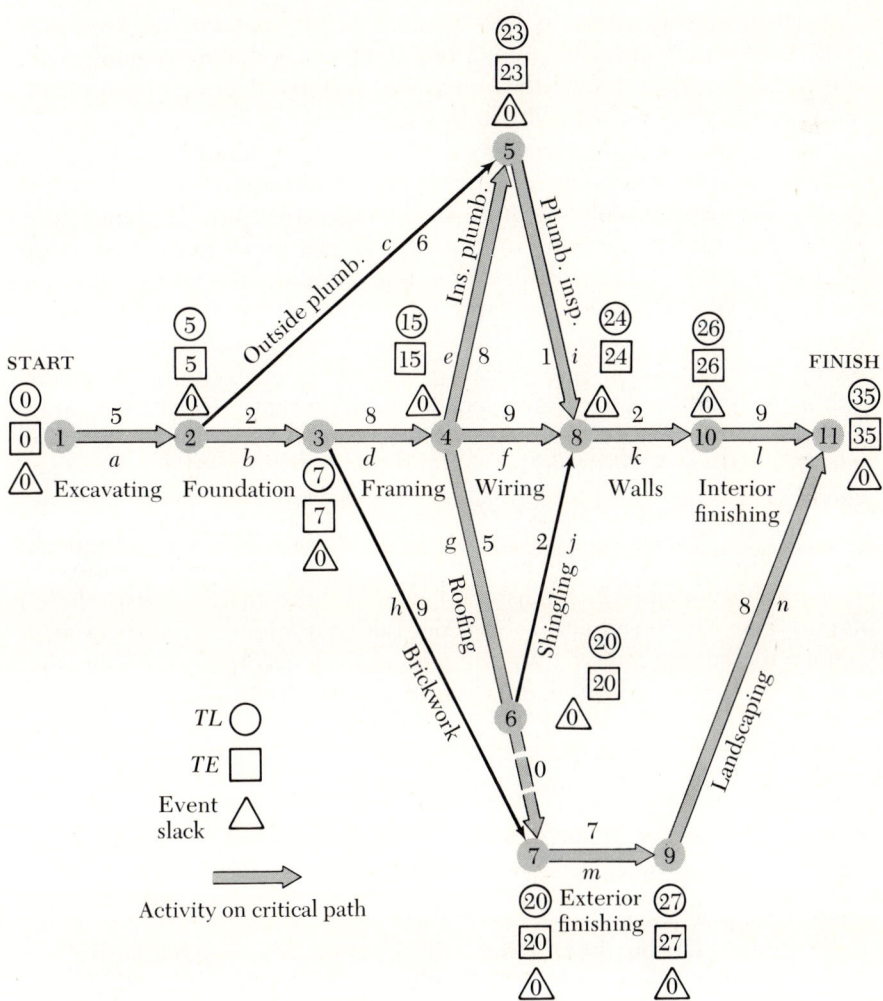

Figure 16-15
PERT network for Plan 4.

16-5 REPLANNING AND ADJUSTMENT WITH PERT

days long. (If inside plumbing were completely crashed all the way to 7 days, the project still would take 35 days, since that activity does not lie on two of these critical paths.)

The next time reduction is complicated by the several critical paths. The durations of all three must be reduced in order to shorten the project further. This might be accomplished in a variety of ways, but one of them is the cheapest. This is to crash interior finishing (*l*) and to partially crash landscaping (*n*), saving one day on each at a combined cost of $250. This fifth plan allows the project to be completed in 34 days at a cost of $17,525.

All three critical paths involve excavating (*a*). Crashing this activity is the next cheapest change, a one-day time reduction costing $300. The resulting plan (the sixth one) reduces the project completion time to 33 days and increases costs to $17,825.

The seventh plan must involve a one-day reduction for activity *e*, since that is the only one remaining in the original critical path that has not been completely crashed. In the other two critical paths, a one-day partial-crash reduction combination for activities *f* and *n* provides the least costly change. Altogether, these time reductions raise total direct costs by $375 to $18,200 and reduce project completion time to 32 days. The PERT network for this plan is provided in Figure 16-16. No further time reductions are possible, since every activity in the critical path *a-b-d-e-i-k-l* is completely crashed. Since that critical path cannot be shortened, further tampering with other crashable activities will only worsen costs with no compensating time savings for the project as a whole.

The time-cost tradeoff curve for the home construction project is provided in Figure 16-17. This provides the builder with a comprehensive summary of possible master plans and indicates the most efficient plan for successive reductions in time. For example, if there is some advantage in shaving 5 days from the regular project completion time, then plan 3 should be adopted if the gain outweighs the added cost. (In-between plans are possible, e.g., a two-day reduction in expected projection completion time by only partially crashing activity *d* by 2 days instead of the full 4 days possible.)

Updating the PERT Network

Once a plan has been established, schedules may be determined and the project can be started. PERT can still be used as the project progresses. The actual completion times of the early activities can deviate, perhaps considerably so, from the expected values identified at the outset. (This could be due to strikes, poor weather, or chance.) Or, the

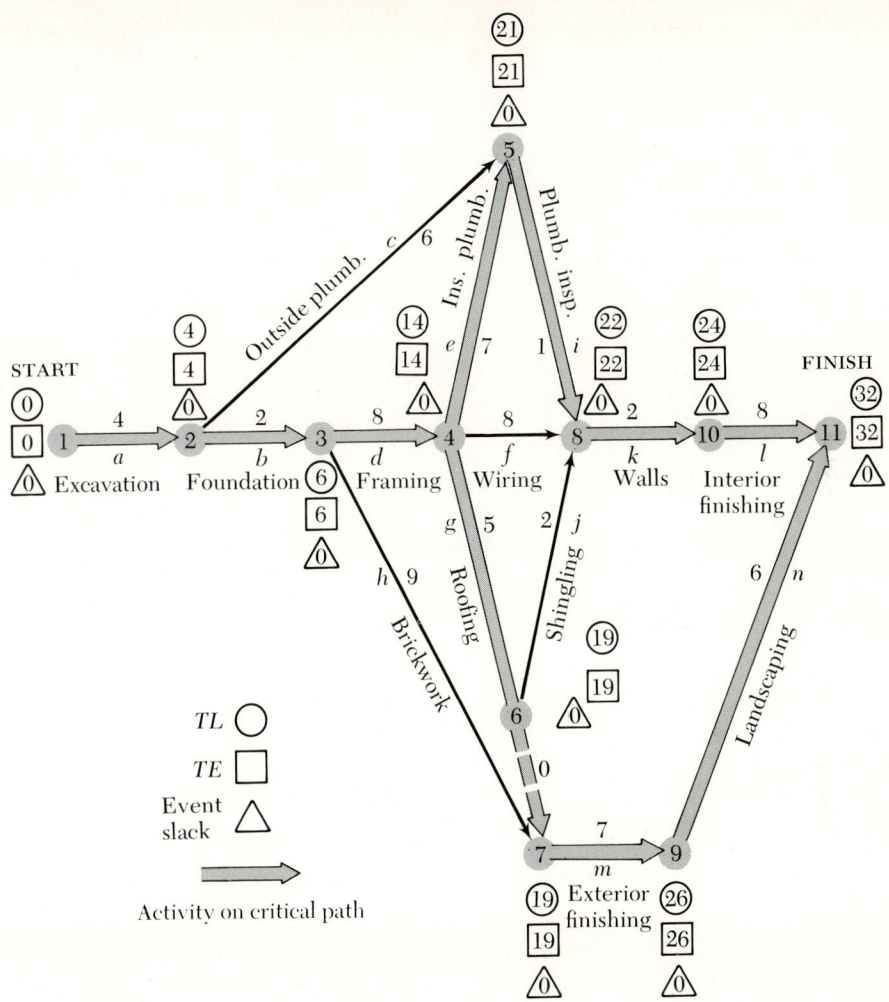

Figure 16-16
PERT network for Plan 7.

expected completion times for some future activities may have to be revised in the light of new information. Or, perhaps a subcontractor simply cannot start working on the scheduled date. Such discrepancies may necessitate revising the PERT network, for much of the earlier analysis would no longer be applicable. (For example, a delay of several days in completion of brickwork can effectively shift the critical path to a portion of the network never considered critical before.)

When the project is well underway, PERT procedures are the same

16-5   REPLANNING AND ADJUSTMENT WITH PERT

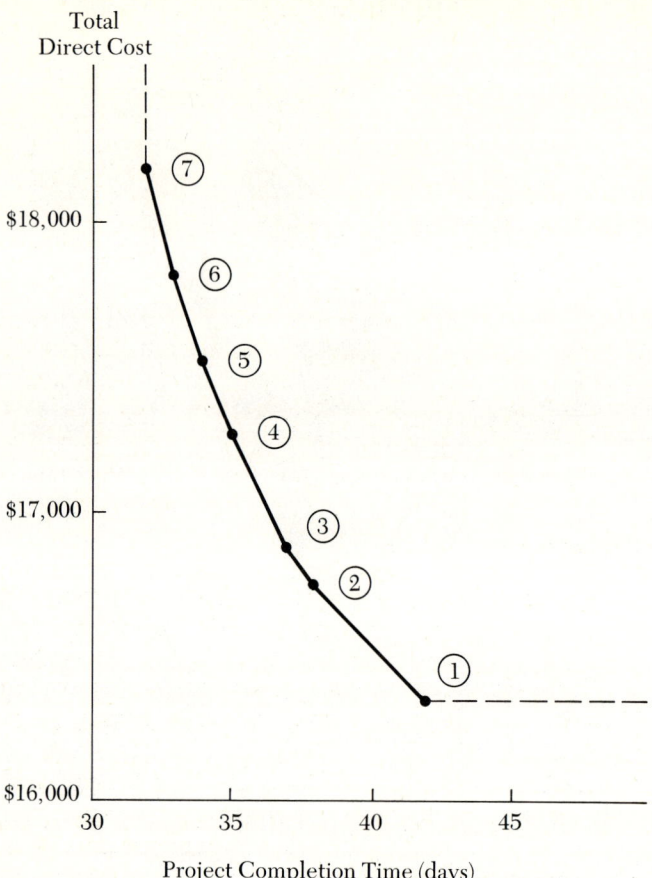

Figure 16-17
Time-cost tradeoff curve for the home-building illustration.

as before, except that completed activities will have actual rather than expected completion times. New time-cost tradeoffs can be made (completed activities, of course, cannot be changed), and a new master plan can be developed that involves revised schedules.

The ability to update PERT networks is especially important in long projects with considerable uncertainties, such as those encountered in weapon system development. Such projects can take more than five years to complete and often involve major technological breakthroughs. In such cases, all activities cannot even be identified in detail before the project starts. Initial PERT planning often begins with educated guesses about the specific tasks that will be required three or four years downstream. As planning becomes better, the PERT network can grow and be based on more sophisticated time estimates. As the PERT network is modified, revised schedules reflecting current planning can be periodically published.

CONCLUDING REMARKS   16-6

This chapter presents the essential concepts of PERT. In doing so, we have barely scratched the surface. For instance, we have not considered how to deal explicitly with the uncertainties about activity completion times nor how the expected values are obtained. The chapter appendix discusses a traditional procedure for probability analysis with PERT. Further treatment involving simulation is provided in Chapter 18.

Although PERT may not appear as such, its mathematical properties place it in an area of linear programming. Establishing *TE*s is a linear programming problem in which the objective is to minimize time. A whole class of linear programming problems involving flows in networks can be analyzed in a manner similar to the PERT network.

Large PERT systems are generally computerized. A variety of programs have been developed to perform various portions of the analysis. Often, these integrate PERT into the structure of broader management information systems. Precursor of these was the Defense Department's PERT/Cost system, which tied cost control and scheduling of activities. The success of that system was limited because of conflicts with contractors' internal accounting systems. In spite of problems with some of the systems associated with PERT, its time-minimization and scheduling aspects are generally accepted to be a very valuable management tool.

APPENDIX 16-1: TRADITIONAL PERT ANALYSIS WITH THREE TIME ESTIMATES*

The body of this chapter does not consider how expected activity completion times are arrived at. Although the techniques presented in Chapter 4 can be used for this purpose, traditional PERT analysis obtains them from a special procedure involving three time estimates:

$$a = \text{Optimistic time}$$
$$m = \text{Most likely time}$$
$$b = \text{Pessimistic time}$$

* Optional section.

These estimates are fairly easy for activity line managers to provide.

The optimistic time a is a value that the activity duration is almost certain of exceeding. Likewise, the actual completion time is almost certain of being below the pessimistic time b. The most likely time m is analogous to the mode in statistics. These three time estimates specify a particular continuous probability distribution that is a member of the *modified beta distribution* family. Such a distribution can be symmetrical or skewed (positively or negatively), depending on the relative positions of a, m, and b. Figure 16-18 shows the frequency curves for each case. The expected activity completion time for the activity may be computed from these three estimates by

$$t = \frac{a + 4m + b}{6}$$

The values calculated for the above may then be used in the main PERT analysis. It may also be useful to have the variance in completion time.

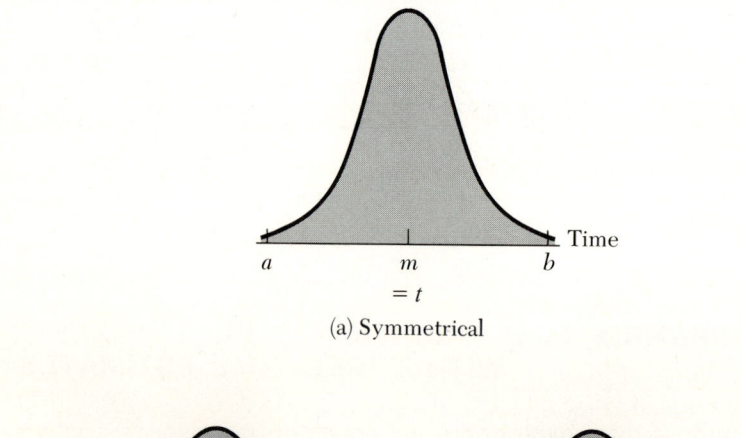

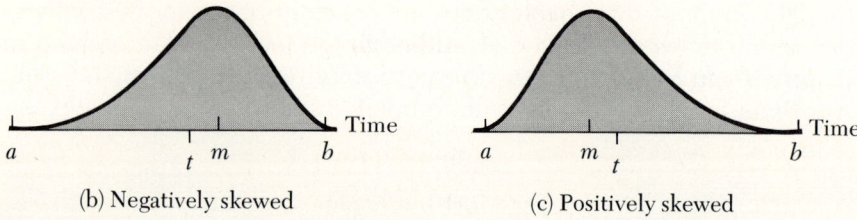

Figure 16-18
Three basic shapes of frequency curves for PERT modified beta distribution.

The variance may be computed from

$$\text{Variance} = \left(\frac{b-a}{6}\right)^2$$

Suppose that the expected regular activity completion times t for each activity used in the home-construction example had been obtained in this manner from the three-time estimate sets provided in Table 16-6.

Table 16-6
THREE TIME ESTIMATES USED TO COMPUTE EXPECTED VALUE AND VARIANCE OF ACTIVITY COMPLETION TIMES FOR HOME-BUILDING EXAMPLE

Activity	Optimistic Time a	Most Likely Time m	Pessimistic Time b	Expected Time $t = \dfrac{a + 4m + b}{6}$	Variance $\left(\dfrac{b-a}{6}\right)^2$
a	3	5	7	5	.444
b	1	1.5	5	2	.444
c	4	5	12	6	1.778
d	8	10	24	12	7.111
e	7	10	13	10	1.000
f	5	9.5	11	9	1.000
g	3.5	5	6.5	5	.250
h	6	8	16	9	2.778
i	1	1	1	1	0
j	1	2	3	2	.111
k	1.5	3.0	4.5	3	.250
l	7	9	11	9	.444
m	6	6.5	10	7	.444
n	5	7.5	13	8	1.778

Notice that possible times for each activity vary considerably. Thus, any of the various events in the PERT network could occur at a wide variety of points in time. The project completion time could be considerably shorter or longer than the 42 days found earlier.

As a result, the duration T of the original critical path a-b-d-e-i-k-l cannot be predicted precisely. We do know that its expected value, which we represent by μ, is the sum of the expected completion times for its component activities:

$$\mu = 5 + 2 + 12 + 10 + 1 + 3 + 9 = 42 \text{ days}$$

If we assume that the activity times are *independent,* we can closely approximate the complete probability distribution for length T of this particular path. Its variance σ^2 is then the sum of the variances of the individual completion times for the critical activities:

$$\sigma^2 = .444 + .444 + 7.111 + 1.000 + 0 + .250 + .444 = 9.693$$

And the standard deviation for T is

$$\sigma = \sqrt{9.693} = 3.11 \text{ days}$$

A general form of the central limit theorem discussed in Chapter 3 indicates that T is approximately normally distributed with mean μ and variance σ. Thus we can establish the probability that 50 days or less will be required to complete path a-b-d-e-i-k-l:

$$z = \frac{50 - 42}{3.11} = 2.57$$

$$P[T \leq 50] = .5 + .4949 = .9949$$

And we get the probability that it will take more than 40 days:

$$z = \frac{40 - 42}{3.11} = -.64$$

$$P[T > 40] = .5 + .2389 = .7389$$

There is one major fallacy in this analysis. *T is the duration for a particular path, not for the project itself.* This point has been widely misunderstood. There is a considerable chance that some path other than the one we identify as critical will actually take longer. Thus, $\mu = 42$ days is not really a measure of how long the *project* may be expected to take, and it can considerably understate the true value for the project's expected length.

A complete probability analysis of the project completion time is beyond the scope of this book. In Chapter 18, Monte Carlo simulation is used to estimate the mean project completion time.

APPENDIX 16-2: THE CPM NETWORK*

The PERT network in this chapter uses a different graphical representation than what is frequently used in some applications. The

* Optional section.

alternative portrayal is generally used in CPM (critical path method). *There each activity is represented by a circle.* The circles are connected with arrows in accordance with the required logical sequence, forming a network like the one in Figure 16-19 for the home-building example. The expected activity completion times appear inside the respective circle. (For convenience, circles are also used to represent the project's start and finish.)

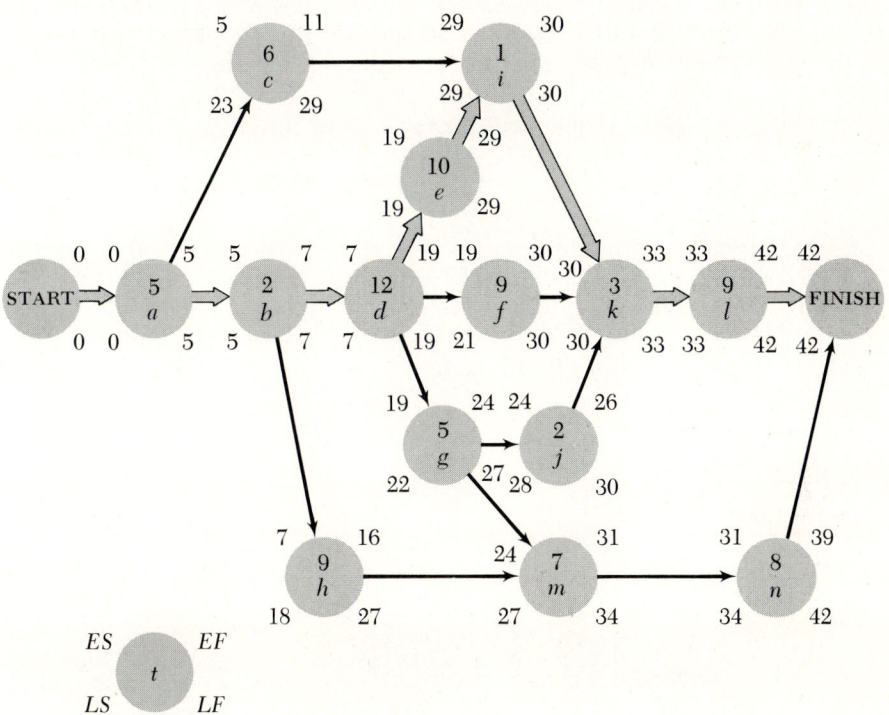

Figure 16-19

CPM network for the home-building example.

The critical path is located by a similar procedure. First, a forward pass is made to obtain the *ES* and *EF* values. A value of zero is used for the start; the *ES* is the largest *EF* of immediately preceding activities. An activity's *ES* value represents the longest path of activities that must be completed before it can start. The *LF* and *LS* values are found in a backward pass. The *LS* used to begin this process is equal to the *ES* for the finish; the *LF* is always the smallest *LS* of immediately succeeding activities. An activity's *LF* is the longest duration from its completion to finish. In doing the above, the relationships on the next page are used.

APPENDIX 16-2: THE CPM NETWORK

$$EF = ES + t$$
$$LS = LF - t$$
$$\text{Activity slack} = LF - EF = LS - ES$$

The critical path is one connecting zero-slack activities.

One distinct disadvantage of the CPM-type network is that it is clumsy for identifying events, which makes it less desirable for milestone scheduling. Each divergence or convergence of arrows corresponds to the standard PERT network event. Earliest possible and latest allowable event times may be obtained from the following:

$$TE = \text{Largest } EF \text{ for preceding activity}$$
$$TL = \text{Smallest } LS \text{ for succeeding activity}$$

Another disadvantage of the CPM-type network is that it is harder to identify activities for computer processing; in standard PERT each activity can be defined in terms of predecessor and successor events. The main advantage of the CPM network is that it is easier to graph than the PERT network because dummy activities are not required.

PROBLEMS

16-1 Find the critical path for the PERT network in Figure 16-20.

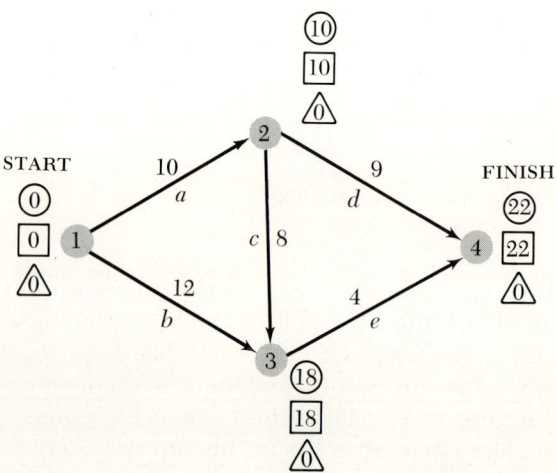

Figure 16-20

16-2 Copy the PERT network given in Figure 16-21 on a piece of paper.

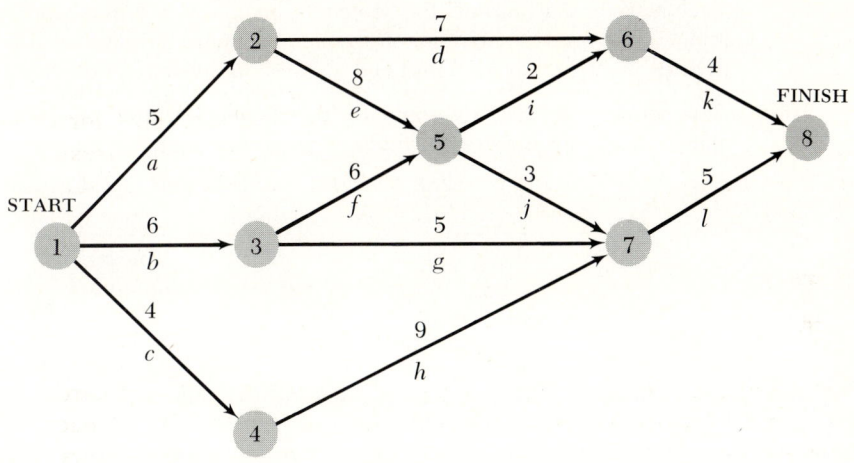

Figure 16-21

Then answer the following:
(a) Determine the TE, TL, and slack values for each event.
(b) Identify the critical path(s). What project duration is indicated?
(c) Find the ES, EF, LS, LF, and slack values for each activity.

16-3 Consider the following activity sequence for a project:

Activity	Activity Immediately Preceding	Expected Completion Time
a	—	2 days
b	—	3
c	—	2
d	b	4
e	a, b	3
f	b	2
g	f, c	5
h	g	4
i	f	3
j	i, d	2
k	j	1
l	e	6

Construct a PERT network and identify the critical path(s).

16-4 Consider the PERT network in Figure 16-20, where the expected completion times are in eight-hour working days. Assuming that the project will start at 8 AM on Monday, September 1, determine a set of mutually compatible schedule dates for starting and finishing each activity that permits the project to be completed in minimum time. (No work is to be done on weekends, ignore holidays, and activities must start at 8 AM and end on 5 PM on the scheduled dates.)

16-5 The following activities apply for the computerization of a company's accounting system, which is presently operated manually:

Activity	Expected Completion Time
(a) Select computer	2 months
(b) Assemble and install computer	6
(c) Design data input forms	2
(d) Design output report forms	2
(e) Write main processing programs	6
(f) Write input routines	4
(g) Write output routines	3
(h) Generate accounting data bank	3
(i) Test and revise system	2

All the program routines can be written independently before the computer is installed and can be debugged using computer time rented from another company. No programs or routines can be written until the particular computer model has been selected, although forms and reports can be designed while alternative computers are being evaluated. No input or output routines can be written until the corresponding forms have been designed. The main processing programs and input routines are required to establish the accounting data bank, which can be created on rental equipment. The final activity before implementation is complete is to test and revise the system.
(a) Construct a PERT network for converting the accounting system.
(b) What is the earliest time that the conversion can be finished, assuming that the above completion times are certain?
(c) Establish the early and late starting and finishing times for each activity. Which ones are critical?

16-6 Consider the PERT network in Figure 16-21. Suppose that the regular and crash data on page 481 apply.

	EXPECTED TIME		DIRECT COST	
ACTIVITY	Regular	Crash	Regular	Crash
a	5 days	4 days	$100	$ 120
b	6	4	200	260
c	4	4	300	300
d	7	5	500	580
e	8	6	700	800
f	6	5	500	560
g	5	5	400	400
h	9	8	950	1020
i	2	2	200	200
j	3	2	250	325
k	4	3	350	440
l	5	3	500	700

(a) Construct the time-cost tradeoff curve for this project. (*Hint:* before starting, make several copies of the PERT network with the activity times left off; use a new network for each plan found.)

(b) Suppose that the project manager values each day saved at $85. Which point on your curve would be optimal? What direct cost and project completion time applies?

16-7 In publishing a textbook, the following simplified sequence of activities applies:

Activity	Preceding Activity	Expected Completion Time
(a) Write book	—	12 months
(b) Design book	a	1
(c) Edit manuscript	a	6
(d) Check editing	c	2
(e) Accept design	b	1
(f) Copy edit	d, e	2
(g) Prepare artwork	d, e	4
(h) Accept and correct artwork	g	1/2
(i) Set galleys	f	4
(j) Check and correct galleys	i	1
(k) Pull page proofs	h, j	2
(l) Check and correct pages	k	1
(m) Prepare index	k	1
(n) Set and correct index	m	1/2
(o) Check camera-ready copy	l, n	1/2
(p) Print and bind book	o	1

(a) Construct the PERT network and determine the critical path. How long should the project take from start to finish?
(b) It is possible through good management to produce such a book in 18 months or less without crashing any activities. This contradicts the findings in part (a). Discuss each of the following.
  (1) Suggest how publishers get the job done so quickly.
  (2) Does this mean that PERT is not applicable to book publishing?
  (3) Publishers usually require an author's complete manuscript before doing any work themselves. In light of your answer to (2), suggest how PERT might be used to shorten the publication time of a book even further.

16-8 *Probability Analysis.* Consider the PERT network in Figure 16-22.

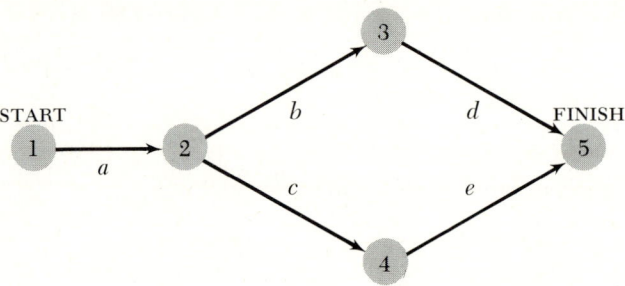

Figure 16-22

Suppose that the following probabilities (in parentheses) apply for the completion times of the various activities:

a	b	c	d	e
8 (1)	5 (1/2)	2 (1/2)	5 (1/4)	8 (3/4)
	6 (1/2)	3 (1/2)	6 (3/4)	9 (1/4)

(a) Use the above data to compute the expected activity completion times. Then determine the critical path and its duration based upon expected values.
(b) What actual durations are possible for the path found above? Assuming activity times are independent events, find the probability for each duration.
(c) Repeat part (b) for the other (noncritical) path.
(d) Using your answers to parts (b) and (c), use the multiplication law to find the joint probability table for the durations of the two paths.

(e) From your joint probability table, identify those situations in which the so-called critical path is actually of shorter duration than the other path. What is the probability that any one of these situations occur?

(f) Using your joint probability table, determine the probability distribution for the length of the longest paths(s) from START to FINISH. This distribution represents the *project* completion time. What is the expected value for this? Is this the same as the duration found in part (a)? Explain.

*16-9 *PERT with Three Time Estimates.* Consider a small project with the following activities:

ACTIVITY	PRECEDING ACTIVITY	COMPLETION TIMES (*days*)		
		Optimistic	Most Likely	Pessimistic
a	—	5	6	7
b	—	4	5	18
c	a	4	15	20
d	b, c	3	4	5
e	a	16	17	18

(a) Determine the expected value and variance for each activity's completion time.
(b) Find the critical path using the expected times from (a).
(c) Assuming that the normal distribution applies, find the probability that the critical path takes between 18 and 26 days to complete.

* Problem marked with an asterisk involves material in Appendix 16-1 to the chapter.

Seventeen

Waiting Lines (Queues)

Quantitative methods have been very successful when applied to waiting line situations. Although it may not seem that anyone cares how long you have to wait in line to cash a check or to buy groceries, most businesses pay a great deal of attention to customer waiting times. Many large retail establishments have actually been designed to achieve an optimal balance between customer inconvenience and operational efficiency. This explains why a supermarket may have 10 checkout stands, even though only two or three are operated most of the time; during Saturday afternoon rush hours, they may all be open. Retailers dare not make their customers wait in line for very long, because in today's world people value their time highly and would rather switch to competing stores than wait for a few extra minutes.

In management science or operations research, a waiting line is called a *queue*. As a field of study, *queuing theory* is one of the richest areas of operations research methodology. The number of models representing specific situations has grown steadily over the years, and new ones are being reported even now. Queuing theory is one of the earliest quantitative methods with its origins in a 1909 paper by a Danish telephone engineer, A. K. Erlang. His name is associated with a large class of probability distributions used with mathematical queuing models. Since then, thousands of articles and numerous books have been written on the subject.

The usual objective of a queuing model is to determine how to provide service to customers in such a way that an efficient operation is achieved. Unlike the inventory or linear programming models encountered earlier in this book, a minimum cost or maximum profit solution is not always sought. Rather, the models aim to find various characteristics of the queuing system, such as the mean waiting time and the mean length of the waiting line. These might then be used in a later cost analysis. Often a targeted level of satisfactory customer service is established instead, and facilities and operations are planned to meet this goal.

To the uninitiated, it may seem that any line is a sign of inefficiency, and that good management should eliminate this nuisance entirely. This viewpoint probably comes from the fact that we are all somebody's customers, but relatively few of us have operated public establishments. If we reflect on this problem, we realize that eliminating waiting lines entirely would be prohibitively costly for banks, stores, or gas stations. The main reason we have to wait in line at the bank is that customers arrive unpredictably (sometimes creating congestion) and seek a variety of services, each of which requires varying amounts of the teller's time. Several times the usual number of tellers might be required to completely eliminate waiting lines, and many tellers would then be idle almost all the time. No bank has fewer tellers than are needed to service its customers within a reasonable time span, and these employees still spend many idle minutes. We never remember the days when we didn't have to wait in a line at all!

BASIC QUEUING SITUATIONS 17-1

All queuing situations involve the arrivals of customers at a *service facility*, where some time may be spent waiting for and then receiving the desired service. Ordinarily we think of customers as persons, but customers may also be things, such as cars being repaired in a garage, unfinished items proceeding to the next stage of production, aircraft waiting to land, or jobs being processed on a computer. A service facility can be a single person—such as a barber or a hairdresser—or several persons, a surgical team, for example. It can also be a machine that dispenses candy bars, stamps parts, or processes data, or a complex entity, such as an airport runway or an oil refinery port facility.

Structures of Queuing Systems

The simplest queuing system involves a single-service facility that takes one customer at a time; any customer arriving while an earlier one is being serviced must wait in line. Such a system may be represented schematically as shown in Figure 17-1.

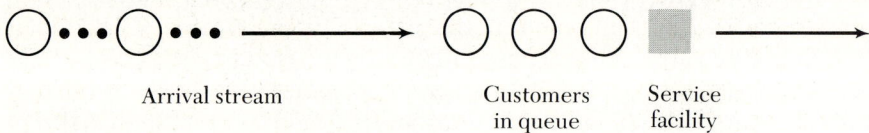

Figure 17-1
Schematic for a single-server single-stage queue.

In a *single-server single-stage queue* all the required services are performed before each customer leaves. The waiting line itself need not be a physical string of customers, as would form at a theater ticket window. It can merely be some identifiable grouping of customers whose sequence of service may or may not be designated (perhaps by a number—often used in a retail store in which physical lines are inconvenient). The customers do not even have to be commingled physically; for example, several inquiries (customers) might stack up in a central computer system, even though they are placed from remote terminals scattered across a huge geographical expanse; or, planes attempting to land at New York might be spread over tens of thousands of square miles of air space.

Somewhat more complicated is the system portrayed in Figure 17-2,

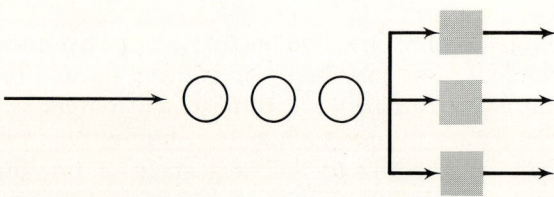

Figure 17-2
Schematic for a multiple-server single-stage queue.

which is a *multiple-server single-stage queue* with several service facilities. In the simplest case, each facility provides identical service, a single waiting line forms, and the leading customer proceeds to the first free server. Such a system is used at many banks, where a single line feeds customers to the teller windows. Slightly different characteristics apply to the old-fashioned scheme, where arriving customers must pick one teller window and wait in separate lines; this is still the case when checking out of a large self-service market.

Another way of viewing queues is in terms of the number of service points or stages a customer must pass through before leaving the system. The simplest of these is represented by the *single-server multiple-stage queue* shown in Figure 17-3.

Figure 17-3
Schematic for a single-server multiple-stage queue.

Before leaving the system, each customer must receive two or more kinds of service. This situation can arise when buying a bulky item, such as a tent, at a department store: first you must wait for a clerk to begin processing your order; second, the clerk checks out your credit by telephoning a central office, which may also have to run quick credit checks for several other customers; finally, a third queue may form in picking up your tent at the loading dock. Such a queue might also apply in manufacturing where semi-finished items await further processing at various stages of production.

Most complex of all is the *multiple-server multiple-stage queue* shown in Figure 17-4.

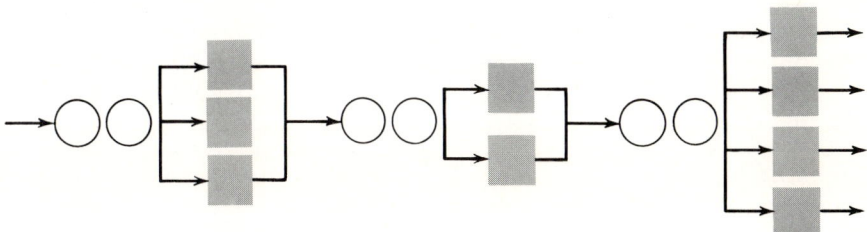

Figure 17-4
Schematic for a multiple-server multiple-stage queue.

17-1 BASIC QUEUING SITUATIONS

Such a system might apply when getting a driver's license: you line up at one of several windows to pay the fee and receive a written test; then you take the exam and wait to get it graded; next, an eye check is made; this is followed perhaps by a behind-the-wheel test administered by one of several possible examiners; finally, you may then wait again to be photographed and to obtain a temporary license.

Queue Disciplines

An important aspect of any queuing situation is the *order* in which customers receive service. We refer to the manner of customer sequencing as the *queue discipline*. The mathematical models developed for essentially the same queuing structure can differ depending on the discipline that applies.

The most common queue discipline is a physical FIFO (first in, first out) scheme where the customers receive service in an order identical to their arrival. Retail establishments and public service agencies usually follow this pattern. Indeed, FIFO has become almost a basic human right—like freedom of speech. In our generally calm modern society, few actions evoke as strong emotions as line cutting.* Many successful establishments rigidly enforce FIFO by issuing numbers to arriving customers. All the queuing models discussed in this book assume that FIFO applies.

Much less common is the LIFO (last in, first out) discipline. There are obvious circumstances, such as using elevators, where LIFO might apply. In most cargo handling situations, the last item in is the first one removed. The queuing aspects of these situations are not of great interest. But one very interesting application of the LIFO discipline has been reported.

> Steel ingots arrive at a rolling-mill from open-hearth shops. They are still hot, but there are still temperature gradients within them. They must therefore be placed in reheating-furnaces ("soaking-pits") before being rolled into slabs or billets, as a more even heat-distribution and a higher temperature are required by the rolling operation. If the soaking-pits are full when the ingots arrive, they must wait. . . . While they wait, they become cooler. The longer they wait, the longer they must eventually remain in the soaking pits.†

To minimize energy costs, the last (hottest) ingot in line should be the first one put in the soaking pits, so that the LIFO discipline applies.

---

* Prior to Christmas, 1973, a man was killed in an altercation that resulted when a family crowded into a line of people waiting to see Santa Claus.
† Lee, A. M. *Applied Queuing Theory* (New York: St. Martin's Press, 1966), p. 16.

Another interesting queue discipline is SIRO (service in random order). A theater refreshment counter during intermission is one of the most exasperating examples of SIRO. Perhaps the most important waiting-line situation involving SIRO occurs at a telephone switchboard. The telephone call that arrives just after a free line is open is the one that gets placed. We may view the waiting line as being comprised of all calls that have encountered the "busy" signal; however, no record has been kept of these calls, so there is no way to determine which was first, and the only way for a call to get through is for it to be redialed. The order of service may thus be considered random. Modern telephone equipment has recently been introduced that places all calls on hold until they can be placed; in such systems the FIFO discipline is generally used.

A variety of other queue disciplines exist. Situations where certain customers have *priority* over others are very common. In a hospital emergency room, for example, patients with the more serious problems are seen earliest. Computer systems often work by priorities, so that the highest priority jobs are processed before all others, regardless of waiting times (and in elaborate systems, jobs may be automatically bumped into successively higher priorities the longer they wait). *Pre-emptive priority* queues arise when service on a lower priority customer is interrupted when a higher priority one arrives. An example is the flat tire job at a service station; the attendant stops working on the tire when a higher priority gasoline customer arrives. Numerous other special queue disciplines have been studied.

Arrival and Service Patterns

The *patterns of arrivals and service* are very important aspects of waiting-line situations. Typically, customers arrive at the system randomly. Various probability distributions may be used to represent the time between arrivals; the most common one is the *exponential distribution*, described later in this chapter. Service time also usually varies (although it may be *constant*), and a variety of probability distributions have been used to characterize it. Queuing models can differ considerably for various combinations of arrival and service patterns.

Queuing models usually assume that customers arrive singly, although some allow for batching of arrivals. The latter might apply when a cross-country bus stops at a roadside restaurant. Most models assume that the same interarrival time distribution applies for all customers throughout the period studied. Obviously, this cannot always be true, as busy periods arise in nearly all waiting-line situations. Thus, a particular model may be appropriate only during peak hours, and another needed for slack periods. Usually the service pattern is presumed to be independent of how customers arrive, which may not be strictly true for some types of service facilities. For example, a supermarket checker may work faster when several persons are waiting than when no one is.

17-2 EXPONENTIAL AND POISSON DISTRIBUTIONS

The most commonly used probability distribution for interarrival times is the exponential distribution, which historically closely fits actual observed data for many queuing systems. The assumptions underlying this distribution are very simple. The central consideration is that *the exponential distribution applies in situations in which events occur randomly over time.* As an illustration, consider cars arriving at a toll collection station. Figure 17-5 illustrates this concept. Each dot represents a car and is positioned so that its horizontal distance from the origin (at 9:00 AM) indicates when it arrives at the station. Such a graph could be constructed from an aerial photograph taken at 9:00 AM of the two miles of highway leading to the station; assuming that all cars are traveling at the speed limit, we could directly translate each car's distance from the station into its arrival time. Notice that the dots in Figure 17-5 are scattered across the page with no apparent pattern, as if placed there randomly.

The Poisson Process

Even though the cars arrive randomly over time, much detailed information can be gleaned from one key characteristic of the arrival stream (of which our graph is but a small sample). Seemingly without pattern, such an arrival stream is an example of a *Poisson process,* named after the eighteenth-century mathematician and physicist Siméon Poisson. And it is the randomness of this pattern that provides the basis for the information it yields. What distinguishes one arrival stream from

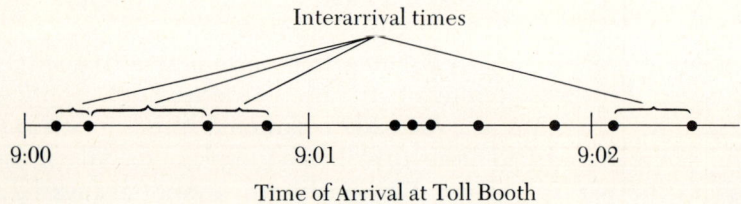

Figure 17-5
Times for random arrivals of cars at a toll booth.

another—and the only thing that can make any two Poisson processes differ—is the *mean arrival rate;* this parameter, denoted by λ (lambda), tells us the mean number of arrivals occurring per minute (or some other unit of time, such as a second or hour). A busy toll station may experience an arrival rate of $\lambda = 100$ cars per minute, whereas an out-of-the-way place may register a rate of $\lambda = 1/2$ cars per minute.

A Poisson process must meet the following conditions:

(1) A Poisson process has *no memory.* That is, the number of events occurring in one interval of time is *independent* of what happened in previous time periods.

(2) The process rate λ *must remain constant* for the entire duration considered.

(3) It is extremely *rare* for more than one event to occur in a small interval of time; the shorter the duration of the interval, the rarer the occurrence of two or more events becomes. And the probability for exactly one event occurring in such an interval is approximately λ times its duration.

The Poisson process provides two very important probability distributions. The most important one in queuing applications is the *exponential distribution,* which provides probabilities for the times between arrivals and, because time is the random variable, is *continuous* (like the normal distribution). The second distribution is the *Poisson distribution,* which provides probabilities for the number of arrivals in any specific interval of time. The Poisson distribution is *discrete* (like the binomial distribution), since the number of cars arriving in any particular minute must be a whole number. As we shall see, *both the exponential and Poisson distributions express the same process in different ways.*

The Exponential Distribution

The gaps between the dots in Figure 17-5 represent the interarrival times, or times between successive arrivals of cars. The exponential distribution is concerned with the size of the gap, measured in time units, separating successive cars. Although the dots are scattered randomly over time, the relative frequency of interarrival times of various sizes is predictable. Suppose that the cars arriving at the toll station were observed for several minutes, and that the time of each car's arrival was noted. Those data would provide a histogram similar to the one in Figure 17-6(a). This approximates the shape of the underlying frequency curve in Figure 17-6(b), the height of which may be determined for any

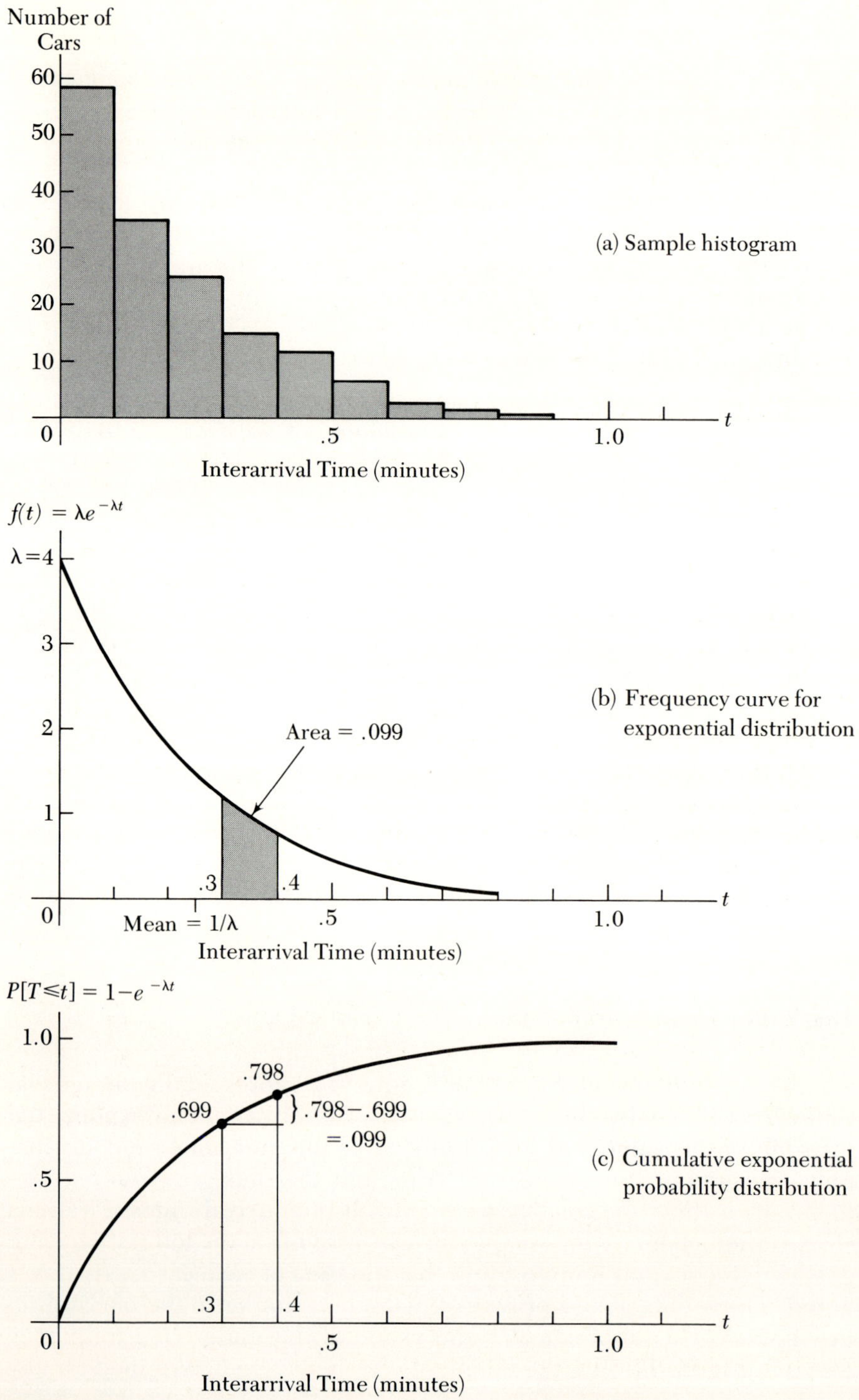

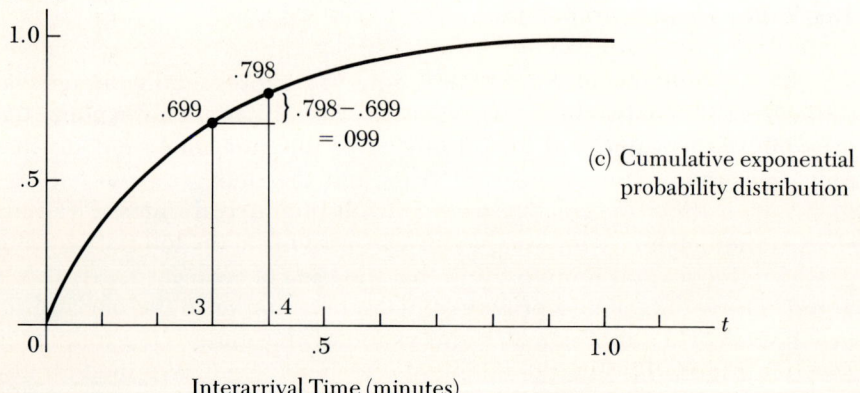

Figure 17-6
Exponential distribution for interarrival times of cars at a toll station.

interarrival time t from

$$f(t) = \lambda e^{-\lambda t}$$

The above expression is the probability density function for the exponential distribution and is based upon the constant e, which serves as the base for natural logarithms (and equals 2.7183). The particular distribution applicable to a specific situation depends only on the level of λ. In our toll-station illustration, a mean arrival rate of $\lambda = 4$ cars per minute applies. Notice that the frequency curve intersects the vertical axis at height λ. The mean and standard deviation of the exponential distribution are identical and may be expressed in terms of λ as

$$\text{Mean} = 1/\lambda$$

$$\text{Standard deviation} = 1/\lambda$$

Notice that the mean time between arrivals is the reciprocal of the mean rate of arrivals. Thus if $\lambda = 4$ *cars per minute*, then the mean time between arrivals is $1/\lambda = 1/4 = .25$ *minutes per car*. Another feature of the exponential distribution is that *shorter durations are more likely than longer ones;* notice that the curve in Figure 17-6(b) decreases in height and the slope becomes less pronounced as t becomes larger. The tail of the exponential curve, like the tails of the normal curve, never touches the horizontal axis, indicating that there is no limit on how large the interarrival time t might conceivably be.

Like those for the normal curve, probabilities for the exponential random variable may be found by determining the area under the frequency curve. The cumulative probability that the time T between two successive arrivals is t or less may be obtained from

$$P[T \leq t] = 1 - e^{-\lambda t}$$

Figure 17-6(c) shows the cumulative probability graph applicable when $\lambda = 4$. Appendix Table D may be used to find values for $e^{-\lambda t}$.

For example, using $\lambda = 4$ cars per minute, we find that the probability that the interarrival time between any two cars is less than or equal to $t = .4$ minutes is (rounded to three places)

$$P[T \leq .4] = 1 - e^{-4(.4)} = 1 - e^{-1.6}$$

$$= 1 - .202$$

$$= .798$$

And the probability that this time is $t = .3$ minutes or less is

$$P[T \le .3] = 1 - e^{-4(.3)} = 1 - e^{-1.2}$$
$$= 1 - .301$$
$$= .699$$

The probability that an interarrival time between .3 and .4 minutes will be achieved is, thus,

$$P[.3 \le T \le .4] = .798 - .699$$
$$= .099$$

The above value is the area under the exponential frequency curve in Figure 17-6(b) between times of .3 and .4 minutes.

The Poisson Distribution

The Poisson distribution expresses probabilities for the number of arrivals in any given time period, such as the one minute between 9:08 and 9:09, the five minutes from 9:09 through 9:14, or the hour between 10 AM and 11 AM. Representing the actual number of arrivals in a period of duration t by the letter X, we may compute the probability that this is equal to one of the possible levels x from

$$P[X = x] = \frac{e^{-\lambda t}(\lambda t)^x}{x!}$$

where $\qquad x = 0, 1, 2, \ldots$

Continuing with our illustration, consider any 1-minute interval, so that $t = 1$ minute. Again, using $\lambda = 4$ cars per minute, we find that $\lambda t = 4$ cars. Appendix Table D provides $e^{-4} = .018316$. The probability that exactly 2 cars will arrive is

$$P[X = 2] = \frac{e^{-4}(4)^2}{2!}$$
$$= \frac{.018316(4)^2}{2}$$
$$= .1465$$

Probability values for other numbers of cars have been calculated in Table 17-1. Notice that for arrivals between 0 and 14 these values sum only to .9999, reflecting the fact that the number of arrivals might be

Table 17-1
POISSON PROBABILITY DISTRIBUTION FOR NUMBER OF ARRIVALS IN ONE MINUTE ($\lambda = 4, t = 1$)

Number of Arrivals x	Probability $P[X = x]$
0	.0183
1	.0733
2	.1465
3	.1953
4	.1953
5	.1563
6	.1042
7	.0596
8	.0297
9	.0133
10	.0053
11	.0019
12	.0006
13	.0002
14	.0001
	.9999

15, 16, or larger, but these unlisted quantities have tiny probabilities that round to zero at four decimal places. Indeed, the Poisson distribution assigns some small probability to any integer value, no matter how large.

The Poisson is completely specified by the process rate λ and the duration t. Its mean and variance are identical and expressed in terms of the parameters

$$\text{Mean} = \lambda t$$

$$\text{Variance} = \lambda t$$

(Here the mean is equal to the variance, not the standard deviation.) In the above example $\lambda = 4$ cars are expected to arrive in any given minute, and the variance in the number of arrivals is also 4. And, because results for any two time periods are independent, the number of arrivals in any minute has no affect on the probabilities for arrivals in the next one. Thus, if 14 or more cars arrive between 9:05 and 9:06, a rare event when $\lambda = 4$, the probability is unchanged for the reoccurrence of that event between 9:06 and 9:07.

17-2 EXPONENTIAL AND POISSON DISTRIBUTIONS

Using Poisson Probability Tables

Like the binomial probabilities, hand computation of Poisson probabilities can be an onerous chore. Cumulative values of these are computed for levels of λt ranging from 1 to 20 in Appendix Table E. As with the binomial, a table of individual probability terms is not provided, because they may be obtained easily from the respective cumulative values.

The table provides values $P[X \leq x]$. For example, to find the cumulative probability values for the number of cars arriving at a toll booth during an interval $t = 10$ minutes, when the arrival rate is $\lambda = 2$ per minute, we look in Table E on the page where $\lambda t = 2(10) = 20$.

The probability that the number of arriving cars is less than or equal to 15 is

$$P[X \leq 15] = .1565$$

whereas the probability that 20 or fewer cars arrive during the 10 minutes is

$$P[X \leq 20] = .5591$$

As with the cumulative binomial tables discussed in Chapter 3, it is possible to obtain the individual term, the greater than, the less than, the greater than or equal to, and the interval Poisson probability values by using Table E.

For example, to find $P[X = x]$, we must determine the difference

$$P[X = x] = P[X \leq x] - P[X \leq x - 1]$$

Thus, the probability that exactly 15 cars arrive in 10 minutes is

$$P[X = 15] = P[X \leq 15] - P[X \leq 14] = .1565 - .1049 = .0516$$

In a like manner, we may obtain the probability that the number of cars arriving lies between x_1 and x_2 from the difference

$$P[x_1 \leq X \leq x_2] = P[X \leq x_2] - P[X \leq x_1 - 1]$$

Thus, the probability that between 16 and 20 cars arrive is

$$P[16 \leq X \leq 20] = P[X \leq 20] - P[X \leq 15] = .5591 - .1565 = .4026$$

To find the greater than or the greater than or equal to probability values, we use the facts that

$$P[X > x] = 1 - P[X \leq x]$$

and

$$P[X \geq x] = 1 - P[X \leq x - 1]$$

For our toll booth illustration,

$$P[X > 20] = 1 - P[X \leq 20] = 1 - .5591 = .4409$$

and

$$P[X \geq 20] = 1 - P[X \leq 19] = 1 - .4703 = .5297$$

Likewise, we may determine the probability that the number of arrivals is less than some amount by utilizing the fact that

$$P[X < x] = P[X \leq x - 1]$$

and, thus,

$$P[X < 16] = P[X \leq 15] = .1565$$

Other Instances of Poisson Processes

The Poisson process is used in queuing analysis mainly for arrivals. As we shall see, it may also be used to represent the completions of customer service when the server is busy. A multitude of other applications exist apart from queuing. The Poisson distribution may be used to represent demands in an inventory situation. The exponential distribution might also apply to times between failures in equipment, so that it may be used in reliability analysis for alternative engineering designs. A Poisson process may be appropriate in some rather bizarre instances; it historically fits well to the number of U.S. Supreme Court vacancies in any year, the deaths of Prussian recruits kicked by horses, and freeze-ups of Lake Zurich.

Although our present application of the Poisson process treats events occurring randomly over *time,* the respective probability distributions may apply when time is not a factor. It may be an appropriate characterization of events occurring in *space* as well. If we consider as events the finding of objects spread randomly over a space, such as misspelled names in a telephone directory, then encountering objects while the space (in this case, pages of the directory) is searched may also be viewed as a Poisson process. This particular application has proven fruitful in quality control and in such esoteric areas as developing search techniques for radar, establishing tactics for ships transiting minefields, and hunting for submarines. Here λ would represent the mean number of events per unit distance (e.g., inch), area (e.g., square mile), or space (e.g., cubic centimeter). More generally, λ may be the mean number of events of a particular kind per observation made of the phenomena in question. Thus λ may be 3 errors per page or it may be 5 bad debts per 1000 installment contracts. The "durations" would be analogous: the space searched, the number of pages scanned, the number of contracts written, etc.

Practical Limitations of the Poisson Process

A very serious mistake in applying one of the distributions associated with the Poisson process is to assume that the mean event occurrence rate λ holds over an extended duration, when it does not. Many queuing situations involve random arrivals whose rate changes with the time of day, day of the week, season of the year, or other circumstances. The mean rate of vehicle arrivals at a metropolitan toll plaza will differ at 9 AM from that at 3 AM; it will differ on Fridays from that on Mondays; and it will be greater in the fall than in the summer, when many drivers are on vacation. It is still proper to treat a variety of such situations as a Poisson process, but care must be taken to keep the durations considered short and to apply the appropriate value of λ. Thus a bank may find it best to keep only a third of its teller windows open at 10:30 AM on Tuesday, when λ is small, but it will probably be optimal to open them all when transaction traffic proves heaviest, say, 5 PM on a Friday.

17-3 SINGLE-SERVER QUEUING MODEL WITH EXPONENTIAL SERVICE TIMES

Basic queuing models are concerned with the state of the system. Under various assumptions regarding the queue discipline and service, a probability distribution may be obtained for the number of customers in the system (either waiting or receiving service) at any future point in time. This probability information can then be used to derive certain useful results mathematically, such as the amount of time a customer can expect to wait in line.

Our initial queuing model considers the single-server single-stage system. We assume that "first come, first served," so the FIFO discipline applies. Arrivals are assumed to be a Poisson process, which means that the arrivals are events that occur randomly over time and meet the other necessary conditions of that process; thus, the interarrival times have an exponential distribution and the number of customers arriving in any specified time interval has a Poisson distribution. Because of the resulting mathematical convenience, our basic model assumes further that *the service times are exponentially distributed.* The *mean service rate* (customers per minute, second, or hour) is represented by the symbol μ (mu). It follows that the mean service time is $1/\mu$. We further assume that *the mean service rate must exceed the mean arrival rate,* $\mu > \lambda$, so that the queuing system must have more than enough capacity to service all customers. (Without this last restriction, a queuing system would be unstable and the waiting line will grow indefinitely.)

Some Important Queuing Results

The queuing model provides the following important results:

(1) *Probability distribution for number of customers in the system.* This distribution is the basis for establishing all the other results listed below. It can also be useful in designing facilities that can physically hold waiting customers.

(2) *Mean number of customers in the system.* This quantity accounts for the number of customers either waiting in line or receiving service. It is useful primarily as an intermediate device for finding the mean customer time spent in the system.

(3) *Mean customer time in the system.* This is an average figure for the total time spent by a customer in the system. When a cost can be associated with each unit of a customer's time, it may be used in making economic comparisons of alternative queuing systems.

(4) *Mean length of the waiting line.* This quantity is similar to the mean number of customers in the system, but only involves those customers actually waiting in line (and not being serviced). It is often useful to know the average number of customers waiting in line. This can help establish the size of holding facilities (e.g., the size of hospital waiting rooms). It is also used in an intermediate step to establish the mean customer waiting time.

(5) *Mean customer waiting time.* This provides an average value that may be used to evaluate the quality of service. Like the mean customer time in the system, this quantity may sometimes be used in economic analysis, but it is unsatisfactory for this purpose if alternative queuing systems involve different service time distributions.

(6) *Server utilization factor.* This is the proportion of time that the server actually spends with customers—the time during which the server is busy. It establishes the expected amount of server idle time that can be devoted to secondary tasks not directly involved with service.

Although discussion of them is beyond the scope of this book, other important results, such as complete probability distributions for a customer's waiting time and the duration of the server's busy period may be obtained from queuing models.

Basic Queuing Formulas

Although many of the mathematical details are beyond the scope of this book, algebraic expressions have been derived for each of the above results. For the present model, all the results are expressed in terms of two parameters:

$$\lambda = \text{Mean customer arrival rate}$$

$$\mu = \text{Mean service rate}$$

We begin with the probability distribution for the number of customers in the system. This distribution may be found by considering each possible number of customers, either waiting or receiving service, as a distinct *state* that can be entered by arrival of a new customer or completion of service on the leading customer. The schematic representation in Figure 17-7 will help to explain this process.

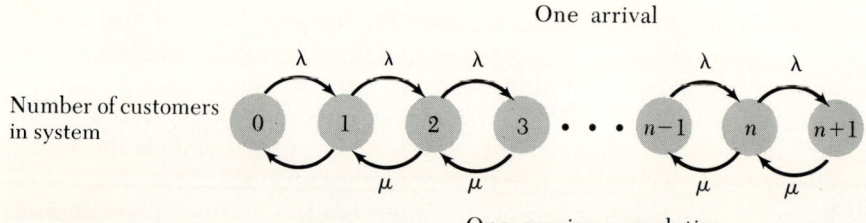

Figure 17-7
Schematic of single-server queuing system states.

Consider a barbershop with a single barber. There are two ways in which it can end up with exactly one customer: it may first have no customers and then a new one arrives; or it may have had two customers, with service completed on the first one. These two cases are represented by the two arrows pointing to 1: at the top leaving 0 and at the bottom leaving 2. Likewise, the barbershop may leave the one-customer state either by the arrival of a new customer or by finishing with the present one. Again, these possibilities are shown as two arrows leaving 1, the top one pointing to 2 and the bottom one to 0. This same feature is exhibited for any number of customers n in the system. Alongside each arrow, the mean rate is indicated for the possible change in state: λ for an arrival and μ for a departure.

For any given instant of time, we define

$$P_n = P[n \text{ customers in system}]$$

Under the assumptions of exponentially distributed arrival and service times, the probability of leaving a state must equal the probability of entering that state, and, in short time intervals, movement is possible only between neighboring states (two to three customers, five to four, six to seven, etc.). For any state except 0, there are two ways to enter and two ways to leave, depending on the preceding number of customers and whether a departure or an arrival occurs first. The probability of one movement (arrival or service completion) is approximately the product of the corresponding rate (λ or μ) with the duration of time considered between changes. These facts lead to the following *balance equations*

$$\lambda P_0 = \mu P_1$$
$$\lambda P_1 + \mu P_1 = \lambda P_0 + \mu P_2$$
$$\lambda P_2 + \mu P_2 = \lambda P_1 + \mu P_3$$

A solution of the balance equations provides the following result:

$$P_n = (\lambda/\mu)^n P_0$$

for

$$n = 1, 2, 3, \ldots$$

which implies that

$$P_0 = 1 - \lambda/\mu$$

The above expressions can be used to derive the remaining queuing formulas. These are provided on page 502.

Mean number of customers in the system:

$$L = \frac{\lambda}{\mu - \lambda}$$

Mean customer time in the system:

$$W = \frac{L}{\lambda} = \frac{1}{\mu - \lambda}$$

Mean length of the waiting line:

$$L_q = \frac{\lambda^2}{\mu(\mu - \lambda)}$$

Mean customer waiting time:

$$W_q = \frac{L_q}{\lambda} = \frac{\lambda}{\mu(\mu - \lambda)}$$

And we define the

Server utilization factor:

$$\rho = \frac{\lambda}{\mu}$$

where the symbol ρ is the Greek rho.

An Illustration

Consider the queuing system involved in the operation of a central supply room for a large office. Employees can pick up needed supplies there, just like customers making purchases at a stationery store. An average of 25 employee customers withdraw supplies each hour of normal operation. A full-time clerk is required to check persons out of central supply, primarily to assure proper accounting control of requisitioned items. Each requisition takes an average of 2 minutes so the clerk can check out 30 customers per hour. We assume that the pattern of arrivals at the checkout counter is a close approximation to a Poisson process and that the checkout times are exponentially distributed. We have

$$\lambda = 25 \text{ customers per hour}$$
$$\mu = 30 \text{ customers per hour}$$

The mean number of customers either waiting in line or being checked out is

$$L = \frac{\lambda}{\mu - \lambda} = \frac{25}{30 - 25} = 5 \text{ customers}$$

while the mean time spent by customers in the system is

$$W = \frac{1}{\mu - \lambda} = \frac{1}{30 - 25} = \frac{1}{5} \text{ hour}$$

or 12 minutes. The above might instead have been calculated by $W = L/\lambda = 5/25 = 1/5$.

The mean number of customers waiting in line is

$$L_q = \frac{\lambda^2}{\mu(\mu - \lambda)} = \frac{(25)^2}{30(30 - 25)}$$

$$= \frac{25}{6} = 4\frac{1}{6} \text{ customers}$$

and the mean customer waiting time is

$$W_q = \frac{\lambda}{\mu(\mu - \lambda)} = \frac{25}{30(30 - 25)} = \frac{1}{6} \text{ hour}$$

or 10 minutes. The above could have been more simply calculated by $W_q = L_q/\lambda = (25/6) \div 25 = 1/6$.

The server utilization factor is

$$\rho = \frac{\lambda}{\mu} = \frac{25}{30} = \frac{5}{6}$$

that is, the supply room clerk is busy five-sixths of the time.

The above results may be used to determine the average daily cost of the waiting-line situation. Suppose that the labor cost for the supply room clerk is $5 per hour, whereas the unproductive time of employee customers is valued at an average hourly payroll figure of $7. The daily cost for the clerk is then

$$\$5 \times 8 = \$40$$

Each customer spends an average of $W = 1/5$ hour in checking out of the supply room, so that the average queuing cost per customer is

$$\$7 \times 1/5 = \$1.40$$

An average of $25 \times 8 = 200$ customers request supplies daily, so that the average daily queuing cost is

$$\$1.40 \times 200 = \$280$$

The average total daily cost for checking out of the supply room is thus

$$\$280 \text{ (queuing cost)} + \$40 \text{ (clerk's cost)} = \$320$$

The above figure does not include the time spent by each employee picking needed supplies off the shelves — that time is independent of the queuing system itself, which considers only the check-out process.

Management should consider the above daily cost figure to be highly excessive, especially since the average cost for the labor lost checking out of the supply room is seven times as great as the cost of the clerk. Two remedies might be considered. The checkout process itself might be speeded by hiring a faster clerk, by making the customers do some of the bookkeeping, or by partially automating the system. Or, one or more extra clerks might be hired to assist the first one; this latter alternative would involve a multiple-channel queue, which is described later in the chapter.

Consider a partially automated system that enables the clerk to double his service rate, up to $\mu = 60$ customers per hour. The mean customer time in the system would be

$$W = \frac{1}{\mu - \lambda} = \frac{1}{60 - 25} = \frac{1}{35} \text{ hour or 1.7 minutes}$$

This considerably reduces the average daily cost of the labor lost in checking out to

$$200 \times \$7 \times 1/35 = \$40$$

Suppose that the special equipment and handling required for automation costs an extra $50 per day, in addition to the clerk's wages. The average total daily cost would be

$40 (queuing cost) + $50 (equipment cost) + $40 (clerk's cost) = $130

Partial automation yields an average savings of $190 per day over manual operation with one clerk.

Management might also be concerned with the amount of traffic through the supply room. If too many people congregate there, it might be too attractive to persons wishing to socialize on company time. For the automated system, the following probabilities apply for the number of persons being checked out:

$$P_0 = 1 - \frac{\lambda}{\mu} = 1 - \frac{25}{60} = \frac{7}{12} = .583$$

$$P_1 = \left(\frac{\lambda}{\mu}\right)^1 P_0 = \frac{25}{60}\left(\frac{7}{12}\right) = \frac{35}{144} = .243$$

$$P_2 = \left(\frac{\lambda}{\mu}\right)^2 P_0 = \left(\frac{25}{60}\right)^2\left(\frac{7}{12}\right) = \frac{175}{1728} = .101$$

Table 17-2 shows the system state probabilities for $n=0$ to $n=9$. We see that there is less than a 10 percent chance that more than two persons will ever be checking out of the supply room at the same time.

Table 17-2

SYSTEM STATE PROBABILITIES FOR NUMBER OF CUSTOMERS IN CHECKOUT PROCESS ($\lambda = 25$, $\mu = 60$)

Number of Customers n	P_n	Cumulative Probability for n or Less	Probability of More than n
0	.583	.583	.417
1	.243	.826	.174
2	.101	.927	.073
3	.042	.969	.031
4	.018	.987	.013
5	.007	.994	.006
6	.003	.997	.003
7	.001	.998	.002
8	.001	.999	.001
9	.000	.999	.001

Interpreting Queuing Formulas and Alternative Expressions

An interpretation of the basic queuing formulas may be helpful. We might view λ as measuring the "demand" for service and μ as expressing the "capacity" of the service facility. The difference $\mu - \lambda$ then represents "excess capacity" of the system to fill demand. Thus, the mean number of persons in the system is the ratio of demand to excess capacity:

$$L = \frac{\text{Demand}}{\text{Excess capacity}} = \frac{\lambda}{\mu - \lambda}$$

When the excess capacity is small in relation to demand, congestion is heavy, and a large number of customers can be expected in the system. In the supply room operated manually by one clerk, demand is $\lambda = 25$ customers per hour, which is five times the excess capacity of $\mu - \lambda = 5$ customers per hour, so that $L = 5$ customers.

The mean customer time spent in the system may be determined by multiplying together the mean time between customer arrivals $1/\lambda$ and the mean number of customers L

$$W = \left(\frac{1}{\lambda}\right)L = \frac{L}{\lambda}$$

Continuing with the example of manual operation with one clerk, we find an average of 5 customers in the system, who arrive once every $1/\lambda = 1/25$ of an hour. Each customer can therefore expect to spend $1/25 \times 5 = 1/5$ of an hour checking out of the supply room. (It may seem perplexing that in getting W from L we multiply by the mean time-between-arrivals $1/\lambda$, not the mean service time of $1/\mu$. But remember that $L = 5$ is only a mean figure, not the actual number in the system, which at any given time might be more or less than 5. If you know in advance that exactly 5 customers are in the system, then the fifth customer would indeed expect to spend $(1/\mu)(5) = (1/30)(5) = 1/6$ of an hour being checked out; but that result is not W, which applies only when the number of customers is unspecified.)

A customer's mean waiting time is simply the difference between the mean total customer time in the system and the mean service time for that customer:

$$W_q = W - \frac{1}{\mu}$$

The above is algebraically equivalent to $\lambda/[\mu(\mu - \lambda)]$. And, the mean customer waiting time also equals the product of the mean time between arrivals and the mean number of customers in the waiting line:

$$W_q = \left(\frac{1}{\lambda}\right)L_q = \frac{L_q}{\lambda}$$

Multiplying both sides of the above by λ, we obtain the expression for the mean number of customers waiting in line:

$$L_q = \lambda W_q$$

We see that all the queuing results can be obtained beginning with L, which we may view as the ratio of "demand" (λ) to "excess capacity" ($\mu - \lambda$). We could instead start with W, L_q, or W_q and obtain the others without having to memorize all four basic formulas. And, some of the relationships described here apply to other queuing situations, where one result may be easier to obtain directly than the others. Other alternative expressions for the queuing results using the server utilization factor are described below.

It is easy to see that under manual operation the checkout clerk will only be busy an average of 5 minutes out of 6. In an eight-hour day the clerk will check out $8 \times 25 = 200$ customers, each taking an average of 2 minutes (1/30 hour), so that altogether 400 minutes will be spent checking customers. Each working day has $60 \times 8 = 480$ minutes. The proportion of busy minutes is therefore $400/480 = 5/6$.

The expression for W_q may be obtained from that for W by multiplying by the server utilization factor:

$$W_q = \left(\frac{\lambda}{\mu}\right) W$$

This same fact applies to L_q and L:

$$L_q = \left(\frac{\lambda}{\mu}\right) L$$

Thus, we see why the values for L_q and W_q, which do not consider that customer receiving service, are both smaller than L and W, which do: Since the clerk is only busy $\lambda/\mu = 5/6$ of the time under manual operation, L_q and W_q are only five-sixths as large as L and W. The expression for L_q may also be arrived at by subtracting the server utilization factor from the mean number of persons in the system:

$$L_q = L - \frac{\lambda}{\mu}$$

This is algebraically equivalent to $\lambda^2/[\mu(\mu - \lambda)]$. One rationale for this result is that L_q does not include the one customer who may be receiving service. Since the server is only busy λ/μ of the time, then, on the average, we can expect that fraction of a customer to be receiving service at any time. Thus, the fraction λ/μ of a customer must be subtracted to provide the expected number of customers who are waiting only.

17-4 MULTIPLE-SERVER QUEUING MODEL

We may now extend the basic queuing model for one service facility to the case of several facilities. Each of these will be assumed identical in all respects, each capable of performing service at the rate of μ customers per unit of time. As before, the pattern of arrivals is assumed to be a Poisson process and the service times are presumed to be exponentially distributed. The queuing formulas given below are based on the FIFO discipline, and we assume that the customer at the head of the line proceeds to the first free server.

Queuing Formulas

The queuing formulas for a multiple-channel system are based on principles similar to those used for a single server. A new parameter is needed to represent the number of channels:

$$S = \text{Number of service channels}$$

Figure 17-8 shows how movement occurs between customer states. As with the single-server model, the arrows represent changes and the quantities alongside the arrows correspond to the applicable rate for that particular change.

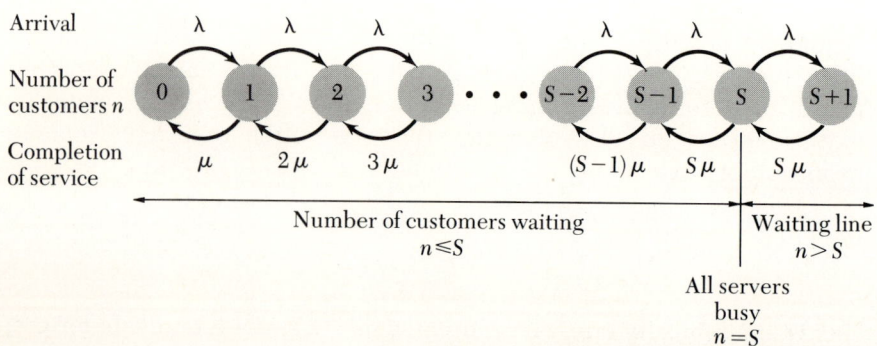

Figure 17-8
Schematic of multiple-server queuing system states.

Notice that when not all servers are busy, that is, when the number of customers n is less than S, no customers are waiting in line and the combined rate of service is $n\mu$. For example, consider a bank with 5 tellers, so that $S = 5$. When $n = 3$ customers are present, each is being served, and the combined rate at which service is being performed is 3μ. In any increment of time, it is thus three times as likely that service will be completed for any one of those three customers as a group as it is individually for any specific customer. When the number of customers is at least as large as the number of servers, $n \geq S$, all servers are busy, and the combined rate of service is $S\mu$. Should our bank have $n = 7$ customers, then two of these are waiting in line and the combined service rate is 5μ. As in our earlier model, we assume that total service capacity must exceed customer requirements, so that $S\mu > \lambda$.

The queuing formulas that result with S service channels are a bit more complex than in the single-channel case. *They are based on the probability that no customers are in the system.*

$$P_0 = 1 \Bigg/ \left[\sum_{n=0}^{S-1} \frac{(\lambda/\mu)^n}{n!} + \frac{(\lambda/\mu)^S}{S!} \left(\frac{1}{1 - \lambda/S\mu} \right) \right]$$

Also important is *the probability that n persons are in the system:*

$$P_n = \begin{cases} \dfrac{(\lambda/\mu)^n}{n!} P_0 & \text{if } 0 \leq n \leq S \\[1em] \dfrac{(\lambda/\mu)^n}{S! S^{n-S}} P_0 & \text{if } n \geq S \end{cases}$$

The remaining expressions are listed below. All of these are based upon first calculating L_q.

Mean length of the waiting line:

$$L_q = \frac{(\lambda/\mu)^S (\lambda/S\mu)}{S!(1 - \lambda/S\mu)^2} P_0$$

Mean customer waiting time:

$$W_q = \frac{L_q}{\lambda}$$

Mean customer time in the system:

$$W = W_q + \frac{1}{\mu}$$

17-4 MULTIPLE-SERVER QUEUING MODEL

Mean number of customers in the system:

$$L = L_q + \frac{\lambda}{\mu}$$

Server utilization factor:

$$\rho = \frac{\lambda}{S\mu}$$

(Notice that the server utilization factor is different than before. In a multiple-server system it is not possible to express the mean customer waiting time as the product of λ/μ and the mean customer time in the system. Thus

$$W_q \neq \left(\frac{\lambda}{\mu}\right)W \quad \text{and} \quad L_q \neq \left(\frac{\lambda}{\mu}\right)L$$

One reason is that λ/μ does not mean the same thing in a multiple-server queuing system.)

An Illustration

A company is considering renting office copying machines. One alternative is to lease two Model A machines that can make 100 copies per minute. However, because of the need for manual placement of items to be copied, the effective rate of copying is quite a bit lower. The actual machine time will also vary from user to user, depending on the number of copies required and originals used. Based upon the manufacturer's historical experience for offices with similar workloads, the total time per user is approximately exponentially distributed with a mean of 2 minutes per job. The effective service rate is therefore .5 jobs per minute. The demand for copying by company employees occurs at the rate of three jobs every 5 minutes, or an average of .6 jobs per minute; historical experience shows that the need for copying occurs randomly over time and that a Poisson process applies for jobs arriving at the copying center.

The parameters of this problem are

$$S = 2 \text{ service channels}$$
$$\mu = .5 \text{ jobs per minute}$$
$$\lambda = .6 \text{ jobs per minute}$$

The probability that no jobs are in the copying system is

$$P_0 = 1 \bigg/ \left[\frac{(\lambda/\mu)^0}{0!} + \frac{(\lambda/\mu)^1}{1!} + \frac{(\lambda/\mu)^2}{2!} \left(\frac{1}{1 - \lambda/2\mu} \right) \right]$$

$$= 1 \bigg/ \left[\frac{(.6/.5)^0}{0!} + \frac{(.6/.5)^1}{1!} + \frac{(.6/.5)^2}{2!} \left(\frac{1}{1 - .6/2(.5)} \right) \right]$$

$$= 1 \bigg/ \left[1 + 1.2 + \frac{(1.2)^2}{2} \left(\frac{1}{1 - .6} \right) \right]$$

$$= 1/[1 + 1.2 + 1.8] = 1/4 = .25$$

The mean number of jobs waiting to be copied is thus

$$L_q = \frac{(.6/.5)^2 [.6/2(.5)]}{2! [1 - .6/2(.5)]^2} (.25) = .68 \text{ jobs}$$

and the mean waiting time per job is

$$W_q = \frac{L_q}{\lambda} = \frac{.68}{.6} = 1.13 \text{ minutes}$$

The mean time each job spends in the copying center is

$$W = W_q + \frac{1}{\mu} = 1.13 + \frac{1}{.5} = 3.13 \text{ minutes}$$

and the mean number of jobs at the copying center at any given time is

$$L = L_q + \frac{\lambda}{\mu} = .68 + \frac{.6}{.5} = 1.88 \text{ jobs}$$

Management is concerned about the average hourly cost of operating with two Model As. Each job is personally processed by the user, whose average hourly payroll cost is $10. Machine rental is a straight 5 cents per copy; an average job involves 12 copies.

The average number of jobs per hour is

$$.6 \times 60 = 36$$

and each employee using the machine spends an average of $W = 3.13$ minutes, or

$$\frac{3.13}{60} = .0522 \text{ hours}$$

17-4   MULTIPLE-SERVER QUEUING MODEL

in the copying center. The average hourly cost of the labor lost in making copies is therefore

$$\$10 \times 36 \times .0522 = \$18.79$$

The hourly rental cost for the two machines is

$$\$.05 \times 12 \times 36 = \$21.60$$

The total hourly average cost of operation is thus

$$\$18.79 \text{ (labor lost)} + \$21.60 \text{ (equipment)} = \$40.39$$

Two Servers Compared to One Twice As Fast

An interesting result arises from queuing theory. To the uninitiated, it may seem that one server twice as fast will produce results identical to those from two separate facilities, each servicing customers at the regular rate. *This is not true* (if it were, we would not need a separate model for multiple-channel queues, and the single-channel case with μ twice as large could be used instead).

Suppose that the Model T has twice the effective service rate as the Model A does. Using $\mu = 1$ job per minute, we find that the single-server model provides a mean number of jobs waiting of

$$L_q = \frac{\lambda^2}{\mu(\mu - \lambda)} = \frac{(.6)^2}{1(1 - .6)} = .9 \text{ jobs}$$

which is more than three times as large as the comparable figure found with two Model As. The mean time each job would spend waiting with one Model T would be

$$W_q = \frac{L_q}{\lambda} = \frac{.9}{.6} = 1.5 \text{ minutes}$$

which is considerably longer than before. Of course, the Model T is twice as fast at service, so the average time spent by a job in the system is smaller than with two Model A's:

$$W = \frac{1}{\mu - \lambda} = \frac{1}{1 - .6} = 2.5 \text{ minutes}$$

Even if the faster Model T rents for a little more per copy than the slower Model A does, it would be cheaper for management to rent the one Model T instead of two Model A's.

CONCLUDING REMARKS 17-5

This book describes only two queuing models in detail. Each presumes the FIFO discipline and exponential distributions for interarrival and service times. As indicated at the outset, many other queuing situations exist and have been studied in detail. Several further models are described in the chapter appendix.

Arrivals occurring *singly* over time often historically fit the Poisson distribution. It is inappropriate to use that distribution when customers arrive in groups—for example, customers picking up their baggage after a flight. Generally, a Poisson process is of limited duration, so that the basic queuing formulas are really only applicable for short periods. As we have seen, a bank or toll station will have different characteristics at different times of the day or days of the week. Thus, several different values of λ may be appropriate for any one of those periods, and different mean waiting times and other queuing results would apply for each.

For mathematical simplicity, the two queuing models discussed are based on exponential service times. This assumption is tenuous and may cause the queuing models to lack credibility. Recall that the exponential distribution assigns the greatest probability to very short times (and a service time of zero is the most likely); theoretically there is no upper limit on how long service can take under this pattern. But few service patterns fit the exponential distribution well. The normal distribution or some other two-tailed non-symmetrical distribution would be more realistic representations in the majority of cases. This raises some serious questions about the usefulness of the basic models except in explaining the underlying queuing concepts. However, although the assumption of exponential service may not be strictly true, the queuing formulas provided in this chapter may often yield satisfactory approximations to the actual results that would be derived using more accurate models.

As we have seen with certain other applications of quantitative methods, the various mathematical models for queues have limited scope and often only approximate reality. This is due to the many simplifying assumptions that must ordinarily be made in order to accommodate the mathematical analysis. To avoid erroneous results, numerical solution procedures are often used instead of standard queuing formulas to evaluate complex queuing situations. One useful procedure is Monte Carlo simulation, discussed in Chapter 18.

APPENDIX 17-1: SOME FURTHER QUEUING MODELS*

A tremendous variety of queuing models exists. Each applies to a particular situation in which any one or a combination of differences occurs in the underlying structure, queue discipline, or patterns of arrivals or service. This appendix provides four additional models with wide application. All the models are based on the FIFO discipline and assume a Poisson process for arrivals; all but the last two also assume that the service times are exponentially distributed.

A Single-Server Model for a Finite Queue

Often the number of customers that a queuing system may handle at any given time is limited. For example, a hospital emergency room may only have enough beds to accommodate a specific number of patients waiting to see the attending doctors; any additional patients must be diverted to other hospitals. A waiting line of limited length is called a *finite queue*. Such circumstances may arise because of physical constraints, as with an emergency room; they may also be apparent, so that customers simply give up when the waiting line is too long. In either case, a turned away customer does not return to the system. Systems involving finite queues differ from those discussed in the chapter, where no limits are placed on the number of customers waiting for service. The underlying queuing formulas must be modified to reflect this structural difference.

The resulting model may be expressed in terms of the constant

$M =$ Maximum number of customers in the system

The probabilities for the number of customers in the system are

$$P_0 = \frac{1 - \lambda/\mu}{1 - (\lambda/\mu)^{M+1}}$$

$$P_n = (\lambda/\mu)^n P_0 \quad \text{for } 0 \leq n \leq M$$

The mean number of customers in the system is

$$L = \frac{\lambda/\mu}{1 - \lambda/\mu} - \frac{(M+1)(\lambda/\mu)^{M+1}}{1 - (\lambda/\mu)^{M+1}}$$

* Optional section.

The remaining queuing results may be found from the above. The mean length of the waiting line is found by subtracting the proportion of time the server is busy, which here is $1 - P_0$:

$$L_q = L - (1 - P_0)$$

The respective mean customer times are

$$W_q = \frac{L_q}{\lambda(1 - P_M)}$$

$$W = \frac{L}{\lambda(1 - P_M)}$$

A Single-Server Model for a Limited Population

A related queuing model arises when the customers arriving at the system represent a small population. Although the situation resembles the last one, the potential customers, rather than the line itself, are limited. Such a situation might arise in a plant that contains several machines that need servicing as they break down. Each malfunctioning machine is treated as an arriving customer, and the breakdowns may be assumed to be a Poisson process.

The model involves the constant

$M =$ Maximum number of customers that may need service

The probabilities for the number of customers either waiting or receiving service are

$$P_0 = 1 \Big/ \sum_{n=0}^{M} \left[\frac{M!}{(M-n)!} \left(\frac{\lambda}{\mu}\right)^n \right]$$

$$P_n = \frac{M!}{(M-n)!} \left(\frac{\lambda}{\mu}\right)^n P_0 \quad \text{for } 1 \leq n \leq M$$

The remaining results are

$$L_q = M - \frac{\lambda + \mu}{\lambda}(1 - P_0)$$

$$L = L_q + (1 - P_0)$$

APPENDIX 17-1: SOME FURTHER QUEUING MODELS

$$W_q = \frac{L_q}{\lambda(M-L)}$$

$$W = \frac{L}{\lambda(M-L)}$$

A Single-Server Model with Poisson Arrivals and Any Service-Time Distribution

The assumption of exponentially distributed service times ordinarily disagrees with the actual service pattern found in many queuing systems. Fortunately, the basic queuing results can be extended to apply to any distribution for service times; all that need be specified are the mean $1/\mu$ and the variance σ^2. The results are only slightly changed from the basic model in the chapter:

$$P_0 = 1 - \lambda/\mu$$

$$P_n = (\lambda/\mu)^n P_0$$

$$L_q = \frac{\lambda\sigma^2 + (\lambda/\mu)^2}{2(1-\lambda/\mu)}$$

$$L = L_q + \frac{\lambda}{\mu}$$

$$W_q = \frac{L_q}{\lambda}$$

$$W = W_q + \frac{1}{\mu}$$

The state probabilities are the same as in the basic model. Notice that L_q and, hence, all the other queuing results depend on the variance σ^2 of the service-time distribution. Regardless of the mean service rate μ, L_q, L, W_q, and W all become larger as σ^2 is increased. Thus, greater variability in service time will result in longer lines and waiting times. This indicates that consistency in service times is very important to the overall quality of the service provided.

A Single-Server Model with Constant Service Times

As a special case, suppose that service times are constant, each taking time $1/\mu$. Since successive customers will all take the same time, the variance is zero. Substituting $\sigma^2 = 0$ into the above model, we find

$$L_q = \frac{(\lambda/\mu)^2}{2(1-\lambda/\mu)^2} = \frac{\lambda}{2\mu(\mu-\lambda)}$$

The other results L, W_q, and W may be calculated from the above. Notice that L_q and, hence, W_q are half as large as in the basic model discussed in the chapter.

PROBLEMS

17-1 On Tuesday mornings, customers arrive at the Central Valley National Bank at a rate of $\lambda = 1$ per minute. What is the probability that the time between the next two successive arrivals will be (a) shorter than 1 minute; (b) longer than 5 minutes; (c) between 2 and 5 minutes?

17-2 During the late Friday rush at the above bank, an average of $\lambda = 5$ customers per minute arrive. What is the probability that no customers arrive during a specified 1-minute interval?

17-3 For each of the following single-channel queuing systems, determine values for L, W, L_q, W_q, and ρ.

(a)	(b)	(c)	(d)
$\lambda = 20$	$\lambda = 8$	$\lambda = 2$	$\lambda = .4$
$\mu = 25$	$\mu = 12$	$\mu = 5$	$\mu = .7$

17-4 Patrons arrive at a small post office at the rate of 30 per hour. Service by the one clerk on duty takes an average of 1 minute per customer.
(a) Calculate the mean customer time: (1) spent waiting in line and (2) spent receiving or waiting for service. Also find the mean number of persons: (3) in line, and (4) receiving or waiting for service.
(b) Construct the probability distribution for the number of persons inside the post office (stopping at that n where the probability rounds to zero to two decimal places).

17-5 For each of the following waiting-line situations give at least one reason why the models provided in this chapter might be inappropriate for determining mean customer waiting time.
(a) Telephone calls placed through a manually operated switchboard.
(b) Customers arriving at a restaurant for dinner.
(c) Patients visiting a dermatologist, who works from appointments only.
(d) A bottling machine filling empties with ingredients.

(e) Plant workers showing their badges to a security guard while passing through the corridor into the main building.

17-6 Sammy Lee operates a barbershop by himself. Between noon and 6 PM on Saturday afternoons his customers arrive on the average of one every 15 minutes. Sammy takes an average of 10 minutes to trim each customer. His little shop only has chairs for 2 waiting customers plus the one getting a haircut.
(a) What is the probability that any particular customer will have to spend part of his wait standing up?
(b) What percentage of an average Saturday afternoon is Sammy busy? How many hours is he idle on an average Saturday afternoon?

17-7 Between 9 and 10 AM on Saturday, the peak business period, customers arrive at Sammy Lee's barber shop at a mean rate of $\lambda = 5$ per hour. During the Thursday slump, between 2 and 3 PM, customers arrive at the rate of $\lambda = 1$ per hour. In either case, the arrivals may be represented as a Poisson process.
(a) Does this mean that there will always be more customers arriving during the peak period than during the slump? Explain.
(b) Compare the probability of exactly two customers arriving during Sammy's slump to that for the same number arriving during his peak period.
(c) If the mean rate of arrivals for the week as a whole is three customers per hour, can Sammy use the Poisson distribution with $\lambda = 3$ to find the probability that next week's arrivals will be between 100 and 150? Explain.

17-8 The final settlement claims filed by policyholders of a casualty insurance company involving amounts of $100,000 or more are events from a Poisson process with a mean rate of $\lambda = 1$ per working day. Funds earmarked for large-claims settlement are invested in short-term government bonds at 8 percent interest, so that the timing of settlements affects company profits. What is the probability that the next large claim must be settled (a) within 5 days; (b) sometime after 2 days; (c) between 2 and 5 days?

17-9 With only partial knowledge of single-channel queuing parameters and results, it is possible to reconstruct the remaining values by using alternative expressions or algebraic manipulation. Using the given data, determine the values of

$$\lambda, \mu, L, W, L_q, W_q, \rho, P_0, \text{ and } P_1$$

for each of the following situations.
(a) $\mu = 40$, $L = 7$, $W = .2$
(b) $\rho = .9$, $W = 1$, $W_q = .9$
(c) $P_0 = .5$, $\lambda = 5$
(d) $W = 5$, $W_q = 3$

17-10 A family receives an average of $\lambda = 2$ pieces of regular mail each day that letters are delivered. Assume that the Poisson distribution applies.
(a) What is the probability that they do not get mail for the next two consecutive days?
(b) What is the probability that, given two days without mail, they will go another two days without mail?

17-11 Mildred's Tool and Die Shop has a central tool cage manned by a single clerk, who takes an average of 5 minutes in fetching and checking parts out to each machinist requesting them. The machinists arrive once every 8 minutes on the average. One hour of machinist's time is valued at $15; a clerk's time is valued at $9 per hour. What are the average hourly queuing system costs associated with the tool cage operation?

17-12 Mildred wishes to improve the costs for the above tool cage operation. Two alternatives are
(1) Use two clerks, each equally fast.
(2) Operate the tool cage with a machinist instead of a clerk. Special knowledge, enables the machinist to provide service twice as fast as the clerk.
(a) Determine for both alternatives the mean machinist time spent in checking out tools.
(b) Find the average hourly queuing system costs for both alternatives. Which one would be cheapest?
(c) Discuss any advantages of each alternative that cannot be measured by applying queuing models.

17-13 C. A. Gopher & Sons is excavating a site requiring the removal of 100,000 cubic yards of material. Mr. Gopher has the choice of using a scoop loader or a shovel crane. He has leased 10 trucks at $20 per hour. A scoop loader costs $40 per hour; a shovel crane, $60 per hour. Once work has been started, the trucks arrive according to a Poisson process with a mean rate of $\lambda = 7$ trucks per hour. The truck-filling times are exponentially distributed. A scoop loader can fill an average of 10 trucks per hour. The shovel crane is faster, capable on the average of filling 15 trucks per hour. (For simplicity, we assume the same truck arrival rate, regardless of equipment used.)

Since the number of truck arrivals required to excavate the site is fixed by the amount of dirt, the optimal choice of filling equipment will be the one minimizing the combined average hourly costs of truck unproductive time plus the cost of the filling equipment. Determine the optimal choice.

17-14 The manager of a WaySafe market with 10 checkout counters wishes to determine how many of these to operate on Saturday morning. His decision will be determined partly by the costs assigned to each additional minute a customer spends checking out of the store. In a special experiment in obsolete stores about to be closed, customers were forced to wait in line for an abnormally long time in order to see what would happen. The study concluded that an average of 5 cents in future profits is lost for every minute a customer spends waiting.

Assume that WaySafe customers' arrivals at the checkout area are approximated by a Poisson process with a mean rate of $\lambda = 2$ per minute and that each attendant can check out customers at a mean rate of .5 per minute (and that the service time is exponentially distributed).

(a) What is the minimum number of checkers needed so that the service capacity *exceeds* the demand for service? Determine the mean customer waiting time when that many employees are providing service.

(b) With the addition of one more checker, what is the mean customer waiting time?

(c) Each checker involves a salary expense of $10 per hour. Which number of checkers minimizes total hourly queuing system cost, that in part (a) or in part (b)? (Ignore time for service, since no penalty applies for time spent in actually checking out.)

17-15 Suppose that a typesetter makes an average of $\lambda = .5$ error per page. What is the probability that there will be no errors in the first $t = 10$ pages? What is the probability that there will be exactly 5 errors in the first 10 pages?

17-16 A California Central Valley tomato grower wishes to protect his crop against destruction by aphids. Two alternatives are open: spray with a powerful insecticide that may harm the local ecology or wait for the ladybugs to eat the aphids. Each spring, massive flights of ladybugs are wafted by wind currents across the California valleys from their Sierra Nevada hibernating points. Unfortunately, where and when a flight of ladybugs lands is purely a matter of chance. Wherever there are plenty of aphids, they lay eggs that rapidly hatch. If at least one flight of ladybugs lands on part of the grower's crop within five days, they and their larva will devour all the aphids. Otherwise the grower will spray, killing all aphids and the unfortunate late-coming aphid-eaters as well, for by that time irreparable crop damage will have been suffered. On any given day 10 percent of the Central Valley is covered by ladybugs. Assume that the arrivals of ladybugs may be considered a Poisson process. (The size of the farm may be ignored.)

(a) Assuming that the mean arrival rate is $\lambda = .1$ flock per day, what is the probability that no flocks arrive during $t = 5$ days?

(b) What is the probability that the farmer won't have to spray?

17-17 In each of the following situations, use Appendix Table E to find the probabilities that the stated number of events occur in a Poisson

process having rate $\lambda = 8$/hour when the duration considered is
(a) $t = 2$ hours, 10 or fewer events
(b) $t = 1.5$ hours, 6 or more events
(c) $t = 1$ hour, exactly 3 events
(d) $t = .1$ hour, between 1 and 5 events

17-18 A typist commits errors at the rate of .01 per word. Assuming that a Poisson process applies, use Appendix Table E to find the probabilities that the number of errors committed in a 500-word letter will be
(a) exactly 5 (b) zero
(c) more than 10 (d) between 3 and 7

* **17-19** A hospital emergency room can accommodate at most $M = 5$ patients. The patients arrive at a rate of 4 per hour. The single staff physician can only treat 5 patients per hour. Any patient overflow is directed to another hospital.
(a) Determine the probability distribution for the number of patients either waiting for or receiving treatment at any given time.
(b) Determine the mean values for: the number of patients in the emergency room; the number of patients waiting to see the doctor; the patient waiting time; and the patient time in the emergency room.
(c) Repeat the calculations in part (b) assuming that there is no restriction on the number of patients to receive treatment.

* **17-20** A machinist services $M = 5$ machines as they breakdown. Machines fail at a rate of 1 per day, and the machinist fixes them at the rate of 2 per day.
(a) Determine the probability distribution for the number of machines down at any given time.
(b) Calculate L_q, L, W_q, and W.
(c) Repeat part (b) for a machinist who services a population of thousands of machines. Assume that the failures and service occur at the same rates given above.

* **17-21** Re-solve Problem 17-4(a) when the service time is normally distributed with a mean of $1/\mu = 1$ minute and a standard deviation of $\sigma = .30$ minutes.

* **17-22** Re-solve Problem 17-4(a) when the service time is constant.

* Problems marked with an asterisk involve material in the chapter appendix.

Eighteen

Simulation

The quantitative methods presented so far in this book involve analytical procedures, in which an algorithm provides a problem solution that can be mathematically proven to be optimal. In decision making under uncertainty, a solution obtained in this manner generally provides maximum expected payoff or minimum expected cost. All such problems therefore involve variables whose values are determined by chance, so that probability distributions must be specified in advance.

We now consider a *numerical solution procedure* that seeks the optimal alternatives through essentially a "trial and error" process. This *simulation* technique may be applied to practically any decision problem involving uncertainty. It is a problem-solving approach with several advantages over traditional analytic methods. The most significant advantage of simulation is that it can provide good answers for problems that are difficult, or even impossible, to solve in a purely mathematical way.

Simulation thoroughly evaluates each alternative by generating a series of values for each random variable at the same frequencies their probability distributions indicate. In effect, this is done by sampling from populations of possible values for the variables. The resulting quantities are combined in accordance with an underlying mathematical model to provide a particular value for the payoff measure. After a number of repetitions, a statistical pattern in the results can be discerned. Simulation is thus a procedure that tries out each alternative "on paper" over and over again; in effect it represents a sample from the future. As in most random sampling procedures, random numbers are used to generate the events and quantities involved, as if they were determined by spins of a roulette wheel. For this reason, the procedure has become known as *Monte Carlo simulation*.

THE NATURE OF SIMULATION 18-1

A simulation only represents reality and can be used for decision-making purposes, for training, or for a variety of other objectives. Monte Carlo procedures use very special kinds of simulations that must be distinguished from the simulations that are most familiar to us.

Other Kinds of Simulation

Often a simulation can be physical in nature, as epitomized by ground flight simulators. These modern pilot training devices duplicate flying conditions as closely as possible. There are several advantages to simulated flight. It provides pilots with exposure to a multitude of conditions over a short period of time, experiences that would be extremely costly to duplicate in actual aircraft. Hazardous situations that would never be created intentionally with real planes can be routinely duplicated in simulated flights; such exposure has proven valuable in training pilots to cope with real emergencies.

Training applications with other nonphysical simulations of a similar nature are encountered with increasing frequency. For instance, the case method used by many business schools asks the student to simulate the decision process of actual managers. Like the mistakes of the airline pilots, student mistakes on cases are not damaging (except to the grade-point average), and the use of such cases allows a concentrated exposure to problems that few managers might otherwise experience in their careers. Growing in popularity are game-type simulations, where students run hypothetical businesses in competition with one another; the interaction of individual decisions in a simulated marketplace produces results that are useful in making later choices and allow for improvements in the decision-making process itself.

Physical simulations are helpful in decisions about the design of buildings, cities, waterways, or aircraft. An architect's three-dimensional model of a design is a simulation; the simulated building provides insights impossible to glean from sketches alone. The U.S. Army Corps of Engineers has a physical model of San Francisco Bay that is helpful in evaluating proposals for such activities as dredging and filling in terms of their overall impact on tides and navigation. The flight characteristics of a proposed aircraft can be determined in advance through simulated flight of a model inside a wind tunnel; the model's aerodynamic properties can lead to refinements in the final design itself.

Features of Monte Carlo Simulation

Monte Carlo simulation differs from the above types in that it is nonphysical in nature and often employs a mathematical model having optimization as the desired end. Thus, Monte Carlo simulation is concerned almost exclusively with decision making itself rather than with training decision makers. Since the procedure is used for decisions under uncertainty, the models are *stochastic* in nature. Because chance elements are involved, an alternative must be evaluated under a variety of conditions generated randomly. Although an architect usually makes just one mock-up of a design, a Monte Carlo simulation repeatedly reconstitutes the situation in variant forms, according to the events and values that turn up each time. With a somewhat changed model, the same process must be started all over again for every alternative. And, when the simulating is finished, all that remains is a history of what happened, which is best analyzed by statistical techniques.

Although Monte Carlo simulation is the more widely used quantitative method, it should not be confused with other types of simulations used in decision making that bear a superficial resemblance. For example, it is possible to simulate stock-market trading strategies by using past data in making hypothetical trades. Such a simulation involves a tremendous amount of data, so that a computer might be used. In this respect, a stock-market simulation resembles a Monte Carlo simulation. However, a stock-market simulation is essentially *deterministic* in nature, since previous market conditions are known and *certain*. In contrast, Monte Carlo simulation is a special procedure that is ordinarily used in conjunction with *uncertain* situations.

A variety of problems have been analyzed with Monte Carlo simulation. The oil-tanker port facility study described in Chapter 1 was analyzed with this procedure. Each design alternative was evaluated by more than 1000 years of simulated operation in order to arrive at a statistically reliable estimate of its expected rate of return. Monte Carlo simulation has been used in establishing baseball batting orders, in selecting rocket combinations to use in launching satellites, and in evaluating starting-time policies at golf courses. It has served in planning restaurant menus, in choosing a car, and in estimating how many tellers a bank should hire. It has determined optimal inventory policies for small retailers and large conglomerates. It has proven useful in production control in the manufacture of automobiles, bicycles, and submarines. Monte Carlo simulation has been used to evaluate queuing systems of all kinds, even those that have neither first-come, first-served policies, nor exponentially distributed service times.

CONCEPTS AND PROCEDURES: 18-2
A WAITING-LINE SIMULATION

To help in discussing the concepts and procedures of Monte Carlo simulation we will apply the technique to a simple waiting-line situation.

A One-Man Barbershop Illustration

Sammy Lee, owner of a one-man barbershop, is contemplating adding a part-time assistant on Saturdays, the busiest day of the week. His daughter Samantha, who is studying quantitative methods at a distant university, has offered to perform a study to aid her father in making his decision. As a first step, Ms. Lee wants to evaluate the characteristics of the present operation.

Ms. Lee knows that customers arrive at Sammy's more or less randomly over time and that the time Sammy spends with a particular customer can vary substantially. To help in performing her final analysis she wants to establish applicable Saturday values for the following:

(1) Mean arrival rate (λ)
(2) Mean time between arrivals ($1/\lambda$)
(3) Mean service rate (μ)
(4) Mean service time ($1/\mu$)
(5) Mean customer waiting time (W_q)
(6) Mean customer time in the system (shop) (W)
(7) Mean number of customers in the waiting line (L_q)

(8) Mean number of customers in the system (shop) (L)
(9) Server utilization factor (proportion of time the barber is busy with customers) (ρ)

Ms. Lee knows the textbook formulas for computing the above values, but she also knows that they depend on a series of crucial assumptions that may not apply in her father's case. Since she is too far away to observe what goes on at Sammy's directly, Ms. Lee will have to simulate the Saturday operations in order to estimate the above parameters.

Duplicating Reality

Any Monte Carlo simulation seeks to duplicate reality as closely as possible within practical limitations. Thus, Samantha Lee wants to conduct a simulation that resembles in all important respects what she would find by actually observing her father's shop in operation.

Were Ms. Lee watching the true operation, what information would she need in order to find the desired parameter values? And, how should she arrange those data to obtain the target results?

The simplest solution is to maintain a log, as illustrated in Figure 18-1, that identifies each customer and records when he arrives, when he receives his haircut, and when he is finished. As we shall see, such a log contains the minimum amount of information necessary to answer the questions.

However, by giving a little additional thought to the design of such a log, we can save work later on. Items 2 and 4 on Ms. Lee's list of parameters are the mean times between arrivals and for service, respectively. The data needed to compute these means exist in the original log, but, by adding two more columns, the bored log keeper can list the times between successive customer arrivals and the service time for each customer. Another new column can record how long each customer must

Customer	Clock Time at Arrival	Clock Time at Beginning of Service	Clock Time at End of Service
Mr. Jones	9:15	9:15	9:30
Mr. Smith	9:25	9:30	9:45
Mr. Green	9:30	9:45	10:00

Figure 18-1
Simple customer log for actual observations at a barbershop.

wait before receiving service. Since a new customer's service cannot begin until the barber is finished with those ahead of him, waiting time is the elapsed clock time between end of service for the preceding customer (and thus beginning for him) and his arrival. Figure 18-2 shows what this more detailed log might look like.

Customer	Time Between Arrivals	Clock Time at Arrival	Clock Time at Beginning of Service	Service Time	Clock Time at End of Service	Waiting Time
Mr. Jones		9:15	9:15	15	9:30	0
Mr. Smith	10	9:25	9:30	15	9:45	5
Mr. Green	5	9:30	9:45	15	10:00	15

Figure 18-2
Detailed customer log for actual observations at a barbershop.

Of course Ms. Lee can't be there, so she must use fictional customers. Her simulated log, discussed later, is very much like the one in Figure 18-2. Because she is only interested in the queuing aspects of the barbershop, it is important that the arrival and service patterns for these customers match the real ones. In this way the interactions between the timing of various events in her simulation will be representative of those occurring in real life.

Probability Distributions

The essential inputs for Ms. Lee's simulation are probability data regarding the patterns of customer arrivals and service. Since much of her analysis involves time, two probability distributions are sought: one for the time between successive customer arrivals and another for service times of individual customers. Although the basic data for generating these distributions can best be determined by clocking customers during actual operation, Sammy can't afford to hire someone to do it. Ms. Lee has, therefore, applied the techniques of Chapter 4 to help her father establish subjective probabilities for these random variables. Although both variables are continuous, Ms. Lee has determined the discrete approximations in Table 18-1 for the underlying probability distributions.

Ms. Lee's hypothetical customers must therefore arrive randomly with the frequency of interarrival times consistent with the probabilities in Table 18-1. The amount of time taken to cut any customer's hair should also be unpredictable and vary according to the respective probabilities.

Table 18-1

PROBABILITY DISTRIBUTIONS FOR CUSTOMER TIMES BETWEEN ARRIVALS AND CUSTOMER SERVICE TIMES

TIMES BETWEEN ARRIVALS		CUSTOMER SERVICE TIMES	
Time	Probability	Time	Probability
5 min	.10	5 min	.05
10	.15	10	.20
15	.25	15	.40
20	.25	20	.20
25	.15	25	.10
30	.10	30	.05
	1.00		1.00

Generating Events Using Random Numbers

A Monte Carlo simulation generates events so they occur with long-run frequencies identical to their probabilities. The process for doing this is very much like a statistical study in which a sample is selected from a population of values by using *random numbers*.

You may recall from an earlier study of statistics that random numbers have no particular pattern and might record the outcomes from successive spins of a wheel of fortune, where any digit between 0 and 9 is equally likely to occur. Appendix Table F contains a list of random numbers created by the RAND Corporation. For convenience, we will use the following partial listings taken from the first two columns of that table.

*12*651   *61*646
*81*769   *74*436
*36*737   *98*863
*82*861   *54*371
*21*235   *15*732
*74*146   *47*887
*90*759   *64*410
*55*683   *98*078
*79*686   *17*969
*70*333   *00*201

Notice that the random numbers listed above contain five digits; since the probability values for the barbershop simulation are accurate to only two places, we can ignore all but the first two digits and use only the italicized portions.

528   SIMULATION

It really doesn't matter how random numbers are picked from the table, so long as the values of earlier numbers do not influence the choice of future ones.

In simulating Sammy Lee's barbershop, each hypothetical customer may be considered a sample observation taken from the population of all future clients seeking a Saturday haircut. In traditional statistics, sample customers would be randomly selected from a master list. But in a simulation the customers are imaginary ones, with all the essential characteristics of real ones; these customers must be created in such a way that they could have come from such a list (like the log in Figure 18-2, which hasn't been and may never be constructed under actual operation). Although used differently than in an ordinary sampling study, random numbers serve this purpose.

In actual barbershop operation the chance events—each customer's arrival and service times—occur randomly. These events are simulated by translating successive entries on the random-number list. Thus, a random number of 67 for the tenth customer could mean that he arrives 20 minutes after the ninth. *A separate random number is used for each variable*. Thus, the next random number on the list might be 19, which might represent a service time of 10 minutes for this customer.

Before the actual simulation begins, exactly which random numbers will correspond to each event or uncertain quantity must be determined. The barbershop study requires two assignments one for each of the time random variables. Consider the time between arrivals first.

Table 18-1 indicates that an interarrival time of 5 minutes occurs with probability .10. This outcome should occur 10 percent of the time in a simulation. Of course, there is no reason why more or less than 10 percent 5-minute outcomes can't occur, just like a sequence of coin tosses can have more or fewer than half heads. But when a large number of cases are considered, the frequency of occurrence for any such event should be very close to its probability. We can let random numbers determine when a 5-minute time will happen. Since any possible number is equally likely to appear in any position on a random-number list, we want to assign exactly 10 percent of these to correspond to an interarrival time of 5 minutes.

Any 10 percent of the random numbers will suffice. But these must be identified in advance. It's easiest if we assign the smallest 10 percent of them to represent 5 minutes. Thus, we will set any two-digit random number between 01 and 10, inclusively, to correspond to a 5-minute interarrival time.

The next possible interarrival time is 10 minutes, occurring with probability .15. Thus the second 15 percent of the random numbers, between 11 and 25, will be assigned to that event. To speed the process of assigning random numbers, it is helpful to first construct a cumulative probability distribution, as in Table 18-2. Each successive set of random

Table 18-2

RANDOM NUMBER ASSIGNMENT FOR TIMES BETWEEN ARRIVALS USING CUMULATIVE PROBABILITIES

Time Between Arrivals	Probability	Cumulative Probability	Random Numbers
5 min	.10	.10	01–10
10	.15	.25	11–25
15	.25	.50	26–50
20	.25	.75	51–75
25	.15	.90	76–90
30	.10	1.00	91–00

numbers begins where the last one left off, ending with that value identical (except for the decimal point) to the respective cumulative probability. This approach guarantees that the proportion of random numbers assigned will always be identical to the probability for the outcome. In doing this, 00 is treated as 100.*

The same procedure is used to assign random numbers to service times in Table 18-3.

Table 18-3

RANDOM NUMBER ASSIGNMENT FOR SERVICE TIMES

Service Time	Probability	Cumulative Probability	Random Numbers
5 min	.05	.05	01–05
10	.20	.25	06–25
15	.40	.65	26–65
20	.20	.85	66–85
25	.10	.95	86–95
30	.05	1.00	96–00

Setting Up the Simulation

Before starting her simulation, Ms. Lee must set it up so that she can create a hypothetical log. She makes up the *worksheet* in Figure 18-3. For convenience, each customer is given an identity number correspond-

---

* An alternative procedure is to use 00 as the low value. In those cases the assignment would be 00–09 for 5 minutes, 10–24 for 10 minutes, . . ., 90–99 for 30 minutes.

Trial or Cust. No.	(1) Rand. No.	(2) Time Betw. Arriv.	(3) Clock Time at Arriv. [last (3) + (2)]	(4) Clock Time at Beg. of Serv. [(3) or last (7)]	(5) Rand. No.	(6) Serv. Time	(7) Clock Time at End of Serv. [(4) + (6)]	(8) Waiting Time [(4) − (3)]
1								
2								
3								

Figure 18-3
Worksheet for the one-man barbershop simulation.

ing to order of arrival. Notice that two additional columns [(1) and (5)] are necessary for entering the random numbers that determine the times between arrivals and the service times. The numbers in these columns may be entered in advance or one-at-a-time as they are needed.

In general, a simulation is a series of *trials*, each of which is a repetition of the basic steps. In our example, the entries made in each customer row constitute a trial. The steps taken comprise a portion of the *simulation model*. In the barbershop simulation, the worksheet itself spells out that part of the overall model in which the trials are generated. Later we will discuss the remaining parts of this particular model.

The model is basically mathematical, so that it is possible to express it in terms of algebraic expressions. It is often more convenient, however, to indicate the model's procedures in a worksheet that clearly indicates each step. In large-scale simulations that must be run on a digital computer, the model is generally imbedded in the programming instructions.

Conducting the Simulation

We are now ready to show how the simulation is conducted. The worksheet entries are made one customer at a time in Table 18-4.

Ms. Lee begins with the first customer, getting the random number 12 from the first list provided earlier. This appears in column (1) and corresponds to a time between arrivals of 10 minutes, entered in column (2). Since there is no prior customer, these minutes are simply added to the shop's 9:00 opening time, providing 9:10 as the clock time at arrival for customer number 1; this time is entered in column (3) and also in column (4) for the clock time when service begins—since Sammy is free to serve that customer immediately upon arrival. The next random number, 61, is read from the second list and entered in column (5); this corresponds to the service time of 15 minutes, which is placed in column (6). Adding the values in columns (4) and (6), we find clock time of 9:25 when service ends and enter it in column (7). Because this customer is served immediately, there is no waiting time.

The second customer gets the random number 81, so that he arrives 25 minutes after the first, at 9:35. Sammy Lee has finished with the preceding customer at 9:25, so service begins immediately at 9:35 with no

Table 18-4
WORKSHEET ENTRIES FOR THE SIMULATION

Trial or Cust. No.	(1) Rand. No.	(2) Time Betw. Arriv.	(3) Clock Time at Arriv. [last (3) + (2)]	(4) Clock Time at Beg. of Serv. [(3) or last (7)]	(5) Rand. No.	(6) Serv. Time	(7) Clock Time at End of Serv. [(4) + (6)]	(8) Waiting Time [(4) − (3)]
Open			9:00					
1	(12)	10	9:10	9:10	(61)	15	9:25	0
2	(81)	25	9:35	9:35	(74)	20	9:55	0
3	(36)	15	9:50	9:55	(98)	30	10:25	5
4	(82)	25	10:15	10:25	(54)	15	10:40	10
5	(21)	10	10:25	10:40	(15)	10	10:50	15
6	(74)	20	10:45	10:50	(47)	15	11:05	5
7	(90)	25	11:10	11:10	(64)	15	11:25	0
8	(55)	20	11:30	11:30	(98)	30	12:00	0
9	(79)	25	11:55	12:00	(17)	10	12:10	5
10	(70)	20	12:15	12:15	(00)	30	12:45	0
11	(14)	10	12:25	12:45	(53)	15	1:00	20
12	(59)	20	12:45	1:00	(08)	10	1:10	15
13	(62)	20	1:05	1:10	(62)	15	1:25	5
14	(57)	20	1:25	1:25	(97)	30	1:55	0
15	(15)	10	1:35	1:55	(90)	25	2:20	20
16	(18)	10	1:45	2:20	(23)	10	2:30	35
17	(74)	20	2:05	2:30	(68)	20	2:50	25
18	(11)	10	2:15	2:50	(16)	10	3:00	35
19	(41)	15	2:30	3:00	(17)	10	3:10	30
20	(22)	10	2:40	3:10	(91)	25	3:35	30
		345				360		255

Elapsed time = 3:35−9:00
= 6 hours and 35 minutes
= 395 minutes

waiting. The next random number, 74, corresponds to a 20-minute service time, so customer 2 is finished at 9:55.

Meanwhile, the third customer arrives 15 minutes behind the second, at 9:50. Sammy is busy with the earlier one until 9:55, so his service cannot begin until then. Customer 3 must wait 5 minutes. In general, the clock time when service begins is the *greatest* of the entries in columns (3) and (7).

The simulation continues until 20 customers have been monitored. It is now possible for Ms. Lee to estimate the various parameters. The procedure for doing this constitutes the remaining portion of the simulation model.

Summing the values in column (2) and dividing by the number of customers 20, we calculate the *estimated mean time between arrivals*:

$$\frac{\text{Total time between arrivals}}{\text{Number of customers}} = \frac{345}{20} = 17.25 \text{ minutes per customer}$$

The reciprocal of this result, in units of customers per minute, is the *estimated mean arrival rate*:

$$\frac{1}{\text{Mean time between arrivals}} = \frac{1}{17.25} = .058 \text{ customers per minute}$$
$$(3.48 \text{ customers per hour})$$

Summing the entries in column (6) and dividing by 20 customers, we compute the *estimated mean service time*:

$$\frac{\text{Total service time}}{\text{Number of customers}} = \frac{360}{20} = 18.00 \text{ minutes per customer}$$

And the reciprocal of this result provides the *estimated mean service rate*:

$$\frac{1}{\text{Mean service time}} = \frac{1}{18} = .056 \text{ customers per minute}$$
$$(3.36 \text{ customers per hour})$$

The true values for the above can be computed from the initial probability distributions, so that it is unnecessary to use these estimates. But some interesting points can be made by comparing our estimates to their true values. The latter are the expected values calculated in Table 18-5 using the probability distributions given initially.

Notice that the true mean time between arrivals is 17.50 minutes per customer, which is quite close to the simulation result of 17.25. However, the true mean service time of 16.25 minutes per customer is considerably smaller than the simulated value of 18.00. We must keep in mind that a simulation is like any sample result, and, like any statistical estimate, sampling errors can be expected. In this particular simulation, the service times were longer than usual, reflecting the fact that the random numbers used were abnormally large. This shouldn't detract from the value of the simulation, since actual observed service times on any particular Saturday may also tend to be longer than usual.

Table 18-5

EXPECTED VALUE CALCULATIONS TO DETERMINE TRUE PARAMETER VALUES

Possible Times	*Probability*	*Time × Probability*
Between Arrivals:		
5 min	.10	.50 min
10	.15	1.50
15	.25	3.75
20	.25	5.00
25	.15	3.75
30	.10	3.00
	$1/\lambda$ = Mean time between arrivals =	17.50 min
For Service:		
5	.05	.25
10	.20	2.00
15	.40	6.00
20	.20	4.00
25	.10	2.50
30	.05	1.50
	$1/\mu$ = Mean service time =	16.25 min

As with any sampling situation, the only protection against sampling error is to increase the precision or reliability of the simulation estimates by conducting a sufficiently large number of trials. Had 200 rather than 20 customers been evaluated, we would expect the estimated mean service time to be much closer to the true parameter value. Later we will consider the question of just how many trials ought to be used.

Ms. Lee's other parameters must be estimated because they cannot be easily computed like the simple expected values found above. Returning to Table 18-4, we divide the total of the column (8) values by the number of customers to determine the *estimated mean customer waiting time:*

$$\frac{\text{Total waiting time}}{\text{Number of customers}} = \frac{255}{20} = 12.75 \text{ minutes}$$

Including the column (6) total of the service times in the numerator, we obtain the *estimated mean customer time in the system:*

$$\frac{\text{Total waiting time} + \text{Total service time}}{\text{Number of customers}} = \frac{255 + 360}{20}$$

$$= 30.75 \text{ minutes}$$

The above calculation reflects the fact that a customer's time in the barbershop must be spent waiting for and then receiving service. The above result is thus equivalent to the sum of the mean waiting and service times:

$$12.75 + 18.00 = 30.75$$

The remaining parameter estimates require some thought. Consider first the problem of finding the average number of customers waiting at any given time. This could be done by taking every five-minute time interval in the simulation and determining how many customers are waiting in each. A relative frequency distribution indicating the proportion of times 0, 1, 2, 3, or 4 persons were waiting could then be found, and their weighted average would provide the desired result. Fortunately, all this extra work is unnecessary. Instead, we take the total waiting time in column (8) and divide this by the simulation's *elapsed time*, its duration from start to finish (calculated in Table 18-4 to be 395 minutes), to get the *estimated mean number of customers waiting:*

$$\frac{\text{Total waiting time}}{\text{Elapsed time}} = \frac{255}{395} = .65 \text{ customers}$$

It may seem a bit odd to get customers by dividing minutes by minutes; yet the above computation is mathematically equivalent to the weighted average approach. We may view total waiting time as the product of the times when customers wait and the number of customers waiting, so that the numerator would be in units of customer-minutes.

In a similar fashion, the totals for columns (6) and (8) can be added and divided by elapsed time to provide the *estimated mean number of customers in the system.*

$$\frac{\text{Total service time + Total waiting time}}{\text{Elapsed time}} = \frac{255 + 360}{395}$$

$$= 1.56 \text{ customers}$$

The above represents the average number of persons either waiting or receiving service at any point in time.

To find the proportion of time the barber is busy with a customer, we divide the total from column (6) by the elapsed time to get the *estimated server utilization factor*:

$$\frac{\text{Total service time}}{\text{Elapsed time}} = \frac{360}{395} = .91$$

We see that Sammy Lee spends about 91 percent of a Saturday actually cutting hair. The above number has another interpretation: it provides the fraction of a customer who may be receiving service at any time. Thus subtracting this from the estimated mean number of customers in the barbershop, we obtain the estimated mean number waiting

$$1.56 - .91 = .65$$

Transient Simulation States

You may have wondered why Ms. Lee stopped her simulation abruptly with the twentieth customer at 3:35, in the midst of a busy period that started about 2 PM. Shouldn't she have continued her simulation until closing time?

All simulations must begin and end some time, and generally the number of trials is established in advance. In the barbershop example, this can lead to distortions near the beginning and the end of the simulation. Sammy Lee opened his shop at 9 AM, and customers started trickling in at 9:10; no opening-time congestion, which might occur in reality, was possible. Also, no successful barber quits for the day when customers are still waiting. The middle of the simulation best matches reality. Distortions encountered at the beginning and the end arise because the simulation is then in *transient states*. An analogy with an automobile engine's performance test may be helpful. An engine exhibits different characteristics while warming up from when it has been running for a while; to get a realistic assessment of performance, only the warm engine results should be considered. Also, slight sputtering or coughing the instant after the ignition switch is shut off should not be reflected in the performance rating.

The impact of transitional distortions can be minimized by running the simulation longer. If Ms. Lee uses 1000 customers (so that 50 or so Saturdays are considered back-to-back), distortions at the beginning and the end can be safely ignored.

It is another matter entirely if the barbershop actually goes through transient states in real operation. This might happen if Sammy has customers lined up at the door when he arrives or if he varies his closing time to accommodate stragglers. Also, arrivals may be more concentrated at 2 or 3 PM than at other times. And, Sammy may slow down in the afternoon, thus, increasing the service times. The simulation model itself must be more complex if it is to reflect varying system characteristics realistically.

Decision Making with Simulation

Ms. Lee's simulation provides a variety of estimates for the key parameters. These can be helpful in any further analysis. Remember that Sammy Lee's basic problem is deciding whether or not to hire a second barber for Saturdays. Evaluation of that alternative requires a second simulation having a somewhat more complex procedure (which is left as an exercise for you to determine). This later simulation will involve a similar set of estimated parameter values that may be compared to the initial ones.

Comparison of two or more simulations can be a demanding task, especially when several kinds of information are available from each. To a certain extent, this presents the same problems encountered in evaluating samples taken from several populations. We next discuss these statistical aspects of simulation.

STATISTICAL ASPECTS OF SIMULATION   18-3

A simulation is completely analogous to a sampling study. Consider the similarities between estimating the mean customer waiting time and estimating a city's mean disposable family income. Each simulation trial provides one randomly chosen waiting time, whereas a randomly selected family yields a sample observation of income. In either case, planning is involved in setting up the study and in deciding how many observations to make. Although the data are collected differently, the results are qualitatively equivalent. In reporting results or deciding what to do, potential sampling error must be acknowledged and contended with. Thus, conclusions in either situation are in the nature of *statistical inferences*.

Required Number of Trials

As indicated earlier, the number of simulation trials determines the precision and reliability of the resulting estimate. This number plays the same role as that of the sample size in traditional statistics. In the planning stage of the simulation the number of trials must be treated as a variable, which we denote by n. Ms. Lee used $n = 20$ in her simulation. How large should n be in estimating mean waiting time? In determining the answer, we will assume that no simulation data are available.

To ease our discussion and transition from traditional statistics, we will adopt the usual notation. Each individual waiting time can be represented by an X with appropriate subscript; thus X_1 represents the first customer's waiting time, X_2 the second customer's, and so forth. The arithmetic mean of these Xs is denoted by $\overline{X}$. The population standard deviation for all future Saturday waiting times is σ. The population mean waiting time is denoted by W_q (instead of μ, which represents the true mean service rate in standard queuing formulas). W_q is the quantity to be estimated. The expected value of $\overline{X}$ is W_q, and, from the central limit theorem, we know that $\overline{X}$ is approximately normally distributed with

$$\text{Mean} = W_q$$

$$\text{Standard deviation} = \frac{\sigma}{\sqrt{n}}$$

when σ is known in advance.

Of course, we don't know the value of σ. We will guess its value, and, to distinguish the true and guessed values for the standard deviation, we use the subscript g:

$$\sigma_g = \text{Guessed value for standard deviation}$$

A rule of thumb for finding σ_g is that it should equal one-sixth the difference between the largest and smallest conceivable values:*

$$\sigma_g = \frac{\text{Largest value} - \text{Smallest value}}{6}$$

---

* Were the individual waiting times to be normally distributed, they would fall within $\pm 3\sigma$ of the true mean about 99.7 percent of the time. This is a range of 6σ. Of course, some other distribution may apply, so the above procedure is not completely accurate.

Suppose that Sammy Lee occasionally keeps a Saturday customer waiting up to 60 minutes, but never any longer; and the smallest waiting time is obviously 0. Thus,

$$\sigma_g = \frac{60 - 0}{6} = 10 \text{ minutes}$$

Before finding n, it is necessary to establish target levels for precision and reliability. These are

$d =$ Target precision level (maximum deviation from true value)

$z =$ Normal deviate for target reliability level

We emphasize that both of the above are essential, since precision and reliability are competing ends. An overly precise estimate, such as $W_q = 2.343$ minutes $\pm .0005$, is almost totally unreliable. Likewise a very imprecise result, such as "W_q lies between 0 and 100 minutes," is perfectly reliable—even if no simulation is conducted.

The target precision level d expresses the maximum deviation to be tolerated between the estimate and its true value—either above or below it—in terms of the units involved (minutes, in the present example). The reliability expresses the probability that the target precision is met. Because such a probability is obtained from a normal curve centered at the true mean and with standard deviation $\sigma/\sqrt{n}$ (represented by $\sigma_g/\sqrt{n}$), for a specific d, z, and σ_g there is a unique n such that*

$$n = \frac{z^2 \sigma_g^2}{d^2}$$

Suppose Ms. Lee wishes to be precise to the nearest whole minute, so that $d = 1$, and that this is done with a .95 reliability, so that the required normal deviate is $z = 1.96$. Using these values and $\sigma_g = 10$ in the above, we find that her required sample size is

$$n = \frac{(1.96)^2 (10)^2}{(1)^2} = 384.16 \text{ or } 385$$

By using only 20 customers, Ms. Lee has *undersampled* and will not meet her targets. Often ns calculated in the above manner are huge, so that hand simulations must then of necessity involve undersampling.

---

* A complete explanation and derivation of this equation is too lengthy for inclusion in this book. See Lawrence L. Lapin, *Statistics for Modern Business Decisions*, 2nd ed. (New York: Harcourt Brace Jovanovich, 1978), pp. 256–70 for a complete discussion.

(In computer simulations the proper n can usually be applied at little cost.) The price paid for undersampling is fuzzy results that make it difficult to compare the alternatives simulated.

The Confidence Interval Estimate

In reporting simulation results, an *interval estimate* is often used, just as with ordinary sample data. When estimating a mean, two values are used in constructing such an interval: the sample mean $\bar{X}$ and the *sample standard deviation*

$$s = \sqrt{\frac{\Sigma(X - \bar{X})^2}{n-1}}$$

The latter statistic may be calculated from simulation data and serves as the estimator of the unknown value of σ. The n used above and in any other statistical calculation involving data must be the *actual* number of trials used. In the barbershop simulation $n = 20$ (not the desired level of 385 found earlier).

Ordinarily some *confidence level*, such as 95 percent or 99 percent, is used to report the results. A normal deviate value z, such as 1.96 or 2.57, corresponds to the level chosen. For the large samples generally used in simulations, the following expression determines the *confidence interval estimate*:

$$\text{True mean} = \bar{X} \pm z\frac{s}{\sqrt{n}}$$

Before computing the confidence interval for the mean customer waiting time, the sample standard deviation must be found; this is calculated in Table 18-6 to be $s = 12.7$ minutes. Ms. Lee desires a 95 percent confidence level, so that $z = 1.96$ is used. Substituting these values, along with $\bar{X} = 12.75$ and $n = 20$, into the above, we determine the following confidence interval for the mean customer waiting time:

$$W_q = 12.75 \pm (1.96)\frac{12.7}{\sqrt{20}}$$

$$= 12.75 \pm 5.57 \text{ minutes}$$

or $\quad 7.18 \leq W_q \leq 18.32$ minutes

The proper interpretation of this result is as follows: *If the twenty-customer simulation were repeated over and over again, using different*

Table 18-6
CALCULATIONS FOR SAMPLE STANDARD DEVIATION OF CUSTOMER WAITING TIMES

Customer i	Waiting Time X_i	Deviation $(X_i - \bar{X})$	$(X_i - \bar{X})^2$
1	0	−12.75	162.5625
2	0	−12.75	162.5625
3	5	− 7.75	60.0625
4	10	− 2.75	7.5625
5	15	2.25	5.0625
6	5	− 7.75	60.0625
7	0	−12.75	162.5625
8	0	−12.75	162.5625
9	5	− 7.75	60.0625
10	0	−12.75	162.5625
11	20	7.25	52.5625
12	15	2.25	5.0625
13	5	− 7.75	60.0625
14	0	−12.75	162.5625
15	20	7.25	52.5625
16	35	22.25	495.0625
17	25	12.25	150.0625
18	35	22.25	495.0625
19	30	17.25	297.5625
20	30	17.25	297.5625
	255	0.00	3073.7500

$$\bar{X} = \Sigma X/n = 255/20 = 12.75$$
$$s = \sqrt{3073.75/(20 - 1)} = \sqrt{161.78} = 12.7$$

random numbers each time, then in about 95 out of 100 cases an interval constructed in the above fashion will contain the true mean waiting time. But about 5 percent of such intervals will lie totally above or below the true value.

Notice that the above confidence interval is quite wide, reflecting the lack of precision due to undersampling.

Further Statistical Considerations

We have barely scratched the statistical surface of simulation. Other kinds of inferences may be made. For instance, Ms. Lee may want to compare the Ws for one-man and two-man barbershops, which brings another set of sample data into the picture. Various hypothesis testing procedures can be employed for this purpose. Should several alternatives be simulated, an analysis of variance might be conducted. A detailed discussion of these procedures is beyond the scope of this book; many good statistical references are provided in the bibliography at the back of the book.

But there are further complications. Ms. Lee wants to estimate nine parameters, and an elaborate report might consider inferences about these as well. Fortunately, the typical simulation involves estimating only one parameter.

Sometimes a simulation involves estimating a probability or a proportion instead of a mean. For example, the optimal number of telephone information operators might be the smallest sized crew providing a .95 probability of rendering service within 10 seconds. In simulating various alternatives, the true probability for a particular crew size could be estimated by the proportion of calls (trials) receiving service within 10 seconds. Although there is not enough space to describe them in this book, equivalent expressions can be used to find n and to compute confidence intervals for such quantities.

18-4 SIMULATION AND PERT

Chapter 17 discussed PERT (Program Evaluation and Review Technique). There we saw that much of the analysis ignores the uncertainties about activity times. Using expected times only, we can provide the project manager with a time-cost tradeoff curve for deciding what activities, if any, should be crashed. Unfortunately, the project completion times obtained in this manner can seriously understate the true expected project completion times.

Consider the PERT network in Figure 18-4, illustrating a project with five activities, each represented by an arrow. The regular activity completion times are provided on the respective arrows. The times shown in boldface for activities b and d are certain and cannot vary; those on the arrows for a, c, and e are *expected* times. Traditional PERT analysis is based upon the *critical path*, which is the longest duration activity sequence from start to finish. Based on the times given in the network, all the paths (a-d, a-c-e, and b-e) are critical, and each is expected to take 20 days.

The continuous probability distributions for the three uncertain activity times are represented in Figure 18-5 by cumulative probability graphs. The project will be simulated using random numbers to determine the times that will be obtained in each trial.

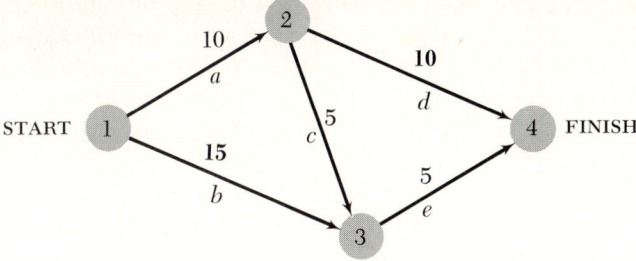

Figure 18-4
A PERT network illustrating a project with five activities.

Using Random Numbers with Continuous Distributions

When a cumulative probability graph is available for a continuous random variable (see Chapter 4 to find out how they are constructed), the graph itself may be used to determine which quantities correspond to the random numbers. As we saw in the barbershop simulation, random numbers can be assigned to trial variable values by establishing the range for the random numbers; the upper limit of that range is identical to the cumulative probability for the value, except for the decimal point. When the variable is continuous, cumulative probability serves the same purpose, except that ranges are not involved—only single quantities. Because fractional activity times are possible, it will be convenient to use all the digits in each random number.

Figure 18-6 illustrates the procedure for generating completion times for activity a. Consider 12651 as the first random number; this corresponds to a cumulative probability of .12651, representing a height on the graph slightly below .13. From the curve we see that the time corresponding to this cumulative probability is roughly 6.8 days. Similarly, we may locate the cumulative probability corresponding to a second random number, 81769; the curve at that height represents a time of approximately 12.3 days. Since any random number between 00000 and 99999 is equally likely, each possible height on the curve is just as likely in each trial. Notice that the steepest portion of the curve occurs around 10 days, indicating that more possible random numbers will yield times falling near 10 than any other time. Likewise, the curve is flatter near 5 days, so that fewer random numbers will lead to times near that level. The graphical procedure will therefore generate times more frequently for the more typical levels and less frequently for the rarer ones. With a large number of trials, the frequencies can be expected

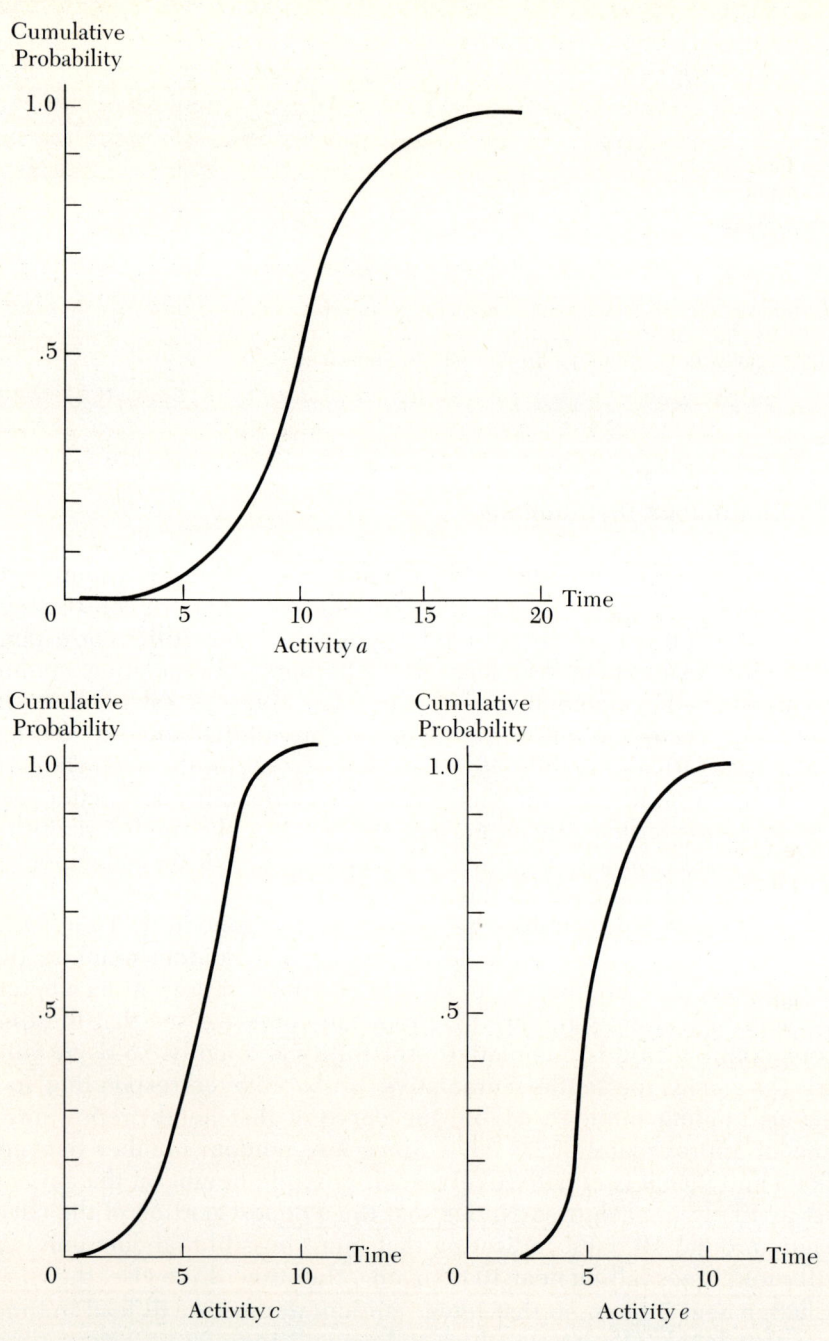

Figure 18-5
Cumulative probability distributions for PERT regular activity completion times.

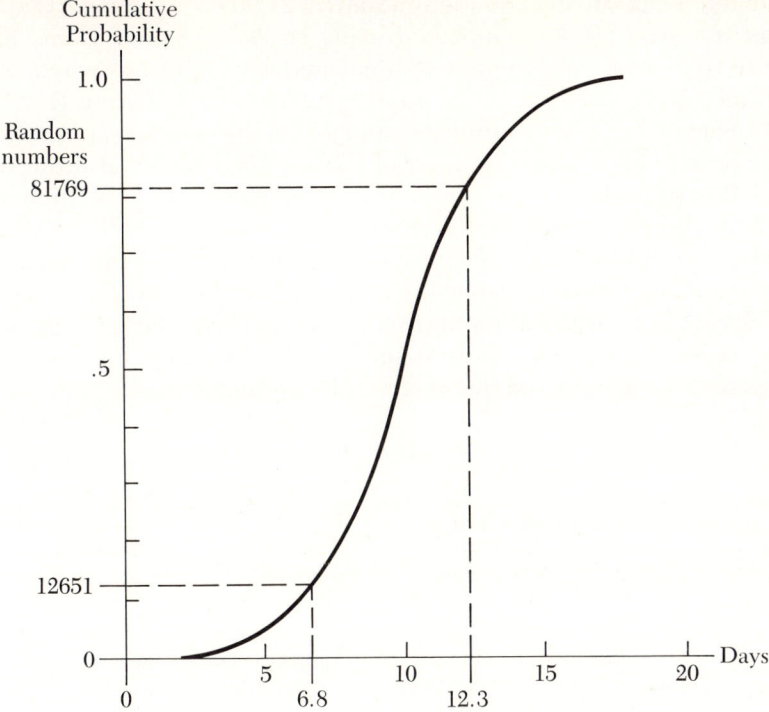

Figure 18-6
Using a cumulative probability curve for assigning random numbers to quantities.

to match the underlying probabilities exactly, which is just what a simulation is supposed to do.

The Simulation

The worksheet for the PERT simulation is provided in Table 18-7, where the results of $n = 20$ trials are shown. Each trial involved reading three random numbers onto the respective cumulative probability graphs for activities a, c, and e to determine the corresponding activity completion times. Then the path with the longest total time through the network was determined, and the duration of that critical path established the project completion time for the particular trial.

The simulation illustrates some interesting results. Notice that the

18-4 SIMULATION AND PERT

simulated mean project completion time of 21.96 days is almost two days *longer* than the 20 days indicated using expected values alone. Since only 20 trials were used, only statistical analysis can tell us whether this difference is significant or the natural result of sampling error. However, studies have established similar results to be the general case in PERT simulations with a larger number of trials. Notice also that if the mean simulation times for the various activities are considered, all three paths based on these averages are shorter than 21.96 days. This illustrates the tendency for traditional PERT procedures — based on average times and individual paths — to understate the mean completion time for the project as a whole. One explanation for this is that no particular path can really be considered singly, for there is some probability that any one of several paths will actually be the longest. Notice that all three paths turned

Table 18-7
WORKSHEET AND RESULTS FOR PERT SIMULATION

	ACTIVITY TIMES (days)								LONGEST (CRITICAL) PATH	PROJECT DURATION
	a		b	c		d	e			
TRIAL	Random Number	Time	Time	Random Number	Time	Time	Random Number	Time		
1	(12651)	6.8	15	(61646)	6.3	10	(11769)	4.2	b-e	19.2
2	(81769)	12.3	15	(74436)	6.8	10	(02630)	2.7	a-d	22.3
3	(36737)	9.4	15	(98863)	8.5	10	(77240)	6.2	a-c-e	24.1
4	(82861)	12.6	15	(54371)	6.2	10	(76610)	6.2	a-c-e	25.0
5	(21325)	7.8	15	(15732)	4.0	10	(24127)	4.6	b-e	19.6
6	(74146)	11.3	15	(47887)	6.0	10	(62463)	5.4	a-c-e	22.7
7	(90759)	13.9	15	(64410)	6.5	10	(54179)	5.1	a-c-e	25.5
8	(55683)	10.2	15	(98078)	8.3	10	(02238)	2.7	a-c-e	21.2
9	(79686)	12.0	15	(17969)	4.2	10	(76061)	6.2	a-c-e	22.4
10	(70333)	11.0	15	(00201)	.5	10	(86201)	6.9	b-e	21.9
11	(14042)	7.0	15	(53536)	6.1	10	(07779)	3.8	b-e	18.8
12	(59911)	10.3	15	(08256)	3.1	10	(06596)	3.6	a-d	20.3
13	(62368)	10.4	15	(62623)	6.4	10	(62742)	6.0	a-c-e	22.8
14	(57529)	10.2	15	(97751)	8.2	10	(54976)	5.4	a-c-e	23.8
15	(15469)	7.1	15	(90574)	7.5	10	(78033)	6.3	b-e	21.3
16	(18625)	7.6	15	(23674)	4.6	10	(53850)	5.1	b-e	20.1
17	(74626)	11.3	15	(68394)	6.7	10	(88562)	7.2	a-c-e	25.2
18	(11119)	6.4	15	(16519)	4.1	10	(27384)	4.7	b-e	19.7
19	(41101)	9.6	15	(17336)	4.2	10	(48951)	4.9	b-e	19.9
20	(32123)	9.0	15	(91576)	7.6	10	(84221)	6.7	a-c-e	23.3
Totals		196.2	300		115.8	200		103.9		439.1
Averages		9.81	15		5.80	10		5.20		21.96

out to be critical in at least one trial, and in no trial was there more than one critical path.

SIMULATING INVENTORY POLICIES 18-5

Simulation has been used to evaluate alternative inventory policies. Figure 18-7 shows the log a retailer might use to record the actual operations of an inventory system for a single product. From this log format a more detailed simulation worksheet might be developed in order to simulate various inventory policies, such as "order 500 items whenever any day starts with less than 60 units."

Day	Starting Inventory	Items Received	Items Demanded	Items Sold	Items Backordered	Items Ordered	Days for Order to Arrive	Holding and Shortage Costs	Ordering Cost
6/7	150	0	100	100	0	0	—	$1.50	—
6/8	50	0	75	50	25	500	2	3.00	$5.00
6/9	0	0	85	0	85	0	—	8.50	—
6/10	0	500	55	55	0	0	—	0.00	—
6/11	335	0	60	60	0	0	—	3.35	—

Figure 18-7
Hypothetical log for the actual daily operation of an inventory system.

Daily demand is one random variable for which a probability distribution must be obtained. Another uncertainty might be reflected in the lead time taken to get the order, and some probability distribution would apply to the number of days until an order arrives. The values for both variables would apply to the number of days until an order arrives and would be generated with random numbers.

The log pictured in Figure 18-7 indicates that all items demanded will be sold, unless the inventory is depleted. In the latter case short items are backordered and will be supplied when the next shipment arrives. Inventory holding costs are presumed to be 1¢ per item held at the start of each day, which represents a daily proration of annual holding costs (usually expressed as a monetary amount per dollar value). A straight penalty of $.10 is assumed to apply for each item short. And the ordering cost is $5.00, regardless of how many items are ordered.

The same approach may be taken for the more elaborate problem that involves several products, each having different demand and lead-time distributions. These products may compete for space and working capital and each has different costs. Some items may involve quantity discounting by the supplier. Shortage penalties may be more elaborate, including added cost for each day the shortage lasts.

18-6 SIMULATION VERSUS THE ANALYTIC SOLUTION

Whenever possible, management scientists prefer to use simulation as a last resort. An analytic solution is preferred if it is valid and can be obtained with less work. One reason is that simulation involves a great deal of effort and expense—even when performed with the assistance of the computer. Separate simulations are required for each alternative—and there could be hundreds or thousands of these. And after the simulating is finished, true values are not available—only statistical estimates. It's no wonder that an algebraic expression providing the exact answer would be more desirable.

Simulation should be put into proper perspective and ought to be used sparingly. But no one has catalogued the situations in which it should and should not be used. In saving ourselves from the tedium of simulation, we must never force a problem to fit a particular analytic solution unless the assumptions underlying the model are closely met by the problem. We may illustrate the pitfalls of doing this by considering Sammy Lee's barbershop one more time.

In Chapter 17, various formulas exist for obtaining the parameters of a single-channel queue. These depend only on the mean arrival rate λ and the mean service rate μ. In the case of Sammy Lee's, the reciprocals of these were computed earlier from the basic probability data:

$$1/\lambda = 17.50 \text{ minutes per customer}$$

$$1/\mu = 16.25 \text{ minutes per customer}$$

Thus,

$$\lambda = 1/17.50 = .057 \text{ customers per minute}$$

$$\mu = 1/16.25 = .062 \text{ customers per minute}$$

Applying the innocuous formula for mean customer waiting time, we have

$$W_q = \frac{\lambda}{\mu(\mu - \lambda)} = \frac{.057}{.062(.062 - .057)} = 184 \text{ minutes}$$

which is over ten times what was obtained in the simulation. Another queuing formula tells us that the mean arrival rate times W_q equals the mean number of customers waiting. Thus,

$$L_q = \lambda W_q = .057(184) = 10.5 \text{ customers}$$

which disagrees with the simulation results by the same factor.

Why these huge discrepancies? The explanation is that Sammy Lee's barbershop does not agree with an assumption of the underlying queuing model. This often overlooked assumption is that the arrival and service times must be *exponentially distributed*. The probability distributions used for the simulation do not even come close to resembling the exponential, which indicates that a time of zero is the most likely one to occur.

The above example was purposely picked to dramatize what can happen by blindly using someone else's analytic solution procedure. Not all of them work so poorly—even when their assumptions are not met exactly. The EOQ (Economic Order Quantity) formulas used to get inventory policies are generally very successful in finding close to optimal answers in such cases. They are said to be *robust* with regard to a variety of violations in the underlying assumptions. It may not be worth the extra work to simulate inventory policies when a very good answer can be found much more simply with a 30-second calculation.

In the quest for analytic solutions, the model itself can so distort reality that the mathematically developed conclusions are not valid and can even be misleading. This happened with PERT. Appendix 16-1 to Chapter 16 describes in detail a popular procedure for obtaining the probability distribution for the duration of that particular path identified as the "critical" one; the traditional label of critical path is somewhat of a misnomer, since traditional methods identify this activity sequence using expected (average) activity completion times. We saw earlier in this chapter why such an analysis based on average times understates the true mean *project* completion time.

The traditional PERT model provides a probability analysis for a variable nobody really cares about—namely, the length of a particular path that may or may not turn out to be the longest one. Project managers are rightly concerned instead with the time it will take to finish the entire project—a totally different variable. Analytic procedures cannot provide a probability analysis of this variable, except in very tiny networks. In conjunction with the PERT network, simulation is the more viable procedure for determining the characteristics of project completion times.

18-7 SIMULATION AND THE COMPUTER

Monte Carlo simulation involves lots of repetition of the same computational steps. This makes the digital computer an ideal tool for applying simulation. Once the computer program has been written, each alternative can be simulated with thousands of trials at a relatively modest cost. Indeed, perhaps no other management science technique has been nurtured so dramatically by the advent of bigger and faster computers.

Simulation Programs and Languages

Simulation has become so integrated with the computer that special languages (similar to Basic, COBOL, and FORTRAN) have been written just to do simulations. One of these is SIMSCRIPT, which is based on FORTRAN. Instructions may be written in this language without detailed knowledge of computers. A special program, called a compiler, then converts the SIMSCRIPT instructions into machine language; compilers exist for a variety of computers.

Another popular simulation procedure applies the General Purpose System Simulator (GPSS). This is really a program developed by IBM for its computers. Versions are also available for computers from other manufacturers. GPSS is more efficient in some respects than SIMSCRIPT, but inferior in others. In choosing a simulation language, the overriding consideration is what system happens to be available.

Should no special simulation software be accessible, it is still possible to use ordinary programming languages, such as FORTRAN, to conduct a computer simulation. All the major languages come with library routines that are useful in computer simulation. These are especially important in generating random numbers.

Random-Number Generation

It would be terribly impractical to prepare random numbers ahead of time and feed them into the computer during a simulation. This would not only slow down the processing, but it might consume too much core memory. Besides, consider the awful job of compiling and keypunching these numbers. Also, computer simulations can involve billions of random numbers—far too many to be taken from published lists.

The random numbers in a computer simulation are invariably generated by the computer itself as they are needed. This is usually done with a seed number, which is multiplied by one constant, divided by another value, with the remainder term being used as the random number. The next number is always found in this fashion from the last one. Of course, all such numbers can be predicted in advance, so they are not really random at all.

Values generated in this way are called *pseudo-random numbers*. They can be used in simulations because *they look like true random numbers*. Pseudo-random number generation schemes yield a stream of numbers that exhibit all the essential properties: nearly equal frequency for all possible values, little serial correlation, and no abnormally long or short runs of any particular type of number.

Disadvantages of Computer Simulation

Using the computer has some disadvantages. Paramount is the programming effort. Unless statistical reliability is very critical or a large number of alternatives must be considered, it is often easier in the long run to "crank it out by hand." The inherent characteristics of the digital computer can create a lot of extra work. For example, computers don't read graphs, necessitating the approximation of continuous probability distributions by a table of typical values and their associated probabilities. Also, some models are pictorial in nature (similar to a PERT network), and it would be especially demanding to write a special program that duplicates the human capacity to make visual inspections.

PROBLEMS

18-1 Consider the following probability distribution for the times between arrivals of cars stopping at a toll booth.

Time	Probability
5 sec	.35
10	.23
15	.15
20	.11
25	.08
30	.05
35	.03

(a) Construct the cumulative probability distribution and determine a random-number assignment suitable for simulation (use two digits).

(b) Simulate the arrival of 20 cars and calculate the estimated mean time between arrivals.

18-2 For the probability distribution in Problem 18-1, make the expected value calculation to find the true mean time between arrivals.

18-3 As part of a simulation to determine response to advertising, you must create trial persons who fall into one of the following categories.

Category	Probability
Urban	.36
Suburban	.47
Rural	.17

Determine a two-digit random-number assignment to generate these events.

18-4 Consider the cumulative probability for demand provided in Figure 4-16 on page 137. Use the following random numbers to generate 20 demands.

```
99582   53390   46357   13244
18080   02321   05809   04898
30143   52687   19420   60061
46683   33761   47452   23551
48672   28736   84994   13071
```

What is the estimated mean demand?

18-5 A staff analyst for the Big-E Corp. has developed a simulation model to estimate the mean annual rate of return for new projects. Separate simulations will be run for the various alternatives, each consisting of several investment lifetime trials. The analyst wants to determine how many trials to create for a particular case where the lifetime annual rate of return might fall between -20 and 40 percent.

How many trials are required to estimate the mean rate of return to the nearest 1 percent when a reliability of 95 percent is desired?

18-6 The mean time required by automobile assemblers to hang a car door is to be estimated. Assuming a guess for the standard deviation of 10 seconds, determine the required n under the following conditions:

(a) The desired reliability probability of being in error by no more than 1 second (in either direction) is .99.
(b) The desired reliability probability for the above is instead .95.
(c) A reliability of .99 is desired, with a target precision of 2 seconds. How does the n obtained compare with your answer to (a)?

18-7 Construct a 95 percent confidence interval for the true means, given the following simulation results:
(a) With $n = 100$, $\bar{X} = 100.53$ minutes, and $s = 25.3$ minutes.
(b) With $n = 200$, $\bar{X} = 69.2$ inches, and $s = 1.08$ inches.
(c) With $n = 350$, $\bar{X} = \$12.00$, and $s = \$7.00$.

18-8 Construct a 95 percent confidence interval estimate for the mean project completion time using the simulation results in Table 18-7 for the PERT illustration in the chapter.

18-9 Consider the alternative of adding a second barber to Sammy Lee's shop on Saturdays. This will attract more customers, so that they will arrive closer together. Suppose the following probabilities apply:

Time Between Arrivals	Probability
5 min	.35
10	.25
15	.20
20	.10
25	.10

Suppose also that the second barber has the same service time distribution as Sammy.
(a) Set up a worksheet for simulating the two-man barbershop. (*Hint:* only one random number is needed for each customer's service time.)
(b) Assuming that a customer will pick Sammy if both barbers are free and the first free barber otherwise, conduct a 20-customer simulation with the random numbers used in Table 18-4.
(c) Find the estimated mean customer waiting time.

18-10 Consider Sammy's barbershop again. Suppose that simulations were conducted long enough to determine the true mean waiting times as follows:

$$W_q = 15 \text{ minutes for one barber}$$
$$W_q = 5 \text{ minutes for two barbers}$$

Suppose that Sammy suffers a goodwill loss of 5 cents for each minute *each* customer spends waiting. The shop is open for 8 hours on Saturdays. Each customer brings an average revenue of $4.00 and the second barber costs Sammy $5 per hour.

Using the probability data in the chapter and in Problem 18-9, compute Sammy's average Saturday earnings in the one-barber and the two-barber cases. What should Sammy do?

18-11 Suppose that the retailer in the chapter experiences a daily demand for items according to the following probability distribution:

Demand	Probability
40	.04
50	.08
60	.15
70	.23
80	.20
90	.15
100	.10
110	.05

and the lead-time distribution for filling an order is

Lead Time	Probability
1 day	.20
2	.25
3	.20
4	.15
5	.10
6	.10

(a) Simulate 25 days of operation to estimate the mean daily inventory cost using an order quantity of 500, with an order placed whenever a day's starting inventory falls below 60. Use a starting inventory of 150.

(b) Repeat your simulation with an order quantity of 1000 and an order point of 100. Use the same random numbers as in (a).

(c) Which of the two inventory policies appears least costly?

18-12 Although not accepted practice, in a pinch you can generate your own random numbers by tossing a coin. For instance, a list of two-digit decimal numbers can be achieved by first generating a list of seven-digit binary numbers from 7 tosses of a coin. This is done by assigning a 0 to tail and a 1 to head. These may then be converted to decimal numbers. For example, the sequence HTHHTTH yields the binary number 1011001. And in decimals this can be expressed as the sum:

$$1 \times 2^6 = 64$$
$$0 \times 2^5 = 0$$
$$1 \times 2^4 = 16$$
$$1 \times 2^3 = 8$$
$$0 \times 2^2 = 0$$
$$0 \times 2^1 = 0$$
$$1 \times 2^0 = \underline{1}$$
$$89$$

Any decimal values greater than 99 can be thrown away.

Generate a list of 10 two-digit random decimal numbers this way.

18-13 The dice game "Craps" provides an interesting example of when not to simulate. The outcome is based on the values achieved tossing two six-sided dice. One way to place a bet involves "playing the field." Here the bettor indicates that he wishes to make a bet with a complicated payoff, depending on which faces of the dice show. If a "field" number, defined by a sum value of 2 through 4 or 9 through 12, occurs, the player wins. Should the roll of the dice yield any other total, he loses. A field gamble is further complicated by a varying payoff. These are 1 to 1 for all field numbers but 2 or 12. The payoff on a 2 is 2 to 1, and for a 12 is 3 to 1. If a bettor wins, he keeps his original bet and is also paid his winnings. If he loses, he forfeits his wager.

(a) For a bet of $1, use the above description and the basic concepts of probability to find the probability distribution for a gambler's net winnings.

(b) Suppose that a system player has an initial bankroll of $7. Beginning with a $1 bet, this player's plan is to place successive field bets until winning once or losing the original $7. Either of these outcomes terminates the play. As long as money remains the gambler will double the last wager lost.

Simulate 10 runs of this system to estimate the gambler's mean winnings per play. (To simplify things, you may roll dice rather than use random numbers.)

(c) Solve the problem in part (b) analytically by determining the appropriate probability values and finding the gambler's expected winnings. Then compare this to the simulated value found in part (b). (*Hint:* a tree diagram might be helpful.)

18-14 A company's computer micro-wave transmission network, connecting 5 cities, is provided in Figure 18-8. Each line represents a channel; transmissions between 2 cities may be routed over any sequence of clear channels. The numbers above each line represents the probability for interference on that channel at any given moment. Management is contemplating adding more channels and

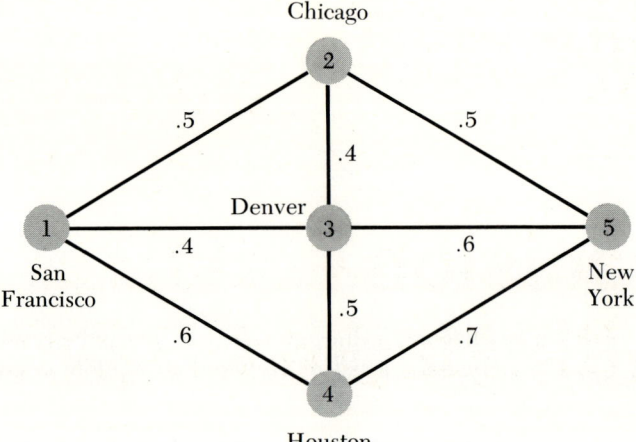

Figure 18-8

wants to estimate the probability that San Francisco and New York communications are completely blocked by interference at any given time.

Simulate this system for 20 trials to estimate the above probability. (*Hint:* you may want to make 20 copies of the network before starting. Then the blocked channels for each trial may be clearly identified.)

Nineteen

Decision Making with Markov Processes

Much decision making is concerned with establishing continuing policies for the various operational aspects of a business or organization. Business functions such as marketing, production, and finance involve uncertainties of a recurring nature. In this chapter, we describe a procedure based on the structure of these uncertainties that can sometimes be used in selecting an operating policy.

THE MARKOV PROCESS 19-1

The particular situations considered fall under the broad category of *Markov processes,* named after the Russian mathematician who helped pioneer modern probability theory. Several features distinguish a Markov process from more general uncertain situations. The basic structure is best described in terms of a *system*. Examples of such systems include the marketplace for a product and its competing brands, the machinery used in manufacturing that product, and the billing, credit, and collection procedures involved in converting accounts receivable from the product's sales into cash. At any given time the respective systems may be in one of several possible *states*. In marketing applications, the states can be expressed in terms of the brand a customer is presently using. In production, the state of concern might be the number of machines in working order. A customer's financial transaction might fall into one of the following states: cash sale, credit sale, or uncollectable.

Characteristics of Markov Processes

The main distinguishing feature of a Markov process is concerned with the *probabilities* of being in the various states at any given time and of going from one state to another. A Markov process is essentially memoryless, so that the probability of moving from one state to another does not depend on what happened before. This feature is sometimes called the *Markovian property*. For example, consider a smoker who is a potential buyer of Lucky Strike cigarettes. Suppose that we view brand switching as a Markov process. If this assumption is valid, the Markovian property tells us that this person will change from Camel to Lucky Strike with a constant probability, such as 1/10 (as determined by marketing research), when making a subsequent cigarette purchase—regardless of whether he or she has been a loyal Camel smoker for decades or has recently switched to Camel from Pall Mall. A further characteristic of a Markov process is that the *long-run* probability of being in a particular state will be constant over time and will hold regardless of the state probabilities that applied in the beginning. This says that the long-run probability that any particular smoker will buy Lucky Strike on the next purchase must be a constant, which sales experience might show to be a value such as 1/20, over time.

As applied to cigarettes, the implications from assuming a Markov process may seem a bit unrealistic. After all, brands come and go. Once Camel, Lucky Strike, Pall Mall, Kool, and Viceroy were leading sellers; today none of them are leaders (and some may be gone forever). How can we realistically assume that today's favorite will not suffer the same fate? The answer is that we can't. What is ignored is that the various probabilities in a Markov process can be changed through *outside action*. For example, advertising and promotion can cause more or fewer persons than before to switch to or from a particular brand. The possibility of such action adds the element of decision making to a Markov process.

State and Transition Probabilities

To illustrate further the concepts of Markov processes, we will expand on the problem of brand switching. Suppose that there are three brands, A, B, and C that all satisfy the same need and may be readily substituted for each other. The product is a convenience item (such as toothpaste or cigarettes) and is bought frequently. Any user is said to be in one of the states A, B, or C, depending on the brand he or she is presently using. Thus, each buyer will be faced from time to time with a buying decision that may result in a change from one state (brand) to another. We will assume that this decision will be made periodically. Changes will thus occur over time. Furthermore, the number of states (brand choices) is finite. Our example thus falls in a class of situations called *Markov chains*, which are distinguished from more general Markov processes in which the states might be continuous (for example, a physical dimension or the level of bulk inventory).

A marketing-research study based on detailed interviews with a sample of several hundred users has determined the frequency at which the customers as a whole have either remained with their present brand or changed brands. These data provide the *transition probabilities* given in Table 19-1.

Table 19-1
TRANSITION MATRIX FOR BUYERS OF THREE BRANDS

From State \ To	State A	B	C
A	.90	.05	.05
B	.10	.80	.10
C	.10	.15	.75

Table 19-1 is sometimes referred to as the *transition matrix*.

The number in the top left-hand corner reflects the research result showing that 90 percent of the users of brand A were found to retain that brand on subsequent purchase; it was therefore concluded that the probability is .90 for going from state A to state A on the next purchase. Likewise, the probability is .05 for going from state A to state B; this same value also applies for a switch from A to C. The above transition probabilities are *conditional probabilities* for entering the state listed on the right given the starting state on the left. As such, the values in each row must sum to 1.

The producers of the various brands want to establish advertising policies. They are concerned not with the above transition probabilities, but rather with their relative shares of the market. More specifically, each producer requires knowledge of the probability that any particular customer will purchase its brand. We refer to such a value as a *state probability*. Such a number is an unconditional probability, and its value may change over time. For convenience, we represent the state probability for state i at period n symbolically:

$$p_i(n) = P[\text{state } i \text{ occurs in period } n]$$

Suppose that further marketing-research data has shown that brand A currently holds 45 percent of the market; brand B, 35 percent; and brand C, 20 percent. These values apply in the initial period of our investigation. Our interpretation of these numbers is that any particular randomly chosen user of the product will have the following state probabilities in the initial period $n = 0$:

$$p_A(0) = .45$$
$$p_B(0) = .35$$
$$p_C(0) = .20$$

How State Probabilities Change over Time

The product manufacturers should be concerned with how permanent the above market shares are and how they might change from period to period. We may determine such changes by looking at the state probabilities in successive periods. As we have noted, a Markov process should have long-run probabilities that are constant over time. Before that equilibrium situation is reached, the process should be given some time to settle down.

Assuming that each customer will make the next brand choice in accordance with the transition probabilities given earlier, we may determine the state probabilities that apply in period $n = 1$ after they have made their initial purchases.

Consider state A. To find the probability that brand A gets chosen, we assume that it might be made by retaining brand A or by switching from either brand B or C. The joint probabilities for these results may be determined by multiplying the respective transition probability in column A of the transition matrix by the corresponding state probability. Summing these products, we obtain the new state probability for A:

$$\begin{array}{c}\text{Old State} \\ \text{Probability}\end{array} \times \begin{array}{c}\text{Transition} \\ \text{Probability}\end{array} = \begin{array}{c}\text{New State} \\ \text{Probability}\end{array}$$

$.45 \times .90 = .4050$
$.35 \times .10 = .0350$
$.20 \times .10 = \underline{.0200}$
$p_A(1) = .4600$

Similar calculations provide the other new state probabilities:

$.45 \times .05 = .0225$ $.45 \times .05 = .0225$

$.35 \times .80 = .2800$ $.35 \times .10 = .0350$

$.20 \times .15 = \underline{.0300}$ $.20 \times .75 = \underline{.1500}$
$p_B(1) = .3325$ $p_C(1) = .2075$

Notice that the period-1 state probabilities have changed. These indicate that more persons will be buying brands A and C than before, while brand B's share of the market drops. We may use the period-1 state probabilities in the same manner as before to find the applicable values for period 2:

$.4600 \times .90 = .41400$ $.4600 \times .05 = .02300$ $.4600 \times .05 = .02300$

$.3325 \times .10 = .03325$ $.3325 \times .80 = .26600$ $.3325 \times .10 = .03325$

$.2075 \times .10 = \underline{.02075}$ $.2075 \times .15 = \underline{.03113}$ $.2075 \times .75 = \underline{.15563}$
$p_A(2) = .46800$ $p_B(2) = .32013$ $p_C(2) = .21188$

We see that the state probabilities have changed further, although not by as much as before. Using our latest results, we find the state probabilities for period 3:

$.46800 \times .90 = .42120$ $.46800 \times .05 = .02340$ $.46800 \times .05 = .02340$

$.32013 \times .10 = .03201$ $.32013 \times .80 = .25610$ $.32013 \times .10 = .03201$

$.21188 \times .10 = \underline{.02119}$ $.21188 \times .15 = \underline{.03178}$ $.21188 \times .75 = \underline{.15891}$
$p_A(3) = .47440$ $p_B(3) = .31128$ $p_C(3) = .21432$

Table 19-2
STATE PROBABILITIES AT SELECTED PERIODS

	$n=0$	$n=5$	$n=10$	$n=15$	$n=20$	$n=25$	$n=30$
$p_A(n)$	.45	.48371	.49466	.49824	.49942	.49982	.49994
$p_B(n)$	.35	.30023	.28970	.28693	.28610	.28584	.28575
$p_C(n)$	.20	.21616	.21564	.21483	.21448	.21434	.21431

Continuing in this fashion, we find further changes in the state probabilities. Table 19-2 shows the results for increments of 5 periods. Notice that the successive changes are smaller. This suggests that the state probabilities may be converging toward a set of constants and that the state probabilities will eventually remain unchanged. At that point the process reaches a *steady state* and will remain the same until outside actions change the transition probabilities.

When reaching a steady state, a Markov process has constant state probabilities from period to period. These values are referred to as the *steady-state probabilities*. From Table 19-2 we see for our illustration that these are approximately .500 for brand A, .286 for brand B, and .214 for brand C. These represent the long-run shares of the market that can be expected for each brand.

19-2 CALCULATION OF STEADY-STATE PROBABILITIES

A considerable amount of work was required to evaluate this problem through $n = 30$ time periods. It is possible to take a shortcut and find the steady-state probabilities algebraically. In doing this, we use the fact that *when the process is in a steady state the probability for leaving any particular state must equal the probability for entering that state*. We may thus ignore the time period n and represent the steady-state probability for state i as p_i. As we have seen, the probability for entering a particular state is found by multiplying the state probability by the respective quantities in the applicable *column* of the transition matrix. For our example, the above fact provides the following relationships

$$p_A = .90p_A + .10p_B + .10p_C$$
$$p_B = .05p_A + .80p_B + .15p_C$$
$$p_C = .05p_A + .10p_B + .75p_C$$

And, the following restriction applies

$$p_A + p_B + p_C = 1$$

The steady-state probabilities must also satisfy the above equations. (Although there are more equations than unknowns, any one of the first three equations is redundant, owing to the fact that the transition probabilities for any starting state must sum to 1.)

We may solve the above equations simultaneously to determine the steady-state probabilities exactly. Solving the first for p_A, we have

$$p_A - .9p_A = .1p_B + .1p_C$$
$$.1p_A = .1p_B + .1p_C$$

and

$$p_A = p_B + p_C$$

Since all the probabilities must sum to 1, using $p_B + p_C$ for p_A we have

$$(p_B + p_C) + p_B + p_C = 1$$

or

$$2p_B + 2p_C = 1$$

Thus,

$$p_B = .5 - p_C$$

and

$$p_A = (.5 - p_C) + p_C = .5$$

Substituting $p_A = .5$ and $p_B = .5 - p_C$ into the second equation, we find

$$.5 - p_C = .05(.5) + .80(.5 - p_C) + .15p_C$$
$$-.35p_C = -.075$$

and

$$p_C = \frac{-.075}{-.35} = \frac{3}{14} = .21429$$

Thus,

$$p_B = .5 - \frac{3}{14} = \frac{7}{14} - \frac{3}{14} = \frac{4}{14} = .28571$$

and the complete set of steady-state probabilities is

$$p_A = .50000 \quad p_B = .28571 \quad p_C = .21429$$

which agrees closely with the result in Table 19-2 for $n = 30$.

19-3 DECISION MAKING WITH A MARKOV PROCESS

We have now set the stage for a decision analysis. Suppose that the manufacturer of product A wishes to consider three different advertising and promotional policies. Policy 1 will increase brand A loyalty through a coupon-redemption plan. Policy 2 involves a series of ads

Table 19-3

TRANSITION MATRICES AND STEADY-STATE PROBABILITIES FOR ALTERNATIVE ADVERTISING AND PROMOTIONAL POLICIES

POLICY 1

From State \ To	State A	B	C
A	.95	.025	.025
B	.10	.800	.100
C	.10	.150	.750

$p_A = 14/21 = .667 \qquad p_B = 4/21 = .190 \qquad p_C = 3/21 = .143$

POLICY 2

From State \ To	State A	B	C
A	.90	.05	.05
B	.15	.75	.10
C	.10	.15	.75

$p_A = 19/34 = .559 \qquad p_B = 8/34 = .235 \qquad p_C = 7/34 = .206$

POLICY 3

From State \ To	State A	B	C
A	.90	.05	.05
B	.10	.80	.10
C	.15	.15	.70

$p_A = 6/11 = .545 \qquad p_B = 3/11 = .273 \qquad p_C = 2/11 = .182$

Table 19-4
EVALUATION OF THREE ALTERNATIVE ADVERTISING AND PROMOTIONAL POLICIES FOR BRAND A

	Market Share p_A	Expected Total Gross Profit $\$10{,}000{,}000 p_A$	Expected Improvement	Added Cost for Policy	Expected Net Payoff
No change	.500	$5,000,000	—	—	—
Policy 1	14/21 (.667)	6,666,667	$1,666,667	$1,500,000	$166,667
Policy 2	19/34 (.559)	5,588,235	588,235	400,000	188,235
Policy 3	6/11 (.545)	5,454,540	454,540	300,000	154,540

aimed at capturing some of the brand *B* market, while Policy 3 is similar and works against brand *C*. Each policy will modify the Markov process, and each change results in a different transition matrix.

The transition matrices for the various policies are provided in Table 19-3. The transition probabilities in each matrix are determined by the policy itself, and they are assumed to apply only if the particular policy is put into operation. The applicable steady-state probabilities that correspond to the respective transition matrices are also shown in Table 19-3; these values were obtained algebraically in the same manner as before, using the entries from the respective transition matrix.

Which policy is best?

Altogether 10,000,000 units of all brands are projected to be sold while the various campaigns are in effect. The brand *A* manufacturer achieves a gross profit of $1 for each item sold. The expected total gross profit experienced by brand *A* is thus $10,000,000 times p_A. This is computed in Table 19-4 for each policy. We may establish each policy's expected improvement over the status quo. Subtracting the costs of the various plans, we determine the expected net payoffs of the policies as shown in Table 19-4. Policy 2 appears to be the best, even though it leads to a smaller market share than Policy 1.

A further illustration involving the setting of an optimal maintenance policy will be helpful in understanding how to analyze decision making with Markov processes.

FINDING AN OPTIMAL MAINTENANCE POLICY 19-4

Questions of equipment maintenance occur in nearly all businesses—even in households. When should you conduct routine maintenance, such as cleaning a typewriter, lubricating a car, or replacing the bearings in a milling machine? Most machines will function a long time without care, but as we well know from personal experience, such neglect can be more costly in the end and might necessitate a major overhaul or even junking of the equipment.

We may view the problem of establishing a maintenance policy in terms of a Markov process with various operating conditions for the states. An optimal decision rule or policy is sought that specifies the remedial action to be taken for each equipment state. Any difference between actions for a given state can be reflected in terms of the cost or payoff and the transition probabilities. Entire policies may be compared in terms of expected costs or payoffs calculated with the applicable state probabilities, themselves obtained from the respective transition matrices.

As an illustration, consider a machine that is classified in one of the following states at the beginning of each day.

Operating Condition States

(1) Good operating condition
(2) Slightly out of adjustment
(3) Operating erratically
(4) Inoperable

Any one of the following actions may be taken before the machine is put into operation at the corresponding cost.

Actions and Costs

(1) Do nothing	$ 0	(n)
(2) Do routine maintenance	100	(r)
(3) Adjust	300	(a)
(4) Adjust and do routine maintenance	350	(a&r)
(5) Overhaul	1000	(o)

For each of the 4 states, any one of 5 actions might be taken. The number of possible distinct maintenance policies is thus $5^4 = 625$. Fortunately, management will consider only a limited number of policies, since many of them would be prohibitively costly or obviously unattractive. Further restrictions limit the possibilities. For instance, an inoperable machine must be overhauled before it can work again, and a machine in good operating condition or needing adjustment should not be overhauled.

The simplest policy is to do nothing until the machine is inoperable; then overhaul it. The transition matrix for this plan, referred to

Table 19-5
TRANSITION MATRIX FOR POLICY 1
— DO NOTHING UNTIL MACHINE IS INOPERABLE

From State \ To State	1	2	3	4	Action	Cost	Steady-State Probability
1	.90	.06	.03	.01	n	$ 0	50/76 = .658
2	0	.80	.10	.10	n	0	15/76 = .197
3	0	0	.50	.50	n	0	6/76 = .079
4	1	0	0	0	o	1000	5/76 = .066

as Policy 1, is given in Table 19-5. Remember, the policy itself establishes the transition probabilities, and they therefore apply only if the policy is adopted. The transition probabilities reflect the daily change in state and were obtained from operating history in which a variety of actions were tried under all operating conditions. The data indicate that doing nothing when the machine is in good operating condition (state 1) results in a .90 probability for that same state occurring on the second day. Smaller probabilities apply in row 1 for ending up in the other states; these values get progressively smaller as the degree of disrepair increases. Should the machine be out of adjustment (state 2), it cannot be restored to good operating condition without human intervention; thus, the probability is 0 for going from state 2 to state 1. The other row 2 probabilities indicate that it is most likely for the machine to remain out of adjustment (state 2) than to revert to erratic operation (state 3) or inoperability (state 4). Row 3 indicates that once the machine is operating erratically (state 3), there is a 50–50 chance of its remaining in that state or becoming inoperable (state 4). Finally, row 4 indicates a probability of 1 for moving the machine from inoperability (state 4) to good operating condition (state 1), since it must then be overhauled.

The steady-state probabilities p_1, p_2, p_3, and p_4 may then be obtained for Policy 1 in the usual manner by solving the following equations:

$$p_1 = .90p_1 + 1p_4$$
$$p_2 = .06p_1 + .80p_2$$
$$p_3 = .03p_1 + .10p_2 + .50p_3$$
$$p_4 = .01p_1 + .10p_2 + .50p_3$$
$$p_1 + p_2 + p_3 + p_4 = 1$$

The first equation tells us that

$$p_4 = .10p_1$$

and the second equation provides the result

$$p_2 = .30p_1$$

Substituting $.30p_1$ for p_2 in the third equation and solving for p_3, we have

or
$$p_3 = .03p_1 + .10(.30p_1) + .50p_3$$
$$.50p_3 = .03p_1 + .03p_1$$
so that
$$p_3 = .12p_1$$

Finally we substitute the above results into the last equation. We have

$$p_1 + .30p_1 + .12p_1 + .10p_1 = 1$$
so that
$$1.52p_1 = 1$$
and
$$p_1 = 1/1.52 = 100/152 = 50/76$$

The other steady-state probability values follow from the above; we obtain

$$p_1 = 50/76 = .658$$
$$p_2 = 15/76 = .197$$
$$p_3 = 6/76 = .079$$
$$p_4 = 5/76 = .066$$

Four other policies are considered by management. The applicable transition matrices for each are given in Table 19-6. The transition probabilities in the *rows* of these matrices reflect the particular action indicated.

Policy 2 involves routine maintenance for states 1 through 3 and overhauling in state 4. The transition probabilities in rows 1, 2, and 3 are different from those in Policy 1, reflecting the fact that routine maintenance reduces the chance of dropping to a worse state of disrepair from what it would be if nothing is done.

Policy 3 involves a different action for each state; row 1 is the same as under the first policy, since the action taken from state 1 is doing nothing in either case. Row 2 applies when the machine is out of

Table 19-6
**TRANSITION MATRICES
FOR THE FOUR REMAINING MAINTENANCE POLICIES**

POLICY 2

From State \ To	State 1	State 2	State 3	State 4	Action	Cost	Steady-State Probability
1	.95	.03	.01	.01	r	$ 100	40/53 = .755
2	0	.85	.10	.05	r	100	8/53 = .151
3	0	0	.60	.40	r	100	3/53 = .057
4	1	0	0	0	o	1000	2/53 = .038

POLICY 3

From State \ To	State 1	State 2	State 3	State 4	Action	Cost	Steady-State Probability
1	.90	.06	.03	.01	n	$ 0	450/554 = .812
2	.80	.10	.08	.02	a	300	30/554 = .054
3	0	0	.70	.30	a & r	350	53/554 = .096
4	1	0	0	0	o	1000	21/554 = .038

POLICY 4

From State \ To	State 1	State 2	State 3	State 4	Action	Cost	Steady-State Probability
1	.95	.03	.01	.01	r	$ 100	900/989 = .910
2	.80	.10	.08	.02	a	300	30/989 = .030
3	0	0	.70	.30	a & r	350	38/989 = .038
4	1	0	0	0	o	1000	21/989 = .021

POLICY 5

From State \ To	State 1	State 2	State 3	State 4	Action	Cost	Steady-State Probability
1	.95	.03	.01	.01	r	$ 100	1500/1585 = .946
2	.80	.10	.08	.02	a	300	50/1585 = .032
3	1	0	0	0	o	1000	19/1585 = .012
4	1	0	0	0	o	1000	16/1585 = .010

19-4 FINDING AN OPTIMAL MAINTENANCE POLICY

adjustment (in state 2) and is adjusted under this policy, so that there is a .80 probability for returning to good operating condition (state 1). The probabilities for achieving the inferior operating conditions from state 2 are substantially lower than before. Row 3, corresponding to an erratically operating machine, has more favorable probabilities than under Policy 2, since both adjustment and routine maintenance will be done.

Policy 4 differs from Policy 3 only in row 1, where routine maintenance is done. This action is identical to what is done when in state 1 under Policy 2. Policy 5 is the same as Policy 4 except when the machine is operating erratically (in state 3) — when an overhaul is made; there the row 3 transition probabilities indicate a certain return to good operating condition (state 1).

The steady-state probabilities under each policy appear to the right of the respective transition matrices. These may be used to determine the expected daily operating cost for each policy. The computations in Table 19-7 indicate the surprising result that Policy 1 — do nothing until the machine is inoperable and then overhaul it — minimizes expected daily cost at a steady-state average of only $66 per day. One explanation for this is that the steady-state probability for the machine becoming inoperable is only .066, so that it is unworkable only 66 out 1000 days, on the average. The costs of routine maintenance and adjustment are just too high to warrant those actions when the machine will still work.

This policy is not far from the one that many Americans use on their cars. We generally abuse our vehicles and — except for oil changes, lubrications, tune-ups, and replacement of batteries and worn tires or brake linings — we make repairs only after the car stops running. One explanation is that mechanical work is very expensive, often costing more than a worn-out and depreciated car is worth. However, airlines go to the other extreme in maintaining planes — replacing engines after several hundred hours of operation and performing extensive preventive maintenance, whether or not it is visibly needed. In the latter case, the cost of failure is huge in comparison to the relatively trivial costs of routine maintenance.

19-5 CONCLUDING REMARKS

We have illustrated the underlying concepts of a Markov process. A class of decisions may be analyzed using the appropriate transition matrix for each alternative policy to find the steady-state probabilities.

Table 19-7

EXPECTED DAILY COST CALCULATIONS FOR THE VARIOUS MAINTENANCE POLICIES

Policy	State	Steady-State Probability	Action	Cost	Cost × Probability
1	1	.658	n	$ 0	$ 0
	2	.197	n	0	0
	3	.079	n	0	0
	4	.066	o	1000	66.00
					$66.00 = Expected cost
2	1	.755	r	100	75.50
	2	.151	r	100	15.10
	3	.057	r	100	5.70
	4	.038	o	1000	38.00
					$134.30 = Expected cost
3	1	.812	n	0	0
	2	.054	a	300	16.20
	3	.096	a & r	350	33.60
	4	.038	o	1000	38.00
					$87.80 = Expected cost
4	1	.910	r	100	91.00
	2	.030	a	300	9.00
	3	.038	a & r	350	13.30
	4	.021	o	1000	21.00
					$134.30 = Expected cost
5	1	.946	r	100	94.60
	2	.032	a	300	9.60
	3	.012	o	1000	12.00
	4	.010	o	1000	10.00
					$126.20 = Expected cost

The latter are then combined with economic data in calculating expected costs or payoffs, which may then be compared to determine the optimal policy.

The validity of this analysis is based on the steady-state behavior of the system under the various policies. Although the adoption of a new operating policy can sometimes result immediately in a new transition matrix, it generally takes a while for any Markov process to settle into the steady state. This is because the individual state probabilities usually differ from their long-run values. Until the equilibrium condition is reached, the system as a whole is in a *transient state*.

19-5 CONCLUDING REMARKS

Thus, a complete analysis should consider what conditions apply in the transient state and how long the revised system takes in reaching a steady state. Should the changes be greater under some alternatives than others or should the durations of the transient phase differ, then these differences ought to also be reflected when selecting the optimal policy.

Analysis of a decision in terms of a Markov process may be more valid in some applications than in others. For instance, this approach has been criticized when applied to brand switching, where the transient state might be quite lengthy in relation to the duration of the alternative advertising policies being evaluated. There is some question whether a steady state is ever reached before the marketplace is perturbed by further competitive forces. Obviously, an analysis based wholly on steady-state behavior would be invalid if that were true. A more fundamental criticism of brand-switching applications pertains to the transition matrix itself. Competitors and shifting customer tastes may cause unanticipated changes in the transition probabilities, so that these values may be uncertain and even short-lived—regardless of what marketing policy a particular manufacturer adopts. The transition matrix that actually results might be viewed as the outcome of a complex interactive decision process involving several parties.

In other applications where outside forces are minimal and where policies are expected to operate under stable conditions for a long time, an analysis based on the Markov process may be the proper procedure. This is often the case in establishing equipment maintenance policies. The same basic approach has been applied with varying degrees of success in a wide variety of applications. These include the designing of port facilities, the planning of political strategies, and the establishment of policies for releasing water from dams.

In this chapter we have barely covered the theoretical aspects of Markov processes, themselves special cases of more general stochastic processes. When the Markov process is combined with decision making, the resulting mathematical procedure falls into the broad category of a *Markovian decision model*. These in turn may fit into a variety of categories described in this book. For instance, decisions involving a Markov process can be solved as a linear programming problem. Others may be expressed as dynamic programs. Thus, the simplex method or a variety of other solution procedures can be used in establishing an optimal policy for a particular situation. Although a detailed discussion of the theory of Markov processes and the more advanced models and procedures used with them in decision making is beyond the scope of this book, several references provided in the bibliography can be used in further study of this rich topic.

PROBLEMS

19-1 A system may be in state 1 or state 2. The following transition matrix applies.

From \ To	1	2
1	1/3	2/3
2	3/4	1/4

Determine the steady-state probabilities.

19-2 A system may be in one of three states. The following transition matrix applies.

From \ To	A	B	C
A	1/2	0	1/2
B	1/4	1/4	1/2
C	1/3	1/3	1/3

(a) Suppose in the initial period that the system will be in state A with certainty. Determine the values $p_A(5)$, $p_B(5)$, and $p_C(5)$.
(b) Compute the steady-state probabilities.

19-3 A system has the following transition matrix.

From \ To	1	2
1	.2	.8
2	.6	.4

(a) Compute the steady-state probabilities.
(b) Suppose that $p_1(0) = .4$ and $p_2(0) = .6$. Compute the successive state probabilities $p_1(n)$ and $p_2(n)$ for $n = 1, 2, 3,$ and 4. In what period does $p_1(n)$ lie within .001 of the steady-state probability for state 1?

19-4 Suppose that the brand A manufacturer discussed in the chapter tries advertising Policy 4, under which 98 percent period-to-period retention applies for brand A, and there is only a 1 percent chance each for switching from A to B and from A to C. Under this policy, the transition probabilities starting from the other brands remain at the original levels. This policy will cost $3 million. If we assume the goal of maximizing expected gross payoff is a valid one, would the manufacturer prefer this policy to the ones discussed in the chapter?

19-5 Reevaluate the maintenance decision discussed in the text when the following costs apply.

$$\begin{array}{ll} \$ \ 0 & (n) \\ 50 & (r) \\ 150 & (a) \\ 200 & (a \ \& \ r) \\ 1000 & (o) \end{array}$$

Which policy yields the minimum expected daily cost?

19-6 Consider a sixth possible policy for the machine maintenance decision described in the chapter. Under this policy, nothing is done until the machine operates erratically, when it is adjusted and routine maintenance is performed, or it is inoperable, when an overhaul is performed.
(a) Determine the applicable transition matrix. (This may be obtained by using the applicable rows from Policy 1 and Policy 3 in Tables 19-5 and 19-6.)
(b) Find the steady-state probabilities.
(c) What is the expected daily maintenance cost of this new policy? Is it better than the original five policies?

19-7 Whenever one state can be reached sometime in a Markov process from another state, the two states *communicate*. Should a state never be left, it is an *absorbing state*.
(a) What can be said regarding the steady-state probability for an absorbing state that communicates with all the rest?
(b) A Hawaiian potato chip is reputed to have a transition matrix like the following for brand-switching in its market.

From \ To	Hawaiian Chip	Mainland Chip
Hawaiian Chip	1	0
Mainland Chip	.01	.99

If the above is true, then eventually one chip will have the entire market to itself. Which chip is it? Verify your answer by computing the steady-state porportion of the market held by each chip. What kind of state is the buyer of the Hawaiian chip in?

19-8 Each sales transaction at Ace Widgets falls into one of the following states:

1. Cash received
2. Account receivable
3. Uncollectable

Suppose the following transition matrix applies for each successive month after a sale.

From \ To	1	2	3
1	1	0	0
2	.80	.19	.01
3	0	0	1

(a) Suppose $p_1(0) = .9$, $p_2(0) = 0$, and $p_3(0) = .1$. Find $p_1(1)$, $p_2(1)$, and $p_3(1)$. Do you notice anything unusual?

(b) What may you conclude regarding the steady-state probabilities with respect to the values of the initial state probabilities?

19-9 Republican Senator Herman Angel is running for re-election against a Democratic challenger, Representative Sheila Saint. The 10,000 voters of Pearly Gates may be categorized in one of five ways.

State	Percentage Who Vote for Angel
(1) Rabid Republican	99
(2) Liberal Republican	95
(3) Fence sitter	50
(4) Straying Democrat	40
(5) Indelible Democrat	10

Angel forces are running a special campaign in that city in an attempt to move the voters into the more favorable categories. Without the special efforts, the following transition matrix now applies for a day-to-day switch in voter sentiment.

From \ To	1	2	3	4	5
1	.95	.05	0	0	0
2	.10	.80	.10	0	0
3	0	.15	.70	.15	0
4	0	0	.20	.70	.10
5	0	0	0	.25	.75

(a) Election day is a long way off. With no special campaign, what is the expected number of Pearly Gates votes for Angel?

(b) The special campaign will focus on fence sitters, making them more favorable to Republican sentiment. This will result in a transition matrix identical to the above except for the new row 3 transition probabilities:

$$0 \quad .40 \quad .50 \quad .10 \quad 0$$

What is the expected number of votes for Angel in Pearly Gates?

19-10 An oil company is evaluating two alternative plans for supplying a remote off-shore drilling platform with drill bits. The first policy involves keeping just one working bit at the site and air-dropping a replacement when it breaks. The alternative is to keep two bits there and to send a replacement by boat only when one of them breaks; the boat will replace all broken bits. A drill bit has only a 10 percent chance of breaking on any day; a bit cannot be replaced on the same day that it breaks. An air-drop takes place the next day—so no avoidable lost production occurs. A sea delivery takes two days longer, and only one boat can be dispatched at a time. Each day's lost production is worth $10,000 in lost future profits, and the two delivery modes have identical costs. A production loss occurs whenever a bit breaks, which we assume happens near the beginning of a working day. When replacements are made or deliveries are received, they occur just before the day's drilling begins. Depending on the delivery policy chosen, some or all of the following states apply at the beginning of any particular scheduled drilling day.

A: No good bits.
B: One good bit; no break yesterday.
C: One good bit; a break yesterday.
D: Two good bits; last replacement was for one bit.
E: Two good bits; last replacement was for two bits.

(a) Construct the transition matrices for the two policies.
(b) Find the steady-state probabilities under each policy.
(c) Consider the air-drop policy. Each transition may involve a production cost (loss). Determine the expected cost for starting in each state by summing the products of these costs with the corresponding probabilities in the applicable row of the transition matrix. Then apply the steady-state probabilities to determine the expected daily policy cost.
(d) Repeat (c) for the sea-delivery policy.
(e) Which policy minimizes expected daily cost?

Bibliography

BASIC CONCEPTS AND SURVEY OF TOPICS

Ackoff, R. L. *Scientific Method: Optimizing Applied Research Decisions.* New York: John Wiley & Sons, 1962.
———, and P. Rivett. *A Manager's Guide to Operations Research.* New York: John Wiley & Sons, 1963.
———, and M. W. Sasieni. *Fundamentals of Operations Research.* New York: John Wiley & Sons, 1968.
Argyris, C., "Management Information Systems: The Challenge to Rationality and Emotionality," *Management Science,* February 1971, pp. B-275–B-292.
Baumol, W. J. *Economic Theory and Economic Analysis.* 3rd ed. Englewood Cliffs, N. J.: Prentice-Hall, Inc., 1972.
Caywood, T. E., et al., "Guidelines for the Practice of Operations Research," *Operations Research,* September 1971, pp. 1127–48.
Churchman, C. W., R. L. Ackoff, and E. L. Arnoff. *Introduction to Operations Research.* New York: John Wiley & Sons, 1957.
Duckworth, E. *A Guide to Operational Research.* London: University Paperbacks, 1965.
Enrick, N. L. *Management Operations Research.* New York: Holt, Rinehart and Winston, 1965.
Hillier, F. S., and G. J. Lieberman. *Introduction to Operations Research.* 2nd ed. San Francisco: Holden-Day, 1974.
Miller, D. W., and M. K. Starr. *Executive Decisions and Operations Research.* 2nd ed. Englewood Cliffs, N. J.: Prentice-Hall, Inc., 1969.
———, and M. K. Starr. *The Structure of Human Decisions.* Englewood Cliffs, N. J.: Prentice-Hall, Inc., 1967.
Rivett, P. *Principles of Model Building.* New York: John Wiley & Sons, 1973.
Sasieni, M., A. Yaspan, and L. Friedman. *Operations Research: Methods and Problems.* New York: John Wiley & Sons, 1959.
Teichrow, D. *An Introduction to Management Science: Deterministic Models.* New York: John Wiley & Sons, 1964.
Turban, E., "A Sample Survey of Operations-Research Activities at the Corporate Level," *Operations Research,* May–June 1972, pp. 708–721.

Wagner, H. M., *Principles of Operations Research*. 2nd ed. Englewood Cliffs, N. J.: Prentice-Hall, Inc., 1975.

———, "The ABC's of OR," *Operations Research*, October 1971, pp. 1259–81.

Woolsey, R. E. D., "Operations Research and Management Science Today," *Operations Research*, May–June 1972, pp. 729–37.

PROBABILITY CONCEPTS (Chapters 2–3)

Feller, W. *An Introduction to Probability Theory and Its Applications*, Vol. 1. New York: John Wiley & Sons, 1957.

Hodges, J. L., Jr., and E. L. Lehmann. *Elements of Finite Probability*. San Francisco: Holden-Day, 1965.

Lapin, L. L. *Statistics for Modern Business Decisions*. New York: Harcourt Brace Jovanovich, 1973.

Laplace, Pierre Simon, Marquis de. *A Philosophical Essay on Probabilities*. New York: Dover Publications, 1951.

Lindgren, B. W., and G. W. McElrath. *Introduction to Probability and Statistics*, 3rd ed. New York: Macmillan, 1969.

Mosteller, F., R. Rourke, and G. Thomas, Jr. *Probability and Statistics*. Reading, Mass.: Addison-Wesley, 1961.

Parzen, Emmanuel. *Modern Probability Theory and Its Applications*. New York: John Wiley & Sons, 1960.

FORECASTING (Chapter 4)

Box, G. E. P., and G. M. Jenkins. *Time Series Analysis: Forecasting and Control*. San Francisco: Holden-Day, 1970.

Brown, R. G. *Smoothing, Forecasting, and Prediction*. Englewood Cliffs, N. J.: Prentice-Hall, Inc., 1963.

Chambers, J. C., S. K. Mullick, and D. D. Smith, "How to Choose the Right Forecasting Technique," *Harvard Business Review*, July–August 1971.

Gross, C., and R. Peterson. *Business Forecasting*. Boston: Houghton Mifflin, 1976.

Holt, C. C., F. Modigliani, J. F. Muth, and H. A. Simon. *Planning Production, Inventories, and Work Force*. Englewood Cliffs, N. J.: Prentice-Hall, Inc., 1960.

Lapin, L. L. *Statistics for Modern Business Decisions*. 2nd ed. New York: Harcourt Brace Jovanovich, 1978.

Makridakis, S., and S. C. Wheelwright. *Forecasting Methods and Applications*. New York: John Wiley & Sons, 1978.

———, *Interactive Forecasting*. 2nd ed. San Francisco: Holden-Day, 1978.

McLaughlin, R. L. *Time Series Forecasting*. Marketing Research Technique, Series No. 6, American Marketing Association, 1962.

Raiffa, H. *Decision Analysis: Introductory Lectures on Choices Under Uncertainty*. Reading, Mass.: Addison-Wesley, 1968.

Schlaifer, R. *Analysis of Decisions Under Uncertainty.* New York: McGraw-Hill Book Co., 1969.

Spencer, M. H., C. G. Clark, and P. W. Hoguet. *Business and Economic Forecasting: An Econometric Approach.* Homewood, Ill.: Richard D. Irwin, 1965.

DECISION THEORY AND UTILITY (Chapters 5–9)

Aitchison, J. *Choice Against Chance.* Reading, Mass.: Addison-Wesley, 1970.

Brown, R. V., A. S. Kahr, and C. Peterson. *Decision Analysis for the Manager.* New York: Holt, Rinehart and Winston, 1974.

Chernoff, H., and L. E. Moses. *Elementary Decision Theory.* New York: John Wiley & Sons, 1957.

Lapin, L. L. *Statistics for Modern Business Decisions.* New York: Harcourt Brace Jovanovich, 1973.

Luce, R. D., and H. Raiffa. *Games and Decisions.* New York: John Wiley & Sons, 1957.

Miller, D. W., and M. K. Starr. *Executive Decisions and Operations Research.* 2nd ed. Englewood Cliffs, N. J.: Prentice-Hall, 1969.

Morris, W. T. *Management Science: A Bayesian Introduction.* Englewood Cliffs, N. J.: Prentice-Hall, 1968.

Pratt, J. W., H. Raiffa, and R. Schlaifer. *Introduction to Statistical Decision Theory.* New York: McGraw-Hill Book Co., 1965.

Raiffa, H. *Decision Analysis: Introductory Lectures on Choices Under Uncertainty.* Reading, Mass.: Addison-Wesley, 1968.

Schlaifer, R. *Analysis of Decisions Under Uncertainty.* New York: McGraw-Hill Book Co., 1969.

———. *Introduction to Statistics for Business Decisions.* New York: McGraw-Hill Book Co., 1961.

GAMES AND INTERACTIVE DECISIONS (Chapter 10)

Davis, M. D. *Game Theory: A Nontechnical Introduction.* New York: Basic Books, Inc., 1970.

Luce, R. D., and H. Raiffa. *Games and Decisions.* New York: John Wiley & Sons, 1957.

Karlin, S. *Mathematical Methods and Theory in Games, Programming and Economics.* Reading, Mass.: Addison-Wesley Publishing Co., Inc., 1959.

May, F. B. *Introduction to Games of Strategy.* Boston: Allyn and Bacon, 1970.

McKinsey, J. C. C. *Introduction to the Theory of Games.* New York: McGraw-Hill Book Co., 1952.

Owen, G. *Game Theory.* Philadelphia: W. B. Saunders Co., 1968.

Rapoport, A. *Two Person Game Theory.* Ann Arbor: University of Michigan Press, 1966.

Vajda, S. *The Theory of Games and Linear Programming.* London: Methuen & Co., Ltd., 1967.

Von Neumann, J., and O. Morgenstern. *Theory of Games and Economic Behavior.* Princeton, N. J.: Princeton University Press, 1947.

Williams, J. D. *The Compleat Strategist.* rev. ed. New York: McGraw-Hill Book Co., 1966.

INVENTORY DECISIONS (Chapter 11)

Arrow, K. J., S. Karlin, and H. Scarf. *Studies in the Mathematical Theory of Inventory and Production.* Stanford, Ca.: Stanford University Press, 1958.

Buffa, E. S., and W. Taubert. *Production-Inventory Systems: Planning and Control.* rev. ed. Homewood, Ill.: Richard D. Irwin, 1972.

Greene, J. H. *Production and Inventory Control Handbook.* New York: McGraw-Hill Book Co., 1970.

Hadley, G., and T. M. Whitin. *Analysis of Inventory Systems.* Englewood Cliffs, N. J.: Prentice-Hall, Inc., 1963.

Hillier, F. S., and G. J. Lieberman. *Introduction to Operations Research.* 2nd ed. San Francisco: Holden-Day, 1974.

Holt, C. C., F. Modigliani, J. F. Muth, and H. A. Simon. *Planning Production, Inventories, and Work Force.* Englewood Cliffs, N. J.: Prentice-Hall, Inc., 1960.

Magee, J. R., and D. M. Boodman, *Production Planning and Inventory Control.* 2nd ed. New York: McGraw-Hill Book Co., 1967.

Starr, M. K., and D. W. Miller. *Inventory Control: Theory and Practice.* Englewood Cliffs, N. J.: Prentice-Hall, Inc., 1962.

Wagner, H. M. *Principles of Operations Research.* 2nd ed. Englewood Cliffs, N. J.: Prentice-Hall, Inc., 1975.

———. *Statistical Management of Inventory Systems.* New York: John Wiley & Sons, 1962.

Whitin, T. M. *The Theory of Inventory Management.* 2nd ed. Princeton, N. J.: Princeton University Press, 1957.

LINEAR PROGRAMMING (Chapters 12-15)

Dantzig, G. B. *Linear Programming and Extensions.* Princeton, N. J.: Princeton University Press, 1963.

Garvin, W. W. *Introduction to Linear Programming.* New York: McGraw-Hill Book Co., 1960.

Gass, S. I. *Linear Programming: Methods and Applications,* 2nd ed. New York: McGraw-Hill Book Co., 1964.

Hadley, G. *Linear Programming.* Reading, Mass.: Addison-Wesley Publishing Co., Inc., 1962.

Hillier, F. S., and G. J. Lieberman. *Introduction to Operations Research,* 2nd ed. San Francisco: Holden-Day, Inc., 1974.

Kim, C. *Introduction to Linear Programming.* New York: Holt, Rinehart and Winston, Inc., 1971.
Kwak, N. K. *Mathematical Programming with Business Applications.* New York: McGraw-Hill Book Co., 1973.
Naylor, T. H., E. T. Byrne, and J. M. Vernon. *Introduction to Linear Programming: Methods and Cases.* Belmont, Ca.: Wadsworth Publishing Co., 1971.
Simonnard, M. *Linear Programming.* Englewood Cliffs, N. J.: Prentice-Hall, Inc., 1966.
Wagner, H. M. *Principles of Operations Research with Applications to Managerial Decisions.* Englewood Cliffs, N. J.: Prentice-Hall, Inc., 1975.

PERT (Chapter 16)

Baker, B. N., and R. L. Ellis. *An Introduction to PERT/CPM.* Homewood, Ill.: Richard D. Irwin, 1964.
Evarts, H. E. *Introduction to PERT.* Boston: Allyn and Bacon, 1964.
Levin, R. I., and C. A. Kirkpatrick. *Planning and Control with PERT/CPM.* New York: McGraw-Hill Book Co., 1966.
Lockyer, K. G. *An Introduction to Critical Path Analysis,* New York: Pitman, 1964.
MacCrimmon, K. R., and C. A. Ryavec, "Analytical Study of the PERT Assumptions," *Operations Research,* January 1964, pp. 16–37.
Moder, J. J., and C. R. Philips. *Project Management with CPM and PERT,* 2d ed. New York: D. Van Nostrand, 1970.
Weist, J. D., and F. K. Levy. *A Management Guide to PERT/CPM.* Englewood Cliffs, N. J.: Prentice-Hall, Inc., 1969.

QUEUES (Chapter 17)

Cooper, R. B. *Introduction to Queueing Theory.* New York: Macmillan, 1972.
Cox, D. R., and W. L. Smith. *Queues.* London: Methuen & Co., Ltd., 1961.
Gross, D., and C. M. Harris. *Fundamentals of Queueing Theory.* New York: Wiley-Interscience, 1974.
Hillier, F. S., and G. J. Lieberman. *Introduction to Operations Research.* 2nd ed. San Francisco: Holden-Day, Inc., 1974.
Lee, A. M. *Applied Queueing Theory.* New York: St. Martin's Press, 1966.
Morse, P. M. *Queues, Inventories, and Maintenance.* New York: John Wiley & Sons, 1958.
Newell, G. F. *Applications of Queueing Theory.* London: Chapman & Hall, Ltd., 1971.
Prabhu, N. U. *Queues and Inventories.* New York: John Wiley & Sons, 1965.
Saaty, T. L. *Elements of Queueing Theory.* New York: McGraw-Hill Book Co., 1961.
Wagner, H. M. *Principles of Operations Research.* Englewood Cliffs, N. J.: Prentice-Hall, Inc., 1975.

SIMULATION (Chapter 18)

Bonini, C. P. *Simulation of Information and Decision Systems in the Firm.* Englewood Cliffs, N.J.: Prentice-Hall, Inc., 1963.

Emshoff, J. R., and R. L. Sisson. *Design and Use of Computer Simulation Models.* New York: MacMillan, 1970.

Evans, G. W., G. F. Wallace, and G. L. Sutherland. *Simulation Using Digital Computers.* Englewood Cliffs, N. J.: Prentice-Hall, Inc., 1967.

General Purpose Simulation System/360: Introductory User's Manual. White Plains, N. Y.: IBM Corporation, 1967.

Kleijnen, J. P. C. *Statistical Techniques in Simulation.* New York: Marcel Dekker, 1973.

Markowitz, H. M. "Simulating with SIMSCRIPT," *Management Science,* June 1966, pp. B-396–404.

Martin, F. F. *Computer Modeling and Simulation.* New York: John Wiley & Sons, 1968.

Meier, R. C., W. T. Newell, and H. J. Pazer. *Simulation in Business and Economics.* Englewood Cliffs, N. J.: Prentice-Hall, Inc., 1969.

Naylor, T. H., J. L. Balintfy, D. S. Burdick, and K. Hu. *Computer Simulation Techniques.* New York: John Wiley & Sons, 1968.

Pugh, A. L. *DYNAMO User's Manual,* 2d ed. Cambridge, Mass.: MIT Press, 1963.

Schmidt, J. W., and R. E. Taylor. *Simulation and Analysis of Industrial Systems.* Homewood, Ill.: Richard D. Irwin, 1970.

Tocher, K. D. *The Art of Simulation.* London: The English University Press, 1963.

MARKOV PROCESSES (Chapter 19)

Derman, C. *Finite State Markovian Decision Processes.* New York: Academic Press, 1970.

Freedman, D. *Markov Chains.* San Francisco: Holden-Day, 1971.

Hillier, F. S., and G. J. Lieberman. *Introduction to Operations Research,* 2d ed. San Francisco: Holden-Day, 1974.

Howard, R. *Dynamic Programming and Markov Processes.* Cambridge, Mass.: MIT Press, 1960.

Kemeny, J. G., and J. L. Snell. *Finite Markov Chains.* Princeton, N. J.: D. Van Nostrand, 1960.

Martin, J. J. *Bayesian Decision Problems and Markov Chains.* New York: John Wiley & Sons, 1967.

Wagner, H. M. *Principles of Operations Research,* 2d ed. Englewood Cliffs, N. J.: Prentice-Hall, Inc., 1975.

Appendix Tables

TABLE **A** Cumulative Values for the Binomial Probability Distribution

TABLE **B** Areas Under the Standard Normal Curve

TABLE **C** Loss Function for Decision Making with the Normal Curve

TABLE **D** Exponential Functions

TABLE **E** Cumulative Probability Values for the Poisson Distribution

TABLE **F** Random Numbers

Table A
CUMULATIVE VALUES FOR THE BINOMIAL PROBABILITY DISTRIBUTION

$$P[R \leq r]$$

$n = 1$

P \ r	.01	.05	.10	.20	.30	.40	.50
0	0.9900	0.9500	0.9000	0.8000	0.7000	0.6000	0.5000
1	1.0000	1.0000	1.0000	1.0000	1.0000	1.0000	1.0000

$n = 2$

P \ r	.01	.05	.10	.20	.30	.40	.50
0	0.9801	0.9025	0.8100	0.6400	0.4900	0.3600	0.2500
1	0.9999	0.9975	0.9900	0.9600	0.9100	0.8400	0.7500
2	1.0000	1.0000	1.0000	1.0000	1.0000	1.0000	1.0000

$n = 3$

P \ r	.01	.05	.10	.20	.30	.40	.50
0	0.9703	0.8574	0.7290	0.5120	0.3430	0.2160	0.1250
1	0.9997	0.9927	0.9720	0.8960	0.7840	0.6480	0.5000
2	1.0000	0.9999	0.9990	0.9920	0.9730	0.9360	0.8750
3	1.0000	1.0000	1.0000	1.0000	1.0000	1.0000	1.0000

$n = 4$

P \ r	.01	.05	.10	.20	.30	.40	.50
0	0.9606	0.8145	0.6561	0.4096	0.2401	0.1296	0.0625
1	0.9994	0.9860	0.9477	0.8192	0.6517	0.4752	0.3125
2	1.0000	0.9995	0.9963	0.9728	0.9163	0.8208	0.6875
3	1.0000	1.0000	0.9999	0.9984	0.9919	0.9744	0.9375
4	1.0000	1.0000	1.0000	1.0000	1.0000	1.0000	1.0000

$n = 5$

P \ r	.01	.05	.10	.20	.30	.40	.50
0	0.9510	0.7738	0.5905	0.3277	0.1681	0.0778	0.0313
1	0.9990	0.9774	0.9185	0.7373	0.5282	0.3370	0.1875
2	1.0000	0.9988	0.9914	0.9421	0.8369	0.6826	0.5000
3	1.0000	1.0000	0.9995	0.9933	0.9692	0.9130	0.8125
4	1.0000	1.0000	1.0000	0.9997	0.9976	0.9898	0.9688
5				1.0000	1.0000	1.0000	1.0000

Table A *(continued)*

$n = 10$

P \ r	.01	.05	.10	.20	.30	.40	.50
0	0.9044	0.5987	0.3487	0.1074	0.0282	0.0060	0.0010
1	0.9957	0.9139	0.7361	0.3758	0.1493	0.0464	0.0107
2	0.9999	0.9885	0.9298	0.6778	0.3828	0.1673	0.0547
3	1.0000	0.9990	0.9872	0.8791	0.6496	0.3823	0.1719
4	1.0000	0.9999	0.9984	0.9672	0.8497	0.6331	0.3770
5	1.0000	1.0000	0.9999	0.9936	0.9526	0.8338	0.6230
6	1.0000	1.0000	1.0000	0.9991	0.9894	0.9452	0.8281
7				0.9999	0.9999	0.9877	0.9453
8				1.0000	1.0000	0.9983	0.9893
9						0.9999	0.9990
10						1.0000	1.0000

$n = 20$

P \ r	.01	.05	.10	.20	.30	.40	.50
0	0.8179	0.3585	0.1216	0.0115	0.0008	0.0000	0.0000
1	0.9831	0.7358	0.3917	0.0692	0.0076	0.0005	0.0000
2	0.9990	0.9245	0.6769	0.2061	0.0355	0.0036	0.0002
3	1.0000	0.9841	0.8670	0.4114	0.1071	0.0160	0.0013
4	1.0000	0.9974	0.9568	0.6296	0.2375	0.0510	0.0059
5	1.0000	0.9997	0.9887	0.8042	0.4164	0.1256	0.0207
6	1.0000	1.0000	0.9976	0.9133	0.6080	0.2500	0.0577
7	1.0000	1.0000	0.9996	0.9679	0.7723	0.4159	0.1316
8	1.0000	1.0000	0.9999	0.9900	0.8867	0.5956	0.2517
9	1.0000	1.0000	1.0000	0.9974	0.9520	0.7553	0.4119
10				0.9994	0.9829	0.8725	0.5881
11				0.9999	0.9949	0.9435	0.7483
12				1.0000	0.9987	0.9790	0.8684
13					0.9997	0.9935	0.9423
14					1.0000	0.9984	0.9793
15						0.9997	0.9941
16						1.0000	0.9987
17							0.9998
18							1.0000

Table A (continued)

$n = 50$

P r	.01	.05	.10	.20	.30	.40	.50
0	0.6050	0.0769	0.0052	0.0000	0.0000	0.0000	0.0000
1	0.9106	0.2794	0.0338	0.0002	0.0000	0.0000	0.0000
2	0.9862	0.5405	0.1117	0.0013	0.0000	0.0000	0.0000
3	0.9984	0.7604	0.2503	0.0057	0.0000	0.0000	0.0000
4	0.9999	0.8964	0.4312	0.0185	0.0002	0.0000	0.0000
5	1.0000	0.9622	0.6161	0.0480	0.0007	0.0000	0.0000
6	1.0000	0.9882	0.7702	0.1034	0.0025	0.0000	0.0000
7	1.0000	0.9968	0.8779	0.1904	0.0073	0.0001	0.0000
8	1.0000	0.9992	0.9421	0.3073	0.0183	0.0002	0.0000
9	1.0000	0.9998	0.9755	0.4437	0.0402	0.0008	0.0000
10	1.0000	1.0000	0.9906	0.5836	0.0789	0.0022	0.0000
11	1.0000	1.0000	0.9968	0.7107	0.1390	0.0057	0.0000
12	1.0000	1.0000	0.9990	0.8139	0.2229	0.0133	0.0002
13	1.0000	1.0000	0.9997	0.8894	0.3279	0.0280	0.0005
14	1.0000	1.0000	0.9999	0.9393	0.4468	0.0540	0.0013
15	1.0000	1.0000	1.0000	0.9692	0.5692	0.0955	0.0033
16				0.9856	0.6839	0.1561	0.0077
17				0.9937	0.7822	0.2369	0.0164
18				0.9975	0.8594	0.3356	0.0325
19				0.9991	0.9152	0.4465	0.0595
20				0.9997	0.9522	0.5610	0.1013
21				0.9999	0.9749	0.6701	0.1611
22				1.0000	0.9877	0.7660	0.2399
23					0.9944	0.8438	0.3359
24					0.9976	0.9022	0.4439
25					0.9991	0.9427	0.5561
26					0.9997	0.9686	0.6641
27					0.9999	0.9840	0.7601
28					1.0000	0.9924	0.8389
29						0.9966	0.8987
30						0.9986	0.9405
31						0.9995	0.9675
32						0.9998	0.9836
33						0.9999	0.9923
34						1.0000	0.9967
35							0.9987
36							0.9995
37							0.9998
38							1.0000

Table A *(continued)*

$n = 100$

P / r	.01	.05	.10	.20	.30	.40	.50
0	0.3660	0.0059	0.0000	0.0000	0.0000	0.0000	0.0000
1	0.7358	0.0371	0.0003	0.0000	0.0000	0.0000	0.0000
2	0.9206	0.1183	0.0019	0.0000	0.0000	0.0000	0.0000
3	0.9816	0.2578	0.0078	0.0000	0.0000	0.0000	0.0000
4	0.9966	0.4360	0.0237	0.0000	0.0000	0.0000	0.0000
5	0.9995	0.6160	0.0576	0.0000	0.0000	0.0000	0.0000
6	0.9999	0.7660	0.1172	0.0001	0.0000	0.0000	0.0000
7	1.0000	0.8720	0.2061	0.0003	0.0000	0.0000	0.0000
8	1.0000	0.9369	0.3209	0.0009	0.0000	0.0000	0.0000
9	1.0000	0.9718	0.4513	0.0023	0.0000	0.0000	0.0000
10	1.0000	0.9885	0.5832	0.0057	0.0000	0.0000	0.0000
11	1.0000	0.9957	0.7030	0.0126	0.0000	0.0000	0.0000
12	1.0000	0.9985	0.8018	0.0253	0.0000	0.0000	0.0000
13	1.0000	0.9995	0.8761	0.0469	0.0001	0.0000	0.0000
14	1.0000	0.9999	0.9274	0.0804	0.0002	0.0000	0.0000
15	1.0000	1.0000	0.9601	0.1285	0.0004	0.0000	0.0000
16	1.0000	1.0000	0.9794	0.1923	0.0010	0.0000	0.0000
17	1.0000	1.0000	0.9900	0.2712	0.0022	0.0000	0.0000
18	1.0000	1.0000	0.9954	0.3621	0.0045	0.0000	0.0000
19	1.0000	1.0000	0.9980	0.4602	0.0089	0.0000	0.0000
20	1.0000	1.0000	0.9992	0.5595	0.0165	0.0000	0.0000
21	1.0000	1.0000	0.9997	0.6540	0.0288	0.0000	0.0000
22	1.0000	1.0000	0.9999	0.7389	0.0479	0.0001	0.0000
23	1.0000	1.0000	1.0000	0.8109	0.0755	0.0003	0.0000
24				0.8686	0.1136	0.0006	0.0000
25				0.9125	0.1631	0.0012	0.0000
26				0.9442	0.2244	0.0024	0.0000
27				0.9658	0.2964	0.0046	0.0000
28				0.9800	0.3768	0.0084	0.0000
29				0.9888	0.4623	0.0148	0.0000
30				0.9939	0.5491	0.0248	0.0000
31				0.9969	0.6331	0.0398	0.0001
32				0.9984	0.7107	0.0615	0.0002
33				0.9993	0.7793	0.0913	0.0004
34				0.9997	0.8371	0.1303	0.0009
35				0.9999	0.8839	0.1795	0.0018

Table A *(continued)*

$n = 100$

P r	.01	.05	.10	.20	.30	.40	.50
36				0.9999	0.9201	0.2386	0.0033
37				1.0000	0.9470	0.3068	0.0060
38					0.9660	0.3822	0.0105
39					0.9790	0.4621	0.0176
40					0.9875	0.5433	0.0284
41					0.9928	0.6225	0.0443
42					0.9960	0.6967	0.0666
43					0.9979	0.7635	0.0967
44					0.9989	0.8211	0.1356
45					0.9995	0.8689	0.1841
46					0.9997	0.9070	0.2421
47					0.9999	0.9362	0.3086
48					0.9999	0.9577	0.3822
49					1.0000	0.9729	0.4602
50						0.9832	0.5398
51						0.9900	0.6178
52						0.9942	0.6914
53						0.9968	0.7579
54						0.9983	0.8159
55						0.9991	0.8644
56						0.9996	0.9033
57						0.9998	0.9334
58						0.9999	0.9557
59						1.0000	0.9716
60							0.9824
61							0.9895
62							0.9940
63							0.9967
64							0.9982
65							0.9991
66							0.9996
67							0.9998
68							0.9999
69							1.0000

Table B
AREAS UNDER THE STANDARD NORMAL CURVE

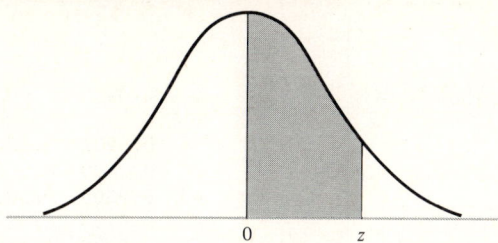

The following table provides the area between the mean and normal deviate value z.

Normal Deviate z	.00	.01	.02	.03	.04	.05	.06	.07	.08	.09
0.0	.0000	.0040	.0080	.0120	.0160	.0199	.0239	.0279	.0319	.0359
0.1	.0398	.0438	.0478	.0517	.0557	.0596	.0636	.0675	.0714	.0753
0.2	.0793	.0832	.0871	.0910	.0948	.0987	.1026	.1064	.1103	.1141
0.3	.1179	.1217	.1255	.1293	.1331	.1368	.1406	.1443	.1480	.1517
0.4	.1554	.1591	.1628	.1664	.1700	.1736	.1772	.1808	.1844	.1879
0.5	.1915	.1950	.1985	.2019	.2054	.2088	.2123	.2157	.2190	.2224
0.6	.2257	.2291	.2324	.2357	.2389	.2422	.2454	.2486	.2518	.2549
0.7	.2580	.2612	.2642	.2673	.2704	.2734	.2764	.2794	.2823	.2852
0.8	.2881	.2910	.2939	.2967	.2995	.3023	.3051	.3078	.3106	.3133
0.9	.3159	.3186	.3212	.3238	.3264	.3289	.3315	.3340	.3365	.3389
1.0	.3413	.3438	.3461	.3485	.3508	.3531	.3554	.3577	.3599	.3621
1.1	.3643	.3665	.3686	.3708	.3729	.3749	.3770	.3790	.3810	.3830
1.2	.3849	.3869	.3888	.3907	.3925	.3944	.3962	.3980	.3997	.4015
1.3	.4032	.4049	.4066	.4082	.4099	.4115	.4131	.4147	.4162	.4177
1.4	.4192	.4207	.4222	.4236	.4251	.4265	.4279	.4292	.4306	.4319
1.5	.4332	.4345	.4357	.4370	.4382	.4394	.4406	.4418	.4429	.4441
1.6	.4452	.4463	.4474	.4484	.4495	.4505	.4515	.4525	.4535	.4545
1.7	.4554	.4564	.4573	.4582	.4591	.4599	.4608	.4616	.4625	.4633
1.8	.4641	.4649	.4656	.4664	.4671	.4678	.4686	.4693	.4699	.4706
1.9	.4713	.4719	.4726	.4732	.4738	.4744	.4750	.4756	.4761	.4767
2.0	.4772	.4778	.4783	.4788	.4793	.4798	.4803	.4808	.4812	.4817
2.1	.4821	.4826	.4830	.4834	.4838	.4842	.4846	.4850	.4854	.4857
2.2	.4861	.4864	.4868	.4871	.4875	.4878	.4881	.4884	.4887	.4890
2.3	.4893	.4896	.4898	.4901	.4904	.4906	.4909	.4911	.4913	.4916
2.4	.4918	.4920	.4922	.4925	.4927	.4929	.4931	.4932	.4934	.4936
2.5	.4938	.4940	.4941	.4943	.4945	.4946	.4948	.4949	.4951	.4952
2.6	.4953	.4955	.4956	.4957	.4959	.4960	.4961	.4962	.4963	.4964
2.7	.4965	.4966	.4967	.4968	.4969	.4970	.4971	.4972	.4973	.4974
2.8	.4974	.4975	.4976	.4977	.4977	.4978	.4979	.4979	.4980	.4981
2.9	.4981	.4982	.4982	.4983	.4984	.4984	.4985	.4985	.4986	.4986
3.0	.49865	.4987	.4987	.4988	.4988	.4989	.4989	.4989	.4990	.4990
4.0	.49997									

SOURCE: © 1970 by Harcourt Brace Jovanovich, Inc., and reproduced with their permission from *Statistical Analysis for Decision Making* by Morris Hamburg.

Table C
LOSS FUNCTION FOR DECISION MAKING WITH THE NORMAL CURVE

$L(D)$

D	.00	.01	.02	.03	.04	.05	.06	.07	.08	.09
.0	.3989	.3940	.3890	.3841	.3793	.3744	.3697	.3649	.3602	.3556
.1	.3509	.3464	.3418	.3373	.3328	.3284	.3240	.3197	.3154	.3111
.2	.3069	.3027	.2986	.2944	.2904	.2863	.2824	.2784	.2745	.2706
.3	.2668	.2630	.2592	.2555	.2518	.2481	.2445	.2409	.2374	.2339
.4	.2304	.2270	.2236	.2203	.2169	.2137	.2104	.2072	.2040	.2009
.5	.1978	.1947	.1917	.1887	.1857	.1828	.1799	.1771	.1742	.1714
.6	.1687	.1659	.1633	.1606	.1580	.1554	.1528	.1503	.1478	.1453
.7	.1429	.1405	.1381	.1358	.1334	.1312	.1289	.1267	.1245	.1223
.8	.1202	.1181	.1160	.1140	.1120	.1100	.1080	.1061	.1042	.1023
.9	.1004	.09860	.09680	.09503	.09328	.09156	.08986	.08819	.08654	.08491
1.0	.08332	.08174	.08019	.07866	.07716	.07568	.07422	.07279	.07138	.06999
1.1	.06862	.06727	.06595	.06465	.06336	.06210	.06086	.05964	.05844	.05726
1.2	.05610	.05496	.05384	.05274	.05165	.05059	.04954	.04851	.04750	.04650
1.3	.04553	.04457	.04363	.04270	.04179	.04090	.04002	.03916	.03831	.03748
1.4	.03667	.03587	.03508	.03431	.03356	.03281	.03208	.03137	.03067	.02998
1.5	.02931	.02865	.02800	.02736	.02674	.02612	.02552	.02494	.02436	.02380
1.6	.02324	.02270	.02217	.02165	.02114	.02064	.02015	.01967	.01920	.01874
1.7	.01829	.01785	.01742	.01699	.01658	.01617	.01578	.01539	.01501	.01464
1.8	.01428	.01392	.01357	.01323	.01290	.01257	.01226	.01195	.01164	.01134
1.9	.01105	.01077	.01049	.01022	.0^{2}9957	.0^{2}9698	.0^{2}9445	.0^{2}9198	.0^{2}8957	.0^{2}8721
2.0	.0^{2}8491	.0^{2}8266	.0^{2}8046	.0^{2}7832	.0^{2}7623	.0^{2}7418	.0^{2}7219	.0^{2}7024	.0^{2}6835	.0^{2}6649
2.1	.0^{2}6468	.0^{2}6292	.0^{2}6120	.0^{2}5952	.0^{2}5788	.0^{2}5628	.0^{2}5472	.0^{2}5320	.0^{2}5172	.0^{2}5028
2.2	.0^{2}4887	.0^{2}4750	.0^{2}4616	.0^{2}4486	.0^{2}4358	.0^{2}4235	.0^{2}4114	.0^{2}3996	.0^{2}3882	.0^{2}3770
2.3	.0^{2}3662	.0^{2}3556	.0^{2}3453	.0^{2}3352	.0^{2}3255	.0^{2}3159	.0^{2}3067	.0^{2}2977	.0^{2}2889	.0^{2}2804
2.4	.0^{2}2720	.0^{2}2640	.0^{2}2561	.0^{2}2484	.0^{2}2410	.0^{2}2337	.0^{2}2267	.0^{2}2199	.0^{2}2132	.0^{2}2067

2.5	$.0^22004$	$.0^21943$	$.0^21883$	$.0^21826$	$.0^21769$	$.0^21715$	$.0^21662$	$.0^21610$	$.0^21560$	$.0^21511$
2.6	$.0^21464$	$.0^21418$	$.0^21373$	$.0^21330$	$.0^21288$	$.0^21247$	$.0^21207$	$.0^21169$	$.0^21132$	$.0^21095$
2.7	$.0^21060$	$.0^21026$	$.0^39928$	$.0^39607$	$.0^39295$	$.0^38992$	$.0^38699$	$.0^38414$	$.0^38138$	$.0^37870$
2.8	$.0^37611$	$.0^37359$	$.0^37115$	$.0^36879$	$.0^36650$	$.0^36428$	$.0^36213$	$.0^36004$	$.0^35802$	$.0^35606$
2.9	$.0^35417$	$.0^35233$	$.0^35055$	$.0^34883$	$.0^34716$	$.0^34555$	$.0^34398$	$.0^34247$	$.0^34101$	$.0^33959$
3.0	$.0^33822$	$.0^33689$	$.0^33560$	$.0^33436$	$.0^33316$	$.0^33199$	$.0^33087$	$.0^32978$	$.0^32873$	$.0^32771$
3.1	$.0^32673$	$.0^32577$	$.0^32485$	$.0^32396$	$.0^32311$	$.0^32227$	$.0^32147$	$.0^32070$	$.0^31995$	$.0^31922$
3.2	$.0^31852$	$.0^31785$	$.0^31720$	$.0^31657$	$.0^31596$	$.0^31537$	$.0^31480$	$.0^31426$	$.0^31373$	$.0^31322$
3.3	$.0^31273$	$.0^31225$	$.0^31179$	$.0^31135$	$.0^31093$	$.0^31051$	$.0^31012$	$.0^49734$	$.0^49365$	$.0^49009$
3.4	$.0^48666$	$.0^48335$	$.0^48016$	$.0^47709$	$.0^47413$	$.0^47127$	$.0^46852$	$.0^46587$	$.0^46331$	$.0^46085$
3.5	$.0^45848$	$.0^45620$	$.0^45400$	$.0^45188$	$.0^44984$	$.0^44788$	$.0^44599$	$.0^44417$	$.0^44242$	$.0^44073$
3.6	$.0^43911$	$.0^43755$	$.0^43605$	$.0^43460$	$.0^43321$	$.0^43188$	$.0^43059$	$.0^42935$	$.0^42816$	$.0^42702$
3.7	$.0^42592$	$.0^42486$	$.0^42385$	$.0^42287$	$.0^42193$	$.0^42103$	$.0^42016$	$.0^41933$	$.0^41853$	$.0^41776$
3.8	$.0^41702$	$.0^41632$	$.0^41563$	$.0^41498$	$.0^41435$	$.0^41375$	$.0^41317$	$.0^41262$	$.0^41208$	$.0^41157$
3.9	$.0^41108$	$.0^41061$	$.0^41016$	$.0^59723$	$.0^59307$	$.0^58908$	$.0^58525$	$.0^58158$	$.0^57806$	$.0^57469$
4.0	$.0^57145$	$.0^56835$	$.0^56538$	$.0^56253$	$.0^55980$	$.0^55718$	$.0^55468$	$.0^55227$	$.0^54997$	$.0^54777$
4.1	$.0^54566$	$.0^54364$	$.0^54170$	$.0^53985$	$.0^53807$	$.0^53637$	$.0^53475$	$.0^53319$	$.0^53170$	$.0^53027$
4.2	$.0^52891$	$.0^52760$	$.0^52635$	$.0^52516$	$.0^52402$	$.0^52292$	$.0^52188$	$.0^52088$	$.0^51992$	$.0^51901$
4.3	$.0^51814$	$.0^51730$	$.0^51650$	$.0^51574$	$.0^51501$	$.0^51431$	$.0^51365$	$.0^51301$	$.0^51241$	$.0^51183$
4.4	$.0^51127$	$.0^51074$	$.0^51024$	$.0^69756$	$.0^69296$	$.0^68857$	$.0^68437$	$.0^68037$	$.0^67655$	$.0^67290$
4.5	$.0^66942$	$.0^66610$	$.0^66294$	$.0^65992$	$.0^65704$	$.0^65429$	$.0^65167$	$.0^64917$	$.0^64679$	$.0^64452$
4.6	$.0^64236$	$.0^64029$	$.0^63833$	$.0^63645$	$.0^63467$	$.0^63297$	$.0^63135$	$.0^62981$	$.0^62834$	$.0^62694$
4.7	$.0^62560$	$.0^62433$	$.0^62313$	$.0^62197$	$.0^62088$	$.0^61984$	$.0^61884$	$.0^61790$	$.0^61700$	$.0^61615$
4.8	$.0^61533$	$.0^61456$	$.0^61382$	$.0^61312$	$.0^61246$	$.0^61182$	$.0^61122$	$.0^61065$	$.0^61011$	$.0^79588$
4.9	$.0^79096$	$.0^78629$	$.0^78185$	$.0^77763$	$.0^77362$	$.0^76982$	$.0^76620$	$.0^76276$	$.0^75950$	$.0^75640$

SOURCE: Reproduced from Robert Schlaifer, *Introduction to Statistics for Business Decisions*, published by McGraw-Hill Book Company, 1961, by specific permission of the copyright holder, the President and Fellows of Harvard College.

Table D
EXPONENTIAL FUNCTIONS

y	e^y	e^{-y}	y	e^y	e^{-y}
0.00	1.0000	1.000000	3.00	20.086	.049787
0.10	1.1052	.904837	3.10	22.198	.045049
0.20	1.2214	.818731	3.20	24.533	.040762
0.30	1.3499	.740818	3.30	27.113	.036883
0.40	1.4918	.670320	3.40	29.964	.033373
0.50	1.6487	.606531	3.50	33.115	.030197
0.60	1.8221	.548812	3.60	36.598	.027324
0.70	2.0138	.496585	3.70	40.447	.024724
0.80	2.2255	.449329	3.80	44.701	.022371
0.90	2.4596	.406570	3.90	49.402	.020242
1.00	2.7183	.367879	4.00	54.598	.018316
1.10	3.0042	.332871	4.10	60.340	.016573
1.20	3.3201	.301194	4.20	66.686	.014996
1.30	3.6693	.272532	4.30	73.700	.013569
1.40	4.0552	.246597	4.40	81.451	.012277
1.50	4.4817	.223130	4.50	90.017	.011109
1.60	4.9530	.201897	4.60	99.484	.010052
1.70	5.4739	.182684	4.70	109.95	.009095
1.80	6.0496	.165299	4.80	121.51	.008230
1.90	6.6859	.149569	4.90	134.29	.007447
2.00	7.3891	.135335	5.00	148.41	.006738
2.10	8.1662	.122456	5.10	164.02	.006097
2.20	9.0250	.110803	5.20	181.27	.005517
2.30	9.9742	.100259	5.30	200.34	.004992
2.40	11.023	.090718	5.40	221.41	.004517
2.50	12.182	.082085	5.50	244.69	.004087
2.60	13.464	.074274	5.60	270.43	.003698
2.70	14.880	.067206	5.70	298.87	.003346
2.80	16.445	.060810	5.80	330.30	.003028
2.90	18.174	.055023	5.90	365.04	.002739
3.00	20.086	.049787	6.00	403.43	.002479

Table E
CUMULATIVE PROBABILITY VALUES FOR THE POISSON DISTRIBUTION

$P[X \leq x]$

λt \ x	1.0	2.0	3.0	4.0	5.0	6.0	7.0	8.0	9.0	10.0
0	0.3679	0.1353	0.0498	0.0183	0.0067	0.0025	0.0009	0.0003	0.0001	0.0000
1	0.7358	0.4060	0.1991	0.0916	0.0404	0.0174	0.0073	0.0030	0.0012	0.0005
2	0.9197	0.6767	0.4232	0.2381	0.1247	0.0620	0.0296	0.0138	0.0062	0.0028
3	0.9810	0.8571	0.6472	0.4335	0.2650	0.1512	0.0818	0.0424	0.0212	0.0103
4	0.9963	0.9473	0.8153	0.6288	0.4405	0.2851	0.1730	0.0996	0.0550	0.0293
5	0.9994	0.9834	0.9161	0.7851	0.6160	0.4457	0.3007	0.1912	0.1157	0.0671
6	0.9999	0.9955	0.9665	0.8893	0.7622	0.6063	0.4497	0.3134	0.2068	0.1301
7	1.0000	0.9989	0.9881	0.9489	0.8666	0.7440	0.5987	0.4530	0.3239	0.2202
8		0.9998	0.9962	0.9786	0.9319	0.8472	0.7291	0.5926	0.4557	0.3328
9		1.0000	0.9989	0.9919	0.9682	0.9161	0.8305	0.7166	0.5874	0.4579
10			0.9997	0.9972	0.9863	0.9574	0.9015	0.8159	0.7060	0.5830
11			0.9999	0.9991	0.9945	0.9799	0.9466	0.8881	0.8030	0.6968
12			1.0000	0.9997	0.9980	0.9912	0.9730	0.9362	0.8758	0.7916
13				0.9999	0.9993	0.9964	0.9872	0.9658	0.9262	0.8645
14				1.0000	0.9998	0.9986	0.9943	0.9827	0.9585	0.9165
15					0.9999	0.9995	0.9976	0.9918	0.9780	0.9513
16					1.0000	0.9998	0.9990	0.9963	0.9889	0.9730
17						0.9999	0.9996	0.9984	0.9947	0.9857
18						1.0000	0.9999	0.9993	0.9976	0.9928
19							0.9999	0.9997	0.9989	0.9965
20							1.0000	0.9999	0.9996	0.9984
21								1.0000	0.9998	0.9993
22									0.9999	0.9997
23									1.0000	0.9999
24										0.9999
25										1.0000

Table E *(continued)*

λt	11.0	12.0	13.0	14.0	15.0	16.0	17.0	18.0	19.0	20.0
x										
0	0.0000	0.0000	0.0000	0.0000	0.0000	0.0000	0.0	0.0	0.0	0.0
1	0.0002	0.0001	0.0000	0.0000	0.0000	0.0000	0.0000	0.0000	0.0000	0.0
2	0.0012	0.0005	0.0002	0.0001	0.0000	0.0000	0.0000	0.0000	0.0000	0.0000
3	0.0049	0.0023	0.0011	0.0005	0.0002	0.0001	0.0000	0.0000	0.0000	0.0000
4	0.0151	0.0076	0.0037	0.0018	0.0009	0.0004	0.0002	0.0001	0.0000	0.0000
5	0.0375	0.0203	0.0107	0.0055	0.0028	0.0014	0.0007	0.0003	0.0002	0.0001
6	0.0786	0.0458	0.0259	0.0142	0.0076	0.0040	0.0021	0.0010	0.0005	0.0003
7	0.1432	0.0895	0.0540	0.0316	0.0180	0.0100	0.0054	0.0029	0.0015	0.0008
8	0.2320	0.1550	0.0998	0.0621	0.0374	0.0220	0.0126	0.0071	0.0039	0.0021
9	0.3405	0.2424	0.1658	0.1094	0.0699	0.0433	0.0261	0.0154	0.0089	0.0050
10	0.4599	0.3472	0.2517	0.1757	0.1185	0.0774	0.0491	0.0304	0.0183	0.0108
11	0.5793	0.4616	0.3532	0.2600	0.1847	0.1270	0.0847	0.0549	0.0347	0.0214
12	0.6887	0.5760	0.4631	0.3585	0.2676	0.1931	0.1350	0.0917	0.0606	0.0390
13	0.7813	0.6815	0.5730	0.4644	0.3632	0.2745	0.2009	0.1426	0.0984	0.0661
14	0.8540	0.7720	0.6751	0.5704	0.4656	0.3675	0.2808	0.2081	0.1497	0.1049
15	0.9074	0.8444	0.7636	0.6694	0.5681	0.4667	0.3714	0.2866	0.2148	0.1565
16	0.9441	0.8987	0.8355	0.7559	0.6641	0.5660	0.4677	0.3750	0.2920	0.2211
17	0.9678	0.9370	0.8905	0.8272	0.7489	0.6593	0.5640	0.4686	0.3784	0.2970
18	0.9823	0.9626	0.9302	0.8826	0.8195	0.7423	0.6549	0.5622	0.4695	0.3814
19	0.9907	0.9787	0.9573	0.9235	0.8752	0.8122	0.7363	0.6509	0.5606	0.4703
20	0.9953	0.9884	0.9750	0.9521	0.9170	0.8682	0.8055	0.7307	0.6472	0.5591
21	0.9977	0.9939	0.9859	0.9711	0.9469	0.9108	0.8615	0.7991	0.7255	0.6437
22	0.9989	0.9969	0.9924	0.9833	0.9672	0.9418	0.9047	0.8551	0.7931	0.7206
23	0.9995	0.9985	0.9960	0.9907	0.9805	0.9633	0.9367	0.8989	0.8490	0.7875
24	0.9998	0.9993	0.9980	0.9950	0.9888	0.9777	0.9593	0.9317	0.8933	0.8432
25	0.9999	0.9997	0.9990	0.9974	0.9938	0.9869	0.9747	0.9554	0.9269	0.8878
26	1.0000	0.9999	0.9995	0.9987	0.9967	0.9925	0.9848	0.9718	0.9514	0.9221
27		0.9999	0.9998	0.9994	0.9983	0.9959	0.9912	0.9827	0.9687	0.9475
28		1.0000	0.9999	0.9997	0.9991	0.9978	0.9950	0.9897	0.9805	0.9657
29			1.0000	0.9999	0.9996	0.9989	0.9973	0.9940	0.9881	0.9782
30				0.9999	0.9998	0.9994	0.9985	0.9967	0.9930	0.9865
31				1.0000	0.9999	0.9997	0.9992	0.9982	0.9960	0.9919
32					0.9999	0.9999	0.9996	0.9990	0.9978	0.9953
33					1.0000	0.9999	0.9998	0.9995	0.9988	0.9973
34						1.0000	0.9999	0.9997	0.9994	0.9985
35							0.9999	0.9999	0.9997	0.9992
36							1.0000	0.9999	0.9998	0.9996
37								1.0000	0.9999	0.9998
38									1.0000	0.9999
39										0.9999
40										1.0000

Table F
RANDOM NUMBERS

12651	61646	11769	75109	86996	97669	25757	32535	07122	76763
81769	74436	02630	72310	45049	18029	07469	42341	98173	79260
36737	98863	77240	76251	00654	64688	09343	70278	67331	98729
82861	54371	76610	94934	72748	44124	05610	53750	95938	01485
21325	15732	24127	37431	09723	63529	73977	95218	96074	42138
74146	47887	62463	23045	41490	07954	22597	60012	98866	90959
90759	64410	54179	66075	61051	75385	51378	08360	95946	95547
55683	98078	02238	91540	21219	17720	87817	41705	95785	12563
79686	17969	76061	83748	55920	83612	41540	86492	06447	60568
70333	00201	86201	69716	78185	62154	77930	67663	29529	75116
14042	53536	07779	04157	41172	36473	42123	43929	50533	33437
59911	08256	06596	48416	69770	68797	56080	14223	59199	30162
62368	62623	62742	14891	39247	52242	98832	69533	91174	57979
57529	97751	54976	48957	74599	08759	78494	52785	68526	64618
15469	90574	78033	66885	13936	42117	71831	22961	94225	31816
18625	23674	53850	32827	81647	80820	00420	63555	74489	80141
74626	68394	88562	70745	23701	45630	65891	58220	35442	60414
11119	16519	27384	90199	79210	76965	99546	30323	31664	22845
41101	17336	48951	53674	17880	45260	08575	49321	36191	17095
32123	91576	84221	78902	82010	30847	62329	63898	23268	74283
26091	68409	69704	82267	14751	13151	93115	01437	56945	89661
67680	79790	48462	59278	44185	29616	76531	19589	83139	28454
15184	19260	14073	07026	25264	08388	27182	22557	61501	67481
58010	45039	57181	10238	36874	28546	37444	80824	63981	39942
56425	53996	86245	32623	78858	08143	60377	42925	42815	11159
82630	84066	13592	60642	17904	99718	63432	88642	37858	25431
14927	40909	23900	48761	44860	92467	31742	87142	03607	32059
23740	22505	07489	85986	74420	21744	97711	36648	35620	97949
32990	97446	03711	63824	07953	85965	87089	11687	92414	67257
05310	24058	91946	78437	34365	82469	12430	84754	19354	72745
21839	39937	27534	88913	49055	19218	47712	67677	51889	70926
08833	42549	93981	94051	28382	83725	72643	64233	97252	17133
58336	11139	47479	00931	91560	95372	97642	33856	54825	55680
62032	91144	75478	47431	52726	30289	42411	91886	51818	78292
45171	30557	53116	04118	58301	24375	65609	85810	18620	49198
91611	62656	60128	35609	63698	78356	50682	22505	01692	36291
55472	63819	86314	49174	93582	73604	78614	78849	23096	72825
18573	09729	74091	53994	10970	86557	65661	41854	26037	53296
60866	02955	90288	82136	83644	94455	06560	78029	98768	71296
45043	55608	82767	60890	74646	79485	13619	98868	40857	19415
17831	09737	79473	75945	28394	79334	70577	38048	03607	06932
40137	03981	07585	18128	11178	32601	27994	05641	22600	86064
77776	31343	14576	97706	16039	47517	43300	59080	80392	63189
69605	44104	40103	95635	05635	81673	68657	09559	23510	95875
19916	52934	26499	09821	87331	80993	61299	36979	73599	35055
02606	58552	07678	56619	65325	30705	99582	53390	46357	13244
65183	73160	87131	35530	47946	09854	18080	02321	05809	04898
10740	98914	44916	11322	89717	88189	30143	52687	19420	60061
98642	89822	71691	51573	83666	61642	46683	33761	47542	23551
60139	25601	93663	25547	02654	94829	48672	28736	84994	13071

SOURCE: The Rand Corporation, *A Million Random Digits with 100,000 Normal Deviates.* New York: The Free Press, 1955. Reproduced with permission of The Rand Corporation.

Answers to Selected Problems

2-1 1/4
2-3 (a) 1/5 (b) 1/10,000 (c) 1/4 (d) 2/3
2-6 (a) Not (b) Not (c) Not
2-8 (a) 2/3 (b) 2/3 (c) 1/3 (d) 1 (e) 0
2-11 (b) .75 (c) Not independent
2-12 (a) 1/13 (b) 1/26 (c) 1/2 (d) 3/13
2-16 (a) P[reject] = .15; P[bad] = .10; P[reject|bad] = .95 (b) .095
2-18 (b) 42/90 (c) No
2-20 (a) .72398 (b) .00051 (c) .25257
2-21 (a) .947 The greens should *not* be watered. (b) .333
2-24 (a) .50 (b) 1/3 (c) 1/4
2-25 (a) No (b) Yes (c) Maybe

3-1

Proceeds	Probability
−$20,000	1/9
− 10,000	2/9
0	3/9
10,000	2/9
20,000	1/9

3-5 Mean = 14.63; Variance = 360.97; Standard deviation = 19.0
3-7 (a) Yes (b) Yes (c) No (d) No (e) No
3-9 (a) .25 (b) .50 (c) 5
3-12 (a) .0490 (b) .2262 (c) .6723 (d) .9687
3-14 (a) .2447 (b) .1597 (c) .9840 (d) .2500 (e) .0510 (f) .8565
3-17 (a) .4332 (b) .1915 (c) .2420 (d) .0062 (e) .0968 (f) .9861 (g) .97585
  (h) .0606
3-20 (a) .9876 (b) .7888 (d) 1 (approximately)

4-1 Winter $72,000 Spring $84,700
     Summer 121,000 Fall   179,685

4-4 (b) $\hat{Y} = 200.67 + 9.673X$ ($X = 0$ at 1970)
     (c) 297.40

4-5 Winter   50.6   Spring 89.8
     Summer 150.9   Fall   108.7

4-6

Quarter		(b) Moving Average	(c) Percentage of Moving Average	Seasonal Index	(d) Deseasonalized Data
1975	W			93.4	4.2
	S			112.0	5.4
	S	6.8	63.2	69.2	6.2
	F	7.8	138.5	125.4	8.6
1976	W	8.7	89.7	93.4	8.4
	S	9.4	112.8	112.0	9.5
	S	10.3	67.0	69.2	10.0
	F	11.6	116.4	125.4	10.8
1977	W	12.6	102.4	93.4	13.8
	S	13.6	111.8	112.0	13.6
	S	14.4	71.5	69.2	14.9
	F	14.4	129.8	125.4	14.9
1978	W	14.3	97.2	93.4	14.9
	S	14.1	102.1	112.0	12.9
	S	13.9	73.4	69.2	14.7
	F	14.3	121.0	125.4	13.8
1979	W	15.3	88.2	93.4	14.5
	S	16.2	112.3	112.0	16.3
	S			69.2	20.5
	F			125.4	16.5

4-8

t	F_t	t	F_t
1	—	11	5,173.2
2	4,890	12	5,191.9
3	4,898.0	13	5,227.1
4	4,926.8	14	5,268.3
5	4,960.1	15	5,313.0
6	5,000.1	16	5,363.8
7	5,040.1	17	5,402.3
8	5,044.1	18	5,449.4
9	5,094.5	19	5,465.6
10	5,128.7	20	5,499.4

4-11 (b) $\hat{Y} = 22.405 + 3.619X$
4-12 (a) 1,100 (b) 900 (c) 700
4-13 $\hat{Y} = -.5595 + .0817X_1 + 1.1605X_2$
4-16 (a) .105 (b) .15 (c) .38 (d) .73
4-20 (b) Answers will vary slightly.
   (1) .06 (2) .40 (3) .68

5-3 Choose either A_1 or A_3.
5-4 Spring-action movement
5-6 A_3 and A_5
5-8 Test market; then if that is successful, market nationally, but if it is unsuccessful, abort.
5-9 Use no test and hire each candidate.
5-12 Market nationally with no consumer testing.
5-13 Use the juvenile hormone.

6-2 (a) A_2 or A_3 (b) A_2 (c) A_2

6-4

EVENTS	ACTS	
	A_1	A_2
E_1	0	10
E_2	70	0

6-5 A_1
6-6 (a) 70/3 for A_1 or A_3 (b) 40 (c) 50/3 (d) 50/3 for A_1 or A_3 (e) They are the same values.
6-8 (a) 10,000 tons for A and 33,333.33 tons for B (b) 80,000 tons (c) Machine A maximizes expected payoff.

(d)

EVENTS	ACTS	
	A	B
$T = 50,000$	$ 0	$150,000
$T = 100,000$	100,000	0

Machine A minimizes expected opportunity loss.
(e) Yes

7-2 (b) The optimal strategy is: Use concrete if test marketing is favorable, but use the wooden hull if it is unfavorable.
7-4 (a) $90,000; No (d) The wildcatter should use the seismic; then if it confirms oil he should drill, and if it denies oil he should abandon the lease.

7-6   (c) The optimal strategy is to retain the old box if sales decrease and to use the new box otherwise.

7-8   (c) The optimal strategy is to not experiment and to market the product.

8-1
	(a)	(b)	(c)	(d)
(1)	A	B	A	B
(2)	$1978	$4166	$35,090	$30,690

8-2   (a) Payoff = $\begin{cases} -\$50{,}000 + \$1000\,\mu & \text{for helmet} \\ \$0 & \text{for no helmet} \end{cases}$

$\mu_b = $ 50 helmets per store

(b) Yes   (c) $833.20

8-5   (a) $55,828
(b) 1.98 gigabits per day
(c) $\mu_1 = 1.782$; $\sigma_1 = .485$; Choose the photographic unit.
(d) .3264

8-7   (a) $114.52

	(1)	(2)	(3)	(4)
(b)	$1.84	$7.63	$23.90	$59.88
(c)	−$.16	$3.13	$11.40	$ 9.88

$n = 25$ is best
(d) Choose A_1 if $\overline{X} = 3.6$ and A_2 if $\overline{X} = 3.9$.

9-3   (a)

EVENTS	ACTS	
	Policy	No Policy
Tornado	−$500	−$40,000
No tornado	− 500	0

(b) −$500 for a policy; −$4 for no policy   (c) No

9-4   (a)

EVENTS	ACTS	
	Buy	Rent
Win contract	$120,000	$50,000
Lost contract	−40,000	0

(b) $40,000 for buying; $25,000 for renting

(c)

EVENTS	ACTS	
	Buy	Rent
Win contract	400	300
Lose contract	0	200

(d) 200 for buying; 250 for renting   (e) Rent

ANSWERS TO SELECTED PROBLEMS

9-7   (a) Willing;   (b,c) Might be willing;   (d) Unwilling;   (e) Willing
9-9   No
9-11 (a) 1/2   (b) 3/4; 1/4   (c) 1/2; inconsistent
9-13 Choose A; then if E_1 occurs, choose D.

10-2 A_3, A_4, B_3, B_4, B_5
10-4 (b) $P = 7/16$; Value of game $= -1/16$ (c) $Q = 7/16$ (d) Unchanged
      (e) Unchanged   (f) 13/20; Yes

10-7

| DRACULA | | UNION | |
Act	Probability	Act	Probability
Tranquil	2/9	Tranquil	4/9
Lock-in	7/9	Strike	5/9
Bite union leaders	0	Wooden stake sabotage	0

Value of game = 100/9 coffins

10-9   (a) No   (b,c) Expand for both   (d) Not expand
10-12 (a) Both players should choose blue; 1¢.   (b) Yes, 5¢

11-1 $Q^* = 200$; order once every .2 year.
11-4   (a) $Q^* = 2620$, $S^* = 2544$, $T^* = .262$ yr   Out of stock .029 of the time.
       (b) $763.23; smaller
11-7   (a) 158.1 tons   (b) .79 yr   (c) .1581 yr
11-9   (a) 632.5 acres; fertilize every .127 year or 7.9 times yearly.
11-11 (a) $\mu = 7.3$ pairs   (b) $r = 9$, $Q = 32$ (c) 1.7 pairs   (d) $68.21

12-2   (a) $X_1 = 7.5$, $X_2 = 2.5$ (b) $X_1 = 1.5$, $X_2 = 1$ (c) $X_1 = -.5$, $X_2 = 2$
       (d) $X_1 = -1.5$, $X_2 = 4.5$
12-3 $X_A = 2.4$, $X_B = 2.4$, $P = 26.4$
12-6   (b) There are two most attractive corners:
           (1) $X_1 = 4$, $X_2 = 4$, $P = 24$;   (2) $X_1 = 12$, $X_2 = 0$, $P = 24$
       (c) $P = 24$; the point represents an optimal solution.
12-8   (a) Let X_R = Quantity of regular models; X_D = Quantity of deluxe models
           Maximize $P = 10X_R + 15X_D$
           Subject to $5X_R + 8X_D \leq 80$ (labor)
                          $X_R + X_D \leq 12$ (frame)
           where $X_R, X_D \geq 0$
       (b) $X_R = 5\frac{1}{3}$, $X_D = 6\frac{2}{3}$, $P = 153\frac{1}{3}$ dollars
12-10 4 forged bits, 6 machined bits, $P = 102$ dollars
12-14 (a) (1) 50   (2) 40   (3) 4000   (4) 4000   (b) $40 for each batch type

13-3 $X_1 = 8$ $X_A = 0$
       $X_2 = 1$ $X_B = 0$
       $X_3 = 0$ $P = 1{,}000$

13-4 (a) $X_1 = 0$, $X_2 = 3$, $P = 9$
(b) Let X_A, X_B, and X_C represent the respective slack variables.

Maximize $P = 2X_1 + 3X_2 + 0X_A + 0X_B + 0X_C$
Subject to $3X_1 + 2X_2 + 1X_A + 0X_B + 0X_C = 6$ (resource A)
             $1X_1 + 0X_2 + 0X_A + 1X_B + 0X_C = 5$ (resource B)
             $0X_1 + 1X_2 + 0X_A + 0X_B + 1X_C = 4$ (resource C)
where   all Xs ≥ 0

(c)

UNIT PROFIT		2	3	0	0	0	
	Var. Mix	X_1	X_2	X_A	X_B	X_C	Sol.
0	$X_A \leftarrow$	3	② ↓	1	0	0	6
0	X_B	1	0	0	1	0	5
0	X_C	0	1	0	0	1	4
	Sac.	0	0	0	0	0	0
	Imp.	2	3	0	0	0	—
3	X_2	3/2	1	1/2	0	0	3
0	X_B	1	0	0	1	0	5
0	X_C	−3/2	0	−1/2	0	1	1
	Sac.	9/2	3	3/2	0	0	9
	Imp.	−5/2	0	−3/2	0	0	—

13-6 64/7 tables, 20/7 chairs, no bookcases; $P = 1,580/7$

14-3 (a) $X_A = 2$, $X_B = 4$, $P = 2.2$

14-5 Using the variables X_E = Number of tons from Eastern, X_N = Number of tons from Northern, X_T = Number of tons from Tom's Lucky, with X_L representing unused labor, and using X_R and X_C as surplus variables for the Northern requirement and copper constraints, and a_R and a_C as the artificials, we obtain the following final simplex tableau:

UNIT PROFIT		280	185	260	0	0	0	−M	−M	
	Var. Mix	X_E	X_N	X_T	X_L	X_R	X_C	a_R	a_C	Sol.
0	X_C	0	0	75	50	80	1	−80	−1	2000
185	X_N	0	1	0	0	−1	0	1	0	100
280	X_E	1	0	2	1	2	0	−2	0	100
	Sac.	280	185	560	280	375	0	−375	0	46,500
	Imp.	0	0	−300	−280	−375	0	−M+375	−M	—

ANSWERS TO SELECTED PROBLEMS

14-7 160 beef, 60 chicken, 80 fish; $C = 490$ dollars

14-9 (a) Unbounded problem (b) $X_1 = 0$, $X_2 = 10$, $X_3 = 0$, $P = 20$

15-1 (b)

From \ To	U	V	W
A	—	50	50
B	—	—	150
C	150	150	—

$C = 4350$

15-4 Ship 100 tombstones to Eldred from Abinger, and ship 50 tombstones to Cedrick and 150 tombstones to Dunstan from Barnesly.

15-6

Brat	Chore
Fritz	Retrieve the Captain's pipe
Hans	Scare cannibals
Gert	Pen ostriches
Zelda	Chase hippos

15-8

Production	Used for Demand
August regular — 25	August — 25
August regular — 75 September regular — 100	September — 175
October regular — 100 October overtime — 50	October — 150
November regular — 100 November overtime — 50	November — 150

$C = \$27,875$

16-1 $a - c - e$

16-3 $b - f - g - h$

16-7 (a) $a - c - d - f - i - j - k - m - n - o - p$ 32 months

16-9 (a)

Activity	Expected Time	Variance
a	6	.11
b	7	5.44
c	14	7.11
d	4	.11
e	17	.11

(b) $a - c - d$ (c) .7568

17-1 (a) .632121 (b) .006738 (c) .128597

17-3

	(a)	(b)	(c)	(d)
L	4	2	.67	1.33
W	.20	.25	.34	3.33
L_q	3.2	1.33	.27	.76
W_q	.16	.17	.13	1.90
	.8	.67	.4	.57

17-6 (a) .20 (b) 66.67%; 2 hr

17-8 (a) .993262 (b) .135335 (c) .128597

17-11 $34

17-12 (a) (1) .0923 hr (2) .0606 hr (b) (1) $28.38 (2) $21.82
One machinist clerk is cheapest.

17-14 (a) 5 checkers; 1.11 min (b) .290 min (c) $56.66 for $S = 5$; $61.74 for $S = 6$

17-16 (a) .606531 (b) .393469

17-17 (a) .0774 (b) .9797 (c) .0286 (d) .5505

17-19 (a)

n	P_n
0	.271
1	.217
2	.173
3	.139
4	.111
5	.089

(b) $L = 1.868$; $L_q = 1.139$; $W_q = .31$ hr; $W = .51$ hr (c) $L = 4$; $L_q = 3.2$; $W_q = .8$ hr; $W = 1$ hr

17-20 (a)

n	P_n
0	.0367
1	.0918
2	.1835
3	.2753
4	.2753
5	.1376

(b) $L_q = 2.11$; $L = 3.07$; $W_q = 1.09$ days; $W = 1.59$ days (c) $L_q = .5$; $L = 1$; $W_q = .5$ day; $W = 1$ day

17-21 $L_q = .295$; $L = .795$; $W_q = .59$ min; $W = 1.59$ min

17-22 $L_q = .5$; $L = 1$; $W_q = 1$ min; $W = 2$ min

18-2 $1/\lambda = 13.05$ sec

18-5 385

18–7 (a) $95.57 \leq \mu \leq 105.49$ min   (b) $69.05 \leq \mu \leq 69.35$ in
(c) $\$11.27 \leq \mu \leq \$12.73$

18–10 $89.142 for one man; $113.191 for two men. Hire the helper.

18–13 (a)

Net Winnings	Probability
−$1	20/36
1	14/36
2	1/36
3	1/36

(c) −$.09

19–1 $p_A = .5294$ $p_B = .4706$

19–3 (a) $p_1 = 3/7$ $p_2 = 4/7$ (b) In period 4.

19–5 Policy 3

19–9 (a) 7977   (b) 9080.2

Index

A

Absorbing states, 574
Act forks, in decision tree diagram, 142-43
Activity, 443-44
Activity completion times, 449-50
Activity scheduling, PERT and, 447-49, 459-61, 465-66
Activity sequence, in PERT network, 447-49
Activity slack times, 461
Acts: admissible, 148; in decision table, 141; in decision tree diagram, 142-43; defined, 140-41; ranking, 143-48; reducing number of, 148
Actual chronology, for probability tree diagram, 195
Addition law, 24-28; application to complementary events, 27-28; errors in use of, 40-42; for mutually exclusive events, 25-26; for mutually exclusive and collectively exhaustive events, 26-27
Admissible acts, 148
Algebraic solutions, in simplex method, 364-66
Algorithm, 12
Analytic solution methods, 325
Area under normal curve, 321-22
Artificial variables, 387-91; in cost minimization problems, 392-93; in infeasible problems, 397; use of, 391
Assignment problem, 359

Attitudes: utility and, 236-37; versus judgment, 251-52

B

Backordering: an optimal inventory policy, 308-11; and shorted items, 316
Backward induction, 156-59, 199
Backward pass, in PERT, 451-53
Balance equations, queuing models and, 501-502
Basic, 550
Battle of Bismarck Sea, game theory and, 268
Bayes decision rule, 167, 180, 184-85; and decision to buy insurance, 236-37; decision criteria and, 172-73; expected utility and, 242; maximization of expected payoff and, 149-50; opportunity loss and, 182-83; revision of probabilities and, 42-47; utility and, 252-53
Bayes' theorem, 43-45
Bernoulli process, 69-70
Beta distribution, *see* Modified beta distributions
Big X method, 407-408
Binomial distribution, 66-77; Bernoulli process and, 69-70; cumulative probabilities and, 72-73; formula for, 70-72; mean and variance of, 77; use of binomial probability tables and, 73-76
Binomial formula, 70-72

Binomial probabilities, 70–72; tables of, 73–76

C

Certain event, 21
Closed-loop path, transportation problem and, 423–25
COBOL, 550
Collectively exhaustive events, 24, 26–27
Column maximums, 270
Column numbers, see Row and column numbers
Communicating states, 574
Complementary events: addition law and, 27–28; errors in identification of, 41–42
Complementary outcome, Bernoulli process and, 69
Composite event, 18
Computer languages, simulation programs and, 550
Computer simulation, 550–51
Conditional probabilities, 28–33, 37, 156; computation from joint probability, 30–31; defined, 28; as posterior probability, 45–47
Conditional values, 143
Confidence interval estimates, 540–41
Constant sum game, 294
Constraint line: determination of valid side of, 337–338; objective function lines parallel to, 353–54; plotting of, 335–37
Constraints: defined, 11–12; in linear program, 332–33, 334; in transportation problem, 414–15; see also Demand constraints, Equality constraints, Mixture constraints, Redundant constraints
Continuity, in utility theory, 244–46
Continuous probability distribution, 77
Continuous random variables, 77, 321–22
Corner points in linear programming, 362, 366–67
Correlation analysis, 126
Cost minimization problem: graphical solution method and, 344–47; simplex method and, 391–96
CPM (Critical Path Method), 443, 471–73
CPM network, 471–73
Crash times, 465–66
Criterion of insufficient reason, 172
Critical activity, 455
Critical path, determination of, 452–56, 457–59, 472–73

Critical value, see Decision rules
Cumulative probabilities, 72–73; in simulation, 543–45
Cumulative probability graph, 129–30
Cycles, 116
Cyclical movement, 96

D

Decision criteria, 167–73; and Bayes decision rule, 172–73; criterion of insufficient reason, 172; maximin payoff, 167–70; maximum likelihood criterion, 170–72
Decision making: attitude and, 235–36; certainty and uncertainty and, 141–42; decision tree analysis and, 150–60; expected payoff and, 149–50; interactive, see Game theory; inventory policy and, see Inventory policy; with Markov processes, 564–65; ranking alternatives and payoff table in, 143–48; using strategies, 173–78; see also Decision making with experimental information, Decision making with Markov processes, Decision making with normal distribution, Utility
Decision making with experimental information, 191–202; posterior analysis and, 198–200; preposterior analysis and, 200–202; revision of probabilities and, 192–98
Decision making with Markov processes, 557–72; see also Markov processes
Decision making with normal distribution, 209–31; decisions regarding sample and, 224–27; decision structure and, 210–12; opportunity losses and, 212–15; posterior analysis for given sample size and, 219–24; prior analysis without sample information and, 215–19; procedures used in, 228–30
Decision making with utility, see Utility
Decision rules: based on sample mean, 219; determining critical value for, 222–24
Decision tables, 141–42
Decision theory: Bayes' decision rule and utility and, 180; decision criteria and, 167–73; elements of decision and, 140–43; expected value of perfect information and, 182–86; opportunity loss and, 180–82
Decision tree analysis, 150–60; assign-

ment of event probabilities and, 154–56; backward induction and, 156–59; decision tree diagram and, 152; determination of payoffs and, 153–54; *see also* Decision tree diagram
Decision tree diagram, 142
Degeneracy, 403–404
Delphi forecasting, 132
Demand, normally distributed, 321–23
Demand constraints, 352; conversion into equality, 388
Dependent variable, 103
Deseasonalized data, 114–15
Diet problem, 359–60; *see also* Feed-mix problem
Dominated acts, *see* Inadmissible acts
Dummy activities, PERT and, 448–49
Dummy plants and warehouses, in transportation problem, 429–31
Dynamic programming, 10

E

Earliest possible event time, *see* TE
Early finishing time, *see* EF
Early starting time, *see* ES
Econometrics, 126
Economic order quantity model, 300–308, 315; non-normal demand and, 321–25; inventory policies and, 549; for uncertain demand, 316–21; *see also* Inventory policy
Economic production quantity, 314–15
EF: activity scheduling for PERT and, 459–61; determination of, 472–73
Elementary events, 17, 19–20
Entering cell: closed-loop path for, 423–25; for transportation solution, 419–23
Entering variable, 373
Entry criterion, 373
EOQ model, *see* Economic order quantity model
Equality constraints, 251–52; conversion of demand constraint into, 388
Equipment replacement, quantitative method and, 10
ES, activity scheduling for PERT and, 459–61, 472–73
Estimation, *see* Confidence interval estimates
Event forks, in decision tree diagram, 142–43

Events: actual chronology of, 195; in decision table, 141–42; decision under uncertainty and, 141; earliest possible times of, *see* TE; generation of, with random numbers, 528–30; probability of, 18–21, 154–56; in probability theory, 15–18; relationships between, 21–24; *see also* Probabilities
Event set, 18
Event slack times, determination of, 457–59
EVPI, 182–86, 202, 217–19, 228
EVSI, 220–21, 228
Exchange coefficients, 371
Exchange ratio, 373
Exit criterion: in cost minimization problems, 395; in unbounded problems, 399
Exiting cell, ties for, 427–28
Exiting variable, 373
Expected activity completion time, estimation of, 468–71
Expected annual holding cost, 317
Expected annual shortage cost, 317
Expected average cycle inventory, 317
Expected mean, prior analysis without sample information and, 215–17
Expected net gain of sampling, 226–27
Expected payoff: maximization of, 149–50; with perfect information, 182–86; under uncertainty, 185
Expected utility: determination of, 243–44; gambles and, 242; *see also* Utility
Expected value: defined, 63–65; of perfect information, *see* EVPI; of sample information, *see* EVSI; and variance of random variable, 65–66
Experimental information, decision making with, *see* Decision making with experimental information
Exponential distribution, 489, 491–94
Exponential smoothing, 116–20; single-parameter, 117–18; two-parameter, 118–20
Extensive form analysis, 175–77
Extrapolation, with time series, 105

F

Feasible solution, 338–39; defined, 12
Feasible solution region, 338–39; constraints and, 352; identification of, 343

Feed-mix problem, 344–47
FIFO queue discipline, 488, 513
Fixed production-rate model, inventory policy and, 312–15
Forecasting, 94–132; with exponential smoothing, 116–20; identifying cycles in, 116; seasonal indexes in, 107–16; trend using regression, 103–107; using causal models, 120–26; using judgment, 126–32; using past data, 95–102
Forward pass, in PERT, 453
Fractile, 128–29

G

Gambles, expected utility and, 242
Game theory, 10, 266–89; Battle of Bismarck Sea and, 260; constant sum game, 294; games with several players and, 288; interactive decision making and, 266–68; mixed strategies in games without saddle points and, 273–78; non-zero-sum games and, 286–88; optimal mixed strategies for zero-sum games and, 278–86; two-person zero-sum games and, 269–73
Game-type simulations, 523–24
General Purpose System Simulator (GPSS), 550
Graphical solution method, 334–43; compared with simplex method, 362; cost minimization problem and, 344–47; equality constraints and, 351–52; feasible solution region and, 338–39; finding valid side of constraint line with, 337–38; line construction problems and, 347–50; mixture constraints and, 348–50; most attractive corner and, 339–41; multiple optimal solutions and, 331–33; plotting constraint lines and, 335–37; summary of, 343–44

H

Horizontal intercept, 336–37

I

Impossible event, 21
Inadmissible acts, 148, 283; elimination of, 276–78
Independent events, 24; multiplication law for, 38–40

Independent variable, 103
Industrial dynamics, 132
Inequality constraint, 332–33; determination of valid side for, 343
Infeasibility, of right-hand side changes, 346–47
Infeasible point, 338
Infeasible problems, 397–99
Infeasible solution, defined, 12
Informational chronology, for probability tree diagram, 195–96
Interactive decision making, see Game theory
Intercepts, see Horizontal intercept, Vertical intercept
Intersection of events, 22
Inventory control, quantitative method and, 10; see also Inventory policy
Inventory costs, 297–98; see also Inventory holding costs
Inventory decisions, see Inventory policy
Inventory holding costs, 297, 323
Inventory items, types of, 298–99
Inventory policy, 295–324; with backordering, 317–21; demand and supply and, 298–99; economic order quantity model and, 300–308; factors influencing, 296–300; fixed production-rate model and, 321–24; importance of, 295–96; inventory cost components and, 297–98; simulation of, 547–48; structure of inventory system and, 298; types of inventory items and, 298–99; uncertain factors and, 315–25
Inventory shortage costs, 297–98
Inventory systems, structure of, 298
Irregular time-series variation, 96

J

Joint events, 22
Joint probabilities, 197; computation of conditional probability from, 30–31; for more than two events, 35–36; multiplication law and, 33–40
Joint probability table, 40, 47; marginal probabilities and, 29–30; used to illustrate posterior probability calculation, 47
Judgmental probabilities, versus attitude, 251–52; see also Subjective probabilities

L

Late finishing time, *see* LF
Latest allowable event time, *see* TL
Lead time, defined, 299–300
Least squares method, 103–105; *see also* Regression analysis
LF: activity scheduling for PERT and, 459–61; location of critical path and, 472–73
LIFO queue discipline, 488
Likelihood, *see* Maximum likelihood act
Linear programming: definition of, 330–32; degeneracy and, 403–404; formulation of program for, 332–34; graphical solution method and, *see* Graphical solution method; infeasible problems and, 397–98; PERT and, 468; quantitative method and, 10; redundant constraints and, 403–404; simplex method and, *see* Simplex method; special problems in, 387–405; ties for optimal solutions and, 401–403; unbounded problems and, 398–401; variables unrestricted as to sign and, 404–405
Linear relationships, defined, 331
Line construction problems, 247–51
LS: activity scheduling for PERT and, 459–60; location of critical path and, 472–73

M

Maintenance policy, Markov processes and, 565–70
Main variables, in linear programming, 363
Management-by-exception principle, 463
Management science, defined, 8
Managerial decision making, *see* Decision making
Marginal probabilities, 29–30
Marginal utility, for money, 238–40
Markov chains, 559
Markovian property, 558
Markov process(es), 10, 557–59; calculation of steady-state probabilities and, 562–63; changes over time in state probabilities and, 560–62; characteristics of, 558; decision making and, 564–65; finding an optimal maintenance policy, in terms of a, 565–70; state and transition probabilities and, 559–60

Mathematical model, defined, 11
Mathematical optimization procedure, defined, 8
Mathematical programming, 10
Maximin payoff act, 167–70, 271
Maximin payoff criterion, 170–72
Maximum expected payoff, 182
Maximum likelihood act, 170–72
Maximum likelihood criterion, 170–72
Mean arrival rate, in waiting line simulation, 525
Mean customer time in system, 499, 502, 506, 509, 525
Mean customer waiting time, 500, 502, 509, 525, 548–49
Mean estimation, *see* Confidence interval estimates
Mean length of waiting line, 499, 502, 509
Mean number of customers in system, 499, 501, 510, 525, 535
Mean of exponential distribution, 493
Mean of normal distribution, 77–83
Mean of Poisson distribution, 495
Mean service rate, 525
Mean service time, 525
Mean time between arrivals, 525
Mean waiting time, 500
Milestone, 446
Milestone scheduling, PERT and, 461–62
Minimax criterion, 274; and games without saddle point, 276; in two-person zero-sum games, 270–71
Minimax loss act, 270–71
Minimum expected opportunity loss act, 183
Mixed strategies, in games without saddle point, 273–78
Mixture constraints, 347–50
Models, in decision making, 11–13; *see also* Economic order quantity model, Fixed production-rate model, Inventory policy, Linear programming
Modified beta distributions, PERT and, 468–71
Money: decreasing marginal utility for, 238–40; utility curve for, risk and, 253–58
Monte Carlo simulation, *see* Simulation
Monthly data, 114
Most attractive corner, 339–41; method for finding, 344; multiple, 331–33
Most attractive edge, 333
Most likely time (PERT), 468

Moving averages, four quarter, 108; percentage of, 112
Multiple optimal solutions, in linear programming, 331–33
Multiple regression analysis, 122–24
Multiple-server multiple-stage queue, 487–88
Multiple-server queuing model, 484–513; compared with single-server models, 512–13
Multiple-server single-stage queue, 486–87
Multiplication law, 33–40; errors in use of, 41
Mutually exclusive events, 23, 26–27; addition law for, 25–26

N

Network planning, *see* PERT
Non-empty cells: required number of, 426; in transportation solution, 419–23
Non-negativity conditions: defined, 334; and feasible solution region, 338–39
Non-zero-sum games, 286–88
Normal distribution, 77–89; and finding areas under normal curve, 79–84; sampling and, 86–88; standard normal random variable and, 84–86; *see also* Decision making with normal distribution
Normal equations, 123
Normal form analysis, 175–77
Normal loss function, determination of EVPI and, 217–19
Normally distributed random variables, probability values for, 79–84
Northwest corner rule, transportation problem and, 331, 416–18
Numerical solution methods, 325; *see also* Simulation

O

Objective function, 307–17; determination of, 344; in linear program, 333
Objective function lines: determining direction of improvement of, 343–44; parallel to constraint line, 331–32
Objective probability, 15
Objectives, 144–45
Operations research: defined, 8; procedures and applications for, 9–11
Opportunity loss: Bayes' decision rule and, 182–83; decision making using, 212, 214–15; defined, 181–82
Opportunity loss acts, minimum expected, 215–17
Opportunity loss table, 181
Optimal corner-point solutions, ties for, 249–51
Optimal decision rule, determination of, 227
Optimal mixed strategies, for zero-sum games, 278–86
Optimal solution: defined, 8, 12; determination of, 341–44; to economic order quantity model, 312–17; multiple, 331–33; with simplex method, 378–81; ties for, 401–403; to transportation problem, 425–26, 428–29
Optimistic time (PERT), 468
Ordering costs, 297, 310
Order level, 308
Order point, defined, 296
Outcomes: assignment of utility values to, 248–53; in decision table, 141; decision under uncertainty and, 140; defined, 140–41; in probability theory, 22; uncertain, *see* Events; without natural payoff measures, 241–42

P

Parameters, defined, 11
Partial cash flows, 154
Payoffs, 144–45; determination of, 153–54; in two-person zero-sum games, 271; utility and, *see* Utility
Payoff table, 143–48
Percentile, *see* Fractile
PERT, 10, 442–79; activity completion times and, 449–50; activity scheduling and, 459–61; activity slack times and, 461; basic concepts of, 443–50; critical path and, 453–55; determination of expected activity completion time and, 473–76; development of, 443; dummy activities and, 448–49; earliest possible event times and, 450–53; importance of time in planning and, 442–43; linear programming and, 473; management applications of, 462–63; milestone scheduling and, 461–62; regular and crash activity plans and, 465–66; replanning and adjustment with, 463–73; research

and development and, 2; simulation and, 542–47; with three-time estimates, 473–76; time-cost tradeoff and, 463–65, 467–70; *see also* PERT network

PERT network, 444–48; analysis of, 450–59; event slack time and, 457–59; latest allowable event times and, 455–57; planning and control using, 459–63; updating of, 470–73

Pessimistic time (PERT), 473

Physical simulations, 524

Pivot element, 375

Pivot operation, 374

Poisson distribution, 491, 494–95

Poisson probability tables, 496–97

Poisson process, 490–91, 498

Portfolio theory, 66

Posterior analysis: decision making with experimental information and, 198–200; determination of critical values and, 222–24; non-optimal strategies and, 199–200

Posterior probabilities: as conditional probabilities, 45–47; defined, 44–45; obtained with probability trees, 192–98; revision of probabilities and, 192–98; for sample mean, 219–22

Preferences, *see* Utility

Preposterior analysis, 200–202; role of EVPI in, 202

Prior analysis: determination of EVPI and, 217–19; minimum expected opportunity loss acts and, 215–17

Prior probabilities, 43; used with probability trees, 192–98

Prisoner's dilemma, 286–88

Probabilities: addition law and, 24–28; assessment through judgment, *see* Subjective probabilities; basic definition of, 18–21; conditional, 28–33; defined, 14–15; errors in applying concepts of, 40–42; event relationships in, 21–24; fundamental concepts of, 15–21; Markov processes and, 560; multiplication law and, 33–40; revision of, 42–47, 192–98; *see also* Probability distribution

Probability distribution: binomial, 66–77; computation of expected value and, 63–66; cumulative, 72; defined, 58; exponential, 491–94; normal, 211–12; for number of customers in system, 499; Poisson, 494–98; random variable and, 61–62

Probability tree diagram, 36–38, 68, 195–98

Production costs, transportation problem and, 433–35

Production decisions: with inventory policies, 321–24; transportation problem and, 433–35

Production problems, 5–6

Profit line, 340–41

Program Evaluation and Review Technique, *see* PERT, PERT network

Q

Qualitative population, defined, 401

Quantitative methods: applications of, 2–8; in decision making under certainty, 93–94; history of, 9; importance of, 13; increasing use of, 1; inventory policy and, 298; models and, 11–13

Queue discipline, 488–90

Queuing formulas, 500–510

Queuing systems, structure of, 486–88

Queuing theory, 484–517; and arrival and service patterns, 489–90; basic queuing formulas and, 500–505; basic queuing situations and, 485–90; exponential distribution and, 491–94; multiple-server queuing model and, 508–13; Poisson probability tables and, 496–97; Poisson process and, 490–91; quantitative methods and, 10; queue disciplines and, 488–90; results of queuing model and, 499–500; single-server model for finite queue and, 514–15; single-server queuing model with exponential service times and, 498–508; structures of queuing systems and, 486–88

R

Raiffa, Howard, 127n

Random factors, decision under uncertainty and, 140

Random numbers: with continuous distributions, 543–45; generation of, 550–51; generation of events with, 528–30; waiting-line simulations and, 531–36

Random sampling, *see* Sampling

Random time-series factors, 97

INDEX 611

Random variable: defined, 58–61; expected value of, *see* Expected value; illustration of, from roulette, 59–61; probability distribution and, 61–62; variance of, 65–66
Ratio-to-moving-average method, 108–13
Redundant constraints, 403–404
Regression analysis, 121, 122–24
Regression coefficients, 103
Regression equation, 103, 122
Regression plane, 123
Relevant costs, defined, 298
Research and development, PERT and, 2
Risk: attitudes toward, utility curve for, 253–58; in decision theory, 179; uncertainty and, 235
Risk averse individual, 250–58
Risk neutral individual, 250–58
Risk seeker, 250–58
Row and column numbers, transportation solution and, 419–23

S

Saddle points, 271–72; games without, 273–78
Saint Petersburg paradox, 239–40
Sample information, *see* Decision making with sample information
Sample mean: critical value for, 222–25; computing the value of, 86–87; posterior probability distribution for, 219–22
Sample space, 15–18
Sampling: expected net gain of, 226; normal distribution and, 86–87; *see also* Decision making with normal distribution
Scatter diagram, 103
Scenario projection, 132
Seasonal fluctuation, 96
Seasonal smoothing, 120
Server utilization factor, 500
Service in random order queue discipline, *see* SIRO queue discipline
Shadow price, *see* Opportunity cost
Shortage cost, 318–19
Simplex, 361–62
Simplex method, 361–83; algebraic solutions and, 364–66; basic concepts of, 363–69; compared with transportation method, 418–19, 435–36; computational aspects of, 405–406; cost minimization problem and, 391–96; defined, 361–62; finding optimal solution and, 378–81; procedures for, 369–81; slack variables and, 363–64; summary of, 373–75, 396; surplus and artificial variables and, 387–91; transportation problem and, 411–12; variable mix and, 366–69; *see also* Simplex tableau
Simplex tableau, 370–73, 391; construction of, 373, 375–77, 406–408; cost minimization problems and, 393–95; for infeasible problems, 398
SIMSCRIPT, 550
Simulation, 10–11, 324–25, 522–51; compared with analytic solution, 548–49; computer programs and, 550–51; confidence interval estimate and, 540–41; decision making with, 537; inventory policies and, 547–58; kinds of, 523–24; Monte Carlo, 524–25; nature of, 522–25; PERT and, 542–47; required number of trials for, 538–40; statistical aspects of, 537–42; *see also* Waiting-line simulation
Single-server queuing systems, 500; with constant service times, 516–17; with exponential service times, 498–508; for finite queue, 514–15; for limited population, 515–16; with Poisson arrivals and any service-time distribution, 516
Single-server single-stage queue, 486
SIRO queue discipline, 489
Slack times: for activities, 461; for events, 457–59
Slack variables, 363–64
Smoothing, *see* Exponential smoothing
Smoothing constant, 117
Standard deviation: of binomial distribution, 77; decision making with normal distribution and, 75–79, 230; of exponential distribution, 493; of Poisson distribution, 495; posterior analysis and, 220–21; prior analysis without sample information and, 215–19; of sample, 224; simulation trials and, 538–39; and variance of a random variable, 65–66
Standard normal curve, finding areas under, 79–86
State probabilities, 560–62
Statistical decision theory, *see* Decision theory
Statistical inferences, 538
Steady-state probabilities, calculation of, 562–63

Stochastic models, 13
Strategies: decision making using, 173–79; defined, 173–74; mixed, 274–76; non-optimal, and posterior analysis, 199–200
Subjective probabilities, 15, 126–31
Subjective probability distribution, approximation of, 126–31
Substitutability, in utility theory, 246–47
Surplus variables, 387–91
System state probabilities, 505

T

TE, 450–53; determination of, 479; determination of event slack times and, 457–59
Time-cost tradeoff, PERT and, 463–65
Time-cost tradeoff curve, construction of, 467–70
Time estimates, 473–76
Time-series analysis, 95; classical model in, 97–102
TL, 455–57; determination of, 479; determination of event slack times and, 457–59
Transient simulation states, 536
Transition matrix, 559
Transition probabilities, 559–60
Transportation method, 411–37; advantages of, 435–36; applications of, 433–35; closed-loop path and, 423–25; determination of optimal solution and, 428–29; dummy plants and warehouses and, 429–31; formulation of, 413–16; location of entering cell and, 419–23; northwest corner rule and, 416–18; optimal solution to, 425–26; required number of non-empty cells and, 426; simplex analogy with, 418–19; simplex procedure and, 411–12; solution to, 418–29; starting solution to, 431–33; ties for exiting cell and, 427–28
Tree diagram, *see* Decision tree diagram, Probability tree diagram
Trend, 96
Trend curve, 105–107
Trend smoothing constant, 119
Trial and error, simulation and, 522
Two-person non-zero-sum games, 286–88
Two-person zero-sum games, 269–73

U

Unbounded problems, 399–401
Uncertainty: experiments and, 191; Monte Carlo simulations and, 524–25; risk and, 235
Utility, 180, 235–58; attitudes, preferences, and, 236–38; attitude versus judgment and, 251–52; Bayes decision rule and, 252–53; determination of values for, 249–53; for money, attitudes toward risk and, 253–58; numerical values for, 238–41; outcomes without natural payoff measures and, 240–41; *see also* Expected utility, Marginal utility
Utility curve, attitudes toward risk and, 256–59
Utility theory, 241–48; *see also* Utility

V

Variable mix, 366–69
Variables: defined, 11; unrestricted as to sign, 404–405; *see also* Artificial variables, Main variables, Slack variables, Surplus variables
Variance: of binomial distribution, 77; of random variable, 65–66; *see also* Standard deviation
Vertical intercept, 336

W

Waiting-line simulation, 525–37; duplication of reality and, 526–27; generation of events using random numbers and, 528–30; probability distributions for, 527–28; procedures for, 530–36; transient simulation states and, 536
Waiting lines, *see* Queuing theory
Warehouses, locating of, 3, 4
World dynamics, 132

Z

Zero-sum games, optimal mixed strategies for, 278–86; *see also* Two-person zero-sum games